THE LAST DAYS OF

Marilyn Monroe

THE LAST DAYS OF

Marilyn Monroe

BY

DONALD H. WOLFE

WILLIAM MORROW AND COMPANY, INC.

NEW YORK

Permissions, constituting an extension of this copyright page, begin on page 513.

Library of Congress Cataloging-in-Publication Data

Wolfe, Donald H. (Donald Hartwig), 1931–
    The last days of Marilyn Monroe / by Donald H. Wolfe.
        p.   cm.
    Includes bibliographical references and index.
    ISBN 0-688-16288-6
    1. Monroe, Marilyn, 1926–1962—Death and burial.   2. Motion
picture actors and actresses—United States—Biography.   I. Title.
PN2287.M69W63   1998
791.43' 028' 092—dc21
[B]   98-36510
                                                                 CIP

Printed in the United States of America

First Edition

1 2 3 4 5 6 7 8 9 10

www.williammorrow.com

for my wife, Ann,
my son, Paul, and
my daughter, Mary

CONTENTS

ACKNOWLEDGMENTS

This book is the culmination of years of research, not only by me but by many authors, biographers, and investigative journalists. I owe all my predecessors a deep debt of gratitude. Fred Guiles, who wrote the Baedeker of all Monroe biographies, was more than helpful in guiding me through the labyrinthine path of Norma Jeane's story. Milo Speriglio also kindly gave of his time and energies in helping me understand the complexities of the cover-up.

I'm especially thankful to Robert Slatzer and his wife, Debbie, for opening up the Slatzer archives to me. A man of rare wit and dedication, Bob Slatzer was uncommonly generous with his time and energies.

Although Anthony Summers was deeply involved in his own project, he took the time to search through his files and run up giant phone bills in lengthy discussions. I'm most grateful to him for guiding me through the forest of disinformation—cheers!

I thank genealogist Roy Turner for sending me his treasure trove of Norma Jeane Baker files, for extensive hours of conversation and guidance, and for his patience.

Peter Brown, who was supportive from the beginning, also shared transcripts of his interviews and files from the Fox archives—thank you, Peter.

Greg Shriner, Roman Hrynjszak, Patrick Miller, and the unique members of "Marilyn Remembered," were very helpful in making contacts with those who knew Marilyn. Their assistance was invaluable.

I want to thank Ted Landreth, the producer of BBC's *Say Goodbye to the President* for his time and generosity.

I owe Kathy Buster very special thanks for her extensive editorial assistance and her frequent attempts to rescue me from the fetid swamp of hyperbolical purple prose.

To Michael Harris, esq., distinguished member of the bar, I owe a deep debt of gratitude for good advice and good friendship.

Lucille Ham and Liz Derby, who burned the midnight oil at their word processors, deserve a million words of praise. I must not forget David Henschel, blessed with the gift of total recall, who was of invaluable assistance. Marilyn's friend forever, Jimmy Haspiel, was endlessly helpful.

I'm grateful to the author James Spada for his assistance and advice. To Gus Russo go many thanks for sharing his wealth of information.

To the staff at the UCLA Special Collections Department; the Psycho-analytic Institute of Los Angeles, New York, and Boston; the FOI office of the FBI; the National Archives at College Park; the Special Collections Department of the University of Texas; the Library of the Academy of Motion Picture Arts and Sciences; and the Kennedy Library—thank you all for your guidance and assistance.

The gold-medal winner of the paper chase is my agent, Alan Nevins of the Renaissance Agency. Alan believed in the book from day one and had the patience and determination to overcome all the obstacles along the path to publication. My special thanks to Alan, Joel Gotler, Irv Schwartz, Brian Upp, and all the remarkable people at Renaissance.

A special word of thanks to Alan Samson of Little, Brown and Company (UK) and Tony Cartano of Albin Michel, who were so helpful and sup-portive from the first word to the last. And I'm indeed grateful to Michael Murphy of William Morrow and Company. His excellent judgment guided the book through the harrows of the publishing process.

I especially want to thank my wife, Ann, who was not only supportive from beginning to end but had so much to do with bringing about an understanding of Norma Jeane and solving so many of the Marilyn mys-teries. Ann was always there—whirling the tumblers of truth.

I must express a special sense of gratitude to a remarkable man who became a true friend in the course of my research—Jack Clemmons. A man of integrity, Jack was a rare breed in pragmatic times. What a far better world it would be if there were just ten more people in it like him. He's gone to the place where all men are honest, and it's the world's loss. I thank Jack Clemmons for being Jack Clemmons.

PART I

1962–1998

Decades of Deception

The Locked Room

Blonde and beautiful Marilyn Monroe, a glamorous symbol of the gay, exciting life of Hollywood, died tragically Sunday. Her body was found nude in bed, a probable suicide. She was 36. The long-troubled star clutched a telephone in one hand. An empty bottle of sleeping pills was nearby.

— The Associated Press, August 5, 1962

Before dawn on Sunday, August 5, 1962, a warm wind swept off the Mojave Desert and rushed into the Los Angeles basin, swaying the tall trees that formed a curtain of privacy around the Brentwood home of Marilyn Monroe. Antique wind chimes that had been a gift from the poet Carl Sandburg softly tolled in the darkness. Strange sounds were carried on the wind during the night—shouting and the crash of broken glass. Neighbors reported that a hysterical woman had yelled, "Murderers! You murderers! Are you satisfied now that she's dead?"

Mr. and Mrs. Abe Landau, who lived to the immediate west of Marilyn Monroe, had returned home from a dinner party late Saturday evening and had seen an ambulance and a police car parked in the cul-de-sac in front of the film star's residence. Near midnight neighbors heard a helicopter hovering overhead. There were other strange sights and sounds before dawn as the city slept. In the crush of time and extremity the film star's home was carefully rearranged, telephone records were seized, papers and notes were destroyed—and a frantic phone call was placed to the White House.

Shortly before midnight a dark Mercedes sped east on Olympic Boulevard in Beverly Hills. Estimating the car to be driving in excess of fifty-five miles per hour, Beverly Hills police officer Lynn Franklin flipped on his siren and lights and gave chase. When the Mercedes pulled to a stop, Franklin cautiously walked to the driver's side and directed his flashlight toward the three occupants. He immediately recognized that the driver was actor Peter Lawford. Aiming his flashlight at the two men seated in the rear, he was surprised to see the attorney general of the United States, Robert Kennedy, seated next to a third man he later identified as Dr. Ralph Greenson. Lawford explained that he was driving the attorney general to the Beverly Hilton Hotel on an urgent matter. Reminding Lawford that he was in a thirty-five-miles-per-hour zone, Officer Franklin waved them on.

At midnight on Saturday, August 4, 1962, Sergeant Jack Clemmons came on duty as watch commander at the West Los Angeles Police Department on Purdue Street. Clemmons's duties proved to be routine until the call that came in shortly before dawn. The caller identified himself as Dr. Hyman Engelberg and said, "Marilyn Monroe has died. She's committed suicide."

Thinking it could be a hoax, Clemmons asked, "Who did you say this is?"

"I'm Dr. Hyman Engelberg, Marilyn Monroe's physician. I'm at her residence. She's committed suicide."

"Give me the address. I'll be right over." Clemmons noted that it was 4:25 A.M. and wrote the time in his logbook. Driving down San Vicente Boulevard, he radioed for a backup patrol car to meet him at 12305 Fifth Helena Drive. He sped down the deserted streets to Carmelina Avenue, then turned down the short cul-de-sac known as Fifth Helena. Finding the address at the end of the street, he pulled through the open gates into the courtyard, where several cars were already parked. Clemmons heard a dog barking as he got out and walked toward the hacienda-style home. After knocking on the front door, he heard footsteps and whispered conversation from inside. A full minute later the porch light came on and a middle-aged woman opened the door. She seemed fearful and nervous as she identified herself as Eunice Murray, the housekeeper. Confirming that Marilyn Monroe had committed suicide, she led Clemmons to a bedroom where a body lay sprawled across the bed. A sheet had been pulled up over her head, leaving visible only a shock of ash-blond hair. A distinguished-looking man sat near the bed, his head bowed, his chin in his hands. He identified himself as Dr. Engelberg, the person who had called the police. Another man, standing near the nightstand, introduced himself as Dr. Ralph Greenson, Monroe's psychiatrist.

"She committed suicide," Dr. Greenson said. Then, gesturing toward an empty container of Nembutal on the nightstand, he added, "She took all of these."

Clemmons could sense the two doctors watching him as he drew back the sheet that covered the naked body. It was indeed Marilyn Monroe, but the face known to millions of moviegoers all over the world was without makeup and splotched with the lividity of death. A telephone cord ran over one side of the bed and lay beneath her. Her body appeared to be bruised.

Clemmons recalled, "She was lying facedown in what I call the soldier's position. Her face was in a pillow, her arms were by her side, her right arm was slightly bent. Her legs were stretched out perfectly straight." He immediately thought she had been placed that way. He had seen a number of suicides, and contrary to the common conception, an overdose of sleeping tablets usually causes victims to suffer convulsions and vomiting before they die in a contorted position.

"Was the body moved?" Clemmons asked.

"No," the doctors replied.

Studying the two doctors, Clemmons noted that Engelberg, the taller and more distinguished-looking of the two, seemed despondent and uncommunicative, while Greenson, who did most of the talking, had a strange, defensive attitude. Clemmons recalled, "He was cocky, almost challenging me to accuse him of something. I kept thinking to myself, What the hell's wrong with this fellow? because it just didn't fit the situation."

"Did you try to revive her?" Clemmons asked.

"No, it was too late—we got here too late," Greenson replied.

"Do you know when she took the pills?"

"No."

In Clemmons's experience, doctors were readily informative and didn't need to be probed—but then, this was the death of a film star. When the sergeant turned to talk to the housekeeper, he found that Murray had left the room.

Searching through the sparsely furnished house, which seemed rather small and inelegant for the home of a film star, he found Murray in the service porch off the kitchen, where both the washer and the dryer were running. She appeared agitated as she folded a stack of laundry on the counter. Clemmons thought it odd that the housekeeper was doing laundry in the middle of the night while her employer lay dead in the bedroom. While she continued folding, he asked, "When did you discover that something was wrong with Miss Monroe?"

"Just after midnight," Murray replied. "Then I called Dr. Greenson, and he arrived at about twelve-thirty. I went to bed about ten o'clock. I had some things to do, and I noticed the light was on under Marilyn's door. I assumed she was sleeping or talking on the telephone with a friend, so I went to bed. I woke up at midnight and had to go to the bathroom. The light was still on under Marilyn's door, and I became quite concerned. I tried the door, but it was locked, you see, from the inside."

"The door was locked?" Clemmons asked.

"Yes," she replied, "I knocked on the door, but Marilyn didn't answer, so I called her psychiatrist, Dr. Greenson, who lives not far away. When he arrived, he also failed to get a response upon knocking on the door, so he went outside and looked through the bedroom window. He saw Marilyn lying motionless on the bed, looking peculiar. He broke the window with a poker and climbed inside and came around and opened the door. He told me, 'We've lost her,' and then he called Dr. Engelberg."

Clemmons felt that her story seemed prepared; she related the events in an even, precise voice and fidgeted with the laundry. The fact that Marilyn Monroe's body had been discovered at 12:30 A.M., but the police had not been called until 4:25 A.M., Clemmons found disturbing. He asked Murray what she had done after the body was discovered.

"I just had so many things to do . . ." she responded. "I realized that there were probably going to be hundreds of people involved, and I had to dress. I had all sorts of things to do. . . . I first called Norman Jefferies, a handyman employed by Marilyn. He had helped with the interior decorating and was a guard at the gate when necessary. So I called him immediately to come over and repair the broken window . . . and then I was doing other things, you know," she added.

"Other things?" Clemmons asked.

"Getting my own things together," she answered, "I've practically lived here most of the time, and I have many personal things besides my clothes, and I have a basket here that's mine, so I filled it with my things."

Returning to the bedroom, Clemmons asked the doctors why they'd waited four hours before calling the police. Greenson caustically replied,

"We had to get permission from the studio publicity department before we could call anyone."

"The publicity department?" Clemmons wondered aloud.

"Yes, the 20th Century-Fox publicity department. Miss Monroe is making a film there."

"What did you do during those hours?" he asked.

The doctors became more evasive, but Clemmons pressed the point.

"We were just talking," Engelberg mumbled.

"About what?" Clemmons queried. "What were you talking about for four hours?"

The doctors shrugged their shoulders and stared at him blankly. Protected by professional confidentiality, they were not compelled to answer, but Clemmons thought their attitude was strange under the circumstances. He noted that there was no drinking glass in the bedroom and wondered how she had swallowed the Nembutal tablets. He recruited the two doctors to help search for the drinking glass, but they found no glass or cup in the bedroom or the adjoining bathroom, where Clemmons discovered that the water had been shut off during remodeling. The sergeant then asked if Monroe was in the practice of using a hypodermic needle or syringe. Engelberg said she was not, and that the medications prescribed were all oral; however, the doctor stated he had been treating her for diarrhea and had recently administered some injections.*

Returning to the bedroom, Clemmons again asked how the body had been discovered. Greenson related the story much as Murray had told it. The housekeeper had called him sometime after midnight. Arriving at about 12:30 A.M., he broke the bedroom window with a poker to gain access to the room, where he found Marilyn on the bed. Greenson stated that her hand was firmly gripping the telephone, and he removed the phone from her hand shortly after discovering the body. He added that she must have been trying to call for help. Clemmons found it curious

---

* This comment by Dr. Engelberg to Sergeant Clemmons has gone unreported for over thirty years. It was discovered in the transcript of a talk given by Jack Clemmons on March 22, 1991, to the Los Angeles organization Marilyn Remembered. He has recently reconfirmed the statement. It has a significance relating to the autopsy. Regarding the digestive tract, Dr. Noguchi states, "The colon shows marked congestion and discoloration." This heretofore unexplained notation has given substance to erroneous speculation that the mode of death was via a suppository or enema infusion of barbiturates. But according to Monroe's New York internist, Dr. Richard Cottrell, she had episodes of colitis brought about by emotional stress, and in 1961 she was diagnosed as having an ulcerated colon.

that Greenson would conclude Marilyn was calling for help when Murray was in the house, and her door was scarcely ten feet down the hall. But it wasn't Clemmons's job to investigate these matters. His duty was to take the initial report and write down what he saw and heard.

Clemmons was relieved by Sergeant Marvin Iannone, and by the time he went off duty, the sun had risen and the desert winds had warmed the morning air. It was going to be a hot day. The police had sealed off the house, but the news had spread quickly, and the streets were soon blocked by the press and a crowd of curious onlookers.

Driving back to the West Los Angeles Division Headquarters, Clemmons was plagued by puzzling thoughts: He believed the body had been moved, and he wondered what the doctors could have been talking about for four hours before calling the police. Why hadn't he found a drinking glass in the locked room, and why had the housekeeper been so anxious to have Norman Jefferies fix the broken window?

By the time he arrived at headquarters to file his preliminary report, Clemmons was convinced that something was very wrong. He felt that he hadn't been told the truth about what happened that night at 12305 Fifth Helena Drive.

"Keep Shooting, Vultures!"

She lies on the couch, asleep, her head turned to one side, hair seeming to flow back upon the pillow. Her blouse is open at the throat, an artery pulses against the pale skin. Her breathing is regular, peaceful. She is a child despite the long artificial eyelashes, the carefully done hair, the voluptuous body; the spirit of the child hangs over her like an innocent light. Her eyelids tremble, a dream perhaps . . . ?

Her eyes open. She asks, fully awake, "What day is it?"

—Norman Rosten

Sunday morning Guy Hockett, owner of the Westwood Village Mortuary, received a predawn call to pick up Marilyn Monroe's body. Hockett drove his dented, nondescript mortuary van to the Monroe residence with his son, Don, a UCLA music student working his way through college by helping his dad pick up bodies on weekends. Arriving at Fifth Helena Drive at approximately 5:45 A.M., they had difficulty getting through the growing crowd of reporters and curious neighbors gathering in front of the entry gates. Ironically, the large wooden gates had just been installed on Friday in compliance with Marilyn Monroe's wish for privacy.

Clemmons's call for backup on the police radio had been picked up by a news junkie and flashed around the world on the wire services. News of the film star's death rolled through communication centers, jolting editors and reporters from their beds. *Time* and *Life* editor Richard Stolley placed an urgent call to Tommy Thompson, then a national news reporter attached to the Beverly Hills office. Thompson and *Life* photographer Leigh Wiener were among the first press people to arrive at the Monroe residence.

Awakened by a predawn call, Joe Hyams, a *New York Herald Tribune* correspondent, telephoned photographer William Woodfield and rousted him out of bed. Woodfield had recently photographed Marilyn Monroe's widely publicized nude swimming scenes on the set of *Something's Got to Give*. Together, Hyams and Woodfield sped to the Monroe house, where they found that the veteran Hollywood columnist James Bacon had beaten them to the scene. Claiming he was with the coroner's office, Bacon had gained entry and gone to the bedroom, where the film star's nude body was being photographed by police photographers. Bacon recalled, "I stayed there long enough to get a good view of the body before the real coroner's staff arrived—then I made a quick exit." Bacon described her body much as Clemmons had. "She was lying facedown on the bed, face slightly turned to the left on a pillow. Her legs were straight. She wasn't holding a phone as some have said. I noticed that her fingernails were dingy and unkempt."

When Hockett entered Marilyn Monroe's bedroom, he collected evidence of the possible cause of death, presumably the pill bottles on the bedside table. He collected eight of them. In one of the police photos there appears to be a water glass on the floor next to the bed. Clemmons stated that it hadn't been there earlier, when the doctors helped him search the room for a drinking vessel.

The police investigators set up temporary headquarters in the kitchen, where Sergeant Robert Byron and his supervisor, Lieutenant Grover Armstrong, commander of the West Los Angeles Detective Division, began interviewing the witnesses. Byron stated that he arrived shortly after 5:30 A.M., and that Marilyn Monroe's attorney, Milton "Mickey" Rudin, was there along with Engelberg, Eunice Murray, publicist Patricia Newcomb, and handyman Norman Jefferies. Apparently Greenson had left sometime between Clemmons's departure and Byron's arrival. In retrospect Clemmons believed that Rudin, Newcomb, and Jefferies were on the premises when he arrived at approximately 4:40 A.M. A number of cars had been parked in the courtyard, and he hadn't entered all the rooms or the detached guest cottage.

When Byron asked Murray about the discovery of the body, she basically repeated the story she had told Clemmons, except that she altered the time frame by three and a half hours. Instead of saying that she had gotten up at midnight and seen the light under Marilyn's door, Murray stated that it was closer to 3:30 A.M., and that she called Greenson at 3:35. Apparently, Murray, Greenson, and Engelberg had decided to change the chronology. Engelberg also advanced the time by three and a half hours, telling Byron that he had pronounced the actress dead at 3:50 A.M.—not "shortly after twelve-thirty A.M.," as he had stated to Clemmons. In a follow-up report dated August 6, 1962, both Greenson and Engelberg reiterated the altered chronology. The time discrepancy wasn't an aberration or an error on the part of one of them—all three had changed their story.

In his report, Byron described Murray as "possibly evasive," and he recalled in a recent interview, "My feeling was that she had been told what to say. It had all been rehearsed beforehand. She had her story, and that was it." As for Engelberg and Greenson, Byron reflected, "There was a lot more they could have told us. . . . I didn't feel they were telling the correct time or situation."

On Sunday morning *Time* and *Life* correspondent Tommy Thompson taped a lengthy interview with Eunice Murray in which she recounted the events surrounding the film star's death in a sincere, soft-spoken voice, carefully measuring her words in a precise manner. In the following decades evidence would contradict her story, and she would ultimately refute many of her statements preserved on the Thompson tapes.

In her initial statements to the police and the press, Murray recalled that she first became concerned about Marilyn when she got up to go to the bathroom and saw the light on under the door. She clearly stated, "It was the light under Marilyn's door that aroused my suspicions that something was terribly wrong." However, Murray's bedroom was adjacent to Monroe's and had its own bath with its own entry from the Murray bedroom. On the way from Murray's bedroom to her bathroom there is no view of Marilyn's bedroom door. Only if Murray had walked out into the hallway would she have had a view of a light under the door. In any case, the "light under the door" would prove to be an impossibility (see floor plan on page 473 of the Appendix).

After Marilyn Monroe's friend Robert Slatzer learned of her death, he went to the Monroe residence with the executrix, Inez Melson, on Thursday, August 9.* Slatzer noted that the recently installed carpeting was so thick that it was difficult to close Marilyn's bedroom door. The door scraped along the surface of the carpet, and it was impossible to see light

---

* In his book *Marilyn Monroe: The Biography*, Donald Spoto accused Slatzer of being merely a fan who once met Marilyn during the filming of *Niagara*. However, evidence and statements made by numerous individuals who knew Slatzer and Marilyn during the decades of their friendship clearly establish their enduring relationship.

beneath it. Murray, who was present during Slatzer's discovery, admitted that he was correct and that she must have been mistaken.

The question remained—what actually led Murray to believe that "something was terribly wrong" in the middle of the night?

In the book *Marilyn: The Last Months*, which Eunice Murray cowrote in 1975 with her sister-in-law, astrologist Rose Shade, she again altered her story. Instead of saying that she got up to go to the bathroom, she attributes the discovery that "something was terribly wrong" to her "Piscean qualities." The book states:

> A highly intuitive and gentle woman, born under a Piscean sign, she [Murray] seemed to sense that nightmare awaited not in sleep, but beyond her bedroom door. She recalls that night vividly:
> "There was no reason I knew of for waking, for turning on the light and opening the door to the hall. There was no evidence of anything amiss until I saw the telephone cord at my feet. I knew then that something was terribly wrong. The cord ran from the spare bedroom [telephone room] across the hall and under Marilyn's closed door. There was no sound from within her room, and thick carpeting made it impossible to tell if her light was on or not. . . . Cautious of awakening her unnecessarily, I did not tap on the door or call her name. Very much alarmed, however, I dialed her psychiatrist on the other line."

In the altered version, Murray tells her readers it was the sight of the telephone cord running under the door that compelled her to call Marilyn's psychiatrist at 3:30 A.M. However, the telephone cord running from the telephone room and under the door into Marilyn's bedroom was not an uncommon sight after midnight; in fact, it was quite routine.

Two telephone lines ran to Marilyn's residence. Her house number, GRanite 24830, was connected to a pink phone in the telephone room and an extension in the guest cottage. Her private number, GRanite 61890, led to the white phone in the telephone room. The pink and the white phone each had a thirty-foot extension cord, allowing Marilyn to take either one into her bedroom. Though Marilyn put the pink house phone under a pillow in the telephone room so its ring wouldn't disturb her, her friends knew that Marilyn kept the private white phone in her bedroom at night. To the annoyance of many, she was a notorious night caller. On sleepless nights she often called people in the small hours of the morning to dispel her anxieties. Her friend Norman Rosten recalled being awakened on numerous occasions in the predawn hours and hearing the whispery voice on the phone saying, "Guess who this is." When the phone rang at 2 A.M. and he fumbled in the dark for it, it didn't take clairvoyance to know that Marilyn was calling. On the night before she died, her friend Arthur James stated that Marilyn left a message at 3 A.M. with his answering service. Obviously, the telephone cord of the private line leading under the door into Marilyn's bedroom was the rule, not the exception.

If neither of Mrs. Murray's stories regarding her suspicion that "something was terribly wrong" had plausibility, the question remains: What did occur in the middle of the night that motivated her to call Dr. Greenson?

Lieutenant Armstrong indicated in his report, "Mrs. Murray was vague and possibly evasive in answering questions pertaining to the activities of Miss Monroe during this time. It is not known whether this is or is not intentional."

In statements made to the press on Monday, Pat Newcomb stated that she had been awakened at her Beverly Hills apartment at approximately 4 A.M. Sunday by a call from attorney Mickey Rudin. According to Newcomb, Rudin told her, "Marilyn has accidentally overdosed." "How is she?" Newcomb inquired. "She's dead," Rudin replied. Newcomb said she then rushed from her Beverly Hills apartment to the Monroe residence, where she met her boss, publicist Arthur Jacobs. Although the police were officially notified of Marilyn's death by Engelberg's call at 4:25 A.M., it becomes evident from Newcomb's statement that both Rudin and Arthur Jacobs had been informed of her death prior to the police. The driving time from Newcomb's Beverly Hills apartment to Marilyn's on a Sunday morning is approximately fifteen minutes. Yet during the time that Clemmons was at the Monroe residence—from 4:40 A.M. until approximately 5:30 A.M.—he didn't see Pat Newcomb or Arthur Jacobs. However, Byron stated that Newcomb was there when he arrived shortly after Clemmons's departure.

Although Newcomb claimed she spent early Sunday morning at Marilyn's dealing with the press and making numerous phone calls, Norman Jefferies described Newcomb as distraught and hysterical. Recalling that the police had difficulty dealing with her, Jefferies stated, "She was looking through drawers and going into Marilyn's bedroom. She had spent Friday night at the house and perhaps she was looking for something she left there. The police had to control her. When they told us to leave because they were going to seal the house, she became unglued. They had trouble getting her out of the door. She kept trying to get back inside.

I don't know if it was because she couldn't find what she was looking for, or if she just couldn't deal with everything that had happened."

According to Murray, "Pat Newcomb didn't want to leave. She was sitting in the third bedroom [the telephone room] where she had so recently spent the night. She had quieted down from her previous hysterical state, but gave no impression of planning to move. . . . The police practically had to forcibly evict her."

In the bedroom, when Guy Hockett and his son placed Marilyn's body on the gurney, he noted, "Rigor mortis was advanced, and she was not lying quite straight, and it took about five minutes to straighten her out. . . . We had to do quite a bit of bending to get the arms into position so that we could, you know, put the straps around her." He added, "She didn't look good, not like Marilyn Monroe. She looked just like a poor little girl that had died. . . ." When the time of death is unknown, it is often determined by the extent of rigor mortis. Over the first four to fourteen hours after death the muscles of the body contract to rock-hardness. Hockett recalled that they placed the body on the gurney sometime between 5:30 and 6 A.M. He estimated that she had died approximately six to eight hours earlier, or sometime between nine-thirty and eleven-thirty Saturday night.

As Marilyn Monroe's body was wheeled out of the house, the mortician's gurney passed over a tile embedded in the entryway, with the Latin inscription "Cursum Perficio," which literally translates, "I have run the course." Reporter Joe Hyams stated, "Mr. Hockett wheeled Marilyn Monroe's body out of the front door at about six-thirty A.M. They wheeled it down to the courtyard near the gates where the mortuary van was parked. Her body had been wrapped from head to toe in a shroud made of a pale blue woolen blanket from the bed. They had placed the body, hands folded across the stomach, on the gurney and tied it down with leather straps at the feet and waist."

Hyams and photographer William Woodfield noted that Captain James Hamilton of the LAPD Intelligence Division was there along with several intelligence officers. Knowing that Hamilton rarely appeared at a crime scene, let alone a suicide, Hyams realized that there was more to be learned regarding the death of Marilyn Monroe. Neighbors told Hyams of the strange sounds heard in the night—a woman screaming, and later a hysterical woman's voice yelling, "Murderers! You murderers! Are you satisfied now that she's dead?" Others said they had heard a helicopter circling overhead shortly before midnight.

Soon after Marilyn's body was placed in the mortuary van, Newcomb, Jefferies, and Murray were escorted by Sergeant Marvin Iannone from the kitchen entrance. Coroner's seals were then placed on the doors of the main house and the guest cottage. Though Newcomb said she had driven to the Monroe residence after Rudin's call, her car wasn't there. Photos and newsreel footage show that she was led from the house and got into the passenger seat of Murray's two-tone Dodge. As Jefferies opened the passenger door of Murray's car and Newcomb stepped inside, photographers scrambled for pictures and reporters bombarded her with questions concerning Marilyn's last hours. Once again becoming hysterical, Newcomb turned on the press and screamed, "Keep shooting, vultures!" As she was driven away from Marilyn Monroe's home for the last time, she yelled out the window, "How would you like it if your best friend died?"

Not long after Murray's car pulled out of the gates, Guy and Don Hockett drove out of the courtyard in the mortuary van with the film star's body. Though Billy Woodfield wasn't ordinarily a press photographer, his instinct grasped the moment. Recently recalling the incident, Woodfield reflected, "Hyams had pressed me into service as a newsy—not my bag— but when the mortician's van drove off I said to Joe, 'C'mon, we've gotta follow the money!' " Woodfield grabbed Hyams and they ran to their car and followed Hockett's van. Not knowing where the van was headed, they followed it to the Westwood Village Mortuary, where Alan Abbott, the mortuary attendant who helped in preparing bodies for embalming, was waiting.

Leaving the body momentarily unattended, the Hocketts and Abbott entered the mortuary building. Woodfield took several photos of the shrouded body in the van, then he and Hyams entered the mortuary to question Hockett. Walking to the office, Woodfield recalled passing the embalming room, where an array of specimen jars had been neatly arranged on a cart beside the embalming table. Name and case number tags were on each jar, and Monroe's name had been written on the embalmer's tags.

Upon removing the body from the van, Alan Abbott became concerned when he discovered that the press had followed Hockett back to the mortuary. "I hid Miss Monroe's body in a broom closet," he recalled. "One of them had offered me ten thousand dollars if they could take a picture of the corpse. I knew it wouldn't be long before they'd be descending on us like locusts, and I urged the Hocketts to call in some security. There was just the three of us there and it was a bit frightening—the lull before a storm. Pinkerton's sent over twenty security guards to keep the press at a distance, and before the day was over we could have used more."

Before leaving, Woodfield was able to get a photo of the shrouded body of one of the greatest motion picture stars of the twentieth century lying in a broom closet cluttered with mops, brushes, rags, and specimen bottles.

"Toodle-oo!"

It was Hollywood that destroyed her—she was a victim of her friends . . .

—Joe DiMaggio

Hollywood was shaken by the news that Marilyn Monroe had committed suicide. Her death was the biggest news story of 1962, ultimately consuming more type space than the Cuban missile crisis, which occurred several months later. MARILYN MONROE A SUICIDE, read the *London Times* headline. The *Los Angeles Times* put out extra editions and rushed them to the newsstands. MARILYN DEAD was the eighteen-point headline in the *Los Angeles Herald-Examiner*.

Joe DiMaggio heard the news early Sunday morning in San Francisco. He took the first plane to Los Angeles. Checking into suite 1035 at the Miramar Hotel, not far from Marilyn's home, he refused to speak to the press and went into seclusion. His friend Harry Hall recalls that he took her death very hard and wept bitterly.

Robert Slatzer was awakened early Sunday morning by a phone call from his friend and neighbor Dr. Sanford Firestone. Dr. Firestone had been present on August 1, when Marilyn had called Slatzer at his home in Columbus, Ohio, from a pay phone in Los Angeles. In an interview with writer Anthony Summers on March 23, 1983, Dr. Firestone discussed his presence along with Slatzer's friend Ron Pataki when Marilyn had called. Dr. Firestone stated, "I know there was some kind of problem. After the call, Bob said she was very nervous, and very afraid . . . as far as Bobby Kennedy, and the Kennedys. . . ."

When Dr. Firestone called Slatzer about Marilyn's suicide, he said, "Bob, I've got some bad news—Marilyn's dead. Sleeping pills, they say."

"She wouldn't do it!" Slatzer exclaimed, "She had too many plans."

He hung up without saying good-bye and turned on the television: ". . . *and authorities report that Marilyn Monroe died at 3:40 A.M. of an apparent overdose of barbiturates . . .*"

When Arthur Miller heard the news, he was quoted as saying, "It had to happen. I don't know when or how, but it was inevitable." He added that he would not be going to the funeral. "She's not really there anymore."

Marilyn's first husband, James Dougherty, was told of her death by Sergeant Clemmons, who called him after filing his report. Dougherty was a fellow police officer in Van Nuys and an acquaintance of Clemmons's. When Clemmons told him, Dougherty replied, "I was expecting it."

Marilyn's friend and mentor, Lee Strasberg, made an unusual statement to the *New York Herald-Tribune*: "She did not commit suicide. . . . If it had been suicide, it would have happened in quite a different way. For one thing, she wouldn't have done it without leaving a note. There are other reasons, which cannot be discussed, which make us [Strasberg and his wife, Paula] certain she did not intend to take her life." Strasberg's perplexing utterance may have been influenced by Marianne Kris, who was Marilyn's New York psychiatrist and a friend and neighbor of the Strasbergs. Kris was in frequent communication with her associate, Dr. Ralph Greenson, and it is likely that he told Kris about the circumstances of Marilyn's death.

Actor Peter Lawford stated to the press, "Pat [Patricia Kennedy Lawford] and I loved her dearly. She was probably one of the most marvelous and warm human beings I have ever met. Anything else I could say would be superfluous."

The public learned little of Marilyn's last hours from the sketchy and often contradictory published statements by the key witnesses: actor Peter Lawford, housekeeper Eunice Murray, psychiatrist Ralph Greenson, publicist Pat Newcomb, attorney Milton Rudin, and physician Hyman Engelberg. There was no coroner's inquest or official investigation, so none of the key witnesses were ever obligated to testify under oath, and many of them, as Murray admitted in 1986, "told what was good to tell at the time."

In an exclusive interview with New York *Journal-American* correspondent Alfred Robbins, Pat Newcomb said, "I had arrived at Marilyn's house on Friday. I was fighting a bad case of bronchitis and had decided to enter a hospital for a complete rest, but Marilyn had called me and said, 'Why don't you come out here? . . . You can sun in the back and have all the rest you want, and you won't have to go to the hospital.' It was typical of Marilyn," she went on, "this concern for friends. So I accepted her invitation. I found her in wonderful spirits. Some furnishings had just arrived from Mexico. She was in a very good mood—a very happy mood. Friday night we had dinner at a quiet restaurant near her home. Saturday she was getting things done inside the house. She loved it. This was the first home she ever owned herself. She was as excited about it as a little girl with a new toy."

Newcomb said that when she left on Saturday, nothing indicated the impending tragedy: "When I last saw her, nothing about her mood or manner had changed." She recalled that Marilyn had waved at her with a smile from the doorway and said, "I'll see you tomorrow. Toodle-oo!" Pat Newcomb left Marilyn's at approximately 5:45 P.M.

Five hours later Marilyn Monroe was dead.

The narrative of events was picked up by Murray, who stated that she stayed at her own apartment in Santa Monica on Friday night and returned to Marilyn's Saturday morning. When she arrived, Norman Jefferies was already at work retiling the kitchen floor.

"I arrived there about eight-thirty Saturday morning," said Murray. "Marilyn was up and dressed in a terry-cloth robe. Pat was asleep in the guest bedroom [the telephone room]. Marilyn and I had some juice; we were sitting in the breakfast nook. We talked for about an hour or so, discussing household things, then Marilyn went back to her bedroom."

Newcomb had slept late, and according to Murray, Newcomb and Marilyn had a disagreement after Newcomb emerged from the telephone room. When asked about the disagreement, Newcomb stated that "the small argument that day was because I had been able to sleep all night and Marilyn hadn't. While I had my door closed and was sleeping, Marilyn had been up wandering around the house. And she just couldn't bear not being able to sleep. Then for her to see someone come out all refreshed, who had been sleeping the night before, you know, that made her furious."

According to Murray, Marilyn didn't eat lunch or dinner that day and spent the afternoon in her bedroom. When Newcomb began walking out to her car at about 1 P.M., Murray stated, "I called to her asking if she wanted something to eat. She said she did, and I fixed her one of my omelets." After lunch Newcomb decided to stay on. Sometime in the afternoon Murray went shopping for about an hour, but she returned before Greenson arrived at about 5 or 5:30 P.M. It was unusual for Greenson to come to Marilyn's. Marilyn almost always met with her psychiatrist at his home, which was only minutes away. When asked if Marilyn had requested that Greenson visit her, Murray replied, "No, I called him late that morning when Marilyn had said something about oxygen. She asked, 'Mrs. Murray, do we have any oxygen around?' I really didn't understand, but it was something that I thought was questionable. It wasn't my habit to call Dr. Greenson about every little thing, but I did call him and asked, 'What's this about oxygen?' And he said, 'Well, I'm not quite sure, but I'll be over later this afternoon.'"

Murray stated that she and Newcomb were talking in the living room when Greenson arrived. After briefly visiting Marilyn in her bedroom, Greenson walked to the living room and told Pat Newcomb she should leave. "When the doctor came, he spoke to Marilyn," Murray said, "and then he asked Pat if she was leaving. She said, 'Yes, I am.' It was part of his plan, evidently, that Pat not stay because Marilyn and she had some kind of disagreement."

According to Murray, Newcomb left between 5:30 and 6 P.M., and the doctor then went back into Marilyn's bedroom. Approximately an hour later he emerged from the bedroom and asked Murray if she would spend the night.

"I said yes," Murray recalled, "There wasn't any feeling of urgency in his request. There wasn't anything that gave me any idea that it was important that I stay." Greenson then left at approximately 7 P.M.

Four hours later Marilyn Monroe was dead.

Not long after Greenson left, one of the phones rang in the telephone room. "I answered the phone and summoned Marilyn, who sat on the floor and talked to Joe DiMaggio, Jr." Murray recalled, "She was in a very gay mood while she spoke with him. He had given her some good news— he had broken off with a girlfriend of whom Marilyn did not approve. She was very pleased about that. I didn't hear what she was saying, but I heard her laughing. After the call, she phoned Dr. Greenson to tell him about it. Then she walked toward her room. I was in the living room facing her bedroom. She turned and said, 'We won't go for that ride after all, Mrs. Murray.' I didn't know what she meant, but the doctor told me later that he had suggested that if she felt restless she should go for a ride. I would take her because I was also her chauffeur."

Murray recalled that Marilyn then took one of the phones into her bedroom and closed the door at approximately 8 P.M. According to Murray, it was the last time she was to see Marilyn alive.

Three hours later Marilyn Monroe was dead.

Though Peter Lawford's story varied in minor details over the years, he held steadfast to the essential elements until his own death in 1984. Lawford said he was having a dinner party at his beach house Saturday night with television producer Joe Naar; Naar's wife, Dolores; and Hollywood agent George "Bullets" Durgom. Lawford said he first telephoned Marilyn at approximately 5 P.M. Saturday, urging her to join them. He recalled that she "sounded despondent over her dismissal from the film *Something's Got to Give* and some other personal matters." She told him she wasn't sure she'd be there and would think about it.

When Marilyn hadn't shown up by seven-thirty, and Lawford called again, he said she sounded depressed and "her manner of speech was slurred." She said she was tired and would not be coming. Her voice became less and less audible, and Lawford began to yell in order to revive her, describing his shouts as "verbal slaps in the face." Then Marilyn stated, "Say good-bye to the president and say good-bye to yourself, because you're a nice guy."

According to Lawford, the telephone then became silent, as if Marilyn had put the receiver down or perhaps dropped it. He called back, but got a busy signal. Deeply concerned, Lawford considered rushing over to Marilyn's, which was only ten minutes away; however, he claimed, he spoke to his manager, Milt Ebbins, who warned, "For God's sake, Peter, you're the president's brother-in-law. You can't go over there. Your wife's out of town. The press will have a field day. Let me get in touch with Mickey Rudin. It's better to let someone in authority handle this!"

Marilyn's attorney, Milton "Mickey" Rudin, resolutely avoided the press, but he summarized his knowledge of what occurred in an interview conducted by Lieutenant Grover Armstrong on August 6:

Mr. Rudin stated that on the evening of 8/4/62 his exchange received a call at 8:25 P.M. and that this call was relayed to him at 8:30 P.M. The call was for him to call Milton Ebbins. At about 8:45 P.M. he called Mr. Ebbins who told him that he had received a call from Peter Lawford stating that Mr. Lawford had called Marilyn Monroe at her home and that while Mr. Lawford was talking to her, her voice seemed to "fade out" and when he attempted to call her back, the line was busy. Mr. Ebbins requested that Mr. Rudin call Miss Monroe and determine if everything was all right, or attempt to reach her doctor. At about 9 P.M. Mr. Rudin called Miss Monroe and the phone was answered by Mrs. Murray. He inquired of her as to the physical well-being of Miss Monroe and was assured by Mrs. Murray that Miss Monroe was all right. Believing that Miss Monroe was suffering from one of her despondent moments, Mr. Rudin dismissed the possibility of anything further being wrong.

Two hours later Marilyn Monroe was dead.

The narrative of the events in Marilyn Monroe's last hours by the key witnesses painted a picture of a rather normal day in which she was in "a very good mood—a very happy mood," save for the "small argument" with Pat Newcomb and the sudden despondency during Lawford's call shortly after 7:30 P.M. However, the narrative was fraught with contradictions and implausible cause-and-effect relations.

If Marilyn had invited Newcomb over "to sun in the back and have all the rest you want," instead of going to the hospital, it seems unlikely that Marilyn would be "furious" about her sleeping late. Both Newcomb and Murray, and at a later date Greenson, confirmed that an argument took place. However, the subject of the argument remains questionable.

Another question arises from Dr. Greenson's visit. Marilyn's inquiry, "Mrs. Murray, do we have any oxygen around?" was allegedly the reason Murray called Greenson. Yet Murray stated that Marilyn was "in very good spirits" that morning; nevertheless, she found the question about oxygen alarming enough to call the psychiatrist. Murray may not have known that oxygen was a well-known Hollywood cure for a hangover, but certainly Dr. Greenson knew this. Yet a call was made that did indeed prompt Greenson's unusual visit. It is the reason given by Murray for the call that remains implausible.

According to Murray, after Marilyn and Newcomb had their disagreement, Marilyn spent most of the afternoon in her bedroom. Murray was specific in stating that Marilyn was in her room when Newcomb left and never said good-bye. That Newcomb stayed on until Greenson arrived and told her to leave seems as inexplicable as Newcomb's recollection of her last view of Marilyn alive—smiling as she waved her last good-bye and saying, "I'll see you tomorrow. Toodle-oo!"

In Peter Lawford's description of his last call shortly after 7:30 P.M., he describes Marilyn as deeply despondent, slurring her words, and uttering the memorable farewell, "Say good-bye to the president . . ." However, Murray stated that at approximately 7:30 P.M., she called Marilyn to the phone to speak to Joe DiMaggio, Jr. DiMaggio confirmed the time in his interview with the police and indicated that Marilyn sounded quite normal and was in good spirits when they spoke. And in Murray's statement regarding DiMaggio's call, she said, "From the tone of Miss Monroe's voice I believed her to be in very good spirits." Murray described Marilyn as being "in a very gay mood while she spoke with him. . . . I heard her laughing."

When the phone went dead during Marilyn's conversation with Lawford, he said that he thought she may have hung up. Lawford maintained that he redialed several times, but the line was busy each time. A telephone operator checked and told him the phone was off the hook. However, Marilyn had two telephone lines, and certainly Lawford had both numbers. If her private line was busy, and he was so alarmed that he tried it several times and had the operator intervene, logically he would have also tried the house phone. Was that busy as well?

Lawford said that he hadn't rushed over to Marilyn's house because Milt Ebbins had stated, "For God's sake, Peter, you're the president's brother-in-law. You can't go over there!" However, Ebbins's statement has a rationale only given the retrospective knowledge of her death.

Responding to Lawford's concerns, attorney "Mickey" Rudin claimed that he called Murray to see if everything was all right. The "highly intuitive" Mrs. Murray assured him that Marilyn was fine. It wasn't until seven hours later that Murray recovered her Piscean qualities and "seemed to sense that nightmare awaited, not in sleep, but beyond her bedroom door where the telephone cord running under Marilyn's doorway indicated 'something was terribly wrong.'"

It was then that she called Dr. Greenson for the second time that day. However, before changing the motivation for calling Dr. Greenson from the "light under the door" to the "phone cord under the door," Murray had already told the press that the last time she'd seen Marilyn alive, "she had turned in the doorway and said, 'We won't be going for that drive after all, Mrs. Murray' and went into her bedroom, taking the telephone with her."

There were many implausibilities in the narrative of events by the key witnesses as to what occured in the last twenty-four hours of Marilyn Monroe's life. Evidence would emerge indicating the depth of the deceptions. Investigative journalists would discover that the alarm concerning Marilyn's death went out as early as 10:45 P.M. Saturday, and that an ambulance arrived at the house while Marilyn was still alive. Years later Murray would once again change her story and refute the "locked bedroom" scenario.

Clearly, in 1962 the key witnesses conspired to conceal information. The haunting question is why six diverse people—an actor, a housekeeper, a psychiatrist, a press agent, an attorney, and a physician—collaborated to conceal the truth regarding the circumstances of Marilyn Monroe's death. What extenuating circumstances could have been so overwhelming that this disparate group conspired in a deception that has endured for over three decades?

Were they the extenuating circumstances of a suicide—or a murder?

Case #81128

Did Marilyn Monroe commit suicide, or were the drugs that killed her injected into her body by someone else?

—Thomas Noguchi, M.D.

While many businesses remained closed on Sundays, it was usually the busiest day of the week at the Los Angeles County morgue, because so many people seemed to die under questionable circumstances on Saturday night. In 1962, the county coroner's office and morgue were in the basement of the Hall of Justice in downtown Los Angeles. The dank, rat-infested facility suffered from limited funding and had a history of mismanagement and corruption. Investigations have revealed thievery, necrophilia, and the acceptance of bribes in the determination of the cause of death. Coroner Theodore Curphey's underpaid and overworked staff consisted of only three full-time medical examiners, four laboratory technicians, and several coroner's aides.

Dr. Thomas Noguchi, a newly appointed deputy medical examiner, arrived for his duties at six-thirty Sunday morning and "discovered something strange." Curphey had left a telephone message: "Dr. Curphey wants Dr. Noguchi to do the autopsy on Marilyn Monroe." Noguchi hadn't heard that Monroe had died and at first didn't realize that the note referred to the movie star. When he learned that it was, indeed, *the* Marilyn Monroe, Noguchi was surprised that he had been the examiner selected. "A more senior medical examiner normally would have performed the autopsy," Noguchi stated, "and yet Dr. Curphey had made a unique call early on a Sunday morning assigning me to the job."

When he didn't find Monroe's name in the necrology of bodies that had arrived at the morgue Saturday night and Sunday morning, he questioned coroner's aide Lionel Grandison, who was responsible for ensuring that anyone who died under questionable circumstances, or without a physician's direct attendance, be directed to the L.A. County Coroner's office. Grandison soon discovered the first of many irregularities that led him to conclude that there had been an attempt to cover up the circumstances of Monroe's death.

"When people die of natural causes in hospitals, the body is generally held there while arrangements are made for transportation to a mortuary," Grandison recalled, "but when the death involved a suspected suicide or murder, or accident, or the causes were simply unknown, the law said the body had to be shipped to the downtown county morgue in the Los Angeles coroner's office for evaluation."

Grandison initiated a search and found the body at the Westwood Village Mortuary. "For that to happen," Grandison related, "someone had to have called the mortuary and specifically asked them to come and pick up the body." He was further surprised to find that the mortuary was preparing the body for embalming and was reluctant to release the corpse to the coroner. "They began to squawk. They didn't want to let us have the body. But ultimately there was nothing they could do because they were under my orders and the jurisdiction of the county." This was an unprecedented situation, and in his subsequent investigation Grandison questioned the Westwood Village Mortuary staff, but he never discovered who had received the call releasing the body from the death scene and directing it to their mortuary.

Shortly after 9 A.M., Grandison had the body removed from the mortuary and driven downtown, where it was placed in crypt #33 of the county morgue in the Los Angeles Hall of Justice. Marilyn Monroe became Coroner's Case #81128. At 10:15 A.M., Eddy Day, a coroner's assistant, wheeled the corpse to stainless steel table #1 to prepare it for autopsy. The table was equipped with a water hose and drainage system, and a scale for weighing human organs.

Marilyn Monroe would be the first of a number of stars to be included in Dr. Thomas Noguchi's cadaverous cast of players. Others would include Sharon Tate, Janis Joplin, William Holden, Natalie Wood, and John Belushi. In 1968 he performed the autopsy on Robert Kennedy. Noguchi went on to publish a book concerning his affinity for the famous and gained the unfortunate title "Coroner to the Stars." After the publication of his book in 1984, he was demoted by the Los Angeles Board of Supervisors and put on probation for allegedly mismanaging his office and sensationalizing his position as medical examiner.

Shortly before the autopsy began, Noguchi was joined by John Miner, a deputy district attorney specializing in medical and psychiatric law. Miner was an associate clinical professor at the University of Southern California Medical School and, along with Dr. Ralph Greenson, a lecturer at the Los Angeles Psychoanalytic Institute.

Also attending the autopsy was the Los Angeles County coroner, Dr. Theodore Curphey. Though the coroner's office has never revealed Curphey's presence at the autopsy, Grandison recently stated, "I do recall the day of that autopsy. And I do know for a fact that Dr. Curphey was there at the autopsy. . . . I know that he personally supervised everything that happened." Grandison's revelation perhaps explains why a newly appointed deputy medical examiner had been assigned to Case #81128. "For Coroner Curphey to attend an autopsy was unprecedented," according to Grandison. "He supervised the entire procedure and orchestrated the final report. It would have been difficult for Curphey to do that with the chief medical examiner, who normally would have received the assignment."

Commenting on Coroner Curphey's handling of the autopsy, Noguchi stated, "As a junior member of the staff, I didn't feel I could challenge the department head on procedures."

At 10:30 A.M. the autopsy began. Miner recalls being profoundly moved when they first viewed the body. "I had looked at thousands of bodies, but Tom and I were both very touched. We had a sense of real sadness, and the feeling that this young, young woman could stand up and get off the table at any moment."

Noguchi and Miner had studied the police reports indicating that Monroe had died in a locked room, and that her doctors believed she died of an ingestion of an overdose. They also had studied the pill bottles gathered by Guy Hockett. Dr. Engelberg had told the police he had given Monroe a refill prescription for fifty capsules of Nembutal on Friday, August 3. Records at the San Vicente Pharmacy indicate that the prescription was filled the day before she died.*

Though no hypodermic needles had been found in the locked room, Noguchi stated that the autopsy began with an external examination for puncture marks indicating that drugs were administered by injection. Miner stated, "We both examined the body very carefully with a magnifying glass for needle marks. There was no indication that the drugs had been administered by way of a hypodermic needle. If there had been marks, they would have been apparent on such a very careful examination of the body."

The autopsy diagram clearly has the notation "No needle marks." However, there are serious questions concerning the findings. It is a matter of record, according to the bill submitted to the Monroe estate, that Engelberg gave her an injection on August 3. The injection was at approximately 4 P.M. on Friday, and according to Guy Hockett she died at approximately 10 P.M. the following day—an elapsed time of thirty hours.

Miner, who was not a physician or a medical examiner, has been the primary defender of the "very careful search for needle marks." However, in his book *Coroner*, Noguchi poses the question, "Were the drugs that killed her injected into her body by someone else?" He states how difficult recent needle marks are to detect, citing the John Belushi case. On examining Belushi's body, the police first ruled out drugs as the cause of death because the coroner's staff at the death scene had been unable to discover needle marks. Also, the chief of the Forensic Medicine Division, Dr. Ronald Kornblum, was not able to discover any needle marks, and neither was Noguchi. But acting on his suspicions, after traces of cocaine powder were discovered at the death scene, Noguchi writes, "I gripped Belushi's upper right arm with both of my hands, then squeezed. . . . Suddenly a tiny drop of blood appeared at the inner elbow, but the very fact that the fresh punctures had been so difficult to discover worried me. . . . A medically clean needle had been used and only drops of blood revealed it."

Another matter for concern in external examinations is the question of lividity, or livor mortis. Lividity is caused when blood pools in the lowest level of the body in the hours after death, producing purplish blotches. In the external report the examiner mentions two such areas: first, the

---

* While only the Nembutal bottle was found and inventoried, Dr. Engelberg had inexplicably erred in stating the number of capsules he had prescribed. The records of the pharmacy indicate that the Nembutal prescription was for twenty-five capsules—not fifty as Engelberg had stated.

face, neck, arms, chest and abdomen; second, "a faint lividity which disappears upon pressure is noted in the back and posterior aspect of the arms and legs." The forensic significance is that when a body is moved during the livor mortis process, which usually extends for the first four hours after death, these "dual lividity" areas are known to occur. For instance, if a body lies on its stomach during a three-hour interval after death, and then is placed on its back by mortuary attendants, a secondary lividity could take place on the posterior during the next hour, or final phase of the process. Noguchi and Miner could have considered this when confronted by the dual lividity, which is mentioned in the autopsy report but not explained. However, it is now known that Marilyn Monroe died at approximately 10:30 P.M. Saturday. Her body was rolled over and placed on the gurney by Guy and Don Hockett eight hours after the time of death, or four hours after the livor mortis process was completed. Therefore, the faint lividity noted on her posterior must have occurred immediately after death, when Monroe's body was on its back for a period of time before being placed facedown on the bed, where it remained until the end of livor mortis.

Without explanation, Noguchi's External Examination Report points out two fresh bruises on Marilyn's body: "a slight ecchymotic area is noted in the left hip and left side of the lower back." However, according to Grandison, more bruises were found on Monroe's body than the official documents reveal. Grandison explained, "When a body is brought into the morgue, it is immediately inspected by a medical assistant. At this time all scars, bruises, cuts, or other trauma are indicated on a special initial examination form. This form becomes part of the official file and is completed before the beginning of the autopsy." Grandison saw this form on the morning of August 5, and he said it included the hip bruises indicated in the autopsy report but also revealed additional bruises on Monroe's arms and the back of her legs. According to Grandison, "This initial examination form was part of a file that disappeared as the case began to expand."

Miner later commented that all of the bruises were small, except for the large bruised area on the left hip. "We saw bruised areas on the body," he recalls, "but nothing that could have contributed to death in any way." However, bruised areas are an indication of violence, and the fact that obvious bruises weren't questioned, and that minor ones weren't even noted, is a disturbing omission.

Noguchi later questioned his own conclusion about the bruises and admitted during an interview in 1982 that the prominent bruise on her left hip should have been looked into. "That bruise," Dr. Noguchi said, "has never been fully explained." When reporters asked what may have caused the bruise, Noguchi replied, "There is no explanation for that bruise. It is a sign of violence."

After completing the external examination, Noguchi proceeded with the internal examination. "The body was opened up," Miner recalls, "the rib cage removed. Then all of the chest organs were examined, weighed, and samples of each dropped in a jar of formalin to preserve them for examination." Noguchi then opened the stomach, and he and Miner examined the contents for signs of the Nembutal tablets. But to their surprise the stomach was completely empty. "There was a small quantity of liquid in the stomach," Miner recalled, "but we did not detect any sign that would indicate it contained any heavy drugs or sedatives."

The examiner's report states, "A smear made from the gastric contents and examined under the polarized microscope shows no refractile crystals." According to Dr. Sidney S. Weinberg, former Chief Medical Examiner of Suffolk County, New York, "It is inconsistent with the mode of death by ingestion of a large amount of barbiturates not to have found refractile crystals in the digestive tract. Under a polarized microscope the smear should have disclosed the exact character of the death-producing drug, as each medication has its own individual crystalline shape." Furthermore, Weinberg and several other prominent medical examiners have pointed out that Nembutal's street name "yellow jackets" derives from the distinctive yellow in the gelatin capsules. If Monroe had swallowed as many as forty or more capsules of Nembutal, as has been estimated, evidence of yellow dye should have been found in the digestive tract—especially in an empty stomach. Noguchi found no trace of yellow dye.

Next, Noguchi and Miner looked at the duodenum, the first digestive tract after the stomach. When pills have been in the stomach for a period of time, sometimes the remains and residue will move on into the duodenum; however, they found nothing. Noguchi said, "I found absolutely no visual evidence of pills in the stomach or the small intestine. No residue. No refractile crystals. And yet the evidence of the pill bottles showed that Monroe had swallowed forty to fifty Nembutals and a large number of chloral hydrate pills."

Noguchi's and Miner's examination is most significant for what they did *not* find.

Marilyn Monroe had attempted suicide on at least four previous occasions; this, of course, made the suicide scenario all the more plausible. And at least twice before, she had ingested a number of barbiturate capsules, and one of those times it was Nembutal.

During Christmas 1950, when she was staying at the apartment of her drama coach, Natasha Lytess, Marilyn became despondent over the death of her mentor, Johnny Hyde. Lytess returned home and discovered a note on her pillow that read, "I leave my car and fur stole to Natasha." She recalled, "I ran to Marilyn's door, which was unlocked, and burst in to find that the room looked like hell on earth. Marilyn was on the bed, her cheeks were swollen, and she was unconscious. There was an ooze of purplish paste in the lip corners. . . . I jammed her mouth open and reached in and took out a handful of wet, purplish stuff she hadn't yet swallowed. On the night table was an empty bottle that contained sleeping pills." Even though she'd used a glass of water, Marilyn had gagged on the pills she tried to consume. Her stomach was pumped, and she revived at the hospital.

In the 1960s, when Marilyn was filming *The Misfits* and was troubled by marital problems with Arthur Miller, she swallowed a number of barbiturate tablets, but she again gagged and regurgitated many of them. When her coach, Paula Strasberg, discovered Marilyn unconscious on a bed, she told of seeing the vomitus on Marilyn's face and described using her fingers to scoop the dissolved capsules out of her mouth. Again, Marilyn's stomach was pumped at the hospital, where she regained consciousness.

These experiences make the absence of vomitus or residue in Noguchi's autopsy even more striking.

Also of significance was the absence of the "odor of pear." Victims who ingest chloral hydrate emit a strong pearlike odor. However, this is not the case when chloral hydrate is injected directly into the bloodstream rather than ingested through the digestive tract.

When Noguchi and Miner were unable to find an indication that death had resulted from the ingestion of barbiturate capsules, the mode of death became the subject of a toxicologist's laboratory examination, to be conducted by Dr. R. J. Abernethy. Before leaving the morgue, Noguchi prepared the brain, blood, urine, and internal organs for examination. On the bottom of his report, he noted, "Unembalmed blood is taken for alcohol and barbiturate examination. Liver, kidney, stomach, and contents, urine and intestine are saved for further toxicological study."

The physical autopsy lasted five hours. The remains of Marilyn Monroe's body were returned to crypt #33.

Sometime after ten o'clock Sunday night, *Life* photographer Leigh Wie-ner snuck into the county morgue. Offering a bottle of whiskey as a bribe, Wiener persuaded a morgue attendant to open up crypt #33 and roll out Marilyn Monroe for a few snapshots. He took a number of photos of the corpse, both covered and uncovered. It was Marilyn Monroe's last photo session.

The Final Verdict

The Coroner's Office is essentially a fact-finding body.
—R. J. Abernethy, 1950

R. J. Abernethy, toxicologist for the Los Angeles County coroner, began his laboratory examination at 8:30 A.M. Monday, August 6, and he quickly concluded that Marilyn Monroe's death was due to a massive overdose of barbiturates. The tests showed 4.5 milligrams percent of pentobarbital and 8.0 milligrams percent of chloral hydrate in the bloodstream. In addition, the liver contained 13 milligrams percent pentobarbital—an abnormally large concentration. Pentobarbital is the chemical nomenclature for the Abbott Laboratories product marketed as Nembutal. Chloral hydrate, sometimes referred to as "knockout drops" or a "Mickey Finn," is a highly potent sedative hypnotic that quickly renders a person unconscious.

After reviewing Abernethy's chemical analysis, Noguchi prepared his preliminary autopsy report. The facts indicated that Monroe's body had been found in a room locked from the inside. No hypodermic needle had been discovered within the locked room. Among eight prescription containers found at her bedside were item #4, an empty container of twenty-five capsules of 1½ grains of Nembutal (pentobarbital) filled by San Vicente Pharmacy on August 3, 1962; and item #5, a chloral hydrate container filled on July 25, 1962—of which ten tablets remained. The toxicologist's report of chemical analysis confirmed the barbiturate over-dose.

Correlating the forensic evidence with the circumstances filed in the police report, Noguchi concluded that the cause of death was "acute bar-biturate poisoning due to the ingestion of an overdose." Under *mode of death* he circled "Suicide"—writing in the word "probable." After filing this report, Noguchi assumed that he had done a thorough examination and reported everything accurately; however, disquieting forensic contra-dictions compelled him to return to the toxicology lab.

Abernethy had furnished laboratory reports on the blood and liver, which indicated death from barbiturate poisoning. However, Noguchi had clearly requested reports on the kidney, stomach, urine, and intestines as well. Examination of these specimens would have revealed how the bar-biturate had entered Monroe's system. But the limited toxicology report contained no analysis of these specimens, and therefore there was no confirmation that the barbiturates had been orally ingested. Neither No-guchi's autopsy nor Abernethy's chemical analysis had furnished substan-tial evidence as to how the barbiturate poisoning took place. When Noguchi again asked for the reports on the kidney, stomach, urine, and intestines, he was amazed to find that the samples he and Miner had prepared under the supervision of Curphey had all mysteriously vanished.

The disappearance of these specimens is perhaps the most disturbing of the long list of irregularities relating to the autopsy. These missing specimens contained vital information definitely determining the mode of death. Laboratory examination of the digestive tract could have con-firmed Noguchi's findings that there was no evidence of the barbiturate or its residue in the stomach or intestines—indicating that the fatal dose had not been orally ingested. If examination of the kidneys had shown no barbiturates, that would also have confirmed that Monroe did not die from an oral ingestion.

Recently, it has been discovered that the specimens "disappeared" at the toxicological laboratory established by Abernethy at the UCLA School of Medicine, where Greenson was an eminent member of the faculty. When questioned, Abernethy refused to discuss what became of the miss-ing organ samples. Westwood Village Mortuary attendant Alan Abbott recently stated, "Knowing Coroner Curphey, and that he had supervised the autopsy, it's difficult to imagine that those specimens just disap-peared. It wouldn't have happened."

Miner observed, "In the entire history of the L.A. County coroner's

office there had never been a previous instance of organ samples vanishing."

Noguchi sent his preliminary report to Coroner Curphey, who reviewed
it along with the police reports. In coroner's cases where suicide is suspected, friends, relatives, physicians, and colleagues of the deceased are
normally interviewed to establish the victim's state of mind. The coroner
then decides if the total evaluation of the victim's death supports a final
verdict of suicide. If there was any doubt as to the cause of death, Curphey's responsibility was to call for an inquest, subpoena witnesses, and
bring about a full-scale inquiry. However, according to coroner's aide Lionel Grandison, Curphey was actually covering up the cause of Monroe's
death. "As I analyze my participation, my conversations with other staff
members, and the things I've seen," Grandison stated, "there's no doubt
in my mind that the Marilyn Monroe case, as we know it now, is not the
true case. Some very sensitive areas have been covered up. Evidence was
suppressed, paperwork was taken from the files, and people who have
knowledge of what happened have not been listened to or sought out."
    Coroner Curphey was an administrator, without an investigative back-
ground, and ordinarily it would have been the job of the coroner's staff
to investigate the circumstances of Monroe's death, but on August 6,
Curphey announced to the press that he would personally question the
star's doctors.
    According to Grandison, Curphey's interference with the normal inves-
tigative procedure was unprecedented, and the little information he
passed on to the staff "changed from day to day, as if it were being tailored
to fit a scenario in need of constant revision by its authors." Grandison
also discovered that someone in the department was removing and rewriting key material from the Monroe file. "I observed information leaving
the file," he later stated, "and much of the information taken out of the
file was never replaced." He claims the file was doctored to support "what
someone wanted the public to think."
    Not until many years later did Grandison fully comprehend the signif-
icance of one item that vanished. This was Monroe's diary, or "book of
secrets." This diary, which was not found among Monroe's effects by the
police or by Guy Hockett, was inadvertently obtained by Grandison when
he was trying to locate Monroe's next of kin. On Monday, August 6, he
sent a driver to Monroe's home to pick up whatever material might give

addresses or phone numbers of relatives. The driver returned with a small red-covered book. The red diary became a matter of controversy, and many have doubted that it ever existed. Only Robert Slatzer and Lionel Grandison claim to have seen it and examined its contents; however, recent discoveries confirm that the controversial diary did exist. In 1994 a CIA document surfaced (see page 469) confirming that Monroe's "book of secrets" was a major national security concern.

Another witness who viewed the diary, or "book of secrets," was former Los Angeles intelligence officer Mike Rothmiller, who worked under Captain Daryl Gates at OCID, the Organized Crime Intelligence Division. In 1978 Rothmiller was assigned to the OCID file room, where floor-to-ceiling shelves housed confidential files. Among them was the Marilyn Monroe file, which Rothmiller states included a copy of her diary.

"It was more like a journal," Rothmiller said. "The majority of the entries were notes about conversations Marilyn Monroe had with John F. Kennedy and Robert Kennedy. The subject matter ranged from Russia and Cuba to the Mafia and Sinatra. I remember she referred to Castro as 'Fidel C.' "

Norman Jefferies also verified the existence of the diary. He recalled that Marilyn kept her red diary either in her bedroom or locked in the file cabinet located in the guest cottage. Jefferies said that on the night she died, her file cabinet was broken into and many of the contents were removed. On Monday, August 6, Jefferies returned to the Monroe residence with Eunice Murray to open the house for Inez Melson, Marilyn's former business manager and executrix of the estate. The driver for the coroner's office arrived while they were waiting for Melson. Jefferies recalled that Murray had the red diary in her possession and gave it to the driver along with one of Marilyn's address books. Jefferies couldn't explain when or how Murray had obtained the diary. Though the diary offered Grandison no clue as to next of kin, he recalled that Bobby Kennedy's name appeared frequently, as did comments about government figures and activities. Grandison remembered seeing the names of both Kennedy brothers, as well as comments about the CIA and the Mafia. He also recalled the names of Jimmy Hoffa, Fidel Castro, and Frank Sinatra. When he left the office that day, he locked the diary in the safe at the coroner's office, but when he opened it the next day, the red diary was gone. According to Grandison only three others knew the combination to the safe: Phil Schwartzberg, the coroner's administrative assistant; Richard Rathman, who was in charge of administration; and Coroner Curphey.

In the meantime, a peckish press was grabbing any tidbit of information regarding Marilyn's last days. Dozens of people claimed they were the last person to speak to her by telephone. The police department received letters containing all sorts of wild allegations. One person "knew for a fact" that Joe DiMaggio had killed his ex-wife in a jealous rage. A stuffed animal she received on the day she died was supposedly connected to a "secret message" that drove her into suicidal despondency.

At a press conference held on Monday, August 6, Curphey revealed that "Marilyn Monroe definitely had not died from natural causes," adding that she may have accidentally taken an overdose of sleeping pills. He announced that her death would be probed not only by the coroner's office but by the Los Angeles Suicide Prevention Team, the independent investigating unit of the Los Angeles Suicide Prevention Center, which had its offices on the campus of UCLA. This investigating team consisted of Dr. Robert Litman, a psychiatrist and professor at UCLA; Dr. Norman Farberow, a prominent psychologist; and Dr. Norman Tabachnick. The *Los Angeles Herald-Examiner*'s evening edition of August 6 referred to them as the "Suicide Squad." Normally, coroner's investigations are conducted by official investigators and the information gathered becomes a matter of public record, but by appointing a private group working free of charge, Curphey made the inquiry an unofficial investigation. No one interviewed would be put under oath, and no interview would ever become a matter of public record. To this day nobody has ever read the full report of the Suicide Squad other than Curphey, who took the findings to his grave. There is no record that the Los Angeles Suicide Prevention Team ever participated in a coroner's office verdict before or after Case #81128.

Litman, Farberow, and Tabachnick were all associates of Greenson, either as faculty of UCLA, as members and lecturers at the Psychoanalytic Institute, or as fellow committee members at the American Civil Liberties Union. Shortly after the Los Angeles Suicide Prevention Team was recruited, it received a sizable grant from the National Institute of Mental Health, under a government welfare program initiated by Robert Kennedy and administered by his intimate friend of many years, David Hackett.

On Monday, August 6, the Suicide Prevention Team, headed by Farberow, held a press conference and announced that they would hold "exhaustive interviews regarding the probable suicide of Marilyn Monroe." On Tuesday, they held another press conference, during which Farberow and Litman announced, "We're interviewing anybody and everybody." Responding to reporters' questions, Farberow stated, "We will seek out all persons with whom Marilyn had recently been associated." On Wednesday, another press conference was held, and Farberow assured the media that there would be "no limitations" to the scope of the inquiry, and that the team would "go as far back in her life as necessary." Yet another hurried press conference was held on August 14. The Suicide Squad had been on the job for scarcely a week, a week largely spent organizing press conferences, and Farberow announced that the Suicide Prevention Team had concluded that Marilyn Monroe was "an emotionally disturbed person who suffered from deep inner conflicts," and their investigation supported the suicide theory.

Because the team's files have never been available to the public, there is no record of who they interviewed or what was discovered, but subsequent investigations have revealed a long list of close friends and associates who were *not* interviewed, among them Peter Lawford, Pat Newcomb, Eunice Murray, Arthur Miller, Joe DiMaggio, Robert Slatzer, Paula Strasberg, Natasha Lytess, Frank Sinatra, and Norman Rosten. The Suicide Prevention Team readily admitted that they had not interviewed John or Robert Kennedy.

Today we know the name of only one person who was interviewed—the most important person of all, Dr. Ralph Greenson. As Marilyn's psychiatrist, he presumably knew more about her state of mind than anyone else. She had been his patient for over two years and had visited him practically every day, often twice a day, during the last two months of her life. Greenson was greatly distressed by his patient's death, and he was reluctant to give interviews. However, in order to complete the informal investigation, Curphey knew he had to interview the victim's psychiatrist. Although John Miner was an attorney, he also held a degree in psychology and lectured at the prestigious Psychoanalytic Institute along with Greenson. They had been friends and associates for many years, and Miner became the logical person to conduct the interview. Miner recalled, "I knew Dr. Greenson personally. Dr. Curphey knew that, and so he asked me to interview Dr. Greenson."

Curphey and Miner expected Greenson to reiterate his opinion that Marilyn Monroe had committed suicide, but Miner was amazed to find that Greenson had totally reversed his opinion. The interview took place on Monday, August 12, 1962, at Greenson's office. Greenson imposed a condition: "A promise was exacted by Dr. Greenson," Miner explained. "I would not reveal the content of anything I learned. He imposed this condition by reason of his professional ethics and consideration for Miss Monroe's privacy. I gave him my word that I would not." However, it was understood that Miner was free to arrive at conclusions and report his opinion as long as he didn't reveal the content of their meeting.

According to Miner, they met for several hours, during which Greenson discussed "not only Marilyn's habits, but also the private confidences she shared with her psychiatrist." Greenson expressed his firm opinion that Marilyn Monroe had *not* committed suicide. Then he played a half-hour tape that Marilyn had made at her home on her own tape recorder. The contents of this tape also led Miner to conclude she had not committed suicide.

Miner later recalled, "Dr. Greenson was very strongly of the opinion that Miss Monroe did not commit suicide. He was very much distressed by her death. The notion that she committed suicide added to that distress, because he firmly felt that she did not commit suicide—very much so, very much so. That I can state. He did not bar me from saying that."

Of all the circumstances, contradictions, and puzzles regarding the death of Marilyn Monroe, perhaps this Greenson interview is the most mind-boggling. It poses two unalterable questions: Why did Greenson reverse his opinion, and what was on the tape played for John Miner?

Without ever having testified under oath about his knowledge of Marilyn Monroe's death, Greenson died in 1979.

Miner stated, "I gave my word to the man and he's dead. So I don't expect ever to reveal it. It's possible that a judge could order me to reveal it and put me in jail for contempt of court if I refused. I hope I never have to cross that bridge."

After the interview, Miner left Greenson's office a shaken man. He too became convinced that Marilyn Monroe had not committed suicide, and he filed his opinion in a memorandum to the district attorney as well as the coroner's office.

When investigative journalist Anthony Summers asked about the contents of the memorandum, Miner recalled that it stated: "As requested by you, I have been to see Dr. Greenson to discuss the death of his late patient Marilyn Monroe. We discussed this matter for a period of hours, and as a result of what Dr. Greenson told me, and from what I heard on tape recordings, I believe I can say definitely that it was not a suicide."

When Summers asked if Greenson thought Marilyn Monroe was murdered, Miner made the significant response, "That is something on which I cannot respond."

When Noguchi learned about Miner's memorandum, he stated, "If Miner's evaluation in 1962 was correct, the only conceivable cause of Monroe's death was murder." Noguchi ruled out an accidental overdose, stating that "an accidental overdose of that magnitude was extremely unlikely. From my forensic experience with suicide victims, I believe that the sheer number of pills Monroe ingested was too many to swallow 'accidentally.' "

The memorandum shocked Coroner Curphey. Two of the most important people in arriving at a probable-suicide verdict were Greenson and Miner, and both had changed their opinion. At this point Curphey should have called for a formal inquest and put witnesses under oath. Instead, he chose to suppress information, and Miner's memorandum soon vanished from the files. Curphey called Grandison into his office and asked him to sign the death certificate, which indicated the cause of death as "probable suicide."

Grandison said, "The standard procedure when we were about to close a case was that all the reports, charts, and other paperwork on the case were there in the file. It would contain the conclusions drawn by the pathologist, the determination of the police, and whatever other agencies made any type of investigation of the case. This file had none of that information in it." Before signing the death certificate Grandison recalled, "I asked Dr. Curphey about the missing paperwork. . . . This was maybe the third or fourth time I had called the missing items to his attention." Grandison also noted that the autopsy report had been altered. "I had seen the initial autopsy report, and this wasn't the same report. The report had been completely changed." When Grandison asked about this, Curphey lost his temper. "He got very angry," Grandison vividly remembered. "He said, 'Listen, you sign the death certificate . . . or else I'm gonna do something!' "

At the time Grandison was a young man with a wife and children, and he believed he would lose his job if he didn't follow Curphey's orders. Reluctantly, he signed the death certificate.

On August 21, 1962, Curphey and the Suicide Prevention Team called a joint press conference to announce the final findings of the "exhaustive investigation" that had lasted a full fifteen days. Farberow announced that Monroe had "suffered from psychiatric disturbances for a long time. She experienced severe fears and frequent depressions; mood changes were abrupt and unpredictable. . . . In our investigation we have learned that Miss Monroe had often expressed wishes to give up, to withdraw, and even to die. On more than one occasion in the past, when despondent or depressed, she had made a suicide attempt using sedative drugs. On these occasions she had called for help and had been rescued. From the information collected about the events of the evening of August 4, it is our opinion that the same pattern was repeated, except for the rescue. . . . On the basis of all the information collected, it is our opinion that her death was a suicide."

Curphey then stepped forward to announce the coroner's verdict: "Probable suicide."

The final verdict, however, has been languishing for over three decades on a dusty shelf in the subcellars of the Los Angeles Hall of Records. The true verdict as to what happened to Marilyn Monroe on August 4, 1962, has always been contained in R. J. Abernethy's toxicology report.

As limited as the report was in 1962, computerized information banks available to the world of forensic medicine in the 1990s allow an analysis of the original report that yields definitive answers to the unanswered questions of decades ago. Abernethy's report clearly states that the blood sample contained 4.5 milligrams (mg) percent barbiturates and 8.0 mg percent chloral hydrate. Computer analysis reveals that Case #81128 had to have swallowed from twenty-seven to forty-two Nembutal capsules (pentobarbital) to reach a blood level of 4.5 mg percent. In addition, she had to have consumed from fourteen to twenty-three chloral hydrate tablets to reach a blood level of 8.0 mg percent. The percentages in the blood, therefore, revealed that a total of from forty-one to sixty-five capsules and tablets had to have been ingested. However, this does not include the 13.0 mg percent pentobarbital that Abernathy's report indicates was also discovered in the liver. Computer analysis reveals that an additional eleven to twenty-four Nembutal capsules had to have been consumed to account for the liver concentration. Therefore, a minimum of fifty-two to a maximum of eighty-nine capsules had to have been consumed for Case #81128, to succumb from the oral ingestion of the lethal dosage. However, in the thousands of fatal cases involving acute barbiturate poisoning due to the ingestion of an overdose, not one case involves the ingestion of over twelve capsules in which no residue has been found in the digestive tract. No case has ever been reported in which the victim has as high as 4.5 mg percent pentobarbital and 8.0 percent chloral hydrate in the blood and no refractile crystals or concentrations found in the stomach or intestinal tract. Yet Noguchi was unable to find capsule residue or any trace of refractile crystals or concentrations of the barbiturates in Monroe's stomach or intestines.

Table 1 illustrates that Marilyn Monroe was on the high end of the mg percentage in the blood. Only Case #4 and Case #1 indicate slightly higher percentages in the blood. (All of the cases indicate stomach concentrations.) However, Monroe also had a high concentration of chloral hydrate, which is synergistic with pentobarbital and greatly increases its lethal effect. The combined dosage was sufficient to kill from nine to twenty people.

TABLE 1.   Tissue Concentrations from Fatal Cases Involving Pentobarbital
Prepared by toxicologist Robert H. Cravey

Case number	Age	Sex	Estimated dose, gm	Dose by weight, mg/kg	Blood, mg/100 ml	Liver, mg/100 gm	Stomach,* mg
1	69	F	6	75	4.7	18.7	130
2	70	F	5	71	3.6	16.0	126
3	43	F	5	45	4.2	22.2	361
4	67	F	3	60	5.0	31.0	108
5	25	F	4	57	4.0	12.0	12
6	42	M	10	101	1.5	42.0	1350
7	26	F	3	60	4.4	26.0	301
8	21	F	3	51	2.3	7.0	40
9	38	F	2	36	1.0	7.5	65
10	54	F	4	83	4.1	19.6	370
11	72	M	5.6	65	1.8	13.5	2300

*Amount recovered from total stomach contents.

The information banks of forensic medicine further establish that there is no case on record of a fatal dose by oral ingestion involving such high concentrations in the blood of both pentobarbital and chloral hydrate. The victim inevitably dies before the fatal concentrations can approach such a high blood level. Monroe would have been dead before even 35 percent of the total barbiturates had been absorbed from the digestive tract into her bloodstream. It is not possible for the remaining 65 percent to have been absorbed from the digestive tract and to vanish without a trace, because when the heart stops beating, the blood stops circulating, and the bodily functions shut down, absorption from the digestive tract into the bloodstream abruptly ceases. The remaining pentobarbital and chloral hydrate could not have entered the bloodstream by ingestion, suppository, enema infusion, or any other absorption process.

How then was the fatal dose administered? It could only have been by needle injection, or what is termed a "hot shot," in which the victim rapidly looses consciousness and succumbs in a matter of ten to twenty minutes.

Sergeant Jack Clemmons was correct that Sunday morning, August 5, 1962, when he returned to division headquarters with the conviction that something was very wrong. Marilyn Monroe did not commit suicide. Technology of the modern world of forensic medicine gives the final verdict— Case #81128 was a homicide victim.

The Disconnected

You know who I've always depended on? Not strangers, not friends—the telephone! That's my best friend. I seldom write letters, but I love calling friends, especially late at night, when I can't sleep.

—Marilyn Monroe to W. J. Weatherby, 1961

Captain Thad Brown, the legendary LAPD chief of detectives, was sleeping in his hideaway trailer in Malibu on Sunday morning when he was awakened by a police messenger pounding on his door with an urgent message. Chief of Police William Parker wanted to see him downtown about "some problems" as quickly as possible. Parker wanted Brown to take over the Marilyn Monroe case, and one of the "problems" was a scribbled note on a piece of crumpled paper found in Monroe's bedcovers.

In 1978, Lionel Grandison disclosed that a scribbled note had once been in the Monroe file. It was rumored to be a suicide note. In a recorded interview with Robert Slatzer, Grandison stated that the note had been turned over to the coroner's office by the West Los Angeles Police Department:

GRANDISON: There was a note—that was basically illegible. . . . It was scribbly, but allegedly in her handwriting. . . . I couldn't determine precisely what the note said, but the fact remains that the note disappeared within one or two days.

SLATZER: Who do you think, in your opinion, confiscated this particular note?

GRANDISON: All I can say is that it was someone who had more authority than I—someone who didn't want this note seen past the couple of days it remained in the coroner's property.
SLATZER: Was Abernethy or Curphey aware of the note?
GRANDISON: Yes, they had to be.

Police investigator Finis Brown, brother of Thad Brown, revealed that the note contained a Kennedy phone number; and the assistant chief of the Intelligence Division, Virgil Crabtree, confirmed that there was a Kennedy number scribbled on it. The significance of the number may lie in a series of telephone calls Marilyn made on Friday, August 3, and Saturday, August 4.

Robert Slatzer spoke to Marilyn Monroe twice shortly before her death. He was in Columbus, Ohio, working on a television series, when she called on Friday, August 3. The call was placed from a pay phone near her home because she feared her phones were tapped. Slatzer's friend Ron Pataki was with him when she called, and he recently confirmed the content of the calls Marilyn placed to Slatzer.

During the conversation on Friday, August 3, Slatzer told Marilyn he'd read in a newspaper that Bobby Kennedy was in San Francisco, where he was scheduled to speak before the American Bar Association on Monday, August 6. Knowing Marilyn was anxious to talk to Bobby Kennedy, Slatzer suggested she call Pat Lawford to find out where he was staying. According to a statement Peter Lawford made in a 1976 *Long Beach Star* interview, Marilyn called him on Friday in an effort to reach his wife, who was staying at Hyannisport. Peter Lawford stated that he reluctantly gave Marilyn his wife's phone number at the Kennedy compound. When Marilyn reached Pat Lawford, she was told that Bobby Kennedy was registered at the St. Francis Hotel in San Francisco. An operator at the St. Francis Hotel confirmed that Marilyn had tried to reach Kennedy there and had left several messages.

The scribbled note found in the bedclothes may have been Marilyn's notations from her attempts to find Kennedy.

The telephone had been an integral part of Marilyn Monroe's life, the immediate tool of communication for a soul who was essentially a loner and frequently suffered from a sense of isolation. The telephone seems to hold the key to her last moments. Peter Lawford had dramatically described Marilyn's last telephone call—her voice fading until there was no response—and Dr. Greenson had painted the too-cinematic picture of Marilyn Monroe's body being discovered with her outstretched hand tightly gripping the telephone. A media maelstrom arose over Marilyn's last call:

Marilyn Mystery Call

Marilyn Monroe got a mysterious telephone call not long before she was found dead from an overdose of barbiturates, The Times was told Monday night. Mrs. Eunice Murray, the blond beauty's housekeeper, said the call came sometime after the actress retired to her bedroom Saturday night.

"I don't remember what time the call came in," she said, "and I don't know who it was from."

Though a number of people claimed to have spoken to Marilyn on the telephone Saturday night, only some of the claims have validity. Henry Rosenfeld, who had been a confidant of Marilyn's since 1949, said he called her from New York on Saturday sometime between 8 and 9 P.M. Pacific time. He recalled that she sounded tired, but very much herself. Though he refused to reveal details of the conversation, he stated that Marilyn discussed plans for the future, including a theater party during a trip to New York the following Thursday.

Shortly before or after the call from Rosenfeld, Marilyn called hairdresser Sidney Guilaroff, whom she had known since the 1940s. Guilaroff told Anthony Summers that the call came at approximately 9 P.M. For decades Guilaroff refused to discuss this conversation, but he recently revealed that Marilyn called him not once but twice that Saturday. The first call came in the late afternoon. "Marilyn was extremely upset. She was in tears and quite hysterical," Guilaroff confided. "She said that Bobby Kennedy had been to her house with Lawford, and that Bobby had threatened her. There was a violent argument. She was afraid—terrified. I tried to calm her down."

The second call came at approximately nine that night. "She was more composed, but I can still hear the fear in her voice. Whatever had happened during Bobby's visit in the afternoon had frightened her. I told her we would talk about it in the morning. I never imagined we would never speak again."

Jeanne Carmen, Marilyn's former next-door neighbor at her Doheny apartment in West Hollywood, stated that Marilyn called her sometime between 9 and 10 P.M. According to Carmen, Marilyn sounded exhausted and nervous, but she was neither groggy nor slurring her words. "She sounded frightened and didn't want to be alone," Carmen recalled. "She wanted me to come over, but I was tired myself and told her I'd call her the next day. My phone rang again about a half hour later. It may have been Marilyn, but I didn't answer."

José Bolaños, a Mexican screenwriter Marilyn met in Mexico City in February 1962, said he called Marilyn from a nearby restaurant at 10 P.M. Bolaños had escorted her to the Golden Globe Awards in March, and they had become romantically involved. He had only recently returned to Los Angeles to see her. Though Bolaños has also refused to disclose the content of their last discussion, he said she didn't hang up the phone but put down the receiver in the middle of their conversation and never returned. Bolaños added, "Marilyn told me something that will one day shock the whole world."

Peter Lawford claimed that Marilyn's last call, in which she slurred her words and faded away, occurred at approximately 7:30 P.M. However, his estimate of the time is inconsistent with the statements of all those who are known to have spoken with her between 7:30 and 10 P.M.: Joe Di-Maggio, Jr., Henry Rosenfeld, Jeanne Carmen, Sidney Guilaroff, and José Bolaños. If Lawford is to be believed, then the call when Marilyn apparently lapsed into unconsciousness must have occurred after 10 P.M.

In 1986 Lawford's guest "Bullets" Durgom confirmed that Marilyn's last conversation with Lawford took place sometime after 10 P.M. Durgom stated, "It was at about ten or eleven that Lawford tried to call Marilyn back and could not get through." According to Durgom it was after that when "the lawyer [Mickey Rudin] and somebody else went over to the house . . . and it was too late." Lawford's maid, Irma Lee Reilly, confirmed "there was no word of worry over Marilyn" before ten o'clock.

According to Joe and Dolores Naar, who were also guests at Lawford's that evening, when they arrived at approximately eight o'clock there was no indication of alarm or concern about Marilyn. The dinner, which turned out to be Chinese takeout, wasn't served until about nine. The Naars recall that Lawford had been drinking heavily, and the party ended early. They left the Lawford house shortly after ten. The Naars are adamant that, during the two-hour time frame when they were with Lawford, no alarm was raised about Marilyn Monroe and not a word was said about a phone call in which she asked Lawford to "say good-bye to the President." Dolores Naar recalled, "It was a very light, up evening. During dinner there was one call from Marilyn that Peter took, but he wasn't gone long, and when he returned, he calmly said, 'Oh, it's Marilyn again'—like she does this all the time. His attitude didn't change. There was no indication that anything was wrong. I picked up on nothing like that."

The Naars knew Lawford and Marilyn well and insist that if anything alarming had happened while they were at the Lawford residence, they would have known about it. The Naars recalled that they returned to their home "well before eleven" and were getting undressed for bed when they received an urgent phone call from Lawford. "He was in a panic about Marilyn," Dolores Naar stated. "Marilyn had called him and was incoherent. He was afraid she had taken too many pills and was in trouble. . . ."

Clearly, this was the call in which Marilyn had lapsed into unconsciousness. The call hadn't occurred at "approximately seven-thirty," as Lawford stated to the press and later to the police. Marilyn's alarming call occurred after the Naars had returned to their home, sometime after ten and "well before eleven."

The Naars recalled that Lawford's urgent call to them occurred at approximately ten-thirty. "We lived near Marilyn's house, and he asked Joe to run over there and see what was wrong." Joe Naar had already undressed for bed, but by the time he had put his clothes back on and was hurrying out the door to drive to Marilyn's house, Lawford called back. "He said that he'd spoken to Marilyn's doctor," Dolores recalled, "and he had said that he had given her sedatives because she had been disturbed earlier and she was probably asleep—'so don't bother going,' Peter told Joe."

The pair of phone calls to the Naars is perplexing. Lawford stated that when Marilyn's voice seemed to fade away, he yelled at her over the phone in an effort to revive her, then the phone went dead. When he called back he received a busy signal. In the 1962 press reports, Lawford said he had the operator check the line, and was told that the phone was off the hook and there was no conversation. Were both of Marilyn's phones off the hook with no conversation on either line? This would have been the case if, as José Bolaños stated, Marilyn didn't hang up the phone, but put down the receiver in the middle of the conversation and never returned.

If Marilyn had left her private line off the hook at 10 P.M., and within the next half hour made the alarming call to Peter Lawford on an extension of the house phone, both lines would have been off the hook and without conversation when Lawford asked the operator to intervene. After

Lawford then placed the urgent call to the Naars at approximately ten-thirty to ask Joe to go over and "see what was wrong," something or somebody prevailed on him to call back in the hope of preventing Joe Naar from discovering what actually had occurred.

Having learned that Marilyn Monroe had died with her hand gripping the telephone, *Herald-Tribune* correspondent Joe Hyams tried to obtain a copy of Marilyn's telephone records. "The morning after her death," recalls Hyams, "I contacted a telephone company employee and asked him to copy for me the list of numbers on her billing tape." Hyams's contact at the telephone company told him, "All hell's broken loose down here. Apparently, you're not the only one interested in Marilyn's calls. The tape's disappeared. . . . I'm told it was impounded by men in dark suits and well-shined shoes. . . . Somebody high up ordered it."

Later a former General Telephone security officer told Hyams that the tapes and toll tabs were confiscated early Sunday morning. "There was just that brief time in limbo, in the very early morning, when you could theoretically get to them before they vanished in the accounting system. After that, they were irretrievable for days, even if J. Edgar Hoover himself wanted them. With the formalities we had then, no ordinary cop could have got to Marilyn's records till nearly two weeks after her death."

However, Captain James Hamilton was no ordinary cop. As head of the LAPD Intelligence Division he wielded a great deal of power and influence. According to former chief Tom Reddin, "Hamilton knew that true power was invisible—that visibility was vulnerability. He was certainly an invisible power in Los Angeles. Hamilton knew where all the bodies were buried, and who buried them."

Former mayor Sam Yorty recalled, "Hamilton's Intelligence Division was Parker's version of the FBI. Parker believed that he was the man who would one day succeed J. Edgar Hoover, and Bobby and Jack Kennedy led Parker to believe he was their choice."

Correspondence between Robert Kennedy and Chief Parker and Captain Hamilton preserved in the Kennedy Library confirms Yorty's observation. Their friendship had gone back to the mid-fifties, when Bobby Kennedy was on the West Coast and Hamilton and Parker assisted him in the Senate rackets investigations. In his book *The Enemy Within*, Robert Kennedy frequently mentions Captain Hamilton as a friend and source of information.

It was Captain James Hamilton, no ordinary cop, who had confiscated Marilyn Monroe's telephone records, and it was Captain James Hamilton who directed the cover-up of information relating to the circumstances of Marilyn Monroe's death for Chief William Parker. *Los Angeles Times* crime reporter Jack Tobin, an acquaintance of Hamilton's, had lunch with him shortly after Marilyn's death and years later revealed, "Hamilton told me he had the telephone history of the last day or two of Marilyn Monroe's life. When I expressed interest, he said, 'I will tell you nothing more.' But it was obvious that he knew more."

Thad Brown disclosed to syndicated Hollywood columnist Florabel Muir that he saw Monroe's phone records on Chief Parker's desk, but that Parker had put the August toll tabs under lock and key. A Muir column that was pulled from afternoon editions of the New York *Daily News* on August 8, 1962, stated:

STRANGE PRESSURES ON MARILYN PROBE

"Strange 'pressures' are being put on Los Angeles police investigating the death of Marilyn Monroe," sources close to the probers said last night.

Police investigators have refused to make public the records of phone calls made from Miss Monroe's home last Saturday evening, hours before she took an overdose of sleeping pills. The police have impounded the phone company's taped record of outgoing calls. Normally in suicide probes here, the record of such phone calls would have been made available to the public within a few days.

The purported pressures are mysterious. They apparently are coming from persons who had been closely in touch with Marilyn the last few weeks.

Thad Brown later told Robert Slatzer that Parker had "called him on the carpet" for mentioning the phone records to Florabel Muir. When Slatzer asked Muir about the records, she said Parker had the phone records in his desk and had flashed them in front of her, stating that they were his insurance of heading the FBI "when the Kennedys get rid of Hoover."

"I asked her what phone calls Marilyn had made during that last billing period," Slatzer said, "and Florabel told me she had learned from Thad Brown that a number of the calls were to Bobby Kennedy." Slatzer then called Parker about the phone records. "He emphatically denied any knowledge of them and hung up on me," Slatzer recalled. He then went down to the Central Division Headquarters and confronted Parker in the hallway about the records. Parker angrily retreated into his office and had Slatzer removed from the building.

Press coverage shows that Robert and Ethel Kennedy had arrived in San Francisco on Friday afternoon, August 3, with four of their children. The San Francisco *Chronicle* reported that Kennedy arrived "without his usual flashing smile and shook hands woodenly with those who welcomed him." After his speech, scheduled for Monday, the attorney general and his family planned a ten-day vacation in the state of Washington.

A special FBI report on the attorney general's activities that weekend specified that he "spent the weekend at the Bates Ranch located sixty miles south of San Francisco. This was strictly a personal affair." The ranch, located in Gilroy, was owned by John Bates, a friend of the Kennedy family. Bates had met John Kennedy when they both served in the navy during the war, and their mutual friend Paul Fay had been named by the president as the undersecretary of the Navy. Bates was a frequent guest at Hickory Hill, Bobby Kennedy's home, and Kennedy had asked him to head the antitrust division of the Department of Justice.

Bates has steadfastly insisted that Bobby Kennedy spent the entire weekend at his ranch. "The attorney general and his family were with us every minute from Friday afternoon to Monday," John Bates maintained to Monroe's biographer Donald Spoto in 1992, "and there is simply no physical way that he could have gone to Southern California and returned." Bates is certain that he would have known about it if Bobby Kennedy had left long enough to reach Los Angeles that day and return. The Gilroy parish priest confirmed that Bobby Kennedy and his family attended the 9:30 A.M. mass at the Church of St. Mary's on Sunday, August 5, approximately when Marilyn Monroe's body was being prepared for autopsy.

In the process of his investigation, however, Thad Brown discovered something startling—the attorney general *had* been in Los Angeles on Saturday, August 4. Thad's brother, detective Finis Brown, related, "I talked to contacts who had seen Kennedy and Lawford at the Beverly Hilton Hotel the day she took the overdose. I went to Thad with the information, and Thad said he had been informed of the fact. He knew Kennedy was in Los Angeles that night, and he told Chief Parker."

Los Angeles is 360 miles south of Gilroy. For the attorney general to fly expeditiously from the Bates Ranch to Los Angeles would have required a ten-minute helicopter commute to either the San Jose Airport or the Naval Air Station, followed by a fifty-minute flight to the Santa Monica Airport and a ten-minute commute to the 20th Century-Fox heliport—where Bobby Kennedy frequently landed during his preproduction meetings at Fox for the film version of his book *The Enemy Within*. Including the five-minute drive from Fox to the Beverly Hilton Hotel, the elapsed time is one hour and fifteen minutes.

Apparently, Thad Brown had done his job too well. Shortly after he relayed his information about Bobby Kennedy to Chief Parker, he was removed from the case. Finis stated that from then on the case was exclusively in the hands of Captain James Hamilton. Under Hamilton, it was handled in an atmosphere of absolute secrecy. Even the department's most trusted employees were cut off from knowing anything about the investigation.

In 1962, Tom Reddin, the deputy chief who later succeeded Parker, recalled, "Where Hamilton and his Intelligence Division were concerned, nobody knew a bloody thing about what was going on. Hamilton talked to only two people—God and Chief Parker." He added, "I was aware of the fact that there was a Hamilton investigation of the Monroe case, but I never knew what it was. I was also aware that there was supposed to be an internal document that never became public."

Though he had officially been removed from the Monroe case, "Thad became somewhat obsessed," recalled his brother, Finis. "He pursued matters privately after Parker removed him. He kept his own extensive Monroe files—including copies he had obtained of her phone records." While Chief Parker considered the Marilyn Monroe file with the telephone records as insurance that he would one day be appointed head of the FBI, Thad Brown considered his private Marilyn file as his own job insurance within the department. Thad Brown stored the file in his garage in Northridge, where copies of Marilyn Monroe's telephone records were to mold in the dark for thirteen years.

Cursum Perficio

Marilyn Monroe will go on eternally.
—Jacqueline Kennedy Onassis

On Sunday, August 5, Marilyn Monroe's body was "posted," or made ready for release to the next of kin. But there seemed to be no loved ones and no immediate family. Her mother, Mrs. Gladys Baker Eley, was confined to the Rockhaven Sanitarium in Norwalk, California. A call to an official of the sanitarium elicited the response, "Mrs. Eley has never heard of Marilyn Monroe." Ultimately, Marilyn's half sister, Berniece Miracle, who lived in Gainesville, Florida, authorized release of the body to Joe DiMaggio.

Arrangements were made by DiMaggio and Inez Melson, Gladys's guardian, with funeral director Guy Hockett of the Westwood Village Mortuary. The funeral was scheduled for 1 P.M. on Wednesday, August 8, at Westwood Memorial Park, where Marilyn had buried two of her surrogate mothers: Grace McKee Goddard, who died in 1953; and "Aunt" Ana Lower, the only person in Marilyn's childhood who had shown her an unqualified degree of love and affection. Hockett recalled that Marilyn frequently spent long hours in the cemetery sitting on a bench near Ana Lower's grave.

Monroe's body arrived at the mortuary at noon on Tuesday, August 7.

That afternoon Allan "Whitey" Snyder, Marilyn's makeup artist, received a call from DiMaggio.

"Whitey, . . . you promised, remember?"

In 1952 Marilyn had undergone an appendectomy at Cedars of Lebanon Hospital in Los Angeles. On the day she was released Whitey arrived and worked his magic—making her radiantly beautiful for the waiting press. Afterward Marilyn elicited a promise.

"Promise me something, Whitey."

"Anything, Marilyn."

"Promise me that, if something happens to me—please, never let anybody touch my face but you. Promise you'll do my makeup, so I'll look my best."

"Sure," he said, jokingly. "Bring the body back while it's still warm, and I'll do it!"

Several weeks later Whitey received a gift package from Tiffany's. Inside was a gold money clip with the engraving:

> Whitey Dear:
> While I'm still warm . . .
> Marilyn

Fortified with a bottle of Smirnoff, Whitey drove to the mortuary, where he did Marilyn's makeup for her final appearance. Sidney Guilaroff was supposed to do Marilyn's hair, but when he saw her body, he collapsed on the mortuary floor. Instead, she wore the wig from *The Misfits*.

On Tuesday afternoon, Mrs. Murray met Inez Melson and Berniece Miracle at Marilyn's house to select what Marilyn would wear. They chose the pale green Pucci dress Marilyn had worn at a press conference in Mexico City earlier in the year.

Hockett's assistant, Alan Abbott, recalled that DiMaggio spent the entire night beside her casket in the Chapel of the Palms. On Wednesday morning, when Whitey Snyder returned to check the makeup job, DiMaggio was still there. "His eyes were red from weeping, and he was transfixed, gazing at her," Whitey recalled. "There were a lot of thought waves bouncing around that silent chapel—a lot of love, regrets, anger, frustration, and sorrow. It was a bit eerie. I think he blamed Hollywood for her death—Hollywood and the Kennedys."

Joe DiMaggio had always been in love with Norma Jeane. His biggest rival was Marilyn Monroe. He felt their relationship had been damaged by her career, and he wanted none of the Hollywood element at her funeral—no stars, producers, agents, Hollywood friends, or press. Only thirty relatives and friends were to be admitted; included were the Strasbergs, Berniece Miracle, Mickey Rudin, Ralph Greenson and his family, Eunice Murray, Whitey Snyder, Ralph Roberts, Inez Melson, and Pat Newcomb. The only newsperson admitted was DiMaggio's friend Walter Winchell. Among those who wanted to attend, but were shut out at the gate, were Frank Sinatra, Dean Martin, Peter and Pat Lawford, the entire Hollywood press corps, and the Who's Who of Hollywood.

Shortly before she died Marilyn Monroe had said, "Everybody is always tugging at you. They'd all like sort of a chunk of you. They kind of like take pieces out of you." Ironically, among the few invited mourners were those who had been the most voracious.

Over fifty Los Angeles police officers controlled the crowds and traffic. Twentieth Century-Fox hired another forty security guards to keep the uninvited out of the cemetery. Bleachers were built along the exterior of the north wall to accommodate the press. Robert Slatzer, who had flown in from Columbus, Ohio, was among the crowd mourning behind the barricades.

Because of the traffic, the services started late. Inside, only the distant drone of media helicopters broke the silence. Eunice Murray recalled, "The handful of mourners seemed to sit withdrawn and remote, each lost in his own thoughts."

As Guy Hockett's wife began playing "Over the Rainbow" on the organ, DiMaggio tearfully sat near the front of the chapel next to his son, Joe Jr. Lee Strasberg then read the brief eulogy:

Marilyn Monroe was a legend.

In her own lifetime she created a myth of what a poor girl from a deprived background could attain. For the entire world she became a symbol of the eternally feminine.

But I have no words to describe the myth and the legend. I did not know this Marilyn Monroe.

We, gathered here today, knew only Marilyn—a warm human being, impulsive and shy, sensitive and in fear of rejection, yet ever avid for life and reaching out for fulfillment.

Despite the heights and brilliance she had attained on the screen, she was planning for the future; she was looking forward to participating in the many exciting things which she planned. In her eyes and in mine her career was just beginning. The dream of her talent, which she had nurtured as a child, was not

a mirage. . . . Others were as physically beautiful as she was, but there was obviously something more in her, something that people saw and recognized in her
performances and with which they identified. She had a luminous quality—a
combination of wistfulness, radiance, yearning—to set her apart and yet made
everyone wish to be part of it, to share in the childish naïveté which was at once
so shy and yet so vibrant.

Now it is all at an end. I hope that her death will stir sympathy and understanding for a sensitive artist and woman who brought joy and pleasure to the
world.

I cannot say good-bye. Marilyn never liked good-byes, but in the peculiar way
she had of turning things around so that they faced reality—I will say au revoir.
For the country to which she has gone, we must all someday visit.

Before the casket was closed, DiMaggio stood and took a long last look.
Eunice Murray remembered Marilyn looking like a child sleeping peace-
fully among the flowers—forever young and beautiful. DiMaggio bent
down and kissed her on the forehead, murmuring, "I love you, I love you,
I love you."

The procession of mourners wordlessly followed the casket to the Corridor of Memories, where her body was entombed. After the rites they
silently dispersed. Soon the frenzied fans and the frustrated press invaded
the cemetery—trampling graves, crushing flowers, grasping souvenirs.

After everyone was gone, that evening, DiMaggio returned and said his
last farewell. For the next twenty years Joe DiMaggio had fresh red roses
placed in the urn beside the crypt where Norma Jeane's body rests today
behind the variegated marble with the simple bronze plaque:

MARILYN MONROE
1926–1962

Answers and Questions

Oh, what is the answer?
what is the answer?
what is the answer?
what is the answer?
what is the question?
—Gertrude Stein

Several days after the funeral, Sergeant Robert Byron of the West Los Angeles Division sought to interview Peter Lawford. He was told by the actor's secretary that Lawford was out of town and would return to the city in several weeks. The day after the funeral, Peter and Pat Lawford along with Pat Newcomb flew to Hyannisport, where they stayed as guests in Robert Kennedy's residence. On Friday, August 10, Peter Lawford gave an interview to Hearst Washington correspondent Marianne Means:

> "I can't believe her death was anything but an accident," Lawford insisted as he leaned back in the soft overstuffed chair and propped mocassined feet on the coffee table in the empty living room of Attorney General Robert Kennedy. . . . "I just can't believe she's not around," he sighed. . . .
>
> It seemed a bit strange that the close friend of America's most famous sex goddess should be detailing his first-hand impressions of her in a room so linked with another kind of fame. In this house where Bobby Kennedy ran the Kennedy "Intelligence Center" on election night 1960.

Jacqueline Kennedy had departed with Caroline on Tuesday, August 7, for an extended holiday in Europe. On August 11 and 12, President Ken-

nedy, the Lawfords, Pat Newcomb, and White House press secretary
Pierre Salinger spent the weekend in Maine at the retreat of former heavy-
weight champion Gene Tunney on John's Island. Sunday the group spent
the day on board the sixty-two-foot coast guard yacht *Manitou*.

Meanwhile, in Los Angeles, reporter Joe Hyams learned that Lawford's
neighbors were upset that a helicopter had touched down on the Santa
Monica shore behind the Lawford residence in the early hours of Sunday
morning, August 5, blowing sand into their swimming pools. Ward Wood,
another neighbor, had told a police department contact that he saw Bobby
Kennedy arrive in a Mercedes at the Lawford mansion "late Saturday
afternoon or in the early evening."

This information led Hyams to contact Billy Woodfield, who had recently been commissioned by Frank Sinatra to take photos of his private
jet from a helicopter rented from the Conners Helicopter Service of Santa
Monica. Woodfield knew that Sinatra's pal Peter Lawford used the same
services, as did many other Hollywood celebrities. Under the pretext of
doing an article on the helicopter service to the stars, Woodfield asked to
review the Conners flight logs listing all of their famous customers. Turning to the pages dated August 4 and 5, he discovered that a helicopter
had been hired to pick up a passenger at the Lawford beach house early
Sunday morning. Woodfield recently recalled, "The time in the log was
approximately two o'clock Sunday morning. It confirmed what the neighbors had told us."

Attempting to piece together Monroe's last hours, Woodfield then
called Dr. Ralph Greenson. According to Woodfield, the psychiatrist
wouldn't discuss what had occurred, ending the call with, "Look, I cannot
explain myself without revealing things I don't want to reveal. You can't
draw a line and say, 'I'll tell you this, but I won't tell you that.' I can't
talk about it, because I can't tell you the whole story. . . . Listen, talk to
Bobby Kennedy."

Woodfield recalls, "Hyams knew he had a powerful news item." "He
called the attorney general's office and asked if Robert Kennedy would
comment on our information. They called back and said, 'The attorney
general would appreciate it if we didn't file the story.'"

Hyams stated, "I filed the article about Bobby and Marilyn with the
Herald Tribune on the Monday or Tuesday after the funeral, but they
killed it. It never ran."

On Thursday, August 9, Robert Slatzer met with executrix Inez Melson
and Eunice Murray at Monroe's house. "Inez was going through what

remained of Marilyn's papers in the file cabinet kept in the guest cottage," Slatzer recalled, "She told me that when she arrived at the house early Sunday morning she discovered the cabinet had been broken into and many of Marilyn's things were missing. It was obvious that the lock had been forcibly broken."

Slatzer remembered Marilyn's concern over the security of her papers. When she had given him a tour of her new house the previous April, she mentioned that things kept disappearing from her files, and she had ordered the lock changed and bars installed on the guest cottage windows. A bill to the Monroe estate from the A-1 Lock and Safe Company of Santa Monica indicates that the locks were changed on March 15, 1962. When Slatzer asked Melson if she had found Marilyn's red diary, Melson said she didn't know anything about the diary. She hadn't seen it.

Before leaving, Slatzer went with Murray to the bedroom where Marilyn's body had been discovered. Though Murray said she had called Norman Jefferies early Sunday morning to repair the broken window, Slatzer noticed that the window was boarded up and hadn't been repaired. He found shards of broken glass lying outside in the dirt of the flower bed, rather than inside where they logically would have fallen.

Slatzer recalls that the last time he had seen Marilyn was just before he left for Ohio in mid-July. She had called from a public phone, and he remembered the unusual urgency to her voice: "Pick me up at six," Marilyn had asked; "I'll meet you at San Vicente and Carmelina." Slatzer remembers driving to the Brentwood corner near her home. Expecting to wait, he was surprised to find her standing on the corner, a lonely figure who went unrecognized—without makeup and wearing large sunglasses, her blond hair pulled back in a ponytail under a scarf. "Hi," she called out as he pulled up to the curb. She hopped in beside him with a big smile, placing her oversize pocketbook on the floor of his Cadillac.

Though she seemed her effervescent self, as they drove north toward Point Dume just beyond Malibu Beach, Slatzer recalls becoming aware of the emotional difficulties she was going through. Shortly after the president's birthday gala in May, Marilyn was suddenly cut off from communication with Jack Kennedy, and the phone number she had to his private line was disconnected. She had been told in a brutal fashion by Peter Lawford that she was never to speak to the president again.

"It was a devastating emotional blow that led to her breakdown on the set of *Something's Got to Give* at 20th Century-Fox," Slatzer recalled. "In her rage and despondency she placed numerous calls to the White House demanding an explanation. Bobby became the emissary to soothe the fury of the woman scorned. I hadn't realized the extent of her involvement with Bobby until she told me that day. When I last saw her she confided to me that Bobby had only recently tried to sever their relationship as well. Like Jack, Bobby offered no explanation." Slatzer perceived that the Kennedys' rejection had touched a raw nerve in Marilyn, and her devastation was turning to anger.

"What Marilyn revealed to me that day on the beach, I found deeply disturbing," Slatzer confides. She removed her small red diary from her bag and showed Slatzer her "book of secrets."

"What is it?" Slatzer asked.

"It's my diary," she replied, "I want you to look through it."

Slatzer remembers thumbing through the pages and finding notes of her conversations with the Kennedys. Some of the topics included government plans to use mobsters to assassinate Fidel Castro, atomic testing, Sinatra's ties to the underworld, civil rights, Bobby Kennedy's efforts to jail Jimmy Hoffa, and a note indicating that Bobby Kennedy had persuaded the president to withdraw American air cover in the Bay of Pigs disaster. Slatzer said he asked her why she had made the notations.

"Mostly because Bobby liked to talk about political things," she replied. "I wanted to be able to talk about things he was interested in. So I'd make notes after our conversations, and then I'd learn as much as I could about the subjects so that I could talk about them intelligently."

"Has anybody else seen this book?" Slatzer asked.

"Nobody." she answered. "But I'm so angry I may just call a press conference and show it to the whole world and let everybody know what the Kennedys are really like!"

Slatzer recalls trying to persuade her to forget about the Kennedys and concentrate on her career—to put away her diary and not show it to anybody. "Obviously Bobby doesn't want anything more to do with you, and for your own good, you'd better forget about him," he advised.

"It's not that easy," she replied.

Several days later, Slatzer left for Ohio, where he received a series of disturbing calls from Marilyn—ending with the one on Friday, August 3, when it seemed so important for her to locate Robert Kennedy.

Odd Men Out

Who killed Marilyn Monroe?—that's a question . . . that was a tragedy.
—Sean O'Casey

Several weeks after the coroner's verdict, Jack Clemmons returned to Fifth Helena Drive to question Marilyn Monroe's neighbors in an unofficial capacity. Elizabeth Pollard, the neighbor directly across the cul-de-sac, told him that Bobby Kennedy had visited the Monroe home in the weeks before her death, and that he had been there late in the day on Saturday, August 4. The neighbors to the immediate west of the Monroe house, Mr. and Mrs. Abe Landau, said they had seen an ambulance and a police car parked at the entry to the Monroe residence when they returned from a dinner party late Saturday night.

Clemmons believed he was the first officer called to the scene at 4:25 Sunday morning, so he was perplexed by the Landaus' statement. He wondered if the police car they saw could have been the patrol car that Sergeant Marvin Iannone checked out of the Purdue Street garage before the 11:30 P.M. roll call Saturday night. Iannone was known to work for Hamilton in Intelligence, and whenever the president or the attorney general visited the Lawfords, Iannone received the special duty assignment from Hamilton to work the Lawford beach house.

In an interview in 1994, Clemmons recalled an encounter with Iannone at the Purdue Street station in the weeks following Monroe's death. "Say, Marv, you know what I think?" asked Clemmons, "I think Marilyn Monroe was murdered, and they're covering up this whole damn thing because the attorney general was involved! What do you think?" Iannone stared at him for a few moments before turning and walking away without uttering a word.

"He really avoided me after that," Clemmons recounted, "Twenty years later, when Marv became police chief of Beverly Hills, and the district attorney's office was putting together the threshold investigation on the Monroe case, I called him several times, but Marv never returned the calls. Maybe he thought I was going to ask him the same question—I was!"

Robert Slatzer also returned again to Fifth Helena Drive to speak to Monroe's neighbors. Elizabeth Pollard told him she remembered having friends over for cards on Saturday, August 4, and one of her guests remarking, "Oh, look, there's Robert Kennedy!" They watched him walk into the Monroe residence with two other men in the late evening. Slatzer then sought out the officer reported to be the first policeman on the scene, Sergeant Jack Clemmons. The two men discovered that they shared the same suspicions.

"Clemmons was convinced from the beginning that Marilyn was murdered," Slatzer remembers. "On a scale of ten he was way over the top on that, but he had nothing to go on other than circumstances at the death scene and his gut feelings. I knew there was motive. After talking to Clemmons and the neighbors, I made up my mind to pursue it."

Following up on the Landaus' statement regarding the ambulance, Slatzer spoke to Walter Schaefer of the Schaefer Ambulance Service, which received most of the emergency calls in the Brentwood area. Schaefer assured Slatzer that none of his ambulances had been called to Fifth Helena Drive on August 4 or 5.

Slatzer also made repeated calls to Peter Lawford that went unreturned. He found that Eunice Murray's phone had been disconnected and was told by neighbors that she had vacated her one-room Ocean Park apartment and left for an extended vacation in Europe. Slatzer found that Pat Newcomb had also suddenly vanished. She moved from her Beverly Hills apartment, leaving no forwarding address. A contact at Arthur Jacobs's public relations firm informed Slatzer that Pat Newcomb had been dismissed and was traveling abroad. In trying to speak to Dr. Ralph Greenson,

Slatzer was told by the doctor's secretary that Greenson had also left Los Angeles for an extended period of time.

The death of Marilyn Monroe was devastating to Ralph Greenson. A colleague at the Los Angeles Psychoanalytic Society and Institute commented, "The fire went out in Dr. Greenson when Marilyn Monroe died. He never really recovered. He went on, but he turned inward after that. . . . He became a bit strange."

"Marilyn's death was extremely painful for him," his wife, Hildi Greenson, confirmed. "Not just that it was so public, which was terrible in itself, but that Marilyn, he felt, was doing much better—and then he lost her. That was quite painful."

Dr. Greenson was suffering to such a degree that he found it impossible to keep his office appointments with his regular patients. "It was awful," he recalled, "But I felt I had to go on. And I went on, and I *was* upset. And my patients saw me upset. . . . With some of them, I had tears in my eyes, and I couldn't hide it."

Actress Janice Rule, who was a patient of Dr. Greenson's at the time, recalled the depth of Greenson's anguish and remembered him stating, "There is no way in my lifetime I will ever be able to answer any of this." A week after Marilyn's funeral, Greenson took a leave of absence to visit his friend and colleague Dr. Max Schur in New York. Schur, a practicing psychoanalyst, had been an associate and personal physician of Sigmund Freud. Schur and Greenson had met when Greenson was a student in Bern and Vienna. In his deep distress, Greenson turned to Schur for emotional support. Their first session lasted twelve hours—the beginning of prolonged therapy in which Greenson hoped to "eventually *begin* to get over this." Seven years later Greenson was still "devastated." He told associates, "I don't know that I will ever get over it really or completely."

In the weeks following the funeral, the press revealed that Marilyn Monroe had left the bulk of her estate to Lee Strasberg, but that she had died broke and in debt. Though columnists Walter Winchell and Dorothy Kilgallen occasionally printed items about the strange circumstances of the film star's death, the tragedy faded from the news, and the Marilyn Monroe story seemed on its way to becoming just another sad chapter in *Hollywood Babylon.* By year's end, the police department closed its file on the case. When asked in later years what happened to the Monroe file,

Captain James Hamilton's former assistant, Lieutenant Marion Phillips, said, "In 1962 Chief Parker took the file to show someone in Washington. That was the last we heard of it."

The records show that Parker's only trip to Washington after Monroe's death was on December 10, 11, and 12, 1962. Correspondence between Parker and Robert Kennedy in the Kennedy Library reveals that Parker met with Kennedy on December 12 at the Park University Motel in College Park, Maryland, about something Parker described in his letter as "a matter of mutual interest."

In June of 1963, Hamilton suddenly resigned his position as chief of the Intelligence Division, and Parker selected Daryl Gates to replace him. "I was astonished," Gates remarked. "Jim Hamilton, the captain of Intelligence, was Parker's man in that position from day one and I had assumed Jim would never leave." But Hamilton went on to a better-paying job as head of security for the National Football League. "Robert Kennedy suggested Jim," Daryl Gates recalled. Before departing, Captain Hamilton promoted Marvin Iannone to lieutenant and transferred him to the downtown office of the Intelligence Division.

When Pat Newcomb returned from her European trip in February of 1963, she relocated to Washington, D.C., where she became liaison officer of the United States Information Agency headed by George Stevens, Jr. George and Liz Stevens were personal friends of Bobby and Ethel Kennedy, as was Pat's immediate boss, Don Wilson. Newcomb served as the liaison between Hollywood and the Capitol, organizing Hollywood participation in film festivals around the world and arranging for motion-picture personalities, such as Kirk Douglas, to travel abroad and make personal appearances at international motion-picture events. In between her worldwide travels Newcomb socialized with the Kennedys; she was frequently a guest at Hickory Hill. In late October 1963 she fell from a horse while riding with Bobby Kennedy and broke her arm. Correspondence between Kennedy and Newcomb in which she refers to herself as "Berthe Bronco" and Kennedy refers to himself as "Charlie Generous" reveals a lighthearted amusement concerning the episode.

On November 22, 1963, when Bobby Kennedy received a call at Hickory Hill from J. Edgar Hoover, stating, "The president is dead," Pat Newcomb helped look after his children while he flew to Dallas to bring back his brother's body.

The Paper Chase

The highest duty of the writer is to remain true to himself and to let the chips fall where they may. In serving his vision of the truth the artist best serves his nation.

—John F. Kennedy, October 1963

Over a hundred and ten books have been published on the subject of Marilyn Monroe since her death. In 1964, Frank Capell's seventy-page booklet, *The Strange Death of Marilyn Monroe*, was the first to say that the film star was murdered, and that the Kennedys were involved. Capell, whom many considered to be a right-wing extremist, was a former FBI agent and publisher of an anticommunist pamphlet, *Herald of Freedom*. He claimed that Marilyn Monroe's murder was part of a communist plot involving Jack and Robert Kennedy. Capell's extremism obscured many of the accurate revelations contained in his slender book.

Though the publication received scant attention, it was reviewed by J. Edgar Hoover. A personal memo from the FBI director to Attorney General Robert Kennedy dated July 8, 1964, states:

Mr. Frank A. Capell is publishing a 70-page paperback book entitled "The Strange Death of Marilyn Monroe," which should be ready for publication about July 10, 1964.

According to Mr. Capell, his book will make reference to your alleged friendship with the late Marilyn Monroe. Mr. Capell stated he will indicate in his book that you and Miss Monroe were intimate and that you were in Miss Monroe's residence at the time of her death.

Any additional information concerning the publication of the above book will be promptly brought to your attention.

Critics scoffed at Capell, but Robert Kennedy took him seriously. When Richard Nixon released a long list of people whose phones had been tapped during previous administrations, Capell appeared on a list of those put under surveillance by Robert Kennedy.

Another writer, Fred Lawrence Guiles, first became intrigued by the Monroe story when he traveled to Reno in September of 1960. He discovered that *The Misfits'* crew was filming nearby and began frequenting the location, where he befriended the film's producer, Frank Taylor, and Marilyn's masseur, Ralph Roberts. Eventually he was introduced to Marilyn. Though he never saw her again after *The Misfits* wrapped production, he was forever captivated and became one of her biographers. Deeply disturbed by the news of her death, in 1963 Guiles wrote a screenplay, *Goodbye, Norma Jean*, envisioned as a motion-picture biography. Frank Taylor brought Guiles's screenplay to the attention of Pat Newcomb, who at that time was assisting Bobby Kennedy in preparing the cinematic eulogy to John Kennedy, *Years of Lightning—Day of Drums*, for the U.S. Information Agency.

With the assistance of Newcomb, *Goodbye, Norma Jean* became enlarged into a *Ladies' Home Journal* magazine series in 1967 called *The Final Summer of Marilyn Monroe*. Newcomb assumed that Robert Kennedy's involvement with Marilyn would not be mentioned; however, Guiles discreetly referred to "An Easterner—a married man not in the [film] industry . . . an Easterner with few ties on the coast . . . a lawyer and public servant with an important political career . . . an attorney who often stayed at his host's beach house." "The Easterner's" identity was readily discernible beneath the disguise, and he was about to run for president. Newcomb had only recently recruited Barbra Streisand, Warren Beatty, and her accumulated coterie of Hollywood friends to support "the Easterner's" campaign. Newcomb was so angered by Guiles's revelation that she hasn't spoken to him since.

Guiles's magazine series was subsequently published as a book in 1969 under the title *Norma Jean: The Life of Marilyn Monroe*. (The correct spelling, as indicated on the birth certificate, is Norma Jeane.) It became a runaway bestseller, and for the first time the general public learned about Marilyn's relationship with a "public servant with an important political career." Guiles accepted the coroner's verdict of probable suicide, but Robert Slatzer did not, nor did he hesitate to reveal the name of "the Easterner." Though Slatzer was a writer of romantic fiction, he found himself becoming an investigative journalist out of necessity—nobody else knew what he knew. Imbued with a love of classic literature, Slatzer had arrived in Hollywood in the 1940s with a young man's high hopes of becoming an important screenwriter. He eked out a living as a journalist for Scripps-Howard, and in time he did well as a Hollywood writer and director.

Initially Slatzer's investigation into Marilyn Monroe's death was an attempt to bring about an official inquiry; however, he soon discovered that the doors in the long marble halls of officialdom were firmly closed to him. In time he joined forces with Frank Capell and Jack Clemmons in the accumulation of investigative information. What started as a small file ended up a vast storehouse of material that now overflows his Hollywood Hills home.

Slatzer began compiling his investigative information in book form in 1964, but it was a long, tortuous odyssey from conception to completion. Death threats, beatings, break-ins, and arson lay along Slatzer's labyrinthine path to publication. At one time in 1972 the monitored death threats became so severe that Slatzer was compelled by the Los Angeles Police Department to have a bodyguard.

When Slatzer's book *The Life and Curious Death of Marilyn Monroe* was finally published in 1974, *Publishers Weekly* termed it "bizarre and disturbing . . . touching and convincing." Briefly on the bestseller list, it was the first major volume to document evidence that Marilyn Monroe was a homicide victim and that Robert Kennedy was implicated. Included in Slatzer's book was the transcript of an interview he conducted with a man named Jack Quinn. Quinn had contacted Slatzer in 1972, after reading about his forthcoming book in a newspaper. Quinn claimed he worked for the Los Angeles Hall of Records and had recently reduced the Monroe police file to microfilm. He gave Slatzer permission to record their conversation, which is preserved in the Slatzer archives:

QUINN: You're right about the coroner's inadequate investigation. . . . Did you see the photographs of her . . . the coroner's photographs taken in her bedroom?

SLATZER: No.

QUINN: She had bruises on her, but they were edited out of the final report. . . .
I saw the reports from the intelligence units. We were supposed to destroy a
lot of their original records and condense everything into a neat package for
microfilming.

SLATZER: So what do you make of it?

QUINN: The bruises? I don't know what they mean. . . . Bobby went to the house
to see her—that's what the police record says. Bobby went to see her on that
last Saturday. That was after he got a call from her at Peter Lawford's house.
Now, the day before, when she was supposed to have been hysterical—I guess
that was sometime in the late afternoon—she was saying how she was going
to do this and that . . .

SLATZER: What else did you spot to make you suspicious?

QUINN: . . . One of the queer things about the Marilyn Monroe case was how
the original folder from the autopsy report happened to get lost . . . and when
they found it all that stuff about the two Kennedy brothers was taken out.
. . . Everything from the investigative report over the ten previous days, going
back from Marilyn's last Saturday to the previous Wednesday, was not there
anymore.

SLATZER: Any idea why?

QUINN: Because of the position of the Kennedy family. Actually, he didn't lie.
He just didn't tell the truth.

SLATZER: Who?

QUINN: Bobby. When he gave his statement to the police—

SLATZER: He clouded it, in other words.

QUINN: Yeah. And did you know about the chloral hydrate? I'm talking about
the discovery of Nembutal and chloral hydrate.

SLATZER: Noguchi was the one who did the autopsy on her.

QUINN: Yeah, that's him. But when they did the autopsy on her, things like
disclosing the shade of her fingernails never came out. I'm trying to tell you
about the effect of chloral hydrate and Nembutal have on the fingernails, like
turning them blue. Well, anyhow, all that was cut out. They did a hell of an
editing job on that damned thing. . . . Do you know the whole record ran 723
pages, and they boiled it down to 54?

SLATZER: But everything's on the microfilm in its original form—right?

QUINN: Well, you can petition the city for a hundred years, and they're going
to deny it exists. And what they'll probably release is the fifty-four pages.

Quinn and Slatzer then met at a Hollywood restaurant. Slatzer brought
along cinematographer Wilson Hong to witness the conversation. Quinn
asserted that an official statement was made by Bobby Kennedy to the
Los Angeles Police Department. "From what I saw in the deposition, it
said that there was almost a divorce pending with Jackie and JFK."

Slatzer asked, "Wasn't there anything about Bobby's having an affair
with Marilyn?"

"No," Quinn replied. "All Bobby said was that JFK was supposed to have been involved with Marilyn and that JFK had dispatched him to come out here and talk to Marilyn because JFK was getting a lot of phone calls from Marilyn and was afraid of the embarrassment it might cause him. Bobby also said that his brother was having wife problems because of Marilyn's calls to the White House. All of this was in Bobby Kennedy's deposition." Quinn then went on to say, "Bobby also said in his deposition that he and Peter Lawford went to Marilyn's house late in the afternoon of August 4. There was a violent argument and Marilyn was grabbed by Bobby and thrown to the floor. . . . Then she was given an injection of pentobarbital in her armpit, which settled her down."

Slatzer then asked, "Does the record show that one of them injected Marilyn with the drugs?"

"No," Quinn replied. "One of them called for a doctor to come over and give Marilyn the injection."

"What doctor?" Slatzer inquired.

"I don't remember his name," Quinn responded. "All I can tell you is that Kennedy's deposition shows that Marilyn went into a tantrum and that she was screaming, 'I'm tired of this whole thing, of being a plaything!' Bobby said that Marilyn complained that she was called over to Lawford's house at times when they had prostitutes and that she was tired of the whole mess."

Quinn then told Slatzer that according to the deposition, Marilyn lunged at Bobby and clawed him. Quinn went on to say, "It's also on the record that the doctor came to the house at five o'clock. There's a statement from him that he gave her a shot. But he didn't say what drug was in the shot. But RFK said in his statement that the doctor gave Marilyn the shot under her left arm. He even named the artery on the tape. He said the shot that went into her was pentobarbital."

Quinn ended by saying that the records also showed that Monroe's death involved a "communist-inspired plot."

Slatzer said these words made him skeptical. Nevertheless, he agreed to meet with Quinn again that night at eight. Slatzer arrived with photographer Wilson Hong ten minutes early, but Jack Quinn never showed up. After several days in which Slatzer vainly waited for Quinn to call, he drove to the Hall of Records and discovered there was no employee by the name of "Jack Quinn," nor did anyone answer to his description. Slatzer never heard from the mysterious Jack Quinn again.

"Frankly, I didn't know what to think about Quinn," Slatzer recalls.

"He seemed genuine, but when he mentioned the 'communist-inspired plot'—as I heard those words spoken, I didn't know what to believe. Quinn came on the scene at the end of ten years of a very frustrating investigation, and I had been lied to so many times I just didn't feel capable of believing anyone anymore. I've tried to forget about Jack Quinn."

However, there's good reason to take a second look at the mysterious Jack Quinn. In 1972 he knew many secrets that have since been verified.

In 1972 only the police and the FBI knew about Marilyn's disturbing telephone calls and letters to the White House and the Justice Department. The phone records weren't made public until investigative journalist Anthony Summers published them in *Goddess* in 1985. Quinn also knew about the bruises on Marilyn's body ten years before Grandison stated that there were bruises excluded from the autopsy report. He also placed Bobby Kennedy and Peter Lawford at Marilyn's home on Saturday afternoon, August 4, 1962, long before witnesses corroborated this. And finally, Quinn knew the effects of cyanosis that had turned Marilyn Monroe's fingernails blue—a fact substantiated in 1993 by photographer Leigh Wiener, who took photos of the body in the morgue. It is therefore clearly possible that the mysterious "Jack Quinn" had access to the 723-page Marilyn Monroe file secreted in the Intelligence Division of the LAPD, the same extensive file that intelligence officer Mike Rothmiller was to view in 1978.

The curiosity of the public and the press was aroused by the many unanswered questions posed by the publication of *The Life and Curious Death of Marilyn Monroe*. Norman Mailer's 1973 bestseller *Marilyn* also alleged a relationship between Marilyn and Jack and Bobby Kennedy. Mailer concluded that "every implication of the evidence was toward murder," and along with Robert Slatzer, publicly called for an official inquiry.

Los Angeles County Supervisor Mike Antonovich supported the growing demand for a grand jury investigation, and the police department was besieged by questions it couldn't answer. Many of those with firsthand knowledge of the Monroe case were deceased: James Hamilton, former head of the Intelligence Division, died in 1964 of a brain tumor; in 1966 Chief William Parker died during a testimonial dinner in his honor; and homicide detective Thad Brown died in 1972.

Scrambling for facts to feed a voracious press, the LAPD asked Hamilton's successor, Captain Daryl Gates, to formulate an in-house report to fend off the call for an official inquiry. Faced with composing an investigative report on Marilyn Monroe, Captain Gates joined the paper chase.

Gates claimed he wasn't able to find anything in the official police files—not even Monroe's death report. However, he followed up on the rumor that Thad Brown had kept his own copy of the Monroe file. Accompanied by Thad's brother, Finis, Gates discovered the unauthorized file Thad Brown had secreted in his garage, where they had moldered for over thirteen years.

The voluminous material comprised over 700 pages of documents, interviews, depositions, photographs, and reports. Gates elected to use only 19 pages of the original files, saying that certain information was withheld as "not part of the public record."

Among the discoveries in Thad Brown's garage were copies of Marilyn Monroe's phone records, which Hamilton had removed from the General Telephone Company on the night of her death—records Chief Parker had denied obtaining. It would be yet another seven years before the LAPD would finally admit having them in its possession.

In 1975, when he was director of operations, Daryl Gates decided to interview Peter Lawford and add his statement to the selected items to be included in his report. While Peter Lawford's recitation of the events had always supported the official version, Lawford had never been officially interviewed by the police. Several days after Marilyn Monroe's death, Sergeant Byron had tried to interview Peter Lawford but was told by his secretary that "Lawford had flown out of the city" and would not be available for several weeks. Six hundred and eighty weeks later, the police interview took place—on October 16, 1975.

Time and circumstances had collected their toll: Jack and Robert Kennedy had been assassinated; Peter and Pat Lawford had been divorced; Lawford's career had plummeted, and he had become a hopeless drunk and drug addict. Having lost his wealth, he moved from the former Louis B. Mayer beach mansion to a small apartment in West Hollywood on the wrong side of the Strip. Everything had changed—except Lawford's story about the night Marilyn Monroe died.

Gates's "in-house" investigation continued until the public outcry for a grand jury investigation had subsided. The final report, issued on October 22, 1975, found "insufficient evidence to warrant an official investigation. Some of the evidence is as thin as Depression food-line soup."

The 165-page report consisted of forty-five pages photocopied from Slatzer's book; a copy of the Lawford interview; a Xerox copy of Monroe's last will and testament; a list of debtors' claims to her estate; a compendium of crank letters sent to the Police Department; a Xerox copy of the autopsy report; and a scrapbook of Monroe's newspaper clippings.

This "exhaustive" report, which undoubtedly required going to the Xerox room on numerous occasions during the year it took to prepare, contained no interviews with the key witnesses—other than Peter Lawford. One of the key witnesses Gates failed to interview was Dr. Ralph Greenson. Photographs of Greenson taken in his later years reveal an extraordinary physical and emotional decline. When he returned to Los Angeles after a lengthy period of analysis with Dr. Max Schur, he shared offices with his friend and associate Dr. Hyman Engelberg at 465 North Roxbury Drive in Beverly Hills. Taking on fewer patients, he immersed himself in teaching and writing.

In his later years Greenson suffered from depression, coronary illness, and an episode of aphasia. "That was very hard for someone who had so many words for everything." recalled his patient Janice Rule. "He became enraged when he found he couldn't express himself." Ralph Greenson died under the care of Dr. Engelberg on November 24, 1979, at the age of sixty-eight.

The death of Ralph Greenson silenced forever the voice of one of the most important of the key witnesses to the circumstances of Marilyn Monroe's death. Whatever he revealed to John Miner was secreted within the hallows of professional confidentiality. However, disturbed by allegations in Donald Spoto's 1993 book, *Marilyn Monroe: The Biography*, that Dr. Greenson was responsible for the actress's death, John Miner obtained permission from Greenson's widow to reveal some of the things he had heard on the tapes Greenson played for him in 1962.

Miner revealed that Greenson told him Marilyn Monroe had recorded the tapes at her home in the days before her death. They were an extension of her free-association sessions with Greenson. Because she had difficulty sleeping, Marilyn suggested she record the tapes at night. She would then give the recordings to Greenson at the following session.

On the tapes played by Greenson during the 1962 interview, Miner stated that Marilyn discussed her relationship with both Jack and Robert Kennedy. "She was very explicit about the sexual relationship," Miner disclosed. Though she had once been in love with Jack Kennedy and couldn't understand why she was suddenly rejected and treated so badly by both Kennedy brothers, she was determined to put the Kennedys behind her and go on with her life.

According to Miner, "The tapes reveal an intelligent woman with a good sense of humor. She had important future plans, and the last thing one could conclude from hearing these tapes was that she was contemplating killing herself.

"Dr. Greenson was of the opinion that she definitely had not committed suicide," Miner continues, "and I don't see how it could have been accidental, with the volume of barbituates that caused death. I don't think she could have swallowed anything like a lethal dose. . . . If there had been an inquest, and I think there should have been, I think there would have been clearer evidence that it was not a suicide."

On the basis of the tapes, Greenson's disclosure, and the toxicology report, Miner believes that the case should be reopened. There is no statute of limitations on a homicide. In June 1997 Miner wrote a formal letter to the Los Angeles district attorney, Gil Garcetti, requesting a new formal investigation into Marilyn Monroe's death. He has recommended that the body be exhumed for reexamination and is prepared to testify about the Marilyn Monroe tapes and what Greenson told him during the interview for Coroner Curphey on August 12, 1962.

Los Angeles District Attorney Gil Garcetti has yet to respond to Miner's request.

The Ambulance Chase

When you have excluded the impossible, whatever remains, however improbable, must be the truth.
—Sherlock Holmes, in A. C. Doyle's "The Adventure of the Beryl Coronet"

In 1982, former coroner's aide Lionel Grandison announced to the press that he had been coerced into signing Marilyn Monroe's death certificate, and he revealed that her diary had been stolen from the coroner's safe.

Grandison's disclosures, along with Robert Slatzer's renewed initiatives, culminated in a second recommendation by the Los Angeles Board of Supervisors for a grand jury investigation. However, District Attorney John Van de Kamp hastily called a news conference on August 11, 1982, and announced that he had an investigation already under way. Though there's no record that an investigation had been initiated before Van de Kamp's announcement, it successfully staved off the Board of Supervisors' action. By preempting the grand jury, Van de Kamp, with his informal "threshold investigation," reduced it to a paperwork shuffle—a rephrasing of material previously dispensed to the public. No one was required to testify under oath, and, predictably, the surviving key witnesses Hyman Engelberg, Pat Newcomb, Peter Lawford, Eunice Murray, and Mickey Rudin chose not to talk to investigators.

In an effort to refute suspicions that the overdose of barbiturates had been injected into her bloodstream via a hypodermic needle, Van de Kamp's 1982 report states:

> The ratio of pentobarbital in the blood to that in the liver suggests more grad-ual absorption of the dose associated with oral ingestion as opposed to hypo-dermic injections. . . . This leads to a reasonable conclusion that Miss Monroe had not suffered a "hot shot" or needle injection of a lethal dose. A needle in-jection would have produced a very high blood level of barbiturate. This would have led to a rapid death, and we would not have seen the evidence of the extended metabolic process which allows time for the liver to absorb the toxic substance.

But contrary to the report's statement, Noguchi said that Monroe had such a massive amount of pentobarbital and chloral hydrate in her blood that he ruled out the possibility of an "accidental" suicide. Computerized comparables of forensic medicine indicate that the high blood levels are totally consistent with a "hot shot" leading to rapid death.

Furthermore, the evidence contradicts the report's claim of an "ex-tended metabolic process which allows time for the liver to absorb the toxic substance." Though 13.0 mg percent of pentobarbital was found in her liver, there was no chloral hydrate—clearly indicating that death oc-curred before the chloral hydrate could be absorbed in the metabolic process. Therefore the pentobarbital in the liver was absorbed earlier from her daily prescription dosage, and from the injection Engelberg gave her the previous day.

Further evidence that Monroe received a "hot shot" is the fact that her body exhibited signs of cyanosis—the classic indication of rapid death. In cyanosis the body takes on a bluish cast due to the rapid depletion of oxygen and reduced levels of hemoglobin. The blue cast of the skin is accompanied by a darkening of the fingernails.

One of the witnesses to the cyanosis was Leigh Wiener, who had taken pictures of the body in the morgue. An interview with Wiener appeared in the September 7, 1982, edition of the *Los Angeles Times* in which he discussed the morgue photographs. Wiener stated, "I had photographed the star five times. The last time was on a refrigerated slab. . . . On this occasion, the body of Marilyn Monroe had a distinctive bluish cast to it." Wiener also noted that the fingernails had darkened.

Just as district attorney investigators Ronald Carroll and Alan Tomich were completing their report, the November 23, 1982, edition of the *Globe* ran a sensational account of ambulance driver James Hall's Code 3 call to the Monroe residence on the evening of August 4, 1962. Hall claimed he was a former ambulance driver for the Schaefer Ambulance Service, and that he and his partner, Murray Liebowitz, were returning to the UCLA Medical Center when they received an emergency call to 12305 Fifth Helena Drive. Hall recalled, "We were real close, practically right around the corner. We were at her house within two minutes."

When they arrived a hysterical woman led them to a small guest cottage, separate from the main house, where they found Marilyn Monroe lying nude, faceup on the bed. Her respiration and heartbeat were slight; her pulse was weak and rapid.

Because CPR requires strong back support, Hall and Liebowitz moved Monroe from the bed to the floor of an adjoining foyer and, placing an airway tube to facilitate breathing, they began resuscitation.

Hall recalled, "The hysterical woman was giving us trouble. She was trying to climb over us to get to Miss Monroe while I was working on her. She was screaming 'She's dead! She's dead!' over and over again. . . . She was hampering what we were doing, but I don't think even a slap in the face would have calmed her down—she was that crazy."

"Soon I was getting a perfect exchange of air from Miss Monroe," he went on. "Her color was starting to come back. I felt she was doing well enough that we could safely take her to the hospital. I said to Murray, 'Get the gurney.' However, at that moment a man carrying a doctor's bag entered the guest cottage and said, 'I'm her doctor. Give her positive pressure.'"

Hall was surprised by the doctor's decision, because the resuscitator was doing its job. "But you never argue with a doctor at the scene of an emergency—never. You'd lose your job," Hall said. "So I took the resuscitator off and began to give her mouth-to-mouth resuscitation while the doctor gave her CPR." Familiar with the "odor of pear" factor in victims of chloral hydrate ingestion, Hall said he did not detect it, nor was there indication of vomitus.

As her vital signs deteriorated, the doctor opened his bag and pulled out a syringe with a heart needle affixed to it. He filled the syringe from a pharmaceutical bottle of adrenaline. The doctor then attempted to inject the stimulant into her heart in an attempt to revive her. "He did it at an incorrect angle," according to Hall, "and the needle hit a rib. Instead of backing it out, he just leaned on it." Hall stated that he believed Marilyn Monroe expired at that moment.*

Placing the stethoscope on her chest, the doctor couldn't find a heart-beat, and according to Hall, he said, "You can leave. I'm going to pro-nounce her dead."

While James Hall was writing his report, a man in a jumpsuit was trying to calm the hysterical woman, who was repeatedly sobbing, "She's dead! She's dead!" Hall noticed that a police officer arrived and briefly spoke to the man in the jumpsuit. The officer then went into the main house before returning to sign Hall's EPA call slip.

Hall later identified the hysterical woman as Pat Newcomb, the man in the jumpsuit as Peter Lawford, the doctor as Ralph Greenson, and the police officer as Sergeant Marvin Iannone.

Hall's revelation was a fascinating but improbable account of events surrounding the circumstances of Marilyn Monroe's death. If his story was to be believed it would explain the neighbor's sighting of the ambulance and police car late Saturday night.†

The story was suspect because it first appeared as tabloid journalism and contradicted the statements of key witnesses. When the press con-fronted Walter Schaefer regarding the tabloid article, Schaefer vehe-mently denied Hall's story and stated that James Hall had never worked for him, and Murray Liebowitz denied having assisted James Hall on the night of the actress's death.

---

* The question arises as to why there was no indication of the puncture mark in the autopsy. There are several possible explanations: 1) It wasn't discovered. 2) It was discovered, but not included in the report because of the problems it presented. 3) The "careful examination for needle marks" occurred *after* the body was opened up and Noguchi was surprised to find that the stomach and small intestine gave no indication of an oral ingestion of the overdose. As Alan Abbott recently stated, "By that time the 'Y' incision in the chest cavity would have obliterated the telling puncture of the heart needle."

† Hall had originally maintained that the Code 3 call to the Monroe residence was between 2 and 4 A.M. Sunday; however, substantial evidence indicates that Monroe died at approximately 10:45 Saturday night. It was late Saturday night that the neighbors saw the ambulance at the residence. The time discrepancy is perhaps explained by Hall's disclosure that he worked a twenty-four-hour shift (a practice now outlawed by the state of California). His shift began at four o'clock Saturday afternoon. Between ambulance calls Hall tried to sleep on a cot provided by Schaefer at the W. L. A. office. On an average twenty-four-hour shift there were often as many as fifteen emergency calls. Hall admitted that it was easy to become time-disoriented on such a schedule. When asked how he had established the time frame of his call to the Monroe residence, he stated that he may have established the time in retrospect, after reading the account in the newspapers on Monday morning.

The ambulance chase came to a screeching halt.

The story, however, alerted the press and the public to the fact that neighbors had seen an ambulance at the death scene. For the first time, Abe Landau and his wife, who still reside next to the former Monroe residence, publicly confirmed that they had seen the ambulance and police car in front of the Monroe driveway late Saturday night, August 4, 1962. At this juncture the ambulance chase resumed and took some hairpin turns.

Compelled by Hall's revelations and the Landaus' statements, the district attorney was forced to address the ambulance story in the 1982 report. Investigator Alan Tomich reviewed the ambulance question with Walter Schaefer, who finally admitted that one of his ambulances had been called to the Monroe residence.

The ambulance story was an inexorable problem for the district attorney. If Hall's statements were correct, and Marilyn Monroe had died in the presence of a doctor in different circumstances and a different location than the coroner had stated, there would be no alternative but to call for an official full-scale inquiry. The solution to the problem was an artful study in the dissemination of disinformation.

While refusing to interview James Hall, the district attorney's office found its solution in interviewing a Mr. Ken Hunter, who said it was he, not James Hall, who had responded to the Schaefer Code 3 call to the Monroe residence. Page 16 of the district attorney's report states:

> Since James Hall's statements surfaced another person, a Mr. Ken Hunter, has been located who claims to have been an ambulance driver who responded to the Monroe residence in the early morning hours of August 5, 1962. He reports that he arrived at the scene in the morning hours with his partner, whom he believes with reasonable certainty to have been a Mr. Murray Liebowitz, and entered the Monroe residence within one or two minutes of their arrival. He observed Miss Monroe in the bedroom, on her face or side. He reported to us that Miss Monroe was obviously dead and exhibited signs of lividity in the neck or front portion of her body. . . . Mr. Ken Hunter reports that after he and his partner made cursory observations of the body, they both left the scene. He reports that police officers were at the scene at the time he and his partner left.

Ken Hunter's story was accepted, and James Hall's story was dismissed without investigation. The report states, "Mr. James Hall's declarations concerning his conduct and observations at the scene of death are not credible." However, there were intrinsic problems with Ken Hunter's story.

Hunter had said that "police officers were at the scene at the time he and his partner left." But according to the official version of events, Sergeant Jack Clemmons was the first officer on the scene, arriving at 4:40 A.M. Clemmons confirmed in 1993, "There was no ambulance or attendants at the house when I arrived, or at any time while I was there." Neither Sergeant Robert Byron, James Bacon, Joe Hyams, nor Billy Woodfield recalls seeing an ambulance in the early hours of Sunday morning after Clemmons's departure.

But there was a bigger problem with Hunter's story: Ken Hunter didn't work for Schaefer in 1962. Carl Bellonzi, vice president of the Schaefer Ambulance Service, who has worked for the company for over forty years, stated in 1993 that Ken Hunter wasn't employed by Schaefer until the mid-1970s, and that Hunter never worked the West Los Angeles area. He was an employee in the 1970s and 1980s in the Orange County office.

Robert Slatzer returned to the offices of Walter Schaefer in 1985 and again questioned him about the ambulance call, and in a recorded interview Schaefer changed his story for the third time. "I guess I can tell it," Schaefer began. "I came in the next morning [Sunday, August 5, 1962] and found on the log sheet we had transported Marilyn Monroe. I understood that she had overdosed. She was under the influence of barbiturates. They took her on a Code Three, an emergency, into Santa Monica Hospital, where she terminated." Again he named Hunter as the driver and Liebowitz as the attendant. When asked why the body was returned to her bedroom, Schaefer replied, "Anything can happen in Hollywood."

Ken Hunter disappeared after his statement to the district attorney's office, but Anthony Summers located him in 1984. He proved to be evasive and refused further contact after an initial call. Murray Liebowitz, who had changed his name and moved, was found in 1985. He told Summers, "I don't want to be involved in this. . . . I wasn't on duty that night. . . . I heard about it when I came to work the next morning. . . . I'm not worried about anything. . . . Don't bother to call me anymore."

In the gridlock of the ambulance chase, one thing becomes clear: an ambulance was called on the night Marilyn Monroe died. However, there have been four ambulance stories: 1) Schaefer's initial story that no ambulance was called; 2) Hall's story of Marilyn dying in the guest cottage;

3) Hunter's story that Marilyn was dead in her bedroom; and 4) Schaefer's second story that Marilyn died at the hospital and was brought back to her house.

Story number one can be eliminated by Schaefer's admission. Stories three and four can be eliminated, not only because of their improbability, but because of their impossibility—Ken Hunter was not employed by Schaefer in 1962. That leaves story number two, James Hall's improbable tabloid account of Marilyn Monroe dying in the guest cottage.

Hall's social security records and Schaefer's payroll deductions indicate that Schaefer wrongfully denied that Hall was his employee. A photo in the *Santa Monica Evening Outlook* shows James Hall transporting a crime victim for Schaefer Ambulance Service in September 1962. Interviews with Hall's father, his former wife, his sister, and his longtime friend Mike Carlson confirm that Hall told them his story shortly after Marilyn's death.

Hall recently recalled, "The *Globe* flew me to Florida and gave me six separate polygraph examinations, and I passed them all with flying colors." Polygraph expert John Harrison stated, "As skeptical as I was when I first heard about Hall's story, I can say, unequivocally, there was no deception on his part during the tests. He was absolutely truthful."

Hall was then put under hypnosis by Henry Koder, a professional forensic hypnotist with more than twenty years of crime investigation experience. "Hall was a good subject," Koder stated. "I was able to take him back to the night of Marilyn Monroe's death under hypnosis and listen to his step-by-step description of his involvement. He was able to vividly recall that night and point out details that he hadn't remembered in earlier questioning." Hall later described the interior of the guest cottage, including the location of the bed, nightstand, and telephone, as well as a partition between the bed and foyer. Few people had seen the cottage's interior during Monroe's lifetime, and when the Monroe estate sold the home to a Dr. Nunez, he had removed the partition that Hall described.

Hall was asked to assist in making an Identi-Kit composite drawing of the doctor. The composite drawing bears a likeness to Dr. Greenson. Hall later positively identified Greenson, Newcomb, and Lawford from photographs.

In 1992, James Hall underwent another series of polygraph tests conducted by Don Fraser of Arcadia, California, a state-licensed polygraph examiner who majored in police science at the University of Southern California. Fraser states, "There's no question that James Hall is telling the truth. His story regarding the scene and circumstances of Miss Monroe's death is absolutely true. He passed every question in several exhaustive polygraph examinations."

Clemmons also believed Hall's story. It explained to him why the death scene in the main house seemed disturbed, and why Monroe's body had the appearance of being placed on the bed. "It wasn't natural," he recently stated. "I knew at the time that the doctors and Mrs. Murray were lying to me. Now I know that they must have moved the body and invented the locked room story. The district attorney wouldn't listen to me. I kept telling them that the death scene was arranged, and they said I was hallucinating."

In 1993, Liebowitz was located in a Los Angeles suburb living under the name Murray Leib. He admitted, after thirty years of denial, that he had been with Hall on the call to Monroe's residence. Stating that Hall's account was accurate, he then confirmed that Marilyn Monroe had died in the guest cottage.

Shortly before Walter Schaefer retired from the ambulance business he was once again visited by Robert Slatzer. Asked why he had not told the truth about the ambulance calls, Schaefer simply replied, "Eighty percent of my business came from the county and government agencies." However, Schaefer's explanation was still less than veracious.

The ambulance chase, which began in 1962, finally came to an abrupt and startling conclusion when Clemmons discovered why Walter Schaefer had been such a willing instrument of artful disinformation.

In 1995, Jack Clemmons met Bob Neuman, who had been a pilot for Walter Schaefer. Neuman revealed that in 1947 Schaefer had initiated an air ambulance service located at the San Fernando Valley Airport. During the period of time Neuman was employed by Schaefer in the late fifties and early sixties, the service occasionally made clandestine flights for the U.S. government. Under the pretext of a medical emergency, the air ambulance service could fly into almost any airport in the world. Though Neuman never knew the true identity of many of his passengers, several were easily recognizable. Among them were the president of the United States, the attorney general, and Marilyn Monroe. He recalls flying Marilyn and Jack Kennedy to a private ranch in Idaho in 1961, as well as other flights with the president and women he couldn't identify. There were also several flights to Cal-Neva and Palm Springs in the early sixties, and Neuman specifically recalls piloting Robert Kennedy and Marilyn Monroe to the Bing Crosby ranch in Cabo San Lucas.

Neuman's revelations may also explain what publicist Arthur Jacobs's wife, Natalie, said to Anthony Summers in 1985, "Arthur absolutely knew about the affair between Marilyn and the president. John Kennedy used to come here—Arthur told me this—very often not in Air Force One, but incognito. . . . God knows how he did it."

Today, the Schaefer Air Ambulance Service still soars into the wild blue yonder—ready for any emergency.

Tumblers of Truth

The failure of the authorities to hold a full and open inquiry into the death of Marilyn Monroe is a violation of the people's right to know the truth.
—Anthony Summers, 1995

While the district attorney's 1982 "threshold investigation" accomplished its purpose in successfully blocking the grand jury inquiry, it proved to be the suasive factor in luring eminent journalist Anthony Summers into "the land of the scorpions." The editor of London's *Sunday Express* magazine commissioned Summers to write an article concerning the district attorney's investigation. Arriving in September 1982, Summers anticipated that the assignment would be concluded within a matter of weeks. Three years later he completed *Goddess: The Secret Lives of Marilyn Monroe.*

Interviewing more than 650 people, Summers created a mesmerizing landmark of investigative reporting telling the revealing story of Monroe's intimate relationships with President John Kennedy and Attorney General Robert Kennedy. At the same time he presented a compassionate view of Marilyn Monroe's tragic life.

Dr. Robert Litman of the Suicide Prevention Team was interviewed in June of 1984, and in *Goddess* Summers writes:

I talked to Dr. Robert Litman, one of the two Suicide Prevention Team members who questioned Greenson. He recalls that Greenson was terribly upset, to the extent that Litman felt as much a bereavement counselor as a formal questioner. He had studied under Greenson, respected him greatly, and 'felt it right not to talk about this until after Dr. Greenson's death.' . . . Referring to his notes taken in 1962, Litman disclosed:

> "Around this time, Marilyn started to date some very important men." Greenson had very considerable concern that she was being used in these relationships. . . . However, it seemed so gratifying to her to be associated with such powerful and important men that he could not declare himself against it. . . . He told her to be sure she was doing it for something that she felt was valuable and not just because she felt she had to do it.

> Dr. Litman says today that Greenson spoke to him of a "close relationship with extremely important men in government," that the relationship was "sexual"; and that the men were "at the highest level." Dr. Litman says that while Dr. Greenson did not actually name the Kennedys, he had "no real doubt" whom he meant by "important men in government." Litman also felt Dr. Greenson had not been "totally candid," even with him.

Monroe's calls to Robert Kennedy at the Justice Department were confirmed by Summers's discovery of the telephone records. The records, which had been recovered from Thad Brown's garage by Daryl Gates, were smuggled from the files of the LAPD Intelligence Division and appeared in *Goddess*. They confirmed Florabel Muir's and Robert Slatzer's allegations of Marilyn's numerous calls to Bobby Kennedy at the Justice Department.

A treasure trove of papers kept by executrix Inez Melson was also found by Summers in a file cabinet stored in the Melson garage. It was the same file cabinet that had been broken into in the guest cottage on the night Marilyn died. Inez had repaired the lock and used it for storing what remained of Marilyn's personal papers. Among the papers in Melson's possession was an undated note to Marilyn from Jean Kennedy Smith that referred to Marilyn and Bobby as "the new item."

While Anthony Summers was preparing *Goddess* for publication, another key witness died. His health destroyed by drink and drugs, Peter Lawford succumbed to liver and kidney failure on Christmas Eve, 1984, at the age of sixty-one. At the end of his life he had been shunned by the film industry, alienated from the Kennedy family, and rebuffed by his friends.

Frank Sinatra went so far as to refuse to do a performance at the Sands Hotel in Las Vegas when he learned that Peter Lawford was in the audience. For all his failings, however, Lawford remained loyal to JFK and stuck to the set piece of his story when interviewed by Anthony Summers several months before his death. However, when Lawford was queried on his deathbed by a *Los Angeles Times* reporter about Marilyn Monroe's involvement with the Kennedys, Lawford offered an interesting addendum.

Suddenly sitting up in his bed, he stated, "Even if those things were true, I wouldn't talk about them. That's just the way I am."

Summers's most significant discovery occurred during his interview with Natalie Trundy Jacobs, widow of Monroe's publicist, Arthur Jacobs. Natalie revealed that the alarm regarding Monroe's death was as early as ten forty-five Saturday night—over five and a half hours before Sergeant Jack Clemmons received the call from Dr. Engelberg at four twenty-five Sunday morning.

Natalie recalled that she and her future husband, Arthur Jacobs, were attending a Henry Mancini concert at the Hollywood Bowl when a staff member came to Jacobs's box with an urgent message from Pat Newcomb—Marilyn Monroe was dead.

"We got the news long before it broke," Natalie Jacobs told Summers. "We left the concert at once and Arthur took me home. He went to Marilyn's house, and I don't think I saw him for two days. He had to fudge the press."

Natalie Jacobs was absolutely certain that the news of Marilyn's death reached them shortly before the end of the concert. Summers checked the *Los Angeles Times* for that date and found that the Mancini concert had begun at 8:30 P.M., and it was established that the concert had concluded by 11 P.M. Because of the Hollywood Bowl's proximity to a residential neighborhood, a local ordinance required that Bowl concerts must conclude by eleven.

While Guy Hockett had estimated the time of death as occurring between nine-thirty and eleven-thirty Saturday evening, Natalie Jacobs's revelation allowed for a more precise time frame. If Marilyn Monroe was known to be speaking coherently and quite normally with Joe DiMaggio, Jr.; Sidney Guilaroff; Henry Rosenfeld; Jeanne Carmen; and José Bolaños between 7:30 and 10 P.M., and the Bowl concert necessarily concluded by eleven, then the fatal dose of barbiturates was administered at some time shortly after ten and she succumbed at some time prior to eleven.

Natalie Jacobs's disclosure coincided with the Naars' statement that there was no alarm regarding Marilyn until they had returned to their home sometime after ten o'clock. According to the Naars, it was approximately ten-thirty when Peter Lawford called in a panic about Marilyn, stating that she was incoherent, her voice was fading away, and the phone was left off the hook. The Naars' statement further narrowed the time frame—Marilyn Monroe died between ten-thirty and eleven.

Allowing for the events that necessarily took place between ten-thirty and eleven—the ambulance arrival, the attempts at resuscitation, Greenson pronouncing her dead, and the message being delivered to Arthur Jacobs at the Bowl—the time of Monroe's death can be established as occurring close to 10:30 P.M.

The passage of time and the many variants of disinformation circulated in the following decades dulled the startling significance of Natalie Jacobs's disclosure. The revelation that the alarm regarding Monroe's death had gone out as early as 10:45 P.M. unalterably confirmed that all the key witnesses had conspired to lie in their statements to the police, the coroner's office, and the press.

Natalie Jacobs's statement in 1984 came forward after the conclusion of the 1982 "threshold investigation" by the district attorney; and in 1986, Ronald Carroll, the district attorney's investigator, stated, "Had we known of Natalie Jacobs's statement at the time, it would have cast an entirely different light on our investigation, and perhaps we would have arrived at different conclusions. If her statement proved to be correct, it would have meant that many of the witnesses had lied and there would have inevitably been a full investigation."

Natalie Jacobs maintains that Pat Newcomb sent the message to Arthur Jacobs at the Hollywood Bowl, but Newcomb stated to the press that she first heard about Marilyn's death when she received a 4 A.M. phone call from Mickey Rudin.

In Donald Spoto's book *Marilyn Monroe: The Biography*, published by HarperCollins in 1993, Newcomb insists that she first heard the news of Marilyn's death when called at her Beverly Hills apartment by Mickey Rudin at five o'clock Sunday morning. However, the 1962 Beverly Hills phone directory reveals that Pat Newcomb and Natalie Trundy, the future Mrs. Jacobs, were next-door neighbors. Newcomb lived at 150 South

Canon Drive, and Natalie Trundy resided at 152 South Canon Drive. When recently asked if she had discussed Marilyn's death with her neighbor when she returned home from the Bowl, Natalie stated, "Pat Newcomb wasn't home Saturday night, and didn't return to her apartment until late Sunday."

Where did Newcomb go after driving off from Marilyn's house at approximately 6 P.M. Saturday? Witnesses attest that she arrived at Peter Lawford's beach house sometime after nine. Bullets Durgom said, "The one thing I remember clearly is Pat Newcomb coming in at maybe nine-thirty. She stood on the step and said, 'Peter, Marilyn's not coming. She's not feeling well.'" In 1985 Patricia Seaton Lawford, who was Lawford's last wife and lived with him for eleven years, also confirmed that Newcomb was at the beach house that night.

Ambulance driver James Hall's identification of Lawford and Newcomb being at the scene when the ambulance arrived establishes an evident sequence of events.

When the alarming call was received by Lawford, and Marilyn apparently lapsed into unconsciousness, he then called back and found both lines busy. The operator then told him that both lines were off the hook with no conversation taking place. The private line in her bedroom had remained off the hook when Marilyn had set down the receiver in the middle of her conversation with José Bolaños "and never returned." The extension of the house phone in the guest cottage was also off the hook because she was clutching the receiver in her hand when she lapsed into unconsciousness.

Lawford then called the Naars in a panic and asked Joe to find out what was wrong. Perhaps it was Newcomb who then cautioned Lawford of the danger of having Naar check on Marilyn. Just as Naar was about to leave, Lawford then called back and defused the alarm.

For years Lawford publicly lamented not having rushed over to Marilyn's house, but that is precisely what he did. He and Newcomb raced over to Marilyn's in Lawford's Mercedes to see what was wrong. On a Saturday night between ten and eleven, it was approximately an eight-minute drive from the Lawford beach house to the Monroe residence. Arriving at approximately 10:35 P.M., they were there minutes before the ambulance.

In 1992 Mickey Rudin finally admitted that he knew about Monroe's death late Saturday night. Rudin recalled having returned from a dinner party at the home of Mildred Allenberg well before midnight when he received a call from Ralph Greenson. "I got a call from Romi [Greenson]. He was over there. Marilyn was dead."

Rudin stated that he drove directly to Marilyn's residence. "Newcomb was there. She was hysterical," he recalled. Rudin's statements further substantiated James Hall's identification of Greenson as the doctor on the scene and Newcomb as the hysterical woman. According to Hall, Newcomb was there when Marilyn died; and as Natalie Jacobs has maintained, it was Newcomb who then called in the message for Arthur Jacobs at the Hollywood Bowl informing him of Marilyn's death.

On Sunday morning, as Pat Newcomb drove away from Marilyn's house yelling, "Keep shooting, vultures!" she was seated in the passenger seat of Mrs. Murray's Dodge because she had driven there with Lawford and her car was still at his beach house.

The question remains, what occurred in the critical thirty minutes between the time that Marilyn set down the phone in her bedroom while talking to José Bolaños at ten o'clock and her conversation with Lawford at approximately ten-thirty, when she lapsed into unconsciousness while grasping the phone in the guest cottage?

What series of events brought her to the guest cottage, where she was given a "hot shot" and died a quick death?

Déjà Vu

I feel an inquiry of evaluation of the new information should be made.
— Thomas Noguchi, 1985

While researching *Goddess*, Anthony Summers crossed investigative paths with Ted Landreth, a former CBS executive who had tried for over three years to convince an American television network to document the true Marilyn Monroe tragedy. The executive seers of network television were reluctant to touch the subject.

In 1983 Summers and Landreth joined forces in an attempt to coordinate their investigative efforts. Summers, with his background in British journalism, persuaded the BBC to produce the documentary *Say Goodbye to the President*, which contained interviews with Jack Clemmons, Robert Slatzer, Eunice Murray, and many of the other principals involved. A totally unexpected revelation occurred following Murray's interview in 1985.

"Initially the interview was quite conventional, in that Mrs. Murray never departed from the story she had recited through the years," Ted Landreth recalls. "However, after the last of the interview and the camera and the lights were turned off, Mrs. Murray made some astounding remarks. Fortunately, the sound tape was still rolling, and we included her comments in the documentary."

Summers, who conducted the interview, recalls, "As the camera crew were starting to clear up, she said suddenly, 'Why, at my age, do I still have to cover up this thing?' I asked her what she meant, and she then astonished us by admitting that Robert Kennedy had indeed visited Marilyn on the day she died, and that a doctor and an ambulance had come while she was still alive."

Asked specifically if Marilyn was still alive when Dr. Greenson arrived, Murray responded, "When he arrived she wasn't dead, because I was there then—in the living room."

Mrs. Murray was then queried about the Kennedy–Monroe relationship.

MURRAY: Well, over a period of time I was not at all surprised that the Kennedys were a very important part of Marilyn's life . . . and, eh . . . so that I was just a . . . I wasn't included in this information, but I was a witness to what was happening . . .
SUMMERS: And you believe that he (Bobby) was there that day?
MURRAY: At Marilyn's house?
SUMMERS: Yes.
MURRAY: Oh, sure!
SUMMERS: That afternoon?
MURRAY: Yes.
SUMMERS: And you think that is the reason she was so upset?
MURRAY: Yes, and it became so sticky that the protectors of Robert Kennedy, you know, had to step in and protect him . . .

When Summers asked Murray why she hadn't told the truth to the police in 1962, she responded, "I told whatever I thought was good to tell."

The highly praised BBC production *Say Goodbye to the President* won numerous awards and was nominated in England as the best television documentary of 1985, but American networks refused to broadcast it. Eventually *Say Goodbye to the President* was syndicated across the United States to wide critical acclaim.

In 1985, Stanhope Gould, a producer for ABC's 20/20, read the early proofs of *Goddess* and concluded that the Monroe–Kennedy story would make an excellent 20/20 segment. He and executive producer Av Westin assigned Sylvia Chase, Geraldo Rivera, and a large staff of researchers to the TV newsmagazine project. Several months and several hundred thousand dollars later, the 20/20 team had completed a half-hour segment, which Hugh Downs and Barbara Walters considered a stunning piece of investigative journalism.

When Sylvia Chase asked Eunice Murray if Marilyn Monroe was romantically involved with Robert Kennedy, she responded, "I would call it a romantic involvement—yes," and cited the details of one of Bobby Kennedy's visits to Marilyn's residence in June 1962. Senator George Smathers told Chase that President Kennedy had told him about Bobby's relationship with Marilyn. Smathers stated that he had learned from the president of problems with Marilyn when she became intoxicated on a flight to meet Bobby Kennedy. Former Los Angeles mayor Sam Yorty disclosed that Chief Parker had told him "that Bobby Kennedy was supposed to be north of Los Angeles in some city making a speech, but that actually he said he was seen at the Beverly Hilton Hotel on the very day she died."

The segment's most stunning revelations came from celebrated Hollywood private eye Fred Otash. Once a Los Angeles police investigator, Otash had gained an international reputation as a private detective and surveillance expert. He said he had been hired by Teamster boss Jimmy Hoffa to place bugs in both the Lawford beach house and Monroe's Brentwood residence. Otash stated the tapes proved that Bobby Kennedy had been at the Monroe residence on the day of her death.

A week before the segment was to air, ABC News president Roone Arledge told Gould and Westin that the thirty-minute segment was to be cut in half. Working day and night, the 20/20 team cut the story to thirteen minutes. Rumors began circulating that the entire segment would be canceled. On October 2, 1985, syndicated columnist Liz Smith wrote, "I just hope ABC isn't going to let itself be a party to suppressing the history of 1962. . . . That, in my opinion, is not the function of a network with a great news gathering arm. . . ."

Westin retorted, "I don't anticipate not putting it on the air. The journalism is solid. Everything in there has two sources. We are documenting that there was a relationship between Bobby and Marilyn and Jack and Marilyn. A variety of witnesses attest to that on camera."

Hours before the October 3 air date, Roone Arledge canceled the segment. The Monroe story was replaced by a segment on police dogs.

The decision created a tumult in the press. Roone Arledge stated that the segment was canceled because it was "a sleazy piece of journalism—gossip column stuff." Outraged by the cancellation, the 20/20 team—Walters, Downs, and Rivera—were bitterly outspoken. Publicly taking issue with Arledge's judgment, Hugh Downs stated to the press, "I am upset about the way it was handled. I honestly believe that this is more carefully documented than anything any network did during Watergate. I lament the fact that the decision reflects badly on people I respect. . . . The Monroe segment was accurate."

Segment producer Stanhope Gould stated, "It was the documentation, coupled with the mob angle, that made it a story—the fact that the president and the attorney general of the United States had put themselves in a position to have the nation's most powerful criminals eavesdrop on their affairs with the nation's most famous actress, and were exposed to blackmail. That was one hell of a story."

Sylvia Chase resigned, Hugh Downs elected to go cable, and Geraldo Rivera was fired for his vitriolic protest.

ABC News President Roone Arledge had often been seen at social functions as Ethel Kennedy's escort, and there were rumors of a romance. Arledge's assistant, David Burke, had been a former Kennedy strategist; and Jeff Ruhe, an Arledge aide, was married to one of Bobby and Ethel's children. Denying that his friendship with Ethel had anything to do with his killing the segment, Arledge stated, "I wouldn't censor anything because it would offend a friend."

However, when Kennedy family member Kerry Kennedy McCarthy appeared on the *Geraldo* show in 1995, she stated, "Quite honestly, Geraldo, you were a victim of the family. . . . The family had become used to hearing the truth about Jack—but when it was Bobby? You see, Ethel had a very close relationship with Roone Arledge. . . ."

Though no copy of the full Marilyn Monroe segment exists outside the ABC vaults, a copy of the thirteen-minute edited version was secreted from the network following the cancellation. Among the surviving elements is a section of Chase's interview with private investigator Fred Otash:

CHASE: How did you get involved in this?
OTASH: Hoffa was very interested in developing a derogatory profile on Bobby Kennedy—not so much Jack Kennedy, but Bobby Kennedy.
CHASE: And then what followed?
OTASH: Bugs were installed in the Lawford house—in the bedrooms and on the phones. There were four bugs all together installed out there.
CHASE: Why the Lawford house?
OTASH: Well, because the information we had was that it was the Kennedy playhouse—that's where Bobby and Jack played. . . . There were numerous tapes made of Marilyn and Jack in the act of love.

CHASE: But you were really trying to obtain information on Bobby Kennedy.

OTASH: Sure.

CHASE: Did you hear Bobby Kennedy on an eavesdropping tape?

OTASH: Yes.

CHASE: Do they confirm that Bobby Kennedy and Marilyn also had an affair?

OTASH: Of course . . . sure . . . Bobby Kennedy and Marilyn were recorded many times.

CHASE: Were there tapes recorded at Marilyn's house right up until Marilyn Monroe's death?

OTASH: They were recorded the day of her death—the night of her death.

CHASE: A conversation with Kennedy?

OTASH: A conversation with *Bobby* Kennedy.

CHASE: And what were they talking about?

OTASH: They had a very violent argument. She was saying, "I feel passed around! I feel used! I feel like a piece of meat!"

CHASE: And this conversation took place on the day of her death?

OTASH: That's right.

Otash described a struggle in the Monroe bedroom and Kennedy yelling, "Where is it? Where the hell is it? I have to have it! My family will pay you for it!" At the conclusion of the struggle, Otash heard physical blows and a door slamming. Later, there was a phone call to Marilyn from Bobby Kennedy, who was at the Lawford beach house. "He tried to reason with her," Otash recalled, "and she angrily shouted, 'Don't bother me! Leave me alone—stay out of my life!' before hanging up the phone."

Hearing of the revelations, the *Los Angeles Times* interviewed Otash, who revealed to the *Times* that shortly after 2 A.M. on the night Monroe died, Peter Lawford drove to Otash's Hollywood apartment. Describing Lawford as drunk, distraught, and very nervous, Otash stated, "He [Lawford] said he had just left Monroe, and she was dead, and that Bobby had been there earlier. He said they got Bobby out of the city and back to Northern California, and would I go out there and remove anything that may be incriminating."

Otash said that Lawford told him Bobby Kennedy and Marilyn had a fight—a violent struggle. "He [Bobby] then went over to Lawford's and was very upset," Otash told the *Times*. "Lawford described Bobby as panicky and quoted him as saying, 'She's ranting and raving. I'm concerned about her and what may come out of this.'" Lawford told Otash that "Marilyn had had it and didn't want Bobby to use her anymore." She had tried to reach Jack Kennedy at the White House, but was told he was in Hyannisport. She kept trying to reach him, but wasn't able to.

Lawford revealed to Otash that Marilyn had called him later Saturday night and was still angry that Jack Kennedy wouldn't talk to her. "Look, do me a favor," she had told Lawford, "Tell the president I tried to reach him. Tell him good-bye for me. I think my purpose has been served." This may have been the 7:30 P.M. telephone call mentioned by Lawford's dinner guests, but hardly the "say good-bye to the president" call Lawford had described to the press. It was the angry good-bye of a woman finalizing a relationship.

Otash told the *Times* that he had remained silent over the years because "I didn't see any purpose in getting involved . . . but I feel it's time for the truth to come out. . . . I'm not getting paid, I'm not writing a book, I'm not making a point. If I wanted to capitalize on my relationship in this matter, I would have written my own book." At the time of the interview Otash was sixty-three, a retired man of wealth with homes in Los Angeles, Palm Beach, and Cannes. Otash died in Los Angeles in October 1992, leaving an estate appraised in excess of one million dollars. At the time of his death the surveillance tapes had not been discovered.

Learning of the revelation on the BBC documentary and the suppressed *20/20* segment, *New York Post* correspondent Jack Schermerhorn arranged an interview with Eunice Murray, which took place at a table in the gardens of the Miramar Hotel in Santa Monica in October 1985.* Murray told Schermerhorn about Bobby Kennedy's visit to Marilyn's house on August 4, 1962, stating that Kennedy had arrived with Lawford in the late afternoon. Revealing that Kennedy and Marilyn were having a disagreement, Murray told Schermerhorn that she was told to leave. She stated that Kennedy and Marilyn were arguing in the rear garden when she left. "I went to the market, and when I returned he was gone. Marilyn was very upset, and I called Dr. Greenson."

Twenty-three years after the fact, Eunice Murray had finally explained why Dr. Greenson had made his unusual visit to Marilyn's residence that afternoon. It wasn't because Marilyn had asked, "Do we have any oxygen around?" It was because Marilyn Monroe had a violent argument with

---

* Mrs. Murray was unaware that Jack Schermerhorn had a tape recorder concealed under a hat on the table. Though the metal table and the hat distorted the sound, her revelations are preserved on the Schermerhorn tape. An edited version of the interview appeared in the New York *Post* on October 16, 1985, but it was not picked up by the press, its significance overlooked.

Bobby Kennedy and she was emotionally upset. Murray's statement, preserved on the Schermerhorn tape, confirms Fred Otash's assertion that an argument took place between Kennedy and Marilyn at her residence and Sidney Guilaroff's disclosure of Marilyn's hysterical call in the late afternoon.

The revelations of *Goddess, Say Goodbye to the President*, Fred Otash's statements to the *Los Angeles Times*, and the furor over the cancellation of the *20/20* segment led to another public outcry for a formal inquiry into the death of Marilyn Monroe. At the instigation of Supervisor Mike Antonovich, the Los Angeles Board of Supervisors once again voted unanimously to call for a grand jury investigation. In the fall of 1985, the Los Angeles grand jury and its foreman, Sam Cordova, concluded that there was reason to doubt the original coroner's verdict of "probable suicide." On Friday, October 25, Cordova called a press conference to announce that there would, indeed, be an official grand jury investigation and that witnesses would be called to testify.

"There is enough evidence to substantiate a special prosecutor to work with the grand jury on the investigation," Cordova told reporters. "A full investigation has never been done by the grand jury. People have not testified under oath. That should have been done a long time ago. It should have been done in 1962."

That evening former Los Angeles Medical Examiner Dr. Thomas Noguchi stated on KABC-TV that he too felt there should be a new investigation. Citing the bruises that had never been explained, and the specimens that had vanished, Noguchi said, "It gives an indication that there was something to hide." Asked if by "something to hide" he meant murder, Noguchi replied, "Could be."

However, on Monday, October 28, District Attorney Ira Reiner announced that Sam Cordova had been fired. While it was the first time in the history of California jurisprudence that a grand jury foreman had been removed from office, Reiner assured reporters that the dismissal had nothing to do with Cordova's investigation into the death of Marilyn Monroe. In fact, Reiner confided that the district attorney's office would undertake its own thorough and impartial investigation as quickly as possible. True to his word, the very next day the district attorney's investigation had been concluded. Reiner announced that he had reviewed the facts in the case, and there wasn't a "scintilla of evidence, new or old, that has been brought to our attention which could support a reasonable belief, or even a bare suspicion, that Miss Monroe was murdered."

When asked about Cordova's findings, Reiner replied, "As far as Cordova's concerned, he's history."

For years Sam Cordova said nothing about his dismissal. In 1995 he disclosed the reason for his silence. He owned a laboratory in Sylmar, California, that was dependent on government contracts, and he had been advised not to speak out or he would put his business at risk. Now retired, Cordova confirmed that his dismissal was a direct result of his determination to have a grand jury investigation of the Marilyn Monroe case.

"The grand jury had discovered a great deal of information that left no doubt there had been a cover-up," Cordova stated. "We had in our possession copies of internal memoranda of the coroner's office calling for the destruction of evidence."

According to Cordova there had been political pressure to scuttle the investigation, but as a jurist representing the people of Los Angeles he felt he had the duty and the right to proceed. "Three days before my press conference my desk had been broken into, and somebody took my Monroe file," Cordova stated. "I still feel very strongly that the grand jury investigation was warranted."

The year 1992 was the thirtieth anniversary of Marilyn Monroe's death. Forests of trees were pulverized to pulp by the publishing industry in an orgy of Marilyn books. Glossy book jackets proclaimed to reveal *The Truth at Last! The Untold Secrets! The Shocking Lies—The Explosive Truth!* Notable among the many publications were Susan Strasberg's *Marilyn and Me*; Robert Slatzer's second Monroe book, *The Marilyn Files*; and the Peter Brown–Patte Barham bestseller *Marilyn: The Last Take*. But perhaps the most significant revelation appeared in Daryl Gates's book *Chief: My Life in the LAPD*. In a chapter on Monroe, Gates wrote, "The truth is, we knew Robert Kennedy was in town on August 4. We always knew when he was here. He was the attorney general, so we were interested in him, the same way we were when other important figures came to Los Angeles. . . . So while we knew Robert Kennedy was in town that day, we paid no attention to where he went or what he did; whether he saw Monroe or not. Frankly, I never bought into the theory that she killed herself because he dumped her."

Gates's statement confirmed once and for all the whereabouts of Bobby Kennedy on August 4, 1962.

As the publishing year celebrating Marilyn Monroe's enduring magic and mystery drew to a close, the strange death of Marilyn Monroe remained an enigma. There had been many revelations, and it became abundantly clear that there was an orchestrated cover-up of the events surrounding Monroe's death, but there was such a deluge of theories, allegations, denials, lies, and disinformation that the general public began to despair of ever knowing the truth. On three separate occasions, Los Angeles County Supervisor Mike Antonovich had been successful in obtaining a majority vote of the Board of Supervisors in recommending a grand jury investigation. Each attempt was subverted by those who didn't want the truth to be known.

Officials in the corridors of power, such as Chief William Parker, Captain James Hamilton, Coroner Theodore Curphey, Chief Daryl Gates, John Van de Kamp, and Ira Reiner, had hoped that the public would grow weary in time—that the clay of mendacity would harden in the aridity of the public's despair. Knowing that time was running out, Robert Slatzer once again prevailed on Mike Antonovich, and on September 8, 1992, for the fourth time, Antonovich presented a motion before the Los Angeles Board of Supervisors calling for an inquiry into the death of Marilyn Monroe.

After an eloquent presentation of the facts to the board by Robert Slatzer, Jack Clemmons, medical experts, and ordinary citizens, a representative of the district attorney's office stepped forward to speak in opposition to the motion. Contrary to his statements in 1986, Assistant District Attorney Ronald Carroll, who had conducted the 1982 threshold investigation, vehemently opposed the motion, stating that the district attorney's office had chased many theories and came up with nothing. "You could have someone from outer space say she was murdered," Carroll stated, "But you have a body that shows no signs of murder."

After Ronald Carroll completed his statement to the board and returned to his chair, the matter was put to a vote. An icy silence pervaded the chamber. This time the motion failed to even obtain a second.

It seemed that the passage of time and the deceptions of officialdom had been successful. Marilyn Monroe's death would forever remain a mysterious enigma. *Probable suicide* would be the official verdict consigned to history. . . .

. . . But in the fall of 1992 the distinguished publishing firm of HarperCollins announced its forthcoming publication *Marilyn Monroe: The Biography*, by eminent biographer Donald Spoto. Revealing that Spoto had been granted access to previously sealed documents, the book was heralded as "The definitive account of her life and death! The Truth! Finally!"

Explosive Revelations

There's a new breed of journalists—and those who call themselves "biographers"—who, in their dash for a swift buck, simply make things up.
—Donald Spoto, 1993

Due to its "explosive revelations," advance copies of *Marilyn Monroe: The Biography* were withheld from reviewers. A prepublishing promo in the tabloid *Star* promised, "For the first time, the truth about her death is revealed—more bizarre and horrifying than anything a Hollywood screenwriter could devise!"

Arriving in the bookstores in March 1993, Spoto's biography denied that there had been a relationship between Bobby Kennedy and Monroe and absolved the Kennedys of any connection with her death. In his acknowledgments, Spoto stated that "Patricia Newcomb offered me unprecedented confidence and detailed many of the fine points of Marilyn's last two years.... Her signal contribution to this book are everywhere evident."

In addition to calling previous Monroe biographers scurrilous journalists who wrote shameful books with "a disregard for the reputations of decent people and a profound indifference to the truth," Spoto accused Dr. Ralph Greenson and Eunice Murray of murdering Monroe by administering a fatal barbiturate-laced enema. The reader was informed that Greenson and Murray's motive was that they had been fired.

Acknowledging that there was a cover-up of Monroe's death, Spoto created a conundrum: the book failed to reveal why the FBI, the LAPD, the district attorney, and the coroner had gone to such lengths for over three decades to protect the reputations of a psychiatrist and a house-keeper.

As Spoto began promoting the book, it became clear that his focus was on exonerating Robert Kennedy. He wrote that "scurrilous accounts" of Marilyn Monroe's affair with Robert Kennedy had "led to the completely groundless assertion of a link between Robert Kennedy and Marilyn's death." Spoto termed the connection hilarious and went on to say, "It is important to establish definitively the truth of this matter."

Spoto's methodology was the systematic elimination of witnesses' state-ments and established facts. He pointedly ignored Murray's statements to the BBC, 20/20, and the New York Post; Marilyn's phone records; Jean Kennedy Smith's note to Marilyn; the helicopter logs; Dr. Robert Litman's notes regarding Marilyn and the Kennedys; Senator George Smathers's statements; Daryl Gates's confirmation that Robert Kennedy was in Los Angeles on August 4, 1962; Mayor Sam Yorty's disclosures; and Fred Otash's statements to the Los Angeles Times.

Rather than refute evidence proffered by investigative journalists, Spoto elected to assassinate the character of those bearing ill news of Camelot. Accusing Anthony Summers of manipulating and misquoting statements of interviewees, Spoto wrote: "In Goddess Summers ignored and/or fre-quently mispresented those he claims to have interviewed." Summers took Spoto to the Queen's Bench division of the English courts. Examination of Summers's recorded interviews revealed the integrity of his research, and in a settlement on March 28, 1994, Spoto agreed to pay Summers a sizable sum as well as print a retraction of his accusations in the paperback and any future editions of his book.

Spoto also maligned Norman Mailer, Fred Guiles, Peter Brown, and a host of other writers before devoting dozens of pages to the denigration of Robert Slatzer, whom he accused of building a "nefarious industry" out of his absurd murder theories and "the nonsense about a love affair between Monroe and Robert F. Kennedy."

Spoto's biography came at the end of decades of deception. Many of the key witnesses had died, and none had ever been required to speak under oath. It seemed that the full story of what happened to Marilyn Monroe would never be known. In her last interview, which appeared in Life the day before she died, Marilyn pleaded, "Please don't make me a joke." But the joke had been on those who wanted to know the truth and had so often been deceived.

In the fall of 1993, however, the remaining tumblers of truth fell into place—unlocking the vault of secrets that had been so firmly shut on August 4, 1962.

In all the accounts of that fatal day, Eunice Murray's son-in-law, handyman Norman Jefferies, vanished from the narrative of events sometime before noon on Saturday. In Eunice Murray's book, *Marilyn: The Last Months*, he is described as working on the remodeling of Monroe's kitchen early that Saturday morning. Jefferies is not identified as being on the scene again until the next day. Murray told Clemmons and the press that the first person she called after Greenson discovered Monroe's body was Jefferies—asking him to come and replace the broken window. In newspaper photos he is pictured at the Monroe residence Sunday morning as he is being led from the kitchen side door, along with Pat Newcomb, by the police. He is next seen opening the car door for Murray as she steps into her Dodge, and also pictured holding the passenger door open for Newcomb.

Inexplicably, Jefferies was never questioned by the police or the press. When Anthony Summers tried to locate him during his research for *Goddess*, he noted that Murray seemed anxious to prevent their meeting. "Murray seemed oddly reluctant to assist me in reaching Jefferies," Summers stated. In 1983 Ted Landreth located Jefferies, living in Laguna Beach, California, but found him reluctant to be interviewed, ultimately refusing Landreth's phone calls.

Ten years later Jefferies was located in Russellville, Arkansas. Terminally ill and confined to a wheelchair, he spoke for the first time about the tragic events that occurred that Saturday—a day he termed "the worst he had ever experienced in his entire lifetime."

Stating, "I guess they can't very well electrocute me in a wheelchair," Jefferies disclosed that he never left the proximity of the Monroe residence on that horrific day. He had remained with his mother-in-law, Eunice Murray, from the time he arrived Saturday morning at about eight o'clock until he departed Sunday morning at approximately seven-thirty. He had been present during all the events that took place. "I was there in the living room with Eunice when Marilyn died, and after that all hell broke loose," Jefferies stated. He was there when Bobby Kennedy and Peter Lawford arrived on Saturday afternoon. He was there when the ambulance arrived on Saturday night. He was there when Dr. Greenson arrived and

Marilyn died in the guest cottage. He was there in the early hours of Sunday morning when Monroe's body was moved to the bedroom. Norman Jefferies had been a key witness.

After years of obfuscation, Jefferies clarified that the reason Murray called Greenson that Saturday night was not "the light under the bedroom door" or "the telephone cord under the bedroom door" or anything to do with Murray's Piscean qualities; it was the sight of Monroe slumped on the bed of the guest cottage in a comatose state, her hand clutching the telephone.

Though many of the puzzling questions surrounding Marilyn Monroe's death were finally answered, new questions evolved. The key witnesses had conspired to conceal Bobby Kennedy's presence at Monroe's residence, as well as the time, location, and circumstances of her death. But why did officials substantiate the key witnesses' statements, and why did the key witnesses corroborate the officials? If it was a "national security matter," as Chief Reddin and Mayor Yorty stated, what was the secret at the heart of the matter? What had locked this diverse group of people into a complex conspiracy to conceal the truth? And why was Marilyn Monroe murdered?

The 1982 district attorney's report on Marilyn Monroe's death concluded:

> If Marilyn Monroe did not commit suicide or suffer an accidental drug overdose, she was murdered. Her murder would have required a massive, in-place conspiracy covering all of the principals at the death scene on August 4 and 5, 1962; the actual killer or killers; the Chief Medical Examiner–Coroner; the autopsy surgeon; and most all of the police officers assigned to the case as well as their superiors at the LAPD. Several variations on this theme can be imagined, but each required the involvement of a significant number of persons. Our inquiries and document examinations uncovered no credible evidence supporting a murder theory.

However, Norman Jefferies's revelations confirm that there was indeed "a massive, in-place conspiracy covering all of the principals at the death scene on August 4 and 5, 1962," and among those seated in the Chapel of the Palms at Marilyn Monroe's funeral were accomplices to her murder and the cover-up.

That the mystery of Marilyn Monroe's death has never been resolved has a great deal to do with the mystery of her life, which was secretive and very private. Norman Jefferies revealed that some of the key witnesses also led very secretive lives and had hidden agendas. In order to comprehend what happened on that fatal Saturday, it is necessary to know and understand the victim and the complex relationships she had with the disparate group of principals at the death scene.

One cannot resolve the secrets of life and death, or know how chance or fate deals with people or understand one of the great crimes of the twentieth century, without knowing the whole story. And while the mystery of Marilyn Monroe's murder will be solved, the mystery of her remarkable life can never be fully explained.

PART II

1926–1946

Gemini Child

Silent Witness

One can't say how life is, how chance or fate deals with people, except by telling the tale.

—Hannah Arendt

Marilyn Monroe's first childhood memory was of being suffocated by her mad grandmother, Della. "I remember waking up from my nap fighting for my life. Something was pressed against my face. It could have been a pillow. I fought with all my strength," she recalled many years later.

Della Monroe Grainger had a history of mental illness, and her first husband, Otis Elmer Monroe, died in a mental institution in 1909. When Della married oil field worker Charles Grainger in 1923, they lived in a bungalow on Rhode Island Avenue in Hawthorne, a suburb of Los Angeles. Grainger soon learned of Della's mercurial moods and was often the object of her irrational rages. Their stormy relationship ended when Grainger arranged to be transferred across the globe to the safety of the oil fields in the wilds of Borneo.

Thrown into despair by her abandonment, Della turned to religion for solace, and joined Sister Aimee Semple McPherson's Church of the Foursquare Gospel, where Sister Aimee would seemingly rise into the air and glow with glory at the end of her illuminating sermons—thanks to the miraculous effects installed by the Otto K. Olesen Illuminating Company of Hollywood. But no amount of illumination could brighten the darkness descending on Della. A manic-depressive psychosis was enveloping her mind.

In December 1925, Della's daughter by Otis Monroe, Gladys, took the Pacific Electric Red Car from Hollywood to Hawthorne to make an uncommon visit to her mother. Informing Della that she was pregnant, and that the father of the child didn't want to marry her, Gladys hoped to stay with her mother until the baby was born. But Della was planning on sailing to Borneo, hoping for a reconciliation with Charles Grainger. A solution was found in Della's suggestion that Gladys stay with Wayne and Ida Bolender, neighbors who lived across the street from Della on Rhode Island Avenue.

The Bolenders were devout Christian fundamentalists who took care of children for a fee. It was arranged for Gladys to stay at their home until the baby was born, and to remain for a few weeks after the birth. Fellow workers at the film laboratory in Hollywood where Gladys was employed chipped in to help pay for the baby's delivery. Norma Jeane was born on June 1, 1926, and baptized by Aimee Semple McPherson several weeks later. In July, Gladys returned to her work at Consolidated Film Laboratories and moved back to her Hollywood apartment. An illegitimate baby was a problem for a single young woman working in Hollywood during the twenties, and Norma Jeane remained with the Bolenders, who were paid five dollars a week.

"I'll come every Saturday and stay over whenever I can, if that's all right," Gladys told them. According to Wayne Bolender, "Gladys would come to visit nearly every Saturday around noon. Sometimes she would spend the night, but she usually had a date on Saturday night or a party to go to and would return to Hollywood after a visit of several hours."

Della's attempt at a reconciliation with Charles Grainger proved to be financially and emotionally draining, and when Della returned from Borneo alone in October 1926, she began drinking heavily. Moving back to her residence across the street from the Bolenders, she soon became fascinated by her grandchild, Norma Jeane, and offered to take care of her. However, Gladys decided that it was best for the baby to stay on with the Bolenders, and it was made clear to Della that Norma Jeane had been placed in their care. Della resented the Bolenders' control over her grandchild, and her frequent visits to see the baby often ended in arguments.

Noting that Della was frequently inebriated and acting strangely, Ida Bolender became concerned when Della began taking Norma Jeane across the street for long periods of time, and it was during the summer of 1927 that the "incident" occurred. Della had taken Norma Jeane for the afternoon and attempted to smother the baby. There was only one tiny, silent witness, and she recalled it from the vague recesses of early traumatic memory.

Sensing that Norma Jeane was frightened by something that had occurred during her stay at Della Grainger's house, the Bolenders began discouraging Della's visits. And in August 1927, Della descended into the snake pit of madness. Wayne Bolender recalled seeing her head up the walk toward the house in a blind rage. She was yelling incoherently, demanding to see her grandchild. He quickly shut the front door and locked it. Hearing the commotion, Ida entered the living room from the kitchen and watched Della through the window. Della was screaming and pounding on the door like a madwoman. Terrified, Ida yelled, "Call the police, Wayne. Hurry!" Before the police arrived Della tried to break down the door. Smashing through a panel with her fist, she injured her hand and blood spurted from the wound. When the police arrived, they subdued Della and forcibly took her away. Wayne vividly recalled his last image of Della as they dragged her off, her head thrown back, screaming to the heavens as she beseeched God's help.

Help soon arrived in the guise of death.

Della Grainger died nineteen days after the incident at the Bolenders' house. Her heart failed during a manic seizure at the Norwalk Hospital for the insane, the same hospital where Norma Jeane's grandfather, Otis Monroe, had died in 1909. Della's death certificate lists "myocarditis" as the cause of death and cites a manic-depressive psychosis as the contributing factor.

On August 25, 1927, Della Grainger was buried in an unmarked grave next to Otis Monroe at Rose Dale Cemetery in central Los Angeles.

Runnin' Wild

Runnin' wild, lost control,
Runnin' wild, mighty bold,
Feeling gay, restless too,
Carefree mind all the time,
Never blue . . .
            —Joe Grey and Leo Wood,
                "Runnin' Wild," 1922

At times the Bolenders boarded as many as five children. One of the children was a boy named Lester. Two months younger than Norma Jeane, he was later adopted by the Bolenders. At fourteen months, Norma Jeane would often mimic Lester, who began calling Ida Bolender "Mama." But Gladys didn't want her baby to refer to Ida as "Mama," and Ida would scold Norma Jeane and say, "I'm not Mama. I'm Aunt Ida—*Aunt Ida!*" Hurt and bewildered that she couldn't call Ida "Mama" as Lester did, Norma Jeane tried to understand, and one of her first complete sentences was "There goes a mama!" when she saw a woman holding a child by the hand.

When Gladys visited on Saturdays she would frequently take Norma Jeane on outings to the beach. Often they would ride the trams that traversed the colorful oceanfront from Venice to Santa Monica, and sometimes they would walk out on Santa Monica Pier, where Gladys would let Norma Jeane ride the merry-go-round; but for years Norma Jeane never knew exactly who the pretty lady with the red hair was.

Though she wasn't to call Ida "Mama," Norma Jeane assumed that Wayne Bolender was her father, and she called him Daddy. "I used to sit on the edge of the bathtub in the morning and watch him shave and ask him questions—which was east or south, or how many people there were in the world?" Marilyn Monroe later recalled. "He was the only one who ever answered the questions I asked."

One day Ida Bolender said to Norma Jeane, "You are old enough to know that I'm not related to you in any way. Neither is Wayne."

"But," Norma Jeane protested, "He's my daddy!"

"No, I'm not your mother, and Wayne is not your father. You just board here. Your mama's coming to see you tomorrow. You can call *her* Mama if you want to."

The next day was Saturday, and the woman she was to call "Mama" arrived. It was the woman with the red hair. "She was the pretty woman who never smiled," Marilyn remembered. "I'd seen her often before, but I hadn't known quite who she was. When I said, 'Hello, Mama' she stared at me. She had never kissed me or held me in her arms or hardly spoken to me."

One Saturday Gladys picked up Norma Jeane and took her for a visit to her rooms in Hollywood. "I used to be frightened when I visited her and spent most of my time in the closet of her bedroom hiding among the clothes," Marilyn remembered.

She seldom spoke to me except to say, "Don't make so much noise, Norma." She would say this even when I was lying in bed at night turning the pages of a book. Even the sound of a page turning made her nervous.

There was one object in my mother's rooms that always fascinated me. It was a photograph on the wall. There were no other pictures on the walls, just this one framed photograph. Whenever I visited my mother I would stand looking at this photograph and hold my breath for fear she would order me to stop looking. My mother caught me staring at the photograph but didn't scold me. Instead she lifted me up on a chair so I could see it better.

"That's your father," she said. I felt so excited I almost fell off the chair. It felt so good to have a father, to be able to look at this picture and know I belonged to him. And what a wonderful photograph it was! He wore a slouch hat a little gaily on the side. There was a lively smile in his eyes, and he had a thin mustache like Clark Gable. I felt very warm toward the picture. . . . I asked my mother what his name was. She wouldn't answer, but went into the bedroom and locked herself in.

The person in the picture with the lively smile in his eyes, who looked like Gable, was a man Gladys had met in Venice Beach. . . .

Known as "the Playland of the Pacific," Venice was a Los Angeles tidal marshland that had been transformed by developers into a plaster facsimile of Venezia, complete with winding canals, Venetian gondolas, arched bridges, and the odor of sewage. In 1917, when the pretty woman with the red hair was only fourteen, she lived there with her mother, Della.

When the oily sulfuric scum that bubbled to the surface of the Venice canals proved to be black gold, one of the wildcatters who arrived in Venice was Charles Grainger. He met Della at a gala New Year's Eve dance on the boomtown waterfront and became a frequent visitor to her apartment at 27 Westminster Street. Though they weren't yet betrothed, Della was soon gondoliered into Grainger's Venice bungalow. Young Gladys, who didn't like the oily Mr. Grainger, proved to be an inconvenience. The problem was solved, however, when Gladys met Jasper Baker, an amusement concessionaire at Pickering's Pleasure Palace on Ocean Park Pier. Attracted by Gladys's beauty and youthful charms, Jasper soon gave Gladys an unanticipated amusement zone gratuity. When it was discovered that Gladys was pregnant with his child, a marriage was quickly arranged.

On May 17, 1917, swearing that her fourteen-year-old daughter was eighteen, Della was witness to Gladys's marriage to the reluctant concessionaire, who was twelve years older than his child bride. Jasper never wanted the child, and demanded that she have an abortion. Nevertheless, Gladys insisted on having her baby, and six months after the wedding, on November 10, 1917, Robert "Jackie" Baker was born. A daughter, Berniece, was born in July 1919.

Gladys was barely out of childhood herself when she married, and her unstable childhood had ill prepared her for marital life and motherhood. From the beginning the marriage was fraught with problems. Jasper was prone to drink and fits of violence, and friends noted that Gladys often wore dark glasses to conceal blackened eyes. In later years, in one of his rare references to his wife, Jasper complained to his daughter Berniece, "She wouldn't cook, and she wouldn't clean house. She wouldn't do anything. She just liked to get out and roam around. . . . She was a beautiful woman, but she was very young—too young to know how to take care of children."

During a trip to visit Jasper's relatives in Flat Lick, Kentucky, Gladys went hiking with Jasper's younger brother. When they returned after dark, Jasper was in a drunken rage and beat Gladys across the back with a bridle until she bled profusely. Townspeople saw her running hysterically down the street, begging to be protected from her husband.

Shortly after the Bakers returned to California, Gladys left her husband. On June 20, 1921, she filed divorce papers accusing Jasper Baker of "extreme cruelty by abusing [her] and calling her vile names and using profane language at and in her presence, by striking [her] and kicking [her]." Taking the children, she moved into Della's Venice bungalow. One weekend Jasper picked up the children for an outing, and little Jackie and baby Berniece never returned. Jasper took them back to his family's home in Flat Lick. Determined to reclaim her children, Gladys hitchhiked to Kentucky, where she found that Berniece had been put in hiding and Jackie was in a Louisville hospital suffering from an unexplained injury. Berniece recalled that Jackie suffered a series of "unfortunate accidents" and had a "never-ending run of bad luck." When Jackie was three and a half, he severely injured his hip. "Daddy told me that Jackie fell out of a car," said Berniece. The truth was that Jasper abused the son he had never wanted.

"Daddy and my grandmother kept me hidden, and they told my mother that she had better not go to that hospital and bother Jackie," Berniece recalled. "Of course, mother went anyway. She visited Jackie, but Daddy had told the doctors not to let her take him out. So she got a job in Louisville as a housekeeper while she waited for Jackie to get better."

Frustrated in her attempts to regain custody of her children, Gladys returned to Venice Beach in May 1923 and moved to the Westminster Apartments, where she met Stan Gifford, a salesman for the Consolidated Film Laboratories in Hollywood. A great deal had changed since she last lived in Venice. Her mother, Della, had married Charles Grainger and moved to nearby Hawthorne, and the Venetian community had become engulfed by oil derricks, roller-coaster rides, and all-night dance halls. The canals of the "Playland of the Pacific" led to speakeasies, jazz joints, brothels, and card rooms frequented by celebrants of the Jazz Age. Among the flaming youth was Gladys Baker, who hoped to forget her melancholy memories in the company of Stan Gifford.

In a 1923 divorce action filed by Gifford's wife, Lillian, she complained:

He associated with women of low character; boasted of his conquests; showed her marks of hypodermic injections of addictive drugs; caroused with fellow workers in the film labs; visited friends in Venice, California, and didn't return for extended periods of time.

Gifford obtained employment for Gladys in the negative-assembly department at Consolidated, where her supervisor was Grace McKee, a young divorcée and casual acquaintance of Gifford's. According to Olin Stanley, a coworker, Grace McKee and Gladys became close friends. "They did, as you'd say, lots of fast living, lots of dates with fellows at the lab or from the studios. They frequently went down to gin joints at Venice with Gifford."

Olin Stanley recalled that Gladys was very much in love with Stan Gifford and hoped to become his wife. But, disillusioned by Gifford's refusal to commit himself, Gladys began seeking the companionship of other men. In the summer of 1924 she met Edward Mortensen, an itinerant laborer of Norwegian descent. Mortensen offered Gladys the stability and security that Gifford denied her, and they were married in a civil ceremony on October 11, 1924. It wasn't long, however, before Gladys realized she had made a mistake. Stating to Grace McKee that her life with Mortensen was unendurably dull, in February 1925 Gladys walked out on her husband of four months and resumed her relationship with Gifford.

In late 1925, many months after she had left Mortensen, Gladys became pregnant with Gifford's child. Grace McKee recalled that Gladys desperately wanted Gifford to marry her and hoped the child would bring about the wedding. But on Christmas Eve there was a confrontation and Stan Gifford refused to marry Gladys.

And so it was that a Gemini child, destined to become the most celebrated film star of the twentieth century, was born on June 1, 1926, at 9:30 A.M. in the charity ward of the General Hospital in Los Angeles— and Martin Edward Mortensen, address unknown, was named as the father. On Norma Jeane's birth certificate it states that the infant was the mother's third child; however, Gladys indicates that the first two born were "no longer living." Perhaps to her broken heart it was as though Jackie and Berniece were, indeed, dead.

Years later, when Gladys lifted little Norma Jeane up on a chair to see the picture of her father, Gladys wouldn't answer when Norma Jeane asked the name of the man with the lively smile in his eyes who looked like

Gable. Instead, she went into her room and locked the door. His name was Stan Gifford.

"It must have hurt my mother very, very much. I don't think she ever got over the hurt," Marilyn Monroe commented in July 1962. "When a man leaves a woman when she tells him she's going to have his baby, when he doesn't marry her, that must hurt a woman very much, deep down inside. A woman must have to love a man with all her heart to have his child under those circumstances—I mean especially when she's not even married to him."

> Always goin', don't know where,
> Always showin', I don't care;
> Don't love nobody, it's not worthwhile;
> All alone, runnin' wild . . .
> —"Runnin Wild"

Into the Abyss

I gave her Christian Science treatments for approximately a year—wanted her to be happy and joyous.

—Gladys Baker

The Bolenders took the children to Sunday school each week, and Norma Jeane learned to sing "Jesus Loves Me, This I Know." It became her favorite song and Ida Bolender recalled her singing it constantly. "Nearly everybody I knew talked to me about God," Marilyn remembered. "They always warned me not to offend him . . . but the only one who loved me and watched over me was someone I couldn't see or hear or touch. I used to draw pictures of God whenever I had time. In my pictures he looked a little like Aunt Grace [McKee] and a little like Clark Gable."

In 1933, Gladys's grandfather on Della's side, Tilford Marion Hogan, committed suicide; but far more devastating was the news that her son "Jackie" had died at the age of fourteen. Though Gladys had tried to blot out the memory of Jackie and Berniece, her son's death was a terrible shock. According to Berniece, Jackie received an injury that led to tuberculosis of the bone, and he was hospitalized. Jasper Baker took Jackie out of the hospital against the doctor's recommendations. When his condition grew rapidly worse, and it became apparent that Jackie was dying, Jasper attempted to catheterize Jackie himself at home. Subsequently the boy died in extreme agony on August 16, 1933.

The news threw Gladys into bouts of depression. Blaming herself for Jackie's death, she turned to Christian Science for spiritual support, spending long hours at night reading her "science" and the Bible. According to Inez Melson, who in later years would become Gladys's conservator, "The underlying problem that led to the deterioration of Gladys's mental state was guilt and self-recrimination."

Recalling an incident that occurred shortly after the news of Jackie's death, Marilyn later related, "One day my mother came to call. I was in the kitchen washing dishes. She stood looking at me without talking. When I turned around I saw there were tears in her eyes, and I was surprised. 'I'm going to build a house for you and me to live in,' she said, 'It's going to be painted white and have a back yard.' "

Determined to establish a conventional home for Norma Jeane, and dreaming of regaining custody of Berniece, Gladys began working double shifts—at Columbia during the day and at RKO in the evening. Grace McKee tried to advise Gladys against taking on the burden of a home at the height of the recession—the economy was in turmoil and employment had become tenuous.

By 1933 the American public had lost faith in the banking system, and Friday, March 3, was marked by a run on the banks. President Roosevelt called a "bank holiday," and with the banks closed the Hollywood studios couldn't meet their payrolls. On March 9, Roosevelt signed the Emergency Banking Relief Act and the banks reopened; however, Hollywood producers announced that all employees' wages would have to be reduced by 25 to 50 percent because of the hard times. The seismic news hit the film industry like the major earthquake that rocked Los Angeles on March 12, 1933—Hollywood trembled. For the first time in the history of Hollywood, on March 13, the IATSE unions went out on strike and the studios were closed.

During the Hollywood labor disputes and prolonged strikes of 1933, Grace McKee elected not to cross the picket lines, but among the strikebreakers was a desperate young woman who was scrimping and saving every penny she could to put a down payment on a house. According to fellow IATSE member Olin Stanley, Gladys was pictured in the newspaper as she jumped over the fence at RKO Studios to avoid the picket line and maintain her employment.

By February 1934, Grace McKee became concerned about Gladys's mental state. Suffering from anxiety and insomnia, Gladys wasn't eating, and she was obviously exhausted and depressed. Grace persuaded Gladys to see a neurologist, who placed her in a Santa Monica rest home where she remained for several weeks before returning to work. Though Grace tried to convince Gladys that the cost of owning a home was beyond her means, Gladys's determination to start a new life for herself and Norma Jeane had become obsessive.

"I told her not to buy it. I begged her not to buy it," Grace stated, but Gladys purchased a six-thousand-dollar house with a down payment of $750 on October 20, 1934. Norma Jeane was told to pack her things. Now eight years old, she was to move to her new home in Hollywood with her mother.

The handsome two-story house in Hollywood had a Georgian portico in front and stood at 6812 Arbol Drive in the Cahuenga Pass, not far from the Hollywood Bowl. True to the promise, it was painted white and had a back yard.

"My mother bought furniture, a table with a white top and brown legs, chairs, beds, and curtains," Marilyn remembered. "One day a grand piano arrived at my home. It was out of condition, but it had once belonged to the movie star Fredric March. It was for me. I was going to be given piano lessons on it. 'You'll play the piano over here, by the windows,' my mother said, 'and here on the sill by the fireplace there'll be a love seat. As soon as I pay off a few other things I'll get the love seats, and we'll all sit in them at night and listen to you play the piano!'"

Faced with economic realities, Gladys rented the upstairs of the house to the Kinnells, a British couple who worked in motion pictures. Murray Kinnell was a character actor who had appeared with George Arliss in the Darryl F. Zanuck production of *The House of Rothschild*. Norma Jeane's move to her mother's house with its Hollywood milieu was a radical departure from the values instilled in her by the Bolenders. She remembered being shocked to see that her mother, Grace McKee, and the Kinnells smoked tobacco and imbibed alcohol.

"Life became pretty casual and tumultuous, quite a change from the first family," Marilyn recalled in later years. "They liked to dance and sing, they drank and played cards, and they had a lot of friends. Because of that religious upbringing I'd had, I was kind of shocked—I thought they were all going to hell. I spent hours praying for them."

The changes in her life were bewildering. She soon learned that not everyone was as devout as the Bolenders. "We're churchgoers, not moviegoers," Ida Bolender had said, but suddenly Norma Jeane was thrust into movieland. The conversation at the dinner table with the Kinnells was often about the movies, and when Norma Jeane wasn't at school she was frequently given a dime to go to one of the opulent movie palaces on Hollywood Boulevard. "There I'd sit all day and sometimes way into the night—up in front, there with the screen so big, a little kid all alone, and I loved it." Marilyn remembered. "I didn't miss anything that happened." She loved musicals and often sat through them two or three times, memorizing the songs, singing them to herself as she wandered home in the dark, late for supper.

But the dream ended abruptly. Though Gladys seemed in better spirits after establishing the home for Norma Jeane, she still had bouts of anxiety and depression. Grace McKee's attempts to help Gladys were of no avail. At times she refused to eat and couldn't sleep, often wandering through the house at night weeping, muttering prayers, and studying her "science." During the day she spent long hours at work to meet the mounting bills that had accumulated to pay for her dream house and its furnishings. Despite all her efforts, it became increasingly evident that the house was beyond her means. She had fallen behind in her payments and was ebbing into the darkness of despair when an incident occurred in December of 1934 that pushed her over the edge and into the abyss of madness.

The only reliable source regarding the incident is Marilyn Monroe. In an interview with Ben Hecht in 1953, she stated very clearly that she was eight years old:

I was almost nine, and I lived with a family that rented a room to a man named Kimmell. He was a stern-looking man, and everybody respected him and called him *Mister* Kimmell. I was passing his room when his door opened and he said quietly, "Please come in here, Norma." I thought he wanted me to run an errand.

"Where do you want me to go, Mr. Kimmell?" I asked.

"No place," he said and closed the door behind me. He smiled at me and turned the key in the lock.

"Now you can't get out," he said, as if we were playing a game.

I stood staring at him. I was frightened, but I didn't dare yell. . . . When he put his arms around me I kicked and fought as hard as I could, but I didn't make a sound. He was stronger than I was and wouldn't let me go. He kept whispering to me to be a good girl.

When he unlocked the door and let me out, I ran to tell my "Aunt" what Mr. Kimmell had done.

"I want to tell you something," I stammered, "about Mr. Kimmell. He . . . he . . ."

My "Aunt" interrupted.

"Don't you dare say anything against Mr. Kimmell," she said angrily. "Mr. Kimmell's a fine man. He's my star boarder!"

Mr. Kimmell came out of his room and stood in the doorway smiling.

"Shame on you!" my "Aunt" glared at me, "complaining about people!"

"This is different," I began. "This is something I have to tell . . . Mr. Kimmell . . . he . . . he . . ."

I started stammering again and couldn't finish. Mr. Kimmell came up to me and handed me a nickel.

"Go buy yourself some ice cream," he said.

I threw the nickel in Mr. Kimmell's face and ran out.

I cried in bed that night and wanted to die. I thought, "If there's nobody ever on my side that I can talk to I'll start screaming." But I didn't scream.

Nine years after relating the incident to Ben Hecht, Marilyn Monroe told the same story to photojournalist George Barris, who photographed her for *Cosmopolitan* just weeks before she died. Again she stated that she was eight years old and referred to Mr. Kimmell as the "star boarder." But instead of saying she ran to her "aunt," Marilyn said, "I ran to my foster mother and told her what he did to me. She looked at me shocked . . . then slapped me across the mouth and shouted at me, "I don't believe you! Don't you dare say such things about that nice man!"

I was so hurt, I began to stammer. She didn't believe me! I cried that night in bed all night, I just wanted to die. . . . This was the first time I can remember stammering. . . . Once afterward when I was in the orphanage, I started to stutter out of the clear blue . . ."

In both recollections Norma Jeane was only eight years old when the molestation incident occurred; therefore it was before June 1935, and before she entered the orphanage. The only boarder she lived with prior to the age of ten, prior to the orphanage, and prior to the onset of stuttering, was at her mother's house. Clearly the "Aunt" and the "foster mother" was Gladys; and Mr. Kimmell, the molester, was Murray Kinnell, the British actor who stayed upstairs at the house on Arbol Drive.

Kimmell is scarcely a disguise for *Kinnell*, but in referring to her mother as her "aunt" or "foster mother" Marilyn was protecting Gladys. The loss of her star boarder would have meant the inevitable loss of the house, and the end of her desperate dream. That her mother hadn't defended her, however, was beyond Norma Jeane's comprehension, and the incident explains to a degree the estrangement Norma Jeane would always feel toward her mother: "If there's nobody ever on my side that I can talk to, I'll start screaming." Though in time Norma Jeane tried to understand and mend the relationship, it was never to be the same. Having failed to protect Norma Jeane, just as she had failed Jackie, Gladys lost the hope of her daughter's love and respect, the only hope remaining to her. In doing so, she lost everything.

Custodial records indicate that it was during the Christmas season of 1934, shortly after the incident with Mr. Kinnell, that Gladys was taken away to a mental institution.

Grace McKee described Gladys's breakdown to Berniece in 1942: "When Gladys bought her own place, she brought in an English family to share the house. They stayed until she found out they were treating Norma Jeane unkindly and we got rid of them. The happy days didn't last long. In a few months Gladys had her nervous breakdown. It seemed like a lot of things happened all at once to put pressure on her. Overwork . . . the trouble with the English couple. One day she was lying on the couch and she—there were steps in the living room leading upstairs—she started kicking and yelling, staring up at the staircase, and yelling 'Somebody's coming down those steps to kill me!'"

Marilyn told Ben Hecht she was having breakfast when

Suddenly there was a terrible noise on the stairway outside the kitchen. It was the most frightening noise I'd ever heard. Bangs and thuds kept on as if they would never stop. "Something's falling down the stairs," I said. The English woman held me from going to see. Her husband went out and after a time came back into the kitchen.

"I've sent for the police and the ambulance," he said.

I asked if it was my mother.

"Yes," he said, "but you can't see her."

I stayed in the kitchen and heard people come and try to take my mother away. Nobody wanted me to see her. The Englishman said, "Just stay in the kitchen like a good girl. She's all right. Nothing serious." But I went out and looked in the hall. My mother was on her feet. She was screaming and laughing. They took her away to the Norwalk Mental Hospital. . . . It was where my mother's father and my grandmother had been taken when they started screaming and laughing."

Gladys was institutionalized at the Norwalk State Hospital for the insane in December 1934, scarcely three months after purchasing her dream house. On January 15, 1935, she was declared legally incompetent. Grace McKee became guardian of the estate and took custody of Norma Jeane.

The dream house was sold along with the furnishings to settle Gladys's debts. The piano was sold to Grace's aunt, Ana Lower.

"All the furniture disappeared. The white table, the chairs, the beds and white curtains melted away, and the grand piano, too. The English couple disappeared also," Marilyn recalled. "Aunt Grace had lost her job at the studio and had to scrape for a living. Although she had no money she continued to look after me. . . . When she ran out of money and had only a half dollar left for a week's food, we lived on stale bread and milk. You could buy a sackful of old bread at the Helms Bakery for twenty-five cents. Aunt Grace and I would stand in line for hours waiting to fill our sack. When I looked up at her she would grin at me and say, 'Don't worry, Norma Jeane, you're going to be a beautiful girl when you grow up. I can feel it in my bones . . .' She was the first person who ever patted my head or touched my cheek. I can still feel how thrilled I felt when her kind hand touched me."

When Grace McKee lost her job at Columbia she had moved in with her mother, Emma Atchinson, who kept an apartment on Lodi Place just off Hollywood Boulevard, and Norma Jeane stayed with Grace at the Atchinson apartment. "I could hear her friends arguing in her room at night when I lay in bed pretending to be asleep," Marilyn remembered. "They advised her against adopting me because I was certain to become more and more of a responsibility as I grew older. This was on account of my 'heritage,' they said. They talked about my mother and her father and brother and grandmother being mental cases and said I would certainly follow in their footsteps. I lay in bed shivering as I listened. I didn't know what a mental case was, but I knew it wasn't anything good. . . ."

It was difficult for Grace to look after Norma Jeane, not only because of her financial situation but because she had fallen in love with "Doc" Goddard, a tall Texan who had also traveled to Hollywood with dreams of becoming a movie star. Goddard and Grace were married in Las Vegas on August 17, 1935, and Norma Jeane hoped she would be able to live with them, but it proved to be impractical. "Doc and Aunt Grace were very poor," Marilyn was to recall, "so they couldn't care for me, and I think she felt that her responsibility was to her new husband."

On the afternoon of September 13, 1935, when Norma Jeane saw "Aunt Grace" packing up her few belongings into a box, she knew she was going away again. Aunt Grace didn't tell her where she was going, but Aunt Grace had been crying all morning, and Norma Jeane had a sense of foreboding. Getting into the car, they silently drove to Vine Street and turned east on Santa Monica Boulevard until they finally came to El Centro Avenue and headed south. Grace stopped the car in front of a stately three-story colonial brick building at 815 North El Centro. A flagpole stood in the midst of the sweeping lawn surrounding the walkway to the front door.

"This is where you will live now," Grace said, "I hope you'll be happy here. I'll come and see you as often as I can. They'll take good care of you—better than I can at home. But I expect soon we'll get a house and then you will come and live with me again."

"Yes, Aunt Gr-Grace," Norma Jeane dutifully said, taking the box of her belongings and walking with Grace up to the front door. As they rang the bell and waited, Norma Jeane read the words of a bronze plaque beside the entry. It clearly stated, "Los Angeles Orphans' Home."

"Orphan!" she exclaimed. "Bu . . . But I'm no orphan! I have a mother! I'm not going in there!" she screamed.

Her body stiffened as the matron opened the door. "I'm not an orphan! My mother's not d-dead! There's been some mistake!" she shouted hysterically as she was dragged inside. It was near dinnertime and the wards of the orphanage were in the dining hall having their supper. "There were about a hundred of them eating," Marilyn remembered. Hearing her screams as she was forcibly ushered into the dining hall, they silently turned to stare at her, and Norma Jeane suddenly became quiet in the paralyzing comprehension that she had become one of *them*.

Throughout her school years Norma Jeane was registered under the last name of Baker, and Norma Jeane Baker was registered as the three thousand four hundred and sixty-third child to be admitted to the Los Angeles Orphans' Home. Ten years later number 3,463 would become Marilyn Monroe.

The Mouse

You see, I was brought up differently from the average American child, because the average child is brought up expecting to be happy.

—Marilyn Monroe

Norma Jeane slept in a dormitory she shared with twenty-six other girls. After dark she often sat in the window and looked out at the city lights. Not far from the orphanage she could see the giant neon sign on top of the stages of a nearby film studio. "At night, when the other girls were sleeping, I'd sit up in the window and cry because I'd look over and see the studio sign above the roofs in the distance," Marilyn later recalled. "It was where my mother had worked as a cutter."

The studio had been named by Joseph P. Kennedy, who entered the motion-picture business in the year Norma Jeane was born. In 1926 Joe Kennedy was a multimillionaire whose bootlegging operations provided a lucrative income and the foundation for his successful stock market manipulations. In 1928 Kennedy had merged the Radio Corporation of America (RCA) and the Keith-Albee-Orpheum (KAO) vaudeville circuit to form a motion-picture studio. It was named Radio-Keith-Orpheum and a monumental reproduction of the studio trademark was erected on top of one of the Hollywood soundstages on the corner of Melrose and Gower— only blocks from the Los Angeles Orphans' Home. The large plaster globe with an enormous radio tower on top was brightly illuminated at night, and flashing neon bolts of electricity emanated from the giant letters RKO.

By 1929 Joe Kennedy had made over five million dollars in his Hollywood ventures, and had established a reputation in the film capital as a shrewd man of numerous business affairs. He was also known for his numerous affairs with budding starlets plucked from the gardens of Hollywood beauties. Stories soon spread of his romances with Marion Davies, Betty Compton, and Gloria Swanson.

Young Jack Kennedy was also "brought up differently from the average American child." Looking back on his childhood, Jack said that he was raised in an atmosphere of "institutionalized living." Surrounded by servants and nannies, the Kennedy children saw little of their mother or father. Joe was frequently busy with his various affairs—always, it seemed, en route to London, or Paris, or Hollywood. When Joe was in London in 1928, Rose wrote him, "I am praying that I shall see you soon. Do pray too, and go to church, as it is very important in my life that you do just that." But Joe was in London with Gloria Swanson and had little time for prayer. Joe's priorities were money and women. In Gloria Swanson he found both. One of Hollywood's top stars, Swanson was beautiful, sophisticated, wealthy—and titled. Her husband was the dashing Marquis de la Falaise de la Coudraye.

In the summer of 1927 Joe Kennedy had acquired the Hyannisport summer house on the east coast of Cape Cod that would one day be expanded into the Kennedy compound. Neighbors recalled the extraordinary event that took place in the summer of 1929 when Gloria Swanson arrived at Hyannis: "Miss Swanson and her party landed in the harbor near the breakwater not far from Kennedy's summer house, in a Sikorsky amphibious aircraft. Hyannisport residents gaped from the beach as Miss Swanson—petite, chic, flawlessly coiffed and a member of the aristocracy since her marriage to the Marquis de la Falaise de la Coudraye—deplaned."

It was a bizarre situation. Swanson found it incredible that Rose Kennedy pretended to know nothing of the affair. Swanson wondered, "Was she a fool, I asked myself with disbelief, or a saint? Or just a better actress than I was?"

The Kennedy children referred to the Hollywood film star as "Aunt Gloria." Aunt Gloria even left her autograph on the wall of the children's playhouse, and Jack wrote her a thank-you note for gifts received. According to children of the Kennedy's neighbors, Joe Kennedy took "Aunt Gloria" sailing in the family sailboat named after Mrs. Kennedy, the "Rose Elizabeth." He and Swanson were interrupted in their nautical lovemaking by young Jack, who had stowed away aboard the *Rose Elizabeth*. When he peeked up from below deck and was surprised to find his father on board "Aunt Gloria," the horrified and bewildered boy panicked and jumped overboard. Joe Kennedy dove in after him and hauled him back to the boat.

What occurred that summer afternoon in 1929, when Jack was twelve years old, was undoubtedly a traumatic event for this young Catholic boy. But Gloria Swanson was only one of the parade of attractive young women who visited the Kennedy compound. Neighbor Nancy Coleman recalled that Rose Kennedy would be driving out to the airport in her Rolls-Royce for one of her frequent trips abroad, and almost simultaneously Joe Kennedy would be driving into the driveway with a girlfriend. Young Jack and the other sons soon learned that promiscuity was an inherent masculine right.

"My own special interest in clothes developed during this period," Rose Kennedy later explained. "Not just from this episode, but from the general circumstances of which it was an especially vivid part. . . . Obviously, I couldn't compete in natural beauty, but I could make the most of what I had by keeping my figure trim, my complexion good, my grooming perfect, and by always wearing clothes that were interesting and becoming."

During the next few years Rose Kennedy would accomplish this by making at least seventeen trips to Europe in which she would haunt the Paris fashion houses, seeking out the latest styles and shopping for particularly interesting diamond jewelry. Rose confided to a neighbor that she made her husband pay for his infidelity. "I made him give me everything I wanted—clothes, jewels, everything!"

Jack Kennedy was particularly sensitive regarding his mother's long absences from home. He confided to a friend that he used to cry each time Rose packed her bags for one of her extended trips abroad, and he protested, "Gee, you're a great mother to go away and leave your children alone." He later angrily exclaimed to one of his school chums, "My mother was either at some Paris fashion house, or else on her knees in some church. She was never there when we really needed her. . . . My mother never really held me and hugged me. Never! Never!"

Rose Kennedy's retreat from her husband and her family was resented perhaps more by Jack than the other children, and he was to tell his friend

Mary Gimbel, "My mother is a nothing!" He grew up with a hostile attitude toward marriage and family. Women were viewed as no more than sex objects. His experience of family life involved "institutionalized living—children in a cell block."

Though the childhoods of Jack Kennedy and Norma Jeane were quite different, the sense of parental isolation and emotional denial was to a certain extent a shared experience.

"In the orphanage I began to stutter," Marilyn recalled. "My mother and the idea of being an orphan—maybe that's the reason. Anyway, I stuttered. Later on in my teens at Van Nuys High School, they elected me secretary of the English class, and every time I had to read the minutes I'd say, 'Minutes of the last m-m-m-meeting.' It was terrible. That went on for years, I guess, until I was fifteen."

She attributed the cause of her speech disorder to "my mother and the idea of being an orphan—maybe that's the reason." However, the chronology of events indicates that the stuttering was related to the molestation incident.

The stammering problem never went away entirely. In 1960 Marilyn Monroe stated, "Sometimes it even happens to me today if I'm very nervous or excited. Once when I had a small part in a movie, in a scene where I was supposed to go up the stairs, I forgot what was happening and the assistant director came and yelled at me, and I was so confused that when I got into the scene I stuttered. Then the director himself came over to me and said, 'You don't stutter.' And I said 'Tha-Tha-That's what you th-thi . . . think!' It was painful, and it still is if I speak very fast or have to make a speech . . . terrible."

The children from the orphanage attended the Vine Street Elementary School several blocks away and walked there in a group. Norma Jeane found it difficult to make friends at Vine Street because the children from the orphanage were considered homeless. "They're from the place for homeless hooligans," it was whispered, and the orphans were never invited to visit and play at the homes of the more fortunate students. In her unhappiness at the orphanage, Norma Jeane made plans for escape. She tried to run away with another girl from the dormitory, but they got only as far as the front lawn before being discovered.

On a homeless child's birthday, the orphanage followed a prescribed ritual. A large, elaborate birthday cake would be wheeled into the dining hall on a tea cart while all the orphans dutifully sang "Happy Birthday" to the celebrant. The birthday child would then blow out the candles. However, the jubilation would often be as wooden as the cake, which had plaster frosting and was carved out of pine. The wooden cake had a triangular divot allowing for one slice of genuine cake, which was ceremoniously served to the orphaned celebrant. Much to the salivary disappointment of the novices, the wooden cake would then be wheeled into a closet where it remained until the next birthday festivities.

Whenever Grace Goddard visited the orphanage, Norma Jeane complained bitterly about her confinement in the hope that "Aunt Grace" would come to her rescue. In the months that followed, her guardian became Norma Jeane's "saving Grace." Grace would often take her away from the orphanage on the weekends for visits to the small Hollywood home she shared with "Doc."

On these special outings Grace permitted Norma Jeane to try her lipstick, and Grace would put her straight light-brown hair in curlers. Sometimes she'd be taken to a beauty parlor on Hollywood Boulevard to have her hair done. Guardianship records indicate that Grace bought dresses and shoes for Norma Jeane with the meager proceeds from the sale of Gladys's few possessions.

In time Norma Jeane was told the truth regarding her mother's mental illness and that Gladys was confined in Norwalk. Gladys was allowed to leave the asylum and lunch with Norma Jeane and Grace, but on these rare occasions Gladys remained withdrawn and uncommunicative, scarcely acknowledging her daughter's presence.

"Grace loved and adored Norma Jeane," a friend and coworker at the studios, Leila Fields, recalled, "If it weren't for Grace there would be no Marilyn Monroe. She raved about Norma Jeane like she was her own. Grace said Norma Jeane was going to be a movie star. She had this feeling—a conviction. 'Don't worry, Norma Jeane, you're going to be a beautiful girl when you get big—an important woman, a movie star!' "

Grace Goddard's compassion for Norma Jeane was entangled with her own frustrations. She had come to Hollywood to be a movie star like Mary Pickford, but ended up being an itinerant assembler of the movie stars' celluloid images. Unable to have children of her own, Grace became a foster "stage mother" and focused the transference of her frustrations on Norma Jeane. In photos taken by Grace during this period, Norma Jeane is seen in Mary Pickford curls and makeup—a lost dream from an earlier generation. By the 1930s, Mary Pickford, the innocent child with the beautiful curls and the petulant pout, was fading into puffy oblivion. She had been supplanted by the overt sexuality of the vamps and the "it" girls. The shimmering platinum-blond sensuality of Jean Harlow in *Hell's Angels*, *Public Enemy*, and *Red Dust* had electrified audiences and catapulted Harlow into instant stardom. Harlow soon became Grace's new idol. She dyed her own hair blond and began divining a young Harlow in Norma Jeane. "There's no reason why you can't grow up to be just like her," Grace would say.

Marilyn recalled, "Time after time Grace touched a spot on my nose and said, 'You're perfect except for this little bump, sweetheart, but with the right hair and a better nose one day you'll be perfect—like Jean Harlow. And so Jean Harlow became my idol, too."

On the weekends Grace frequently took Norma Jeane to lunch and a movie show at the Grauman's Chinese, where Norma Jeane remembered "trying to fit my feet into the footprints—but my school shoes were too big for the stars' slim high-heeled ones." In 1935 she saw *China Seas* with Clark Gable and Harlow. Gable reminded her of the man with the mustache and the jaunty smile in the photo of Stan Gifford her mother had kept on the wall. When Gladys had been taken away, Gifford's photo was packed in a trunk by Grace, and it would be many years before Norma Jeane would see it once again. But in her dreams Gable became "the man I thought was my father."

It was during her confinement at the Orphans' Home that a sleep disorder had its onset. The affliction was to haunt her the rest of her life. Marilyn Monroe suffered from "night terrors." While insomnia is characterized by a restless wakefulness that prevents sleep, night terrors are characterized by the victim's sudden arousal from deep sleep by the "fight or flight" syndrome—the rush of adrenaline that accompanies panic and fear. In extreme cases the victim wakes in a cold sweat—screaming, trembling, and in mortal terror.

At the orphanage Norma Jeane would suddenly wake up at night screaming and shivering in the darkness. Anxieties and a sense of isolation may have been momentarily forgotten in merciful play, sports, and the duties of the day, but when she lay sleeping in the dark of the dormitory, her heart would race, her pulse quicken, her mind and body surge with adrenaline as the suppressed memory of her mad mother, her "heritage," and the sudden severance of relationships engulfed her. Orphans often vanished from their beds after dark, when the "night people" came and took them away before dawn.

Norma Jeane's world brightened when Grace McKee appeared one weekend and held out the hope of rescue. She indicated that one day she might be able to provide a home for her. Doc Goddard had three children from a previous marriage, and Grace was faced with her own practical considerations. However, the directress of the orphanage felt that Norma Jeane needed to be placed in a family situation, and it was arranged for Norma Jeane to be temporarily placed in a foster home until a more permanent arrangement could be made.

"Suddenly, I wasn't in the orphanage anymore," Marilyn remembered.

I was placed with a family who were given five dollars a week for keeping me. I was placed with nine different families before I was able to quit being a legal orphan. I remember one where I stayed for just three or four weeks. I remember them because the woman delivered furniture polish made by her husband. Every morning we'd load up the backseat of her car with the bottles and she'd take me along. We'd bump along the roads and the car smelled like polish, and I'd get *so* carsick. I can still hear the awful sound of the car starting and her yelling, "Norma Jeane! Get in the car! Let's go!"

After that I only lived in the orphanage off and on. The families with whom I lived had one thing in common—a need for five dollars. I was also an asset to have in the house. I was strong and healthy and able to do almost as much work as a grown-up. And I had learned not to bother anyone by talking or crying. I learned also that the best way to keep out of trouble was by never complaining or asking for anything. Most of the families had children of their own, and I knew they always came first. They wore the colored dresses and owned whatever toys there were. My own costume never varied. It consisted of a faded blue skirt and white waist. I had two of each, but since they were exactly alike everyone thought I wore the same outfit all the time.

Every second week the Home sent a woman inspector out to see how its orphans were getting along in the world. She never asked me any questions, but would pick up my foot and look at the bottom of my shoes. If my shoe bottoms weren't worn through, I was reported in a thriving condition. I never minded coming "last" in these families except on Saturday nights when everybody took a bath. Water cost money, and changing the water in the tub was an unheard of extravagance. The whole family used the same tub of water. And I was always the last one in. One family with whom I lived was so poor that I was often scolded for flushing the toilet at night. "That uses up five gallons of water," my new "uncle" would say, "and five gallons each time can run into money."

I was always very quiet, at least in front of the adults. They used to call me "the mouse." I didn't say very much except to other children, and I had a lot of imagination. The other kids liked to play with me because I could think of things. I'd say, "Now we're going to play murder . . . or divorce," and they'd say, "How do you think of things like that?" No matter how careful I was, there were always troubles. Some of my troubles were my own fault. I did hit someone occasionally, I'd pull her hair, and knock her down . . . and I was often accused of stealing things—a necklace, a comb, a ring, or a nickel. I never stole anything. When the troubles came I had only one way to meet them—by staying silent. Aunt Grace would ask me when she came to visit how things were. I would tell her always they were fine because I didn't like to see her eyes turn unhappy. In a way they were not troubles at all because I was used to them. When I look back on those days I remember, in fact, that they were full of all sorts of fun and excitement. I played games in the sun and ran races. I also had daydreams, not only about my father's photograph but about many other things. I daydreamed chiefly about beauty. I dreamed of myself becoming so beautiful that people would turn to look at me when I passed. And I dreamed of colors— scarlet, gold, green and white. I dreamed of myself walking proudly in beautiful clothes and being admired by everyone and overhearing words of praise.

Norma Jeane, the Human Bean

Side by side with the exigencies of life, love is the great educator.
—Sigmund Freud

When Norma Jeane had her "troubles" she was often sent back to the orphanage until Grace Goddard could find another foster family to take care of her. Many of the families were among those who had been lured to the golden dream of Southern California in the roaring twenties, only to find themselves stuck in their stucco crackerboxes in the desperate thirties. While the foster families had a common need for five dollars, they also had in common a family relationship to Grace Goddard. The five dollars a week that Grace's relatives received from the state for looking after Norma Jeane went a long way in the midst of the Depression: in 1936 gasoline was nine cents a gallon, hamburger was eight cents a pound, movies were fifteen cents, oranges were a dime for three dozen. As the court-appointed guardian, Grace received $325 a year, comparable in purchasing power to approximately $3,500 in the mid-1990s—enough to buy groceries rather than wait in line at Helms Bakery for stale bread.

That Norma Jeane was farmed out by Grace Goddard to numerous foster homes, but never stayed for any period of time with Doc and Grace, may be attributed to Grace's practicality. While Grace was quick to do a kindness, she drew the line at any inconvenience to her private life. Her coworker Leila Fields stated, "Grace was fun, outgoing and generous, but ultimately Grace never did anything unless it was right for Grace." However, shortly after Norma Jeane's eleventh birthday, she moved into the Goddards' small house on Barbara Court in Hollywood's Cahuenga Pass. On June 12, 1937, Norma Jeane left the orphanage for the last time.

After twenty-one months of being shuttled from orphanage to foster home and back, Norma Jeane believed she had finally found a permanent home with the Goddards. The house on Barbara Court was not far from Hollywood Boulevard, where Grace would take her to the beauty shop, C. C. Brown's Ice Cream Parlor, and the movie palaces.

"Grace could have no children of her own, and so she lavished her affection on Norma Jeane, whom she considered to be as much or more hers than Gladys's," Doc's daughter Bebe Goddard observed. "Grace was very perceptive. From this very early time she had the idea that Norma Jeane was going to be a movie star, and she did everything in her power to bring it about."

According to Grace Goddard's friend Olin Stanley, Grace would bring Norma Jeane to the studios and show her off. She'd be wearing a pretty dress and shiny Mary Jane shoes, and have her hair done up in curls. Grace would fuss over her and exclaim, "Olin, isn't she pretty? Norma Jeane, turn around and show the nice man the big bow on the back of your dress. Now walk down that way and turn around . . . Good! Now walk back here again. Tell Olin what you're going to be when you're all grown up. Say, 'a movie star,' baby! Tell him you're going to be a movie star!"

Norma Jeane loved the attention: "Grace was always wonderful to me," Marilyn Monroe commented in later years. "Without her, who knows where I would have landed?"

But the idyll at the Goddards' Barbara Court home came to a sudden end. In November 1937, scarcely five months after her arrival, Norma Jeane was again uprooted and sent to the house of Ida Martin and "Aunt Olive" Monroe in nearby Lankershim.

Marilyn Monroe stated in 1960 that the move took place because "Doc and Aunt Grace were very poor, so they couldn't care for me." But the truth was that Doc drank too much. By 1937 both Doc and Grace were well on their way to becoming confirmed alcoholics, and according to Norma Jeane's first husband, James Dougherty, Doc got roaring drunk one night, causing a scene that convinced Grace to send Norma Jeane away.

"At first I was waking up in the mornings at the Goddards' and thinking

I was still at the orphanage, then, before I could get used to them, I was with another 'Aunt' and 'Uncle,' waking up and thinking I was still at the Goddards'. . . . It was all very confusing," Marilyn recalled.

Aunt Olive and Ida Martin's home in Lankershim was on Oxnard Street, not far from Laurel Canyon Boulevard. Olive Monroe was a true aunt, having been married to Gladys's younger brother, Marion Monroe. Shortly before the birth of the couple's third child, Marion walked out of the house for a newspaper and never returned. Left destitute, the family moved in with Olive's mother, Ida Martin, at the house in Lankershim.

While it was gratifying to meet relations, Norma Jeane found her new home a difficult experience. "I don't think Ida Martin was a very nice person, as I remember," Bebe Goddard confided. "And Olive kind of gave Norma Jeane a bad time because she wasn't too fond of Marion's family after his disappearance."

Norma Jeane shared a bed with Ida Mae, who was ten years old. They also shared lively imaginations. Ida Mae recalled years later, "Norma Jeane and I were just kids. We did things kids do. I remember the time we decided to make wine. We had a big tub in the back yard. We gathered grapes and piled them into the tub and tromped them with our bare dirty feet. When my mother called we hid the tub under the back porch and forgot about it. For weeks the house and yard reeked of rotten grapes and nobody knew why except Norma Jeane and I, and we were afraid to tell my mother. Once we decided to run away from home. We were going up to San Francisco to look for my father, who was Norma Jeane's uncle, because someone said they had seen him there, but we never really went, of course. But I'll never forget Norma Jeane. She stayed with us until the San Fernando Valley flood."

The flood, which caused the Los Angeles River to overflow and flood Lankershim, occurred in March 1938, and Norma Jeane was again uprooted—this time by an act of God. It proved to be the beginning of more fortunate circumstances.

"I had a real happy time while I was growing up when I went to live with a woman I called 'Aunt Ana,' " Marilyn remembered. "She was Grace McKee's [Goddard's] aunt. She was a lot older. She was sixty, I guess, or somewhere around there, but she always talked about when she was a girl of twenty. There was a real contact between us because she understood me somehow. She knew what it was like to be young. . . . And I loved her dearly. I used to do the dishes in the evening and I'd always be singing and whistling, and she'd say, 'I never heard a child sing so much!' So I did it during that time. Aunt Ana . . . I adored her."

"Aunt Ana" was Edith Ana Atchinson Lower, the sister of Grace's father. She was fifty-eight years old when Norma Jeane moved into the duplex she owned at 11348 Nebraska Avenue in West Los Angeles. Like Grace and Gladys, she was a Christian Scientist. In her devotion to the belief formulated by Mary Baker Eddy, she had advanced to the level of healing practitioner.

Norma Jeane was loving by nature and responded to the concept of God as love, and every Sunday she accompanied Aunt Ana to the Christian Science Church, whose essential transcendental belief was that God the Creator is Love—the only Reality. Mary Baker Eddy believed that the passing material world was unreal, and therefore evil and corruption had no reality. Norma Jeane's lifelong ability to become aloof from the evils that surrounded her and remain forever the guileless child perhaps stemmed from her early protective belief in Mary Baker Eddy's creed that "evil is the awful deception and unreality of existence."

Aunt Ana's duplex was in the Sawtelle district of West Los Angeles, and when Norma Jeane moved there, she entered the seventh grade at Emerson Junior High School, a two-mile walk from Sawtelle. "The other girls rode to school in a bus, but I had no nickel to pay for the ride. Rain or shine, I walked the two miles from my aunt's home to school. I hated the walk, I hated the school. I had no friends. The pupils seldom talked to me and never wanted me in their games. . . . The first year at Emerson, all I had was the two light-blue dress outfits from the orphanage. I sure didn't make any best-dressed list. In school the pupils often whispered about me and giggled as they stared at me. . . . I was very quiet. They called me dumb and made fun of my orphan's outfit. You could say I wasn't very popular. Nobody ever walked home with me or invited me to visit their homes. This was partly because I came from a poor part of the district where all the Mexicans and Japanese lived. It was also because I couldn't smile at anyone."

According to Norma Jeane's classmate Gladys Phillips, "In the thirties Los Angeles was a very divided, class-conscious society, and this was unfortunately true of school life, too. All the students were immediately, unofficially classified according to where they lived, and Sawtelle was simply not the place to be from." Her teacher, Mary Campbell, remembered, "Norma Jeane was a nice child, but not at all outgoing, not vibrant. . . .

She looked as though she wasn't well cared for. Her clothes separated her a little bit from the rest of the girls. In 1938 she wasn't well developed."

By the age of twelve, when Norma Jeane entered the seventh grade, she was tall for her age—five feet five inches, almost her full height. But she was skinny. The boys at Emerson jokingly referred to her as "Norma Jeane, the human bean." But "Norma Jeane, the human bean" was trembling on the evanescent vine of adolescence, and the faded orphan's outfit became the chrysalis of nature's revenge.

"My body was developing and becoming shapely, but no one knew this but me," she recalled.

> I still wore the blue dress and ragged blouse, and I started to look like an overgrown lummox. I tried to cheer myself up with daydreams. I dreamed of attracting attention, of having people look at me.... This wish for attention had something to do, I think, with my trouble in church on Sundays. No sooner was I in the pew with the organ playing and everybody singing a hymn than the impulse would come to me to take off all my clothes. I wanted desperately to stand up naked for God and everyone else to see.
>
> My impulse to appear naked and my dreams about it had no shame or sense of sin in them. Dreaming of people looking at me made me feel less lonely. I think I wanted them to see me naked because I was ashamed of the clothes I wore—the never-changing faded blue dress of poverty. Naked, I was like the other girls....

One morning Norma Jeane found that her last ragged blouse was torn, and she borrowed a sweater from a friend. "She was my age, but smaller," Marilyn later remembered, "I arrived at school just as the math class was starting. As I walked to my seat everybody stared at me as if I had suddenly grown two heads, which in a way I had. They were under my tight sweater. At recess a half dozen boys crowded around me. They made jokes and kept looking at my sweater as if it were a gold mine.... After school four boys walked home with me, wheeling their bicycles by hand. I was excited but acted calm." Norma Jeane had brought a new equation to the math class.

> I didn't think of my body as having anything to do with sex. It was more like a friend who had mysteriously appeared in my life, a sort of magic friend. A few weeks later, I stood in front of the mirror one morning and put lipstick on my lips. I darkened my blond eyebrows. I had no money for clothes, and I had no clothes except my orphan rig and the sweater. The lipstick and the mascara were the clothes, however. I saw that they improved my looks as much as if I had put

on a real gown. . . . My arrival in school with painted lips and darkened brows, and still encased in the magic sweater, started everybody buzzing.

By the time she entered the eighth grade in September 1939, "Norma Jeane, the human bean," had become the hubba-hubba-*mmmmmmm* girl. One of the older students who had noticed Norma Jeane's magical metamorphosis was Chuckie Moran. "There's the *mmmmmmm* girl!" he'd inevitably comment as they passed in the hall. Her renown in the halls of Emerson as "the *mmmmmmm* girl" had its origins in a humming sound Norma Jeane used for suggestive emphasis. It was undoubtedly borrowed from her idol Jean Harlow, who frequently used the sensual *mmmmmmm* sound to good effect on Clark Gable in *Red Dust* and *China Seas*. What worked on Gable apparently also worked on Chuckie Moran. Chuckie, a popular ninth-grader, had an old jalopy he was turning into a hot rod, and he often took Norma Jeane to the school dances, or the drive-in. Sometimes they'd go to the Aragon Ballroom on the Ocean Park Pier, where Pickering's Pleasure Palace once stood, and dance to one of the popular big bands like Artie Shaw, Glenn Miller, or Benny Goodman. Norma Jeane loved to do the Lindy, the Big Apple, and the Rumba, and she and Chuckie could out-jitterbug anybody on the dance floor.

> We danced until we thought we'd drop, and then, when we headed outside for a Coca-Cola and a walk in the cool breeze, Chuckie let me know he wanted more than just a dance partner. Suddenly his hands were everywhere! But I thought, well, he isn't entitled to anything else. Besides I really wasn't so smart about sex, which was probably a good thing. Poor Chuckie, all he got was tired feet. . . .

By the end of the 1930s the Depression was on the wane and the New Deal was in full power. If war clouds were looming over Europe, Hollywood was preoccupied with making movies and making money: 1939 was the year of *Gone With the Wind*, *Ninotchka*, *Wuthering Heights*, and *The Wizard of Oz*. But while Hollywood was grinding out politically innocuous fantasies, Hitler's Gestapo was rounding up Jewish "undesirables," Mussolini was gassing Ethiopians, Stalin was launching a series of deadly purges, and the Japanese were invading Manchuria. Fascism, communism, and militarism were vanquishing humanism, but according to Dorothy Parker the only "ism" Hollywood was interested in was plagiarism.

Many of those in the film business who had genuine concerns over the plight of the oppressed joined the Anti-Nazi League, which was organized by Hollywood communists John Howard Lawson and Donald Ogden Stewart. The growing threat of fascism formed an alliance of Hollywood liberals and communists, and the Anti-Nazi League attracted a wide spectrum of supporters, including Eddie Cantor; actress Florence Eldridge; Ring Lardner, Jr.; Fredric March; and Ernst Lubitsch.

Among Communist Party front organizations, the Hollywood Arts, Sciences, and Professions Council was perhaps the most influential. It combined artists, writers, lawyers, and physicians. One of the zealous members in the 1940s was Dr. Hyman Engelberg, who many years later would be Marilyn Monroe's physician at the time of her death.

Engelberg had joined the Communist Party in the early thirties when he was a medical student at Cornell University. After marrying Esther Goldstein in 1933, Engelberg became an intern at Cedars of Lebanon Hospital in Hollywood, where he met fellow internist Romeo Greenschpoon (later to be known as Ralph R. Greenson). According to Dorothy Healey, who was chairman of the Los Angeles Communist Party, both Hy Engelberg and his wife Esther became active communists in the party heyday of the thirties. Archives of the Los Angeles Communist Party document the Engelberg's attendance at numerous party meetings and fundraisers. Brochures of the Communist People's Education Center list Hyman Engelberg as an instructor. In testimony before the House Un-American Activities Committee, Dr. Oner Barker stated that Hyman Engelberg was an active member of the Doctors Unit of the Hollywood Arts, Sciences, and Professions Council.

"I remember," said a former member of the council, "that whenever you were at a meeting at a home, you always had to have a drink so that in case anyone walked in, you'd look as if you were at a party. I recall one writer saying, 'What do you think of my great Marxist library?' and there wasn't a book around. Then he pushed a button and the bar swung out and there was indeed a great Marxist library. But I think he used the bar more than the books."

In Hollywood the secrecy of the Communist Party offered a sense of excitement for some who suffered from the ennui of fame and success. According to Dorothy Healey, "The biggest mistake we made was in the party's staying underground—the cult of secrecy. The thrill came in the sense of the forbidden, of international intrigue—the secret names, aliases, underground meetings, and double identities."

Hollywood's close-knit group of communists, like communists everywhere, had insisted that the rumors of a Hitler–Stalin pact were fascist propaganda. But when German Foreign Minister Joachim von Ribbentrop flew to Moscow to sign the Hitler–Stalin Non-Aggression Treaty on August 21, 1939, the news that the pact was a fait accompli brought about bitter recriminations within the Hollywood circle of liberals and party members.

The difference between the dedicated red and the progressive liberal was quickly delineated with the announcement of the pact. The bitter debate that soon followed splintered the Anti-Nazi League, which quickly changed its name to "The Hollywood League for Democratic Action." The loyalists followed the new party line of neutrality, as it became increasingly clear that war in Europe was inevitable. Several days after the signing of the Hitler-Stalin pact, the German army began massing on the Polish border, and on September 1, Nazi troops and tanks swept into Poland.

On Saturday morning, September 3, David Niven was sleeping aboard a yacht Douglas Fairbanks, Jr., had anchored off Catalina Island on the coast of Southern California. Lawrence Olivier, Vivien Leigh, and a number of other Britons in exile were also on board. They woke to hear the news flash on the radio that Britain had delivered an ultimatum to Germany, and Hitler had rejected it. The two nations were at war. Fairbanks raised a glass to toast victory, and Olivier reportedly raised his glass, and raised his glass—and raised his glass—until, Fairbanks observed, he became "smashed as a hoot owl." Olivier began ranting and raving, "This is the end! You are finished—all of you—finished! Finished! You are relics! Done for! Doomed relics!"

But just twenty-six miles across the sea Norma Jeane Baker neither felt doomed nor looked like a relic as she walked on the sands of Ocean Park. On that sunny day at the beach the war seemed far away.

"By the summertime I had a real beau," Marilyn remembered.

He was twenty-one, and despite being very sophisticated he thought I was eighteen instead of thirteen. I was able to fool him by keeping my mouth shut and walking a little fancy. . . . I practiced walking languorously. My beau arrived at my home one Saturday with the news that we were going swimming at the beach. I borrowed a bathing suit, which was too small, and put on an old pair of slacks and a sweater. The skimpy bathing suit was under them.

It was a sunny day, the sky was blue, and the sand was crowded with people. I stood and stared at the ocean for a long time. It always had sort of a hypnotic effect on me. It was like something in a dream, full of gold and lavender colors, blue and foaming white. "Come on, let's get in!" my beau suddenly yelled.

"In where?" I asked.

"In the water," he laughed, thinking I had made a joke.

So I removed my slacks and sweater and stood there in my skimpy suit. I thought, "I'm almost naked," as I started walking across the sand. I was almost at the water's edge when some young men whistled at me. I closed my eyes and stood still for a moment. Then, instead of going into the water, I turned and walked down the beach. The same thing happened that had happened in the math class, but on a larger scale. It was also much noisier. The men whistled, and some jumped up from the sand and trotted up for a better view. Even the women stopped moving and stared as I came nearer.

I didn't pay much attention to the whistles and whoops. In fact, I didn't quite hear them. I was full of a strange feeling, as if I were two people. One of them was Norma Jeane from the orphanage who belonged to nobody. The other was someone whose name I didn't know. But I knew where she belonged. She belonged to the ocean and the sky and the whole world. . . .

Lucky Jim

Marilyn Monroe and I were married four years, and if we had stayed married, it's a cinch that today I'd be Mr. Monroe.

—Jim Dougherty

In 1940 America hovered between peace and war. Following the Hitler–Stalin pact, the left and the right joined in a strange mixed marriage of neutrality. "Keep America Out of War" was the rallying cry of Charles Lindbergh, Joseph Kennedy the ambassador to Britain, and the isolationists. "The Yanks Are Not Coming" was the slogan of John Howard Lawson, Frederick Vanderbilt Field, and the voices of the Comintern. Keeping America out of the war became a central objective of the Communist Party (CP). Frederick Vanderbilt Field, known as the "silver-spoon communist," traveled the country campaigning for neutrality and organizing the American Peace Mobilization, a CP front with over three hundred committees from the East Coast to Hollywood.

"All-out aid to the British Empire means total war for the American people," Field stated. "Men in high places are dragging us into a war three thousand miles away. Americans don't want their sons to die—mangled scraps of flesh—in order to enrich Wall Street. America, keep out of the war!"

As the Battle of Britain was being waged, Hollywood still held to the belief that the business of Hollywood was Hollywood business. "Hollywood made three hundred and fifty pictures last year," commented Walter Wanger. "Fewer than ten of these pictures departed from the usual westerns, romances, and boy-meets-girl story." Hollywood's big musical event of 1940 was Walt Disney's *Fantasia*, and the comedy riot of the year was the first pairing of Bob Hope and Bing Crosby in *Road to Singapore.*

But America was gearing up for war, and among those working on the assembly lines at Lockheed Aircraft in Burbank was the man destined to marry Norma Jeane—James Dougherty. Jim Dougherty lived with his parents on Archwood Street in Van Nuys, and Doc and Grace Goddard lived just behind them. Doc had found a job as a salesman for Adel Precision Products, and the Goddards moved from Cahuenga Pass to a small house in the Valley owned by Ana Lower. In the spring of 1941, Ana Lower, who suffered from heart disease, was unable to continue caring for Norma Jeane, who was sent to live with Doc and Grace, where she shared a room with Doc's daughter Bebe.

"I was thirteen when I first met Norma Jeane, who I called 'Normie,' " Bebe recalled, "but we really didn't live together until she moved into the house in Van Nuys. We were both born in 1926, and we became good friends. Jimmy Dougherty lived next door and was five years older than Norma Jeane, but Normie went for older men and thought Jimmy was a dreamboat."

It wasn't long before Dougherty noticed that another pretty girl was living with the Goddards. "I discovered her name was Norma Jeane," Dougherty recalled, "but I didn't have enough interest to find out her last name."

Dougherty worked the graveyard shift and he remembers an afternoon when he was trying to sleep and Norma Jeane was in the nearby backyard whooping and hollering with laughter. Annoyed, he went to his bedroom window and saw her playing with Grace's spaniel.

"The dog had got the best of Norma Jeane and had her down on the ground, licking her face. She was giggling and shrieking," Dougherty recalls. "I got up—I think it was the second time this had happened—and I was a little angry. But when I asked her to can the loud noise, Norma Jeane was so angelic, you might say, all I could say was, 'Well, don't worry about it. Forget it.' After that we'd talk and shoot the breeze, but she was much younger than she looked. She was just a kid—a charity case, having just gotten out of an orphanage."

In September 1941, the Goddards moved to a more spacious California ranch house set back from the street in a grove of pepper trees on Odessa Avenue. The new Goddard home was farther away from Van Nuys High, but the transportation problem was solved when Grace asked Jim Dougherty's mother, Ethel, if her son would mind picking "the kids" up from school. Jim volunteered because "it seemed like the neighborly thing to do." Norma Jeane was pleased with the arrangement. Jim was a gentleman, with a lively, outgoing personality and a handsome, happy-go-lucky Irish face to go along with his uncomplicated manner. His friends called him Lucky Jim.

"As I recall, there was quite a flirtation when Jimmy was bringing us home from school," Bebe said. "We'd ride home from school with Jimmy and hang around the house. After school sometimes we'd have quite a crowd. . . . Jimmy and a couple of guys that played guitar would hang around and teach us to play craps and stuff like that. Then he finally asked her for a date."

Dougherty, who occasionally sported a mustache, bore a faint resemblance to the photo of Norma Jeane's father. "Norma Jeane was fascinated by my mustache," Dougherty remarked. The mustache made him look older and more mature than his twenty years. Norma Jeane often referred to him as "Daddy," just as she would later call DiMaggio "Pa" and Arthur Miller "Pappy." "What a Daddy!" Norma Jeane once exclaimed to Bebe after returning from a date with Lucky Jim.

"She was real nice company, but awfully young," Dougherty recalls. "Still, the message was clear enough each day—Norma Jeane liked me. It was in her expression as she got out of the car, in her smile, the warmest smile I'd ever seen in a girl."

During the fall semester at Van Nuys High School, Dougherty recalled that Bebe was frequently sick and absent from school. On these occasions he'd be alone in the car with Norma Jeane, and she would sit extra close to him. Sometimes the car ride home would end up in the Hollywood Hills. After an early movie on the weekends they'd park up on the notorious Mulholland Drive and do what was innocently referred to as "necking—a lot of kissing and a lot of hugging." In those days young people weren't as promiscuous and, according to Dougherty, Norma Jeane knew when to stop. "She very neatly held things in check," Dougherty stated.

On December 7, when the Japanese launched a surprise attack on Pearl Harbor, it was feared that they would next bomb Los Angeles, where two-thirds of the nation's aircraft production was centered at Douglas, North American, and Lockheed. Some people were so terrified of an attack by

Japanese planes that they vacated their homes and moved inland. People in the movie colony suddenly took extended vacations in Palm Springs, and Los Angeles real estate took a nosedive.

On Wednesday, December 10, Los Angeles had its first complete blackout. People in Hollywood were having dinner when the sirens wailed. A voice over the radio announced, "This is the Fourth Interceptor Command. Unidentified planes in the sky. Complete blackout ordered immediately." The lights went out in Chasen's, the Brown Derby, Ciro's, the Trocadero. As the city became dark, patrons poured out of restaurants and nightclubs eager to get home or head for the desert. It seemed like the end of the world—except on Hollywood Boulevard, where they couldn't find the switch to turn off the lights on the Christmas trees that lined "Christmas Tree Lane."

Unable to drive to the midnight shift at Lockheed because of the blackout, Jim Dougherty waited until the all-clear, which came in the early hours of the morning. Though Norma Jeane begged him not to go, Dougherty drove on to the Lockheed plant in Burbank, where the business of building bombers received new impetus. Despite the war jitters, Doc Goddard's company, Adel Precision Products, decided to hold its annual Christmas dance. Knowing that something was going on between Norma Jeane and Jimmy, Grace suggested to Jimmy's mother Ethel that Jimmy invite Norma Jeane to the dance and find a date for Bebe. Jimmy still remembers how fantastic Norma Jeane looked that night in a beautiful red party dress she had borrowed for the occasion. He recalls that during the slow numbers like "Everything Happens to Me" and "Dream," Norma Jeane leaned extra close to him, eyes shut tight in a romantic reverie. "Even Grace and Doc noticed that I wasn't being just 'Good Neighbor Sam,' so to speak. I was having the time of my life with this little girl, who didn't seem or feel so little any more."

In January of 1942 Adel Precision offered Doc Goddard a position as the head of its burgeoning East Coast Sales Department. Doc eagerly accepted the promotion, which involved relocating in West Virginia. Grace and Bebe were to accompany him, but it was decided that Norma Jeane, who was still a ward of the court, would have to remain. When Norma Jeane learned of the Goddards' plans, she was devastated. Just as she began to feel that she had a real home and a real family and a budding romance, there was to be another sudden wrenching of relationships.

As Norma Jeane prepared herself for the Goddards' departure and an uncertain future, Ethel Dougherty approached her son with a blunt suggestion. "Sometime in the early part of 1942," Dougherty recalled, "Mom called me aside and said, 'Doc and Grace are going to move to West Virginia for his company. They're going to take Bebe, but they can't take Norma Jeane. Mrs. Lower isn't well enough to look after her, and that means she goes back to the orphanage until she's eighteen.' "

"I'm listening," Dougherty responded.

"Grace wants to know if you would be interested in marrying Norma Jeane. She turns sixteen next June."

After contemplating the alternatives, and thinking about Grace's suggestion, Dougherty said yes. When Grace presented the idea to Norma Jeane, she confided, "Jim's such a wonderful person. I want to marry him, but I don't know anything about sex. Can we get married without having sex?"

"Don't worry about that," Grace said. "Jim'll teach you."

The marriage was planned for mid-June, after Norma Jeane turned sixteen. In March Norma Jeane temporarily moved back to Aunt Ana's home in Sawtelle and transferred from Van Nuys to University High School in Santa Monica, where she was in her junior year. In April the Goddards moved to West Virginia, taking Bebe with them, and there were painful good-byes. Norma Jeane and Bebe had become close friends. "We were both just heartbroken," Bebe Goddard confided, "And after we moved to Huntington, West Virginia, I was very lonely for Normie, but we corresponded, and I still have some of her letters."

When Doc and Grace Goddard left Norma Jeane behind, Dougherty recalled that she went through a period of feeling rejected. Once again she had been abandoned, and on this one occasion Norma Jeane tearfully complained that Grace "had let her down and always thought of herself first." But that was the past. In the future Jim Dougherty would be there for her.

Ethel Dougherty and Ana Lower planned the wedding, which took place on Friday evening, June 19, 1942. The Bolenders were sent an invitation by Norma Jeane and were among the twenty-five guests in attendance. The Goddards wired their love and best wishes from West Virginia. There seemed no possibility that Gladys would attend. Having left the Norwalk State Hospital, she was institutionalized at the Agnew State Hospital near San Francisco.

The ceremony was conducted by a nondenominational Christian minister at the Brentwood home of the Chester Howells, friends of the Goddards. Norma Jeane descended the spiral staircase in a beautiful wedding dress that had been a gift from Aunt Ana. Dougherty's brother, Marion, was the best man; a girl friend from "Uni High" was her matron of honor; and Dougherty's nephew, Wesley, was the ring bearer. It was Aunt Ana who gave the June bride away. Lucky Jim fondly reminisced, "When she smiled at me after the ceremony, her sweet smile would have melted a stone. It seemed to say, 'I trust you, I believe what you say, I love you.' And her eyes were so expressive.... While it's hard not to sound senti-mental about it, she had offered me her heart—nobody else was going to have it. That was it."

Norma Jeane, "who belonged to nobody," now belonged to Lucky Jim. But Dougherty didn't know about the other person, the one who made Norma Jeane feel as if she were two people—"the other . . . whose name I didn't know. But I knew where she belonged. She belonged to the ocean and the sky and the whole world. . . ."

Mr. and Mrs. James Dougherty moved into a new studio apartment on Vista Del Monte in the Valley. "Norma Jeane was delighted with the place," Dougherty remembered. "It was the first time in her life she'd had a real place of her own. It had a pull-down Murphy bed, which she thought was great fun.... She began our married life knowing nothing, but absolutely nothing, about sex. But Norma Jeane loved sex. It was as natural to her as breakfast in the morning. There were never any problems with it."

Dougherty went back to work at Lockheed the Monday following the wedding and found a note in his lunch box: "Dearest Daddy—When you read this, I'll be asleep and dreaming of you. Love and kisses, Your Baby." With the Goddards gone and his "Baby's" mother in an institution, Dougherty realized he had taken on a great responsibility. "I was very much in love," Dougherty recalled. "She had a quick wit and a beautiful face and body. She was the most mature sixteen-year-old I had ever met when we married.... There was something mature and terribly proper about her, which she may have inherited. I later noticed this trait in her mother, even though she was emotionally disturbed. Then at other times she was like a little girl. She had no childhood and it showed. There were two Norma Jeanes—one was the child whose dolls and stuffed animals were propped up on top of the chest of drawers 'so they can see what's going on.' The other Norma Jeane had moods in her that were unpre-dictable and often a little scary. You'd catch glimpses of someone who had been unloved for too long, unwanted too many years."

After staying in the studio apartment for six months, the Doughertys rented a small house on Bessemer Street in Van Nuys. It was at the Bessemer Street house that Dougherty came home one rainy day to find Norma Jeane trying to lead a cow from a nearby field into the living room because she had heard it mournfully mooing out in the rain.

According to Dougherty, she tried very hard to be a grown-up housewife. She kept the house very neat, always packed him a lunch box with a love note, and tried to learn to be a good cook. Dougherty confessed that the stories of her frequently cooking peas and carrots because she liked the color combination are true. He confided that in those days Norma Jeane trusted everybody. While Dougherty was out she would buy encyclopedias from men in their thirties who told her they were working their way through college. She had a thirst for knowledge and thought she could buy it on the installment plan. At one time they had three sets of encyclopedias, and another one on the way.

The Doughertys had a mutual understanding that they would practice birth control. Dougherty admits that he was the one who insisted on it and talked her into the decision. There were the insecurities of the war to consider, and Dougherty felt that Norma Jeane was too young to be a mother. He described Norma Jeane as a girl who "thoroughly enjoyed sexual union," and that their lovemaking was pure joy. "We both had trim bodies and the sight of hers and mine nude excited both of us. Getting undressed for bed was almost unfailingly erotic and almost before the light was out we were locked together. If I took a shower and she opened the door, it was the same thing all over again—instant sex."

He once confided to a friend that Norma Jeane's sexual appetite at times seemed insatiable. "The most vivid memory I have of Norma Jeane is of her hand reaching over as we were driving along a country road, and I knew it meant that she wanted me to stop wherever we were and make love. Sometimes I'd say, 'Honey, we've got a home and a beautiful bed,' but she would lean against my chest and look up at me and sigh, 'It's more romantic out here.' So we'd park right there and do it. . . . Sometimes this impulse came over her while we were driving through a built-up section of the San Fernando Valley, which was well populated. And Norma Jeane would say urgently, 'Pull off here! Pull off here!' And away we went."

But Norma Jeane's emotional demands could also be insatiable.

"She was so sensitive and insecure, and I realized I wasn't prepared to handle her," Dougherty admitted. "Her feelings were very easily hurt. She thought I was mad at her if I didn't kiss her good-bye every time I left the house. When we had an argument—and there were plenty—I'd often say, 'Just shut up!' and go out and sleep on the couch. . . . I thought I knew what she wanted, but what I thought was never what she wanted."

Though the Selective Service had called in many of Dougherty's friends and former classmates, he was exempt from the draft as long as he held his strategic employment at Lockheed. But without saying anything to Norma Jeane, Dougherty admits, "I went out and began the process of enlisting in the navy." When Norma Jeane heard of Dougherty's plans she became distraught.

"Oh, honey," Dougherty recalls her crying, "Please don't do this! Your job at Lockheed is important! Please don't!"

Disturbed by her hysteria, Dougherty asked the enlistment officer to tear up his application papers, and he continued working at Lockheed.

Dougherty claims that he "felt guilty about not being more involved with the fighting and taking the risks nearly all my schoolmates were taking." But his next attempt at seeking sanctuary from Norma Jeane's demands had little relationship to the war: "I went down to the local fire department and asked if there were any openings. There were, and I filled out an application."

Fighting fires instead of the Axis powers offered the best of both possible worlds. Lucky Jim would spend several days a week at home with the wife he loved but "wasn't prepared to handle," and he would spend several sequential days and nights on duty at the fire department—where all he might have to fight were infernos. But when Norma Jeane learned about the application at the fire department, she was burning mad.

"She was angry about it," Dougherty said, "She seemed to think we'd got all that settled when I applied for the navy."

"You'll lose your deferment!" she bitterly complained, and he asked the fire department to tear up that application as well.

Dougherty has memories of Norma Jeane's unpredictable mood swings. Sometimes she would be quiet and withdrawn; at other times she would be aggressive and extroverted. "With friends she was often quiet and more of a listener, far more of an introvert than I could ever be," he recalls. But Dougherty would see another aspect of his wife when they had friends over and Norma Jeane asked them to bring dance records. After dinner the carpet would be rolled back, and Dougherty would be amazed to see the instant metamorphosis that would take place. As soon as the needle hit the shellac she'd be transformed into an erotic bombshell of rhythmic grace. Dougherty would grow increasingly jealous as she cut in and danced with all the male guests, giggling and obviously enjoying the attention she received.

Buddies told Dougherty about the merchant marine. He had learned that there were frequent home leaves between trips, and in midsummer of 1943, a little more than a year after their wedding, Dougherty told Norma Jeane that he had definitely made up his mind—he was joining the merchant marine. That night there was a terrible scene. "It was a bad one, the worst I could remember since we were married," Dougherty reluctantly recalled. "Norma Jeane threw herself frantically at me, begging me to make her pregnant so that she 'would have a piece of me, in case something happened.' She seemed to fear, now that she had me and her life had a direction for the first time, that it would end suddenly—that she would be cheated again by life the way she had been so many times before. I explained to her that if anything did happen, the child might end up like she did—with a mother who couldn't support it because of the pressures, and it would wind up in an institution. But she wouldn't agree, and she cried and wept all night. Perhaps I was too harsh—too insensitive to her needs. . . ."

The day Dougherty left to report to the merchant marine in San Pedro, California, Norma Jeane was hysterical. She was so distressed that Dougherty feels he wouldn't have been able to leave her had she not been left in the care of his mother, Ethel. After a couple of days at the Maritime Training Base on nearby Catalina Island, Dougherty was allowed to phone home, and Norma Jeane was thrilled to hear the sound of his voice. "You would have thought I'd been gone for a year," he vividly remembered.

When he called Norma Jeane to tell her that he was to be stationed with a training unit on Catalina and she could live with him in Avalon, he recalled that she let out a shout of joy that could have been heard from Van Nuys to Catalina without the aid of a telephone.

In September of 1943 they found an apartment in Avalon, on the side of the bay that overlooks the harbor. Dougherty had been assigned as a physical instructor to new recruits, and he worked regular hours and was able to return to the apartment in the evenings. The wartime population on the island was predominantly male. The merchant marine, the OSS, and the marines had virtually commandeered Catalina as a training ground, and the few women who lived there were either old ladies who remained in their homes for the duration, or the few wives of officers and instructors in permanent training companies. Ninety percent of the wartime population consisted of virile males isolated on an island where the few women were mostly old, plain, and married. "Those hordes of sex-starved marines and sailors crowded onto that small island with us suddenly loomed as a major threat," Dougherty said.

He remembers the Saturday night Stan Kenton and his band came over to play at a dance for the servicemen in the Avalon Casino Ballroom. "Norma Jeane was very excited and got into a tight white summer dress and spent hours over her hair. This drawn-out getting-ready ritual had begun soon after we were married. She could spend an hour deciding what to wear and just as long bathing. Norma Jeane would drive me crazy getting ready. I don't think she really knew how long a minute was, or an hour. She thought time was a rubber band. Well, when we finally got to the dance, I swung into a few steps of a swing version of 'The Peanut Vendor' with Norma Jeane, and almost immediately felt a tap on my shoulder. A marine cut in and I lost sight of Norma Jeane for more than an hour. She was having a ball, of course. Hell, she was the belle of the ball.

"I couldn't be sure, but Norma Jeane must have danced with every one of those guys at the dance during the three or four hours we were there, because they were all cutting in on each other. It was the first taste I'd had of her appeal to a large group, and I must admit I was shaken by the experience. I'll even grant I got a bit jealous. . . . I felt threatened."

But for Norma Jeane it was a dream come true, and there was no way that Lucky Jim could have fully comprehended his young bride's cache of daydreams—dreams she scarcely understood herself.

Eighteen months after their wedding, Jim Dougherty shipped out. Though he could have stayed on as a physical trainer at Catalina, he admits that he requested sea duty. He would like to believe that Norma Jeane never learned that it was his decision and not the merchant marine's. In December he sailed for the South Pacific on the freighter *Julia S. DuMont*. He had signed up for over a year at sea.

In the winter, when the damp fog rolls in and enshrouds Catalina, the island takes on a surreal sense of separation from time and circumstance, even in the best of times and circumstances. But the Christmas season was always a difficult time for Norma Jeane, who was left alone in the apartment overlooking Avalon Bay. The mournful wail of the foghorn must have echoed her resounding sense of rejection by the man she had once given her heart to. In a letter that was postmarked in Avalon six weeks before Dougherty received it in Townsville, Australia, Norma Jeane told him she couldn't bear the thought of him being so far away, and that she could "see nothing from the porch at Avalon but fog."

Norma Jeane from the orphanage belonged to nobody again, and she couldn't see her way. But on a clear day, when the sun shimmered on the ocean and the seas danced with gold and lavender colors, she could see the nearby mainland's glimmering shore. When the fog lifted she could see that it was on the mainland's golden strand that the other person belonged, that other person whose name she still didn't know.

Did You Happen to See...?

> There's something addicting about a secret.
> —J. Edgar Hoover

Though his back condition and a history of unstable health should have disqualified him from military service, Jack Kennedy's father used his influence to have his son granted a commission as an ensign in the naval reserve. Ensign Jack Kennedy's first active duty assignment was at ONI, the Office of Naval Intelligence in Washington, D.C.

When her brother arrived in the capital in October 1941, Kathleen "Kick" Kennedy was a reporter for the *Washington Times-Herald*, and it was "Kick" who introduced Jack to the *Times-Herald* columnist Inga Arvad. Arvad's column "Did You Happen to See . . . ?" was a gossipy interview piece with varied Washington personalities. When Arvad happened to see Ensign Jack Kennedy of ONI, she recalled being enthralled: "He had the charm that makes birds come out of the trees. And when he walked into a room you knew he was there, not pushing, not domineering, but exuding animal magnetism. . . . His best-seller *Why England Slept* had been published and my boss Cissy Patterson said, 'Get an interview for your column with young Jack Kennedy'—I did!"

The "Did You Happen to See Jack Kennedy?" column appeared in the *Washington Times-Herald* of November 27, 1941. It read:

If former Ambassador Joe Kennedy has a brilliant mind and charm galore, then son no. 2 has inherited more than his due. . . . The 24 years of Jack's existence on our planet have proved that here is really a boy with a future. He speaks eloquently, and he is the best listener I have come across. . . .

Another good listener was J. Edgar Hoover. The FBI chief suspected that Inga Arvad had been sent to Washington as a Nazi spy. "We had microphones planted in her apartment and a tap on her telephone," Hoover's assistant, William Sullivan, stated.

John White, Kick Kennedy's beau of the hour, said of Arvad, "She was very smart—certainly smart enough to be a spy—but also extremely loving. . . . She was adorable, just adorable. She looked adorable and was. She was totally woman. She was gorgeous, luscious—*luscious* is the word. Like a lot of icing on the cake. . . . What was it that attracted Jack? Oh . . . sex!"

Initially, the FBI had no idea of the identity of the Nordic beauty's mysterious lover, who was seen frequently staying the night in her apartment at 1600 Sixteenth Street. The surveillance agent described him as "a Naval Ensign who wore a gray overcoat with raglan sleeves and gray tweed trousers. He does not wear a hat, and has blonde curly hair which is always tousled . . . known only as 'Jack'." Bugs planted in the apartment revealed that he called her "Inga Binga," and she called him "Jacko Tobacco."

When it was discovered that the suspected Nazi spy's lover was Ensign Jack Kennedy of ONI, the FBI chief's alarm sounded. Jack's assignment at Naval Intelligence was decoding secret naval dispatches and preparing a daily update and position report of operations for Naval Command. J. Edgar Hoover sent out an urgent request for strict surveillance, which included interception of Inga Arvad's mail, twenty-four-hour visual surveillance, phone taps, room bugs, burglary, and the solicitation of information regarding her past.

According to the voluminous Arvad/JFK FBI files, it was during her acting and modeling days in Germany that Inga became socially involved with the Nazi hierarchy—becoming a close friend of Rudolf Hess and an acquaintance of Heinrich Himmler, Hermann Göring, and Joseph Goebbels. It was at Hermann Göring's wedding that she met the best man— Adolf Hitler. Hitler, who referred to her as "the perfect Nordic beauty," invited her to sit with him in his box at the 1936 Olympic Games.

When Rear Admiral Wilkinson, the director of Naval Intelligence, was informed by the FBI that Ensign Jack Kennedy was having an affair with a suspected spy, he became "so upset over the situation that you might say he was really frantic," revealed Captain Hunter, Jack's ONI section chief. "He wanted to get Kennedy out as quietly as possible. . . . He was very frightened at the time—very upset over the whole situation."

Rear Admiral Wilkinson wanted to have Ensign Kennedy discharged from the Navy; however, it was ultimately decided to quickly transfer him to a less sensitive assignment, and he was told to report to a desk job at the navy base in Charleston, where he was restricted from traveling beyond a seventy-mile radius. Jack Kennedy later confided to *PT-109* author Robert Donovan, "They shagged my ass down to South Carolina because I was going around with a Scandinavian blonde, and they thought she was a spy!" But the move to Charleston didn't put an end to the relationship. Continued surveillance revealed that "Inga Binga" was visiting "Jacko Tobacco" in South Carolina. Using the alias "Barbara White," she traveled to Charleston on February 6, 1942, and checked in at the Fort Sumter Hotel. Both the FBI and naval security were trailing them and reported that Ensign Kennedy arrived at the hotel at 5:30 P.M. in his 1940 Buick convertible and went to Inga's room, where he remained until the next morning.

When J. Edgar Hoover learned that Jack Kennedy's transfer hadn't ended the affair, he called Joe Kennedy and warned him that his son was in serious trouble. According to Hoover's assistant William Sullivan, the FBI chief had Ensign Kennedy transferred to the South Pacific "for security reasons"; however, when Kennedy returned from the South Pacific as a war hero, it helped launch his political career—not exactly what Hoover had in mind.

In July 1942, Kathleen Kennedy took over Inga Arvad's column at the *Times-Herald*, and through the machinations of Joe Kennedy it was arranged for Inga to move to Southern California, where she became a ghostwriter for Sheilah Graham's syndicated *Los Angeles Times* gossip column about Hollywood—where secrets were more banal.

While Pearl Harbor had been a disaster for some, it was a boon for the movie industry. Gas rationing allowed the average American family to go little farther than the neighborhood theater for entertainment, and in the pre-TV era every movie was accompanied by a newsreel that rendered the war visually comprehensible to the home-front audience. In the 1940s moviegoing was still cheap and had become an American habit, leading to big film grosses and big profits. Films affected morale, and the Roosevelt administration considered Hollywood film production as crucial to the war effort as some of the war production industries. "E for Effort" pennants proudly waved from the rooftops of the studio soundstages.

Hal Roach Studios in Culver City, once the home of the Laurel and Hardy and Our Gang comedies, was invaded by the army's First Motion Picture Unit and became the center of production of public-information films. One of the commanding officers was Lieutenant Ronald Reagan, who while drilling the troops jokingly threatened to attack MGM and capture the Thalberg Building. Reagan referred to the studio as Fort Roach, and many of Hollywood's talented artists and technicians were stationed there. In the fall of 1944, Lieutenant Reagan sent out a crew from Fort Roach to photograph women contributing to the war effort in strategic jobs. One of the photo assignments was at the Radioplane Company, located at the Glendale Metropolitan Airport. Among the photo crew sent to Radioplane was still photographer Corporal David Conover. Conover's keen eye irised in on a shapely young girl whose overalls seemed to complement the alls they were over. He was so taken by her attractiveness that he unhesitatingly approached her and introduced himself. When asked if she had done any modeling, "Just clay" was Norma Jeane's response.

When Norma Jeane closed up the Avalon apartment, she had moved in with Dougherty's mother, Ethel, who had helped her obtain her job at Radioplane, where Norma Jeane worked a ten-hour shift inspecting parachutes used in the recovery of target drones.

"I wore overalls in the factory," Marilyn later recalled. "I was surprised that they insisted on this. Putting a girl in overalls is like having her work in tights, particularly if a girl knows how to wear them. . . ."

Conover noticed that she knew how to wear them, and it was at Radioplane that a flash-gun wedding took place between Norma Jeane and the camera.

"Her response to the camera then was amazing," Conover recalled. "I was so excited I could hardly hold my camera steady."

"Am I really photogenic?" she asked.

Not only was she photogenic, she was "a hummmm-dinger!" Conover recalled. Returning to Radioplane with the prints, Conover noted in his diary that she had a problem with stuttering, just as he did, and even with her face smudged by dirt, her eyes held something that he found intriguing. It struck him as "incongruous that such a lovely creature was working on an assembly line."

"Say, you d-don't belong here," Conover stammered when he returned with the photos.

"Just where do I be-b-belong?" she asked with a puzzled look.

"On a magazine cover!" Conover unhesitatingly replied.

Norma Jeane wrote Grace Goddard:

The first thing I knew the Army photographers were taking pictures of me . . . and some of them asked for dates, etc. (Naturally I refused!) . . . After they finished with some of the pictures, an Army Corporal by the name of David Conover told me he would be interested in getting some color shots of me. He used to have a studio on "The Strip" on Sunset Blvd. He said he would make arrangements with the plant superintendent if I would agree, so I said okay. He told me what to wear and what shade of lipstick, etc., so the next couple of weeks I posed for him at different times. . . . He said all the pictures came out perfect. Also, he said that I should by all means go into the modeling profession . . . that I photographed very well and that he wants to take a lot more. Also he said he had a lot of contacts he wanted me to look into.

He is awfully nice and is married and is *strictly* business, which is the way I like it. . . .

> Love,
> Norma Jeane

But "strictly business" was not the way Corporal Conover recalled it in his memoirs. According to Conover, who was adept at retouching faded images, they had a brief affair.

Norma Jeane's half sister, Berniece, recalls hearing about the army photographer when Norma Jeane visited in the fall of 1944. Norma Jeane took the money she was saving for the future Dougherty house and spent it on a trip east to see Grace Goddard and Berniece. Grace had left West Virginia, where Doc was working, and had taken a temporary job in Chicago at a film laboratory. "She had developed a drinking problem and had to get away from Doc," according to Bebe Goddard.

"One of the reasons Norma Jeane blew her savings and went to Chicago to visit Grace," Bebe believes, "was that after Jim left she was sort of lost and having a bad time. Normie and Jim's mother didn't get along all that well and she felt very much alone." Norma Jeane knew that Grace held the answers to questions she had never been able to formulate as a child, and many of them had to do with the picture that had once hung on the wall of her mother's room, which Grace had carefully packed away. According to Bebe, during the trip to Chicago, Grace gave Norma Jeane the picture of her father, Stan Gifford.

After visiting Grace, Norma Jeane went to Detroit to see Berniece, the half sister she had never seen. "It was really Grace who coordinated this visit," Berniece remembers. "When Grace wrote me that a visit was possible, I answered, 'Sure, I'd love to have Norma Jeane, love to!' And then Norma Jeane wrote me and told me that she'd be there, what train, what time—everything."

Berniece had married Paris Miracle and moved from Kentucky to Detroit during the war, where Paris found employment in the Ford assembly line building military vehicles. "Paris and I walked out to the tracks and stood waiting while the train screeched to a stop. . . . All the passengers stepping off looked so ordinary, and then all of a sudden there was this gorgeous girl—so pretty and fresh. Well, there was no chance of missing her!"

As they drove to the Miracles' apartment, Berniece recalls that she and Norma Jeane perched on the edge of their seats and stared at each other. "Every now and then our arms would fly around each other in a hug, and we'd look in each other's eyes and say how happy we were. We didn't have anything very original or profound to say. We were both so excited we were almost out of our minds. . . . We were overwhelmed at finally getting to see each other."

During the short visit, Berniece had many questions about Gladys, the mother she had so briefly known, and Norma Jeane wanted to know about Jackie, the dead half brother she had never seen. "You know, I don't think Mother can believe that Jackie is really dead," Norma Jeane said. "Grace told me that she still refuses to believe it." Berniece observed that in her letters from Gladys, their mother never mentioned Jackie's name.

In a letter to Grace after their visit, Norma Jeane noted that David Conover wanted to take more pictures; however, Dougherty was coming home over the Christmas holidays, and Norma Jeane wrote, "I would rather not work when Jimmie was here. So he [Conover] said he would wait . . . I love Jimmy so very much, honestly I don't think there is another man alive like him! He really is awfully sweet."

Norma Jeane was waiting for Dougherty at the Glendale Depot when his train arrived from San Francisco, and for a while things were as they used to be. That first night they headed for "the most luxurious motor lodge on Ventura Boulevard, the La Fonda," Dougherty remembered. "Norma Jeane had bought a black nightgown for the occasion, and we rarely left our room."

Over the holidays they went to familiar places—movies at the Grauman's Chinese, Pop's Willow Lake, the Coconut Grove, or the homes of old friends, but as his Christmas leave ran out Norma Jeane was becoming distant and more and more melancholy. "She grew increasingly morose and a kind of dread took hold of her. She didn't want to talk about or think about my leaving," Dougherty observed. "I knew that she considered my shipping out again as another rejection."

"On one of those last days, she suddenly announced that she was going to call her father, a man she had never been in touch with before. Her illegitimacy was something we had talked about on a few occasions. It was something she accepted without any apparent bitterness." But after Norma Jeane had returned from Chicago with the picture of Stan Gifford, she discovered where he lived and had gotten his phone number.

Dougherty vividly remembered the call: " 'This is Norma Jeane' she said in a trembly voice, 'I'm Gladys's daughter.' "

Gifford said he had nothing to say to her, told her not to call again, and hung up.

Dougherty recalls how totally devastated she was by Gifford's refusal to speak to her. He tried to ease her pain by explaining that perhaps a call out of the blue may have been difficult for him, especially if Gifford was married and had another family. But nothing he could say or do was of consolation, and she wept for days.

Dougherty lamented, "When I was getting ready to return to the ship, it was another very emotional experience for her. It was just sad, very sad—sad for me because I didn't want to leave her, and sad for her because every time I left, it was a destructive thing that hit her extremely hard." When Norma Jeane went with Dougherty to the dock at San Pedro and waved good-bye, he didn't realize she was waving good-bye to the past as she stood on the brink of the future.

> I could have loved you once, and even said it,
> But you went away,
> A long way away.
> When you came back it was too late
> And love was a forgotten word,
> Remember?
>
> —Norma Jeane

This Way Out

When Miss Dougherty came to us, the first thing we tried to do was change that horrible walk. That wiggle wasn't good for fashion models.
—Emmeline Snively

Corporal David Conover was awakened by a scream "so shrill and pen-etrating" that he jerked upright on the sofa where he slept. He looked around the dingy motel room and saw Norma Jeane sitting on the bed shivering and bathed in perspiration.

"It's that n-nightmare," she stammered.

"What happened?" he asked.

"They force me into a straitjacket and carry me out of the house. I'm screaming, 'I'm not crazy! I'm not crazy!' When we come to a brick bu-building that looks like my old orphanage, we go through one black iron door after another and each door slams shut behind me. 'I don't belong here!' I shout. 'What are you doing to me?' They pu-put me in a bleak room with barred windows and they go out and lock the iron door, leaving me in a straitjacket. 'I don't belong here!' I scream again and again, until I have no more breath."

The night terror struck on the last night of a photo safari in which Conover was trying to capture Norma Jeane on film in the Mojave Desert during the spring of 1945. She had taken sick leave from Radioplane while Conover helped her put together a portfolio she could take to modeling agencies. On the way back to Los Angeles they had shared a motel room in Barstow to save money. When they got back to L.A., Conover found that orders were waiting for him at Fort Roach—he was to be shipped out the next day to a combat photo unit in the Philippines. When Conover called Norma Jeane and broke the news about his orders, he advised, "Take the pictures to the Blue Book Modeling Agency and talk to Miss Emmeline Snively."

But she was uncertain what she should do and felt very much alone. In June 1945 Norma Jeane would turn nineteen, and it was a difficult time for her. With Grace in Chicago and Jim gone she felt trapped in a limbo of loneliness. "I had been sort of a 'child bride' and now I was sort of a 'child widow,' " she observed. At Radioplane she had transferred from the parachute room to the "dope room" because of animosity from girls she worked with who resented the attention and wolf whistles she received. She wasn't getting along well with Jim's mom, Ethel, who disapproved of Norma Jeane's idea of becoming a model. Ana Lower was frequently ill, her mother was in an institution, and her father wouldn't speak to her.

"Sundays were the loneliest," she later reflected,

> but I discovered a place to go on Sundays. It was the Union Station. All the trains from all over the country came in at the Union Station. It was a beautiful building, and it was always crowded with people carrying suitcases and babies. . . . I would watch people greeting each other when the train crowds entered the waiting room. Or saying good-bye to each other.
>
> They seemed to be mostly poor people. Although, now and then some well-dressed travelers would appear. But chiefly it was the poor people who kept coming in and going away on trains.
>
> You learned a lot watching them. You learned that pretty wives adored homely men and good-looking men adored homely wives. And that people in shabby clothes, carrying raggedy bundles and with three or four sticky kids clinging to them, had faces that could light up like Christmas trees when they saw each other. And you watched really homely men and women, fat ones and old ones, kiss each other as tenderly as if they were lovers in a movie. . . . Union Station—I used to go there on Sunday and stay most of the day.

As she watched the smiling faces of reunited families and friends leaving the station beneath the sign that said "This Way Out," she wondered what the way out was for her. Where was the exit from the loneliness and isolation, where familial communication could be observed only vicariously? It was in this caldron of loneliness that the ingredients were mixed into the potion that brewed up a goddess. The remote childhood hope that Grace had instilled in her of becoming a movie star like Jean Harlow became burning ambition.

"You don't have to know anything to dream hard," she stated. "I used to think as I looked out on the Hollywood night, 'There must be thousands of girls sitting alone like me dreaming of becoming a movie star. But I'm not going to worry about them. I'm dreaming the hardest!' I knew nothing about acting. I had never read a book about it, or tried to do it, or discussed it with anyone. I was ashamed to tell the few people I knew of what I was dreaming. But there was this secret in me—becoming an actress, a movie star! It was like being in jail and looking at a door that said, 'This Way Out.' "

Without telling Ethel, she made an appointment with Miss Emmeline Snively, the proprietor of the Blue Book Modeling Agency, for 11 A.M., August 2, 1945.

The night before, she was too excited to sleep. She got up before dark and took a long bath and massaged cologne into her skin. It took over an hour to make up her face. Had she made her lips too large? Was the mascara line right? Should she wear the suit or the dress? She put on the dress. She brushed her white suede shoes, her only good pair. Whatever she wore would have to match the shoes. The suit went best with the shoes. So off went the dress and on went the suit—too tight—back to the white dress.

She had called in sick at Radioplane, and Ethel had guessed she was up to something. They didn't speak as Norma Jeane put on her dark glasses and walked out the door—a vision in white as she got into Doughertys' old Ford coupe and drove off to Miss Snively's office at the Ambassador Hotel.

It was only a few minutes after eleven when Norma Jeane arrived at the glass door of the Blue Book Modeling Agency. Taking a deep breath, she became "the other person" as she walked languorously into the reception room where large photos of beautiful, successful models hung on the walls. It wasn't long before she was ushered into the inner sanctum, Miss Snively's office. She tried with all her might to calm her nerves and hoped she wouldn't stutter. Miss Snively, a small, effervescent lady in her fifties, had been in the business for decades. She could distinguish a model from a wanna-be at a glance.

"My dear, please walk to the door and back." Miss Snively noted that the walk was unsteady and wiggly, the hair was too thick and too curly, the upper lip was too short, and there was a slight bump on the nose—but the smile was good, the legs were shapely, the bosom was superb. What caught Miss Snively's attention, however, was the air of wholesome sweetness about her. In the white dress, Miss Snively recalled, "She looked like a cherub in a church choir."

"Do you really want to be a model, dear?"

"Yes, I'd like to try."

"Try—that's the spirit, dear. If you've got the willpower you'll make it. There are a lot of pretty girls like you in this town, but you've got one thing, dear, that beats 'em all, and that's charm. Charm—that's what you've got!"

"Thank you, ma'am."

"But you've got to have the know-how, dear. We offer a three month course of training for one hundred dollars."

"I guess that lets me out," Norma Jeane said dejectedly, "I d-don't have one hundred dollars."

"You don't have to pay me now, dear. You can pay it out of what you earn as a model. Do you want to get down to work?"

"Oh, yes!" was the immediate reply.

The next day Norma Jeane quit her job at Radioplane. When Ethel Dougherty learned of her plans and complained that Jim wouldn't approve of a modeling career, Norma Jeane took her things and moved back to Ana Lower's home.

Looking back at the days when Norma Jeane was just beginning her career, Miss Snively commented, "She was the hardest worker I ever handled. She never missed a class. She had confidence in herself, and did something I've never seen any other model do. She would study every print a photographer took of her. I mean she'd take them home and study them for hours. Then she'd go back and ask the photographer, 'What did I do wrong in this one?' or 'Why didn't this come out better?' They would tell her. And she never repeated a mistake. Photographers liked her because she was cooperative. She knew how to take directions."

Norma Jeane's first modeling job was as a hostess at the Los Angeles Home Show in the Pan-Pacific Auditorium. The ten dollars a day she earned was almost enough to pay back Miss Snively for her training. By the end of the summer, she was becoming a photographer's dream, earning enough money to pay rent to Aunt Ana and the repair bills on Dougherty's Ford, which she had smashed into a streetcar when she was enthralled by a daydream.

At first she may have thought that the car horns that reached a crescendo in the Los Angeles basin on the afternoon of August 14, 1945, were honking at her. But the persistent honking of horns throughout the city was the first cacaphonic news flash to most Angelenos that World War II had come to its sudden conclusion. The noisy celebrations of peace reached jubilant crescendos on Hollywood Boulevard, Times Square, and the Main Streets of America, but the euphoria was soon chilled by the fall of the Iron Curtain and the onset of the cold war. With the defeat of the Axis powers, the unity of purpose that had united East and West came to an end as the Soviets aggressively sought world domination.

Following Lenin's dictum "Capture the cinema, and you capture the hearts and the minds of the people," the Comintern focused on Hollywood, where a concerted effort was made to infiltrate the film industry. The full extent of the Comintern's covert activities has only recently been documented, with the opening of the Central Party Archives in Moscow. Many of the Hollywood fronts were orchestrated by the Comintern headquarters under directives from the Kremlin.

Money was always a problem, and the "silver-spoon Communist" Frederick Vanderbilt Field was frequently relied upon by the Comintern to put together funding for CP fronts. It was Field who financed the Russian Institute; the Arts, Sciences, and Professions Council; and the People's Education Centers, where John Howard Lawson and Dr. Hyman Engelberg were instructors along with Hollywood labor leader Herb Sorrell.

Another shadowy figure along with Dr. Hyman Engelberg in the Arts, Sciences, and Professions Council was Eunice Murray's husband, John M. Murray. Eunice Murray's son-in-law, Norman Jefferies, stated that John Murray was a devoted member of the Communist Party who had several identities and led a double life. Both lives would have ended in the shadow of obscurity were it not for brief mention of Eunice Murray's husband by Monroe biographers. In the addenda of Frank Capell's book, *The Strange Death of Marilyn Monroe*, Capell refers to John Murray as "a left-wing labor organizer" who often came home "messed up from his strike and organizing activities." In *Marilyn Monroe: The Biography* Donald Spoto refers to John Murray as a Yale divinity student who became a Hollywood studio carpenter, "which Eunice took for an imitation of the Lord Jesus Himself."

However, there is no academic record of John Murray's having attended Yale Divinity School, and according to Norman Jefferies, Murray's faith was drawn from the well of Marx and Engels, and he revered Joseph Stalin.

Murray was far from being a simple carpenter who worked at the studios; his tools were the hammer and sickle, and he worked diligently with Herb Sorrell in following Lenin's dictum to capture the cinema. John Howard Lawson's declared objective was to introduce Marxist thought into the content of Hollywood films, while John Murray's task was to communize the Hollywood trade unions.

In 1940 John Murray and Herb Sorrell had made a concerted effort to gain control of the motion-picture unions by forming the CP-oriented United Studio Technicians Guild to supplant the International Alliance of Theatrical Stage Employees (IATSE). Together they organized the bitter jurisdictional strike against the Walt Disney Studio in 1941. When World War II ended they formed a leftist coalition of anti-IATSE studio employees called the Conference of Studio Unions, and the surrender of Japan marked the beginning of renewed labor wars in Hollywood orchestrated by Murray and Sorrell.*

Selecting Warner Bros. as the field of jurisdictional battle, Murray and Sorrell placed 750 pickets around the Warner Bros. lot in Burbank. When the IATSE employees tried to enter the studio gates the pickets overturned their cars as Jack Warner angrily looked on from a soundstage roof. The Burbank police and studio guards beat back the pickets with clubs and fire hoses, and by the end of the next day over eighty people had been injured in a pitched battle between the rival unions before additional police called from nearby towns could restore a semblance of order. The matter was turned over to the National Labor Relations Board (NLRB), which in October 1945 ruled in favor of the Conference of Studio Unions. The victory inflamed Murray and Sorrell's ambition to take over all the Hollywood locals, and the labor wars quickly spread to the other Hollywood studios.

Norman Jefferies recalled that it was during the time of the strikes that he was dating John and Eunice Murray's daughter, Patricia, a student at Santa Monica High School. The Murrays had built a large and comfortable home in Santa Monica at 802 Franklin Street, and according to Jefferies it was the scene of numerous meetings involving the communist labor movement in Hollywood. Fifteen years later it would be to this same house on Franklin Street that Marilyn Monroe would be driven by Mrs. Murray for her appointment with her psychoanalyst, Dr. Ralph Greenson.

---

* The IATSE filed a civil suit against Murray and Sorrell, which is in the Los Angeles Hall of Records under civil case #446193.

Jefferies described John Murray as a bright, well-educated man versed in history and the arts who spoke six languages. "Jack [John] Murray was a strange man—so was his brother Churchill," Jefferies observed. "Jack wasn't home much, or even in Los Angeles, unless it was on party business. That was his life. The Murrays didn't have much of a marriage because he was gone most of the time. He was either in Mexico or on the East Coast.

"During the strikes the Murrays frequently had cell meetings, or what they called 'club' meetings there at the house," Jefferies recalled. "Herb Sorrell was there a lot, but Jack Murray was the strategist along with his brother Churchill and people he brought up from Mexico. Sorrell was the organizer and the street fighter, but Jack and Churchill were the brains. Eunice was part of all this, but I never got the idea that she was an organizer."

The prolonged postwar Hollywood labor strikes of 1945 and 1946 caused economic hardship for the studios as well as the unions. After over a year of walkouts and litigation, the Conference of Studio Union's strike funds were totally depleted, and many of those who had supported John Murray and Herb Sorrell lost everything when the NLRB reversed its position and ultimately ruled in favor of the IATSE. As Norman Jefferies recalled, the Murrays could no longer meet their mortgage payments and lost the home that had been built on Franklin Street by unemployed studio carpenters. It was ultimately purchased by a man Jefferies had occasionally seen at the meetings held in the Murray home, a man they looked to for party directives—Ralph R. Greenson.

Los Angeles Limited

Hell must be like Los Angeles....
—Bertolt Brecht

Sigmund Freud was twelve years old when his father told him the story of how an arrogant gentile had knocked his new fur cap into the muddy gutter and shouted, "Jew! Get off the pavement!" . . . "And what did you do?" asked young Sigmund. "I stepped into the gutter and picked up my cap," said Jacob Freud.

For centuries after the destruction of Solomon's temple and the Diaspora, the Jews suffered and endured persecution that became ingrained into their culture as a way of life. But when Hitler came to full power with the burning of the Reichstag in 1933, hate and intolerance revealed their demonic face.

Dr. Henry Lowenfeld, a Freudian psychoanalyst working with mental patients in a Berlin asylum, noticed a strange change taking place among the inmates. "As the threat of the Nazis coming to power became greater," he said, "You could see its effect even on the mental patients. They began to play at being Nazis themselves. Of course, a few really were Nazis. But the others—they would pretend that they were Nazis too. Some of them, when I went to talk to them, even tried to threaten me."

When insanity became a system of government, the fortunate few fled from the European madhouse that had been taken over by the inmates. Hitler's rise to power brought to America some of its finest scientists, musicians, teachers, and artists.

The Jewish immigrants hoped for assimilation, and while there was, indeed, widespread anti-Semitism in America during the thirties, it wasn't genocidal, and the hope was that if a Jew worked hard and behaved like a good American, his family could at least live in peace. Many of them took innocuous new names, cut off their earlocks and trimmed their noses, listened to Lum and Abner, took off their yarmulkas and put on fedoras and cowboy hats. In West Los Angeles some even tried to join the Bel Air Country Club.

Most of the Freudian psychoanalysts seeking refuge in America were Jewish, and many of them were Marxists. For those who had abandoned their faith in Judaism, Freud and Marx offered a leap of dissent to dogmatic empiricism and a means of interpreting human aggression.

To many Americans in the thirties psychiatry was regarded as esoteric and foreign. Because of its sexual context, practitioners of Freudian analysis were suspect in a culture with Puritan roots. Some immigrant analysts remained in New York, and others went to Boston, Chicago, and Topeka, but the ultimate destination for many of the Freudian exiles was Hollywood, the sun-filled oasis of golden opportunity—with its pools and palms and a plethora of meshugas, who seemed to find safety in numbers in Movieland.

Freud's student Ernst Simmel was one of the first refugee analysts to arrive in Hollywood. Simmel and the highly respected Freudian Otto Fenichel had been among the founders of the prestigious Berlin Psychoanalytic Institute. But they were members of the Communist Party, and when Hitler came to power they compounded their sins against the Reich by being Jews who espoused Freudian-Marxism. When Simmel heard that the Nazis were coming to get him, he jumped out of the rear window of the Berlin Psychoanalytic Institute and didn't stop running until he reached Hollywood and Vine.

Otto Fenichel's route was more circuitous. It was his desperate dream that Freudian-Marxism would prevail over Nietzschean facism, and Fenichel first fled to Oslo and then Prague, where he led underground movements against the Nazis and secretly published his *Rundbriefe*— mimeographed circulars that he sent to a select group of intellectuals who endorsed Freudian-Marxist solutions to mankind's problems.

As Hitler's armies overwhelmed Europe, and Fenichel was forced to flee, Ernst Simmel arranged for Fenichel's immigration to Los Angeles in 1938. Though many of Simmel and Fenichel's fellow Freudians held Marxist views and were members of the Communist Party, the situation in America didn't provide a climate for a political concept of psychoanalysis.

The rather pragmatic medicalization of analysis in the United States tended to undermine the zealous cultural and political heritage of the Freudian exiles. Some of the early Los Angeles analysts, such as May Romm and Francis Deri, began making big bucks on Bedford Drive with monied clients from the film industry who were willing to pay plenty to hear themselves talk.

The majority of the immigrant psychoanalysts didn't want to be overtly political. They wanted to get established and make money. The burning intellectualism that had lit the fires of the European Freudian movement became the fifty-minute-cash-and-carry-on hour in the United States. Though Fenichel and Simmel tried to keep the Marxist flame burning, they found that it wasn't politic for them to publicly espouse pro-Soviet sympathies.

Suspecting that he was under surveillance by the FBI, Fenichel elected to be private in his political statements. His thick FBI file reveals that he was correct in his decision. Little of Fenichel's published writing reflects his dedication to the communist cause, but he did continue circulating his *Rundbriefe* in America in an attempt to keep Marxist political psychoanalysis alive. Though he recommended that the recipients burn the *Rundbriefe* after reading them, many crumpled and faded copies have been salvaged for the archives of psychoanalytic history.

Shortly after he arrived in Los Angeles, Fenichel joined Simmel's study group of European exiles who shared Marxist sympathies. The study group included Max Horkeimer, T. W. Adorno, and occasionally Leo Lowenthal—all key figures in exile of the Frankfurt school. The group of intellectual sociologists known as the Frankfurt school devoted themselves to psychoanalysis as part of their larger neo-Marxist "critical theory."

Meetings of the study group took place at the homes of various members. They were open to analysts and nonanalysts alike. The lecture by a participant was usually followed by heated discussions, which often went on well past midnight and ended in spirited arguments held out on the sidewalk. A wide range of topics was presented—education, the cinema, jazz, radio, literature. The nonanalysts in the group often included Thomas Mann, Christopher Isherwood, Bertolt Brecht, Peter Lorre, Bruno Frank,* Fritz Lang, Hanns Eisler, Otto Katz, Leon Feuchtwanger, and Leo Rosten. Rosten, who was to become a prominent humorist and the author of *Captain Newman, M.D.*, had journeyed to Hollywood in the late thirties in the hope of becoming a screenwriter.

Another person who attended Simmel's study group and frequently carried the heated discussions out to the curb was a young doctor who had recently arrived in Los Angeles—Ralph Greenson. Greenson became Fenichel's close friend and disciple, and in a brief biography of Fenichel written by Greenson for the *Encyclopedia of Psychoanalysis*, Greenson states,

> I met Otto Fenichel early in 1938, shortly after he had settled in Los Angeles, and I knew him until his untimely death in 1946. In that short span of less than eight years, I had the opportunity of knowing him as a therapist, teacher, supervisor and for a brief period, as friend. He was by far the most important influence in my psychoanalytic life, and I consider myself most fortunate to have had so extraordinary an opportunity. It is true that my many-sided emotional involvement with him has limited my objectivity, but it has also afforded me many first-hand insights into the man and his work. . . .

Greenson became his analysand and went through four years of didactic analysis under Fenichel. According to Hildi Greenson, "Otto Fenichel became Romi's inspiration, trusted mentor, colleague, and friend."

Ralph Greenson's background was quite different from his mentor's. Born on September 20, 1911, in Brooklyn, he was the fraternal twin to Juliet and was named Romeo by his parents Joel O. Greenschpoon and Katharine Greenschpoon (née Goldberg.) It was Papa Greenschpoon who chose to name the twins Romeo and Juliet. "My father liked Shakespeare and was a romantic," Greenson later explained. "My mother was too weak from delivering twins to argue." Both parents were Russian Jewish emigrants, having escaped the czarist pogroms of 1903, and when Romeo was born they lived in a tenement on Miller Avenue in the Brownsville section of Brooklyn.

The majority of the Russian Jews who fled to America during the mass migrations between 1880 and 1920 settled in Brownsville and on the Lower East Side of Manhattan. Though the Jewish communities in New York had a multitude of nationalities, they were closely unified by their

---

* The German novelist Bruno Frank became a refugee immigrant in 1936. His wife would become Marilyn Monroe's drama coach in 1948.

cultural background, their Yiddish language, and the need to protect themselves from widespread bigotry. Many of the Russian Jews who had survived the slaughters of the czarist pogroms took spiritual refuge in Orthodox Judaism. Others found faith and hope in Zionist-Marxism, which they followed with a burning zeal. On the sabbath in Brownsville, residents went either to the Sholem Alechem Temple on Pitkin Avenue or to the Labor Lyceum on Sackman Street. The Greenschpoons attended the Labor Lyceum, where Lenin was revered.

According to family lore, Papa Greenschpoon had seen his father murdered by a Cossack in their *shtetl* outside of Minsk. Young Joel Greenschpoon was a promising chemistry student, and the family raised the money to send him to America, where he opened a pharmacy in Brownsville at 373 Bradford Street. Joel first met his wife, Katharine Greenberg, when she answered his ad for a pharmacist. Kate was a feisty and intelligent woman who had also been educated as a chemist in Russia. Joel and Kate found that they made good chemistry, and they married in 1910. Recognizing her husband's gifts at diagnosing the customers' aches and pains, Kate urged Joel to study medicine while she took over the pharmacy. In 1914, three years after Romeo and Juliet were born, Papa Greenschpoon earned his medical degree.

Romi's younger sister, Elizabeth, was born in 1913; and a younger brother, Washington Irving, was born in 1916. It was the mother, Kate, who was the central figure in the household. A woman of indomitable will and energy, she raised her rather eccentric and volatile family in a warm environment of Yiddish culture with a measure of Tolstoy and Rachmaninoff mixed in a Marxist mortar. An accomplished pianist herself, Kate prompted the children's interest in music. Elizabeth proved to be a gifted pianist and went on to the concert stage, and Romi became a proficient violinist.

Growing up in Brownsville with the name of Romeo was a decided detriment. Brownsville was the home of Louis Lepke Buchalter of Murder, Inc. Former Brownsville resident Al Lewis remembers, "There were plenty of Jewish gangsters—Meyer Lansky, Abe Rellis, Pittsburgh Phil Straus, Banjo Bernstein, the boys in Murder, Inc. They hung out on the streets. We didn't know—or didn't want to know—the infamous acts they were involved in, that they were murderers for hire, would ice-pick a guy to death for two hundred dollars. All we knew was they were not so *oy-oy-oy!*"

The taunting cry of "Wherefor art youse Romeo?" frequently echoed down Miller Avenue and prompted the young Greenschpoon boy to stay inside and dutifully practice his violin. It was to this trauma that Romi later wryly ascribed his early interest in psychoanalysis. Unknown to his parents, when he was in the fifth grade he changed his name to Ralph, after a hero he had read about in *Ralph of the Roundhouse*. Friends and family, however, always called him Romi. The Greenschpoon children attended P.S. 149, where Romi's school records show that he was an A student. P.S. 149 was renamed the Danny Kaye School in the 1960s after one of its illustrious graduates. A number of artists in the entertainment world were raised in Brownsville: George Gershwin, Steve Lawrence, Shelley Winters, Joey Adams, Phil Silvers, Henny Youngman, Jerry Lewis, Joe Papp, and the impresario Sol Hurok were among those whose ambitions were formed in the crucible of Brownsville's streets.

When Hurok's family moved from Russia to Brownsville in 1905, he became a partner of Kate Greenschpoon's brother, Alex Goldberg, in directing the Brownsville Labor Lyceum at 219 Sackman Street. Hurok's start as a manager of musical artists began at the Labor Lyceum, where he and Alex Goldberg and his sister, Kate Greenschpoon, booked speakers and concert artists. Knocking on Efrem Zimbalist's dressing room door at Carnegie Hall, they persuaded Zimbalist to appear at the Labor Lyceum, and among the speakers that Kate Greenschpoon brought to Brownsville was a young man with a growing voice in the labor movement—Frederick Vanderbilt Field.

In his memoirs Sol Hurok recalled, "Brownsville in those days was a steaming microcosm of culture in the heart of Brooklyn, alive with intellectual striving and artistic hungers. I was becoming more and more active in the labor movement at the Lyceum, and there was never any lack of audience for speakers or concerts. With my partners the Goldbergs, we were busy supplying the artists and organizing the events. Music thrived in Brownsville."

Marxism also thrived in Brownsville. The waves of immigrants from Eastern Europe seethed with social protest. Socialists, radicals, and communists vied to make the masses cognizant of the deplorable social and economic conditions under which they lived. By 1919 Brownsville, "The Garden District of Brooklyn," became known as "The Red District," and many party leaders and activists grew up on its teeming streets. There was no such thing as a Republican in Brownsville, and every Saturday evening before election day an extraordinary event took place at the intersection of Pitkin and Saratoga Avenues. It was called "politics night." Al Lewis recalls, "On each of the four corners at Pitkin Avenue, there'd be speakers up on soap boxes, an American flag beside them as they screamed out their party's slogans. On one corner there'd be the Liberal Party, on another corner was the American Labor Party, across from them would be the Socialist Party, and then the Communist Party. That was it!"

Joel and Kate Greenschpoon stood on the corner with the communists, who were screaming the loudest and echoed the pain and frustrations the Russian Jews had endured at the hands of the "ruling class." It was in this environment of dialectical materialism endemic to the Marxist creed—so carefully taught every Saturday at the Labor Lyceum—that young Romeo Greenschpoon lost his instinctive belief in a Creator and adopted the Marxist atheistic dogma that he expounded until his death.

Though Ralph Greenson later claimed to have been raised in a *hoo hoo* house in the more affluent area of Williamsburg, described as a "large Colonial home situated majestically behind a high gate which reflected the family's growing prosperity," the fact is that the census records, the school records, and Brooklyn directories clearly establish that the Greenschpoon family lived in a tenement house that still stands at 393 Miller Avenue in Brownsville, and that they lived there from the time Romeo and Juliet were born until the family moved to Los Angeles in 1933.

After graduating from P.S. 149 midschool in 1927, Ralph Greenson later stated, he completed his undergraduate and premedical studies at Columbia University, but that wasn't exactly true, either. He never attended classes on the Columbia campus but attended Seth Low Junior College in Brooklyn. In the 1920s and well into the 1930s, Columbia maintained a quota for Jewish students, and it was very difficult for Jews to attend Columbia unless they came from an influential family. A solution to the problem of the many Jewish applicants was the establishment of Seth Low in Brooklyn by the Columbia regents. As a result the student body at Seth Low was 95 percent Jewish. That it became a hotbed of Zionist-Marxism was ultimately a problem for the Columbia regents, who disbanded Seth Low in 1937.

Graduating from Seth Low in June of 1929 with an A-B grade average, Romi found it equally difficult to attend the medical school of his choice in the United States because of the prevalent quota system. His father helped him enroll at the Medical School in Berne, Switzerland, where he stayed at a boarding house run by the Troesch family. It was there that he met Hildegard Troesch, who would become his lifelong companion and devoted wife. Hildi's older brother had been a member of the Communist Youth movement in Berne and later became a leader of the Communist Party in Switzerland.

After completing medical school in 1932, Romi traveled to Vienna and studied psychoanalysis under the imaginative but somewhat erratic Wilhelm Stekel. Stekel, who was one of Freud's earliest adherents and a founding member of the Vienna Psychoanalytic Society, was also a Freudian-Marxist and had much in common with Romeo Greenschpoon. The grandiloquent Viennese analyst was described by Freud's biographer, Peter Gay, as "intuitive and indefatigable . . . Though entertaining company, he alienated many with his boastfulness"—traits that could one day equally describe Dr. Ralph Greenson.

Romi married Hildi Troesch in 1935, and by the time he had completed his studies in Vienna and returned to the United States, Papa Greenschpoon had moved the family to Los Angeles, where he opened an office as a general practitioner on Fairfax Avenue. Romeo's twin, Juliet, had married a successful pediatrician with an office in Beverly Hills, Dr. Max Belous; and his younger sister, Elizabeth, had become a concert pianist and was dating a young promising Los Angeles attorney by the name of Milton "Mickey" Rudin.

In 1936 Romi and Hildi moved into a small apartment at 633 North Berendo Street, not far from the Cedars of Lebanon Hospital in Hollywood, where he did his internship along with a fellow intern, Dr. Hyman Engelberg. Mickey Rudin recalls that it was at this time, when Romi Greenson and Hy Engelberg were interns at Cedars, that he first became an acquaintance of Engelberg and his wife, Esther.

It was following the completion of his internship in 1937 that Romeo Greenschpoon and his brother Washington Irving Greenschpoon legally changed their names to Ralph and Walter Greenson, and Dr. Ralph R. Greenson opened his office and set up his couch at 1930 Wilshire Boulevard. He had ingratiated himself with Ernst Simmel and Francis Deri at the Southern California Psychoanalytic Study Group, and it was Simmel who introduced him to Otto Fenichel upon Fenichel's arrival from Europe in 1938. A close friendship began.

The war interrupted Ralph Greenson's career just as it was beginning. "I was just getting to earn some money," Greenson recalled. "I got an office in Beverly Hills and was going to pay back Fenichel, and pay for the furniture in the office, and by this time I was drafted."

Entering the United States Army in 1942, he was assigned to a psychiatric ward at the Army Air Force Convalescent Hospital at Fort Logan, Colorado, and it was there that Greenson discovered he had a gift for teaching. He began giving seminars to psychiatrists and medical personnel on how to treat the mental casualties of war. Leo Rosten's popular book, *Captain Newman, M.D.*, which was made into a motion picture starring Gregory Peck in 1964, was largely modeled on Captain Greenson's wartime experiences. In describing Captain Newman (Greenson), Rosten stated, "The mannerisms he had always displayed, that unpredictable interplay between the wry, the weary, the impatient, the disenchantment—he was spilling over with responsiveness. . . . His seminars were jammed from the beginning, and they were about as lively, unorthodox, and illuminating as any I ever heard. He loved to teach. He loved to perform."

In describing his experiences at Fort Logan, Greenson states, "At this time Colonel Murray comes to the post from the Air Force in Washington, and he says, 'Look, Greenson, I want to tell you something. Do you know why I'm here?' I said, 'no.' He said, 'I'm looking where to set up a teaching hospital in psychiatry. I've just made my decision.' He said, 'I'm going to set it up at Fort Logan, and I'm setting it up and you're going to be my assistant.' And by God he came. A few months later and there he was. Colonel John M. Murray was Commanding Officer of the Psychiatric Unit, and I was his assistant."

Was it the same John M. Murray who was married to Eunice? The same labor organizer whom Norman Jefferies described as a strange "well educated man versed in history and the arts and spoke six languages"? The same John M. Murray who "wasn't home much, or even in Los Angeles unless it was on party business"?

In the many books and biographies on the subject of Marilyn Monroe very few facts are revealed of the relationship between Dr. Greenson and John and Eunice Murray. The unlikely "friendship" between Dr. Greenson and Eunice Murray has never been clarified. In her book, *Marilyn: The Last Months*, Eunice Murray scarcely mentions her husband, or the circumstances of her association with Dr. Greenson. The coauthor of that book, her niece Rose Shade, states, "She was drawn to psychology, feeling a need to work with people and their problems. Eunice read and studied, and when an opportunity came to care for a psychiatric case in the patient's home, Eunice was prepared with enough knowledge and understanding to work under the guidance of a psychiatrist as his aide, helping in any kind of therapy that seemed indicated. She worked with many kinds of patients."

Yet this is among the many bewildering contradictions in the strange life of Eunice Murray. There is no documentation of any eductional qualifications in the psychatric field, nor any evidence of any cases in which she may have been involved. Deepening the mystery, neither Hildi Greenson nor the Greenson children, nor the Murray children, will discuss the relationship between Dr. Greenson and John and Eunice Murray.

The military records of Colonel John M. Murray indicate he was born in 1897, the same year as Eunice's husband. Colonel Murray studied psychiatry in Vienna in 1932, the same year that Romi Greenschpoon was a student. They both apparently knew Otto Fenichel, who was a frequent lecturer in Vienna, and who was brought to Fort Logan for seminars.

All that could be attributed to coincidence, but Colonel Murray was a founder of the Boston Psychoanalytic Institute, and a photograph of him at the Institute taken in 1942 bears a striking resemblance to the one extant photograph of Eunice Murray's husband taken in 1957. Handwriting samples of the two John M. Murrays are strikingly similar.

Norman Jefferies said John M. Murray was frequently on the East Coast or in Mexico on party business. Did one of the John M. Murrays lead a double life as a frequent flier on the Comintern triangle?

Nymph Errant

By the time you swear you're his,
  shivering and sighing,
And he vows his passion is
  Infinite, undying—
Lady, make a note of this:
  One of you is lying.
                    —Dorothy Parker

Another exile who had sought refuge from the European storm was Andre de Dienes, a young Transylvanian with a Gypsy heart, who had traversed the nomadic trails of European café society before settling down in New York City as a *Vogue* fashion photographer. Romantic by nature, he was a fervent sensualist and had an epicurean eye for the female form. His wanderlust took him to Hollywood, where he called the Blue Book Modeling Agency and requested a shapely model.

Yes, Miss Snively did have a young girl on the books, who had little experience but might fill the bill. An hour later Norma Jeane Dougherty was knocking at de Diene's door at the Garden of Allah. She wore a tight pink sweater, her light-brown curly hair was tied with a ribbon to match her outfit, and in her hand she carried a hatbox containing a skimpy swimsuit.

"My name is Norma Jeane," she said. "Are you Mr. d-de Di-Dienes?"

He wasn't prepared for what stood on the threshold. "In one fell swoop I was intrigued, moved and attracted by her," de Dienes recalled, "the firm, well-rounded breasts, a trim waist set off by the perfect curve of her hip, long, lithe legs."

He picked her up early the next morning at Aunt Ana's home. It was a bright November morning in 1945 on a beach in Malibu that Norma Jeane, without makeup, danced in the golden freshness of the dawn—whirling, prancing, sinking to the sand, jumping to her feet, brimming over with the joy of life in a ballet with the camera choreographed by Andre de Dienes.

What had been captured on film that day was developed that night in the photographer's darkroom. "As I watched the prints appear in the developing bath, I became more convinced of her great future, and more determined to do some extended location work with her," de Dienes remembered.

Mrs. Snively observed, "She still seemed a scared, pretty lonely little kid who wore mostly fresh white cotton dresses, and wanted somebody somewhere to think she was worth something." De Dienes made her feel special, buying her clothes and jewelry to be used in the photo sessions. His energetic liberating spirit took Norma Jeane out of her pit of loneliness. To de Dienes she could reveal her wild heart and share her tumultuous daydreams.

Driving off in de Dienes's black Buick convertible early one morning in the first week of December, they headed for the Mojave Desert and Death Valley. That first night they stayed at Furnace Creek, and much to de Dienes's disappointment, Norma Jeane insisted on her own room. When he knocked on her door in the middle of the night, she smiled and calmly asked him to be good and go back to bed.

It was well past daybreak when he awoke, and de Dienes's favorite time for shooting was eluding him as the sun rose in the cloudless sky. He found Norma Jeane was already up and dressed, looking as bright as the dawn. "There she was fresh as a daisy, wearing a polo-neck sweater, slacks, and a smile," de Dienes remembered. "I felt I could not photograph her too often that day."

"Run!" *click* "Leap!" *click* and he talks to her of wild things and daydreams *click* of mountains of gold and riches *click* fame *click click* "Turn! Arch your back!" *click* The firm, well-rounded breasts *click* and tousled hair in the golden sun *click* "Jump!" *click* the perfect curve of the hips *click click* and the eagles soar against the cobalt sky as she laughs and kisses the sunshine amid the endless vistas and infinite freedom of youth *click* and nature *click* and beauty *click click click*!

It was dark when they arrived in Portland. Norma Jeane had spoken to Grace Goddard on the phone and learned that her mother, who had been released from the institution in Agnew, was living alone in a hotel room in Portland, Oregon. Annoyed with himself for allowing Norma Jeane to persuade him to drive so far north, de Dienes accompanied her to the hotel in the center of town, where they found Gladys in a stark, depressing room on the top floor. He recalls that the meeting was awkward, and that they had nothing to say to each other. Norma Jeane unpacked the presents she had bought and put on a cheerful front. She tried to engage her mother in conversation but Gladys didn't respond. "Mrs. Baker buried her face in her hands and seemed to forget all about us," de Dienes recalled. "It was distressing. She had obviously been released from the hospital too soon."

When they left, they headed south again. It was raining and growing dark, and de Dienes could see that Norma Jeane was depressed. It was again the holiday season, eleven Christmases since Gladys had been taken away, and it was seven years since Norma Jeane had last visited her mother. According to de Dienes, a veil of sadness seemed to envelop her, and there was nothing he could say or do to lift her spirits.

Soon the icy rain turned to snow and the dark road was becoming impassable. Not far from Mt. Hood they made out some lights shining from an old brick hotel called Government Lodge. According to de Dienes there was only one vacancy—a room with a double bed.

When de Dienes and Norma Jeane returned to Los Angeles there was a message waiting from Jim Dougherty. His ship had docked on the East Coast. He was heading home by train and wired the time of his arrival. Learning of her husband's return, Andre de Dienes informed Norma Jeane that a friend in New York had died unexpectedly, and he suddenly left town, having added another shapely model to his portfolio.

When Dougherty arrived at Union Station, his wife wasn't there to greet him. "She was an hour late," Dougherty remembers. "When she did show up—with *my* car—she said she had been at a modeling job and it had taken longer than she figured. Before, I always had received a warm homecoming, a genuine feeling of love and a sense that she had missed me terribly. Now it was a little cool. There was an embrace and a kiss, but it was different."

Though he was home for two weeks, Dougherty recalls that they had only two or three evenings together during his leave. "She was busy modeling, earning good money. It was my first inkling of her ambition, and instead of me being the center of her attention the way it had been on my first trip home, now I was incidental. I was squeezed into her busy day, and resentment set in early. Norma Jeane wasn't talking about our future anymore either. It was her career nearly all the time."

When Dougherty looked at his bankbook, he noted that all the savings had been drawn out—most of it spent on clothes for modeling. "She would show me her new dresses and shoes as though I cared about such things," Dougherty reflected. "She had a collection of all these magazines she'd appeared in. She was beginning to appear on a number of covers and was very proud of that. She expected me to be, too, but all I was, was queasy. I had a sinking feeling in my gut."

Apparently Grace Goddard and Norma Jeane had discussed the distressing visit with her mother in Portland, and it was arranged for Gladys to stay with the Goddards in Van Nuys until Norma Jeane could find a place for her mother to stay. Dougherty has a vivid memory of going with Norma Jeane to the Greyhound bus station in downtown Los Angeles to pick up Gladys. Dougherty had never seen Gladys before, and it was something of a shock. "She was wearing an all-white outfit and looked more like a nurse," Dougherty said. "She was polite enough, but she didn't seem to connect with me at all. Her mind was out in left field somewhere. I never saw her angry, and I never saw her laugh."

Recalling the showdown he had with Norma Jeane in January, shortly before he was to report back for sea duty, Dougherty said, "I saw myself losing out, little by little, and I thought, 'Hell, this is no way to live!' . . . I thought I'd given her modeling career a fair trial, well over a year, and she was letting our home life slide more and more. So I just told her that she would have to choose between a modeling career or a home life with me like we had in Catalina. Then she got very emotional. She said I was gone too much. How could I expect her to be a housewife when I was at sea more than half the time? 'Catalina was wonderful,' she said, 'but when are you coming home to stay?' I knew I was losing the fight to keep us together," Dougherty acknowledged. "She knew what she wanted, and I couldn't offer her anything except promises. When I shipped out again, she must have figured that the most important one had been broken."

Jim was gone again, and not knowing when he would return, Norma Jeane concentrated on her career. With the de Dienes photos, Emmeline Snively had an exceptional portfolio of pictures to circulate, and Norma Jeane became very much in demand. In February and March 1946 she posed for photographer Joe Jasgur and artist Earl Moran. Moran took snapshots of her in a variety of poses, and would then do pastels of them for Brown and Bigelow, a major calendar-art and postcard company. She became Moran's favorite model, and he paid her ten dollars an hour for posing on numerous occasions over the course of the next four erratic and hungry years. Commenting on her talent, Moran later stated, "She knew exactly what to do; her movements, her hands, her body were just perfect. She was the sexiest. Better than anyone else."

By February 1946, Norma Jeane was earning enough money to rent Ana Lower's downstairs apartment on Nebraska Avenue, and have her mother move in with her. The expediency of the move may have had its origins in problems enveloping the Goddard household. According to Bebe, by the time Grace and Doc Goddard had moved back to Van Nuys they had both succumbed to alcoholism, and their life was at times chaotic.

Though living with Gladys presented emotional and practical difficulties, Norma Jeane had a real desire to know her mother and mend their estrangement. On most Sunday mornings Aunt Ana, Gladys, and her daughter attended Christian Science services together in Westwood Village. Emmeline Snively had a vivid recollection of an unexpected visit by Norma Jeane's mother at the Blue Book Modeling Agency. An apparition in white, Gladys suddenly appeared at Miss Snively's door wearing her white dress, white shoes, white stockings, and white hat. The two ladies spent an hour discussing Norma Jeane's career. When Gladys got up to leave she took Emmeline's hand and said, "I only came so I could thank you personally for what you've been doing for Norma Jeane. You've given her a whole new life!"

Emmeline Snively felt that Norma Jeane could be more successful as a blonde, and she frequently suggested lightening her hair, but Norma Jeane protested that she wouldn't look natural. Miss Snively pointed out to her, "If you intend to go places, you've got to bleach, dear. The biggest demand is for blondes. A blonde can be photographed light, medium, or dark by controlling the light. The way your hair is now you'll always come out more dark than light." Nevertheless, Norma Jeane remained stubborn about not changing her hair.

In the spring of 1946 commercial photographer Raphael Wolff called

Emmeline Snively to say that he wanted to use Norma Jeane for a series of Lustre Creme shampoo ads at ten dollars an hour, but he wouldn't hire her unless she became a blonde. He added that he would pay for the bleach job himself. Norma Jeane gave in and was sent to the Hollywood hairstyling salon of Frank and Joseph, where her hair was bleached golden blond and styled in a sophisticated upsweep.

At first she thought it looked artificial. "It wasn't the 'real me,'" she said, and she had difficulty getting used to the other woman whose strange, exotic image stared back at her from the looking glass. But she soon recognized the image as the same friend who had disrupted the math class at Emerson and caused incidents of whiplash on the beaches of Southern California. As a blonde she noted that heads turned a little faster and wolf whistles were a little shriller.

But to be a blonde demanded a certain commitment. Blondes are different. Shapely blondes fall into a mythological morphology. They dress differently, think differently, act differently. Studying the reflection of the blonde in the mirror, she must have recognized something that was true to herself—something that was blond inside.

And as she stared at the strange, exotic image of the other woman, Norma Jeane stepped through the looking glass and became a blonde forever.

"*MM* . . ."

The patient stated that he felt a constant pleasant humming sensation in his lips. He felt as though he were making the sound "Mm . . ." The "Mm" sound was a pleasantly toned auto-erotic expression.

—Dr. Ralph R. Greenson, 1953

Hollywood, it has been said, is a state of mind, a celluloid city that extends from the back lots of the dream factories and has no boundaries— its false fronts and plaster streets wending endlessly through Oz, Shangri-la, the Casbah, and Jurassic Park to the darkened cinema palaces, multiplexes, and living rooms around the globe.

A visitor to the real Hollywood of today is often shocked by the dichotomy between the dream and the reality. Hollywood Boulevard, once a magical mecca, has become the street of busted dreams where panhandlers, grifters, psychos, and life's disenfranchised gather to commiserate in the silent scream of social rejection. The day of the locusts has come and gone, leaving the few vestiges of Hollywood's glory days in ruin and decay.

But there was a day and an arc-lit night when Hollywood was in a better state of mindlessness—the plaster was fresh, the tinsel was real tinsel, and the unrecycled dream was an honest simulation of genuine illusion. There were real stories, and there were real stars. Legendary stars such as Valentino, Gable, Harlow, Pickford, Fairbanks, and Garbo had an aura unknown to the stars of today. The star system and the stars' distinctive larger-than-life individuality placed them in an outer orbit where they burned stronger, burned brighter.

To Norma Jeane, they were the beacons of a promised land—the land of Ingrid Bergman, Claudette Colbert, Joan Crawford, Bette Davis, Gene Tierney, and Jennifer Jones—and she thought,

All actors and actresses were geniuses sitting on the front porch of Paradise— the movies. Acting became something golden and beautiful. It wasn't an art. It was like the bright colors I used to see in my daydreams—like a game that enabled me to step out of a dark and dull world, into worlds so bright they made my heart leap just to think of them. From time to time I took drama lessons, when I had enough money. They were expensive. I paid ten dollars an hour, and I often used to say my speech lesson out loud:

Ariadne arose from her couch in the snows in the Akrakaronian moun- tains. . . . Hail to thee, blithe spirit, bird thou ne-never wert.

I got to know a lot of people, people different from those I'd known, both good and bad. Sometimes when I was waiting for a bus a car would stop and the man at the wheel would roll down the window and say, "What are you doing here? You should be in pictures." Then he'd ask me to drive home with him. I'd always say, "No, thank you. I'd rather take the bus." But all the same, the idea of the movies kept going through my mind.

Early in 1946 Norma Jeane spoke with Emmeline Snively about her ambition to be a movie actress, and Miss Snively recommended that she see her friend Helen "Bunny" Ainsworth, the West Coast representative of the National Concert Artists talent agency. A huge woman, Bunny Ainsworth weighed in at well over two hundred pounds and jokingly re- ferred to herself as the biggest agent in Hollywood. Impressed by Norma Jeane, Ainsworth signed her to the agency on March 11, 1946, and Harry Lipton was appointed as her motion-picture representative.

But Norma Jeane was only one of thousands dreaming the same dream, following the same road sign, THIS WAY OUT. They packed up their hopes and hitchhiked, grabbed the bus, or jumped on the train for movieland, each one dreaming with all her heart that she would be the one who would make it to the top: hundreds and hundreds of smiles and capped teeth and dye jobs, fixed noses, electrolysis—all bumps and warts re- moved; thousands of brunettes, redheads, blondes with lithe legs, full firm breasts, and the perfect curve of the hip—or excellent falsies and bun pads; thousands and thousands of photos and head shots and résumés—

"Broadway experience," can sing, tap-dance, do the hula, play piano, double-jointed, "Miss Wyoming," studied with Meisner, Abbey Players, Pocono Playhouse, slept with Zanuck (has special wink and walk), has large expressive eyes; "Bright as hell, Jack, studied in London—*class*, but look at those jugs!" . . . "exudes confidence, charm and allure!" . . . "and listen, Harry, get this—she's J. Paul Getty's sweetie pie" . . . Thousands and thousands of babes and dolls and lays and lookers, schemers and dreamers with gams and grins, boobs and kissers, and—and then there was Norma Jeane.

She followed the prescribed trail from Schwab's Drugstore to the studio casting offices, portfolio and résumé in hand. She read big books to improve her mind while waiting long hours on hard benches, only to be told, "We can't see you today." She had heard through the grapevine at Schwab's that no major studio would put her under contract, in any event, if she was married. Her agent, Harry Lipton, confirmed that the studios felt they would be wasting money and time in training a starlet who might get pregnant. According to Lipton, he spoke to Norma Jeane about her marriage of four years to Dougherty, and realizing that the marriage was in fact over, persuaded her to go to Nevada and obtain a quickie divorce.

She filed for a divorce from James Dougherty in Las Vegas on May 14, 1946. Though she was legally required to live in Nevada until the divorce was finalized, she frequently commuted between Hollywood and Vegas, gambling on the odds that she wouldn't be caught.

Dougherty recalls that his ship had docked in Shanghai when the mail arrived from the states. Norma Jeane hadn't written for a long time, and he didn't really expect a letter. But his name was called out and one of the sailors handed a letter back to him and said, "Hey, your old lady's divorcing you!" It was from a Las Vegas attorney. "It was a Dear John," Dougherty remembers, "and all kinds of crazy thoughts went through my mind. I thought about jumping over the side, about doing away with myself any way I could manage. But that feeling passed within minutes." Despair quickly turned to anger as Dougherty saw that a movie contract meant more to his wife than a marriage contract. Instead of doing away with himself, Dougherty stated, "I immediately went to the captain and said, 'I want my wife's allotment cut off as of *right now!*'"

In July, Norma Jeane appeared on the cover of four "girlie" magazines—*Click, Pic, Laff,* and *Sir.* Packing her bulging portfolio, she headed for 20th Century-Fox, determined to see the casting director, Ben Lyon.

In the wartime boom years and pre-TV days, Fox had become the largest and most successful of the Hollywood majors. Invariably, the studio empires had been built on the vision of individuals rather than executive boards, agents, and Wall Street lawyers; and it was Darryl F. Zanuck, an idiosyncratic man of dauntless will and energy, who had turned the ailing William Fox Corporation into a vast empire encompassing the worldwide Fox theater chain and the Westwood Studio, with its sixteen soundstages, three hundred acres of lakes and forests, western towns, New York City streets, medieval castles, railway stations, jungles, and Oriental bazaars—all on prime real estate bordering Beverly Hills.

With a stable of stars that included Betty Grable, Tyrone Power, Gene Tierney, Dana Andrews, June Haver, and Clifton Webb, Fox made seventy-five films in 1945, and Zanuck ran the studio like a Prussian general. An ex–polo player, Zanuck had been barred from playing polo in Brentwood because he had swung his mallet at a horse in a fit of anger. He then turned his mallet into a swagger stick, and it was said that he swung it at yes men who said "yes" before he was finished talking.

In the summer of 1946 a nineteen-year-old journalist from Ohio was waiting in the crowded lobby of Fox Studios, hoping for an interview with Gene Tierney, when an attractive blonde carrying a bulging portfolio pushed open the large entry doors. Catching her heel, she stumbled and her pictures scattered on the linoleum floor. As the young journalist helped her pick up the pictures, she smiled at him with her bright blue eyes and said, "Thank you!" before walking to the receptionist's window.

Young Robert Slatzer tried to return to his book, but the blonde's perfume lingered, and he found it hard to concentrate on his reading. He glanced once more at the shy, beautiful blonde as the receptionist asked her to take a seat. Slatzer recalls feeling fortunate that there was only one place left for her to sit—next to him.

"What kind of book is that?" she asked as she sat down.

"*Leaves of Grass,*" Slatzer said.

"What's it about?" she asked with wide-eyed wonder.

"It's a collection of poems by Walt Whitman," he told her as he handed her the book. "Are you an actress?" Slatzer inquired.

"No, I'm a model," she responded enthusiastically, as she began thumbing through the book's pages. "But I hope to be an actress someday. My name is Norma Jeane."

When he introduced himself, she began asking Slatzer about movie stars he had interviewed: What were they like? Were they the same in person as they were on the screen? Where did they print his interviews? And as they spoke Slatzer realized there was something special about this shy, beautiful blonde. "We had an instant affection towards each other," he recalled. "She had a certain magic about her that was quite different. I guess you could say my heart went out to her from that very first day— and she sensed that."

Before he knew it they had made a date for that very night. He was to pick her up at the apartment on Nebraska, and they would have dinner up in Malibu at a place she liked that overlooked the ocean. He hadn't told her he was broke and didn't have a car. Slatzer was staying at the home of character actor Noble "Kid" Chissell, whom he had met on location in Ohio when Fox was filming *Home in Indiana*. Fortunately, Chissell wasn't using his car that night and let Slatzer borrow his car and ten bucks.

While Slatzer never got his interview that day with Gene Tierney, he did have an entrancing evening with the beautiful blonde. Gene Tierney was filming *Dragonwyck* with Walter Huston, and too busy to see the young journalist; however, there was another young man from the east who had no trouble in meeting Gene Tierney on the set of *Dragonwyck*, a charismatic man who had recently arrived in Hollywood—Jack Kennedy.

In June of 1946 Jack Kennedy had won the Boston primary in the Eleventh Congressional District by a landslide. Flush with his first political success, he packed his bags and headed for a vacation in Hollywood, where he could work on his tan and his image before launching the November election campaign. Following in the footsteps of his old man, he was intent on mingling with the stars and "knocking a name," as he put it to his friend Chuck Spalding, who worked for Gene Tierney's agent, Charles Feldman.

Recalling meeting Jack on the set of *Dragonwyck* at Fox, Gene Tierney stated, "I turned and found myself staring into the most perfect blue eyes I had ever seen on a man. He smiled at me. My reaction was right out of a ladies' romance novel. Literally, my heart skipped." Though she was married at the time to Oleg Cassini, Gene Tierney became enamored of Jack Kennedy and believed he was in love with her.

"I'm not sure I can explain the nature of Jack's charm," she said, "but he took life just as it came. He didn't try to hide. He never worried about making an impression. He made you feel very secure. I don't remember seeing him angry. He was good with people in a way that went beyond politics, thoughtful in more than a material way. Gifts and flowers were not his style. He gave you his time, his interest."

But Gene Tierney was not the only woman to whom Jack gave his time and his interest. She was only one of many married women, divorcées, stars, and starlets he pursued on his Hollywood escapade.

"News from the Hollywood love front!" Sheilah Graham coyly revealed in her gossip column of August 15, 1946. "Peggy Cummins and Jack Kennedy are a surprise twosome around town during this Congressman-for-Boston's visit here!"

According to his *PT-109* shipmate Red Fay, Jack also had an affair with Sonja Henie, whom he had met at the Hollywood home of his friend actor Robert Stack. Fay recalls Jack stating, "Making it with the ice-skating star was one of my greatest triumphs." It was that summer, when Jack was eyeing the stars and starlets at Hollywood parties, that Robert Stack remembers seeing a pretty model named Norma Jeane.

"I first met Norma Jeane Dougherty before she changed her name, when a good-looking Hungarian actor named Eric Feldary took her to one of our swimming parties," Stack recalled. Feldary, who was also a friend of Sonja Henie, appeared in *For Whom the Bell Tolls* and *Hold Back the Dawn*. Stack noted that Norma Jeane wore a white bathing suit, "which she filled beautifully, but then so did many of the other pretty girls. I remember that she appeared to be shy and somehow on the outside of everything taking place at the party. I tried being a good host, and every time I'd ask if she wanted anything she'd say, 'No, everything is fine.' "

In the summer of 1946, Norma Jeane appeared in her bathing suit on the cover of *Laff*, a girlie magazine that Howard Hughes found more than amusing. On July 7, Hughes had narrowly escaped death when the experimental plane he was testing crashed into a Beverly Hills residence. He was semicomatose for days and encased in a plaster cast, but signs of life returned when he spotted Norma Jeane's photo on *Laff*'s cover. Hughes called his office at RKO and told one of his associates to find out who the cover girl was and arrange a screen test. Learning of Hughes's interest, but savvy enough to know that a Hughes screen test for a starlet often meant a command performance between the call sheets, Bunny Ainsworth planted an item in Hedda Hopper's syndicated movie column of July 29:

Howard Hughes is on the mend. Picking up a magazine, he was attracted by the cover girl and promptly instructed an aide to sign her for pictures. She's Norma Jeane Dougherty, a model.

Miss Ainsworth then called 20th Century-Fox casting director Ben Lyon and told him Norma Jeane hadn't signed the Hughes contract yet, and she'd give Fox a chance, but they'd have to act fast. "Bring her right over," Ben Lyon said.

Norma Jeane was at Aunt Ana's when she got the call. Nebraska Avenue was only minutes away from the Fox lot, but there'd be little time to fix her makeup, put on the right dress, and do her hair. Nevertheless, she was ready for this moment. When she arrived, Miss Ainsworth was there waiting for her, and this time there'd be no long wait on the hard chairs, culminating with "I'm sorry, no more interviews today." The receptionist ushered them through the doors and they hurried down the hall of the administration building to Ben Lyon's office. Lyon didn't ask her to read a scene. He didn't recall asking about her experience. He didn't remember whether he asked about her education, her age, or whether she was married. He was struck by what he saw and sensed. Seeing was believing. He recalled saying something inane to Bunny Ainsworth like, "I think she's got good bones in her face."

"Can you test her tomorrow, Ben?" Miss Ainsworth asked.

"Mr. Zanuck has to approve every test. It will take a little time to get his okay on it."

"Do it fast, Ben," Miss Ainsworth said. "We're on our way over to RKO from here."

"Give me two days—just two days," Ben Lyon asked. "I'll set it up."

Two days later Lyon arranged an unauthorized screen test. Not wanting to run the risk of Zanuck's saying no, Lyon gambled that once Zanuck saw the test he'd sign her. They went on the set at five-thirty on an August morning with a skeleton crew to film the silent test. Lyon told Norma Jeane to start walking across the set when he said "Action." Then she was to sit down and light a cigarette . . . put it out . . . get up . . . walk upstage . . . cross . . . look out the window . . . turn . . . come downstage, and exit.

Norma Jeane stood waiting in the dark, nervously shaking her hands as if to shake out the demons. The electrician's grip threw the knife switch that turned false dark into false day, and cameraman Leon Shamroy indicated he was ready. As Lyon said "Action," Norma Jeane began her silent dialogue with the transfiguring eye of the camera. "I know few actresses who had the incredible talent for communicating with the camera lens as she did," photographer Philippe Halsman once said. "She would try to seduce a camera as if it were a human being." But the unerring eye of the camera to Norma Jeane was millions and millions of eyes—the cyclops of the whole world, the world where the other person, whose name she didn't know, belonged. It was the lens that had the power to divine the voluptuous waif who had wandered somnambulently into the wrong world—the dreaming child with the wide-eyed Technicolor gaze of wistful incertitude. In recalling that morning when they made the test, Leon Shamroy stated, "Later, I got a cold chill. This girl had something—something I hadn't seen since silent pictures. She didn't need a soundtrack to tell her story."

There was a prescribed ritual at Fox when Darryl F. Zanuck entered a projection room. The secretary would call the projectionist when the studio boss was on his way, and he would then buzz the theater when Zanuck entered the outer corridor. Everyone stood up for Zanuck's entrance and waited until he was seated before sitting down. When Zanuck took his seat on the afternoon he was to see the Norma Jeane Dougherty test, Ben Lyon sat down uneasily, knowing what was to come.

After the dailies ended, Norma Jeane's silent Technicolor test unexpectedly came on the screen. The room was deadly quiet. When it ended, Zanuck barked, "Who's that girl?"

"Her name's Norma Jeane Dougherty, Mr. Zanuck. She's a model."

"I don't know her. Did I authorize this test?"

"No, sir," Lyon said, anticipating a devastating Zanuck tirade.

"It's a damn fine test. Sign her up!"

Several days later Norma Jeane rushed to the Goddards' house waving her contract in the air, shouting, "I've got it! I've got it! I'm with the finest studio in Hollywood! They liked my test. I'm actually on the payroll! Look!" Grace Goddard and Norma Jeane embraced and wept with joy.

"I told you, honey!" Grace exclaimed, wiping away the tears. "I said one day you're going to be a movie star! I told you!"

"The people are all wonderful, and I'm going to be in a movie! It'll be different now for all of us," Norma Jeane exclaimed as she excitedly told Grace all the details about the test. She mentioned that the casting director had suggested "she think up a more glamorous name than Norma Dougherty."

"Haven't you any ideas for a name?" Grace asked.

"The man at the studio suggested 'Marilyn,'" she said.

"That's a nice name," Grace replied. "And it fits with your mother's maiden name. She was a Monroe."

"That's a wonderful name," Norma Jeane exclaimed. "Monroe . . . Marilyn . . . Marilyn . . . Monroe . . . Marilyn   Monroe . . . Marilyn   Monroe!" She repeated it over and over and over to herself and wrote it down again and again . . .

. . . until it looked comfortable and sounded familiar—like a friend. And she decided it would be the name of the other person.

PART III

1946–1954

All the Bright Colors

Rara Avis—With Options

I had a new name, Marilyn Monroe. I had to get born. And this time better than before.

—Marilyn Monroe

Ten years after entering the Los Angeles Orphans' Home, orphan number 3,463 became Marilyn Monroe. Reborn on August 24, 1946, in the 20th Century-Fox legal department, she entered the celluloid world of dreams as a starlet earning seventy-five dollars a week, "subject to the terms of a seven-year contract, hereinbefore amended with options of the aforesaid agreement and subject to renewal, as herebefore agreed."

For the wide-eyed starlet it was like being a refugee escaping to the promised land, and the rolling hills of 20th Century-Fox became her adopted home. Though she wasn't required to be at the studio every day, she regularly attended the studio classes in voice, acting, and dance. In the hairdressing department she learned the tricks of being a blonde, and heard the latest hair-curling studio gossip. Visiting the editing rooms and soundstages, she learned the boiler-room mechanics of the Fox film factory. Allan "Whitey" Snyder, who first met Marilyn at Fox in 1946, recalled that she was "desperate to absorb all she could."

Everyone seemed to notice the attractive and personable new starlet except the head of the studio, Darryl F. Zanuck. In the fall of 1946, Zanuck was producing *Gentleman's Agreement*, starring Gregory Peck. Directed by Elia Kazan, it was to be an award-winning, heartfelt statement about anti-Semitism. At the same time Zanuck was supervising postproduction of *The Razor's Edge* and *The Late George Apley*. He was the overseer of the entire output of the studio, which produced fifty-three films in 1946. Fox had over forty contract players, and Marilyn was only one of a dozen starlets. Zanuck seldom saw a starlet unless it was on the screen or on the chaise of his studio chateau. Seldom seen by the ordinary studio employee, Zanuck was a night person. Marilyn belonged to the day.

Studio publicist Roy Craft was sent to interview Marilyn and put together a brief bio for the studio files. He recalled being deeply moved by her Dickensian story concerning the orphanage and the series of foster homes. Grace Goddard had advised Marilyn not to reveal her mother's history of mental illness. And so Marilyn told Roy Craft what she once suspected to be true in her early days at the orphanage—that her mother was dead.

At the time of the interview, however, Gladys was staying with Marilyn at Aunt Ana's. Shortly after Marilyn had signed her Fox contract, Berniece and her daughter Mona Rae came to visit for several months. It was the first time Berniece had seen her mother since they said good-bye in Kentucky in 1923.

According to Berniece, there was always friction between Marilyn and her mother, who frequently was argumentative and critical of her daughter. "I keep telling myself," Marilyn confided to her half sister, "that mother will act better when she has been on the outside longer. I still feel as if we're strangers. I'm still trying to get acquainted with her. When I went to see her in Portland, I drove up there thinking it would be a joyful occasion—all those years I had waited and wished . . . but then she was so cold. I felt so let down." Berniece noted that Marilyn went to great lengths to try and heal the relationship and was ingeniously inventive in trying to divert Gladys's urge to be argumentative. But Marilyn ultimately confided to Berniece, "Mother and I could never live together."

Shortly after Berniece and Mona Rae ended their visit, Gladys moved from the Nebraska Avenue apartment she shared with Marilyn and returned to Oregon with an itinerant salesman, John Stewart Eley, whom she later married. In the fall of 1946, Marilyn moved from Aunt Ana's to a rented room in the Hollywood Hills on Temple Hill Way. It would be one of many rooms and small apartments she would live in during the difficult years of her early career.

In her first weeks as a Fox starlet, Marilyn occasionally met with the young Ohio journalist, Bob Slatzer, who was a fountain of film lore. He took her to Hollywood landmarks and loaned her books to fill her insatiable appetite for knowledge. Slatzer recalled that one Sunday they visited the old John Barrymore estate on Tower Grove, which had been put up for auction after Barrymore's death. The fifty-five-room mansion had fallen into decay, but it still contained many relics from Barrymore's eclectic collections—totem poles, shrunken human heads, armor, paintings, and stuffed rare birds. Slatzer remembered that Marilyn found the sight of the stuffed birds distressing, and that she quickly tuned in to the tragedy that lingered in the halls of the Barrymore estate. When they visited the room where Barrymore had lain near death, hemorrhaging from the ravages of alcoholism, Marilyn said, "This place is a nightmare of everything that went wrong with a man." Slatzer observed that Marilyn was instinctively repelled by possessions, and when they drove out of the rusting Barrymore gates, she remarked, "I never want to own anything pretentious in my life—especially not a big home." She then blurted out, as if Norma Jeane were making a vow to Marilyn Monroe, "Remember that you're here for just a little while. And don't you damn well forget it!"

Slatzer left Los Angeles in September to resume his college studies in Ohio, but he was determined to return to Hollywood to pursue his career and learn more about the fascinating creature who had stumbled into his life in the lobby of 20th Century-Fox.

In November, Marilyn played her first bit part, as a telephone operator in *The Shocking Miss Pilgrim*. Because she's barely seen the film is seldom mentioned in her filmographies; nevertheless, it was her first professional motion-picture experience.

Reminiscing about her early days at Fox, Marilyn recalled attending a party at the home of agent Charles Feldman, whose Famous Artists Corporation was one of the top agencies in Beverly Hills.

One night a bit player, a male, invited me out for dinner.

"I haven't any money," I warned him. "Have you?"

"No," he said. "But I've received a sort of invitation to a party. And I would like to take you along. All the stars will be there."

We arrived at the Beverly Hills home at nine o'clock. It was a famous agent's house. I felt as frightened entering it as if I were breaking into a bank. My stockings had a few mends in them. I was wearing a ten-dollar dress. And my shoes! I prayed nobody would look at my shoes. I stood as straight as I could and put on the highest-class expression I knew, but the best I could manage was to walk stiff legged into a large hall and stand staring like a frozen blonde at dinner jackets and evening gowns.

My escort whispered to me, "The food's in the other room. Come on!" He went off without me. I remained in the hall, looking into a room full of wonderful furniture and wonderful people. Jennifer Jones was sitting on a couch. Olivia de Havilland was standing near a little table. Gene Tierney was laughing next to her. There were so many others I couldn't focus on them. Evening gowns and famous faces drifted around in the room laughing and chatting. Diamonds glittered. There were men, too, but I only looked at one. Clark Gable stood by himself holding a highball and smiling wistfully at the air. He looked so familiar that it made me dizzy.

A voice spoke.

"My dear young lady," it said, "do come and sit by my side."

It was a charming voice, a little fuzzy with liquor, but very distinguished. I turned and saw a man sitting by himself on the stairway. He was holding a drink in his hand. His face was sardonic like his voice.

"Do you mean me?" I asked.

"Yes," he said. "Pardon me if I don't rise. My name is George Sanders."

I said, "How do you do."

"I presume you also have a name," he scowled at me.

"I'm Marilyn Monroe," I said.

"You will forgive me for not having heard it before," said Mr. Sanders. "Do sit down—beside me."

"May I have the honor of asking you to marry me?" he said solemnly. "The name, in case you've forgotten, is Sanders."

I smiled at him and didn't answer.

"You are naturally a little reluctant to marry one who is not only a stranger, but an actor," Mr. Sanders said. "I can understand your hesitancy—particularly on the second ground. An actor is not quite a human being—but then, who is?"

Mr. Sanders's handsome and witty face suddenly looked at me, intently.

"Blonde," he said, "pneumatic, and full of peasant health. Just the type for me!"

I thought he was going to put his arm around me, but he didn't. Mr. Sanders put his glass down and dozed off.

Despite George Sanders's ennui, Charlie Feldman was known for giving some of the best parties in Hollywood. Originally a New Yorker, Feldman knew Joe Kennedy, and it was through the Kennedy family connection that Jack's friend Chuck Spalding was working for Feldman at Famous Artists in 1946. When Jack Kennedy went to Hollywood on his "hunting expeditions" he was often a guest at the Feldman house, and he was dating two of Feldman's clients, Gene Tierney and Peggy Cummins. According to Feldman's ex-wife, Jean Howard, Kennedy stayed at Feldman's house in 1946, and Chuck Spalding's wife, Betty, confirmed that it was Charlie Feldman who introduced Jack Kennedy to Marilyn Monroe.

By Christmas of 1946 Marilyn had performed as a bit-extra in only two films, and she soon realized that one of her problems at Fox was that the studio had too many blondes. Betty Grable was the star of the lot, and June Haver and Vivian Blaine were already being groomed for stardom. As the superfluous blonde, Marilyn rode on floats, appeared at premieres with studio dates, did grand openings of supermarkets, and posed for photos, but she didn't see her name on the call sheets. Discouraged, she turned to Ben Lyon and said, "What do I do to become a star, Ben? Tell me how to become a star!" Lyon detected the tone of raw determination in her voice. "She had her heart set on becoming the queen of the lot," Lyon reflected. "Fox had become a home to her, a replacement for the family she never had." He advised her to be patient and study. But among the aging bit players, Marilyn noted many who *had* studied and *had* been patient.

In the hair-raising studio gossip mill, Marilyn undoubtedly heard the wave of stories about the seventy-year-old Fox studio czar, Joe Schenck. One of the founding fathers of Hollywood, Schenck had been convicted of perjury during government investigations into bribes he and other studio bosses had paid to Willy Bioff, Johnny Rosselli, and union racketeers connected with the Mafia. Schenck served a six-month prison term at Danbury in 1942. But in 1947, as an executive at 20th Century-Fox, he still wielded considerable power in the film capital.

Schenck had a shrewd eye for business and a connoisseur's eye for attractive women. In his waning years he maintained his keen appreciation of the feminine mystique and collected beautiful young specimens who raised his flagging spirits—if nothing else. Among the studio gossips they were known as "Schenck's girls," young beauties who congregated at Schenck's Holmby Hills Mediterranean mansion for cocktails, dinner, screenings, and card parties.

In early 1947, Joe Schenck was driving from the Fox lot when his limousine encountered an exotic *rara avis* wiggle-walking across a studio street. Perhaps it was more than coincidence that she happened to be wiggling by at the propitious moment and gave Schenck a wide-eyed smile. Telling his chauffeur to stop the car, Schenck motioned Marilyn over and asked her name. Learning that she was a contract player, and knowing that contract players were usually hungry, he ensnared the beautiful creature with the suggestion, "Why don't you call me about dinnertime?" and handed her a card with his home number. If, as Ben Lyon stated, Fox had become Marilyn's surrogate home, then Joe Schenck became her surrogate father. Within weeks she became one of Schenck's girls, and a regular at his dinner parties.

Marion Wagner, who had known Marilyn from the Blue Book modeling days, was also one of Schenck's girls, and she vividly recalled those evenings when Schenck's limousine brought the girls up to his elegant mansion at 141 South Carolwood Drive. After cocktails and dinner they'd either see a movie in his private projection room or play cards. "He used to get a kick out of backing us when we played gin rummy against his male pals, and if we won it pleased him," Marion Wagner remembered. "He was like a father figure, a father confessor, a very wise, lovely old man. When the evening was over, I would simply be taken home in the limousine, and so far as I know it was the same for Marilyn."

Among the card sharks and male pals were mafiosi Johnny Rosselli and Bugsy Siegel, and Columbia Pictures boss Harry Cohn. Rosselli, Siegel, and Cohn were associated with Schenck in a number of Los Angeles Mafia gambling operations as well as partners in the Aqua Caliente Race Track in Baja California. Siegel dropped out of the game when he was fatally shot in the eye at his home on June 22, 1947.

Soon it was Marilyn Monroe who was the subject of the studio gossip mill. "The first fame I achieved was a wave of gossip that identified me as Joe Schenck's girl," Marilyn lamented. "Mr. Schenck had invited me to his Holmby Hills mansion for dinner one evening. Then he fell into the habit of inviting me two or three evenings a week. I went to Mr. Schenck's mansion the first few times because he was one of the heads of the studio. After that I went because I liked him. Also the food was very good, and there were always important people at the table—Mr. Schenck's personal friends. The fact that people began to talk about me being Joe Schenck's girl didn't annoy me at first. But later it did annoy me. Mr. Schenck never so much as laid a finger on my wrist, or tried to. He was interested in me because I was a good table ornament and because I was what he called an 'offbeat personality.' . . . I liked sitting around the fireplace with Mr. Schenck and hearing him talk about love and sex. He was full of wisdom on these subjects, like some great explorer. I also liked to look at his face. It was as much the face of a town as of a man. The whole history of Hollywood was in it."

In February 1947, the studio renewed her contract for another six months at an increased salary of one hundred dollars per week. Several weeks later her name appeared on the call sheets for *Scudda-Hoo! Scudda-Hay!* starring June Haver and Lon McCallister. In what is generally considered her screen debut, she played the bit part of Betty, with two words of dialogue: "Hi, Rad!"

"Now just walk up to Miss June Haver, smile at her, say hello, wave your right hand, and walk on. Got it?" Marilyn recalled the assistant director telling her. "The bells rang. A hush fell over the set. The assistant director called, 'Action!' I walked, smiled, waved my right hand, and spoke. I was in the movies! I was one of those hundred to one shots—a 'bit player.'"

In the brief scene, June Haver and child actress Natalie Wood are engaged in conversation in front of a small-town church in Paducah. Parishioners are exiting the church behind them. Among them is a pretty young blonde who walks by, turns to Miss Haver and waves as she says, "Hi, Rad!" Miss Haver then responds, "Hi, Betty!" In the next reel there's a scene by a lake where blond Betty is seen in the background with another bit player paddling a canoe.

"There were a dozen of us on the set, bit players, with a gesture to make and a line or two to recite," Marilyn recalled. "Some of them were veteran bit players. After ten years in the movies they were still saying one line and walking ten feet toward nowhere. A few were young and had nice bosoms. But I knew they were different from me. They didn't have my illusions. My illusions didn't have anything to do with being a fine actress. I knew how third rate I was. With the arc lights on me and the camera pointed at me, I suddenly knew myself. How clumsy, empty, uncultured I was! A sullen orphan with a goose egg for a head. I could actually feel my lack of talent, as if it were cheap clothes I was wearing inside. But my God, how I wanted to learn! To change! To improve! I didn't want anything else. Not men, not money, not love, but the ability to act!"

It would be a long and bumpy ride for blond Betty of Paducah before she arrived at *Bus Stop*.

Smog

There is something in corruption which, like a jaundiced eye, transfers the color of itself to the object it looks upon, and sees everything stained and impure.

—Thomas Paine

Shortly after Shelley Winters hitchhiked from Brooklyn and arived in Hollywood, she began hanging around Schwab's Drugstore on the Sunset Strip because she had heard that it was where Lana Turner had been discovered. Though Lana Turner was discovered elsewhere, it was at Schwab's that Shelley met movie columnist Sidney Skolsky and his chauffeur, Marilyn Monroe.

Winters recalled that when she met Marilyn in 1946, "she was driving Skolsky around to interviews in her old Ford, since he had never learned to drive." Skolsky was one of the more colorful members of the Hollywood press corps. A diminutive man, he also had a short temper and once fiercely bit columnist Louella Parsons on the arm in a fit of anger during a dinner party at Chasen's.

Though he wasn't afraid of Louella Parsons, Skolsky had many phobias. He was afraid of automobiles, cats, dogs, children, and germs. Perhaps his hypochondria as well as his love of show business led him to establish his office in a drugstore. His balcony office in Schwab's commanded a dramatic view of the Hollywood struggle pit below, which he called the "Schwabadero"—the wanna-bes' Trocadero. The Schwabadero served as a jitney stop for volunteer drivers who took Skolsky wherever he wanted to go. It was said Skolsky didn't drive because his feet couldn't reach the pedals; however, he was truly afraid of cars. At various times his chauffeurs included almost everyone in the star system—from Marlene Dietrich to Humphrey Bogart to Marilyn Monroe. Shelley Winters recalled that one day Skolsky took Marilyn and Winters out to the parking lot behind the drugstore and pointed to a long low building where his daughter, Stefi, was a drama student. " 'That's the Actors Lab,' he told us. 'It's the new Hollywood home of the Group Theatre, and some of the best actors in the world teach there!' We almost knocked the poor man down in our rush to get to the front door."

The Group Theatre had been organized in New York by Hannah Weinstein, executive director of one of the Comintern fronts, the Arts, Sciences, and Professions Council. Under its directors Harold Clurman, Cheryl Crawford, and Lee Strasberg, the Group Theatre presented some remarkably innovative productions in the 1930s: *Success Story* by John Howard Lawson; *Men in White* by Sidney Kingsley; *Awake and Sing* by Clifford Odets. In 1932 the Group presented *Night Over Taos* by Maxwell Anderson, the story of a revolt against landowners. The production starred Morris Carnovsky, J. Edward Bromberg, Phoebe Brand, Clifford Odets, and an attractive young actress, Paula Miller, who would later marry the play's director, Lee Strasberg.

During the thirties, the Group Theatre made no pretense of burying the Marxist message in its presentations—it was loudly projected to the cheap seats by gifted, dedicated artists. Morris Carnovsky and his wife Phoebe Brand became coaches at the Actors Lab, where Marilyn and Shelley Winters studied in 1947. There was a deep dichotomy between the mind-set of the Group Theatre, with its roots in Stanislavsky's Method, and the West Coast endocrine system of acting. Exercises in sense memory, animal improvisations, and searches for motivation were unlike anything Marilyn had previously been exposed to. Anthony Quinn, Lee J. Cobb, Joe Papp, Lloyd Bridges, John Garfield, Larry Parks, and Walter Bernstein were among the talented students. Walter Bernstein would one day become the screenwriter called in by Fox to rewrite *Something's Got to Give*.

Phoebe Brand, one of Marilyn's teachers, remembered her as a self-conscious girl who never spoke up in class. "I never knew what to make of her," she said. "She didn't tell me what her acting problems were. . . . I tried to get through to her, but I couldn't. She was extremely retiring.

What I failed to see in her acting was wit, her sense of humor. It was there all the time—this lovely comedic style, but I was blind to it. Frankly I never would have predicted she would be a success." Joe Papp remembered her as a young girl who came to class with a small dog that sat in her lap. He recalled that she was so shy she barely spoke at all.

Remembering her days at the Actors Lab, Marilyn said, "All I could think of was this far, faraway place called New York, where actors and directors did very different things than stand around all day arguing about a close-up or a camera angle. I had never seen a play, and I don't think I knew how to read one very well. But Phoebe Brand and her company somehow made it all very real. It seemed so exciting to me, and I wanted to be part of that life."

The list of Actors Lab sponsors was a who's who of Hollywood Stalinism: John Howard Lawson; Alvah Bessie; Ring Lardner, Jr.; Albert Maltz; Dalton Trumbo; Waldo Salt; Donald Ogden Stewart; J. Edward Bromberg; Abe Polonsky. But the majority of students, many of whom attended under the G.I. Bill, were merely ambitious young innocents like Marilyn Monroe who had a fierce determination to learn their craft.

Once, asked how she felt about communists, Marilyn said, "They're for the people, aren't they?" But Marilyn wasn't a political person. Her opinions were opinions of the heart, not dialectics. She didn't take part in the political and artistic arguments that raged in the Actors Lab commissary, at the Schwabadero, or at Greenblatt's Deli across the street. Her golden dreams had little to do with ideology, revolution, or a new social order. Her dreams had to do with the quiet revolution going on within herself.

In May, Marilyn Monroe was cast by Fox in *Dangerous Years*, a B movie produced by Sol Wurtzel. It would be a best-forgotten film of 1947 had Marilyn not played Eve, a waitress in a hangout for delinquent teenagers. She was on the screen for only a few minutes; nevertheless, it was the first real bit part in which she could do a portrayal. Though the director, Arthur Pierson, admired her performance and Ben Lyon saw promise, the studio didn't renew Marilyn's contract when the option fell due in August of 1947.

"I got called into the casting department and informed that I was being dropped by the studio and that my presence would no longer be required," Marilyn recalled. "I went to my room in Hollywood and lay down in bed and cried. I cried for a week. I didn't eat or talk or comb my hair. I kept crying as if I were at a funeral burying Marilyn Monroe."

Several days later, she was invited to the Schenck home for dinner, and Marilyn remembered sitting at the dinner table feeling too ashamed to look into anyone's eyes. She remarked,

That's the way you feel when you're beaten inside. You don't feel angry at those who've beaten you. You just feel ashamed.

When we were sitting in the living room Mr. Schenck said to me, "How are things going at the studio?"

I smiled at him because I was glad he hadn't had a hand in my being fired.

"I lost my job there last week," I said. Mr. Schenck didn't try to console me. He didn't take my hand or make any promises.

"Keep trying," he told me.

"I will," I said.

"Try Columbia," Mr. Schenck said. "There may be something there."

I called Columbia two days later. The casting department was very polite. Yes, they had a place for me. They would put me on the payroll and see that I was given a chance at any part that came up. Max Arnow, the casting director, smiled, squeezed my hand and added, "You ought to go a long way here. I'll watch out for a good part for you."

I returned to my room feeling alive again. And the daydreams started coming back—kind of on tiptoe. The casting director saw hundreds of girls every week, whom he turned down, real actresses and beauties of every sort. There must be something special about me for him to have hired me right off, after a first look.

There was something special about me in the casting director's eyes, but I didn't find it out till much later. Mr. Schenck had called up the head of Columbia and asked him as a favor to give me a job.

But the truth was that Harry Cohn was reluctant to put Marilyn under contract until pressure was put on him by Joe Kennedy's occasional golf partner, Johnny Rosselli. There were other odd contingencies to Marilyn's sudden departure from Fox and her new arrangement with Columbia. Though one would conclude from reading Marilyn's account that it all happened very quickly—a matter of a few days and a phone call—actually there was an extended period of time between Marilyn's departure from Fox in August 1947 and her new contract with Columbia in March of 1948. Marilyn dropped from sight for seven months.

Uncharacteristically, there are no known photographs taken of Marilyn from July 1947 until her career resumed in early 1948. Normally she would have been busy modeling and appearing in ads and on the covers of girlie magazines. Some biographers have stated that she performed at the Bliss-Hayden Playhouse in *Glamour Preferred* in October 1947, but there's no advertising, clippings, or programs to document her appearance.

The source of the play date was based on the hazy recollections of the theater manager, Lila Bliss, twenty years later.

At Harry Drucker's barber shop in Beverly Hills—where film moguls and mafiosi talked business, broads, and horses—the hot rumor wafting in the cigar smoke was that Fox had dropped Marilyn Monroe because she was pregnant. The rumor was in later years supported by Marilyn's own revelation to several friends that she had given birth to a baby girl when she was barely twenty, and that the baby had been taken away from her.

When Marilyn lived with Milton and Amy Greene in 1955, she told Amy that she had given birth to a baby when she was barely out of her teens and felt very guilty about letting the baby go for adoption. In 1961 she told her New York maid, Lena Pepitone, about having a baby before she became a film star. "I had the baby—my baby!" Marilyn said to Pepitone. "It was wonderful, but the doctor and the nurse came in with Grace. They all looked strange and said they'd be taking the baby from me. . . . I begged them, 'Don't take my baby!' "

During the time Marilyn dropped from sight, she stayed at the San Fernando Valley ranch of Rosselli's Golf and Turf Club buddy, actor John Carroll, who, it was said, looked after Marilyn for Rosselli.

A baby girl born in November of 1947 was placed with the Maniscalcos, a family of Sicilian descent living in Brooklyn. When the girl grew up, she took on the name Nancy Maniscalco Greene and insisted she was the daughter of Marilyn Monroe. Appearing on *Hard Copy* in 1991, she stated that a "pretty woman" used to visit her on Long Island in the late 1950s. She knew the woman as "Mrs. Greene." Later, Nancy was told by her grandmother that the "pretty woman" was Marilyn Monroe, and that Marilyn was her birth mother. Subsequently, Nancy learned that she had been placed with the Maniscalco family by New York mafia boss, Vito Genovese.

Though Nancy's sincerity on *Hard Copy* was evident, her story was unsubstantiated by documentation and dismissed as another aberration of tabloid television. But Nancy Greene has now become central to the legal arguments and looming court battles over the controversial Cusack papers, which the Kennedy family and *20/20* have dismissed as forgeries.

The Cusack papers comprise over three hundred documents, many of them handwritten, regarding legal matters between Jack Kennedy and Marilyn Monroe. Allegedly found among the papers of Kennedy attorney Lawrence Cusack, the papers refer to a financial settlement in the form of a trust to be established for Marilyn's mother, Gladys, and her half sister, Berniece, in compensation to Marilyn Monroe for "wrongs and broken promises" by JFK.

A handwritten document among the Cusack papers, allegedly written by Jack Kennedy in 1960, expresses his concern regarding "Nancy Greene" and that "MM claims to make this public." Highly respected Kennedy handwriting expert, Charles Hamilton, attested that the document is genuine. If so, the implication is that Jack Kennedy was the father.

Beauty and the Beast

We make money when we make good pictures. And what are good pictures?
Good pictures are those that make money.

—Harry Cohn

Columbia Pictures was one of the minor Hollywood majors. Once the
place of employment of Marilyn's mother and aunt Grace, the studio was
located at "Gower Gulch," the corner of Gower and Sunset Boulevard—at
one time the casting corner for cowboy extras. Its ill-conceived lot was a
rambling maze of stages, offices, bungalows, and cutting rooms that
seemed to be linked by dead-end corridors—a Frankenstein built by a
monster, Harry Cohn. A bald, beefy ogre of a man, Cohn had fought his
way up to the bottom of the majors with forthright ruthlessness. Hedda
Hopper once commented, "You had to stand in line to hate him." Agents
referred to him as "White Fang."

Columbia may have been on the bottom rung of the majors, but Harry
Cohn was in the top echelon of studio lechers. He was noted for inviting
attractive starlets aboard his yacht, where careers could be launched or
scuttled overnight. When Marilyn arrived at Columbia, Rita Hayworth
was Cohn's major star, and he was preparing to launch Kim Novak.

It was Cohn's casting director, Max Arnow, who sent Marilyn to Natasha Lytess, the studio's drama coach. In her unpublished memoirs, Lytess recalls Marilyn appearing twenty-five minutes late at her bungalow

office wearing a knitted wool hip-clinging dress that was cut too low. Lytess referred to it as a "trollop's outfit." She said of that first meeting, "She was utterly unsure of herself. Unable even to take refuge in her own insignificance."

When Marilyn first encountered Lytess, she recalled that the woman who opened the bungalow door was "unsmiling and Slavic looking, with large and challenging eyes, thick graying hair, and an emaciated figure that suggested some illness." The "illness" could be attributed to the human condition. Having lived through two world wars, Lytess had been a refugee for a good portion of her difficult lifetime. Somewhat neurasthenic, she ate like a bird, and her inner hysteria expressed itself in a burning intensity that was at times overwhelming.

Natasha Lytess (née Liesl Massary) tutored her students in a book-lined bungalow that was located next to the Three Stooges' stage. The walls were lined with books, many of them in German and signed by the authors. A photograph of her mother, Viennese operetta diva Fritzi Massary, hung on the wall along with a large autographed photo of Max Reinhardt, with whom she had studied in Austria and Germany and had a brief affair.

Born in 1903 in Vienna, Natasha was the widow of the left-wing Austrian novelist and poet Bruno Frank (*Sturm im Wasserglass*). Bruno and Liesl Frank were among the exiles who fled Nazi Germany, where they had been close friends of Thomas Mann and his wife Katia. In 1925 the Franks had moved next door to the Manns in Herzogpark, Munich. The Manns and the Franks fled to Switzerland in 1933 before journeying to Southern California in 1938, where they were again neighbors in Santa Monica.

A daughter, Barbara, was born to the Franks in 1943, shortly before Bruno became seriously ill. When he died in 1945 in Los Angeles, he left Liesl and the child destitute. Agent Paul Kohner had helped Frank's widow obtain employment as a film actress. Because of her onerous Germanic background, during the war she attempted to take on a Russian identity. Under the professional name of Natasha Lytess she appeared in featured roles in a number of motion pictures, which included *Comrade X* (MGM, 1940), *Once Upon a Honeymoon* (RKO, 1942), *House on Telegraph Hill* (Fox, 1951), and *Anything Can Happen* (Paramount, 1952). Through his friend Max Arnow, Kohner placed Lytess as drama coach at Columbia, where her oasis of knowledge and learning within Cohn's kingdom at Gower Gulch seemed out of place next to the Three Stooges' stage.

For Marilyn, Lytess's bungalow was an asylum in the land of the Philistines. Here was a woman who represented all Marilyn wanted to be—an accomplished actress and a person of knowledge and brilliance. She had known the greats of theater and literature, including many of the distinguished authors and artists whose books and photos lined the bungalow walls. Marilyn immediately perceived in Lytess a knowledgeable mystagogue who could dress up "the cheap clothes she was wearing inside."

"She was like a waterfall pouring out impressions and images," Marilyn observed. "I just sat there watching her expressive hands and flashing eyes, and listening to her confident voice. She told me what she had been through and made clear how much she knew. But she gave me the impression I was something special too."

Lytess was forty-four when they met, Marilyn only twenty-one. Marilyn's needs were obvious, but she was too young to realize Lytess's needs, which were germane to their relationship. Natasha's own youthful ambition for a great career as an actress had been subverted by world calamity. She had been denied both a career and the gift of beauty and lithesome grace so generously bestowed on the neophyte in the "trollop's outfit" who had knocked on her door.

They began with basics: speech and breathing. "Marilyn was inhibited and cramped, and she could not say a word freely," Natasha reflected. "Her habit of barely moving her lips when she spoke was unnatural. The keyboard of the human voice is the gamut of emotion, and each emotion has its corresponding shade of tone. All this I tried to teach Marilyn."

Natasha was embittered by her own circumstances, and her restless brilliance found an outlet in controlling and dominating her students. Sensing Marilyn's special qualities and eagerness to learn, Lytess found the perfect subject. In a transference of needs, they became locked in an intense working relationship that was destined to burn out under Hollywood's acetylene sun within seven years. The devotee's rite of passage would inevitably lead to the casting out of the sibylline oracle who had perceived a goddess—and a meal ticket.

In mid-March Marilyn received a call from Grace Goddard, who told her that Aunt Ana had died. Though Ana had been ill for several years with heart disease, the news came as a terrible shock. "She changed my whole life," Marilyn said. "She was the first person in the whole world I ever really loved and she loved me. She was a wonderful human being. I once wrote a poem about her. It was called 'I Love Her.' She never hurt me, not once. She couldn't. She was all kindness and all love. She was good to me."

Ana Lower's death became a source of deep grief that Marilyn seldom discussed. It was a private grief expressed in frequent visits to Ana Lower's grave site at the Westwood Cemetery. The Atchinson family had purchased the first burial plot sold (#5) at Westwood Memorial Park, and Ana Atchinson Lower's ashes were interred close to the Chapel of the Palms, where, many years later, mourners would gather around Marilyn's casket.

According to Bebe Goddard, Marilyn attended Ana Lower's services on March 18, 1948, with Doc and Grace Goddard. Jim Dougherty and his second wife, Patricia, were at the viewing in the chapel but didn't attend the funeral. In her will, Aunt Ana left Marilyn the black baby grand piano, the last tangible vestige of Gladys's dream. Having no place to put it in her one-room apartment in Hollywood, Marilyn put the piano in storage until the day she could afford a place large enough to keep it.

Many years later Arthur Miller recalled that he and Marilyn were once looking out at the New York skyline from their Fifty-Seventh Street apartment, and apropos of nothing they had been discussing, Marilyn began talking about Aunt Ana, and how terrible the shock of her death had been: "I went and lay down in her bed the day after she died . . . just lay there for a couple of hours on her pillow. Then I went to the cemetery and these men were digging somebody's grave and they had a ladder into it, and I asked if I could get down there and they said sure, and I went down and lay on the ground and looked up at the sky from there. The ground is cold under your back, but it's quite a view."

After Aunt Ana died, Marilyn often turned to Lytess for guidance. "She opened up, and leaned on me like a child for comfort and advice," Lytess recalled. "One day she told me she was in love, and that 'Freddy' was the man of her dreams."

"Freddy" was Fred Karger, a composer and arranger who had been working in the Columbia music department when Marilyn first met him during that limbo in her career between the Fox and Columbia contracts. Ten years older than Marilyn, Freddy Karger was quite different from any other man she had met, and for the first time in her life she fell hopelessly in love.

Karger was a handsome man with dark wavy hair who bore a slight resemblance to Jack Kennedy. His soft, sardonic smile betrayed intelligence and sophistication beneath an intriguing reserve. He had been raised in the new-money atmosphere of old Hollywood; his father, Max Karger, was one of the founding fathers of the Metro Company, which later became Metro-Goldwyn-Mayer. His mother, Anne Karger, was a warm and gregarious woman of Irish Catholic heritage.

When Marilyn canceled a date with Karger because she wasn't feeling well, he decided to pay her a visit and discovered she was living in a dark, depressing room off Hollywood Boulevard. When he realized that the cause of her illness was hunger compounded by a sense of failure, he invited her to come home with him for dinner. Since his divorce he had lived in his mother's apartment on Harper Avenue, not far from Schwab's and the Sunset Strip. When he brought Marilyn home, Karger told his mother, "This is a little girl who's very lonely and broke."

"Nana" Karger, who had the motherly warmth of Aunt Ana, and even bore a resemblance to her, was instinctively drawn to Marilyn, or "Maril," as Nana called her. They maintained a close friendship until the day Marilyn died.

Through the efforts of Freddy Karger, Marilyn was accepted as a resident at the Studio Club on June 3, 1948. Located at 1215 North Lodi Street, the residence hotel for women was only blocks away from Columbia Studios, and she was an official resident in room 334 until March 13, 1949. The four-story Moorish-style building had bright, well-furnished rooms, and there were parlors in which residents could receive guests, an excellent restaurant, and a spacious patio with a fountain set amid tropical foliage. Founded by Mary Pickford in 1915 and operated by the YWCA, the Studio Club was intended as a wholesome home away from home for young women seeking careers in Hollywood.

For Marilyn the Studio Club was a "safe house" where she often sought refuge, but like a cat, she always had another home or two in reserve. During the brief time she was officially a resident at the Studio Club, she also stayed at Joe Schenck's, the Kargers', and Natasha Lytess's, and she was a frequent guest at the Hollywood Hills apartment of Bob Slatzer, who had returned from Ohio to pursue his screenwriting career.

The corny-copia of B-movie scripts being prepared for production at Columbia were routinely sent by Max Arnow to Lytess, who would spot contract players into auditions for bit parts. When Lytess read *Ladies of the Chorus*, she saw an opportunity for Marilyn to play one of the chorus girls. Upon reading the script, Marilyn focused on a featured part—Peggy

Martin, a chorus girl who proves to be the love interest for the leading man, Rand Brooks.

There were several factors that ultimately led to Marilyn's being cast for the part. When Lytess learned that the part was still uncast, she asked the producer to wait for Marilyn to audition. While Lytess worked with Marilyn on her portrayal, Freddy Karger was recruited to prepare her for the two songs she was to sing, "Anyone Can See I Love You," and "Everybody Needs a Da-Da-Daddy." But the most important factor in the casting of Marilyn Monroe in *Ladies of the Chorus* was Marilyn Monroe. She was cast because of her impressive audition. Filmed in July 1948, *Ladies of the Chorus* suffered from a cliché-ridden script riddled with banal dialogue. Nevertheless, Marilyn glowed on the screen, and her obvious talent rose above the mediocrity of the material.

"Marilyn Monroe is cute and properly naive," the *Hollywood Reporter* reviewer stated. Tibor Krekes in the *Motion Picture Herald* commented, "One of the bright spots is Miss Monroe's singing. She is pretty and, with her pleasing voice and style, she shows promise."

But despite her standout performance on the screen, her career at Columbia was scuttled when she refused to perform off-camera for "White Fang."

Warned by Lytess, Marilyn did her best to avoid Harry Cohn, but shortly before her option for renewal fell due the inevitable occurred. Marilyn received a call from casting director Max Arnow requesting her to come to his office at 4 P.M. Under the impression that Mr. Arnow wouldn't have called her himself unless it was important, Marilyn spent the day bathing and fixing her hair. She felt that this must be her big chance for a good part in a major film. She told herself, "I mustn't act overeager or start babbling, or grin with joy. I must sit quietly and have dignity every minute."

When she arrived at the casting director's office at exactly 4 P.M., she was surprised to find that Mr. Arnow wasn't there. "But his secretary smiled at me and told me to go inside and wait for him," she recalled.

> I sat straight in one of Mr. Arnow's chairs waiting and practicing dignity. A door at the back of the office opened and a man came in.
>
> "Hello, Miss Monroe," Harry Cohn said.
>
> He came over to me, put his hand on my arm, and said, "Come on, we'll go in my office and talk."

"I don't think I can leave," I said. "I'm waiting for Mr. Arnow. He telephoned me about a part."

"The hell with Mr. Arnow!" he said. "He'll know where you are." I hesitated and he added, "What's the matter with you? You stupid or something? Don't you know I'm the boss around here?"

I followed him through the back door into an office three times larger than Mr. Arnow's.

"Turn around," Mr. Cohn said. I turned like a model.

"You look all right." He grinned. "Nicely put together."

"Thank you," I said.

"Go ahead, sit down," Mr. Cohn said, "I want to show you something."

He rummaged through his oversized desk. I looked at his office I had never seen an office like this before—the office where the head of an entire studio presided. Here was where all the great stars, producers, and directors came for conferences, and where all the decisions were made by the great man behind his battleship of a desk.

"Hold all calls," Mr. Cohn said into a box on the desk. He beamed at me. "Here's what I want to show you."

He brought a large photograph to my chair. It was a picture of a yacht.

"How do you like it?" he asked.

"It's very beautiful," I said.

"You're invited," he said. He put his hand on my neck.

"Thank you," I said. "I've never been to a party on a yacht."

"Who said anything about a party?" Mr. Cohn scowled at me. "I'm inviting *you*—nobody else! Do you want to come or not?"

"I'll be glad to join you and your wife on your yacht, Mr. Cohn," I said.

"Leave my wife out of this!" he said. "There'll be nobody on the yacht except you and me—and some expensive sailors. We'll leave in an hour. And we'll take a cruise overnight!"

He stopped and scowled at me as I stood there motionless.

"What's the idea of standing there and staring at me like I insulted you?" he demanded to know.

He put his arms around me. I didn't move.

"I'm very grateful to you for the invitation, Mr. Cohn," I said, "but I'm busy this week, and so I shall have to refuse it."

His arm dropped from me. I started for the door, and I thought to myself I mustn't act as if I thought he was some kind of monster. I turned in the doorway. Mr. Cohn was standing glaring at me. I had never seen a man so angry. I made my voice as casual and friendly as I could. . . .

"I hope you invite me some time again on an occasion when I can accept your invitation," I said.

"This is your last chance!" he said fiercely.

I walked through the door and out of the office where movie stars are made. "Maybe he's watching me," I thought. "I mustn't let him see me upset."

He cursed and yelled after me, "What makes you think you're so special!?"

I drove to my room in my car. Yes, there was something special about me, and I knew what it was. I was the kind of girl people expect to find dead in a hall bedroom with an empty bottle of sleeping pills in her hand. But things weren't entirely black. They really never are. When you're young and healthy you can plan on Monday to commit suicide, and by Wednesday you're laughing again.

On Monday she received word that Columbia would not be picking up her option.

The Ways of the Cross

Love is eternal—until it ends.
—Dorothy Parker

Being dropped by a major for the second time was a long fall. From the depths of the Hollywood deep it was difficult to see the bright colors— the gold and shining white, the greens and violets—that danced on the surface, where King Cohn's yacht sailed in the blue with expensive sailors.

"I lay in bed again day after day, not eating, not combing my hair," Marilyn remembered. "I kept remembering how I had sat in Mr. Arnow's casting office controlling the excitement about the great luck that had finally come to me, and I felt like an idiot. There was going to be no luck in my life. The dark star I was born under was going to get darker and darker.

"I cried and mumbled to myself. I'd go out and get a job as a waitress or clerk. Millions of girls were happy to work at jobs like that. Or I could work in a factory again. I wasn't afraid of any kind of work. I'd scrubbed floors and washed dishes ever since I could remember."

Marilyn didn't know what to do with her life. She was still in love with Freddy Karger, and she could have been content being Mrs. Karger; but Freddy, who had just gone through a divorce, wasn't ready to marry again. In her quandary she turned to Nana Karger for advice. Seeing her deep distress, Nana, who was a Roman Catholic, suggested she go to a church and ask God what she should do, "Any church. It's good. You'll get some comfort out of it. . . . Just pray to God and give your thoughts to Him." It was to St. Victor's Church in West Hollywood that Nana often went for comfort and inspiration, and Marilyn went there and sat quietly for nearly three hours before the altar with the large cross.

"I sat alone thinking a lot about the past and understanding the frosty-hearted child, Norma Jeane. . . . When I looked back on all the years I could remember, I shuddered. I knew now how cold and empty they had been. I had always thought of myself as someone unloved. Now I knew there had been something worse than that in my life. It had been my own unloving heart. I had loved myself a little, and Aunt Grace and Ana. How little it seemed now!"

She concluded that if she could make just one person happy by loving him her life could find some meaning and fulfillment, and she realized how deeply in love she was with Freddy Karger. "It was while I lay on the ocean bottom, figuring never to see daylight again, that it hit me, hoisted me into the air, and stood me on my feet looking at the world as if I'd just been born. . . . A new me appeared in my skin—not an actress, not somebody looking for a world of bright colors. . . . When Freddy said 'I love you' to me, it was better than a thousand critics calling me a great star—all the fame and bright colors and genius I had dreamed of were suddenly in *me*!"

Marilyn told Natasha Lytess, "The only security I hope for is to be married, and Freddy is the man I want to be married to." Karger had said that he loved her. He was charmed by the love she had for him and by her beauty, and he delighted in answering her questions about life and music and art. He took her to concerts at the Hollywood Bowl and outings at the beach, and they went dancing at the Palladium. But Karger's love was not the open-hearted surrender of Marilyn's. His heart bore the safety bars of cynicism. His sardonic smile expressed a world-wary skepticism, and he doubted the depth and sincerity of Marilyn's emotions. The protective barrier he put up was something she was unable to fathom, and sometimes he teased Marilyn about her ignorance of culture and history, laughed at her malapropisms, and said, "Your mind isn't developed. Compared to your body, it's embryonic."

Lytess had moved with her daughter Barbara to an apartment on Harper not far from Karger's. Often Marilyn would stay there and look out the window, anxiously waiting for Karger to stop in on the way to work, or on the way home. When Karger had left and Lytess returned, she frequently found Marilyn with tears in her eyes. Aware that Marilyn and Karger were carrying on an affair in her apartment, Lytess advised her not to see him anymore. "She was in love with someone who was treating her miserably, as a convenience," Lytess said years later. "He was only interested in her physically—not as a human being, not as an actress. . . . All the time, she was so nice to his family and to his daughter. Marilyn would have loved to marry him, even though he was impossible. She thought love would change him. I hoped she would be distracted from this relationship."

While Lytess made it clear that she didn't like Freddy Karger, at the same time Karger distrusted Natasha Lytess, who he felt had too great an influence over Marilyn and was trying to dominate her life.

One night when Karger and Marilyn were in bed together, they started talking about the future.

"I've thought of us getting married," Karger said. "But I'm afraid it's impossible."

Marilyn didn't say anything.

"It would be all right for me," he observed, "but I keep thinking of my daughter. If we were married and anything should happen to me—such as my dropping dead—it would be very bad for her."

"Why?" she asked.

"It wouldn't be right for her to be brought up by a woman like you," Karger said. "It would be unfair to her."

After Karger left, Marilyn recalled that she cried all night, "He didn't love me," she said. "A man can't love a woman for whom he feels half contempt. He can't love her if his mind is ashamed of her."

In the holiday season of 1948, Marilyn bought Karger an expensive watch as a Christmas present. It was meant as a token of her eternal love, but proved to be very much involved with time. Engraved with the date 12/25/48, the watch cost five hundred dollars—far more than Marilyn could afford. She purchased it on time, with installment payments of twenty-five dollars a month. After wrapping the gift she hurried over to Karger's apartment and gave it to him.

Marilyn recalled that he was quite overcome by the beauty and generosity of the gift. Nobody had ever given him such an expensive watch before. But he wondered why she had only engraved the date and hadn't included something like "From Marilyn to Freddy, with love," or a sentiment like that. She responded, "Because you'll leave me someday, and you'll have some other girl to love. And you wouldn't be able to use my present if my name was on it. This way you can always use it, as if it were something you'd bought yourself."

She hoped he would contradict her and say that her fears were silly and unfounded, but he didn't. "I cried again all night," she remembered. "To love without hope is a sad thing for the heart, and I knew what I had to do. I had to leave him. The moment I thought it, I realized I'd known it for a long time. That's why I'd been sad—and desperate. That's why I had tried to make myself more and more beautiful for him, why I had clung to him as if I were half mad. Because I had known it was ending."

It took her two years to pay off the five hundred dollars for the watch. By the time Marilyn had paid the last twenty-five-dollar installment, Karger had married Jane Wyman in the Catholic church with the large cross above the altar.

And in the new moon of 1949 all the fame and bright colors and genius Marilyn Monroe had dreamed of moved to the plenilune alignment that eclipsed the dark star. . . . She went on an interview for a Marx Brothers movie:

"This is the young lady for the office bit," said the producer, Lester Cowan.

Groucho stared thoughtfully at her.

"Can you walk?" he demanded to know.

She nodded.

"I am not referring to the type of walking my Tante Zippa has mastered," said Groucho. "This role calls for a young lady who can walk by me in such a manner as to arouse my elderly libido and cause smoke to issue from my ears."

Harpo honked the horn on the end of his cane and gave her a cross-eyed leer.

Marilyn demonstrated her walk.

Harpo's horn honked three times, and he stuck his fingers in his mouth and blew a piercing whistle.

"Does your chiropractor know about this?" Groucho inquired.

"Walk again," said Mr. Cowan.

She walked up and down in front of the three men. They stood grinning.

"Does your chiropractor's wife know about this?" Groucho asked.

"What do you think?" Mr. Cowan asked Groucho.

"She's Mae West, Theda Bara, and Bo Peep all rolled into one," said Groucho. "You've got the part, Miss Peep. We're going to shoot you tomorrow at dawn for stealing this picture. Come early, unless you'd like to spend the night with me rehearsing. And don't forget your lines—I certainly can't."

"And don't do any walking in any unpoliced areas!" said Harpo. (*Honk-honk!*)

They shot the scene the next day in a stage on the Goldwyn lot. Groucho directed her in a "walk on" that walked off with the picture—*Love Happy*.

Golden Dreams

I've been on calendars, but never on *Time*.
—Marilyn Monroe

Photographer Tom Kelley's call came at a propitious moment. He asked Marilyn if she would pose nude for a calendar photo.

"What does it pay?" she asked.

"Fifty dollars," Kelley responded.

Though Marilyn Monroe bore no misgivings about nudity, she had never posed *des nuda*. But the mean slapstick of poverty had recently delivered a stinging blow. After her brief scene in *Love Happy*, which had yet to be released, Marilyn made the rounds of the casting offices in her secondhand car, but found no work and no prospects. Soon she wasn't able to keep up with her car payments or rent.

In their travels along the perilous path of the Hollywood fringe, Marilyn and young Bob Slatzer pooled their poverty and moved in together, sharing an apartment beneath the shadows of the Hollywood sign on Primrose Path. Bob occasionally resorted to picking cotton in the fields of Indio in order to buy the groceries. After the cotton season, the pickings were still poor in Hollywood, and Marilyn received a repossession notice on her automobile. One night when the two of them returned to their apartment, they found that the landlady had changed the lock on their door for nonpayment of rent.

After waiting for the landlady to leave the building, Slatzer crawled through the window while Marilyn drove her car up the driveway. They quickly loaded their few worldly belongings into the car. Opening the apartment door from the inside, Bob and Marilyn then entered the hallway and exited the building like respectable tenants—only to see Marilyn's car pull out of the driveway and roar off down the street with their things. The car had been repossessed. It would cost fifty dollars to get it back.

"What did you say it pays?" Marilyn asked photographer Tom Kelley.

"Fifty dollars is the best I can do," Kelley replied.

On May 25, 1949, Marilyn arrived at Kelley's Hollywood studio. Located at 736 North Seward, it was virtually across the street from Consolidated Film Laboratories, where Gladys, Grace Goddard, and Stan Gifford once worked. While Marilyn certainly needed the fifty dollars, posing nude for the camera also held a certain appeal—an extension of her childhood dream of appearing for all to see in the attire bestowed upon her at nature's finest boutique. The photos Tom Kelley took that day proved to be incredibly unique. Posed on red folds of velvet, such as one might see lining a Tiffany jewelry box, Marilyn Monroe appears less erotic than iridescent, the pièce de résistance in the master jeweler's sample case. The Baumgarth Calendar Company paid Tom Kelley five hundred dollars for the world publishing rights. Baumgarth made a small fortune on the *Golden Dreams* calendar. Marilyn got her fifty dollars, and the return of the priceless possession a Hollywood starlet with golden dreams can't possibly live without—her car.

While making the rounds of the agencies and casting directors, Marilyn was waiting in an office of the William Morris Agency when she was spotted by Johnny Hyde, a onetime child juggler and acrobat in the Loew's vaudeville circuit who had become one of Hollywood's top agents. A diminutive man, he had had a special chair made that gave him stature as he sat behind his large executive desk, staring at the luscious blonde with the lost look.

"You're going to be a great star," Hyde said. "I know. Many years ago

I discovered a girl like you and brought her to Metro—Lana Turner. You're better. You'll go farther. You've got more!"

"Then why can't I get a job?" Marilyn asked. "Just to make enough to eat on."

"It's hard for a star to get an eating job," said Johnny. "A star is only good as a star. You don't fit into anything less."

Marilyn recalled that she laughed for the first time in months, but that Johnny Hyde didn't laugh with her—he just kept staring and staring.

Johnny began squiring Marilyn around town, showing her off. They attended Hollywood parties, had dinner at Chasen's and Romanoff's, danced at Ciro's, the Mocombo, and the Troc. Sometimes there would be dinner parties at Johnny Hyde's big house on North Palm Drive near Charlie Feldman's. Marilyn called Johnny's dining room "my own private Romanoff's" because it had booths and café tables just like Mike Romanoff's famous restaurant. Johnny bought her clothes, put her up in a small efficiency apartment at the Beverly Carlton Hotel on Olympic Boulevard, and took her to the Beverly Hills plastic surgeon to the stars, Michael Gurdin, who rounded her chin and took the bump off her nose—the bump Grace had always said was her only imperfection.

While Johnny went to Europe on business, Marilyn went on a multiple-city tour for the opening of *Love Happy*. When she arrived in New York, Andre de Dienes located her at the Sherry-Netherland Hotel, and they had a reunion on the strand of Long Island, where he photographed her cavorting on the beach. "She was radiant," de Dienes recalled. "She had the presence and ease of an established star." But de Dienes no longer clicked with Marilyn, and the ashes of their fiery romance were never reignited.

Marilyn suddenly abandoned the *Love Happy* tour when Johnny called to say she had landed a role in *Ticket to Tomahawk* at Fox. Hoping it would be her ticket to a new contract, Marilyn played a chorus girl in a western musical. But *Ticket to Tomahawk* went nowhere, and it again revealed that Marilyn's talents were far above the mediocrity of the material.

Though Darryl F. Zanuck continued to ignore the blonde, whom he referred to as "strawhead," MGM talent director Lucille Ryman alerted Marilyn to a role Metro was casting.

"There's a part in John Huston's picture *The Asphalt Jungle* that's perfect for you," Lucille said. "It's not a big part, but you'll be bound to make a big hit in it. Tell your agent to get in touch with Mr. Huston."

Johnny Hyde brought me to Mr. Huston's office, and Mr. Huston gave me a copy of the script. Unlike Mr. Zanuck, he did not believe that actresses shouldn't be allowed to know what they were going to act in. I took it home and my friend Natasha Lytess agreed to coach me. . . . I studied the part for several days and then returned to Mr. Huston's office to read for him.

I felt sick. I had told myself a million times that I was an actress. I had practiced acting for years. Here, finally, was my first chance at a real acting part with a great director to direct me. And all I could do is stand there with quivering knees and a quivering stomach. . . . I felt desperate. Mr. Huston caught my eye and grinned.

"We're waiting, Miss Monroe," he said.

"Would you mind if I read the part lying on the floor?" I blurted out.

"Why, not at all," Mr. Huston replied gallantly.

"I stretched myself out on the floor. . . . I had rehearsed the part lying on a couch, as the directors indicated. There wasn't any couch in the office. Lying on the floor was almost the same thing, however. I went through the part and when I finished I said, "Oh, let me do it again."

"If you want to," said Mr. Huston, "but there's no need."

I did it again.

When I stood up Mr. Huston said, "You got the part after the first reading. Go fix yourself up with the wardrobe department."

During the shooting Johnny Hyde was as excited as I was. He kept telling me, "This is it, honey. You're *in*. Everybody is crazy about your work."

When the picture was previewed, all the studio heads went to see it. It was a fine picture. I was thrilled by it. The audience whistled at me. They made wolf noises and laughed happily when I spoke. They liked me very much.

It's a nice sensation to please an audience. I sat in the theater with Johnny Hyde. He held my hand. We didn't say anything on the way home. He sat in my room beaming at me. It was as though *he* had made good on the screen, not me. His heart was happy for me. I could feel his unselfishness and his deep kindness. No man had ever looked on me with such kindness. He not only knew me, he knew Norma Jeane, too. He knew all the pain and all the desperate things in me. When he put his arms around me and said he loved me, I knew it was true. Nobody had ever loved me like that. I wished in all my heart I could love him back. My heart ached with gratitude. But the love he hoped for wasn't in me. You might as well try to make yourself fly as to make yourself love. But I felt everything else toward Johnny Hyde, and I was always happy to be with him. It was like being with a whole family and belonging to a full set of relations.

Johnny found Marilyn bit parts in a number of films: she was a roller-derby fan in *The Fireball*, a model who dodges a flirtatious feint from a has-been boxing champ in *Right Cross*, and a receptionist ogled by her boss in *Home Town Story*. But it wasn't until Hyde placed her in the role of Miss Caswell of the "Copacabana School of Dramatic Art" in *All About Eve* that the dotted line was rolled out for her return to 20th Century-Fox.

Written and directed by Joseph L. Mankiewicz, *All About Eve* was produced by Darryl F. Zanuck, and though he never fully understood the special appeal of the starlet, he realized at the preview of *Eve* that nobody was looking at Bette Davis, George Sanders, Celeste Holm, or Anne Baxter when "strawhead" was on the screen. Zanuck arranged a new screen test for Marilyn, and she was offered a new seven-year contract.

Another person whose star was rising in 1950 was Captain William Parker of the LAPD. Known as "Whisky Bill" to those in the know at Los Angeles Police Headquarters, Bill Parker was an ambitious man who had his eye on the chief's badge. By 1950, Parker had become the hard-drinking buddy of the hard-drinking interim chief, William Worton. When Worton retired and recommended "Whisky Bill" Parker as his replacement, it raised some ire and eyebrows in City Hall. The powers that be had assumed the chief's badge would go to Norman Chandler's favorite, Captain Thad Brown, chief of detectives.

Thad Brown was expected to nose out Parker because Brown was Chandler's choice. As head of the *L.A. Times*, Chandler held the power; however, in the summer of 1950 intrigue of the highest Machiavellian order shifted the balance of power from Thad Brown to "Whisky Bill" Parker.

Parker's friend Lieutenant James Hamilton was assigned by Parker's mentor, Chief Worton, to be the investigator for the Police Commission. But instead of investigating *for* the Commission, Hamilton became an investigator *of* the Commission. It was the five police commissioners, political friends of Chandler, who would ultimately vote on the appointment of the new police chief. In the course of his duties, Lieutenant Hamilton observed Norman Chandler picking up one of the Police Commissioners, Mrs. Curtis Albro, on the steps of the L.A. City Hall. Mrs. Albro, an attractive member of the Southern California social set, was the wife of a prominent Los Angeles businessman.

Sensing an auspicious career move for himself within the power structure of the LAPD, Lieutenant James Hamilton tailed Chandler and Mrs. Albro to a luxurious Malibu beach house and staked out the home until the curvaceous Commissioner Albro left the next morning with Chandler.

Recruiting the assistance of two detectives, Archie Case and James Ahearn, Hamilton put Albro and Chandler under surveillance. Cameras and bugs were installed in the Malibu beach house, and the tide soon changed in the power struggle for the chief's badge. The detectives assured Hamilton that they had enough evidence to ensure "Whisky Bill's" appointment. Chandler, however, had already come out with a story in the L.A. *Times* stating that Thad Brown would be appointed the next chief of police. According to the *Times* article, three of the five commissioners, including Mrs. Albro, supported Brown.

The majority would ensure Brown's appointment, but shortly after Parker and Hamilton revealed to Norman Chandler the compromising surveillance gathered by the two detectives, Mrs. Albro suddenly died. While her mysterious death was mourned by high society, low society persuaded Chandler's friends on the Police Commission to vote unanimously for "Whisky Bill" Parker as the new police chief.

In an act of noblesse oblige, Parker promoted Hamilton and made him captain of the newly formed Intelligence Unit. The two detectives Archie Case and James Ahearn were also promoted and became Hamilton's key lieutenants. Later they would serve dutifully under Captain Daryl Gates, who was to be appointed Hamilton's successor when Bobby Kennedy arranged for Hamilton's executive position within the National Football League in 1963.

Parker served as chief for sixteen years, from 1950 until his untimely death in 1966. He was buried wearing the badge.

Red Scare

Well, we were Reds, and we sure were scared.
—Sylvia Thompson

After three marriages, three divorces, and a throng of affairs, Johnny Hyde was hopelessly in love. He wanted Marilyn to marry him. She told him she couldn't, that it wouldn't be fair. Marilyn knew she could be faithful only to the one man she could love with all her heart.

"The person I wanted to help most in my life—Johnny Hyde—remained someone for whom I could do almost nothing," Marilyn stated. "He needed something I didn't have—love. And love is something you can't invent, no matter how much you want to." But Hyde was having heart trouble of another kind. He had been hospitalized with a heart attack in 1948 and was popping nitroglycerin tablets to fight off angina. He told Marilyn that his doctor said he didn't have long to live.

"I'm rich," Hyde said. "If you marry me you'll inherit it when I die."

"I had dreamed of money and longed for it," Marilyn recalled, "but the million dollars Johnny Hyde offered me meant nothing. 'I'll not leave you,' I told him. 'I'll never betray you. But I can't marry you, Johnny. Because you're going to get well. And who knows, sometime later I might fall in love.' He smiled and said, 'I won't get well, and I want you to have my money when I'm gone.' But I couldn't say yes."

"He was right. He didn't get well," Marilyn said. "A month later he went to the hospital. In the hospital he kept begging me to marry him, not for his sake anymore, but for mine. He wanted to think of me as never having any more hunger or poverty in my life."

Johnny Hyde died on December 18, 1950. His ex-wife and her children requested that Marilyn be excluded from the funeral held at Forest Lawn. But a heavily veiled blonde with an unusual walk, accompanied by Natasha Lytess, sat in the back of the church sobbing uncontrollably during the service. She later recalled, "When I passed by his coffin I felt such a sadness for Johnny Hyde that I forgot myself. I threw myself on the coffin and sobbed. I wished I was dead with him.

"My great friend was buried," Marilyn lamented. "I was without his importance to fight for me and without his love to guide me. I cried for nights at a time. I never regretted the million dollars I had turned down. But I never stopped regretting Johnny Hyde—the kindest man in the world."

Eerily, Johnny Hyde's generous Christmas presents, which he had purchased for his friends shortly before his fatal heart attack, began arriving right after the funeral. Marilyn received a mink stole. On Christmas Eve, Natasha Lytess arrived at the apartment on Harper and found a note, "I leave my car and fur stole to Natasha." When Natasha hurriedly entered the apartment she found another note on Marilyn's bedroom door warning that Lytess's daughter, Barbara, shouldn't enter. Lytess burst in to discover that "the room looked like hell on earth. Marilyn was on the bed, her cheeks puffed out like an adder's."

Lytess recalled shouting, "Marilyn! What have you done?" and she forced open Marilyn's mouth, which was caked with capsule residue, and reached in and gouged out "greenish stuff she hadn't been able to swallow." Her stomach was pumped, and she recovered in the hospital.

Shortly before his death, Johnny had secured a role for Marilyn in *As Young As You Feel*, a Paddy Chayefsky story filmed at Fox in January of 1951. Marilyn was twenty-four years old, and it was her twelfth film—the first for Fox under her new contract, which specified that her name appear above the title. When production began in January of 1951 she was still mourning Johnny. "She can't stop crying," complained director Harmon Jones. "Every time we need her in front of the cameras she's crying, and it puffs up her eyes." When they needed her on the set she was often found by the assistant director off in some dark corner of the soundstage trying to pull herself together. And it was there, in the corner of the stage, that Arthur Miller met Marilyn Monroe.

"From where I stood, yards away, I saw her in profile against a white light," Miller recalled. "She was weeping under a veil of black lace that she lifted now and then to dab her eyes." Introduced to Marilyn by Elia Kazan, Miller recalled that when they shook hands "the shock of her body's motion sped through me, a sensation at odds with her sadness amid all this Hollywood glamour and technology and the busy confusion of a new shot being set up."

Miller's wife, Mary, had stayed in Brooklyn while Miller went to Hollywood. Fresh from his Broadway hits *Death of a Salesman* and *All My Sons*, Miller had been brought to Hollywood by Charlie Feldman, who was trying to put together a film deal based on *The Hook*, a screenplay Miller had written about labor strife on the Brooklyn waterfront. Intending to stay as a houseguest at Feldman's for a week, Miller stayed for a month, having been captivated by "the saddest girl I've ever seen."

Miller saw Marilyn again at one of Feldman's parties, and the next day she tagged along with Kazan and Miller at a story conference in Harry Cohn's Columbia studio office. Masquerading as a secretary, Marilyn wore glasses and adopted a prim and businesslike demeanor as she made notations in her steno pad of Miller and Kazan's meeting with her old nemesis "White Fang."

"Cohn could hardly keep his eyes from Marilyn," Miller observed. "Trying to recall where he had seen her, he marched around in front of her hitching up his pants like a Manhattan cab driver getting ready for a fight. He peered at her growling, 'Wait a minute, I think I know whose goil you were, maybe!'" But he couldn't quite place the curvaceous secretary, and the production meeting continued with Kazan talking about directing Miller's screenplay. Miller remembered looking over at Marilyn and finding her staring at him, smiling secretively about her joke on Cohn. "I desperately wanted her," Miller stated, "and I decided I must leave that night, if possible, or I would lose myself."

But Miller stayed on. And when he ran out of excuses for not returning to his wife and children, Kazan and Marilyn took Miller to the airport. Many years later he remembered that "her hair hung down to her shoulders, parted on the right side, and the sight of her was something like pain, and I knew that I must flee or walk into a doom beyond all knowing. With all her radiance she was surrounded by a darkness that perplexed me. I could not yet imagine that in my very shyness she saw some safety, release from the detached and centerless and invaded life she had been given. . . . When we parted I kissed her cheek and she sucked in a surprised breath, and I hurried backwards toward the plane. I had to escape her childish voracity. I was retreating to the safety of morals, to be sure, but not necessarily to truthfulness. Flying homeward, her scent still on my hands, I knew my innocence was technical merely, and the secret that I could lose myself in sensuality entered me like a radiating force."

Arthur Miller's screenplay *The Hook* was never produced. Cohn became leery of the project when he was warned that Miller was a Marxist. With America's entry into the Korean conflict, the cold war was heating up, and the world was becoming increasingly divided into armed camps of opposing political and philosophic principles. In a nuclear age the dichotomy grew more perilous as the Western world became encircled by countries that had fallen under Soviet domination.

In the 1950s the Un-American Activities Committee was focusing much of its attention on Hollywood, where it was suspected there was a Commie hidden under every plaster rock. Suddenly, it was no longer fashionable to be a member of the Marxist intelligentsia. The Hollywood HUAC hearings became the great purgative power that separated the hardened Marxist from the dilettante fellow traveler, who was quite willing to jump off the Hollywood Red car at the first stop. There were those who lied and denied, and those who committed suicide. There were those who quickly confessed and named names, like Edward Dmytryk, Clifford Odets, and Miller's friend Elia Kazan. And there were those who went to jail, and those who remained silent and went underground.

When John and Eunice Murray lost their home on Franklin Street during the Hollywood labor wars, they moved to a small home in Santa Monica Canyon at 431 West Rustic Canyon Road. Norman Jefferies had married the Murrays' daughter Patricia, and they lived in an upstairs unit of the Murrays' new home, where, he said, communist cell meetings were held. Jefferies recalled that many of those who attended the meetings were nameless or had party names, but he recognized Dr. Ralph Greenson, Herb Sorrell, and Churchill Murray, who would arrive from Mexico with people Jefferies assumed were Comintern agents.

While Dr. Greenson had always been secretive about his Marxist affiliations, Dr. Hyman Engelberg and his wife Esther had been quite open in their support of communist causes. Dr. Engelberg continued teaching at the People's Education Center and remained prominent in the activities of the Arts, Sciences, and Professions Council. In 1947 Engelberg was one of the principal speakers at the ASPC Thought Control Conference in Los Angeles. But with the advent of the HUAC investigations, Engelberg, along with many people who remained loyal to the Communist Party, went underground. The "red scare" had made it scary to be a red.

Arthur Miller observed, "Jews were embracing Catholicism, socialists were joining the Communist witch-hunt with no regard for its civil liberties implications, and lifelong pacifists were banging the cold war drums." Though much of Miller's writing had its inspiration in Marxism, he began to have doubts about Stalinism. He commented that in the early fifties he began to question "whom or what was I writing for. I needed the benediction of something or someone, but all about me was mere mortality. I had always assumed I was writing in the service of some worthy cause in which I no longer believed."

It was at this juncture in his life, when the absolutes of Stalinism failed him, that he met Marilyn. He stated, "Even after those few hours with Marilyn she had taken on an immanence in my imagination—the vitality of a force one does not understand, but that seems on the verge of lighting up a vast surrounding plain of darkness. . . . A youth was rising from a long sleep to claim the feminine blessing that was the spring of his creativity, the infinite benediction of woman, a felicity in the deepest heart of man as needful as the sky."

In other words, Arthur was dropping Stalinism like a hot kartofl, and embracing Marilyn Monroe.

In his memoir, *Timebends*, Miller states that after he had last seen Marilyn in 1951, occasionally he got notes from her that "warmed my heart." They were written "in strangely meandering slanted handwriting that often curled down margins and up again on the other side of the paper, using two or three different pens with a pencil thrown in. She talked about hoping we could meet again when she came east on business, and offered to come without any excuse if I gave her some encouragement. I wrote back a muddy, formal note saying that I wasn't the man who could make her life happen as I knew she imagined it might, and that I wished her well. Still, there were parched evenings when I was on the verge of turning my steering wheel west and jamming the pedal to the floor."

Though public perception was that Marilyn Monroe and Arthur Miller didn't become romantically involved until her move to New York in the mid-fifties, there were secret rendezvous and occasions when Miller did jam the pedal to the floor—times when Marilyn jetted to the East Coast and met Miller at their hideaway in Sandsfield, Massachusetts, near Richard Widmark's old farm.

The two plays Miller wrote after he had first met Marilyn, *The Crucible* and *A View from the Bridge*, reflect an acute personal crisis that the author went through between 1950 and 1955, which paralleled the collapse of his marriage. Marilyn is an identifiable character in both plays. She is the spirit of Abigail in *The Crucible* and Catharine in *A View from the Bridge*. Though critics prefer to underline the political overtones of *The Crucible*, the play's central concern is the guilt of a married man, John Proctor, who has betrayed his wife in having an affair with Abigail, a young servant girl. The love triangle and the problem of guilt repeat themselves in *A View from the Bridge*—between Eddie Carbone, his wife, and their young ward Catharine.

In the introduction to the 1957 edition of his collected plays, which is dedicated "To Marilyn," Miller wrote that both *The Crucible* and *A View from the Bridge* are concerned with "the awesomeness of a passion which, despite its contradictions, despite the self-interest of the individual it inhabits, despite every kind of warning, despite even the destruction of the moral beliefs of the individual, proceeds to magnify its power over him until it destroys him."

As for Marilyn, she told Louella Parsons that Arthur Miller attracted her "because he is brilliant. His mind is better than that of any other man I've known. And he understands and approves my wanting to improve myself."

As she listened to conversations between Kazan and Miller, it dawned on Marilyn that she often had no idea what they were talking about. "There was no hiding from it," she said. "I was terribly dumb. I didn't know anything about painting, music, books, history, geography. I didn't even know anything about sports or politics." And in the fall of 1951 she enrolled at UCLA in an art history class and began reading the classics as well as buying books about Freud and his disciples. "I promised myself I would read all the books and find out about all the wonders there are in the world," she stated. "And when I sat among people I would not only understand what they were talking about, I'd be able to contribute a few words."

Much to Natasha Lytess's annoyance, at the suggestion of Elia Kazan, Marilyn began taking separate acting classes with Michael Chekhov, nephew of the great playwright. Chekhov had studied under Stanislavsky in Moscow. Marilyn told him, "I want to be an artist, not an erotic freak. I don't want to be sold to the public as a celluloid aphrodisiac. It was all right for the first years. But now it's different." Chekhov, who had a great appreciation of Marilyn's talent, responded, "But Marilyn, you are a young woman who gives off sex vibrations, no matter what you are doing or thinking. Unfortunately, your studio bosses are only interested in your sex vibrations."

Kazan was also interested in her sex vibrations, and he later acknowledged that he had an affair with Marilyn after his friend Arthur Miller returned to New York.

When Marilyn had signed with Fox, she insisted that the contract include a provision for Natasha Lytess, who was put on salary at the studio as a drama coach. Lytess guided Marilyn through her brief role in *Let's Make It Legal,* which was filmed in April. Though the film was a flop, Marilyn was not. She was luscious and vivacious and knew how to get laughs. Though her special appeal was still lost on Zanuck, the public was beginning to keep an eye out for her.

With her steady income, Marilyn became generous to a fault. She paid for Lytess's expensive dental bills and helped her buy a house on Rexford Drive in Beverly Hills. Marilyn sold the mink stole Johnny Hyde had given her to help make the down payment. In the fall of 1951, when the studio option was renewed and her paycheck rose to five hundred dollars a week, Marilyn hired business manager Inez Melson to look after her finances and take care of her mother, who was transferred from the state institution in Norwalk to the more comfortable country-club atmosphere of Rockhaven Sanitarium in Verdugo, California. A portion of Marilyn's income was set aside each month toward her mother's care, and Inez was appointed the conservator.

Hiring a private investigator, Marilyn tracked down her father, Stan Gifford. She hadn't spoken to him since he hung up on her in 1944. Her father had retired from Consolidated and purchased a dairy farm in Hemet, a desert community south of Riverside, where he lived with his third wife and several children.

Marilyn hoped her father would be happy to hear from his daughter. Driving out to Hemet with Marilyn, Lytess had a foreboding that Stan Gifford wouldn't necessarily be overjoyed by a visit from his illegitimate daughter—even if she happened to be Marilyn Monroe.

"You could be hurt by this," Lytess tried to warn her.

"After all these years, I'm sure he's not the same man who walked out on my mother and refused to talk to me," Marilyn responded. "You agree that I must see him, don't you? Tell him who I am and everything?"

Believing that Marilyn was determined to see her father in any case, Lytess remained silent and made no further attempt to dissuade her.

Stopping at a gas station near Riverside, Lytess persuaded Marilyn to telephone first, reminding her that Gifford was a married man with children: "You can't just arrive without calling," she advised. As Marilyn dialed the number written on a scrap of paper she held in her trembling hand, Lytess said a silent prayer.

Mrs. Gifford answered the phone. She wanted to know who was calling.

"This is Marilyn . . . the little girl he knew years ago—Gladys Baker's daughter. He's sure to know who I am."

Marilyn was asked to wait, and Lytess observed her trembling in silence, her head thrown back with her eyes closed in the pain and anxiety of the emotional wound endured for a lifetime.

Mrs. Gifford returned to the phone with the message, "He doesn't want to see you. He suggests you see his lawyer in Los Angeles if you have some complaint. Do you have a pencil?" Marilyn slowly hung up and walked back to the car and slumped over the wheel in tears. There was nothing Lytess could say or do that could comfort her.

Gifford's stepdaughter, Susan Reimer, now a nurse in Hemet, was nine years old at the time and vividly recalls the incident when Marilyn called the house in 1951. It caused a furor, and when she asked her mother about the caller, she was told, "We're not supposed to tell. It was Marilyn Monroe." Susan's half sister Lorraine stated, "I heard all my life that Stan was Marilyn's father. It's something the family always talked about. It was always told to me as fact."

On the long drive back to Los Angeles, Marilyn remained locked in a brooding silence.

Fame

The studio didn't make me a star. If I am one, the people did it.
—Marilyn Monroe

To the surprise of Darryl F. Zanuck, Marilyn's bit parts and cameo roles brought her a flood of fan mail—over three thousand letters each week. But it was when she made her entrance into the 1951 20th Century-Fox sales convention that she crossed the threshold of stardom.

The sales and publicity forces had gathered in the Café de Paris to mingle over cocktails with Fox executives and the studio's stable of stars— Tyrone Power, Betty Grable, Gregory Peck, June Haver, Susan Hayward. But the salespeople were looking out of the corner of their eyes for Marilyn Monroe.

She made a calculated late entrance, and all eyes were riveted on her as she paused in the doorway, breathtaking in a strapless black cocktail gown. The room became silent, and in that hushed moment the president of 20th Century-Fox, Spyros Skouras, felt the vibrations and heard the melody of cash-register bells. Skouras insisted that Marilyn sit next to him at the executive table. Zanuck issued orders the next day that Marilyn Monroe be given the star treatment. Philippe Halsman photographed her for *Life,* and she soon appeared in *Look, Colliers,* and *Quick* as Hollywood's new anatomic bombshell.

Earlier in the year, Marilyn had been loaned out to RKO to play a supporting role in an adaptation of Clifford Odets's play *Clash by Night*. Starring Barbara Stanwyck and Robert Ryan, the film was directed by the formidable Fritz Lang. Natasha Lytess recalled that Lang made Marilyn so nervous that she'd throw up before each scene and red blotches blossomed on her face and neck. Lang hadn't wanted Lytess on the set, but Marilyn insisted. "She fought Lang to have me there," Lytess remembered. "I was glued to her, working in her tiny dressing room all day long. She was so nervous, she missed some of her lines, and then Lang took her on like a madman." Marilyn was shivering with fright, and only her iron will and determination to succeed got her from the dressing room to the bright lights in front of the camera.

When *Clash by Night* was released in 1952, Marilyn received favorable notices. In the *New York World-Telegram* Alton Cook proclaimed, "Marilyn Monroe is a forceful actress, a gifted new star, worthy of all that fantastic press pageantry. Her role is not very big, but she makes it dominant."

Having seen the rough cut of *Clash by Night*, Zanuck tested Marilyn for the lead in *Don't Bother to Knock*. "I didn't think she was ready for so demanding a role," Lytess stated, "but she made such a beautiful test that even Zanuck had to write her a glowing note."

Marilyn played a psychotic baby-sitter who threatens to kill her bratty ward at a downtown New York City hotel, and her career could have been easily scuttled by this mediocre melodrama. But from her first appearance through the revolving door of the hotel, there was something captivating about her that sailed high above the murky script. There were intricate prisms of nuance to her portrayal of a psychotic woman who has been emotionally broken by tragic loss.

But just as Fox was preparing to release Marilyn's starring vehicle, the executive offices received the news that the photograph of the entrancing nude popularized on the widely circulated calendars of the Baumgarth Company was a photo of their new star. Marilyn was summoned to the front office by Harry Brand, head of publicity, who demanded to know if the story was true. When Marilyn admitted it was, Brand screamed, "How could you do such a thing! Don't you know how offensive this is to the public? This could ruin your career if it comes out, don't you know that?"

"Well," Marilyn began to sob, "I needed the money, and I di-didn't think I'd ever be identified."

"There's only one thing to do," Brand exclaimed. "Deny it! You never posed for any calendars, understand! Just stick to your story and we may get out of the woods!"

As Brand slammed the door behind her, Marilyn began to panic. She didn't want to lie, nor did she want to lose her career. Telephoning Sidney Skolsky to ask his advice, she sobbed, "I'm so mixed up and scared, Sidney. I don't really feel ashamed. I didn't do anything so b-bad, did I? I needed the money to get my car back. I wouldn't have done it if it was bad. They're trying to make me feel ashamed but I'm not. What should I do?"

"Just tell everybody what you just told me," Sidney advised, "and you've solved your problem."

Marilyn disclosed the simple truth to UPI reporter Aline Mosby, and the story broke on March 13, 1952. It was picked up by almost every newspaper in the United States. To Brand's amazement, no civic, pious, or public guardian of morality denounced the Monroe calendar. It was generally perceived as a lovely photograph of a naked Venus, and those who may have found it immodest didn't find it offensive. Fox's publicity department was deluged by requests for a copy of the calendar, and crowds stood in line to see the naked Venus perform in RKO's *Clash by Night*. Marilyn soon began to receive star billing above Barbara Stanwyck on the theater marquees.

"Success came to me in a rush," Marilyn said. "It surprised my employers much more than it did me. . . . I knew what I had known when I was thirteen and walked along the sea edge in a bathing suit for the first time. I knew I belonged to the public and to the world, not because I was talented or even beautiful, but because I had never belonged to anything or anyone else. The public was the only family, the only Prince Charming and the only home I had ever dreamed of."

She soon found her Prince Charming.

"Miss Monroe, this is Joe DiMaggio," said David March, a friend of hers and DiMaggio's who had set up a blind dinner date at the Villa Nova on the Sunset Strip.

"I'm glad to meet you," DiMaggio said with a warm smile.

Marilyn recalled that she thought she was going to meet "a loud, sporty fellow." Instead she found herself smiling at a reserved gentleman in a gray suit, with a gray tie and a sprinkle of gray in his hair. "We smiled and sat down next to each other at the table," Marilyn remembered, "and hardly said two words to one another. There was no denying I felt attracted, but I couldn't figure out by what. Somehow he was exciting. The excitement was in his eyes. They were sharp and alert."

When it was time to leave the restaurant, DiMaggio turned to Marilyn and explained that he was just a visitor in Hollywood and didn't have a car. "Would you mind dropping me at my hotel?" he asked. As she drove DiMaggio to the Hollywood Knickerbocker, Marilyn began to get anxious when she realized that Joe DiMaggio might be stepping out of her life when they arrived, and she'd never know what had attracted her to him. She slowed her car to a crawl as the hotel came into view, and Joe spoke up just in time.

> "I don't feel like turning in," he said. "Would you mind driving around a little while?" We rode around for three hours. I had never seen a baseball game, and I really didn't know what it was exactly that Mr. DiMaggio did. After the first hour I began to find out things about Joe DiMaggio. He was a baseball player and had belonged to the Yankee Ball Club in New York, and he always worried when he went out with a girl in Hollywood. He didn't mind going out once with her. It was the second time he didn't like. As for the third time, that very seldom happened. He had a loyal friend named George Solotaire who ran interference for him and pried the girl loose.
> "Is Mr. Solotaire in Hollywood with you?" I asked. He said he was.
> "I'll try not to make him too much trouble when he starts prying me loose," I said.
> "I don't think I will have use for Mr. Solotaire's services on this trip," he replied.
> My heart jumped, and I felt full of happiness. Something was starting between Mr. DiMaggio and me.

During the filming of *Monkey Business*, which costarred Cary Grant, Marilyn began suffering abdominal pains and was running a fever. Diagnosed with appendicitis, Marilyn checked into Cedars of Lebanon Hospital on April 28, 1952, to have her appendix removed. In the operating room the surgeon was amazed to find a handwritten note taped to her abdomen:

> Dear Dr. Rabwin,
>   Cut as little as possible. I know it seems vain but that doesn't really enter into it. The fact that I'm a woman is important and means much to me.
> For God's sake Dear Doctor—No ovaries removed!
> Thanking you with all my heart.
>
> Marilyn Monroe

Mobbed by the press when she left the hospital several days later, she relied on Whitey Snyder to make her look the picture of health. It was then that she exacted Whitey's promise to make her up for her funeral, if she should die.

In May she recuperated at her new apartment on the corner of Doheny Drive and Cynthia Street, where DiMaggio was a frequent visitor. The press was soon on to the budding romance between two of America's most publicized celebrities. It was a match made in movie-mogul heaven, and Zanuck didn't hesitate to renew Marilyn's option, which raised her salary to $750 a week—one of the lowest salaries paid to an important star. Marilyn was already scheduled to film *Niagara* with Joseph Cotten, and it was announced on her birthday that she would have the plum role of Lorelie Lee in the musical comedy *Gentlemen Prefer Blondes*. Originally planned for Betty Grable, the part went to Marilyn because of her increasing box-office draw.

On her way to the *Niagara* location in Buffalo, Marilyn visited Joe DiMaggio in Manhattan, sparking rumors of their romance. But at the time he wasn't Marilyn's only romantic interest. She was also having an affair with Nico Minardos, a young Greek actor she had met at Fox, and she frequently saw Bob Slatzer. When Marilyn flew to the *Niagara* location, she called Slatzer and suggested he meet her. When he arrived, he found that Marilyn had arranged accommodations for him in the choicest room at the hotel—the one next to hers.

After celebrating their reunion with several glasses of champagne, Slatzer recalls Marilyn giggling, "Wouldn't this be a wonderful place to get married? We wouldn't have to go to Niagara for our honeymoon because we're already here!" Very much aware of her romance with DiMaggio, Slatzer wondered if it was just the bubbles talking. After several more glasses of champagne, they decided to go ahead with the honeymoon, and talk about marriage later.

When *Niagara* finished filming, Slatzer and DiMaggio both followed Marilyn back to Hollywood. "I saw Marilyn as much as DiMaggio did," Slatzer commented. "When he was out of town I saw her practically every night. Sometime I'd be at the apartment when DiMaggio would phone, and there were times when I would call late at night and DiMaggio would be there—then she'd call back sometimes at three o'clock in the morning, and say, 'Bob, I can talk now.'"

Dorothy Kilgallen picked up on Marilyn's affair with Slatzer, and wrote in her column of August 16, 1952, "A dark horse in the Marilyn Monroe romance derby is Bob Slatzer, former Columbus, Ohio, literary critic. He's been wooing her by phone and mail, and improving her mind with gifts of the world's greatest books."

Three weeks later, Kilgallen invited Slatzer to do a guest column about

Marilyn, and on September 12 his column appeared under Kilgallen's "Voice of Broadway" byline. Slatzer wrote of supplying Marilyn with literary classics in her quest for knowledge. *Confidential* followed up with a cover story on Slatzer's romance with Marilyn. "DiMaggio was jealous," Slatzer said, "and Marilyn told me she couldn't see any way she could be happy with him, because he was always so jealous. Not only over me—he would become jealous of anyone she paid attention to. If someone asked for an autograph or took her picture, he'd get bent all out of shape and give her hell. Back in the fall of 1952, I'd never have thought she'd marry him."

Slatzer claims she decided to marry him instead.

After a long night of talk and champagne, Slatzer and Marilyn headed for Rosarita Beach, just south of the Mexican border. Stopping at the Foreign Club in Tijuana for a few more drinks, they suddenly decided to get married. Finding a lawyer who performed marriages, they were told to come back in an hour. On the Avenida, they encountered Kid Chissell, who had loaned Slatzer and Marilyn his car on their first date in 1946.

"It was pure chance," Chissell said. "I was down in Tijuana with an old navy buddy, and I saw Bob and Marilyn coming out of a shop. I gave him a shove and he swung around, looking mad. When they realized who I was, we all laughed, and they said, would I be their witness at the wedding?"

Chissell recalled that Marilyn wanted to visit a church before the ceremony, and they went to a nearby Catholic church off the main street. He remembered seeing Marilyn cover her head with her sweater and light a candle near the altar. Afterward they went to the lawyer's office, filled out the forms, and were married.

On the way back from the border, the champagne bubbles began to burst. Marilyn was having second thoughts. When Slatzer turned the car radio on to hear some music, there was Joe DiMaggio announcing the World Series, and Marilyn began to cry. When they got back to Hollywood, Marilyn decided she had made a mistake. The next day they returned to Tijuana and bribed the lawyer to tear up the marriage certificate, which hadn't yet been officially filed. Bob and Marilyn had been married on Saturday, October 4, 1952. By Monday the marriage had ended. Actress Terry Moore, who knew Marilyn well during her years at Fox, stated, "I remember very well her being excited about going out with Bob. She wanted so much to have culture, and she respected Bob because he was well-read. She did tell me she had married him, right after they did it." Interviewed by Anthony Summers in 1982, Kid Chissell also confirmed his involvement as a witness on that wedding day.

By the end of 1952, Marilyn had become the most publicized star in Hollywood and was receiving over five thousand fan letters a week. She shared top billing with Jane Russell in one of the major musicals of the fifties, *Gentlemen Prefer Blondes*. Her option was renewed and her salary increased. But she wasn't happy: "I was making more money a week than I had once been able to make in six months. I had clothes, fame, money, a future, all the publicity I could dream of. I even had a few friends. And there was always a romance in the air. But instead of being happy over all these fairy tale things that had happened to me, I grew depressed and finally desperate. My life suddenly seemed as wrong and unbearable to me as it had in the days of my early despairs."

She attended the studio's annual Christmas party and put on a smiling face. Afterward, she left the festivities with nothing to do but return to her empty Doheny apartment. DiMaggio had said he was going to spend the holidays in San Francisco with his family, and she hoped he might call. When she entered her apartment, she was surprised to see a Christmas tree and a large cardboard sign—MERRY CHRISTMAS TO MARILYN. Joe was sitting in a chair in the corner. "It's the first time in my life anyone ever gave me a Christmas tree," Marilyn later remarked to Sidney Skolsky. "I was so happy, I cried."

How to Marry a Millionaire costarred Marilyn, Betty Grable, and Lauren Bacall. Nunnally Johnson, who tailored the script for Marilyn, said, "It was the first time she had a chance to act in a role that was somewhat like she really was, and the first time anybody liked Marilyn for herself in a picture. She herself diagnosed the reason for that very shrewdly. She said that this was the only picture she'd been in, in which she had a measure of modesty—not physical modesty, but modesty about her own attractiveness."

Director Jean Negulesco observed, "She may have been late and difficult at times, but in the end I adored her because she was a pure child who had this 'something' that God gave her, that we still can't define or understand. It's the thing that made her a star. We did not know whether she'd been good or bad, and then when we put the picture together there was one person on that screen who was a *great* actress—Marilyn."

Shortly after her twenty-seventh birthday, Marilyn and Jane Russell, her costar in *Gentlemen Prefer Blondes,* placed their imprints in the cement of the Grauman's Chinese Theatre forecourt. The gala event took place not far from the spot where eight-year-old Norma Jeane had once tried to fit her shoes into the prints of the stars. DiMaggio was conspicuously absent. He hated the Hollywood hoopla and abhorred the way Marilyn flaunted her "sexual vibrations." He refused to attend the ceremonies at Grauman's, the Photoplay Awards when Marilyn was named "Fastest Rising Star," and the glittering premiere of *How to Marry a Millionaire.* Jealous of any rivals for Marilyn's attention, DiMaggio was often seething with anger beneath his image of the strong, silent hero of American baseball legend. Commenting on his temper, Natasha Lytess observed, "All during these months of 1952 and 1953, Marilyn would phone me day and night, sometimes in tears, complaining about the way he misused her."

During the filming of *River of No Return,* Marilyn began having conflicts with her director, Otto Preminger. Filmed in the wilds of the Canadian Rockies, the picture required scenes of a raft caught in the rapids of a raging river. Preminger insisted that Marilyn do the perilous scenes herself, and there were a series of accidents in which Marilyn hurt her leg. Perhaps exaggerating the extent of her injuries, the press painted the director as a sadist, and DiMaggio rallied to Marilyn's defense. DiMaggio arrived at the location accompanied by a doctor, and Preminger became uncharacteristically subdued in the presence of "the slugger." DiMaggio and Marilyn vanished for a weekend, and rumors began spreading of a secret marriage.

When Marilyn returned to Hollywood, Joe virtually moved into what was referred to in the press as their Doheny "love nest." Marilyn learned to cook spaghetti the way Joe's mother did, and she tried to influence him to read the classics. Joe preferred television. There were visits to the DiMaggio family home on Beach Street in San Francisco, where Joe's sister Marie lived. There were fogbound days when Marilyn would bundle up in a leather jacket and jeans and go surf fishing with him up the coast.

During the years of Marilyn's sudden fame, she had kept in touch with Aunt Grace. It was a difficult time in the Goddards' life. Because both Doc and Grace Goddard had become confirmed alcoholics, the visits were painful. Much of Marilyn's success was lost on Grace, who was often incoherent. In October 1953, Grace died from an overdose of barbiturates. She was buried in the Westwood Village Mortuary, not far from Aunt Ana.

Toward the end of 1953, Marilyn was scheduled to begin filming *Pink Tights*, costarring Frank Sinatra, but neither Joe nor Marilyn liked the script. Marilyn thought her role stupid and ill-motivated, and Joe thought her part risqué. Zanuck demanded that Marilyn fulfill her contractual obligation, but Marilyn and Joe disappeared. Fox suspended Marilyn on January 5, 1954, for failing to appear for work. When the press discovered that Joe and Marilyn were in San Francisco, the DiMaggio family home became the scene of media frenzy. Marilyn recalled Joe's anger.

"I wonder if I can take all your crazy publicity?" Joe said.

"It's part of my career," I said. "Do you want me to hide in a basement?"

"We'll see how it works out," he said. "You're having all this trouble with the studio and not working, so why don't we get married now?"

I had never planned on or dreamed about becoming the wife of a great man. Any more than Joe had ever thought about marrying a woman who seemed eighty percent publicity. The truth is that we were very much alike. My publicity, like Joe's greatness, was something on the outside. It had nothing to do with what we actually were.

On January 14, 1954, the private marriage ceremony took place in the chambers of San Francisco Judge Charles Peery. The marriage would last less than nine months.

Red-Eye

It's no fun being married to an electric light.
—Joe DiMaggio

Before the marriage, DiMaggio had already agreed to accompany his friend Frank "Lefty" O'Doul to an exhibition baseball game in Japan. It was decided that the business trip would also become an extension of the DiMaggios' honeymoon. When they arrived in Tokyo, Marilyn's fans turned out in the thousands and stormed the airplane. Joe and his bride had to escape through the baggage hatch. Two hundred police were called in to restore order when they checked into their hotel. At a press conference arranged in DiMaggio's honor, the Yankee Clipper was ignored, and all the questions were fielded to Marilyn.

According to Lefty O'Doul, Joe became angry when he realized just how popular his wife had become. When Marilyn was invited by the Far East Army Command to entertain the troops in Korea, a miffed DiMaggio exclaimed, "Go ahead, if you want to. It's your honeymoon—not mine!" Lefty O'Doul accompanied Marilyn to Korea, where she did a four-day whirlwind chopper tour, entertaining thousands of troops.

"We took a helicopter for the front," she recalled. "I didn't see Korea and its battlefields and beaten-up towns. I left one landing field and came down on another. Then I was put in a truck and taken where the 45th

Division was waiting. It was cold and starting to snow. I was backstage in dungarees. Out front the show was on. I could hear music playing and a roar of voices. The roar I'd been hearing was my name being yelled by the soldiers. An officer came backstage. He was excited. 'You'll have to go on ahead of schedule, Miss Monroe, I don't think we can hold them any longer.' "

Thirteen thousand men of the Forty-Fifth, waiting in the freezing cold, roared their approval as Marilyn stepped out of her makeshift dressing room onto the stage and sang "Diamonds Are a Girl's Best Friend," "Do It Again," and "Bye Bye Baby." It was the first time she had performed before a large audience, and it was far from Hollywood and far from Joe's critical attitude. Feeling the love and admiration of thousands of smiling soldiers, she gave brilliant, spontaneous performances. But Joe wasn't smiling. DiMaggio was enraged by the hoopla over the Korea visit and threatened to divorce her on their honeymoon.

During the tour, Marilyn was hiding an injured hand. Her right thumb had been broken. Hidden most of the time under a mink coat Joe had given her as a wedding present, the injury drew the curiosity of a reporter. "I just bumped it," Marilyn explained. "I have a witness. Joe was there. He heard it crack."

When the newlyweds returned to Hollywood, Sidney Skolsky paid Marilyn a visit and recalled that Marilyn "dropped a baffling bombshell."

"Sidney, do you know who I'm going to marry?" she asked.

"Marry!" Skolsky exclaimed. "What are you talking about?"

"I'm going to marry Arthur Miller," Marilyn responded.

"But you just got married! I don't understand," Skolsky said.

"You will," Marilyn commented without further explanation.

When the DiMaggios returned from their honeymoon, the twosome rode on such a high crest of international adulation that Fox was quick to forgive its million-dollar baby. She was cast in *There's No Business Like Show Business*, and one Fox executive jubilantly exclaimed, "We haven't lost a star—we've gained a center fielder." The studio hoped DiMaggio would be present at Marilyn's publicity events, but Joe was quick to disappoint them.

Though Joe preferred living in San Francisco, they rented a house at 508 North Palm Drive in Beverly Hills. The house was across the street from Marilyn's agent, Charlie Feldman, who was Jack Kennedy's host on his frequent forays to Hollywood. Feldman's secretary, Grace Dobish, remembered Marilyn and Jack Kennedy being together at the Feldmans' house in 1951. Alain Bernheim, who worked with Feldman, recalled that Marilyn was at a dinner party Feldman gave for JFK in the early fifties.

In the summer of 1954, Jack and Jacqueline Kennedy were invited to Charlie Feldman's home for a dinner party, and among the guests were Peter and Pat Lawford and Feldman's neighbors the DiMaggios. Marilyn told Slatzer that she felt uncomfortable at the party because Jack kept staring at her and Jackie had noticed. When DiMaggio saw what was happening, he became angry, grabbed his wife by the arm, and said, "Let's go! I've had enough of this!" Marilyn didn't want to leave, and Feldman recalled, "They had words about it!"

A good friend of Marilyn's, Arthur James, a prominent real estate agent in Malibu, stated that he was aware of an ongoing affair between Marilyn and Jack Kennedy during the fifties. "He was unknown here, relatively speaking. He and Marilyn could get away with a great deal. They sometimes drank at the Malibu cottage, which was the raunchiest place you've ever seen in your life." James stated he saw Jack and Marilyn walking near the Malibu pier sometime in the mid-fifties, and that he was aware she stayed with Jack at the Holiday House, a romantic hideaway on the Malibu coast.

When Jack Kennedy was hospitalized for back surgery several months after the Feldman dinner party, visitors to his room were amused to see a poster of Marilyn Monroe hanging on the wall next to his bed. Marilyn was wearing blue shorts and stood on the beach with her legs spread wide apart. Jack had hung the poster upside down.

There's No Business Like Show Business and Billy Wilder's *The Seven Year Itch* were filmed back to back. Anxious to have their box-office bombshell keep the cash registers ringing, Fox gave Marilyn no respite between pictures. In August 1954, without one day off, Marilyn stepped out of the role of Vicky on the *Show Business* stage and walked to the *Itch* stage, where she became "the girl" who lived above Tom Ewell. On September 9 she flew alone to New York for the *Itch* location sequences, and there were rumors that the DiMaggios' marriage was breaking up. "Everything's fine with us," Marilyn told the press. "A happy marriage comes before anything." But the marriage was anything but happy.

Five days later, Wilder was preparing to film the sequence in which a

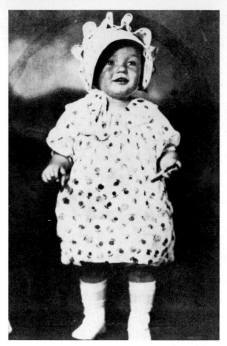

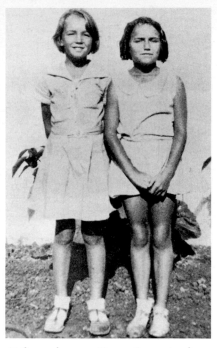

Baby Norma Jeane in a matching hat and dress made by Ida Bolender. *Robert Slatzer Collection*

At the orphanage, Norma Jeane stands next to an unidentified friend. *Robert Slatzer Collection*

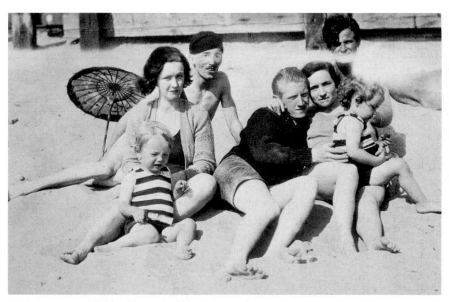

On the sands of Ocean Park: To the left is Gladys Baker behind Norma Jeane. Sitting next to Gladys is her brother Marion and his wife, Olive, with their baby, Ida May. Marion disappeared several years after this photo was taken. *Fred Guiles Collection*

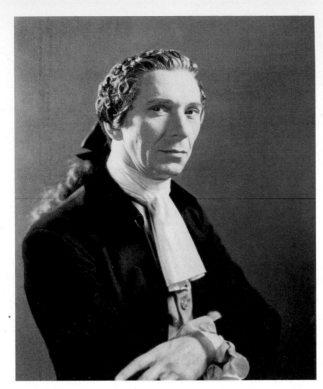

Actor Murray Kinnell. He was the boarder at Gladys's home when Norma Jeane was molested. *Courtesy of the American Film Institute*

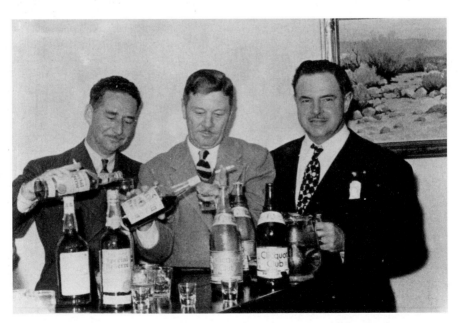

Norma Jeane's father, Stan Gifford, stands to the right at a Consolidated Laboratories party. *Fred Guiles Collection*

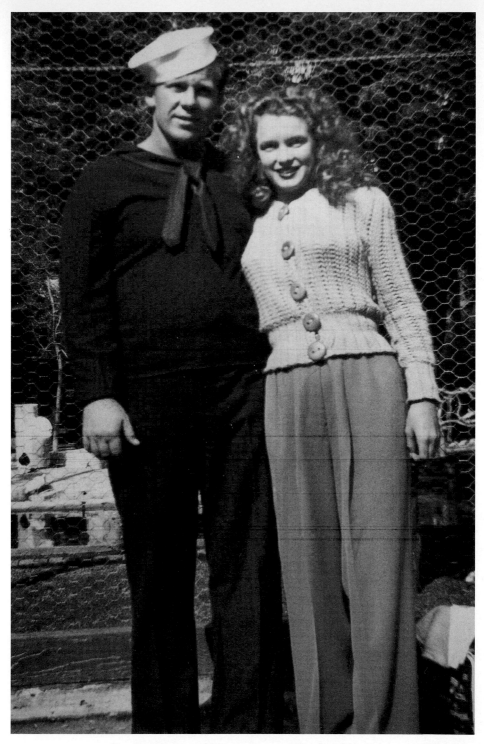

Jim Dougherty and Norma Jeane on Catalina Island.
George Zeno Collection, courtesy of James Dougherty

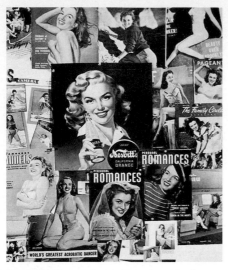

By 1946 Norma Jeane Dougherty had become one of the Blue Book Agency's most popular models. *George Zeno Collection*

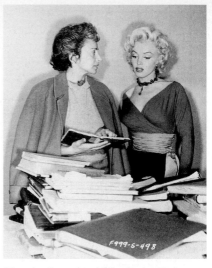

Natasha Lytess and Marilyn at Fox in the early 1950s. Marilyn insisted that Natasha be hired by the studio as a drama coach. *Robert Slatzer Collection*

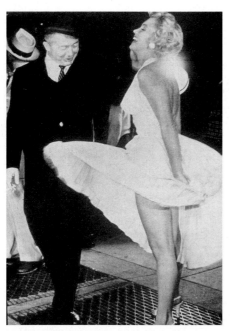

Director Billy Wilder looks on during rehearsals for the famous scene above the subway grate in *The Seven Year Itch*. *Retna Ltd.*

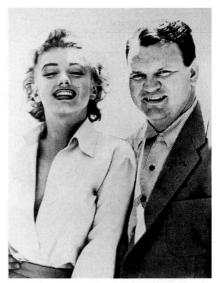

Marilyn and Robert Slatzer in 1952. *Robert Slatzer Collection*

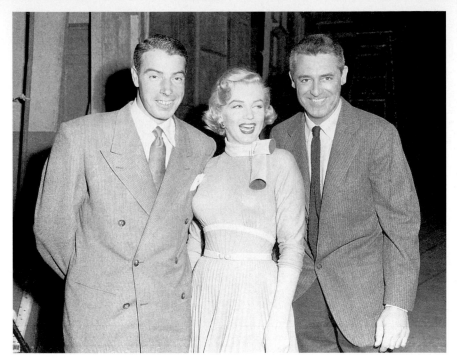

Joe DiMaggio in one of his rare studio visits, on the set of *Monkey Business* with Marilyn and costar Cary Grant. *Robert Slatzer Collection*

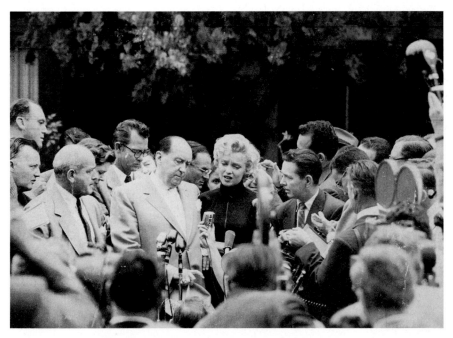

Marilyn, in front of her home, with attorney Jerry Geisler as he announces the end of the DiMaggio marriage. *MPTV Archives*

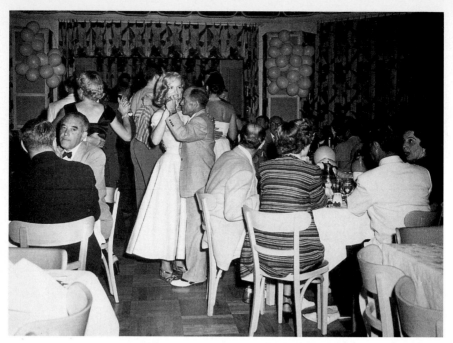

Dancing with a big man in Hollywood, Johnny Hyde, who offered Marilyn $1 million to marry him. *Bruno Bernard, courtesy of Susan Bernard*

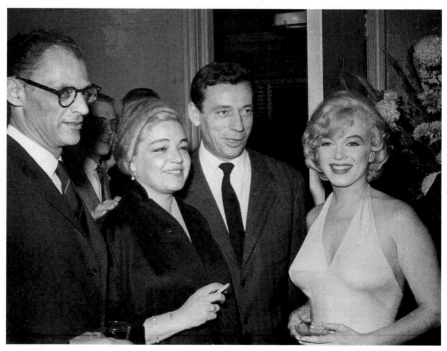

The Millers with Simone Signoret and Yves Montand at a studio party, celebrating Montand's arrival in Hollywood for *Let's Make Love*. *George Zeno Collection*

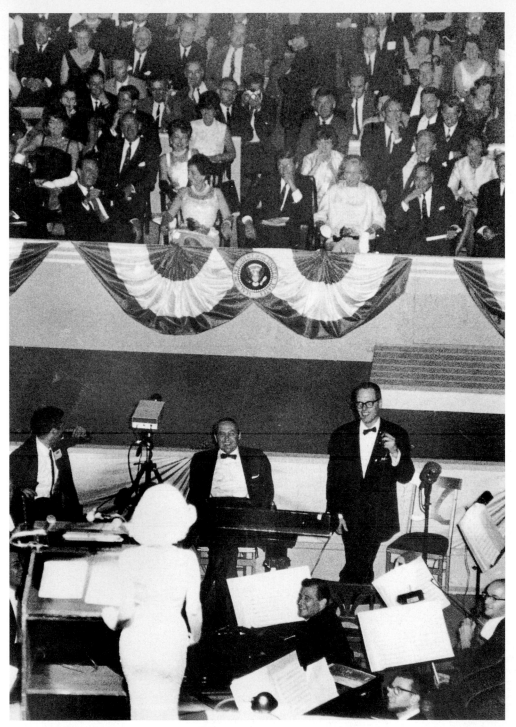

At the president's birthday gala in Madison Square Garden, Marilyn sings "Happy Birthday" to Jack Kennedy, who can be seen behind the Presidential Seal. Bobby Kennedy is seated two rows behind him, several seats to the right. *Foto File*

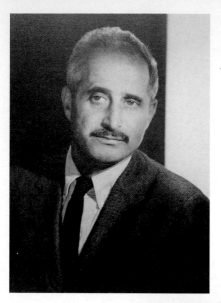

Dr. Ralph Greenson, who began treating Marilyn in January 1960. *Courtesy of the Los Angeles Psychoanalytic Institute*

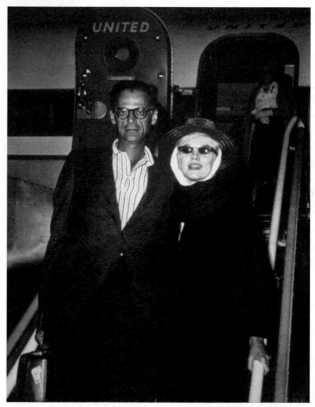

After her stay at the West-Side Hospital in Los Angeles, Marilyn returns to Reno to resume filming *The Misfits*. Miller clearly shows the strain of the production and their marital problems. *MPTV Archives*

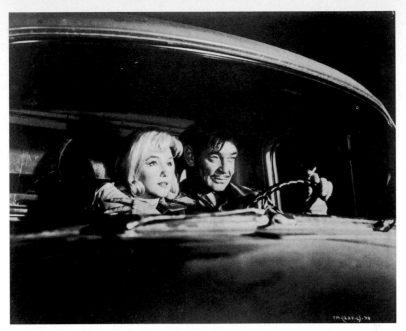

Marilyn and Gable look to the stars in the final scene of *The Misfits*. It would be the last day of their last completed picture. *George Zeno Collection*

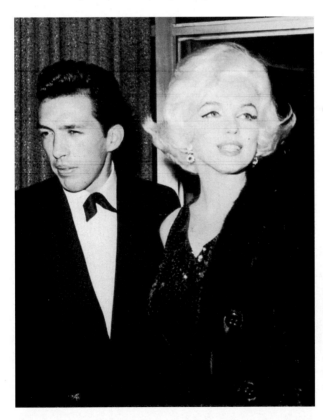

José Bolaños escorts Marilyn to the Golden Globe Awards in March 1962. Marilyn is wearing the diamond-and-emerald earrings given to her by Frank Sinatra. *George Zeno Collection*

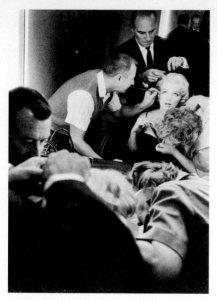

Makeup artist Whitey Snyder and hairdresser Sidney Guilaroff prepare Marilyn for a scene in *Let's Make Love*.
Robert Slatzer Collection

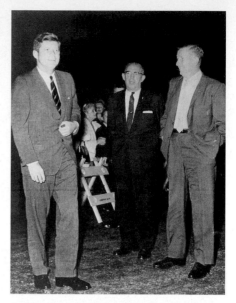

Left to right: Jack Kennedy, Los Angeles Police Chief William Parker, and Captain James Hamilton of the Intelligence Division. *Robert Slatzer Collection*

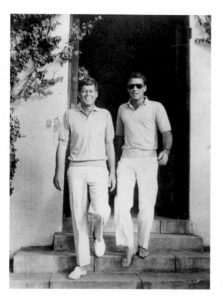

Jack Kennedy and Peter Lawford at Lawford's Santa Monica beach house.
Robert Slatzer Collection

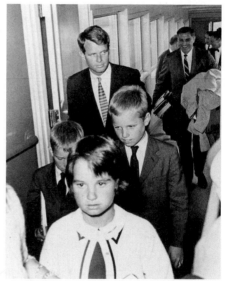

Robert Kennedy and three of his children as they arrive in San Francisco with Ethel on Friday, August 3, 1962. *Robert Slatzer Collection*

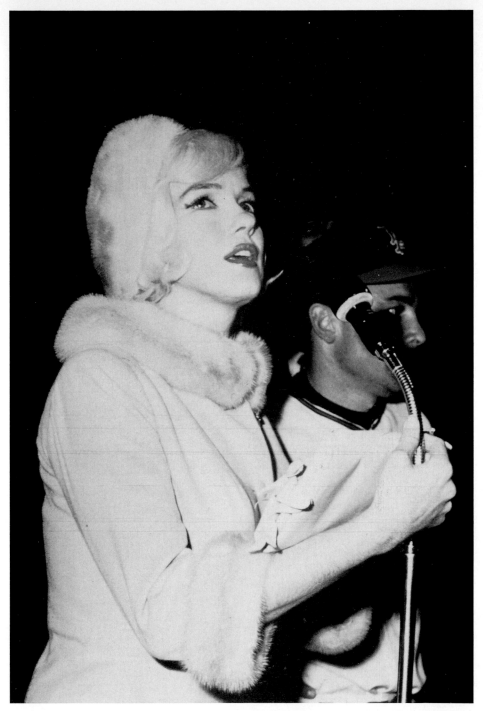

Marilyn's last public appearance, at Dodger Stadium on June 1, 1962. *Robert Slatzer Collection*

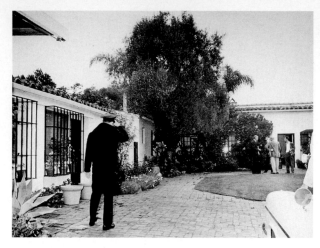

A Los Angeles police officer stands in the forecourt of the Monroe residence. To his left is the door to the guest cottage. Reporters stand near the entrance of the home. *Robert Slatzer Collection*

A view of Marilyn Monroe's bedroom from the window Dr. Greenson used to gain entry. Mrs. Murray can be seen standing in the entry to the telephone room beyond the officer. *Globe Photos— Don Tompkins*

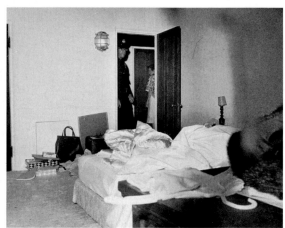

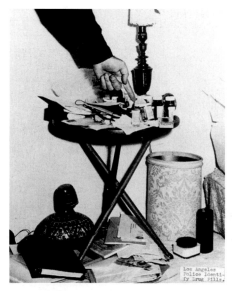

Marilyn's bedside table, where the pill bottles were found. On the floor to the right is what could be a drinking glass. Sergeant Jack Clemmons stated it was not there when he searched the room. *Foto File—Walter Fisher*

Pat Newcomb exits the house, followed by Norman Jefferies, Eunice Murray's son-in-law, who was employed at the house as a caretaker. *Foto File— Walter Fisher*

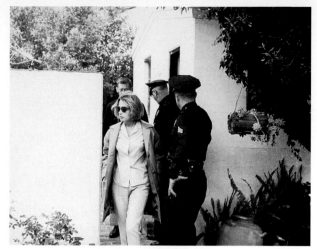

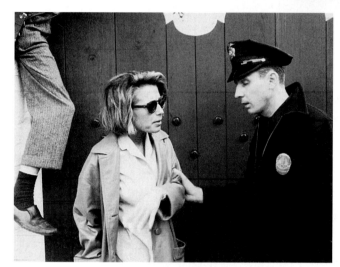

A police officer restrains Pat Newcomb near the wooden entry gates as the coroner's van prepares to leave. *Foto File—Walter Fisher*

Hockett prepares to drive out of the gates while the officer leads Pat Newcomb aside. Behind the officer is the guest cottage. *Foto File—Walter Fisher*

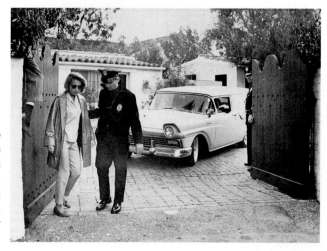

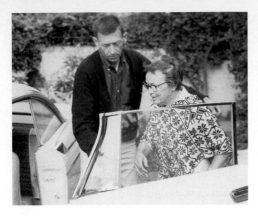

Norman Jefferies helps his mother-in-law, Eunice Murray, into her Dodge.
Foto File—Walter Fisher

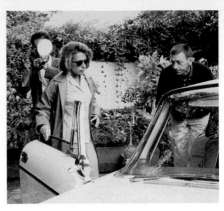

Norman Jefferies assists Pat Newcomb into the passenger side of Mrs. Murray's car. Though Newcomb claims she drove to Marilyn's that morning, her car was not there. *Foto File—Walter Fisher*

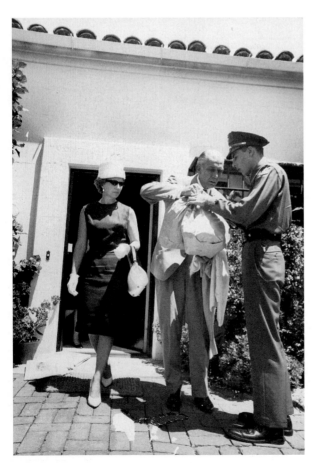

On Tuesday, August 7, Marilyn's half sister Berneice Miracle exits the house with mortician Guy Hockett, who hands his son, Don, the dress and wig that would be used to prepare Marilyn's body for the funeral.
Black-Star—Eugene Anthony

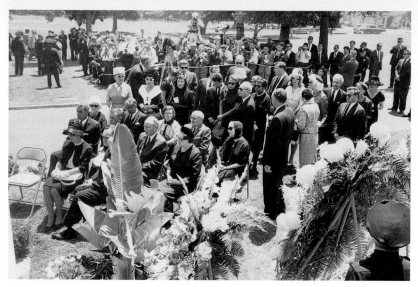

The invited mourners gather by Marilyn's tomb. Joe DiMaggio refused to invite the many Hollywood friends who wanted to attend. *Black-Star—Eugene Anthony*

Among the mourners were the Greenson family. *Left to right:* Danny, Dr. Ralph Greenson, Hildi, and Joan.
Black-Star—Robert Smith

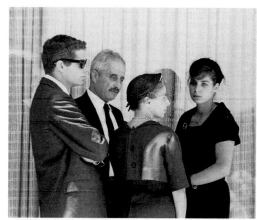

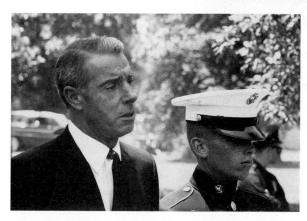

A grieving Joe DiMaggio with his son, Joe Jr.
Black-Star—Eugene Anthony

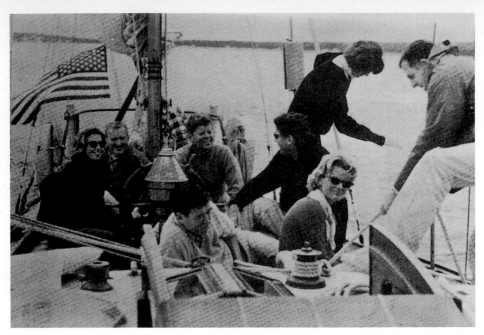

Pat Newcomb yachting with President Kennedy aboard the *Manitou* off the coast of Maine on August 12, 1962—four days after Marilyn's funeral. *Left to right in the wheel well:* Pat Newcomb (wearing the president's jacket), Paul "Red" Fay, JFK, Peter Lawford, Patricia Lawford (standing). *Robert Slatzer Collection*

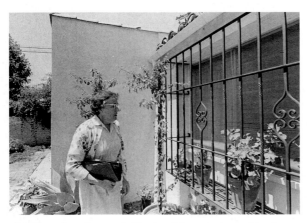

On Thursday, August 9, Eunice Murray returned to the house for the last time. Before leaving, she gazed into the guest cottage. It was on the floor, just beyond the window, that Marilyn died. *Robert Slatzer Collection*

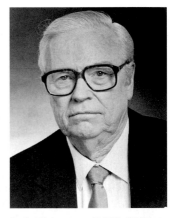

Jack Clemmons (1922–1998), the officer called by Hyman Engelberg early on Sunday, August 5, 1962. Clemmons always believed that Marilyn Monroe was a homicide victim. *Robert Slatzer Collection, courtesy of Eileen Clemmons*

draft from a subway grate blows Marilyn's skirt into the air. Joe arrived in New York that day and was drinking with Walter Winchell and George Solotaire at Toots Shor's, which was just around the corner. The scene was filmed after midnight to avoid crowds of onlookers, but thousands of people were ogling Marilyn when DiMaggio arrived at two in the morning. The mob whistled and hooted every time Marilyn's skirt went up, and DiMaggio got madder and madder. Turning to Winchell, he angrily exclaimed, "What the hell's going on here! I don't go for this. Let's get the hell outta here!"

Later that morning, Marilyn's neighbors at the St. Regis heard DiMaggio and Marilyn having a violent argument. There were screams and the sound of a scuffle. The next day on the set Marilyn's bruises had to be covered by heavy makeup before she could go before the cameras. Whitey Snyder stated, "They loved one another, but they just couldn't be married to one another. . . . Sometimes he'd hit her up a bit."

When the *Itch* company returned to Hollywood, Marilyn called Billy Wilder and said she wouldn't be coming to work because "J-Joe and I are going to get a d-divorce." Harry Brand and the 20th Century-Fox publicity office carefully orchestrated the announcement. Accompanied by attorney Jerry Geisler, Marilyn emerged from her house, where a horde of newsmen had gathered. There was an obvious bruise on her forehead. Marilyn tried to speak to the press before driving off, but, racked with sobs, she was unable to say more than "I'm sorry . . . I'm sorry . . ."

The day after her separation from DiMaggio, Marilyn went back to work with a vengeance. She drove through the Pico Boulevard studio gates at 7 A.M. and was ready for the first take by 9:40 A.M. She had her lines down cold; her voice was clear; her concentration was good. Quickly grasping Wilder's suggestions, she followed them precisely, and each scene was printed by the second or third take.

Natasha Lytess had never liked DiMaggio, and she believed that Marilyn's difficulties on the set were related to her marital problems. "Now she does everything better," Lytess exclaimed. "She concentrates better. She remembers lines better. She's much easier to work with. Sometimes now with one word I will make her know what Mr. Wilder wants from her."

The Seven Year Itch finished filming on Friday, November 4, 1954. The production ran three weeks over schedule and $150,000 over budget, but Billy Wilder knew he had delivered a superb comedy, and Charlie Feldman and Zanuck knew they had a box-office bonanza. Marilyn's performance projected delightful nuances of humor that perfectly underscored her unique blend of naïveté and sexuality. Fox assured Marilyn that she would receive a $100,000 bonus for *Itch* and that her next vehicle for Fox, *How to Be Very, Very Popular*, was going to be a "high-class screenplay" written especially for her by Nunnally Johnson.

To celebrate, Feldman hosted a party in Marilyn's honor at Romanoff's. It was a significant event for Marilyn—Hollywood's A list had finally accepted her. Those lining up to sign a huge souvenir portrait of Marilyn included Humphrey Bogart and Lauren Bacall, Claudette Colbert, William Holden, Jimmy Stewart, Gary Cooper, Doris Day, and Clark Gable. Zanuck was there, as were Jack Warner and Sam Goldwyn. Marilyn showed up an hour late. Tastefully dressed in a subtle black tulle gown, she looked every bit the ravishing star she had become. She danced with Gable.

"I've always admired you and wanted to be in a picture with you, Mr. Gable."

"Call me Clark."

"Well, I would, really, I would, Clark."

There was a late supper, chateaubriand, champagne, more champagne, after-dinner dancing. She dazzled them all. She had arrived. But she was about to say good-bye.

Marilyn was unhappy with the scripts Fox was giving her. She was tired of playing the dumb blonde, and wanted to appear in more challenging roles. When Marilyn received the "high-class screenplay" of *How to Be Very, Very Popular*, she discovered it was about a *very, very* dumb blonde, this time a burlesque dancer. Marilyn wouldn't do it. Zanuck insisted. Marilyn refused. Fox threatened to put her on suspension and reneged on her $100,000 bonus for *Itch*.

She had been discussing her problems with her friend Milton Greene, the *Look* magazine photographer. He advised her to leave Fox and set up her own production company in New York. Greene suggested a partnership, and he put together potential investors for their independent film ventures. While the lawyers drew up the papers, Marilyn was trying to make up her mind to break with Fox. The New York lawyers Frank Delaney and Irving Stein were growing increasingly skeptical that the corporate papers for Marilyn Monroe Productions would ever be signed.

Greene flew to Los Angeles on November 16 and reiterated the advantages of establishing her own corporation—the power to choose her own scripts, directors, and costars.

"But, Milton," Marilyn said, "suppose those New York lawyers are wrong. Suppose we can't break my contract?"

"We're not breaking it, Marilyn," Greene recalled telling her. "*They* broke it. They can't hold you to a slave contract!"

While the lawyers and the agents argued, Marilyn disappeared. MARILYN VANISHES! WHERE'S MARILYN? the trade papers headlined. She had, in fact, moved into the apartment of Nana Karger on Harper until she could decide what to do. It was the reviews of *There's No Business Like Show Business* that helped her in making a decision. Mild by today's standards, *There's No Business Like Show Business* went into national release over the Christmas holidays, and it was roundly criticized for its bad taste. Both Hedda Hopper and Ed Sullivan were among those that lashed out at Marilyn for appearing in a "cheap and tawdry film." Sullivan wrote, "The 'Heat Wave' number is frankly dirty—easily one of the most flagrant violations of good taste this observer has ever witnessed. . . ."

There were many who echoed Sullivan's sentiments, and Marilyn, who sought the love and admiration of the average people who went to the Bijous on the Main Streets of America, was mortified. Sullivan's column was her boarding pass for the red-eye to Manhattan. She called Milton Greene and told him she was on her way. Marilyn Monroe Productions was a go.

Putting on a black wig, dark glasses, and a plain dress, she bought a one-way ticket on a night flight to New York under the name of "Zelda Zonk." As the mystery woman in the dark glasses and the black wig boarded the plane, she said good-bye to the dumb blonde. She had only celluloid ties to the West Coast, so there was no family to see her off. Grace and Ana were in their graves. Gladys was in the institution. Stan Gifford had disavowed her. Doc Goddard had gotten remarried, and Marilyn had lost touch with Bebe Goddard. She didn't tell DiMaggio, Skolsky, or Slatzer she was going away. Only Natasha Lytess and Nana Karger knew.

As the plane took off from the L.A. airport it headed out over the ocean toward the setting sun. If she looked out the window she could see the last rays dancing on the shimmering sea surrounding Catalina Island, where Norma Jeane had once dreamed her golden dreams. She always had a way of making dreams come true. Beyond will and determination, there was an insightful intuition at play that divined all the bright colors. But what was in the deep, where colors drop off into darkness and only the eyes of bitter experience can see?

She usually slept well on airplanes at night. In the limbo of transition there was little sense of time or place, only the drone of the engines and the luxury of disconnection. As the plane approached New York a crimson ribbon of light arched across the horizon. The future held bright promise, and something Marilyn Monroe had always found entrancing—a new beginning.

PART IV

1955–1959

The Danger of

All Dreams

Zelda Zonk

She longed for privacy, but she had murdered privacy, as Macbeth had murdered sleep. Her time was not hers. And her personality was not hers.

—Maurice Zolotow

Norma Jeane was nineteen when she moved into a room in Hollywood to live by herself, because "I wanted to find out who I was." She never did. Instead she became Marilyn Monroe. In the kinetic whirlwind of becoming a movie star—the acting lessons, modeling, photo sessions, interviews—much had been postponed. Marilyn later said of Norma Jeane, "This sad bitter child who grew up too fast is hardly ever out of my heart. With success all around me, I can still feel her frightened eyes looking out of mine. She keeps saying, 'I never lived, I was never loved.' "

She was twenty-eight when she arrived in New York, and the person who stepped off the plane was still the shy and frightened girl who looked out of Marilyn Monroe's eyes. She needed to find out who she was.

Milton and Amy Greene were waiting at LaGuardia Airport and drove Marilyn to their eighteenth-century farmhouse in Weston, Connecticut. It was rumored in the gossip columns that she had flown to the East Coast, but a baffled press searched for her in vain. "Where's Marilyn?" queried Walter Winchell. Marilyn was in the Greenes' little purple guest quarters, where she sat in a tub full of bubbles. It was the Christmas season and everybody came to the Greenes' on the weekends. The entrance was a revolving door full of visitors like Joshua and Nedda Logan, Gene Kelly, Leonard and Felicia Bernstein, Truman Capote, Richard and Dorothy Rodgers, and Mike Todd. They knew that Marilyn was the hush-hush house guest, but she seldom appeared.

"When do we get to see Marilyn?" they asked.

"Oh, she's very nervous about new people," Amy would say. "She's shy and afraid to come out. She's been in the bathtub for an hour."

One of the Greenes' guests, Joyce Saffir, recalled, "She finally did come out. She didn't wear any makeup, I remember. She was scrubbed clean and looked like a child. She was just beautiful in pants and a sweater. She sort of sat off in a corner and didn't speak. While the others were gossiping, laughing, catching up on the latest nonsense, she would go off by herself and sit on the stairs, kicking her leg, just sitting there. I thought, frankly, there was something wrong with her. I started thinking she was out of it." Indeed, Christmastime brought painful memories to Norma Jeane. It was exactly twenty years since Gladys's breakdown. Marilyn confided to the Greenes' cook, Kitty, that her mother had been institutionalized. "She used to tell me how her mother was sick, and that used to touch my heart," Kitty said. She remembered Marilyn frequently talking about her days in foster homes. Being in another strange place with a surrogate family brought back painful memories. Kitty recalled that Marilyn would go to the kitchen and help her snap beans and peel potatoes. She would take the Greenes' children out for walks and baby-sit when Milton and Amy went out. When Marilyn lamented to the cook about the breakup of her marriage to DiMaggio, Kitty said, "Well, look how lucky you are, Marilyn. You got to be a star!"

"Yeah, Kitty," Marilyn responded, "but there are other things in life, too, that you need while you're getting to be a star. And if you don't get them, you'll miss them."

Marilyn frequently ventured forth from the little purple guest room to browse through the Greenes' extensive library, where she began reading about Napoleon and Josephine. "She was fascinated by women who made it," recalled Amy Greene. "We had a number of volumes about Emma, Lord Hamilton's mistress. She was intrigued by the story of the servant girl who became Lady Hamilton." Amy Greene remembered Marilyn keeping a diary, which she carried around the house, making notes on conversations and subjects that interested her in her reading. In the afternoons she would go for long walks alone in the woods surrounding the farmhouse.

Shortly after her arrival on the East Coast, Marilyn appeared on Edward R. Murrow's *Person to Person*, telecast from the Greenes' farmhouse. She seemed overcome by shyness and spoke in monosyllables, interrupted by an effusive Amy Greene, who delighted in explaining to America what Marilyn was trying to say.

"With us she had something entirely new," Amy Greene observed. "She had a structured life in an organized house. She had her own little room. But soon we were in the New York social whirl. We were invited everywhere and were doing everything. She wanted to become an educated lady, but she also wanted to be a star! That was a conflict, but in the beginning she was very happy—functioning well, fighting with Zanuck, feeling her oats."

On Friday, January 7, 1955, a press conference was held at the residence of lawyer Frank Delaney and the incorporation of Marilyn Monroe was announced. "I feel wonderful! I'm incorporated," said Marilyn, who was to be president of Marilyn Monroe Productions.. "We will go into all fields of entertainment," Marilyn stated. "I'm tired of the same old sex roles. I want to do better things. People have scope, you know. . . ."

Her announcement caused shock waves on Pico Boulevard, where there was a sudden run on legal pads. Fox was under the impression that Marilyn Monroe was contractually obligated to the studio for four more years. Zanuck was furious. Marilyn was ecstatic. That night she invited the Greenes and a party of friends to celebrate at the Copacabana, where Frank Sinatra was entertaining.

"We won't be able to get a table at the Copa," Amy Greene warned. "It's been sold out for weeks."

"Don't worry," Marilyn said. "If you want to hear Frank, follow me."

Sinatra's show had already started when they arrived, but the maître d' recognized Marilyn and had extra tables and chairs brought in and placed on the dance floor in front of the stage. Sinatra stopped the show, smiled, and winked at Marilyn while the crowd stared in hushed amazement. Looking astonishingly lovely in a borrowed white ermine stole, Marilyn took her place at the table with the party of celebrants.

"She knew precisely the power and influence she had," Amy Greene recalled.

With the help of Joe DiMaggio, who had followed her to the East Coast, Marilyn became an official New Yorker when she moved into the Gladstone Hotel on East Fifty-Second Street. Sparking speculation that she and DiMaggio were reunited, Marilyn stated that they were separated, but still friends. "I'm madly in love with New York," she exclaimed. "This will be my home from now on!"

She was enchanted by the city. Removing all her makeup and putting on a black wig, she explored Manhattan as Zelda Zonk. Friends and acquaintances often commented on Marilyn's special beauty when she was without makeup, and how different she appeared. There were multiple personalities at large within her that she could seemingly bring to life at will.

Eli Wallach was amazed by the metamorphosis that could turn Zelda Zonk into Marilyn Monroe. Wallach described walking down the street in midtown Manhattan with her: "Nobody noticed who she was because she was just being herself—suddenly her walk, attitude and appearance would change and in moments everyone would be ogling her and asking for autographs. 'I just wanted to be Marilyn Monroe for a moment,' she said."

On the streets of New York she liked exploring the possibilities of being an ordinary human being. After years in the Hollywood dream factory, she wanted to close the doors on the past and live like a normal person. Brooklyn poet Norman Rosten described his first meeting with this ordinary human being. She was brought to his Brooklyn apartment by a mutual friend, Sam Shaw.

Now they reach my landing. Photographer Sam Shaw mumbles her name: it sounds like Marion. She murmurs, "Pleased to meet you," and enters the living room, finds a chair and sits at once, rather stiffly, but her eyes are mischievous. She snuggles into the chair with a shy smile. . . . My wife Hedda enters to say hello and nonchalantly goes out to put up some coffee. Then we chat, small talk about the weather and Brooklyn Botanical Gardens. She listens more than she speaks; the sentences are short, breathless. . . . Now my wife rejoins us with coffee and cake. While Sam and I are gossiping, my wife sits next to our other visitor, and I catch part of their conversation.

"No, I'm not from New York," she is saying. "I've been here for about a month. I'm going to study acting."

"That's wonderful," replies Hedda, impressed. "Then you must have been in theater. What plays have you been in?"

"No, I've never been on the stage. But I have done some movies."

"Oh? What was your movie name?"

In a timid voice: "Marilyn Monroe."

Rosten related that later in the evening they took her to a neighborhood party where few people recognized her. "She was totally, mysteriously unrecognizable, as if she had stepped into the reality of her true self."

Norman Rosten and his wife were among the few friends she acquired on the East Coast who weren't interested in Marilyn Monroe the actress. They appreciated her for herself. "We didn't really give a damn who she was," Rosten said. "With us she was herself and she was thoroughly enchanting—such an odd human being. . . ."

For a brief period of time she studied with Constance Collier, to whom she was introduced by Truman Capote. Constance Collier had become a unique drama coach, who worked only with stars, such as Audrey Hepburn and Vivien Leigh. She took on Marilyn Monroe as "my special problem." Reporting to Truman Capote on Marilyn's progress, she said, "Oh, yes, there is something there. She is a beautiful child. . . . I don't think she's an actress at all, not in any traditional sense. What she has—this presence, this luminosity, this flickering intelligence—could never surface on the stage. It's so fragile and subtle, it can only be caught by the camera. It's like a hummingbird in flight: only a camera can freeze the poetry of it." And in a prophetic moment she said to Capote, "Somehow I don't think she'll make old bones. Absurd of me to say, but somehow I feel she'll go young. I hope, I really pray, that she survives long enough to free the strange lovely talent that's wandering through her like a jailed spirit."

Marilyn met Broadway producer and Actors Studio cofounder Cheryl Crawford at a dinner party in March. Together they discussed the Actors Studio, and Cheryl Crawford suggested that Marilyn meet with the Actors Studio artistic director, Lee Strasberg, to discuss her acting problems. Marilyn first met Strasberg in his book-lined apartment at Broadway and Eighty-Sixth Street. After a brief conversation he agreed to take her on as a private pupil. Strasberg was fascinated by Marilyn, and at times his enthusiasm would rise to a high hyperbolic boil. "She was engulfed in a mystic-like flame," he exclaimed, "like when you see Jesus at the Last Supper and there's a halo around him. There was this great white light surrounding Marilyn!" Lee Strasberg was broke at the time, and may have been speaking in the unconscious metaphor of mendicancy when he exuberantly stated, "It was almost as if she had been waiting for a button to be pushed, and when it was pushed a door opened and you saw a treasure of gold and jewels!" Strasberg pushed the button, and Marilyn's arrival at the Actors Studio proved to be an "open sesame" that ultimately led to riches beyond Strasberg's dreams.

Marilyn consented to be an usherette at the Actors Studio's benefit and world premiere of *East of Eden*, starring James Dean. With the news of Marilyn's participation the benefit was an instant sellout. The magic name of Monroe caused a run on tickets, which were being scalped at triple their sales price. One of the crowd at the Astor Roof who was anxiously waiting to see the usherette was Arthur Miller, who had attended the Actors Studio benefit with his sister, actress Joan Copeland. Marilyn had been very much on Miller's mind. He stated, "I no longer knew what I wanted—certainly not the end of my marriage, but the thought of putting Marilyn out of my life was unbearable."

Pink Elephants

1955 was a year of growth and discovery for Marilyn. It was also the time when she started swallowing too many pills and drinking too much champagne.
—Truman Capote

They painted the elephant pink, and Marilyn was to ride it around the arena in Madison Square Garden for Mike Todd's Celebrity Circus benefit on March 30. A dazzling circus costume of feathers and spangles was made for Marilyn, but it didn't fit properly and had to be resewn at the last minute. The costume was ready only moments before she was to make her appearance. She hurriedly put it on and quickly climbed the scaffolding to mount the elephant for her entrance. Ringmaster Milton Berle announced, "Ladies and gentlemen, boys and goils, here comes the only goil in the world who makes Jane Russell look like a boy!" *Ta-dum dum!*

Grabbing the rope harness, she sat down bareback on the elephant, and suddenly felt a sharp pain in her derriere. As the circus band played a fanfare and the spotlights illuminated the beautiful blonde on the pink elephant, it lurched forward and began circling the packed arena to thunderous applause, cheers, and whistles. Effervescently beautiful, Marilyn smiled and waved at the jubilant crowd. But with each step the elephant took, she suffered a searing pain. A pin left in the costume had sunk deep into her flesh. It took twenty minutes for the elephant to parade around the arena, and Marilyn smiled and waved to the ecstatic crowd for the full distance. No one was aware of what happened until she dismounted backstage in agony, her costume blotched with blood.

Another pain in the derriere proved to be Walter Winchell. Winchell had discovered that Marilyn was seeing Arthur Miller, and he planted a blind item in his column, "America's best known blonde moving picture star is now the darling of a pro-lefto. . . ."

Marilyn had moved to suite 2728 in the Waldorf Towers, where Arthur Miller became a frequent visitor. Arthur observed, "I would be with Marilyn in her subleased apartment high up in the Waldorf Tower, while below in the streets the *Daily News*, the *World-Telegram* and the *Journal-American*, each running all the pictures of her they could as many times a week as they could get them, were indignantly calling me a subversive, un-American."

In order to avoid discovery by the press, Marilyn and Arthur met in obscure places—bicycling in Coney Island, walking in Battery Park, or spending quiet evenings in Brooklyn at Rosten's poetry readings. Arthur Miller reminisced, "She was a whirling light to me then, all paradox and enticing mystery, street-tough one moment, then lifted by a lyrical and poetic sensitivity that few retain past early adolescence. Sometimes she seemed to see all men as boys—children with immediate needs that it was her place in nature to fulfill. Meanwhile, her adult self stood aside observing the game. . . . She had no common sense, but what she did have was something holier, a long reaching vision of which she herself was only fitfully aware: humans were all need, all wound. What she wanted most was not to judge but to win recognition from a sentimentally cruel profession, and from men blinded to her humanity by her perfect beauty. She was part queen, part waif. . . . For myself it was beyond rationalizing— she was finally all that was true. I was in a swift current, there was no stopping or handhold."

Only Winchell seemed to be on to their romance, and when it was later revealed that J. Edgar Hoover often fed information to Winchell for his column, some suspected that Winchell's source was the FBI chief, who by 1955 had both Arthur Miller and Marilyn Monroe under surveillance. Another friend of Winchell's who was keeping an eye on Marilyn was Joe DiMaggio. He was carrying the torch in dark doorways on the wintry streets of Manhattan. Jimmy Haspiel, who with a half-dozen avid Monroe fans dubbed "The Monroe Six" stood vigil awaiting her appearance, often spotted DiMaggio keeping watch on "Mazzie"—their code name for Marilyn.

"Easily the most curious personage standing out there on street corners and lurking in dimly lit doorways was none other than Monroe's recent ex, Joe DiMaggio himself!" Haspiel remembers. "Yes, on a number of occasions I observed Joe as he secretly watched Marilyn's comings and goings." Marilyn told friends that one night DiMaggio "came into the Waldorf and almost broke the door down. Police had to be called to calm him down. He was very, very jealous."

Marilyn was seeing many different men other than Arthur Miller. She was frequently in the company of Henry Rosenfeld, a wealthy dress manufacturer she had met in New York during the *Love Happy* tour. It was Rosenfeld who arranged for Marilyn to move into the Waldorf Towers, where she was also visited by a frequent date referred to as "Carlo"— Marlon Brando. Freddy Karger was also a suitor. After being divorced for the second time from Jane Wyman, Karger journeyed to New York and made a date with Marilyn at the Waldorf. Proving that timing is everything, she stood him up. Did she imagine Karger looking at the very expensive watch with the date 12/25/48 and wondering where the hell she was? Another visitor was Senator John F. Kennedy, whose father's apartment was conveniently located at the Waldorf. Rumors that Marilyn also visited Jack Kennedy at the Carlyle Hotel are supported by Anthony Summers's interview with Jane Shalam. The windows of Shalam's apartment looked down on the back entrance of the Carlyle, and she stated, "I saw Marilyn coming and going at that time, and she was certainly in and out enough to notice her. Most times people wouldn't know who she was— when she took her makeup off and had her hair back, you wouldn't know it was Marilyn Monroe."

Having made the decision to move away from Hollywood, Marilyn couldn't go forward with another film until her legal position with Fox was resolved. In the meantime her living expenses were high. Milton Greene purchased a new black Thunderbird sports car for Marilyn, in addition to a new wardrobe. Among Marilyn's expenses were: $1,000 a week for the Waldorf apartment, $100 a week for Gladys's care, $125 a week for Marilyn's psychoanalyst, $500 a week for "beautification," $50 a week for perfume, $200 a week for a private secretary, and $300 a week for her press agent.

It was costing over $100,000 a year to maintain Marilyn while Greene renegotiated her Fox contract. Somewhat in limbo, she did public appearances, studied at the Actors Studio, saw a number of Broadway shows, dated a number of men, took a number of pills, and drank too much champagne. Both the president and the vice president of Marilyn Monroe

Productions dabbled in pharmaceuticals. Marilyn's benefactor and vice president, Milton Greene, who had her hooked on the idea of producing her own pictures, was also known to be a pill pusher.

"It was an awful cycle," Amy Greene revealed. "Milton's brother was a doctor, and we had tons of pills—anything we wanted, uppers, downers, it was all available."

Marilyn's habit of taking barbiturates began early in her career when under-the-counter prescriptions at the Schwabadero were readily available and samples were freely handed out by drugstore journalist Sidney Skolsky. In the New York theater world, pharmaceuticals were relied upon to get through the day—up for performances or interviews when one was exhausted, hung over, or depressed; or down when the heart was racing at midnight.

Marilyn once said that she was all superstructure without a foundation, and she confided to Susan Strasberg that every day was an identity crisis. Susan replied that she, too, at times didn't know which person she was and sometimes heard another voice clamoring inside her head. Marilyn remarked, "You have only one voice? I have a whole committee!"

One day a member of the committee recalled that Norman Rosten had suggested a visit to the Rodin exhibit at the Metropolitan Museum of Art. Rosten sensed that Marilyn would have a special appreciation for Rodin, who also had an abstract sense of time (Rodin was always late). Several months after Rosten had suggested that they visit the Metropolitan, his phone rang:

"It's me," said the breathless voice. "I'm ready, C.B., if you are . . ."

"Ready for what? And where? Not to mention with whom?"

"The Rodin. You promised, remember? I'm free this afternoon."

So that afternoon they met at the museum. Norman recalled that she wore one of her disguises—dark glasses, crazy hat, no makeup, and a loose coat to uncurve her. He noted that she was awed by the exhibit of marble figures, which almost seemed to breathe. She found one Rodin particularly fascinating: *The Hand of God*, a dazzling white marble depicting a huge hand curving upward in which a man and woman are entwined in a lyrical and passionate embrace. Rosten remembered Marilyn walking around and around *The Hand of God*. Removing her dark glasses, she stared at it transfixed in wide-eyed fascination. Rosten realized that the entwined couple in *The Hand of God* had a special significance to her, a coded meaning that he hoped in time she would decipher.

A Madness to the Method

Anyone who goes to a psychiatrist ought to have their head examined.
                                                —Sam Goldwyn

Lee Strasberg never directed a distinguished play or gave an extraordinary performance, yet he became one of the leading visionaries of the American theater. His unique gift was in the discernment of talent and the teaching of technique. Strasberg's forebears were Talmudic scholars, and he brought to the theater a patriarch's zeal that transcended knowledge. There was a mystic quality to his burning intensity that superseded theory. The laser cast of his eyes betrayed a penetrating intelligence, a unique ability to see into the heart of a matter—the discernment of temperament, the hidden nuggets of talent or a gift, the truth behind the pretext, the origins of aberration and self-deception, the nature of a psychic wound.

Strasberg became the Dalai Lama of Dream Street, and among those artists starving for enlightenment who made pilgrimages to his walk-up West Side kitchen-temple were Julie Harris, Paul Newman, James Dean, Ben Gazzara, Shelley Winters, Dustin Hoffman, Maureen Stapleton, Al Pacino, Rod Steiger, Patricia Neal, Eli Wallach—and Marilyn Monroe.

Elia Kazan observed, "Actors would humble themselves before his rhetoric and the intensity of his emotion. The more naive and self-doubting the actors, the more total was Lee's power over them. The more famous and the more successful these actors, the headier the taste of power for Lee. He found his perfect victim-devotee in Marilyn Monroe."

Actor Kevin McCarthy recalls hardly noticing Marilyn at the Actors Studio at first as they sat side by side watching a badly acted scene from Chekhov's *Three Sisters*. "This tousled piece of humanity was sitting to my right, and I didn't recognize her. Then as I glanced at her I saw this metamorphosis take place. I looked again and I realized that a breathing, palpitating Marilyn Monroe had transcended out of that nothing. . . . I remember looking and thinking, 'My God, it's her'—she'd just come to life!"

Lee Strasberg, who had never seen a Marilyn Monroe movie, was astonished at the Monroe magic—the "mystic-like flame," the size of the crowds she drew, and the sizable monetary benefits to the Actors Studio. Her appearances at Studio fund-raisers proved to be a financial windfall, and critics accused Strasberg of being an opportunist. Marilyn gave her Thunderbird to Strasberg's son, John, who observed, "The greatest tragedy was that people, even my father in a way, took advantage of her. They glommed onto her special sort of life, her special characteristics, when what she needed was love."

Marilyn's classes were on Tuesdays and Fridays at the Studio, which was then located in the Paramount Theater building on Broadway. There were exercises in "sense memory" in which Marilyn would close her eyes and recapture a childhood experience in all its sensory immediacy. She would try to recall objects and surroundings in detail, as well as the sequence of events that occurred and—most important—the emotional content of the experience. Another exercise would be to sing a song without gestures, so that the emotion and context would be projected solely by voice. When the blond refugee from Hollywood did her first exercise, the blue-jeaned disciples of Stanislavsky were laying in wait. MM was a tinseltown moovie stah. The *sans culottes* of Shubert Alley were of the *Théâtre*.

She was to sing a song.

Most students chose a simple song like "Happy Days Are Here Again" or "Give My Regards to Broadway." Marilyn chose "I'll Get By." She stood limply on the stage, rag-doll arms at her sides, head tilted up in surrender to the muse.

This old world was as sad a place for me
As could be,
I was lonely and blue
Until I met you.
Although wealth and power I may never find
Still as long as I have you, dear, I won't mind.

Though there was a trace of a brave smile, tears began streaming down her face, and the familiar refrain seemed to take on new meaning. . . .

For I'll get by as long as I have you.
Tho there be rain and darkness too,
I'll not complain, I'll laugh it through.
Poverty may come to me that's true.
But what care I?
Say, I'll get by as long as I have you.

Not wiping away the tears, she kept her concentration, singing in surrender to the song—its victim. The most cynical studio observers were swept up in the emotion. Susan Strasberg recalled that when Marilyn finished her song there wasn't a dry, jaundiced eye in the house. Everyone wanted to run onstage and hold her. It was said that Lee Strasberg nudged Paula and said, "I told you she was great—now even I believe it!"

Strasberg maintained that some students couldn't benefit from the Method unless they unblocked emotions dealing with their past through psychoanalysis. He suggested to Marilyn that she open up her unconscious through psychotherapy, and she began visiting Dr. Margaret Herz Hohenberg, who was recommended to her by Milton Greene. Margaret Hohenberg had studied medicine in Vienna and practiced in Prague before fleeing to America in 1939. Milton Greene had been her patient for several years, and in the spring of 1955, Marilyn began commuting several days a week to Hohenberg's office at 155 East Ninety-Third Street.

Not long after the windfall of Marilyn's arrival on the East Coast, the Strasbergs moved from their walk-up on West Eighty-Sixth Street to a spacious apartment at 135 Central Park West, where Marilyn was a frequent guest. Strasberg was an avid reader, and several of the rooms were stacked with books from floor to ceiling. Marilyn referred to the decor as "early Brentano's." The family rented a house on Fire Island for the summer, and Marilyn was often there on weekends, when champagne would bubble on Saturday nights and Marilyn would dance to phonograph records. "She was like a child," Susan Strasberg recalled. "She'd fill the room with her full laughter, sensual movements, and high spirits. My father loved it. He had this smile of pleasure on his face. He got that smile around children and animals. Marilyn made him laugh."

Susan Strasberg, who was only sixteen at the time, remembered many whispered conversations about "Arturo," a married man Marilyn was having a heavy romance with. Marilyn and Paula Strasberg would have long discussions about "Arturo" far into the night. "Arturo" didn't like Lee Strasberg. In 1967 Arthur Miller interrupted Fred Guiles when the subject of Strasberg came up: "Don't talk to me about Lee Strasberg because I can't stand the man!" he exclaimed. "My sister, Joan Copeland, who is an actress, believes Strasberg is a great man.... I think there is something false about him. Lee became a guru to these people and unless he is there, they can't move. I never blasted him to Marilyn because she needed him. I recognized that dependency, and as long as she got something out of it, I never said anything. We just didn't discuss him."

Miller wrote of Marilyn's double-edged vulnerability in an unpublished play in which the character modeled on Marilyn has a purgatorial effect on three dedicated research physicians. The researchers are employed by a wealthy pharmaceuticals maker who inspires them with social idealism, while, in fact, using them for raw capitalistic ambition. "They typified what I then saw as the captive artist-creator," Miller stated. Into their midst comes Lorraine, the mistress of one of the doctors, who Miller admitted was a character modeled on Marilyn:

> With her open sexuality, childlike and sublimely free of ties and expectations in a life she half senses is doomed, she moves instinctively to break the hold of respectability on the men until each in his different way meets the tragedy in which she has unwittingly entangled him—one retreats to a loveless and destructive marriage in fear of losing his social standing; another abandons his family for her, only to be abandoned in turn when her interests change. Like a blind, godlike force, with all its creative cruelty, her sexuality comes to seem the only truthful connection with some ultimate nature, everything that is life-giving and authentic. She flashes a ghastly illumination upon the social routiniation to which they are all tied and which is killing their souls—but she has no security of her own and no faith, and her liberating promise is finally illusionary.

Miller stated that the play remained unfinished because he couldn't accept the nihilistic spiritual catastrophe it persisted in foretelling: "That is, I believed it as a writer but could not confess it as a man. I could not know, of course, that in the coming years, I would live out much of its prophecy myself."

In mid-May thousands watched as a fifty-two-foot-high image of Miller's "godlike force" was lifted into place in Times Square, advertising the opening of *The Seven Year Itch* at the Loew's Broadway; and on June 1, all five feet five and three-quarters inches of the real thing showed up for the premiere on the arm of Joe DiMaggio.

"We're just good friends. We do not plan to remarry. That's all I can say," she told the press. It was Marilyn's twenty-ninth birthday, and after the premiere DiMaggio hosted a party for her at Toots Shor's. She and Joe had a violent argument and Marilyn went home early. "Marilyn was afraid of Joe," said Arthur Jacobs's New York publicist, Lois Weber. "She was physically afraid. He was obviously rigid in his beliefs. There must have been a great ambivalence in his feeling toward her. . . . There were times she made it clear he had hurt her very badly, maybe even struck her in some jealous rage."

The Seven Year Itch was a giant success both for Marilyn and Fox. *Variety* termed *Itch* the hottest ticket seller of the summer. Bosley Crowther of the *New York Times* said, "From the moment she steps into the picture Miss Monroe brings a special personality to the screen." The *New York Daily Mirror* stated, "Marilyn's a fine comedienne. Her pouting delivery, puckered lips—the personification of this decade's glamour—make her one of Hollywood's top attractions."

But Hollywood no longer had its "top attraction," and the giant success of *Itch* had Fox attorneys scratching their heads. Marilyn Monroe was earning a fortune for Fox and they were newly motivated to appease their runaway star. For directing *Itch*, Billy Wilder received half a million dollars plus a share of the profits, and producer Charles Feldman, who was also paid as Marilyn's agent, received $318,000 plus guarantees. Marilyn received $1,500 a week plus a $100,000 bonus, which Fox had failed to pay. During the summer, when Milton Greene and Irving Stein were negotiating a new agreement with Fox, the studio was forced to recognize the inequity of her contract. And in November word rippled through the Fox lot that the studio had agreed to a new nonexclusive contract with Marilyn Monroe Productions.

The "dumb blonde" had won.

The agreement called for Marilyn Monroe to appear in four Fox pictures over the next seven years. She was to receive at least a hundred thousand dollars per picture. In addition, she was given director approval. A Fox executive commented, "There was only one topic of conversation today in the producers' dining room, and that was Marilyn's fantastic deal. I've been in the business a long time, and when I tell you a deal is fantastic, you know I mean *fantastic!*"

The holiday season of 1955 ended happily for Marilyn. Her life seemed to be coming together. She had learned a little bit more about herself; moreover, she had won her war with Fox. Zanuck, in fact, had resigned and was being replaced by Buddy Adler. And in private Marilyn and "Arturo" were talking about marriage. According to Norman Rosten, Marilyn brought about a transformation in Arthur Miller, who had always been a staid, introspective loner. "Miller was in love, completely, seriously in love. It was wonderful to behold."

New Year's Eve was celebrated at the Greenes' home in Connecticut among a small group of Marilyn's friends. Snow was falling, and at midnight a champagne toast was made to the future, which held bright promise. Truman Capote later wrote to a friend, "Saw Marilyn M. and Arthur Miller the other night, both looking suffused with a sexual glow. They plan to get married, but can't help feeling this little episode is called, 'Death of a Playwright.'"

Black Bart and Grushenka

Reporter: They say you want to play *The Brothers Karamazov*.
MM: No, I don't want to play the brothers. I want to play Grushenka.

Fresh from her victory over the Hollywood philistines, President Monroe announced a glittering array of projects for Marilyn Monroe Productions. She would be returning to Fox to star in the Broadway hit *Bus Stop*, to be directed by Joshua Logan. And on February 9, 1956, a press conference was held at the Plaza Hotel, where more than 150 reporters and photographers converged for the joint announcement by Marilyn Monroe and Sir Laurence Olivier of their forthcoming production of *The Prince and the Showgirl*.

Perhaps as a portent of things to come, Olivier, who insisted on top billing, was all but ignored by the clamorous press. When the reporters finally got around to Sir Laurence, he was about to reply to their queries when one of the straps on Marilyn's dress broke. The simultaneous *poff* of dozens of flashbulbs exploded any illusions Sir Laurence may have had as to who was really going to be the star of *The Prince and the Showgirl*. Olivier looked on in astonishment at the frenzied scene in the Terrace Room of the Plaza before retreating to his Rolls limo. As he drove off with the film's writer, Terence Rattigan, Olivier made the comment, "I wonder if I've made a mistake getting involved in this?"

Either thou art most ignorant by age, or thou wert born a fool.
—*A Winter's Tale*, Act II, Scene 1

Shortly before Marilyn was to depart for Hollywood to do *Bus Stop*, word got around that she was going to do a scene from *Anna Christie* at the Actors Studio with Maureen Stapleton. Marilyn was playing the part of Anna, which Garbo had made famous: "Gimme a whiskey, ginger ale on the side—and don't be stingy, baby!"

After weeks of rehearsal Maureen Stapleton recalled that Marilyn called the day before they were to do the scene and said, "Maureen, I don't think we should rehearse tomorrow. I hear somebody is going to do a very interesting scene at the studio tomorrow morning, and I don't want to miss it."

"Marilyn!" Maureen said with alarm, "the important scene is *Anna Christie*. It's *our* scene!"

"Tomorrow's the d-day we . . . we do the scene?" Marilyn exclaimed. "God, I thought it was *next* Friday!"

It was standing room only on Friday, February 17, at the Actors Studio.

"She was so terrified," Susan Strasberg recalled. "I didn't know how she was going to get herself up there. She also knew as many people were there to see her fail as succeed."

Recalling her terror before she went on stage, Marilyn said, "I couldn't see anything before I went on stage. I couldn't remember one line. All I wanted was to lie down and die. I was in these impossible circumstances and I suddenly thought to myself, 'Good, God, what am I doing here?' Then I just had to go out and do it."

The scene was set in a bar, and when Marilyn came onstage many were under the impression she was too afraid and sick and wouldn't be able to do it. Her hands were trembling when she picked up a glass, and she seemed to be exhausted, ill, and in despair. But the audience quickly realized that it was the character—it was Anna's despair, exhaustion, and fear that had seemed so real.

The scene was particularly poignant for Marilyn when Anna talked about the father who'd abused and betrayed her:

It's my old man I got to meet, honest! It's funny, too, I ain't seen him since I was a kid—don't even know what he looks like. . . . And I was thinking maybe, seeing he ain't done a thing for me in my life, he might be willing to stake me to a room and eats till I get rested up. But I ain't expecting much from him. Give you a kick when you're down, that's all men do. . . .

When the scene ended there was silence. Then the studio burst into applause—a rare occurrence. Actress Kim Stanley, who was among the skeptics in the audience, recalled, "We were taught never to clap at the Actors Studio—it was like we were in church—and it was the first time I'd ever heard applause there." Kim Stanley felt some resentment toward Marilyn because it was Cherie, the role Stanley had created in *Bus Stop* on Broadway, that Marilyn would be doing on film in Hollywood—yet she found herself applauding with the others.

According to most of the people present, Marilyn Monroe was astonishing. Actress Anna Sten found her performance "very deep and very lovely, giving and taking at the same time—and that's a very rare quality."

Afterward Marilyn and Maureen Stapleton went to the corner bar for a stiff drink—"and don't be stingy, baby." Stapleton was amazed to discover that Marilyn believed she had been terrible. But the Strasbergs were ecstatic and assured her she had been excellent. In a discussion with Joshua Logan, who was about to direct Marilyn in *Bus Stop*, Strasberg said, "I have worked with hundreds and hundreds of actors and actresses, and there are only two that stand out way above the rest—number one is Marlon Brando, and the second is Marilyn Monroe."

Not long after doing the scene at the Actors Studio, Marilyn returned to Hollywood. It had been over a year since Zelda Zonk took the red-eye out of town. Her dressing room at Fox had remained empty, a dusty reminder of the lot's missing star. Books, scripts, old memos, and call sheets littered the shelves and floor along with cartons of unopened fan mail. In her absence she had been receiving over six thousand fan letters a week. A smiling picture of Joe DiMaggio still stood on the dressing table. With the news of her impending arrival, the dressing room was cleaned and painted, and all the old debris was removed, as the studio awaited the appearance of the new Marilyn Monroe.

But it was the same old Marilyn Monroe who arrived at the airport and kept thousands of fans and hundreds of photographers waiting for her to emerge from the airplane. When she finally appeared, looking very New Yorkish in a smart black cocktail dress and gloves, she was greeted by a tumultuous reception. The ovation she received from the thousands who came to greet her was tremendous—a triumph. "Hollywood turned out to meet her as few women have been met," *Time* reported. Reporters bombarded her with questions about her new production company and plans. One reporter queried, "When you left here last year you were dressed quite differently, Marilyn. Now you have a black dress and a high-necked blouse. Is this the new Marilyn?"

"No," she replied. "I'm the same person—it's just a new dress."

It took her two hours to get through the crowds at the airport and off to the house the Greenes had rented in Holmby Hills at 595 North Beverly Glen Boulevard.

Learning of her whereabouts from the studio, Natasha Lytess tried to reach Marilyn by telephone, but her calls were refused. Many of Lytess's letters to Marilyn when she left Hollywood had gone unanswered. Though it had been made clear to Lytess that things would be different for her when Marilyn moved to New York, she was able to keep her job at Fox during Marilyn's absence. But when Marilyn returned Lytess unexpectedly received a dismissal notice from the studio. She desperately tried to contact Marilyn, and after dozens of phone calls and notes went unanswered, Lytess drove to the Beverly Glen address and was turned away. She was bitterly disappointed. On March 3 she received a telephone call from attorney Irving Stein, and in a legal memorandum of the call Stein stated:

I identified myself as Marilyn Monroe's lawyer and instructed her firmly not to call Marilyn Monroe or visit or attempt to see Marilyn Monroe. These instructions must be obeyed to avoid trouble. Natasha, whom I'd never met, called me "Darling" and asked if I'd listen. The following are exact quotes:

"My only protection in the world is Marilyn Monroe. I created this girl—I fought for her—I was always the heavy on the set. I was frantic when I called the house and she would not speak to me. I am her private property, she knows that. Her faith and security are mine. I'm not financially protected, but she is. Twentieth told me on Friday, 'You don't have your protection any more, we don't need you.' . . . But my job means my life. I'm not a well person. I would like very much to see her even with you if only for one half-hour." I told her no. Marilyn wouldn't and didn't intercede and we didn't want to speak to or see her. I told her she must not call Marilyn or I would have to use other means to stop her.

But the oracle who had divined the goddess couldn't believe that Marilyn would refuse to help her. Lytess again appeared at the Beverly Glen house on March 5. Agent Lew Wasserman answered the door and barred her from entering. "Your engagement at the studio is none of Miss Monroe's concern," he stated, and threatened to obtain a restraining order if she returned or attempted to contact Marilyn again. As she was leaving, Lytess glanced up and saw Marilyn watching her impassively from a second-story window. "It was the last time I ever saw her," she recalled. "In Marilyn's powerful position she had only to crook her finger for me to keep my job at the studio. Had she any sense of gratitude for my contribution to her life, she could have saved my job."

That Marilyn Monroe could have ignored "so humble a plea" has often been cited as an incident exemplifying her ruthless use of people before discarding them. But Marilyn was fiercely loyal to those few who were loyal to her. However, she couldn't abide disloyalty, and once trust was broken she was quick to sever the relationship. Marilyn had learned through Arthur Miller's friend Maurice Zolotow that Natasha Lytess was writing a Marilyn Monroe exposé.

When Zolotow began his Monroe biography, he interviewed Marilyn on three occasions at the Waldorf Towers. Zolotow's researcher on the Monroe book was Jane Wilkie, a writer with *Photoplay*. After Marilyn left Hollywood, Jane Wilkie began working with Natasha Lytess on an exposé of Marilyn that was originally intended for *Photoplay* and later planned as a book. Never completed, the unpublished manuscript remains in the Zolotow Collection at the University of Texas. When Marilyn learned from Zolotow what Natasha was doing, it ended their friendship.

After her dismissal from Fox, Lytess tried to survive on income from students she coached at her home. But she was unable to meet the mortgage payments for the house on Rexford Drive that Marilyn had helped her purchase, and it was lost in foreclosure. Robert Slatzer recalls Marilyn showing him a letter from Lytess that arrived from Rome in April of 1962. "She was begging for money and Marilyn said, 'Natasha always writes me when she's broke.'"

The new Marilyn had hoped that Lee Strasberg would accompany her to Hollywood and coach her through *Bus Stop*, but it was impossible for him to leave his students, and he suggested that Paula go in his stead. Though Greene complained and Fox fumed, Marilyn insisted that Paula Strasberg be put on the payroll at $1,500 a week—the salary Marilyn earned on *The Seven Year Itch* as its star.

Bus Stop is the poignant story of Cherie, a second-rate cabaret singer from the Ozarks. After a series of disappointing love affairs, Cherie meets a rodeo cowboy (Don Murray) who has come to the big city (Phoenix) in pursuit of an angelic wife to take home to his ranch. He chooses Cherie. She resists but ultimately is charmed by the cowboy's bumbling devotion.

As the start date for *Bus Stop* approached, Marilyn worked long hours with Paula, going through the script scene by scene. She immersed herself in the character of Cherie, drawing on sense memory and emotional recall, analyzing dialogue and motivation, thinking out body language and gesture. She studied Cherie's Ozarks drawl, and once she was into it seldom departed from Cherie's dialect in her daily conversations until production ended. Strasberg urged his students to sum up a character's central motivation in one key sentence: the key sentence Marilyn chose for Cherie was "Will this girl who wants respect ever get it?"

Marilyn felt that the dominant characteristic of the character's appearance lay in her weariness. Seldom out in the sunlight because she works in bars until 4 A.M., Cherie wouldn't get much sleep or sunshine, and Marilyn and Milton Greene conceived a chalky white makeup that startled the front-office staff when they saw the makeup tests. If they were going to pay her more, shouldn't she look better?

"To me Marilyn's attitude toward her makeup and costuming was courageous," Joshua Logan stated. "It was incredible, really. Here you have a well-established star and she was willing to risk her position with a makeup many stars would consider ugly. She wasn't afraid. She believed she was right in her analysis of the character, and she had the courage to commit herself to it completely."

Logan recalled that Marilyn also plotted out Cherie's costuming. She liked William Travilla's design for the long gown she was to wear during her ballad number in a Phoenix bar, but to Travilla's dismay she began yanking off spangles and tore the gown in several places. She then had the tears crudely sewn up with mismatched thread. Recalling her own days when she only had one pair of stockings, she had the net stockings worn during "That Old Black Magic" number ripped and then poorly darned back together.

"Let's not have my clothes made to order," she told Logan. "Let's find them in wardrobe." She and Logan rummaged through clothing racks and picked out the tawdry dresses and cheap clothes that a second-rate cabaret singer would wear.

Logan, who was a good friend of Lee Strasberg and the only prominent American director who had actually studied with Stanislavsky in Moscow, agreed to allow Paula Strasberg to coach Marilyn—with the understanding that Strasberg not appear on the set. But in the first week of shooting on the stage at Fox, Logan's proviso was ignored. Despite the director's instructions, Paula lurked in the shadows behind the camera. She wore black, hoping to be less noticeable, but her witchlike outfits only served to attract attention, and it was on the set of *Bus Stop* that Marilyn gave Paula the nickname that was to stay with her: "Black Bart."

The Fox gossip centers crackled with Black Bart and Grushenka stories, and La Monroe became the favorite conversation hors d'oeuvre at Hollywood cocktail parties. It was said that the Fox star had changed and was throwing her newfound power around. Now that she was queen of the lot, it seemed that her attitude toward all the "little people" on the set had changed. She was showing her true colors. No longer friendly with the grips and electricians and the crew who waited endlessly for her to get ready, she was said to treat coworkers with an air of disdain. The new Monroe was "cold and rude."

But the new Monroe was fighting off the demons of "indicating"—that fatal actor's flaw of performing rather than *being*. It took extraordinary concentration. While Paula was supportive, she also forced Marilyn to reach for concepts in her portrayal that seemed beyond her experience. Only with determination and a focused will could she dance on the high wire and never fall despite the emotional strain and exhaustion it entailed.

The trick, of course, was concentration—a transference by immersion into character, and she was often so into her character and prepped for the moment when the director said "Action" that all else around her was oblivion. Conversation was distraction. To those on the set who had known the old Marilyn, she seemed "cold and aloof." But the truth was that Cherie didn't know they were there.

Billy Wilder had said that Marilyn was one of the few stars who possessed "flesh impact," that there was an immediacy to her image on the screen that made the audience look at Marilyn no matter who she was playing a scene with—whether it be Tom Ewell, Jane Russell, Cary Grant, dogs, babies, or the Marx Brothers. It was Marilyn who commanded the frame. But it wasn't just "flesh impact," it was "body and soul impact." It was the totality of her being that projected its curious immediacy.

This magic trick of transference, however, went beyond will and concentration. Her performance was drawn intuitively from the well of her
secret depths. It has often been said that her concentration was poor, that
she frequently forgot her lines or missed her marks. Her concentration
was, in fact, extraordinary, but born in the realm of intuition and emotion
rather than deliberation. Paula was often mystified that Marilyn would
forget her lines during a take, when Paula knew she had known the lines
cold for days. Actors would fulminate in their dressing rooms that she
hadn't arrived prepared. But it wasn't the lines she forgot—it was the
character. She'd lose touch with Cherie, and just stop. The immersion
had to be total to get through a take, and with each take she got closer
to Cherie. In *Bus Stop* she *was* Cherie.

Joshua Logan said, "Marilyn is as near a genius as any actress I ever
knew. She is an artist beyond artistry. . . . From the start, she visualized
playing Cherie in a tender area that lies between comedy and tragedy.
This is the most difficult thing for an actor to do well. Very few motion
picture stars can do it. Chaplin achieved it. Garbo, too, at times, in *Cam-
ille* and *Ninotchka*. And you know, I believe Marilyn has something of
each of them in her. She is the most completely realized and authentic
film actress since Garbo. Monroe is pure cinema."

It had been a bumpy ten-year ride from blond Betty's "Hi, Rad!" in
front of the church in Paducah to Cherie's memorable soliloquy on the
bus to Phoenix:

I've been goin' with boys since I was twelve—them Ozarks don't waste much
time—and I've been losin' my head about some guy ever since. . . . Of course I'd
like to get married and have a family and all them things. . . . Maybe I don't
know what love is. I want a guy I can look up to and admire. But I don't want
him to browbeat me. I want a guy who'll be sweet with me. But I don't want
him to baby me, either. I just gotta feel that whoever I marry has some real
regard for me—aside from all that lovin' stuff. You know what I mean?

Tempus Fugit

One should make haste slowly.
—Marilyn Monroe

According to Arthur Miller, there came a juncture when Marilyn became interested in time as a concept—or perhaps a curiosity. She began wearing a watch as a locket around her neck as well as two wristwatches—one set for West Coast time, the other for New York time. But this was like collecting encyclopedias in the hope that their voluminous presence would impart knowledge: the watches didn't improve her ability to cope with time. On March 12, she missed the plane by twenty minutes when the *Bus Stop* company flew from Los Angeles to Phoenix, Arizona, where the annual rodeo was to be held on March 15. She did manage to arrive on time, however, for Logan to shoot the location sequences amid the crowd of twenty-five thousand people who attended the street parade and rodeo.

As a rule it is more difficult for actors to work on location than in the studio, but directors found that Marilyn worked better al fresco. Like a flower, she did better in the sunshine and fresh air than in the artificial light of Hollywood's soundstage hothouses. In the sunshine her energy and concentration were always up. She'd usually appear on the set on time and things went smoothly. Logan could get his print on the first or second take when she was working in the sunlight.

The press was kept at bay during the filming of *Bus Stop*, and few interviews or photos were allowed. Only Milton Greene seemed to have free access to Marilyn with a camera. When she accidentally fell from a rodeo-stadium ramp, Milton Greene, who was standing nearby with his Rollie, took pictures of her writhing in pain on the ground rather than rushing to her aid. When Logan asked why he hadn't helped her, Greene said, "Look, I was a photographer before I was a producer!"

Billy Woodfield, who was then a photographer for *This Week* magazine, recalled that Greene wouldn't let him get near Marilyn. He commented, "During the rodeo location it got so bad that we were all hiding out and taking pictures with telephoto lenses from under the stadium stands. I got some pictures of Marilyn throwing up under the bleachers. I had the pictures printed, set them down in front of Milton Greene, and said, 'This is what we have to go with unless you let us take some pictures!' Finally he broke loose, and I got my shots."

Arthur Jacobs's Beverly Hills office was handling the publicity for Marilyn Monroe Productions, and while Rupert Allan was Marilyn's personal publicist, Pat Newcomb was sent along with other members of the Jacobs staff to Phoenix. Only twenty-five years old at the time, the spin doctor was merely an intern in the practice she would soon master. Margaret Patricia Newcomb was born and raised in the shadow of the Capitol, and her grandfather had been a prominent Washington judge. Her father, Carmen Adams Newcomb, was a lobbyist for the coal industry, which included the Great Lakes Coal and Coke Corporation, owned by Ethel Kennedy's father, George Skakel, Jr.

After living in Chevy Chase, Maryland, Pat Newcomb moved with her family to Los Angeles in 1946, when her father became West Coast representative of the extensive Skakel family real estate holdings in Southern California. Pat attended Immaculate Heart High School in Hollywood, and in 1948 she enrolled at Mills College, an exclusive girls' school in Oakland, where she took a liberal-arts course, majoring in psychology.

One of Pat Newcomb's lecturers at Mills College was Pierre Salinger, who would later become President John Kennedy's press secretary. In the early fifties Salinger was an investigative journalist for the *San Francisco Chronicle*. When Newcomb graduated from Mills in 1952, she became a researcher for her mentor, Salinger, who was writing a series of articles on corruption within the Teamsters Union. Three months were spent researching the articles, first at Dave Beck's union headquarters in Seattle, and then in Detroit, where Jimmy Hoffa ran the affairs of the Central

States Conference of Teamsters. Salinger uncovered incidents of corruption and brutality and found that Beck was lining his pockets with union funds, while Hoffa was recruiting ex-convicts and racketeers to enforce his policies.

When Salinger learned that Arkansas Democratic Senator John L. McClellan was preparing to convene a Select Committee on Improper Activities in the Labor and Management Field, it was through Pat Newcomb and her father, Carmen, that an appointment was made for Salinger to meet the chief counsel for the committee—Ethel Skakel's husband, Robert F. Kennedy, the younger brother of Senator John F. Kennedy, who also served on the committee.

"I shall never forget my first meeting with Bob," Pierre Salinger stated. "It was a two-hour lunch in the Senate dining room. Although I was there as a reporter to interview him, I spent most of the time answering his questions on Beck and Hoffa. . . . Bob and I hit it off from the very beginning."

In 1956 Pierre Salinger was asked by Bobby to become an investigator for the McClellan Committee, and in November they set up shop in Los Angeles while investigating Teamster activities on the West Coast. In *The Enemy Within*, Bobby Kennedy wrote, "We arrived in Los Angeles on November 14, 1956, and got in touch with Captain James Hamilton of the Intelligence Division of the Police Department. We interviewed union officials, employers and employees and several confidential informants."

According to former Los Angeles police chief Daryl Gates, "At the invitation of Chief William Parker, Bobby Kennedy set up his offices in the LAPD Intelligence Division. Their desks were next to Captain James Hamilton's. Bobby Kennedy and Hamilton became close friends, and Bobby often relied upon Hamilton for information and guidance during the Select Committee investigations." Two of Hamilton's most trusted officers, the detectives Archie Case and James Ahearn, were assigned to assist Bobby in the investigations.

Pat Newcomb decided that show business was her field, and it was through an intimate friend that she joined Arthur Jacobs Public Relations. However, her first assignment, on *Bus Stop*, proved to be short-lived. On the location in Phoenix she had a conflict with Marilyn Monroe, and Arthur Jacobs told her to return to Los Angeles. When questioned by Anthony Summers about the conflict with Marilyn, Newcomb stated,

"We had this terrible falling out almost immediately. I didn't know why for years, but it turned out to be over some guy that Marilyn thought I liked, someone I didn't have any interest in at all. I didn't know how to cope with it, and Arthur Jacobs told me I'd better get out of there at once."

The truth was that Marilyn had heard rumors that the spin doctor was a lesbian and having an affair with another woman connected with Arthur Jacobs. According to Rupert Allan, who had been in Phoenix when Newcomb's proclivities were called to Marilyn's attention, she telephoned Arthur Jacobs and requested that Newcomb be taken off *Bus Stop*. The moral climate was quite different in the fifties, and Allan observed that Marilyn didn't want a situation that could indirectly involve her in scandal. Several years after *Bus Stop*, Newcomb would become Marilyn's publicist and one of the last people to see Marilyn on the day she died—a day on which they were to have another "terrible falling out."

When the *Bus Stop* company returned to Los Angeles, Marilyn moved from the Beverly Glen house to the Chateau Marmont on the Strip, where she stayed in the former Jean Harlow suite. Manager Corrinne Patten recalled that Arthur Miller was a frequent weekend visitor: "His weekend visits to the Marmont were *very* hush-hush. He was supposed to be in residence in Reno, obtaining his divorce. Instead, he was sneaking away to be with Miss Monroe."

In March of 1956, Arthur Miller had traveled to Reno to establish a six-week residency for his divorce. He stayed in a small motel cottage at Pyramid Lake, fifty miles northeast of Reno. While waiting for his divorce he frequently visited the Stix house, which was in nearby Quail Canyon. The Stix house had been rented to an attractive divorcée who had befriended two cowboys. They were itinerants who made their living by searching the surrounding mountains for wild mustangs and selling them for dog food. Both were confirmed bachelors and heavy drinkers and fancied themselves lady-killers. Miller became intrigued with these two Wild West throwbacks to a vanishing frontier, and they would evolve into the central characters of *The Misfits*.

"Once a week I would fly into Los Angeles, a technical illegality, since my period of residency in Nevada had to be unbroken," Miller remembered. "Marilyn's coach, Lee Strasberg's wife, Paula, had the next room in the Chateau Marmont and was acting as Lee's proxy, with daily phone calls to him in New York on Marilyn's problems."

Amy Greene recalled that Joshua Logan began dreading Mondays at the studio, knowing that Marilyn would have difficulty getting back in touch with Cherie after a weekend with Arthur. "She was a wreck after those weekends," Amy Greene reflected. "She couldn't bring Arthur to see us, he couldn't leave the hotel, and then suddenly on Sunday night or Monday morning, he skipped back to Nevada. This left her confused, guilty, lonely—and all that brought on a cycle of pills and sickness."

Marilyn didn't get along well with her leading man, Don Murray, who was appearing in his first film. But Marilyn's problem with Don Murray was on a professional level, not a personal one. An accomplished stage actor, Murray was a bright, well-educated, cultured young man, whom Logan had spotted on Broadway in the ANTA revival of *The Skin of Our Teeth*. In *Bus Stop* Murray had trouble in reaching for Bo's crude behavior toward Cherie. His gentle approach worked against the animalistic sexual tension between Cherie and Bo—so essential to the thin story.

Logan often sided with Murray in his less aggressive concept of the character, and Marilyn found herself alone in her struggle to uncivilize Murray while Cherie was trying to civilize Bo. Don Murray, who never topped his performance in *Bus Stop*, apparently was totally oblivious of what Marilyn managed to accomplish.

"Like a child, she said and did things impulsively from a self-centered viewpoint," according to Murray. "When she thought I'd ruined a scene of hers, she continued the action as rehearsed, taking her costume and hitting me across the face with it. Some of the sequins scratched the corner of my eye and she ran off. But she wasn't deliberately mean."

The scene Murray was referring to was the first encounter in the Blue Dragon Café, when Cherie tries to escape Bo's advances and runs off the cabaret floor. Bo clutches at her costume and rips off the sequined train. Cherie grabs it back, angrily saying, "Give me back my tail," and hits Bo across the face with it.

Cherie's spunky anger and the blow across the face are totally unexpected, and this shows in Bo's reaction. The scene proved to be essential in establishing the undercurrent of their relationship, but Murray hadn't wanted to play the scene that way. He felt that Bo should be playful, rather than "vulgar and aggressive." He wanted to toy with the tail of her costume and have it come off accidentally rather than yank it off—and Logan was going along with him. Murray was so upset that Marilyn had struck him so hard with the tail that he went to Logan and said that he refused to work with her any longer unless she apologized. Logan took up the matter with Marilyn, who agreed to offer her apologies, but when the moment came and the two were face to face at the end of the day, Marilyn burst into tears and said, "Damn it, damn it—I won't apologize to you, no, *no!*"

Cherie had her way, and that's what ended up on the screen—but Marilyn paid the price.

After the incident on the set with Murray, Arthur Miller was awakened in the middle of the night by his motel manager, who told him he was wanted on the phone. It was near midnight when Miller put on his robe and ventured forth to the phone booth outside the motel office. It was Marilyn. "Her voice, always light and breathy, was barely audible," Miller recalled:

> "I can't do it, I can't work this way. Oh, Papa, I can't do it!" she said in the shorthand of breathless hysteria. ". . . says I did the scene with vulgarity . . . can't stand women—none of them can. They're afraid of women, the whole gang of them. . . . Vulgar! *Vulgar!* Supposed to rip off my tail—this thing I have sticking out of my costume in the back. . . . But angrily, so it makes a mockery of me so I can *react*, instead of just lifting it away. I didn't even know he'd done it. So I said, 'Rip it off! Be rough with me so I can make it real when I react.' But they're afraid to act nasty because the audience might not approve—you see what I mean? I'm no trained actor, I can't pretend I'm doing something if I'm not. All I know is real! I can't do it if it's not real. And he calls me vulgar because I said that! Hates me! Hates me! Oh, Papa, I can't do it anymore! I can't make it!"

Miller had never heard her so unguardedly desperate before, and he tried to calm and reassure her.

"Oh, Papa, I can't fight them alone. I don't want this!" she sobbed. "I hate it! I want to live quietly in the country and just be there when you need me, and be a good wife. I can't fight for myself anymore."

She had never revealed this dependency before, and Miller recalled feeling the rush of trust she was expressing in him and their future together: "I suddenly saw that I was all she had, and then I realized that I was out of breath, a dizziness was screwing into my head, my knees unlocked, and I felt myself sliding to the floor of the phone booth, the receiver slipping out of my hand. I came to in what was probably a few seconds, her voice still whispering out of the receiver over my head. After a moment I got up and talked her down to earth, and it was over: she would try not to let it get to her tomorrow, just do the job and get on with it. Lights were still revolving behind my eyes. We would marry and start a new and real life once this picture was done."

Mazel Tov!

When you're in love, the whole world is Jewish.
—Paula Strasberg

Marilyn once remarked that she had appeared on calendars "but never on *Time*," In May 1956, however, she made the cover of *Time* magazine. A lengthy cover story by Ezra Goodman hinted at her romance with Arthur Miller.

With *Bus Stop* completed, she returned to her Sutton Place South apartment in New York, where she was besieged by reporters seeking confirmation of the romance rumors. Marilyn declined to comment. Miller's divorce was granted on June 11, and the next day he returned to the East Coast, where he found the press camping on Marilyn's doorstep—along with a representative of the House Un-American Activities Committee, who handed him a subpoena. He was to appear before the committee in Washington on June 21.

Miller wasn't surprised at being called before HUAC. So many of his friends and associates had already been subpoenaed—Elia Kazan, Lee J. Cobb, Clifford Odets, Lillian Hellman, Dashiell Hammett, Hannah Weinstein. But the timing was bad. Arthur and Marilyn were planning on going to London for the production of *The Prince and the Showgirl*, and he needed a passport.

The evening before Miller was to leave for Washington for the HUAC hearing, Spyros Skouras, the Greek immigrant who had become president of 20th Century-Fox, paid a surprise visit to Arthur and Marilyn in an attempt to encourage Miller to cooperate with the committee as Kazan, Odets, and Lee J. Cobb had done. If the rumors that Fox's top star was going to marry a "pro-lefto" were true, Skouras's concern was that patriotic organizations would boycott Marilyn Monroe movies. Miller described the meeting:

> When I opened our apartment door to let Skouras in, I saw that he was tired, a weary old man in a dinner jacket. . . . Marilyn immediately came into the foyer, and they embraced, almost tearfully on his part. . . . "Won'erful, won'erful," he kept repeating with eyes closed, his nose in her hair. . . . Her nearness could make old men actually tremble, and in this was more security for her than in a vault full of money or a theater echoing with applause. Holding her hand to his lips, Skouras took her to the couch and sat beside her.
>
> "Hones'-to-Gah dahling, I worry about you personally. I can't help what some of those people out there doin' to you these years. I'm not *Twentieth*, I'm only the president. I speakin' to you from my heart, Mahlin, dahlin'."
>
> Out of the blue, he took Marilyn's hand, and with an envelopment of privacy between them asked, "You in love, Switthar'?"
>
> She nodded that she was.
>
> "Gah-bless you—won'erful!" he said, patting her hand with fatherly benediction . . . turning to me he said, "Gah-bless you Artr—won'erful. I know you fine man, you goin' take good care this girl. She's like my own daughter, hones'-to-Gah!"
>
> Now that he had to believe we were not merely shacking up, the Company was inevitably and menacingly involved. With two pictures still owing them before she was totally free, her marrying at all was bad enough for her image of sexy availability, but to marry me in my situation was disaster. He sighed, "Artr, I hopin' very much you not goin' to make some terrible mistake with the Committee."
>
> He came wide awake now, watching for my reaction. 'I know these congressmen very well, Artr, we are good friends. They are not bad men, they can be reasonable. I believe personally, Artr, that in your case they would take you privately in executive session, you understand? No necessity to be in the public at all. I can arrange this if you tell me?"

In the subtext of the times, Skouras meant that in exchange for "clearing" himself by naming names and cooperating with the committee, Miller would be questioned *in camera* instead of in open hearings, which would be widely reported by the press. Miller was tempted, but the committee members didn't want to hear him *in camera*. They wanted to question him in open hearings.

When Miller was called he was represented by attorney Joseph Rauh, who had also represented Lillian Hellman. Miller's appearance before the committee was on June 21, 1956, in the Caucus Room of the Old House Office Building. Miller's clash with the committee came when he refused time and again to name others he had met at communist gatherings. "I could not use the name of another person and bring trouble on him," he stated to his interrogators. "These are writers, poets, as far as I could see, and the life of a writer, despite what it sometimes seems, is pretty tough. I wouldn't make it any tougher on anybody. I ask you not to ask me that question."

Miller's words had an effect on all who listened. Even the committee was taken aback by the sense of honor revealed; however, according to one source, the words were Marilyn's. In 1961, Marilyn related to Danny Greenson, the son of psychiatrist Ralph Greenson, that Arthur Miller had been afraid. He had seen the careers of many writers destroyed by the committee. Miller had been very tempted to name names. It was Marilyn who told him he mustn't make any writer's or poet's life tougher than it already was. Marilyn revealed to Danny that she had told Miller, "You can't let those bastards push you around. You've got to stand up to them." When she related this in 1961 it was of great interest to Danny, because at the time he was a student at the University of California at Berkeley, and as a political leftist and a member of SLATE* he had been demonstrating against the Un-American Activities Committee. Danny Greenson later commented, "She really was unsophisticated politically, but her instincts were always with the underdog and—to me—on the side of right. There was more to Marilyn than met the eye."

Marilyn was suspicious of any doctrinaire political theories, and her sentiments, which were drawn from her own experience, were with the downtrodden and people in emotional and material need. Though she disagreed with Stalinism or any form of tyranny, she respected the individual's right to embrace what he or she believed in.

At the hearings, Marilyn stood by the man she loved, and in doing so played one of her better roles. She wisely played the role of the loving

* SLATE was identified by the California Senate Fact Finding Committee as a Communist front organization. It was SLATE that organized the violent demonstrations against the House Committee on Un-American Activities in San Francisco in May 1960.

ingenue waif and engendered sympathy for Miller. When asked by reporters about Miller's testimony, she smiled sweetly and replied, "I don't know much about politics. I'll have to have a good talk with him, and I think he's very tired." However, Marilyn's New York maid Lena Pepitone later revealed that when Marilyn was mad at Arthur, she would refer to him as "that damned communist!"

While Arthur Miller was before the committee being interrogated about his leftist leanings, he made a rather left-handed proposal of marriage. Asked by an interrogator why he wanted a passport to go to England, Miller replied, "The objective is double. I have a production which is in the talking stage in England, and I will be there with the woman who will then be my wife." Besieged by reporters as he left the hearing, he announced that he would marry Marilyn Monroe "very shortly." Soon afterward, Norman Rosten received a hysterical call from Marilyn, "Have you heard?" she gasped. "He told the whole world he was marrying Marilyn Monroe—me! Can you believe it? You know he never really asked me! I mean *really* asked *me* to marry *him*! We talked about it, but it was all very vague."

The committee voted to give Miller ten days to present it with names of communists he had known within the front organizations he had joined. On June 25, 1956, he was cited for contempt for noncompliance. A contempt conviction meant a thousand-dollar fine and one year in jail. Almost all the similarly cited witnesses—such as Dashiell Hammett, Ring Lardner, Jr., and Howard Fast—had been convicted and went to prison. Miller's attorney, Joseph Rauh, filed an appeal, however, and not only was Miller not jailed, but he was quickly granted a passport, while the passports for Paul Robeson and other witnesses were denied. The leniency Miller received was unprecedented.

Many believed that the benevolence on the part of the Passport Office could be attributed to concern over the bad press it would receive as a naysayer to Miller's romance with America's favorite ingenue waif. However, the Passport Office had indeed decided to deny Miller's passport. Someone within the State Department subsequently ordered its issuance. It was rumored in Washington that Senator John Kennedy and Kennedy family friend Averell Harriman had intervened.

When Arthur introduced Marilyn to his parents in their Flatbush apartment, he stated, "This is the girl I want to marry." Marilyn embraced her new surrogate parents, Isadore and Augusta Miller, and they all wept with happiness. Mrs. Miller said, "She opened her whole heart to me and Marilyn was like my own daughter." Marilyn felt a particular fondness toward Arthur's father, Isadore, a retiring man of gentle disposition. She knew he had lost everything during the Great Depression and had never recovered emotionally or economically. Marilyn was to remain close to and supportive of Isadore Miller for the remainder of her life.

Marilyn asked Arthur's mother, Augusta, to teach her how to cook the Jewish dishes that Arthur enjoyed. Perhaps knowing that Augusta Miller had been unhappy because Arthur's first wife was not Jewish, Marilyn announced that she was going to enter the Jewish faith, and she studied with Rabbi Robert Goldberg, who later performed the wedding ceremony. Her conversion to Judaism took Arthur by surprise. He had long ago abandoned the tenets of Judaism when he embraced Marxism. When Susan Strasberg asked Marilyn why she wanted to become Jewish, Marilyn replied, "I believe in everything a little, and if I have kids, I think they should be Jewish. Anyway, I can identify with the Jews. Everybody's always out to get them, no matter what they do."

Susan Strasberg recalled that Marilyn began injecting Jewish expressions in her conversations: "Hi, bubuleh! Oy vay! Wotta shlep!—It's all bashert!" And she was constantly making chicken soup with matzo balls (an apocryphal joke at the time had her asking Arthur what they did with the rest of the poor matzo).

Public interest in the couple and their betrothal received more press coverage than anything since King Edward VIII abdicated to marry Wallis Simpson. As stalwart reporters stood vigil outside Marilyn's Sutton Place South apartment waiting for confirmation of the wedding plans, the door opened and the announcement came from an unexpected source: An air-conditioner repairman had overheard Marilyn talking about the wedding on the telephone. Emerging from the apartment he announced to the anxious crowd, "I heard her say she was going to marry Miller!" To escape the growing camp of reporters on their doorstep, Miller and his betrothed fled to his Connecticut farm. The press followed en masse, and Marilyn's enraged fiancé promised to hold a press conference on June 29 if the reporters would leave them in peace until then.

On Friday, June 29, scores of automobiles lined the roads leading to the intersection of Old Tophet and Goldmine Road, where the Miller farm was located. More than four hundred reporters and photographers from all over the world wandered about the property, looking through windows, knocking on doors, hoping that Monroe and Miller would appear. There was no food, no coffee, no sanitary facilities. There were rumors and gossip: *They're already married . . . No, they're in the house . . . They're getting married in London . . . They're in New York—the wedding's off . . . No, it's tomorrow . . .*

Suddenly a green Oldsmobile sped into the driveway to the farm and stopped on the hill. Arthur Miller and Marilyn jumped out from the backseat and ran for the house. The man at the wheel, Miller's cousin Morton, cried hysterically, "There's been an accident! It's bad! This car was following us, there's a turn in the road. We heard a crash behind us. Oh, God, there was a photographer and a woman—their car hit a tree. She was thrown through the windshield. She's bleeding—all cut up! We tried to do what we could. Marilyn's all upset. Arthur's calling the hospital now!"

Correspondent Myra Sherbatoff of *Paris-Match* died before she got to the hospital. Marilyn was horrified and had to be reassured by Lee and Paula Strasberg that it hadn't been her fault. But privately Paula said to Lee and Susan, "This is an ill omen. It's all bashert!"

While she was trying to comfort the dying woman, Marilyn's sweater had become stained with blood. As she changed and tried to recover from the catastrophe, the reporters swarmed to the scene of the accident, took their grisly photos, and returned to the farm—waiting, smoking, gossiping. The heat was relentless. A photographer fell from a tree.

Marilyn and Miller emerged from the house with his parents and Milton Greene. Greene took command—twenty minutes for newsreels, twenty minutes for stills, thirty minutes for interviews. Miller looked like a man in shock. Marilyn tried to appear serene.

"Stand a little closer! . . . *click* . . . Please smile, Mr. Miller! . . . *click* . . . Would you put your arm around him, please? . . . *click* . . . Smile, Mr. Miller! . . . Look this way . . . *click* . . . Please smile, Mr. Miller—*big* smile now . . . *click* . . . This way now! . . . *click, click, click* . . .

That night there was a double-ring civil ceremony in White Plains, conducted by a municipal judge. Arthur gave Marilyn a ring engraved with the ambiguous sentiment "Today Is Forever."

On Sunday, July 1, the nuptials were to be performed by Rabbi Goldberg at the nearby home of Arthur's literary agent, Kay Brown, in Katonah, New York. Away from the press, twenty-five friends and relatives gathered for the traditional Jewish wedding ceremony. But while the jubilant guests arrived downstairs, Marilyn was in the upstairs guest room having second thoughts.

According to Amy Greene, Marilyn decided she had made a mistake and didn't want to go through with the ceremony. "Marilyn was in a terrible state," Amy Greene recalled, and she and Milton tried to comfort her.

"You don't have to go through with this marriage, you know," Milton Greene said to Marilyn.

"No, I don't want to go through with it," Marilyn said, her eyes filled with tears.

"We can put you in a car and we'll deal with the guests," Greene suggested, and he telephoned attorney Irving Stein, asking him "to stand by in case of immediate difficulty about Marilyn's marriage."

The last-minute change of mind was dramatized in the wedding scene of Miller's 1964 play *After the Fall*, in which it is apparent that the character of Maggie is based on Marilyn and Quentin is based on Miller:

On the second platform Maggie appears in a wedding dress. Carrie, a colored maid, is just placing a veiled hat on her head . . .

Quentin enters.

QUENTIN: Oh, my darling. How perfect you are.

MAGGIE: Like me?

QUENTIN: Good God!—To come home every night—to you!

(He starts for her open-armed, laughing, but she touches his chest, excited, and strangely fearful.)

MAGGIE: You still don't have to do it, Quentin. I could just come to you whenever you want.

QUENTIN: You just can't believe in something good really happening. But it's real, darling. You're my wife!

MAGGIE: *(With a hush of fear in her voice.)* I want to tell you why I went into analysis.

QUENTIN: Darling, you're always making new revelations, but . . .

MAGGIE: But you said we have to love what happened, didn't you? Even the bad things.

QUENTIN: *(seriously now, to match her intensity.)* Yes, I did.

MAGGIE: I . . . I was with two men . . . the same day . . . I mean the same day, see . . . *(She has turned her eyes from him. The group of wedding guests appear on first platform.)* I . . . I don't really sleep around with everybody, Quentin . . . I was with a lot of men, but I never got anything for it. It was like charity, see. My analyst said I gave to those in need. *(She almost weeps now, and looks at him, subservient and oddly chastened.)* I'll always love you, Quentin. But we could just tell them we changed our mind . . .

QUENTIN: Sweetheart . . . The past is not important—it's what you took from it. Whatever happened to you, this is what you made of it!

MAGGIE: (With hope now.) Maybe . . . it would even make me a better wife, right?

QUENTIN: (With hope against the pain) That's the way to talk! You're a victory, Maggie! You're like a flag to me, a kind of proof, somehow, that people can win.

WOMAN GUEST: Ready! Ready! (The guests line up on the steps, forming a carrison for Maggie and Quentin.)

QUENTIN: Come, they're waiting. (He puts her arm in his, they turn to go.)

MAGGIE: Teach me, Quentin! I don't know how to be! (Moving along the corridor of guests as the wedding march begins.) I'm going to be a good wife. I'm going to be a good wife. I'm going to be a good wife. . . .

"Ready! Ready!" someone yelled from downstairs, where the guests had gathered. Prepared for the awkward task of telling the guests that the marriage was off, Greene knocked on the door where Marilyn and Miller were having their discussion.

"Five minutes!" Marilyn said. And twenty minutes later, the radiant smiling bride descended the stairs. Miller's brother Kermit was the best man; Hedda Rosten was the bridesmaid. At the end of the traditional Jewish ceremony, the groom crushed the crystal betrothal goblet beneath his heel. It symbolized trust—once broken, impossible to mend. And later, Marilyn was to write on the back of their wedding photograph, "Hope, Hope, Hope!"

Norman Rosten described the wedding party:

On this day, all was serene and sunny. The day everywhere spoke of life: the long table behind the house with guests seated and drinking, bride and groom moving among friends, everyone exchanging good wishes and embraces. The bride was both beautiful and nervous. Really ecstatic. She gave off a luminosity like the Rodin marble; she was the girl in "The Hand of God." It was the culmination of a dream and carried within it the danger of all dreams.

Mazel tov!

Bashert!

Double, double, toil and trouble;
Fire burn, and cauldron bubble.
—*Macbeth*, Act IV, Scene 1

Logan tried to prepare Sir Laurence Olivier. As an old friend of Olivier's, he wrote to him shortly before Marilyn and Miller were to leave for London for *The Prince and the Showgirl*. "First of all," Logan said, "be sure that you do *not* have Paula on the set. I'm sure she's going to be with Marilyn on your picture, and I think it would be most disturbing for you to have anyone there in authority except you." He described to Olivier Marilyn's special beauty and unique talent, but added, "Please do not expect her to behave like the average actress you have worked with. For instance, don't tell her exactly how to read a line. Let her work it out some way herself no matter how long it takes."

Logan remembered getting a polite response to his suggestions. Olivier assured Logan he would be patient with her. "I will not get upset if I don't get everything my way," he stated. "I will iron myself out every morning like a shirt, hoping to get through the day without a wrinkle."

THUNDER: Enter the three WITCHES.
Yet, was thrice a wrinkle and double trouble
Though starch like hell-broth boil and bubble.

Round about the cauldron go;
In the poisen'd starch do throw
Lizard legs and Black Bart hat,
Writer's pen and tail of cat
Tongue of Red and toady Greene
Eyes of snake and words so mean
Gall of star with strap that falls
Peas and carrots and Matzo's balls.
ALL. Double, double toil and trouble;
        Starch gruel thicken, boil and bubble.
Exeunt WITCHES
[ALARUM:]

Enter piston plane:

Mr. and Mrs. Arthur Miller arrived at London's Heathrow airport on July 14, 1956. They were met by Sir Laurence Olivier and his wife, Vivien Leigh, over three hundred photographers and reporters, seventy-five policemen, and thousands of adoring fans. Giggling with disbelief, Olivier called it "the largest reception and press conference in English history." Describing the awesome moment when they emerged from the plane, Miller wrote, "The camera flashes formed a solid wall of white light that seemed to last for almost half a minute, a veritable aureole, and the madness of it made even the photographers burst out laughing."

Olivier and Leigh were swamped in the hysterical mob of reporters and movie fans that forced the celebrities and police to retreat behind the protection of a ticket counter. One photographer who fell at Marilyn's feet was trampled by the stampeding mob, and had to be rushed to the hospital.

"Are all your conferences like this?" Leigh inquired.

"Well," Marilyn replied, "this is a little quieter than some of them."

At this point in her life Marilyn Monroe had evolved beyond celebrity; orphan 3,463 had become the most famous woman in the world.

The Millers' asylum from the madding crowd was to be Parkside House, at Englefield Green. Adjoining Windsor Park, the Georgian mansion had been rented for the duration of the filming. It was there that the Millers' honeymoon, such as it was, would be eclipsed by rehearsals, wardrobe fittings, and press conferences, at which Miller again found it difficult to smile. One British journalist referred to him as "Cold as a refrigerated fish in his personal appearance. Not like a hot lover—more like a morgue keeper left with a royal cadaver."

Costarring with Sir Laurence Olivier in *The Prince and the Showgirl* had been Marilyn's inspiration. In 1953 Olivier had costarred with Vivien Leigh in the London production of Terence Rattigan's play, which was entitled *The Sleeping Prince*. Vivien Leigh had received less than rave notices. She was obviously miscast as the ingenue American chorus girl. But the part was perfect for the younger, more voluptuous Marilyn Monroe, a requisite that prompted Leigh's most gracious disdain.

Terence Rattigan's play was a stylish light comedy that floated on the buoyancy of its theatrical charm. The dated atmosphere was thick, the plot was not:

FADE IN: The very mannered and dispassionate prince regent of Carpathia (Olivier) is in London in 1911 for the crowning of King George V. Despite his rigid reserve, he falls in love with an entrancing American chorus girl, Elsie Marina (Marilyn). Duty calls the prince regent to return to Carpathia, but he promises to come back and marry the beauteous chorus girl: FADE OUT.

Such slight and boneless plots are fleshed out by the abracadabra of ingenious situation, artful staging, sparkling dialogue, and bravura performances. Joshua Logan believed that the combination of Sir Laurence Olivier, Earl of Notley, and La Monroe of Dickensiana would be magical: "The best combination since black and white and salt and pepper." But it proved to be more like Earl and water. There was thrice a wrinkle.

When Olivier first met Marilyn in New York in February he observed, "By the end of the day one thing was clear to me: I was going to fall most shatteringly in love with Marilyn, and *what* was going to happen? There was no question about it, it was inescapable, or so I thought; she was so adorable, so witty, such incredible fun and more physically attractive than anyone I could have imagined. I went home like a lamb reprieved from the slaughter just for now, but next time . . . Wow! For the first time now it threatened to be 'poor Vivien'!"

But the next time it was "poor Larry": Marilyn was on her honeymoon, and Vivien had gone "round the bend." It was not the best of times for Olivier and Leigh. Despite appearances, their marriage was all but over. In 1953, Vivien Leigh was to have starred in Paramount's *Elephant Walk* with Peter Finch. On location in Ceylon, she and Finch had an affair. She suffered a nervous breakdown and was removed from the film and replaced by Elizabeth Taylor. On returning to London, Leigh was placed in the Netherne psychiatric hospital, where she underwent electroshock therapy. Diagnosed as a manic-depressive, she made a partial recovery and returned to Notley Abbey, where Olivier tried to nurse her back to health. But the shock treatments had somehow made her a stranger to her husband, who observed to friends that she seemed a changed woman. Olivier confessed with sadness that he had difficulty understanding the woman who had come back to him. He found himself viewing her increasingly distantly and dispassionately—as an observer rather than a husband. She was no longer the same woman he had loved and married.

Believing that going back to work together would be the best thing for Vivien and their troubled marriage, Olivier had their friend Terence Rattigan tailor the slight and undemanding *Sleeping Prince* for their appearance together at the Phoenix Theater. Designed as a courtier's offering to Queen Elizabeth II in her coronation year, *The Sleeping Prince* opened on November 5, 1953, Leigh's fortieth birthday.

While *The Sleeping Prince* received generally good reviews, critics noted Olivier's rather wooden performance and felt that Leigh was "strident and a shade too old for the ingenue, and Olivier was a mite too dull for the Don Juan." Few knew of the unhappiness, bickering, and daily crises that were going on in the wings of their private life, which would later be echoed in Olivier's brilliant performance as Archie Rice in *The Entertainer*. Though she appeared to be normal, if strident, onstage, Leigh was suffering from manic-depressive episodes. Between performances she would often become incoherent, partying all night with friends, only to vanish on all-day buying sprees—appearing at the theater just before curtain. During her manic phase, Leigh often hissed to Olivier onstage, sotto voce, "You shit—you absolute shit!"

By the summer of 1956, the relationship of the fabled theatrical couple had deteriorated to feeble attempts at keeping up appearances and sustaining their professional partnership. Their lives were in crisis.

LIGHTNING FLASH: Enter Marilyn
Monroe with Black Bart and entourage—
Milton and Amy Greene, Arthur Miller,
Hedda Rosten, and "Whitey" Snyder.

Marilyn's entrance was late. Olivier had assembled the cast of *The Prince and the Showgirl* on a stage at Pinewood Studios for several days of rehearsals before filming began. Shadowed by Black Bart, Marilyn Monroe was tardy by forty-five minutes. Olivier was extremely distressed to see Paula Strasberg at Marilyn's side. "Paula's presence alarmed me considerably," Olivier commented. "I had rarely thought that coaches were helpful. . . . Paula knew nothing. She was no actress, no director, no teacher, no adviser—except in Marilyn's eyes. For she had one talent—she could butter Marilyn up."

On many occasions Olivier had voiced criticism of Lee Strasberg's Method, which he viewed as "deliberately anti-technical." The Method, he felt, dictated "an all-consuming passion for reality, and if you didn't feel attuned to exactly the right images that would make you believe that you were actually IT and IT was actually going on, you might as well forget about the scene altogether." For Olivier, acting was pretending, and after all, *The Prince and the Showgirl* was a fairy tale. Olivier was very good at pretending.

The first day of rehearsals proved to be a disaster, and from there things grew steadily worse.

Marilyn had a way of idolizing certain men—putting them on the pedestal of her high hopes until they inevitably toppled. Olivier wasted no time in shattering her illusions. Marilyn was the odd girl out. She had never worked in films beyond the perimeter of the Hollywood environment, and the London cast and crew were Olivier stalwarts—Dame Sybil Thorndike, Esmond Knight, Richard Wattis, and cameraman Jack Cardiff. They had all been Olivier's friends and associates for many years. On the first day of rehearsals, when Olivier introduced Marilyn to the assembled cast and crew, he took her hand and in the most condescending manner suggested that everyone be patient with their guest—that it might take their Hollywood visitor some time to learn "*their* method," but how pleased they were to have "such a delightful little thing" among them. His attitude toward her was strangely patronizing, and none of his demeaning subtleties escaped Marilyn Monroe's finely tuned vibe barometer. It was a storm warning of the tempest to come.

An icy frost hung over the rehearsals, which began on July 30, and Olivier noted Paula Strasberg's critical glares and Marilyn's pronounced lack of enthusiasm. "Marilyn was not used to rehearsing and obviously had no taste for it," he observed. "She proclaimed this by wearing very dark glasses and exhibiting an overly subdued manner which I failed miserably to find the means to enliven."

In a daily diary kept during production, Colin Clark, the third assistant director, noted that Marilyn Monroe arrived two hours late on the first day of filming.* The call was for 6:30 A.M. She arrived at eight-thirty for makeup and wardrobe, and subsequently arrived on the set at eleven-thirty, which is when British crews normally call lunch. Colin Clark noted:

MONDAY, 6 August
    Finally at 11:30 A.M. MM did emerge, fully dressed and looking, I am bound to say, ravishing. What a beautiful creature she is, to be sure. . . . Everyone is simply hypnotized when she appears, including me. Everything revolves around her, whether she likes it or not, and yet she seems weak and vulnerable. If it is deliberate, it is incredibly skillful, but I think it is a completely natural gift. All the people round her want to control her, but they do so by trying to give her what they think she wants. . . . Paula takes a firm grip of MM on one side and Milton Greene on the other. They hardly bother to conceal their battle for control. And not just them—Arthur Miller wants control too. . . . We are all really thinking of what they want underneath. "Oh, what a nice pot of gold you are. Can I help you, pot of gold?"

In his first days of directing the film Olivier said to her, "All you have to do is be sexy, dear Marilyn." She was devastated. The demeaning remark indicated that he had no intention of recognizing her sensibilities as an actress and no interest in her method of making contact with her role. Her disappointment with Olivier turned to a burning resentment, and the asbestos fell between the star and the director, never to rise again. She avoided him whenever possible. Directions had to be given circuitously through Paula Strasberg; and whenever Olivier spoke to Marilyn directly, she would stare at him with indifferent eyes, suddenly turning away in midconversation and walking off to discuss the scene with Paula or to telephone Lee Strasberg in New York.

Olivier recalled, "Her manner to me got steadily ruder and more insolent; whenever I patiently labored to make her understand an indication for some reading, business or timing she would listen with ill-disguised impatience, and when I had finished would turn to Paula and petulantly demand, 'Wassee mean?' A very short way into filming, my humiliation had reached depths I would not have believed possible."

When she was to begin filming a scene with Dame Sybil Thorndike, one of the legendary actresses of the British theater, Marilyn arrived an hour late. Regarding it as a great discourtesy, Olivier became livid. Upon her arrival, he strode over to Marilyn, took her by the hand, led her over to

---

* Clark, son of art historian Kenneth Clark, kept a fascinating diary of the production, which was published in England under the title *The Prince, the Showgirl, and Me*.

Dame Sybil like a naughty schoolgirl, and through clenched teeth demanded that the president of Marilyn Monroe Productions apologize for her tardiness. Having no comprehension that she was late, Marilyn began an abject apology. Much to Olivier's displeasure, Dame Sybil interrupted and said, "My dear, you mustn't concern yourself. A great actress like you has other things than time on her mind, doesn't she?"

Marilyn realized that she had at least one friend on the set, and she and Thorndike became quite close during the production. While watching dailies in the projection room, Thorndike turned to her old friend Olivier and said, "You did well in that scene, Larry, but with Marilyn up there nobody will be watching you. Her manner and timing are just too delicious. And don't be too hard about her tardiness, dear boy. We need her desperately. She's really the only one of us who knows how to act in front of the camera."

> WEDNESDAY, 15 August
>
> I suppose you could say that today was a red-letter day. This morning I definitely saw more of MM that I ever expected to, and she went up in my estimation in more ways than one. She arrived really early for her, and nearly caught us on the hop at 7:30 A.M. She was in a jolly mood.
>
> As lunchtime drew near the A.D. caught me in the corridor, and told me to look for MM's marked script which was missing. I assumed this meant that MM was on the set, so I just barged into her dressing room . . . There she stood— MM completely nude, with only a towel around her head.
>
> I stopped dead. All I could see were beautiful white and pink curves. I must have gone as red as a beetroot. I couldn't even turn and rush out, so I just stood there and stared and stammered. MM gave me her most innocent smile. "Oh, Colin," she said. "And you an old Etonian!" How did she stay so cool? And how did she know my name and which school I had gone to and what it meant?
>
> When I managed to get out of the room and pull myself together, I realized MM could be a bit brighter than we think. . . . What fun it might have been to make a movie with MM when she felt everyone around her was her friend.
>
> Dream on Colin . . .

During her sleepless nights at Parkside House, Marilyn began to believe that Olivier was deliberately trying to undermine her performance, and it occurred to her that Milton Greene had made an enormous mistake in allowing Olivier to be both star and director.

When Marilyn expressed distrust of Olivier to her husband, Arthur Miller was put in the awkward position of both pacifying his wife and at the same time alleviating her suspicions. "She came to believe that he was trying to compete with her like another woman, a coquette drawing the audience's attention away from herself," Miller recalled. "Nothing could dissuade her from this perilous vision of her director and co-star. . . . It was simply impossible to agree that he could be the cheap scene-stealer she was talking about. . . . I occasionally had to defend Olivier or else reinforce the naivete of her illusions. The result was she began to question the absoluteness of my partisanship on her side of the deepening struggle."

Could Marilyn have been correct in her assessment of Olivier? Was it possible that the legendary star of stage and screen could be trying to undermine and upstage the ingenue neophyte from Hollywood? When Marilyn and her entourage arrived on the scene, not only was Olivier's private life in crisis, but so was his career. He was turning fifty and his ham was well cured. There weren't many leading-men parts left for him, and he was very sensitive about his age. The makeup and attire he wore as the prince was so heavy that at times he was barely recognizable behind his monocle. Vanity and the fight to justify top billing went with the prince of Carpathia's territory.

Both Marilyn and Olivier had what is known to cameramen as a "good side"—the side of the face that photographs best. For both of them it was the right side. Olivier, the director, always made sure that the right side of Olivier the actor was to camera, which meant that Marilyn's "bad side" was to camera when they faced each other.

Despite the letters received from Joshua Logan, Olivier elected to ignore his advice, stating, "I refused to treat Marilyn as a special case—I had too much pride in my trade—and would at all times treat her as a grown-up artist of merit, which in a sense she was."

If there was any doubt that Marilyn was an artist of merit, it was dispelled by the reviews of *Bus Stop*, which opened on August 31 to critical acclaim. "Hold onto your chairs, everybody, and get set for a rattling surprise. Marilyn Monroe has finally proved herself an actress in *Bus Stop*," raved Bosley Crowther of the *New York Times*, who had never been a Marilyn fan. "Effectively dispels once and for all the notion that she is merely a glamour personality," said the *Saturday Review of Literature*. The London *Times* observed, "Miss Monroe is a talented comedienne, and her sense of timing never forsakes her. She gives a complete portrait, sensitively and sometimes even brilliantly conceived. There is about her a waiflike quality, an underlying note of pathos which can be strangely moving."

"Brilliant," said *Variety*.

"She's a troublesome bitch!" Olivier was heard to mumble.

Arthur Miller soon discovered that the Marxist boy from Brooklyn and the Earl of Notley had something in common—difficult wives. At the end of an exhausting day at Pinewood dealing with a very difficult actress, Olivier would go home to Notley Abbey and face another very difficult actress. Vivien Leigh would often be in her manic phase, and Olivier would frequently arrive to find a house full of her animated guests and hangers-on who would party all night, when what he desperately needed was sleep and tranquillity. There were times when he would lock his door, only to be awakened in the middle of the night by Leigh pounding on it. On one occasion when he had neglected to lock the door he was awakened by Leigh beating him across the face with a wet towel at three in the morning. Few knew of his private hell. But there were days when Olivier would brace himself with a stiff drink in his Pinewood dressing room before going home, and Arthur Miller would join him for commiseration and a bracer.

One evening the two of them went to the theater together; Miller wanted to see John Osborne's *Look Back in Anger* at the Royal Court Theater, and Olivier reluctantly went with him. Osborne was then a new-wave playwright—an ideological adversary who, it seemed, was out to discredit the British traditionalist world that Olivier was so much a part of. Yet that world was vanishing. Its institutions were as old hat as Rattigan's play and the gold-braided light-opera ghosts of Carpathia—as old hat, perhaps, as the aging Olivier, whose career was in a rut.

After the play Miller and Olivier went backstage to congratulate the stars, Mary Ure and Alan Bates, and were introduced to the rebellious author, the dreaded John Osborne. When they were leaving, Miller was amazed to hear Olivier hesitantly say to Osborne, "Do you suppose you could write something for me?" Osborne could. He would. He did. And out of that evening on the town with Miller was born *The Entertainer* and Archie Rice, the illegitimate child of the wooden prince of Carpathia.

Realizing that *The Prince and the Showgirl* had gotten off to a rather rotten start, Olivier suggested that Terence Rattigan throw a party at which the film's principals could socialize away from the pressures of Pinewood, and perhaps mend antagonisms in a relaxing atmosphere.

SUNDAY, 19 August
Terry Rattigan's party last night was as formal and artificial as his plays. He has a typical expensive show-business house on Wentworth golf course—1920's classical, and very *nouveau riche*; thick carpets, crystal chandeliers, flowers. I got

there early and alone. . . . Terry Rattigan was in a white dinner jacket beaming urbanely at everyone (though not at me, the 3rd A.D.)

Milton was there with Amy—small and attractive, both of them. . . . Milton's boyish, very slight, dark brown eyes always smiling. He must be extremely shrewd to have got control of the most famous film star in the world. SLO was brimming over with bonhomie—always a bad sign. When he is irascible is when he's sincere.

Finally Arthur Miller and MM. A. Miller looked very dashing, also in a white dinner jacket—strong jaw, intense gaze, the perfect he-man intellectual. I fancy he is very vain indeed. MM looked a bit straggly. She had done her hair herself and she had not been made up by Whitey. She even seemed a bit scared, not of us, but of AM. He really is unpleasant. He struts around as if MM were his property. He seems to think his superior intelligence puts him on a higher plane, and treats her as if she is just an accessory. Poor MM. Another insensitive male in her life is the last thing she needs. I can't see the romance lasting long. She's the one who could be forgiven a little vanity, but, strangely enough, that's not in her make-up at all.

The party just never gelled . . . Sir Laurence surrounded by people of great assured self importance . . . Viv is discretely [sic] catty . . . Hedda Rosten drinks too much . . . Arthur raids the Hors D'oeuvre platters . . . Milton plays the ugly American—no one really friendly. A bit stiff. I bet it would have been another matter if we were all queer. (Gaiety, everyone!)

In his autobiography *Hollywood in a Suitcase*, Sammy Davis, Jr., talked about an affair Marilyn was having during the filming of *The Prince and the Showgirl*. In the summer of 1956 Davis was living in London, and he wrote, "When she was making *The Prince and the Showgirl* with Laurence Olivier, she was going through one of the most difficult periods of her life. She was having an affair with a close friend of mine. . . . They met clandestinely at my house. . . . We had to get up to all sorts of intrigues to keep the affair secret. I used to pretend we were having a party, and Marilyn would arrive and leave at different times from my pal. Once they were in the house, of course, they went off to the swimming pool, which had its own self-contained bungalow."

Sammy Davis, Jr., was often the beard for Jack Kennedy. Was it JFK Marilyn met in the pool bungalow? According to Colin Clark's diary, Marilyn went to London incognito on Saturday, August 25. She failed to show up at all at Pinewood on the following Monday. The diary indicates that just prior to the weekend in question Marilyn and Miller had a falling-out over his behavior at the Rattigan party. Jack Kennedy was in Europe at the time. Immediately following the July 1956 Democratic Convention, in which Jack had lost the vice-presidential nomination to Estes Kefauver by thirty votes, he flew to the French Riviera with his brother Teddy—

leaving behind Jacqueline, who was pregnant. In Cannes, Jack and Teddy Kennedy connected with George Smathers and chartered a forty-foot yacht, complete with skipper, galley cook, and blondes, according to a *Washington Star* correspondent who interviewed the skipper.

On August 23, while still recuperating from the strain of the convention, Jacqueline Kennedy was rushed to Newport Hospital in Rhode Island, where an emergency cesarean was performed. The child, an unnamed girl, was stillborn. The Kennedy family tried in vain to contact Jack. He couldn't be reached on the yacht by transatlantic phone, though it had a ship-to-shore radio. His passport application indicates that he planned to travel to England, France, Italy, and Sweden.

Kennedy was finally located and flew home on Tuesday, August 28. His prolonged absence at this critical time brought about a breach with Jackie. "There was certainly talk of divorce between Jack and Jackie," Peter Lawford acknowledged. "But it was only talk." *Time* later reported a meeting between Jackie Kennedy and Joe Kennedy in which he purportedly offered her a million dollars not to divorce her husband.

It was on Tuesday, August 28, the day Kennedy flew back to the states, that an incident occurred marking the turning point in the Miller marriage. At a time when Marilyn desperately needed her husband's support, she discovered Arthur's notebook open on his desk to a page containing a passage so devastating to her that the fragile trust of their betrothal shattered like glass.

The notebook revealed that Arthur was having second thoughts about their marriage. Sobbing to Paula Strasberg about what Arthur had written, she said, "Olivier was beginning to think I was a troublesome bitch, and Art said he no longer had a decent answer to that one." The notations in the notebook went on to say that she was an unpredictable, forlorn child-woman to be pitied, but that he feared his own creative life was threatened by her endless emotional demands. "Art once thought I was some kind of angel," Marilyn cried to Strasberg, "but now he guessed he was wrong—that his first wife had let him down, but I had done something worse." Arthur had referred to Marilyn as a "whore."

Arthur Miller didn't discuss the incident in his memoirs, but it became the fulcrum of the climactic scene in *After the Fall*.

QUENTIN: (*Grasping her wrist, but not trying to take the pill bottle out of her hand.*) Throw them in the sea, no pill can make you innocent! See your own hatred . . . and life will come back, Maggie. Your innocence is killing you!

MAGGIE: *(Freeing her wrist)* What about *your* hatred? You know when I wanted
to die? When I read what you wrote, Kiddo. Two months after we were married, Kiddo. *(She moves front and speaks toward some invisible source of justice
now, telling her injury.)* I was looking for a fountain pen to sign some autographs. And there's his desk . . . and there's his empty chair where he sits and
thinks how to help people. And there's his handwriting. And there's some
words, 'The only one I'll ever love is my daughter. If I could only find an
honorable way to die!' *(she turns to him)* Now, when you gonna face that,
Judgey? Remember how I fell down, fainted? On the new rug? That's what
killed me, Judgey. Right?

Perhaps Miller was drawing from the evening at Rattigan's party: in the
play Quentin tells Maggie he made the notations, "Because when the
guests had gone, and you suddenly turned on me, calling me cold, remote,
it was the first time I saw your eyes that way—betrayed, screaming that
I'd made you feel you didn't exist." After she angrily tells him not to mix
her up with his previous wife, Quentin says, "That's just it. That I could
have brought two women so different to the same accusation—it closes
a circle for me. And I wanted to face the worst thing I could imagine—
that I could not love. And I wrote it down, like a letter from hell."

The "letter from hell" in Miller's black notebook damned their marriage, left Marilyn distraught, and marked a turning point in her life.
"Hope, hope, hope" seemed beyond her grasp, and she increasingly turned
to barbiturates to mask the emotional pain.

MONDAY, 27 August
  No MM today. Frantic calls to Parkside were to no avail, although dark hints
that AM and MM were not on such friendly terms. I thought so on Saturday at
the party. . . . Finally AM calls to say that MM wasn't well. A fever. Hmmm.
Apparently MM and AM had a row last night, and AM could not control MM
at all. She was wandering around the house in a very distressed state. There had
been a lot of phone calls, many of them transatlantic. Finally Milton had gone
over with extra pills. . . . In the end one of the doctors in New York talked to
her until she was calm enough to go to sleep. (Imagine what that cost?)

Recognizing Marilyn's deep distress and Paula's difficulty in coping with
the situation, Lee Strasberg flew to London, and Milton Greene arranged
for Dr. Hohenberg to arrive for supportive therapy. Calming Marilyn,
Hohenberg was successful in getting her back to work, and he introduced
her to Anna Freud, who had a practice in London. Marilyn had several
sessions with Anna Freud after Hohenberg returned to New York.

Marilyn found herself surrounded by people she could no longer trust. Dismayed at her husband, belittled by her director, she received little support from Milton Greene, whose priority was to mediate between her and Olivier in his efforts to get the film completed. Hedda Rosten was drinking so much she was little help to anyone. Miller couldn't stand the Strasbergs. To him they were "poisonous and vacuous." He resented Marilyn's "nearly religious dependency" on them, which undermined his own influence and control. The relationship between Miller and Milton Greene was equally strained. "Greene thought he would be this big-shot producer and she would be working for him," Miller observed. "But she saw that he had ulterior aims." Miller accused Milton and Amy Greene of buying expensive antiques that were charged to Marilyn Monroe Productions and shipped to their home in Connecticut.

WEDNESDAY, 19 September
    AM arrived at midday with MM and has been universally cast as the villain of the piece. SLO is cross because he had hoped AM would help MM turn over a new leaf, and this clearly has not happened. She arrived at the studio late and demanding.
    In fact she is clearly fed up with AM and also disenchanted with Milton whom she cuts dead. . . . Milton blames AM for the change in MM's attitude, both to her work and to him. Milton is in a very difficult position. He wants to control MM and her career, but has to get his film finished on time and on budget if MMP, and he, is to make money. And this means he has to cooperate with SLO and all of us, even at the risk of upsetting MM. So it is easy for someone (AM) to poison MM's mind against him.
    Paula is treated by AM with extreme disdain. I have heard him describe Paula as a charlatan to Milton in SLO's dressing room, and I'm sure he does it in front of MM. This is hard luck on MM since she totally depends on Paula. She has no one else except the tipsy Hedda. Finally AM is not above snide remarks about Milton to Paula, which quickly get repeated.
    This evening MM told Milton that she was not satisfied with her new car. She wants it replaced with a new Jaguar (a MK VII saloon). . . . But Milton sees the dark hand of AM at work. "He is trying to pull a fast one. He wants us (MMP) to buy it and then he will ship it over to the USA for his own private use." Milton was livid, but I think it's funny that a left-wing intellectual should want to drive round in a Jaguar with Marilyn Monroe. (Although didn't Lenin have a Rolls-Royce?)

FRIDAY, 12 October
    It has been a tough week. At the end of the day I went into SLO's dressing room with fresh whisky and cigarettes. SLO and Milton are shattered. So is AM.
    'I've had it,' said SLO. 'I think I'll go off to China for a month.'

'I'll come with you,' said Milton.

'So will I,' said AM grimly.

'Come now, dear boy,' said SLO, 'Your new bride!'

'She's devouring me,' I heard AM say as I left.

The golden opportunity to make a delightful film with a magnificent cast had become a hellish nightmare from which there would be no exit until the last frame of *The Prince and the Showgirl* passed through the narrow gate of the Technicolor camera—Marilyn's true loyalist.

THUNDER and LIGHTNING: ENTER WITCHES

WITCH 1: When shall we witches meet again?
          In thunder lightning and backlit rain?

WITCH 2: When the hurly burly film flam's done
          'Neath the arc light's merciless
          spurious sun.

ALL: Double, double, toil and trouble,
          Fire burn and cauldron bubble.

EXEUNT ALL.

Please Don't Kill Anything

She could rise to hope like a fish swimming up through black seas to fly at the sun before falling back again. And perhaps those rallies—if one knew the sadness in her—were her glory. But England, I feared, had humbled both of us.

—Arthur Miller

Before their marriage Arthur Miller had kept a studio at the Chelsea Hotel on West Twenty-Third Street in New York, which was a writers' haven. Writers and intellectuals had all the modern twentieth-century conveniences at the Chelsea—Communist Party headquarters were just across the street, along with a Marxist library and bookstore. And for those disenchanted with Stalinism, a synagogue was right next door, and a Catholic church only a stone's throw away. Taking his books and typewriter from the Chelsea, Miller moved his study to the more fashionable East Side, where the Millers leased an apartment at 444 East Fifty-Seventh Street, just around the corner from Marilyn's old Sutton Place South address. On the thirteenth floor, it was a large and spacious apartment with a view of the East River. Marilyn had it redone in movie star moderne—Harlow white with plenty of mirrors. Still protective of her mother's unrealized dream, Marilyn had the Franklin baby grand hoisted from the street and placed in the living room, where it remained until Marilyn's death.

Marilyn told Milton Greene that she "didn't want to work for a while because she wanted to have a baby," and she and Miller divided their time between Manhattan and a cottage they rented near the shore at Amagansett, Long Island. The Millers were going to take time to recover the understanding that had been lost in the witch's brew of *The Prince and the Showgirl.*

"Soon there was a routine," Arthur reminisced, "with Marilyn off to her analyst in the mornings and to the Strasbergs' apartment in the afternoons for hours of private lessons with Lee. Occasionally we went out to Brooklyn to visit my parents, who would bring in the neighbors to shyly adore Marilyn. The street out front would be full of kids who cheered her when she came out of the little house. She took much pleasure in these ordinary folk and especially loved my aging father, who simply lit up at the sight of her."

At Amagansett their lives took on more normal rhythms. They would go for long walks on the shore, and Marilyn tried cooking the recipes passed on by Arthur's mother. Deciding to make homemade noodles, she would hang them on chair backs and dry them with a hair dryer. The Rostens were frequent visitors and Norman observed, "Upon their return to the States toward the end of the year, a change was discernible in Marilyn. The tone of the marriage had changed. Something new and mysterious had arisen between them, which close friends would recognize: the honeymoon cruise was over, the real voyage had begun. Storm and heartbreak ahead."

It was during the spring of 1957 that Marilyn's longing to have children intensified. A number of her friends recalled how she yearned to be a mother, even if it meant temporarily putting films aside. She desperately wanted fulfillment. Having a child would increase her sense of a place in the world and provide stability and the promise of continuity. In a sense, motherhood was an extension of her childlike mystical reverence for life, and it was the same life force, so intense within her, that she projected into all living things. As Norman Rosten observed of her, "The survival of an unprotected shrub on a windy hillside, through rain and frost, is to her a source of trembling joy. She knew her own battle to survive and could appreciate the triumph in nature."

Miller's short story "Please Don't Kill Anything" is based on Marilyn's sensitivity to the life-and-death struggle of all living creatures. The story concerns a husband and wife walking along a beach who observe fishermen hauling in a net through the surf. The wife becomes distressed at the thought of the fishes' doom. As the net is pulled ashore she exclaims, "Oh, dear, they're going to be caught now! Each one is wondering what

happened!" She convinces her husband they must toss back into the water all the discarded smaller fish flopping on the beach struggling to
breathe. In *Timebends* Miller recounts the incident that inspired the
story:

> We walked the empty Amagansett beach in peace, chatting with the occasional
> commercial fishermen who worked their nets from winches on their rusting
> trucks. These local men, Bonackers, so-called, greeted her with warmth and re-
> spect, even though she perplexed them by running along the shore to throw back
> the gasping "junk" fish they had no use for and had flung from their nets. There
> was a touching but slightly unnerving intensity in her then, an identification that
> was unhealthily close to her own death fear. One day, after throwing a couple
> of dozen fish one by one back into the water, she was losing her breath, and I
> finally had to distract her and draw her away to keep her from working the
> shoreline until she dropped.

Jimmy Haspiel mentions her concern over the pigeons in a small New
York City park at the end of Fifty-Seventh Street, where Marilyn often
went to sit on a bench incognito. "Marilyn went over there one night and
came upon two young boys who were capturing pigeons, trapping the birds
in nets, then caging them. Marilyn asked the lads why they were doing
this, and they informed her that they made money by catching pigeons
and selling them to a meat market as squab for fifty cents apiece. Marilyn
asked the boys, 'If I give you the money, will you free the birds?' They
agreed, the cage was opened, and the pigeons were freed. Marilyn then
arranged to meet the kids on the nights they worked catching pigeons,
and at the end of the evenings she could pay them for the birds, then
ecstatically watch as they were released back into the air over the East
River."

According to her New York driver, Peter Leonardi, Marilyn didn't limit
her concern for God's creatures. He remembered that she often went
down to the Bowery as Zelda Zonk and handed out money to the sad
humanity who had neither fins nor wings to carry them from misfortune.

One person who failed to be a recipient of Marilyn's benevolence, however, was Milton Greene. In April the Millers viewed a temp-dub version
of *The Prince and the Showgirl.* Having viewed a rough cut of the film in
New York in December, which she liked, Marilyn was bitterly disappointed
by the changes that had been made. She blamed Milton Greene for allowing the film to be ineptly reedited.

In a bid to gain full control over MMP, and further his own position,

Miller encouraged Marilyn to sever her ties with Greene, and on April 11, a statement was issued through Arthur Miller's attorney, Robert H. Montgomery, Jr., accusing Greene of mismanagement. Several days later it was announced by Marilyn Monroe Productions that Milton Greene's attorney, Irving Stein, had been replaced by Miller's attorney, Robert Montgomery, and that the treasurer would be Miller's brother-in-law, George Kupchik.

In a statement that avoided rancor, Milton Greene was quoted in the *Los Angeles Times* as saying, "It seems that Marilyn doesn't want to go ahead with the program we planned. I'm getting lawyers to represent me. But I don't want to do anything now to hurt her career. I did devote about a year and a half exclusively to her. I practically gave up photography." After a lengthy legal battle, MMP bought out Milton Greene's stock for $100,000, and he abandoned his career as a movie producer. Arthur Miller took his place as vice president of MMP.

Defying circumstance, *The Prince and the Showgirl* proved to be vastly entertaining, giving no hint of its hellish origins. It received mixed reviews, but high praise for Marilyn's radiant performance, and even Olivier was forced to admit, "She gave a star performance. Maybe I was tetchy with Marilyn and with myself, because I felt my career was in a rut. . . . She was quite wonderful—the best of all." Indeed, the film was flawed by Olivier's sodden performance. He was the same wooden prince in reel ten as he had been in reel one, and the delight of seeing the transition from the staid prince of Carpathia to the impassioned romantic who had fallen hopelessly in love with the showgirl was denied.

Despite their differences, Milton Greene's instincts for Marilyn were certainly correct. He had an insight into what was right for her as an actress, and two of Marilyn Monroe's best films were made under his guidance. After he was removed from MMP, Greene and Marilyn never met again. He attempted to return to photography but became increasingly addicted to alcohol and drugs. Later, Marilyn was to admit to Amy Greene, "Arthur took away the only person I ever trusted—Milton."

Shortly before he succumbed to cancer in 1989, Milton Greene reminisced, "She was ultrasensitive, and very dedicated to her work, whether people realize this or not. She came through magnificently in *Prince* and she was great in *Bus Stop*. All I did was believe in her. She was a marvelous, loving, wonderful person who I don't think many people understood."

Because Marilyn's psychoanalyst, Margaret Hohenberg, had been recommended by Milton Greene, Arthur advised Marilyn to change analysts. Arthur's analyst, Rudolph Loewenstein, recommended Marianne Kris, as did Anna Freud in a telephone call from London.*

Marianne Rie Kris was born and raised in Vienna, where she had been a childhood friend of Sigmund Freud's daughter, Anna Freud. Kris studied and practiced in Vienna, and later Berlin, where she became an associate of the Berlin Psychoanalytic Institute along with the Freudian-Marxists Franz Alexander, Otto Fenichel, Ernst Simmel, and Rudolph Loewenstein. It was in Berlin that she married Ernst Kris, a prominent psychoanalyst and art historian who published many of Otto Fenichel's papers.

Simmel and Fenichel fled to Hollywood to escape the Nazis, and Ernst and Marianne Kris escaped to London in 1938 with Sigmund and Anna Freud. While Anna remained in London after her father's death, Ernst and Marianne Kris were among the exiles who immigrated to America, where they continued their practice in New York.

Dispersed by the Nazi terror, the close-knit group of Freudian-Marxist exiles kept in touch through letters and reunions at psychoanalytic seminars. Many were on the mailing list of Otto Fenichel's *Rundbriefe*, which kept them up to date on current activities and theory. Ernst Kris died in New York a few weeks before Marilyn began her sessions with Marianne Kris, whose office/residence was conveniently located down the hall from the residence of Lee Strasberg at the Langham, 135 Central Park West.

Marilyn initially liked Kris and was pleased to be a patient of someone so closely allied with the Freud family. More than ever, Marilyn wanted to understand herself and her donative relationships with men. She wanted to be "a good wife," and she wanted her marriage with Arthur Miller to succeed. Both Marilyn and Kris saw motherhood as her salvation.

For Marilyn to have a child of her own would have been "a crown with a thousand diamonds," Miller said, and in June of 1957 their doctor confirmed that she was pregnant. Marilyn was so elated that she was deaf to the warning that it could be an ectopic pregnancy. Privately, the doctor told Miller of that danger. "But the very idea of her as a mother ultimately

---

* For many years Miller had been a patient of Loewenstein, who was on the Communist Party's "approved list" of Marxist analysts. Loewenstein, a friend of Ralph Greenson, was also a disciple of Otto Fenichel. When Fenichel died it was Loewenstein who wrote his eulogy: see "In Memorium—Otto Fenichel" by Loewenstein in *Psychoanalytic Quarterly* 15 (1946): page 140.

swept me along with her," Miller stated, "for already there were moments of a new kind of confidence, a quietness of spirit that I had never seen in her. She was beginning to feel a safe place around herself, or so it seemed. If a child might intensify anxieties, it would also give her, and hence myself, a new hope for the future."

On Thursday morning, August 1, Arthur was working inside the Amagansett cottage when he heard her screaming. He found her in the garden doubled over in pain. Carrying her into the house, he laid her on the couch and called the doctor. He was told to call an ambulance at once and rush her to Doctors Hospital in Manhattan. He held her hand and tried to comfort her as she writhed in agony during the three hours it took to get to the hospital, where she was given sedation and rushed into surgery.

The loss of her baby was a great sorrow. "Hope, Hope, Hope!" had once again been deferred. Arthur recalled the seemingly endless ride from the hospital back to Amagansett. "She lay there sad beyond sadness, and there were no words anymore that could change anything for her."

Every Day I Have the Blues

Most marriages, after all, are conspiracies to deny the dark and confirm the light.
—Arthur Miller

Speaking to Fred Guiles on the veranda of Miller's Roxbury farm in 1983, Miller said, "This farmhouse is located in the Litchfield Hills. I have nearly four hundred acres. Right now I'm starting a tree farm on the place. When Marilyn and I were first married, I had another old house about a mile and a half down this road. I sold it in 1956 and bought this. I had my eye on it for a long time and always wanted it, but I couldn't get it until the farmer's mother died here and he gave up the place."

Agrarian reform in the guise of death enabled Miller to purchase the farm in the summer of 1957 with Marilyn's money. As Marilyn described it, the eighteenth-century farmhouse was "a kind of old saltbox with a kitchen." Though the house was over a hundred and fifty years old and in a decrepit state, the Millers ignored friends' advice to tear it down. The Millers' need to repair their marriage became exteriorized in the tangible hope of restoring "Arthur's farm."

Determined to become the woman her husband needed, Marilyn helped Miller renovate the old farm building, a task that Marilyn never considered completed. The original beams and ceilings were left intact, but walls were removed and rooms enlarged. A new wing was added, which

Marilyn christened "the nursery," in the hope that she would still have a baby. There were broad verandas that overlooked the sweeping meadow and the manmade pond. Despite his Brooklyn origins, Miller was genuinely drawn to the land. For him it was where the perspective of cultured people could be regained and where psychic renewal had its roots. Arthur said, "It's the place where we hope to live until we die."

Marilyn discovered that the farm was a place where she could indulge her love for all living things, and she acquired an array of animals and birds. Worried about how birds feed during migration, she fixed a feeding station in a maple tree. She adopted Cindy, a half-starved mongrel who had wandered into the yard; and Hugo, the Millers' basset hound, would often wander with rain-soaked muddy feet over the living room's white carpeting. Marilyn's concern for animals was compulsive. Inez Melson, her Los Angeles business manager, was once awakened at four o'clock in the morning with an urgent call from Marilyn in Connecticut informing her that they were having a thunderstorm and that "the animals and birds were very frightened."

In a newspaper interview at the time Marilyn said, "Marriage makes me feel more womanly, more proud of myself. It also makes me feel less frantic. For the first time I have a feeling of being sheltered. It's as if I have come in out of the cold. . . ." She told another interviewer, "I need to be here to get my husband's breakfast and make him a cheerful mid-morning cup of coffee. Writing is such a lonely kind of work."

Recognizing her husband's need to put some distance between his role as paternalistic lover to the "forever child" and his needs as a writer, Marilyn had a split-shingle cabin built for him on a knoll not far from the farmhouse where he could write.

On weekdays Miller was in the habit of writing from 9 A.M. to 1 P.M. In the year since his marriage he had only published one short story, "The Misfits," which appeared in *Esquire*, and he was still revising his unfinished play concerning the research physicians and Lorraine, the godlike force "who moves instinctively to break the hold of respectability on the men until each in a different way meets the tragedy in which she has unwittingly entangled him."

Miller was now himself deeply entangled in the real-life tragedy. According to him, he had written over a thousand pages of the Lorraine play, but he burned them in the summer of 1957 because he couldn't deal with the implications of what he was writing. Lorraine went up in flames, but Miller's reality remained.

It was when Marilyn was recuperating from the loss of the baby that Miller began working on a screenplay of *The Misfits*, which was based on the lives of the two rodeo cowboys and the divorcée he had met in Reno. Expanding the role of the woman, Miller made "Roslyn" the key character in the screen version and wrote the part for Marilyn. Miller stated that he hoped the film project would draw Marilyn out of her sadness, and she expressed delight that he was writing something especially for her. Yet this was a business and career project—something exterior to their private life. Marilyn became increasingly suspicious of Miller's motives and often found him disapproving, cold, and distant.

Norman Rosten recalled a dinner party at the farm. After dinner,

there was dancing and quite a bit of merriment. Marilyn left the room at one point without a word to anyone. I followed several moments later and discovered her on the porch sobbing quietly.

"What is it, dear?" I asked, sitting next to her.

She hurriedly dried her eyes. "I can't tell you. I feel terrible, maybe it's the weather." She was plainly evasive.

"Why don't you come in and dance?"

"Well, maybe a little later."

"I don't want to leave you here to cry."

She sniffed, straightened her hair. "Make believe I just was out here powdering my nose or something, Okay? Arthur will only get upset."

"Right," I nodded. We went back inside."

The Millers divided their time between the farm and the East Fifty-Seventh Street apartment, which was only a two-hour drive in the Jaguar MK VII Saloon. But as the months progressed Marilyn spent more time in the city and less in the country. Her New York maid, Lena Pepitone, described Marilyn's life as "incredibly monotonous. . . . Her doctor's appointments and her acting lessons were virtually all she had to look forward to." May Reis, who had been Elia Kazan's secretary, then Miller's before the marriage, handled the mail, appointments, and phone calls from a small office in the apartment. Neither Miller nor Marilyn was very social, and when she was in the city she spent a good deal of time in her room talking on the telephone, which according to Lena Pepitone seemed to be her greatest pleasure. "But the calls she enjoyed the most—and talked the longest on—came from two men who were very, very special to her: Joe DiMaggio and Frank Sinatra."

When Miller was in the city, he spent most of his time in his study working on the screenplay of *The Misfits*. Miller observed, "With *The Misfits* I was preparing to dedicate a year or more of my life to her enhancement as a performer—I would never have dreamed of writing a movie otherwise. I was sometimes apprehensive and unspontaneous with her. This she might interpret as disapproval, but it was simply that I was off balance and could no longer confidently predict her moods. It was almost as though the fracture of her original idealization of me in England had left no recognizable image at all, and if what remained was to humbly accept reality, it meant junking the ideal, a difficult thing to do when, paradoxically, her energy rose out of her idealizations of people and projects. Still hope was by no means fading; most marriages, after all, are conspiracies to deny the dark and confirm the light."

Though many had blamed Milton Greene for involving Marilyn with drugs, it was during her marriage to Miller, and months after Miller had deposed Milton Greene, that Marilyn's slide into drug dependency became a life-threatening problem. To kill the pain of her unhappiness she had begun to prick her barbiturate capsules with a pin to make them work faster, and for the first time since the death of Johnny Hyde, Marilyn overdosed. Miller was at the apartment when the incident occurred. He stated, "There is no word to describe her breathing when she was in trouble with the pills. The diaphragm isn't working. The breathing is peaceful, great sighs. It took me an awfully long time before I knew what was coming on."

Describing Maggie's overdose in *After the Fall*, Arthur Miller wrote:

She falls asleep, crumpled on the floor. Now deep, strange breathing. He quickly goes to her, throws her over onto her stomach for artificial respiration, but just as he's about to start, he stands. He calls upstage.

QUENTIN: Carrie? Carrie! (*Carrie enters as though it were a final farewell*) Quick! Call the ambulance! Stop wasting time! Call the ambulance! (*Carrie exits. He looks down at Maggie, addressing listener.*) No-no, we saved her. It was just in time. Her doctor tells me she had a few good months; he even thought for a while she was making it. Unless, God knows, he fell in love with her too. (*He almost smiles.*) Look, I'll say it. It's really all I came to say. Barbiturates kill by suffocation. And the signal is a kind of sighing—the diaphragm is paralyzed . . . And her precious seconds squirming in my hand, alive as bugs; and I heard those deep, unnatural breaths, like the footfalls of my coming peace—and knew . . . I wanted them. How is that possible? I loved that girl!

Describing Marilyn's overdose to Fred Guiles, Miller stated that once he realized what was happening, he wasted no time trying to revive her himself, but sought medical help. When the doctor arrived, her stomach was pumped out and she was saved. Miller stated, "After she was revived, she would be extremely warm and affectionate to me because I had saved her. . . . You might trace it [the overdose] to something someone said or did, but it could come out of nowhere, too."

"Nowhere," Marilyn later related to Dr. Greenson, was Miller's coldness and indifference.

Recounting the growing rift between Miller and Marilyn, Lena Pepitone said that it was as if the apartment had two wings, his and hers. When they dined together they would "sit at the table without speaking for the longest time. Marilyn looked at her husband admiringly and longingly, as if she was dying for some attention. However, he just ate quietly and did not look at her."

Marilyn often listened to Frank Sinatra records in her bedroom. One of her favorite records was "All of Me," and Lena recalled that when she was unhappy she would play the record and stare at a full-length picture of Joe DiMaggio that she kept on the back of her closet door. "She seemed to be looking at Joe's picture, but her eyes would have the faraway expression I had seen many times when Marilyn was unhappy," Lena recalled. "I remember the one song she played most often on the small record player next to her bed. It was a number called 'Every Day I Have the Blues.' "

> *Nobody loves me, nobody seems to care*
> *Speaking of bad luck and trouble*
> *Baby you know I've had my share*
> *You see me worried baby*
> *Because it's you I hate to lose*
> *Every day . . . every day I have the blues*
> *Every day . . . every day I have the blues*

Nobody's Perfect

Making a picture with her was like going to the dentist. It was hell at the time, but after it was over, it was wonderful.

—Billy Wilder

Scripts arrived daily for Marilyn Monroe's consideration, but Marilyn wasn't in a rush to make another movie. Arthur Miller and May Reis reviewed the various proposed productions, carefully going over the screenplays and occasionally passing on to Marilyn the few they thought had possibilities. According to Lena Pepitone, Marilyn would read a couple of pages, toss the script in a corner, and complain, "Another stupid blonde. I can't stand it!"

Arthur read a synopsis submitted by Billy Wilder called *Some Like It Hot*, a wacka-doo Roaring Twenties comedy about two musicians who accidentally witness the Chicago St. Valentine's Day massacre. To hide from the killers they dress up as women and jump on a train headed for Florida with Sweet Sue's Society Syncopaters, an all-girl jazz band. Wilder wanted Marilyn to play Sugar Kane, the band's lead singer who befriends the two new "girls."

When Marilyn read the synopsis she was incensed. "I've played dumb blondes before, but never *that* dumb. How couldn't I recognize that they were men? I won't do it!" she told Miller. "Never!"

But Miller had been idle professionally for some time. The better part

of his royalties were consumed by alimony payments and legal fees connected with his contempt citation. He had been living on his wife's income from *The Prince and the Showgirl*, which was rapidly diminishing.
They needed money. She was offered $100,000 for starring in *Some Like
It Hot*, plus a historic ten percent of the gross profits.

Lena Pepitone observed that Miller tried very calmly to convince Marilyn what a great opportunity the film would be, and suggested that "they
could make a fortune from the project." Despite the fact their resources
were dwindling, the mere mention of money sent Marilyn into a rage. She
complained, "Money! All he cares about is money. Not me! I can't take
another one of these parts. This is the dumbest ever! Why doesn't *he* try
to write something *he* hates? Then he'd see!"

Miller persuaded her to at least discuss the film with Wilder, who flew
to New York with Jack Lemmon and Tony Curtis to convince her that
the part would be a milestone in her career. When Marilyn read the
completed screenplay by Wilder and I. A. L. Diamond, she appreciated
the humor and saw an opportunity to do a portrayal, but ultimately it
was Lee Strasberg who opened the door for Marilyn to pick up the ukulele
and jump aboard the Pullman with Sweet Sue's Society Syncopaters.

"I've got a real problem, Lee," she told him. "I just can't believe in the
central situation. I'm supposed to be real cozy with these two newcomers,
who are really men in drag. Now how can I possibly feel a thing like that
without just being too stupid?"

Strasberg considered her quandary for several moments before replying,
"Well, that shouldn't be a problem. You know, Marilyn, it's very difficult
for you to have a relationship with other women. They're always jealous
of you. When you come into a room, all the men flock around, but women
kind of keep their distance. So you've never really had a girlfriend."

"That's almost true," Marilyn replied.

"A lot of men have wanted to be your friend," Strasberg continued,
"But you haven't ever had friends who were girls. Now suddenly, here are
two women, and they want to be your friend! They like you. For the first
time in your life, you have two friends who are girls!"

Strasberg said that Marilyn's eyes glowed with appreciation. Sugar had
a *need* to believe in the friendship. It was something Marilyn could use.

On July 8, 1958, Marilyn and her entourage, May Reis and Paula Strasberg, arrived in Los Angeles and checked into the Bel Air Hotel. That
afternoon she appeared at a press conference with Billy Wilder and costars
Tony Curtis and Jack Lemmon. It was her first public appearance in Hol-

lywood since *Bus Stop*, and the press clamored for interviews. Stunning in a diaphanous white silk dress, she announced she was back in Hollywood to star in *Some Like It Hot*.

Producer Harold Mirisch gave Marilyn a lavish dinner party to celebrate her return to Hollywood. Some eighty guests on the Hollywood A list were invited for cocktails at seven, which was to be followed by dinner at nine. The guests were beginning to leave when Marilyn arrived at eleven-twenty.

Shortly before the film was scheduled to start production, the United States Court of Appeals in Washington reversed Miller's contempt citation, and he flew to Los Angeles and joined Marilyn at her Bel Air Hotel suite. She greeted him with the news that she was pregnant. Overjoyed at the prospect that this time she might become a mother, Marilyn contemplated dropping out of Billy Wilder's production, but Miller felt she should proceed with the film, which was scheduled to wrap by the end of September. Marilyn called Norman Rosten to ask his advice:

"Should I do my next picture or stay home and try to have a baby again? That's what I want most of all, a baby, I guess, but maybe God is trying to tell me something, I mean with all my pregnancy problems. I'd probably make a kooky mother, I'd love my child to death. I want it, yet I'm scared. Arthur says he wants it, but he's losing his enthusiasm. He thinks I should do the picture."

Rosten's response was in the form of a poem he sent in July:

> *Of Gemini born, the twin stars,*
> *Twin demons of her cold sky,*
> *The body aflame, the soul in dread.*
> *Round her the Furies in their black ring*
> *Obscenely mocked, crying Give us love.*
> *We watched and bought her anguish with our coins.*

The prophetic anguish began shortly after the start date of *Some Like It Hot*, August 4, 1958. The film had a relatively short schedule for a major film—forty-five days. Most of it was to be shot on the soundstages of the Samuel Goldwyn studios. Though Billy Wilder had had many problems working with Marilyn on *The Seven Year Itch*, he wasn't prepared for the three-month ordeal that faced him.

Wilder approached his films with kinetic force. Many writers wouldn't work with him because he could be ruthless, bombastic, and insulting in

the manic process he went through to perfect a screenplay. All was preparation for Wilder—putting together the right script and the right cast.
By the time he got to the soundstage, the entire film was already cut in
his mind. He seldom shot masters or close-ups all the way through a scene
because he knew just where he wanted to cut from the long shot and just
when he wanted a two shot or a close-up. He gave editors few choices in
the cutting room. Buoyant and humorous when things were going his way,
he could be a bit of a sadist when crossed. Wilder's mind crackled with
wit, and he enjoyed firing humorous barbs at cast and crew. The rollicking
wisecracks and jokes that bounced between Tony Curtis, Jack Lemmon,
and Wilder on the set were as funny as anything that happened on the
screen, and the production started off with a sense of great camaraderie.
Marilyn's first scene in the shooting schedule was her entrance in the film
as she boards the train for Florida with Sweet Sue's Society Syncopaters.
Wilder recalled, "She had a tremendous sense of joke, as good a delivery
as Judy Holliday, and that's saying a lot. She had kind of an inner sense
of what will play, what will work. She called me after the first daily rushes
because she didn't like the way her introductory scene played. . . . We
made up the new introduction with her new entrance."

In the revised version Sugar is late for the train, which is about to pull
out of the station. She rushes down the platform, wiggle-wobbling on her
high heels. A blast of steam from the engine hits her in the fanny, and
she's impelled forward through the vapor toward the "girl" musicians. It
was an artfully amusing entrance and Wilder observed, "She was absolutely right about that."

The problems began several days later. On the swaying Pullman headed
for Florida, the jazz girls rehearse "Runnin' Wild" with Josephine (Curtis)
on sax, and Daphne (Lemmon) on string bass. As Sugar finishes her lyric,
a flask of booze falls out of her garter onto the floor in front of the distaff
bandleader, who has a strict "no liquor" rule. Wilder wanted Marilyn to
show alarm and fear over the blunder. After several takes Wilder said,
"You aren't surprised or worried enough, Marilyn dear."

They rolled again and Marilyn gave a little more surprise. "Cut!" Wilder
called in the middle of the take. "Let's try it again, dear—a *big* surprise,
this time. You're alarmed and worried and Daphne covers for you—that's
the gag. Now, once more! *Big* surprise!"

What Marilyn had feared was happening: Wilder was painting Sugar
with broad strokes. But Marilyn was determined not to be the Betty Boop

floozy foil for the drag gags. If she had to do a dumb blonde, it was going to be a portrayal. Sugar was going to be three-dimensional, with a heart and soul and motivation, beyond making a gag work.

As the camera rolled once more and the flask fell, she reacted with chagrin and an embarrassed giggle.

"Cut! You still haven't got it, dear. The flask drops. Sue sees that it's booze. And you're alarmed. You're afraid of what might happen. It's a very simple reaction, dear." And Wilder did a demonstration—showing her the broad reaction he wanted. Marilyn began trembling and walked out of the Pullman set to where Black Bart was waiting in the dark. It was one of those moments on a set when crew people pretend not to notice what's happening and make themselves busy doing nothing. Marilyn and Strasberg walked off to a corner of the stage and whispered and nodded for over twenty minutes, while Wilder, the script clerk, and the assistant director, Sam Nelson, exchanged nervous glances.

It was the beginning of the behind-the-scenes battle of *Some Like It Hot*—a cold war waged between star and director. It was to be a *guerre à mort*. The public heard battle reports from the director's camp and those that preferred to play the Wilder card, but they never got a briefing from Marilyn. She was too discreet. The true story of Marilyn Monroe's battle for a character never became public knowledge.

Marilyn's technique was quite different from Curtis's and Lemmon's. They could be joking on the set one moment and step before the cameras the next, giving Wilder Cary Grant or Donald Duck on take one or two. But Marilyn needed total concentration. She knew her limitations and was determined to rise above them. She relied on Paula Strasberg to help her with the character. Commenting to Hedda Hopper on Strasberg's presence on the Wilder set, she said, "Paula gives me confidence and is very helpful. You see, I'm not a quick study, but I'm very serious about my work and am not experienced enough as an actress to chat with friends and workers on the set and then go into a dramatic scene. I like to go directly from a scene into my dressing room and concentrate on the next one and keep my mind in one channel. I envy these people who can meet all comers and go from a bright quip and gay laugh into a scene before the camera. All I'm thinking of is my performance, and I try to make it as good as I know how."

When Wilder realized that Marilyn was toning down Sugar Kane, he kept trying to punch up her performance. Calling "cut" when she wasn't playing a scene the way he envisioned it, he pushed for the exaggerated gesture, the broader reaction, and the underlined dialogue. He was asking her to do things she didn't feel were right for the character, and it broke her concentration.

"I never heard such brilliant direction as Billy gave her," Jack Lemmon stated, "but nothing worked until she felt right about it. She simply said over and over, 'Sorry, I have to do it again.' And if Billy said, 'Well, I tell you, Marilyn, just possibly if you were to . . .'—then she'd reply, 'Just a moment now, Billy, don't talk to me, I'll forget how I want to play it.' That took me over the edge more than once. Nobody could remind her she had a professional commitment."

But Marilyn's commitment was to Sugar Kane. Her instincts told her that Wilder's broader approach was wrong, not only for her, but for the picture. She fought for the character with the only weapon at her disposal—attrition. If Wilder was going to call "cut" on what she brought to the character, she was going to wear him down. If he was going to break her concentration, he'd have to pay for it. When Wilder tried to change her portrayal, she'd flub the scene and never give him enough to use. The constant flubbing, and drying up, and forgetting lines was the exhaustive process Marilyn went through until Wilder gave up. By take twenty-nine, Marilyn's way began looking good to the frustrated director.

Wilder publicly complained, "Marilyn was constantly late, and she demanded take after take—the Strasbergs, after all, had taught her to do things again and again and again until she felt she got them right. Well, now she had us doing things again and again and again. Our nice sane budget was going up like a rocket, our cast relations were a shambles, and I was on the verge of a breakdown. To tell the truth she was impossible—not just difficult."

Another thorn in his side was Paula Strasberg. Black Bart stood in the dark behind the camera making gestures and signals to Marilyn, and after each take Marilyn would look to her rather than Wilder for approval. The stress of the battle led to muscle spasms in Wilder's neck and back, and he was often forced to direct from a reclining board next to the camera. Jack Lemmon and Tony Curtis were among the casualties. Walking around in high-heeled shoes in take after take gave them blisters along with battle fatigue. They grew resentful. In their scenes with Marilyn they were worn out and dry by take twelve, and Marilyn was just getting started. In a moment of pique, Tony Curtis made the widely publicized statement, "Kissing Marilyn was like kissing Hitler."

"Well, I think that's his problem," Marilyn responded. "If I have to do intimate love scenes with somebody who really has that feeling toward me, then my fantasy has to come into play—in other words, out with him, in with my fantasy. He was never there."

Many years later Tony Curtis stated that the "Hitler" remark was taken out of context. They were on take forty-seven of the kissing scene before Wilder gave up and let Marilyn do it her way. When the company was watching the dailies in the projection room, Curtis made the remark, "You know, after take forty, kissing Marilyn is like kissing Hitler."

For many working on the set of *Some Like It Hot*, it seemed that there was no rational basis for Marilyn to constantly blow her lines. In one scene she enters the "girls'" hotel room in quest of some booze. As she opens and closes bureau drawers in search of a hot-water bottle filled with booze, her line was "Where's the bourbon?" Wilder wanted her to play it frantic. But frantic wasn't the way she felt it should be played. He kept calling "cut!" and insisting on a wacka-doo urgency. She gave him twenty-seven frantic takes, but never got the line right—"Where's the whiskey?" "Where's the bureau?" "Where's the booze?" "Where's the bonbons?" "Where's the bottle?" "Where's the bromo?" Wilder resorted to posting the line "Where's the bourbon?" on the back of the door and inside each of the bureau drawers. Still she went up on the line. Finally, when everyone was exhausted and Wilder was getting spasms, she did the scene her way, got the line right, and Wilder said, "Good—that's a print." The scene is on the screen for perhaps fifteen seconds and took half a day to shoot.

Wilder, of course, knew what she was doing, but didn't believe she was right. She knew she was right and believed that a star of her stature had the prerogative of playing a scene the way she felt it. There was a method to her madness, but unfortunately cinema mythology preferred to repeat the myriad stories of Marilyn Monroe's inability to remember a simple line—a myth that was unearthed once again during the debacle of *Something's Got to Give*.

Marilyn was frequently late in arriving at the studio. Sometimes very late. If she had a 9 A.M. set call, it meant getting up at 5 A.M. to get to the studio by six-thirty and go through hairdressing, makeup, and wardrobe by nine. But she couldn't sleep, and she didn't want to take sedatives during her pregnancy. Sometimes it would be 2 or 3 A.M. before she fell asleep, and if she got up at five she'd be no good on camera. So she would sleep the sleep of exhaustion. And she would be late. Quite late. I. A. L.

Diamond, who cowrote the screenplay with Billy Wilder, ascribed Marilyn's lateness to an attempt by the star to throw around the power she had gained following her Fox walkout. "Having reached the top she was paying back the world for all the rotten things she had had to go through," said Diamond. "There were mornings when nine A.M. rolled around and Marilyn was not on the set or anywhere near it. Ten A.M. comes—no Marilyn. She is now in makeup. She is now in hairdressing. Ten forty-five A.M. and she walks in. Everybody has been waiting all morning. Not a word of greeting. Not a word of apology. She's carrying a copy of Thomas Paine's *Rights of Man*, personally given to her by Arthur to read while she's keeping us waiting. Billy waits some more and finally sends the assistant director to her dressing room to knock on the door, and she yells out, "Fuck you!"

Not everybody who worked with Marilyn knew the private ordeal she went through to make the metamorphosis from Norma Jeane to Marilyn Monroe to Sugar Kane. It was a transcendental trick that didn't happen instantaneously. Not only did the Marilyn Monroe image depend on the meticulous way she looked—her makeup, her hair, her wardrobe—but she also had to make up her inner psyche and steel her concentration to fend off the director.

Twenty-nine days over schedule, *Some Like It Hot* completed filming on November 6, 1958. Marilyn got the "fuzzy end of the lollipop" and wasn't invited to the wrap party Wilder gave for the cast and crew. But Marilyn had won the battle. Sugar Kane was etched in silver, and there was nothing Wilder could do about it. The animosity and bitterness would one day be forgotten, but what was on film would endure. The heartfelt and seamless performance of Marilyn Monroe was the substance that glued the film together and kept it from falling into the kinetic mayhem of Wilder's subsequent farce *One, Two, Three*.

She had paid a price. She was suffering from exhaustion and checked into Cedars-Sinai Hospital. A week later she traveled by ambulance to the airport, "so as not to jar the baby," and flew back to New York with Miller.

Some Like It Hot was sneak-previewed at the Village Theater in Westwood on December 17, 1958, and the audience started laughing in the first scene and didn't stop until the fade-out gag when Joe E. Brown discovers that the girl he wants to marry (Jack Lemmon) is not, after all, a girl. He shrugs off the dilemma with the remark, "Nobody's perfect." Audiences have continued laughing ever since, and to date *Some Like It*

Hot has grossed over $47 million and earned over $4,500,000 for Marilyn Monroe's heirs—the majority of it going to Ana Strasberg, a woman Marilyn never knew.

We watched and bought her anguish with our coins.

On the day of the hilariously successful preview, December 17, Marilyn had a miscarriage. She went into a period of deep mourning. Her sessions with Dr. Kris offered little comfort, and over the Christmas holidays she lapsed into a depression which she tried to alleviate with sedatives. She blamed losing the baby on *Some Like It Hot*, on Billy Wilder, and on Miller. She felt she never would have made the movie if Miller hadn't encouraged her. According to her maid, Lena Pepitone, she was terribly upset.

It was shortly after the miscarriage, while she was trying to recuperate, that an interview with Billy Wilder written by Joe Hyams appeared in newspapers across the country. Criticizing Marilyn's lateness and lack of professionalism, Wilder stated, "I'm the only director who ever made two pictures with Monroe. It behooves the Screen Director's Guild to award me a purple heart." Complaining that her behavior had made him ill, Hyams inquired whether Wilder's health had improved after completing *Some Like It Hot*. "I'm eating better," Wilder replied, "My back doesn't ache any more. I am able to sleep for the first time in months, and I can look at my wife without wanting to hit her because she's a woman." Asked if he would like to do another picture with Marilyn Monroe, Wilder replied, "Well, I have discussed this with my doctor and my psychiatrist, and they tell me I'm too old and too rich to go through this again."

When Marilyn read the syndicated interview, she was furious. She couldn't believe that Wilder would publicly joke about her in the press. Lena Pepitone recalled her shouting, "I made *him* sick?" as she shredded the newspaper into tiny pieces. "I made *him* sick!!" She leapt out of bed and ran into Miller's study screaming, "It's your fault! It's your damn fault!" Pepitone could hear her shouting at Miller from the far end of the apartment, "You damn well better do something about it, you bleeding-heart bastard! Now everybody in the world'll take me as a fool—a joke! You've got to say something! People'll listen to *you. You've* got respect!"

Miller suggested she forget about it.

"Forget it? *Forget* it!" she shrieked. "I'll never forget it! How could I ever forget my baby? . . . My *baby*!"

Marilyn began crying hysterically, and Pepitone recalled that Miller helped her back to her room. He couldn't deal with noise and arguments, and he hoped she would take a sedative and go to sleep and forget the whole thing. But several times that day she became hysterical once again and ran to his study screaming, crying hysterically, and pulling at her hair. Miller retreated to the farm. Several nights later Norman and Hedda Rosten received a phone call from May Reis at 3 A.M. Marilyn had overdosed.

Pepitone found her unconscious on the bedroom floor, her face caked with vomit. Unable to awaken her, Pepitone called the doctor whose number was on the emergency list in May Reis's office. The doctor rushed to the apartment, pumped Marilyn's stomach, and put her in bed. When May Reis arrived, she called Miller and then the Rostens.

It had been another close call. Norman Rosten recalled that toward dawn she regained consciousness and began weeping quietly in her bed. As Rosten leaned over in the half-light, he asked, "How are you, dear?"

"Alive . . . bad luck," she weakly replied. "Cruel, all of them *cruel*, all those bastards. Oh, Jesus . . ."

On the Ledge

Never give all the heart
For everything that's lovely is
But a brief, dreamy, kind delight
*O never give the heart outright. . . . **
                                    —W. B. Yeats

Though he hadn't completed a play in five years, on January 27, 1959, Arthur Miller was awarded one of the nation's most prestigious literary awards, the gold medal for drama of the National Institute of Arts and Letters. Marilyn Monroe, on the other hand, thought some of his writing on *The Misfits* was "dreck."

Norman Rosten observed, "The pupil/student had now become a critic. The shadow that had fallen between them in England was increasing, deepening. Their evenings with friends were often played out in a facade of marital harmony. Miller was more and more living with her in the third person, as it were, an observer."

Miller looked down on screenwriting, and he insisted that writing *The Misfits* was a sacrifice on his part, made for Marilyn. Yet Marilyn wasn't at all sure she wanted to appear in *The Misfits*. "She would read parts of

---

* One evening at a poetry reading at the Rostens', a copy of Yeats was passed around for each person to open and read at random. At Marilyn's turn, she opened to "Never Give All the Heart." "She read the title, paused, and began the poem," Rosten said. "She read it slowly, discovering it, letting the lines strike her, surprised, hanging on, winning by absolute simplicity and truth. When she finished, there was a hush."

the screenplay and laugh delightedly at some of the cowboy's lines," Miller stated, "but seemed to withhold full commitment to playing Roslyn. . . . I was constructing a gift for her. In the end, however, it was she who would have to play the role, and this inevitably began to push the project into a different coolly professional sphere. If my intention was as authentic as I wished to believe it was, she had a right to decide not to play the part—after all I was not writing it to enslave her to something she had no excitement about doing. Nevertheless, her caution had to hurt a bit."

Arthur Miller was to receive $250,000 from Marilyn Monroe Productions in compensation for the "gift" of *The Misfits*, which he wrapped in bright ribbons: Arthur brought in John Huston as the director, the part of Gay was written especially for Clark Gable, and Marilyn's friends Montgomery Clift, Kevin McCarthy, and Eli Wallach would be included in the cast.

Lena Pepitone reported, "Marilyn was getting a terrible chip on her shoulder against her husband and she said, 'All he cares about is himself, his own writing . . . and money—that's all!' " According to Lena, it never occurred to Marilyn just how much money was necessary to keep the two households going: the staff, the rent, the attorneys, the clothes, the beauticians, and the doctors—Miller was undergoing psychotherapy with Dr. Rudolph Loewenstein, while Marilyn was having almost daily sessions with Marianne Kris. "Marilyn assumed that plenty of money was there," Lena recalled. "If she was so famous how could she be poor, she thought. 'I worried about money for too long,' she said. 'I'm sick of it. I'm never going to worry about it again.' " When Arthur, or Mr. Montgomery, or May Reis tried to discuss finances with Marilyn, she would put her hands over her ears and turn away. "I don't want anything. Not money! Not things! I've got things," she said. "I just want to act. I want friends. I want to be happy! I want some respect! I don't want to be laughed at. Doesn't anyone understand?"

Jack Kennedy understood. Gene Tierney had once said, "I'm not sure I can explain the nature of Jack's charm. He made you feel very secure. He gave you his time, his interest." Kennedy's attentiveness, wit, and directness, along with his ability to make you feel secure, were certainly not lost on Marilyn.

Peter Lawford and others observed that Jack Kennedy merely regarded Marilyn as another trophy to be added to his extensive collection, but Kennedy and Marilyn had a unique relationship that ultimately endured for over a decade. Few of his casual affairs with women could claim such longevity. Unlike his relationships with Inga Arvad and Gene Tierney, the relationship with Marilyn endured despite geographic separations, marriage, and other inconveniences, and when all hope of her relationship with Arthur Miller came to an end, she continued seeing Jack Kennedy.

Lena Pepitone, who was at the Manhattan apartment from 9 A.M. to 6 P.M., said that Marilyn spoke much more about Jack Kennedy than Bobby Kennedy, and "referred to him as 'that big tease.' He was always telling her dirty jokes, pinching her, squeezing her, she said. She told me that he was always putting his hand on her thigh. One night, under the dinner table, he kept going. But when he discovered she wasn't wearing any panties, he pulled back and turned red. 'He hadn't counted on going that far,' Marilyn laughed."

According to Pepitone, Marilyn thought that Jack Kennedy had married Jacqueline Bouvier "because their families made them. . . . I feel sorry for them, locked into a marriage I bet neither of them likes. I can tell he's not in love—not with her."

Jack Kennedy had told Marilyn that he was in love with *her*, and she revealed to Bob Slatzer, who had visited her in New York, that she and Kennedy would one day be married. Kennedy had led Marilyn to believe he would seek an annulment of his marriage with Jacqueline.

According to Susan Strasberg, "Marilyn seemed bored with the part-time role of country housewife," and in 1959 she seldom visited the Roxbury farm, where Miller was preoccupied with *The Misfits*. In March the Millers attended the New York premiere of *Some Like It Hot*. Newspaper photos taken of Marilyn on Miller's arm at the premiere party show her radiant and smiling, giving no hint of domestic discord or her intense dissatisfaction with any aspect of *Some Like It Hot*. Uncharacteristically, she went to Chicago on a promotional tour—something she had not done since *Love Happy*.

Jack Kennedy was another visitor to the Windy City at the same time. In meetings with Sam Giancana and Mayor Daley, JFK was soliciting assistance for his forthcoming election campaign. According to Sam Giancana's brother, Chuck, meetings were held at the Ambassador East and both Sam Giancana and Mayor Richard Daley were there. FBI surveillance confirms that a deal was struck in which the Mafia would assist JFK's campaign. One of Mayor Daley's aides was surprised to find that Marilyn Monroe was also a guest at the Ambassador.

Returning to New York, Marilyn resumed her classes with Lee Strasberg at the Actors Studio, and while Miller was preoccupied with the cinematic iconography of his wife, she was pursuing her own literary interests: lunching with Carson McCullers at her Nyack home, having poetry discussions with Isak Dinesen, visiting with the Pulitzer Prize–winning author of *Profiles in Courage* at the Carlyle, and having literary discussions with Carl Sandburg, who became an occasional visitor at the Fifty-Seventh Street apartment. Sandburg found Marilyn to be "warm and plain" and asked for her autograph. "Marilyn was a good talker and very good company," he stated. "We did some mock play acting and some pretty good, funny imitations. I asked her a lot of questions. She told me how she came up the hard way, but she would never talk about her husbands."

Marilyn's contract with Fox required her to fill a studio commitment before she could proceed with the MMP production of *The Misfits*. Fox producer Jerry Wald had suggested *Let's Make Love*, a Technicolor musical comedy written by Norman Krasna, which was to be directed by George Cukor and costar Gregory Peck.

Though the script had obvious problems, Marilyn agreed to do the film in order to fulfill her Fox commitment, and Miller agreed to rewrite the screenplay. Miller recalled, "I had all but given up any hope of writing: I had decided to devote myself to giving [Marilyn] the kind of emotional support that would convince her she was no longer alone in the world— the heart of the problem, I assumed. I went so far as to do some rewriting on *Let's Make Love* to try and save her from a complete catastrophe, work I despised on a script not worth the paper it was typed on."

In September, Marilyn flew to the West Coast for studio conferences on *Let's Make Love* and met Soviet Premier Nikita Khrushchev at a reception held at Fox Studios. "You're a very lovely young lady," Khrushchev said. Her response made newspaper headlines around the world: "My husband, Arthur Miller, sends you his greetings. There should be more of this kind of thing. It would help both our countries understand each other." And in a rare tribute from the gentlemen of the fourth estate, as she boarded the plane to return to the East Coast the crush of reporters broke into applause instead of bombarding her with questions.

While Marilyn was in Hollywood, Yves Montand and his wife, Simone Signoret, had arrived in New York, where Montand was to open his highly successful one-man show at the Henry Miller Theater. Marilyn went to the opening night with Montgomery Clift and was so impressed by Montand's performance that she returned the next night with Miller and Norman and Hedda Rosten. Rosten recalled that the audience snickered at unlikely moments because it was obvious Montand's pants were unbuttoned—a recurring problem.

When Gregory Peck became aware that Arthur Miller was rewriting Norman Krasna's script for Marilyn, and his part was diminishing day by day, he dropped out of the film. Arthur suggested that Peck be replaced by Yves Montand, and Marilyn agreed. After Jerry Wald and George Cukor saw Montand's show, he was signed by Fox as Marilyn's costar, and Arthur began rewriting the Peck role for Montand.

In November and December, Marilyn commuted between New York and Hollywood for wardrobe fittings, color tests, and rehearsals of the musical numbers, which were choreographed by Marilyn's friend Jack Cole. According to the British singing star Frankie Vaughan, who played a supporting role, "She was always on time for rehearsals. There were none of those notorious late starts. When she arrived, everybody smartened up, as if her presence was the light that fell on everyone. Certainly she seemed to be very professional."

By the end of 1959, many of Marilyn's dreams had become realities. Having received rave reviews in four successive motion pictures, she had earned the film industry's respect and had become the world's top box-office attraction—the most celebrated film star of the twentieth century. But when George Belmont of *Marie Claire* asked her if she was happy, she said, "If I can realize certain things in my work, I come the closest to being happy. But it only happens in moments. I'm not just generally happy. If I'm generally anything, I guess I'm generally miserable, but since I'm only thirty-three and have a few years to go yet, I hope to have time to become better and happier, professionally and in my personal life. That's my one ambition. Maybe I'll need a long time, because I'm slow. I don't want to say that it's the best method, but it's the only one I know and it gives me the feeling that in spite of everything life is not without hope."

Though she knew her marriage to Arthur Miller was all but over, she had her career, and she dreamed that one day she might be Mrs. John Kennedy. "You have to remember that Marilyn worked and lived in a dream world," confided her friend Henry Rosenfeld. " She began to live in her dreams, and her dream was to marry Jack Kennedy—and supplant Jackie."

But during the holiday season of 1959, Marilyn's dream reached the rainbow's end. In December it was made clear that Jack Kennedy would never divorce his wife. Jack was going to run for president. Divorce was out of the question.

At a dinner party in Manhattan Norman Rosten noticed the sadness that enveloped her.

> I watched her seated on the windowsill sipping her drink, staring moodily down to the street below. I knew that look more and more. She was floating off in her personal daydream, out of contact, gripped by thoughts that could not be pleasant. I went up to her and said softly, "Hey, pssst, come back."
>
> She turned. "I'm going to have sleep trouble again tonight. I get that way now and then . . . and I'm thinking it's a quick way down from here." I nodded because it was a fact, but it was the first time she spoke of this. She continued, "Who'd know the difference if I went?" I answered, "I would—and all the people in this room who care. They'd hear the crash." She laughed. Right then and there we made a pact. If either of us was about to jump, or take the gas, or the rope, or pills, he or she would phone the other. We each committed ourselves to talk the other out of it. We made the pact jokingly, but I believed it. I felt that one day I would get a call. She'd say, "It's me. I'm on the ledge," and I'd reply, "You can't jump today, it's Lincoln's birthday," or something unfunny, like that.

According to Dr. Ralph Greenson's correspondence with Marianne Kris, Greenson first met Marilyn in bungalow 21 of the Beverly Hills Hotel when the actress had a nervous collapse. Though it has been variously written that Marilyn's breakdown took place because she was distraught over her brief love affair with Yves Montand, Dr. Greenson's correspondence with Kris establishes that he first visited Marilyn Monroe in January 1960, which was prior to the affair with her *Let's Make Love* costar but soon after Jack Kennedy announced he was running for president.

According to Ralph Greenson's wife, Hildi, Marilyn's New York psychoanalyst had called Greenson to ask if he would see her patient for a few sessions to help her over a "difficult situation." Dr. Kris explained that Marilyn was suffering "severe anxiety stress." But there were unusual circumstances that brought Otto Fenichel's disciple, the former Romeo Greenschpoon, to Norma Jeane's door. When Greenson first visited Marilyn, he had become well established in the Freudian couch culture of Hollywood. Among his more illustrious clients were Peter Lorre, Celeste Holm, producer Dore Schary, Vincente Minnelli, Inger Stevens, and Frank Sinatra. When Sinatra had become despondent over the breakup of his marriage to Ava Gardner and slashed his wrists, his lawyer, Mickey Rudin, suggested that Sinatra see Rudin's brother-in-law, Dr. Ralph Greenson. Rudin was an attorney for Gang, Tyre, and Brown, which often represented entertainment personalities under investigation by the Un-American Activities Committee, and insiders would joke as to which brother-in-law had the more star-studded clientele, the lawyer or the analyst. Dr. Greenson was on the Communist Party's secret list of analysts approved for party members, and often their clients overlapped.

Mickey Rudin was both Frank Sinatra's and Marilyn Monroe's lawyer, and Rudin and his wife, Elizabeth Greenschpoon Rudin, were privy to Marilyn's intimacy with the presidential candidate, as of course were Marianne Kris and Miller's analyst, Rudolph Loewenstein. Marianne Kris and her late husband Ernst were good friends of Ralph and Hildi Greenson, as well as friends of Greenson's former Air Force commander, John M. Murray.*

It was an odd set of circumstances and relationships that had brought Marilyn Monroe into this close-knit circle of Freudian-Marxists, and when Greenson knocked on Norma Jeane's door he arrived with an uncommon knowledge of Marilyn's relationship with JFK and an insight into the problems that had led his patient into her "severe anxiety stress."

Dr. Greenson found the film star heavily sedated. Marilyn slurred her words and had poor reactions. She seemed remote and failed to understand simple conversation. When she proceeded to recite the litany of drugs she had been taking—Demerol, sodium pentothal, phenobarbital, amytal—he became alarmed. Greenson's immediate problem was to bring her drug abuse under control. Later, he was to express his anger at the "stupid doctors" who had caved in to Marilyn's prescription requests. Marilyn had a long list of doctors in her phone book whom she could ply with her needs. In the future Dr. Greenson would try to make sure she used only one physician, and he strongly recommended a prominent Beverly Hills internist—Dr. Hyman Engelberg.

Dr. Greenson's visit to Marilyn's bungalow lasted several hours, and by the time he departed Marilyn felt much better. Impressed by Greenson's warmth and understanding, she asked him to return on a regular basis. So began what would prove to be a very unusual doctor-patient relationship which ended in Marilyn Monroe's death two and a half years later.

* The Krises' son, Anton, became John M. Murray's analysand and delivered the eulogy at Dr. Murray's funeral.

After several visits with Greenson, Marilyn returned to rehearsals for *Let's Make Love*. Although she was officially a patient of Marianne Kris's, while she was on the West Coast she was under Greenson's care. In the ensuing months, Greenson and Kris would correspond and compare notes. Greenson wrote that his goal was to wean Marilyn from her array of drugs and help her with her sleeping problems. He reported listening to her "venomous resentment" toward Arthur Miller. She claimed her husband was "cold and unresponsive" to her problems and attracted to other women. He also noted symptoms of paranoia and observed signs of schizophrenia. He wrote, "As she becomes more anxious, she begins to act like an orphan, a waif, and she masochistically provokes [people] to mistreat her and to take advantage of her. As fragments of her past history came out, she began to talk more about the traumatic experience of an 'orphan child.' " Undoubtedly they discussed the problems which had precipitated her breakdown, and he observed her acute sense of rejection.

Marilyn was very impressed by the analyst's knowledge and understanding. She began to refer to him as "My Jesus—My Savior." When Marilyn telephoned Lena Pepitone in New York she raved about her new analyst and said, "Lena, Lena, I've finally found him. I've found a Jesus for myself!"

"A Jesus?" asked Pepitone.

"Yes, I call him Jesus. He's doing wonderful things for me."

"What?" Pepitone inquired, "What does he do?"

"He listens to me."

"What exactly does he do for you besides listen?" Pepitone asked.

"He gives me courage. He makes me feel smart, makes me think. I can face anything with him. I'm not scared anymore."

However, Marilyn was unaware of the curious set of circumstances that had brought Dr. Ralph Greenson to the door of the fascinating woman who knew many secrets about the man who was destined to be president of the United States.

A case history for the files of the Kremlin was on the couch.

PART V

1960–1962

Rainbow's End

Let's Make Love

If Marilyn is in love with my husband, it proves she has good taste.

—Simone Signoret

At a press reception held by Fox for Yves Montand in January 1960, Marilyn was the smiling, beautiful hostess. "She still has the old glamour, the magic," wrote Sidney Skolsky. Making a toast to Montand, Marilyn stated, "Next to my husband and Marlon Brando, I think Yves Montand is the most attractive man I've ever met."

When asked how he felt about working with Monroe, Montand commented, "Everything she do is, how you say?—'original'—even when she stand and talk to you." Montand added in his best manufractured Franglaise, "She help me, I try to help her."

But he didn't know just how much help she needed. He didn't know that her marriage to Arthur Miller was all but over, and he didn't know about Jack Kennedy. Montand had a morphological resemblance to Miller, but none of Miller's coldness; he had the warmth and charm of Jack Kennedy, but none of the calculating duplicity. Montand didn't know that everything she do was, how you say?—on the rebound.

Shortly after the Millers moved into bungalow 21 at the Beverly Hills Hotel, Fox arranged for Yves Montand and his wife, Simone Signoret, to move into bungalow 20—just next door. The two couples became immediate friends and joined each other for home-cooked meals and late-night discussions. The Montands had starred in the French production of *The Crucible*, and they shared Arthur's political convictions; Simone Signoret appreciated Marilyn's humor and eccentricities. She didn't see Marilyn as a threat.

Montand was so totally preoccupied with trying to learn English and master his lines that he was oblivious to *le piège amoureux* he had fallen into. "If I was thinking of falling in love with anything," he said, "it was the English language. I was a million miles from thinking that anything whatsoever could happen between Marilyn and me. In the beginning Marilyn and I had only one thing in common—our obsession with our work. She worked, worked, worked."

One evening in February after filming had begun, the Montands and the Millers had gone to La Scala for dinner and were driving back to the hotel when Marilyn whispered to Yves, "You know, Cukor's not such a hot director."

"What?"

"Cukor's a lousy director."

"Sorry, don't say that. Is not true," Montand replied, already in a bit of a panic because he couldn't understand a word Cukor said. "Cukor great director—you look beautiful, but I think you're afraid of acting. You need—how you say?—rehearsals."

"Yes, you're right. I think maybe we should rehearse," Marilyn replied.

Montand recalled that was how they began to work together, seeking to calm their respective fears. "I would knock at her door, or she would come to me. We would sit facing each other and rehearse. She corrected my English, and I did my best to get her to trust herself. The image that comes back to me is of Marilyn in jeans, a plaid shirt open at the neck, and those incredibly blue eyes that maintained the clarity other women's only rarely possess."

Arthur Miller observed, "I guess it [our marriage] was deteriorating. . . . Marilyn was looking at Montand rather idolatrously, and she couldn't realize that he was not this tower of strength. At any period of her life, the oncoming stranger was vitally important. He or she was invested with immense promise, which of course was smashed when this person was discovered to be human."

Always in search of the man she could rely on, Marilyn found that Montand's assurance and *joie de vivre* had a way of giving her confidence. Montand took pride in his professionalism, and it soon became apparent to those on the set of *Let's Make Love* that Marilyn was responding to his influence—becoming more cooperative and showing up on schedule. Her new punctuality came as a gratifying surprise to Cukor and producer Jerry Wald.

"She's got so she'll do whatever I ask her to do on the set," Montand confided, "and everyone's amazed at her cooperation." Much to Paula Strasberg's displeasure, Cukor noticed that Marilyn was often turning to Montand for approval after a take rather than Black Bart, who was now making two thousand dollars a week as Marilyn's coach.

There were bad days, however, when Marilyn would leave the set early in the afternoon to visit Dr. Ralph Greenson, and Cukor would have to shoot around her. Following the initial sessions with Greenson at the hotel bungalow in January, Marilyn continued her visits with the psychoanalyst at the office he shared with Dr. Milton Wexler at 405 North Bedford Drive—the libido lane of Beverly Hills. The doctor's office was conveniently located between Fox Studios and the Beverly Hills Hotel, and Marilyn visited it as often as her schedule allowed—sometimes on a daily basis.

In a letter Greenson wrote to Marianne Kris, he describes Marilyn as "such a perpetual orphan that I felt even sorrier as she tried so hard and failed so often, which also made her pathetic." He encouraged her to telephone each day when she was out of town or unable to see him "so that she would understand his values and translate them into the things she needed to survive."

Another Ralph in Marilyn's life was Ralph Roberts. While Ralph Greenson massaged the minds of the movie stars, Ralph Roberts was known as the physical "masseur to the stars." He had studied physiotherapy and was familiar with the unique muscular problems of performers. An actor himself, Ralph Roberts had first met Marilyn at Lee Strasberg's apartment in 1955 when he was studying with Strasberg and appearing on Broadway in *The Lark* with Julie Harris and Boris Karloff.

In 1959 he traveled to Hollywood as Judy Holliday's masseur during the filming of *Bells Are Ringing*. Learning that Ralph Roberts was in Hollywood, Marilyn called him when the rigorous dance rehearsals for *Let's Make Love* began. They became close friends, and from the beginning she referred to him as "Rafe" (as in waif). Though he was well over six feet tall and had a rather forbidding appearance, Roberts was a gentle soul— a soft-spoken, cultured gentleman from North Carolina.

———

At the end of February, production of *Let's Make Love* was put on hold for several weeks by an actors' and writers' strike over television residuals. During the hiatus, Miller and Marilyn planned to fly back east for meetings with her attorney Aaron Frosch. "I'll miss you," Marilyn whispered affectionately in Montand's ear—adding a special good-bye. Not understanding what she said, he noted down the words and later asked a friend what they meant. When the phrase was translated he was touched, but "thought no more about it." Just before Arthur and Marilyn departed, the Academy of Motion Picture Arts and Sciences announced the Oscar contenders. Among the nominees were Shelley Winters as best supporting actress in *The Diary of Anne Frank* and Simone Signoret as best actress in *Room at the Top.*

"Good luck! I know you're going to get it!" Marilyn shouted to Signoret as the Millers left for the airport. But she was in fact a bit jealous and disappointed that her performance as Sugar Kane in *Some Like It Hot* hadn't received a nomination. It was regarded by critics nationwide as one of the best comedic performances in years. But Hollywood Academy voters were somewhat peeved by what they perceived as the East Coast parvenu pretenses of the valley girl, and while Doris Day was nominated for her performance in *Pillow Talk,* Marilyn wasn't considered.

On the starry night of the Thirty-Second Academy Awards, Shelley Winters won the Oscar for best supporting actress, and later in the ceremonies Fred Astaire introduced Yves Montand, who sang and danced a tribute to Astaire, *"Un Garçon Dansait."* As he took his bows to thunderous applause and went to the wings, Montand was told by director Vincente Minnelli to return to his seat. "No, no," Yves said. "The next Oscar is for best actress, and Marilyn say my wife is going to get it." Rock Hudson opened the envelope and proved Marilyn correct. Simone had a picture commitment in Europe, and several days later she flew off to Rome with her Oscar—and Marilyn was bestowed with her Yves.

Shortly after the Millers had returned to Hollywood, Arthur flew to Ireland for *The Misfits* preproduction meetings with John Huston, and Montand wondered if his halting English was playing tricks on him when Miller said good-bye to him and muttered, "What will happen will happen."

Doris Vidor, a friend of Montand and the Millers, recalled that Montand telephoned her in "an absolute state." Montand exclaimed to Doris, "He's leaving me with Marilyn, and our apartments are adjoining. Do you think that Arthur doesn't know that she is beginning to throw herself at me?" Doris Vidor recalled telling Montand, "Yves, I think this is getting very complicated. . . . I would be suspicious of Arthur's leaving at this time. How do you know that he isn't deliberately going? Maybe he's tired of the burden that he's had, and maybe he's glad someone is around to step in."

Montand recalled in his memoirs:

I had Marilyn all to myself. But it was as a partner and a friend that I called on her to rehearse with. Every night after getting back from the studio we worked for an hour or two. When we got up after it was over, we were both still living in the tension of the rehearsal. I'd be smoking a cigarette, and then she'd smile and say, "Okay, now we'll eat." Then I look at her, and I think she is amazingly beautiful, healthy, desirable. I felt this powerful radiation, the impact of the amazing charisma!

One day she was really, how you say?—"wiped out!"—much too tired to rehearse and not feeling well. And I had a tricky scene the next day. I was getting ready to leave the studio and go work on my own, when I bumped into Mrs. Strasberg. "Go and say good-night to Marilyn," she said. "It'll make her feel better. It's bothering her that she can't rehearse." I went. I remember that the living room was all white—white chairs, white curtains—with the exception of a black table. There was caviar and, as usual, a bottle of champagne. I sat on the side of the bed and patted her head.

"Do you have a fever?"

"A little, but it'll be okay. I'm glad to see you."

"So am I. I'm glad to see you."

"How was your day?"

"Good, good."

It was the dullest exchange you can imagine. I still had a half-page to work on for the next day. I bent down to put a good-night kiss on her cheek. And her head turned, and my lips went wild. It was a wonderful, tender kiss. A kiss of fire. I was half stunned, stammering, I straightened up, already flooded with guilt, wondering what was happening to me. I didn't wonder for long.

It soon became obvious on the set of *Let's Make Love* that the stars were taking the title seriously, and the love affair that developed between Marilyn Monroe and Yves Montand quietly became a matter of Hollywood gossip.

Columnist Dorothy Kilgallen gave the first hint to the public when she commented, "An actress whose name came up at this year's Oscars is currently having marital problems." Soon a Beverly Hills Hotel room-service waiter was telling bedroom stories to journalist James Bacon, and the Montand-Monroe affair became public knowledge. It was feeding time at the paparazzi zoo. Some reported that the star turned up at bungalow 20 "naked beneath her mink coat." Arthur Miller was reported to have left his pipe behind at the hotel and returned to discover the lovers in bed. Hedda Hopper confidentially advised Marilyn in her widely syndicated column, "You have still to prove that you are a great actress. Your success is due only to publicity. I beseech you, Marilyn, stop this self-destruction."

Amid the tabloid feeding frenzy, Marilyn Monroe was presented with the Golden Globe Award as the Best Actress of 1959 for *Some Like it Hot*. And *Life* and *Look* were preparing stories on the on-screen/off-screen lovers of *Let's Make Love*.

By the time Miller returned to Hollywood and rejoined Marilyn at the Beverly Hills Hotel, news of the Monroe-Montand affair filled the gossip columns and had become a public drama. In recalling his feelings at the time, Miller stated, "I couldn't help her. By this time I represented betrayals and misplaced trust. And there was no possibility of erasing that from her mind. It was just there."

According to Norman Rosten, "Montand wasn't the only one. There had been others. She hadn't been totally faithful to Arthur for some time. Marilyn had this terrible neediness. When she felt insecure she went with other men simply for something to hold on to."

The extended shooting schedule of *Let's Make Love* was slated to end in mid-June, and Marilyn wanted to believe that her relationship with Montand was more than a passing affair scheduled to end with the production. But as filming neared its conclusion, Montand admitted hovering between "intoxication and panic." Marilyn, he said, "clung to me . . . and the light in her eyes indicated such joy was meant to last."

In his memoirs, Montand recalled, "I was touched—touched because it was beautiful, and it was impossible. Not for a moment did I think of breaking with my wife, but if she [Simone] had slammed the door on me, I would probably have made my life with Marilyn, or tried to. That was the direction we were moving in. Maybe it would have lasted only two or three years. I didn't have too many illusions. Still, what years they would have been!" But when the shooting schedule drew to a close and *Let's Make Love* completed filming, both the on-screen and the off-screen romance were a wrap.

Marilyn left Hollywood for *The Misfits* wardrobe tests in New York, while Montand stayed on the West Coast for contract negotiations. On June 30, Montand flew to New York on his way back to Europe. Marilyn met him at the airport for what she hoped would be a rendezvous, but ended up being a tearful *adieu*. They said good-bye in the back seat of a Cadillac limousine parked at the terminal, while Montand waited to board his plane for France. He told her he had been happy with her and hoped that he had occasionally made her happy too, but he had no intention of leaving his wife.

He flew off to Paris, where Simone and the paparazzi were waiting. "The Montands have survived Hurricane Marilyn," headlined *Paris-Match*. And Marilyn was left, how you say?—*on the lurch*.

The Jack Pack

You must remember—it's not what you are that counts, but what people think you are.

—Joseph P. Kennedy

By the time Joseph P. Kennedy turned sixty in September 1948, the man from the east docks of Boston had amassed a fortune in excess of $400 million. He decided to give himself a birthday present worthy of the occasion, and a bevy of Boston beauties were paraded through his suite at the Ritz-Carlton. He chose Janet Des Rosier, a twenty-four-year-old graduate of Leicester High School with a timeless hourglass figure. Des Rosier was bright, funny, and beautiful. In her photos she has a striking similarity to Rose in her bloom.

"He was very taken with me," Des Rosier recalled. "He made up his mind right then and there that I would be his." She became Joe Kennedy's mistress, secretary, and companion.

A decade later, when Kennedy became a septuagenarian and the flagging ambassador began hearing the echoing refrains of "September Song," he arranged for his mistress to become an executive of General Dynamics Corporation. When it was decided that Jack Kennedy was going to run for president, Joe Kennedy discussed leasing a General Dynamics Convair twin-engine turbo prop for his company, and Janet Des Rosier arranged for a demo flight for the candidate and his entourage from Washington to New York. Ten days later, Joe Kennedy called Des Rosier and exclaimed, "Hell, Janet, Jack isn't going to rent a plane from you. We're going to buy him one."

Christened the *Caroline* after Jack Kennedy's daughter, the Convair was purchased for $385,000 and came with many custom-built luxury appointments and plush features—along with Janet Des Rosier, who became Jack Kennedy's stewardess, secretary, and masseuse. When Kennedy lost his voice during the campaign, he wrote notes on a legal pad instead of talking. Des Rosier kept the pad and later sold some of the more unusual notations from the rigors of the campaign. One of the notes read, "I got into the blonde."

On February 7, 1960, the *Caroline*, with Kennedy and his brother Teddy on board, arrived in Las Vegas for a meeting with Frank Sinatra, the "chairman of the board," and Sam Giancana, the "boss of bosses." Kennedy was gambling on winning the nomination, and his plans for the primaries were being made at the Sands Hotel, where Sinatra and the "Rat Pack" were performing nightly.

While there was a credo that every young American had an opportunity to become president of the United States, Sam Giancana's credo was that every young mafioso had an opportunity to *own* the president of the United States. Giancana was well aware of the Kennedy *hamartia*, or fatal flaw. He had observed it in the father, and knew that Jack Kennedy too was a womanizer. If they could catch the presidential candidate in a compromising situation, the Mafia would be holding a Kennedy marker. Through Sinatra, Giancana believed he could not only enrich Mafia coffers by having access to some of Hollywood's biggest entertainers, but also add to his collection of Kennedy markers by utilizing Sinatra's association with the presidential candidate.

Perhaps only Sinatra's psychiatrist, Dr. Ralph Greenson, could have explained Sinatra's aberration concerning power and the Mafia. Eddie Fisher once commented, "Frank wanted to be a hood. He once said, 'I'd rather be a don of the Mafia than president of the United States.' I don't think he was fooling." Sinatra and Giancana had a lot in common: both had a mercurial temperament, wild mood swings, and a giant ego; both loved to gamble and fornicate; both could be lavishly generous and lavishly cruel; both suffered from bottomless greed and had bottomless pockets— price was no object when it came to a flashy suit, a pretty girl, or a great toupee.

Shortly after it became apparent that Jack Kennedy was a viable candidate, Sinatra began cultivating the friendship of "brother-in-Lawford," and he became solicitous of Marilyn, whom he knew to be intimate with his new friend, Kennedy. Suddenly, Sinatra found himself with a pal who was headed for the White House, and a blonde acquaintance who occasionally slept in his pal's bed. It was a strategic position of subtle power and influence. In 1983, in an unguarded moment shortly before his death, Peter Lawford made the statement, "I'm not going to talk about Jack and his broads because I just can't . . . and, well, I'm not proud of this, but all I will say is that I was Frank's pimp, and Frank was Jack's. It sounds terrible now, but then it was really a lot of fun."

The FBI's files reveal information regarding several of the women Sinatra brought to Kennedy's attention in Palm Springs, Las Vegas, and New York. One FBI file contains the statement, "It is a known fact that the Sands Hotel is owned by hoodlums, and that while the Senator, Sinatra and Lawford were there, showgirls from all over the town were running in and out of the Senator's suite."

It was at the Sands that Sinatra introduced Jack Kennedy to Judith Campbell Exner, an attractive divorcée with dark hair and sparkling blue eyes. Exner frequented the nightclubs in Los Angeles and Las Vegas and was frequently seen on the arm of West Coast Mafia boss Johnny Rosselli. According to her friend Patricia Breen, "Judith was absolutely the most gorgeous thing you've ever laid eyes on and had a subtle resemblance to Jackie Kennedy."

Describing the visit, Judith Exner recalled that Sinatra invited her, along with a group of friends, to be his guest. The entourage included Dean Martin's wife Jeanne, agent Mort Viner, Gloria Romanoff, and publicist Pat Newcomb, who was a friend of Sinatra, the Lawfords, and the Kennedys.

Sinatra's guests flew to Las Vegas on Friday afternoon, February 5, 1960, and it was on Sunday afternoon at Sinatra's table in the Sands' lounge that Judith Exner was introduced to Senator Jack Kennedy and his brother Teddy. That evening Judith Exner, Pat Newcomb, and Gloria Romanoff were guests at Sinatra's table in the Copa Room for the late show starring Sinatra, Dean Martin, Peter Lawford, and Sammy Davis, Jr. "I sat next to Teddy, and Jack sat across from me," Judith Exner noted. "Jack looked so handsome in his pinstripe suit. Those strong white teeth and smiling Irish eyes. . . . I must say I was tremendously impressed by his poise and wit and charm."

Many years later, Judith Campbell Exner wrote about her affair with Jack Kennedy in her autobiography, *My Story*. She described dozens of trysts in hotel rooms around the country and in the White House. Though her revelations were initially met with skepticism, the subsequent release of FBI files and White House telephone logs confirmed over seventy phone conversations, some of extended duration, between Judith Campbell Exner and the president between February 1961 and April 1962. An additional call to JFK was logged on August 5, 1962, when Marilyn Monroe's death hit the news.

Judith Exner became the liaison for meetings between Giancana and JFK, and she told of arranging a meeting between the "boss of bosses" and the senator at the Fountainebleu Hotel in Miami, where plans were finalized to "get out the vote" in the West Virginia primaries. While Kennedy had beaten Hubert Humphrey in the New Hampshire and Wisconsin primaries, West Virginia was ninety-five percent Protestant. In order to become the presidential candidate, Kennedy would have to prove to the Democratic Party that he could win the Protestant vote despite his Catholicism. The Kennedy forces entered the West Virginia primary with all the energy, determination, and cash at their disposal. FBI wiretaps later revealed that Giancana contributed a war chest of $150,000, which was distributed by Sinatra and Giancana's friend Paul Emilio "Skinny" D'Amato. More than $50,000 was disbursed to convince the West Virginia sheriffs, who controlled the political machine, how important it was for Kennedy to win.

Kennedy swept West Virginia by a three-to-two margin, amassing 219,246 votes to Humphrey's 141,941. The *New York Times* termed the victory a "smashing upset," and Democrats all over the nation were impressed. Hubert Humphrey tearfully dropped out of the presidential race and confided to a colleague, "The way Jack Kennedy and his old man threw money around, the people of West Virginia won't need any public relief for the next fifteen years."

According to Kennedy's friend Senator George Smathers, Kennedy was concerned about the "Marilyn Monroe problem." With the nomination looming ahead, he was worried that she might talk about their relationship, and other private matters that could damage his candidacy. But Marilyn joined the Kennedy bandwagon and was at the top of the list of celebrities endorsing JFK's nomination—celebrities that Sinatra organized to support the Democratic candidate, with the help of his friends Henry

Rogers and Pat Newcomb. And while Marilyn was on the East Coast during the Hollywood strike, she become the Democratic Party's alternate delegate to the Fifth Congressional District of Connecticut.

The selection of Los Angeles as the site for the 1960 Democratic National Convention was propitious for JFK. It put Kennedy's show-business supporters in close proximity to the action. On July 10, the eve of the convention's opening, the Democratic Party gave a one-hundred-dollar-a-plate fundraiser at the Beverly Hilton Hotel. Sinatra rounded up a host of celebrities, including Milton Berle, Janet Leigh, Tony Curtis, Judy Garland, Mort Sahl, and the entire "Jack Pack" to mingle with the crowd of twenty-eight hundred supporters. Jacqueline Kennedy, who was six months pregnant, did not attend.

When Jack, Bobby, and Teddy Kennedy arrived in Los Angeles, they checked into the Biltmore Hotel. The Kennedy suite, which was down the hall from Chief Bill Parker's private apartment, was Bobby's boiler room for the convention. The Kennedy security team included Captain James Hamilton, Lieutenant Daryl Gates, Officers Frank Hronek and Marvin Ianonne, and the two intelligence officers Archie Case and James Ahearn.

Though Joe Kennedy never set foot on the convention floor, he remained in the wings of the Marion Davies mansion behind the Beverly Hills Hotel, where "he was the mastermind of everything," according to Kennedy aide Joe Timilty.

Officially a resident at the Biltmore, Jack Kennedy stayed at an apartment belonging to entertainer Jack Haley on Rossmore Boulevard, near the Wilshire Country Club. This hideaway was discovered by an alert member of the fourth estate, and Kennedy was observed by an apartment resident climbing down the fire escape to avoid being caught in a compromising situation. The press caught up with him as he was spotted climbing over a fence and getting into a car. He shouted to the perplexed reporters, "I'm going to meet my father!" as he hurriedly drove off. The compromising situation may have been with Marilyn Monroe, who was visiting Kennedy on her way to the Reno location of *The Misfits*, which was to begin filming on July 21.

On the second night of the Los Angeles convention, Jack Kennedy and Marilyn had dinner at the Jack Pack's favorite restaurant, Pucini's, along with Peter Lawford and Kennedy's media campaign manager, Peter Summers. Pucini's was owned by Sinatra, Lawford, and Mickey Rudin. According to Detective John St. John of the Los Angeles Police Department, Pucini's was frequented by the Mafia, and there was a private room upstairs designated for VIP assignations. Peter Summers recalled seeing Kennedy and Marilyn together the next morning emerging from a shower at the Lawford beach house. "Jack was really very, very fond of Marilyn," Summers stated. "She was delightful. . . . I did feel she was so impressed by Kennedy's charm and charisma that she was almost starry-eyed."

During the final days of the convention, it was still uncertain whether Kennedy would prevail over Adlai Stevenson. By the time the roll call had reached Wyoming, Kennedy was within a few votes of a first-ballot victory. Joe Kennedy instructed Teddy to sew up the Wyoming delegation. Pushing his way through the crowded floor to the Wyoming chairman, Teddy Kennedy shouted above the roar, "You have in your grasp the opportunity to nominate the next president of the United States. Such support can never be forgotten by a president." A short time later, Wyoming cast all fifteen votes for John F. Kennedy, and the convention hall erupted into a frenzy of acclamation for the Democratic nominee. Frank Sinatra and the Jack Pack patted each other on the back and were totally ecstatic. "Brother-in-Lawford" had never seen Sinatra so jubilant. It was almost as if he were the one going to the White House. Indeed, he had one alligator shoe in the back door.

Two days later at the Los Angeles Coliseum, Jack Kennedy, who had learned so well from his father the importance of winning, declared to a jubilant crowd, "We stand today on the edge of a New Frontier—the frontier of the 1960s—a frontier of unknown opportunities and perils. . . . I am asking each of you to be new pioneers on this New Frontier!"

After the Coliseum victory speech, Peter Lawford threw a party for Jack Kennedy at the beach house, and borrowed the head bartender from Romanoff's, Ross Acuna. Acuna recalled seeing Sammy Davis arrive at the party with Marilyn Monroe. "I couldn't get the drift, but I was a bartender—you see a lot of things, you keep your mouth shut. But pretty soon here comes the Kennedy boy, from making that speech at the Coliseum. . . . Soon I saw that Monroe and the Kennedy boy were pretty close together. Sammy Davis? I think they just asked him to bring Monroe in, you know what I mean? He was a black beard."

Peter Summers confirmed that Marilyn and Jack Kennedy were together that evening at the Lawfords'. The celebration went on into the early hours of the morning, while Case and Ahearn and Parker's security officers stood watch. Frank Hronek was the senior officer, and he recalled that in the course of the evening the party became raucous. From the beach they observed a bevy of nude party girls, supplied by a well-known Hollywood madam, cavorting around the pool. As one of the officers put it, "several of the girls were stark ass naked." Indeed, the frontier of the 1960s was to be "a frontier of unknown opportunities and perils."

Snake Eyes

This is an attempt at the ultimate motion picture.
—Frank Taylor

No experience can be quite as ephemeral as working on a motion picture. Over a period of weeks, or months—or what can seem an eternity—a group of diversely egocentric, engaging, neurotic people are thrown together in an intense crucible of cinematic activity. Members of a film company on location live and work together for long hours in a gathering of crafts and talents—working in unison until the last shadowy image is captured on the last frame. Friendships and bonds form. Love affairs and hate affairs begin and end—end and begin. Secrets are shared, promises made, loyalties avowed, animosities affirmed. There's a sense among cast and crew that they're involved in something special—something beyond the ordinary and above the commonplace. *Important* people and *big* money are involved in something *big* and *important*. The *now* takes on special significance *above* and *beyond* and . . .

Suddenly it's over.

They all go their separate ways—off to other pictures, vacations, the unemployment line. Cast and crew members seldom see each other again. For Marilyn it must have been reminiscent of going from foster home to foster home, school to school. Perhaps that's why she had accumulated her "family" of trusted friends and coworkers who went with her from picture to picture.

The Misfits was Marilyn's twenty-ninth and final completed film in an astonishing career that spanned sixteen years. The motion picture was to be a tribute to Marilyn from her husband, one of the world's most distinguished dramatists. Not only was it to be directed by one of Marilyn's favorite directors, John Huston, but her costar would be her lifelong idol, Clark Gable, and the film was to be produced by the Millers' friend Frank Taylor. All her favorites—her family, as she called them—would be behind the camera supporting her: coach Paula Strasberg, masseur Ralph Roberts, secretary May Reis, makeup artist Allan "Whitey" Snyder, hairdressers Sidney Guilaroff and Agnes Flanagan, limousine driver Rudy Kautzky, stand-in Evelyn Moriarty, and publicist Rupert Allan. What could go wrong?

Everything.

On the afternoon of July 20, 1960, Marilyn Monroe arrived in Reno on a United DC-7 from Los Angeles. She was met by Arthur Miller, Frank Taylor, Rupert Allan, the Reno press, and hundreds of fans who waited patiently for a half-hour for her to finally emerge from the plane. It was explained that she had been changing her clothes in the ladies' room, but Sidney Guilaroff later disclosed that she was having trouble with her wig. Because the start date of *The Misfits* was delayed by the actors' and writers' strike, which had interrupted production of *Let's Make Love*, she was rushing from one production to another with only three weeks' respite between pictures. According to Guilaroff her hair had been damaged by the constant bleaching and setting during the production at Fox, and it was decided at the last minute that she would have to wear a wig during filming of *The Misfits*. She never liked the idea of the wig, which was being restyled on the plane from L.A. to Reno.

She now faced a lengthy and difficult production schedule on a very rigorous film, shooting six days a week in the intense heat of the desert. She arrived exhausted and suffering from physical and emotional pain. The three most important men in her life had deceived her: Montand had made *le grand sortie*, JFK had charmingly taken advantage of her naïveté, and Miller, she felt, had used her. She was also suffering from a persistent pain in her right side and bouts of indigestion. But the production gears of *The Misfits* had been set in motion. Any further delay, she was told, risked the danger of losing Gable and Huston, who had other commitments. She arrived with a purse full of painkillers. But nothing would kill the pain of filming *The Misfits*.

Rupert Allan commented that Marilyn was "desperately unhappy at having to read lines written by Miller that were obviously documenting the real-life Marilyn." Though Roslyn was supposed to be based on Marilyn, and much of the dialogue and situations had been drawn from the Millers' life together, Marilyn felt that the character of Roslyn had inconsistencies—she was too passive, voiced platitudes, and needed to be humanized. Marilyn had never been satisfied with the script, and when she arrived in Reno Miller was still making revisions on the screenplay he had been working on for over three years. When production finally started she found herself faced with playing the most difficult role of her career—a misconstrued concept of herself. Miller had begun *The Misfits* as an homage to his wife, a testimonial of his enduring love, but it ended as a painful reminder of their failed marriage.

Rumors quickly spread on the set that the president of Marilyn Monroe Productions wasn't so lovey-dovey with the vice president—that they were headed for divorce. Though the Millers shared a suite at the Mapes Hotel, where the rest of the cast and crew were also staying, they were rarely seen together and drove to locations in separate cars.

John Huston wasn't fully prepared for the problems he encountered with Marilyn. "I first noticed her condition when we started production," Huston recalled. "She was very late, and apparently she had been on narcotics for some time. . . . Her eyes had a strange look, and as time went on her condition worsened."

Huston had met with Marilyn only once, briefly, since filming *The Asphalt Jungle*, and neither person was exactly the same. Huston's cynicism had blossomed into flowers of artful sadism, and Marilyn had blossomed into a consummate actress, while the sadness of her private life had reached the lower depths. She looked different in *The Misfits*. The wig subtly subtracted from her vibrancy, and her heavily mascaraed eyes, which hid some of the "strange look," may have worked for the character of Roslyn the Reno divorcée, but it wasn't exactly the same Marilyn—not the Marilyn of *The Seven Year Itch*, *Bus Stop*, and *Some Like It Hot*. Exhaustion, pain, and disappointment were taking their toll. The lumens had imperceptibly dimmed, though it wasn't apparent to the constant flow of reporters and photographers who visited the set.

Alice McIntyre of *Esquire* described Marilyn as "astonishingly beautiful.

Like nothing human you have ever seen or dreamed!" Photographer Henri Cartier-Bresson saw her radiant beauty as "a certain myth of what we call in France *la femme eternelle.*" One of the photographers who may have noted a less than eternal *femme* was Inge Morath of Magnum, who arrived in Reno with Cartier-Bresson and stayed on to become the next Mrs. Arthur Miller.

Marilyn looked forward to working with Gable, who had arrived in Reno with his wife Kay. Gable had a special understanding of and feeling for Marilyn. Always a gentleman, he treated her with paternal concern throughout the production, though privately he complained about her lateness. A thorough professional, he couldn't comprehend what took Marilyn so long to get onto the set. Gable said to his agent George Chasin that he appreciated Marilyn's work as an actress but wondered, "What the hell is that girl's problem? I like her, but I damn near go nuts waiting for her to show."

He never showed his impatience on the set, however. When she was late, he was heard to remark jokingly, "Why is it that sexy women are never on time?" Or sometimes he would pinch her, wink, and say, "Get to work, beautiful." Sensing her distress and exhaustion, Gable always made sure she had a chair, and often they would sit side by side on the set talking about his vast experience in the film business. But she soon learned that her fantasy father had a flaw—Gable drank up to two quarts of whiskey a day, and he occasionally got the shakes. Though he had a heart condition, and his doctor had told him to stop smoking and drinking, they were lifelong habits that continued during the strenuous filming in the hot Nevada desert. Several of his close-ups had to be reshot because Gable could be seen trembling in the hundred-degree heat.

John Huston was a perfectionist who was known to lose interest in a film when he discovered that the formula for his cinematic chemistry was flawed. He soon perceived that no sorcerer could divine a magic solution for *The Misfits,* and early on he mentally walked off the picture and into the Reno casinos, where he turned to his old reliable solution—booze. He spent his nights at the craps table, drinking and losing money and sleep. During the day he walked through the picture on the quicksand of benzedrine, not always successfully managing to direct the bizarre traffic of characters assembled on the set.

Alcohol was only one of Montgomery Clift's myriad problems. He had been such a heavy drinker that by May of 1960 he had developed alcoholic hepatitis and had been institutionalized at Mount Sinai Hospital in New

York City, where a resident recalled, "He didn't seem to know who or what he was. He seemed to be subject to free-floating anxiety. He was afraid of sex, and he was afraid of authority." Marilyn had made the comment to a friend that Clift was the only person she knew who was in greater trouble than she was. On the set of *The Misfits* he kept very much to himself, systematically drinking vodka and grapefruit juice from a thermos; and in the role of Perce, the thump-drunk bronco buster, he proved once again that he was one of the most brilliant actors in American films.

According to Whitey Snyder, no teetotaler himself, most of the cast and crew made a beeline to the bars after the horrors and heat of filming during the day. "They'd wake up in the morning with screaming headaches, hoping to God Marilyn would be late again."

During production the film company became polarized into two disparate factions by the seeds of discord sown by the Miller camp. Early on, Frank Taylor, John Huston, and Arthur Miller planned a strategic ambush on Black Bart. Prior to Paula Strasberg's arrival in Reno, Frank Taylor, who had been briefed by Miller, held a meeting of key production personnel. "I told them that Paula's previous tactics of divide and conquer— such as she had done with George Cukor on *Let's Make Love*—would not work if we would band together against it," Taylor recalled. "We were to be civil to her, say good morning and good night, but no conversation with her. She was to be frozen out."

When Miller's camp began freezing Strasberg out, and it became evident what they were doing, Marilyn was livid. It was the final betrayal, and what was left of the Millers' cordial professional relationship disintegrated into outright and open contempt. On one occasion, when Miller missed his ride back to the Mapes Hotel from location and attempted to get into Marilyn's limousine, she slammed the door in his face—leaving him stranded in the desert. They didn't speak for days afterward.

Screenwriter Arnold Schulman, who visited the set of *The Misfits*, observed, "I went to Reno and it was just awful. The tension. And Miller was sulking around like a two-year-old, glowering at everybody, particularly at Paula. If he'd looked at me like that, I would have withered and died on the spot. I don't know how Paula got through those days. Everybody hated her. Here she was trying to hold this whole thing together, and everybody kept saying 'what a pain in the ass' and making jokes about her."

The strategy of the Miller camp reduced Paula Strasberg to tears, and when it became apparent what she was going through, Marilyn called Lee Strasberg in New York. Lee and Susan Strasberg made an unexpected journey to Reno, where Lee appeared in cowboy boots and a ten-gallon hat for a showdown with Arthur Miller at Quail Canyon.

"I can't tolerate this behavior toward Paula," Lee snarled up to the lanky Miller. "She's an artist. She's worked with many stars and never been treated like this. If something doesn't change, I'm afraid I'll have to pull her off the picture. She has to be shown some respect!"

Faced with the inevitable repercussion of their ill-conceived tactics, Miller's camp became more conciliatory. Sidney Guilaroff observed that Huston would occasionally flash one of his "snake-eye smiles at Paula." A candlelight champagne victory celebration of sorts was held by Marilyn's camp. Ralph Roberts, Susan Strasberg, Agnes Flanagan, May Reis, and Whitey Snyder circled the flagons and drank to success, while brush fires ringed Reno. Ralph Roberts remembered, "The brush fires had caused a power failure, and we were in darkness except for candles. We were sitting in a wardrobe department we had set up on the ninth floor of the Mapes Hotel, and Marilyn slipped out of the suite she shared with Arthur and had a split of champagne with us."

Recalling the evening, Susan Strasberg said, "Marilyn sat on a wardrobe trunk and was having a drink in the dark with her friends. Grabbing a wig, she got up and did a razor sharp imitation of Mitzi Gaynor—singing and dancing in the dark, faceless, anonymous, she gave off blue sparks of lifelight."

Using Estelle Winwood's wig as a prop, she sang "I'm Going to Wash That Man Right Out of My Hair," and everyone knew which man she was referring to.

Shortly after the conclusion of the Democratic National Convention in Los Angeles, Frank Sinatra opened at the Cal-Neva Lodge at Lake Tahoe and invited Marilyn along with the other *Misfits* stars to see his show on Saturday, August 13. Gable said he wouldn't go unless the entire company was invited—and everyone was. The entire cast, production staff, and crew were transported to Cal-Neva to be wined and dined and see Sinatra's show—including Arthur Miller.

Marilyn was struck by the kindness and generosity of Sinatra's offer, but there were contingencies to the invitation. According to FBI Agent Bill Roemer, who had Sam Giancana under surveillance, among the guests at Cal-Neva that weekend were Joe and Jack Kennedy, Sam Giancana, and Johnny Rosselli.

Sinatra was in the process of acquiring the Cal-Neva Lodge with partners Sam Giancana and Mickey Rudin. The manager was to be Skinny
D'Amato, fixer of the West Virginia primaries and former pit boss of the
Havana Thunderbird for Giancana. For many years Cal-Neva had been
one of the favorite haunts of Joe Kennedy, who had often vacationed there
with Janet Des Rosier. Following Jack Kennedy's nomination at the Democratic convention, Joe Kennedy went to Cal-Neva for a two-week working
holiday while laying plans for the campaign with Sinatra and Giancana.

According to Senator George Smathers, things weren't going well between Marilyn and Jack Kennedy. Now that Kennedy had won the nomination, Marilyn's silence about her relationship with the presidential
candidate became vital. Smathers stated that an effort was made to "talk
to Marilyn Monroe about putting a bridle on herself and on her mouth
and not talking too much, because it was getting to be a story around the
country."

Whatever occurred at Cal-Neva had its devastating effect on Marilyn
in the following days on location in Reno, when she returned to the professional agony of filming *The Misfits*. Cameraman Russell Metty told
Huston that they couldn't shoot close-ups because Marilyn's eyes had that
"strange look." She began slurring dialogue and missing cues. On Friday,
August 26, Paula Strasberg discovered Marilyn unconscious in her room
at the Mapes. She had overdosed. Scooping out the dissolving capsules
still in her mouth, Strasberg called for an ambulance. Marilyn was rushed
to the hospital, where she had her stomach pumped. On Saturday she
was taken to the Westside Hospital in Los Angeles, where she was placed
under the care of Dr. Ralph Greenson and internist Dr. Hyman Engelberg.
Recalling the incident, Jack Kennedy's friend Chuck Spalding stated that
he had been asked to fly from New York to Los Angeles to make sure she
was okay. "I got out there, and she was really sick. With Lawford's help,
I got her to the hospital," Spalding said. Marilyn spent a week in the
Westside Hospital, where Greenson and Engelberg quickly withdrew her
from her barbiturate regime. Greenson said later, "Although Marilyn re-
sembled a hard-core drug addict, she was not the usual addict. She could
stop cold with no physical symptoms of withdrawal."

On her way back to Nevada to finish filming *The Misfits*, Marilyn
stopped over in San Francisco to visit Joe DiMaggio. Marilyn told
DiMaggio that she was getting a divorce from Arthur Miller when *The
Misfits* was completed, and it may have raised his hopes of a reconciliation.

Marilyn returned to the Reno location on September 5, determined to finish the film. She resumed work "looking wonderfully self-possessed," Arthur Miller related. "Her incredible resilience was heroic to me, but by this time we both knew we had effectively parted."

In a moment of frustration Marilyn angrily stated, "It was to be 'our movie!' But Arthur changed the script. She's [referring to Roslyn] not like me at all! She's almost incidental to the story. All he cares about are the men. . . . All Arthur wanted was to use me to regain his prestige! I'll never forgive him—never!"

During October, the production company finished its location shooting and returned to Paramount Studios in Hollywood to film the last scene of *The Misfits*, which also proved to be the final scene in the careers of both Gable and Monroe.

On November 4, 1960, on Paramount's stage 7, Clark and Marilyn were seated in a truck in front of a process screen:

INT. TRUCK—DUSK
TWO SHOT
Gay puts his comforting arm around Roslyn as he drives off into the desert, and the rapidly descending night.
ROSLYN: How do you find your way back in the dark?
Gay looks ahead at the expansive desert, and fixes his eye on a bright distant star.
GAY: Just head for that big star straight on. The highway's under it—it'll take us right home.
Roslyn stares at the star before snuggling into the safety of Gay's shoulder. They both keep their eyes on the star that shines above and beyond—the bright star of hope.
FADE OUT

But "Hope, Hope, Hope!" was gone.

The agony of filming *The Misfits* had come to an end, and so had the externals that remained of the Millers' marriage; however Marilyn had one more big scene to play out that day. When the Millers returned to their bungalow at the Beverly Hills Hotel, Marilyn released all her pent-up, seething rage at her husband. Arthur Miller hurriedly packed his belongings and fled into the night.

"Today Is Forever" had terminated.

"Today" had been one thousand five hundred and fifty-eight days.

"Forever" had been *The Misfits*.

The Blues

It would be nice to have a president who looks
so young and good-looking.
                                    —Marilyn Monroe

On November 8, 1960, Marilyn Monroe was too despondent over the breakup of her marriage to go to the polls and vote for her friend John F. Kennedy. However, his narrow margin of victory over Richard Nixon succeeded in any event. Kennedy had other friends.

By the early morning hours of November 9, it was still undetermined whether Kennedy had won the election. California, Michigan, and Illinois were still uncertain. Before retiring, Kennedy telephoned his father's long-time friend Mayor Richard Daley of Chicago, voicing his concern. Daley made a knowing reply: "Mr. President, with a bit of luck and the help of a few close friends, you're going to carry Illinois." Mayor Daley's own initial victory in 1955 had been decided by the vast Chicago West Side river wards, which were dominated by Sam Giancana and the Mafia. Voter fraud was a way of life in Cook County. By the time Kennedy awoke the next day, he had won the election by a mere 118,574 votes out of more than 68 million cast. In Illinois, Nixon had won 93 of the state's 102 counties, but he lost Illinois by 8,858 votes because of the huge Kennedy majority in Cook County, which included Chicago.

After checking only 699 paper ballot precincts, Nixon came up with a net gain of 4,539 votes; however, Mayor Daley stepped in and blocked an official recount. After the election, Sam Giancana often bragged to Judith Campbell Exner, "Listen, honey, if it wasn't for me your boyfriend wouldn't be in the White House."

At his first formal news conference on November 10, the president-elect announced the reappointment of J. Edgar Hoover as FBI director. The news came as a shock to Kennedy friends and supporters who were well aware of the animosity Kennedy felt for the bureau chief. The night before the reappointment, Ben Bradlee, editor of *Newsweek*, had urged Kennedy to dismiss Hoover and assumed that he would; however, he didn't know about Hoover's expanding accordion file of Kennedy indiscretions.

Quite cognizant of his son's peccadilloes as well as the antipathy that J. Edgar Hoover held for the Kennedys, Joe Kennedy told Jack to appoint Bobby Kennedy attorney general. Only Bobby, as head of the Justice Department, could keep Hoover in check. Aware that the appointment would be controversial, Jack Kennedy tried to dissuade his father in the matter. However, Joe Kennedy was adamant.

One of the problems with the decision was the fact that the Justice Department had thirty thousand employees and a $130 million budget, and young Bobby Kennedy had never practiced law. When Ben Bradlee heard about the appointment, he asked Jack how he was going to announce it. "Well," Jack responded, "I think I'll open the front door of the Georgetown house some morning at about two A.M., look up and down the street and if there's no one there I'll whisper, 'It's Bobby.' "

When Jack actually made the announcement from the front door of his Georgetown house, it was high noon, and he was faced with a mob of reporters. Just before stepping forward, he was heard to say to Bobby Kennedy, who was standing by his side, "Damn it, Bobby, comb your hair, and don't smile too much or they'll think we're happy about this."

J. Edgar Hoover seethed with anger when he received the news regarding his new superior. Conservative Hoover had become FBI director a year before Bobby Kennedy was born, and now "that skinny squealing little liberal shit" was going to be his boss. The animosity increased when, shortly after Jack Kennedy took office, Bobby Kennedy forced the FBI, for the first time, to clear its press releases and speeches with the attorney general. He also mandated that all press releases be issued in the name of the Department of Justice, rather than the FBI. More vexing, Bobby Kennedy insisted that all FBI directives from the bureau chief also cross his desk. The antagonism between Hoover and the Kennedys would climb to icy new heights during the brilliance of the thousand days and the shadows of the thousand nights.

After the election, Marilyn referred to Jack Kennedy as "Prez," and she told Bob Slatzer that her concern that the election would end her relationship with JFK was unfounded. Her New York friend Henry Rosenfeld told Anthony Summers, "When he became president, she became very excited. Her opinion was that this was the most important person in the world and she was seeing him. She was so excited you'd have thought she was a teenager."

Senator George Smathers observed, "What happened was that she, like naturally all women, would like to be close to the president. And then she began to ask for an opportunity to come to Washington and come to the White House, and that sort of thing. . . . She made some demands."

Smathers recalled seeing Jack Kennedy and Marilyn together on the presidential yacht on the Potomac, and Chuck Spalding vividly recalled a private visit by Marilyn to Hyannisport, where she was welcomed as an intimate of Kennedy's.

As Arthur Schlesinger later observed, "If anything untoward happened at all, it did not interfere with Kennedy's conduct of the Presidency." Nor, apparently, did the presidency interfere with anything untoward. Marilyn oftentimes had to outwit the Secret Service and the press who surrounded Kennedy by wearing a black wig and horn-rimmed glasses. Carrying a steno pad and disguised as a secretary, she visited Kennedy incognito at the Carlyle and on Air Force One. Her calls to the White House were placed through the president's appointments secretary, Kenny O'Donnell, using the code name "Miss Green." And, according to Schaeffer Air Ambulance pilot Bob Neuman, there were untoward emergency flights to clandestine rendezvous in Palm Springs and Cabo San Lucas.

In November 1960, a series of publicity stills for *The Misfits* were taken at the Paramount Studios still gallery. Standing in the shadows behind the bright lights was Pat Newcomb. A Byzantine series of events and relationships had brought the spin doctor back into Marilyn's employ after the *Bus Stop* incident: Rupert Allan, who was associated with Pat Newcomb at the Arthur Jacobs public relations firm, handled the press relations for some of Hollywood's top stars. Allan's clients had included

Sinatra and Grace Kelly as well as Marilyn. Sinatra was a close friend of Princess Grace, and frequently visited her in Monaco and participated in her charity galas. When Princess Grace complained to Sinatra about her European press representatives, it was arranged that Rupert Allan would take over Monaco's press relations. Allan was made an offer he couldn't refuse, which included considerable tax advantages, provided that he maintained residency in Monaco for the majority of the year. Though it has been written that it was Allan who suggested Newcomb as his replacement with Marilyn, Allan later stated that he disliked Newcomb. He referred to her as a "pill-pusher" and said, "Pat Newcomb is the last person I would have recommended." With Allan gone, it was Sinatra who persuaded Marilyn to hire Newcomb. Sinatra knew she was close to the Kennedys, and that his pal Jack Kennedy was worried about Marilyn's knowledge of dark secrets concerning important people in high and low places. Having majored in psychology at Mills, and being a protégée of Pierre Salinger and a close friend of Bobby's, Newcomb was the perfect person to keep an eye on Marilyn.

When Marilyn returned to New York she had to announce the breakup of her marriage, and Newcomb traveled east with Marilyn to handle the press. The imminent divorce was revealed on November 11, and Marilyn was beseiged by newsmen for comments. She emerged tearfully from her apartment with Newcomb at her side to say there would be a friendly divorce. Miller, meanwhile, had moved his blank paper and pipe cleaners back to the convenience of the Chelsea, and several days after the divorce announcement he arrived at the Fifty-Seventh Street apartment to pick up his typewriter and books. Marilyn remained in her room. After he gathered his things, Lena Pepitone recalled, Miller left without saying a word. When he had gone, Marilyn emerged from the bedroom and entered Miller's study, which had been closed for nearly the entire time the Millers occupied the apartment. The room was bare. Only a photo of Marilyn remained hanging on the wall. "He really wants to forget," she said. "I guess I'm gonna have to forget, too."

On November 17, Marilyn was awakened at 4 A.M. by a journalist with the news that Clark Gable had died from a massive heart attack. She was too grief-stricken to speak, and when Pepitone arrived at the apartment in the morning she found Marilyn alone in a state of shock. "Oh, God, why is he dead?" she sobbed. "I loved him, Lena. He was so nice to me.

He was always smiling, always encouraging. He was the biggest star of all, but he respected me. I just saw him. He kissed me good-bye. My friend . . ."

Vicious rumors began circulating in the press that Marilyn was responsible for Gable's death. A fallacious item in a gossip column stated that Kay Gable believed Marilyn had contributed to her husband's condition: "The tension and exhaustion Marilyn had caused by her lateness and unprofessionalism had prolonged the picture for weeks and brought on Gable's fatal heart attack." Feeling that there might have been some truth to the rumor, Marilyn began suffering remorse.

Pepitone said, "She was so gentle, so sad. But somehow she got it into her head that she was responsible for Gable's heart attack. It became impossible for her to sleep without ever-increasing doses of sleeping pills. For days she would lie on the bed, her eyes bulging out, wringing her hands in frustration."

Having lost Montand to Signoret, Miller to his farm, Jack Kennedy to his ambitions, and her fantasy father to the grim reaper, Marilyn felt totally alone. To try to cheer her up, Pepitone talked her into getting out of the apartment—to go shopping. It seemed like a good idea. It wasn't. It was Christmastime again, and the brightly decorated streets highlighted her gloom. Aglow with the Christmas spirit, tourists and families and lovers were out buying presents for relatives and friends. Not much had changed since Union Station, when Norma Jeane was the isolated observer of the human family.

When Marilyn got back to the apartment, Pepitone recalled, she was weeping. There was no tree, no gifts, no relatives. Worried about Marilyn, Pepitone decided to stay on until she had gone to bed. When she checked on Marilyn later in the evening she found her at the bedroom window, which was wide open—her hands grasping the outside molding. It looked as though she was about to jump to the street thirteen floors below.

Pepitone described running toward Marilyn and grabbing her around the waist.

"No, no—let me die! I want to die! I deserve to die!" Marilyn screamed.

As Pepitone restrained her and tried to quiet her down, Marilyn sobbed, "I can't live anymore. It's Christmas! Who do I have? I have no one! What have I got to live for?"

Pepitone held Marilyn for a long time, until she stopped shivering and sobbing. Christmas Eve was spent watching out for the film star.

On Christmas day, Joe DiMaggio sent Marilyn several large poinsettia plants, and that night he appeared at her door. Pepitone recalled that DiMaggio stayed in New York for several days, and Marilyn's spirits began to improve. He frequently appeared at dinnertime and would leave early the next morning in the service elevator to avoid being seen.

"She was happy just to have Joe around," Pepitone said, "and it was obvious to me that they still loved each other. So one day I came out with what was on my mind and said, 'Why don't you marry Marilyn again? She loves you. It would be wonderful for her.'" Pepitone recalled DiMaggio saying that he loved Marilyn more than any other woman, but they had too many differences that they just couldn't work out as long as she had her career.

After DiMaggio returned to Florida, Pat Newcomb suggested that the best day for Marilyn to get a Mexican divorce from Arthur Miller would be January 20, 1961. It was President Kennedy's inauguration day and the press would have its attention distracted by this momentous event. Newcomb and Marilyn, along with her attorney Aaron Frosch, flew to Juarez, hoping the news wouldn't leak out until she returned to New York.

At eight in the evening, a Mexican judge was persuaded to reopen his office, which had closed for the day. He quickly granted the divorce on the grounds of "incompatibility of character." Marilyn signed the papers without reading them. By the time Marilyn left the judge's office the building was surrounded by paparazzi, and she had to fight her way through the crowd to the car that would drive her back to the airport.

During a stopover in Dallas, Marilyn and Newcomb watched a telecast of the inauguration as they waited in the terminal for the flight back to New York. Among those who had received invitations to the inaugural ball was Arthur Miller. Arthur attended with Inge Morath and Joe and Olie Rauh. Miller's single most vivid memory of the historic event was the sight of "Frank Sinatra and his pack in a special box overlooking the festivities. Lounging in magisterial isolation above the excited crowd, Sinatra seemed not so much to rise to the honor of presidential favor as to deign to lend his presence to the occasion."

In the divorce settlement, Miller waived his right to contest a unilateral filing. He took custody of their dog, Hugo, and Marilyn gave him the Roxbury farm, where for almost four decades Miller has lived with his third wife, Inge Morath, whom he married in 1962.

After DiMaggio's visit, Marilyn had no one to turn to except her psychiatrists. While she continued to visit Marianne Kris in New York, she often telephoned Ralph Greenson in Los Angeles. Paula Strasberg became deeply concerned about her, and Susan Strasberg recalled that Marilyn was "withdrawing like a sick animal into a kind of semihibernation." She no longer visited the Strasbergs to escape her pain and sense of hopelessness, but stayed in her apartment listening to the blues on her record player:

> Because it's you I hate to lose
> Every day . . . every day I have the blues.
> Every day . . . every day I have the blues.

Escorted by Montgomery Clift, Marilyn attended the New York premiere of *The Misfits* at the Capitol Theater on January 31. She hated the film. She hated her performance. She hated the way she looked—the wig, the black and white. She hated the story. She hated the memories.

The critics didn't hate it quite as much as Marilyn. *The Misfits* received mixed reviews. Viewers found the story puzzling and abstract—a cowboy story told within the proscenium archness of Group Theatre. It was an eastern western. Viewing *The Misfits* threw Marilyn into a deeper vale of depression. In her visits to Marianne Kris she expressed suicidal thoughts. Subsisting on barbiturates for several days, she stayed in her bedroom, didn't speak to anyone, and stopped eating. Alarmed, Kris suggested that she check into a private room at a New York hospital where she could rest, withdraw from the barbiturates, and have every comfort provided.

On Sunday, February 5, Marilyn was driven by Dr. Kris to New York Hospital–Cornell Medical Center, where she was admitted under the name of "Faye Miller." Expecting to be consigned to a conventional hospital room, she was escorted to the Payne Whitney psychiatric ward, where she was locked in a padded cell reserved for the most critically disturbed patients.

For Marilyn, it was Kafkaesque. It was the true nightmare that had often precipitated her night terrors—the repetitive nightmare of her childhood that she had once related to photographer David Conover: "I'm screaming, 'I'm not crazy! I'm not crazy!' They p-put me in a bare room with bars on the windows and they go out and lock the iron door, leaving me in a straitjacket. 'I don't belong here!' I scream and scream again, until I have no more breath . . ."

But the nightmare was real. The fear that she would end up like her mother was suddenly coming true. Becoming hysterical, she screamed and shouted. Demanding to be released, she pounded on the locked steel door until her hands bled. Throwing a chair across the room, she smashed the small window on her locked door.

To the nursing staff, she indeed appeared to be a seriously disturbed psychiatric case, and they proceeded to put her in the dreaded straitjacket. Relating her horrifying experience to Gloria Romanoff months later, she said, "It was like a nightmare. . . . They had me in a restrainer. They had me sedated, but not so sedated that I didn't know what was going on. . . . At night there was a steady procession of hospital personnel, doctors and nurses, coming to look at me. There I was, with my arms bound. I was not able to defend myself. I was a curiosity piece, with no one who had my interests at heart."

She spent forty-eight hours in a padded cell, unable to communicate with the outside world until a sympathetic nurse's aide supplied her with paper and pencil and agreed to deliver it to the Strasbergs' apartment. It was received on Wednesday, February 8:

Dear Lee and Paula,
  Dr. Kris has put me in the hospital under the care of idiot doctors. They both should not be my doctors. I'm locked up with these poor nutty people. I'm sure to end up a nut too if I stay in this nightmare. Please help me. This is the last place I should be. I love you both.

Marilyn

P.S. I'm on the dangerous floor. It's like a cell.

On Thursday the ninth, Marilyn was allowed to make one call. It was to the person she could always rely on—Joe DiMaggio. He arrived in New York that evening and went to Payne Whitney, where he demanded that Marilyn be released into his custody. The doctors refused, saying that Marilyn couldn't be released without the approval of Dr. Kris. Joe telephoned Kris and told her that if Marilyn was not released by Friday he would "take the hospital apart brick by brick."

Stating that Marilyn needed hospitalization to withdraw from barbiturates, Kris agreed to release her from Payne Whitney—if Marilyn would agree to enter a hospital more to her liking. To avoid the press, Joe waited in Marilyn's apartment while Ralph Roberts and Dr. Kris picked Marilyn up at Payne Whitney, where she exited from the delivery entrance. After the car pulled away from the hospital, "Marilyn began screaming at the doctor as only she could," Roberts remembered. "She was like a hurricane unleashed. I don't think Dr. Kris had ever seen her like that, and she was frightened and very shaken by the violence of Marilyn's response at their meeting. I wound up driving the doctor home, and Dr. Kris was trembling and kept repeating over and over, 'I did a terrible thing, a terrible thing. Oh, God, I didn't mean to. I didn't mean to, but I did.' "

Marilyn never saw Marianne Kris again. Ironically, Kris remained a beneficiary in Marilyn's will, which had been signed only the previous month.

On the afternoon of Friday, February 10, Joe DiMaggio helped Marilyn check into a more accommodating room at the Columbia-Presbyterian Medical Center, where he visited her daily during her three-week stay.

After twenty-three days of rest and rehabilitation at the Columbia-Presbyterian Hospital, Marilyn Monroe returned to her Fifty-Seventh Street apartment. One of the first things she did was to call the "Prez." While the cold war raged, men raced for the moon, and fallout shelters were being built, JFK was kept within arm's reach of the nuclear apocalypse phone—and apparently instructions were left at the White House switchboard that all calls from "Miss Green" be put right through to the Oval Office.

Other pressing White House matters at the time included planning for the assassination of Fidel Castro and the Bay of Pigs invasion. President Kennedy had confided to aide Tad Szulc that "he was under terrific pressure from advisors to okay a Castro murder," and the president asked, "What would you think if I ordered Castro to be assassinated?" But, according to the records of the Church committee, the plan had already been put in place. It was a disturbing subject that JFK debated with Bobby Kennedy and other confidants. Senator George Smathers and Jack Kennedy were discussing the subject of Castro and the Cuban problem at the dinner table in Miami and Smathers recalled, "I remember that he took his fork and just hit his plate and it cracked, and he said, 'Now, damn it, let's quit talking about this subject. Do me a favor—I don't want you to talk to me anymore about Cuba!' "

But it was a subject destined not to go away.

Pierre Salinger referred to the Bay of Pigs disaster as "the least covert military operation in history," and added, "The only information Castro didn't have was the exact time and place of the invasion." However, there's every indication that Castro did. Fidel Castro seemed to know far more about the invasion plans than many people in the White House who were close to the president. Adlai Stevenson, the United States delegate to the United Nations, was among many of the top government officials taken by surprise. However, as early as January 1961, shortly after

Kennedy's inauguration, Castro had denounced the American invasion plans and was making diligent preparations. Castro knew that an attempt would be made on his life shortly before the covert invasion was to take place. Frank Sturgis, a.k.a. Frank Fiorini, testified to the Church committee in 1975 that a Mafia/CIA assassination plot involving Santo Traficante, Sam Giancana, and Johnny Rosselli had arranged for Castro's mistress, Marita Lorenz, to drop botulism tablets supplied by Giancana into Castro's drink. Shortly before the Bay of Pigs invasion on April 17, 1961, the Havana press reported that Castro was "seriously ill." Castro suddenly vanished from public view, and the CIA concluded that their efforts may have met with success. However, Castro was in hiding as he prepared to rout the invaders.

Another person who may have known of the invasion plans and assassination plot was Marilyn Monroe. In July 1962, Marilyn showed her red diary or "book of secrets" to Robert Slatzer. In the diary were notes regarding her early knowledge of the CIA plot to kill Castro, and a statement that Bobby Kennedy was adamant about withdrawing United States military support from the Bay of Pigs invasion forces.

Marilyn had kept a daily diary and memo book for many years. Reporter James Bacon recalled her keeping a diary back in the 1950s and was amused to see her scribbling notes about what he said. Susan Strasberg remembered her as "a great note taker." Amy Greene confirmed that Marilyn kept a notebook when she was a patient of Dr. Margaret Hohenberg. Many psychoanalysts ask patients to keep a journal, and according to Janice Rule and several other former analysands of Dr. Ralph Greenson, it was something Greenson requested of his patients. The analyst would then review the journal notes during the analytic session.

Being the analyst to an intimate of the president of the United States put an apparatchik of the Comintern in a unique position. On the analyst's couch was a source of compromising secrets regarding the private life of the President of the United States as well as insights into world matters discussed with "the Prez" and recorded in his patient's journal— the same journal, or "book of secrets," that became a matter of concern to CIA counterintelligence chief James Jesus Angleton. (See CIA document in Appendix, page 469.)

According to Lena Pepitone, Marilyn spent long hours with her unfailing friend, the telephone, talking to Dr. Greenson. Pepitone sensed that Marilyn was becoming "completely dependent upon him. It was like an addiction," she said. "And she never talked of being well, so that she wouldn't need him again." Marilyn told Pepitone that Dr. Greenson had made her realize that her marriage to Miller was the cause of many of her problems. "As a great intellect and playwright, he was too big a challenge for her," Greenson told Marilyn. "In trying to win his [Miller's] respect, she had become obsessed with the 'serious dramatic actress' goal. This was false, it wasn't her. She should continue her acting lessons, and gradually improve her skills, but the movies she should concentrate on now were those that came most naturally to her—comedies, musicals, 'fun' movies, nothing too serious." Greenson had told her, "Above all, she had to be herself."

"Whoever that is," Marilyn added with a giggle and a slightly puzzled look.

Marilyn told Pepitone that Greenson was by far "the nicest, kindest doctor she had ever had." He believed in her, buoyed her self-confidence, and she believed in him.

Marilyn took frequent weekend flights to the West Coast for sessions with Greenson and dates with Frank Sinatra. On one of the return trips Marilyn brought back a white French poodle Sinatra gave her. "This is my baby, mine and Frankie's," Marilyn exclaimed to Pepitone as she cuddled the dog in her arms. Marilyn named the poodle "Maf," short for Mafia; and, indeed, "Maf" witnessed many clandestine events and kept the Sicilian code of *omertà*.

In April 1961 the center of Marilyn Monroe's life moved from right to left. After more than six years as a New Yorker, she moved back to Los Angeles. In a sense the move was a defeat—a retreat from a dream. As early as the days at the Hollywood Actors Lab she had dreamed the dream: "All I could think of was this far, faraway place called New York. . . . It seemed so exciting to me, and I wanted to be part of that life." She had become a part of the life she had longed for—studied with Strasberg, married one of America's leading playwrights, became a consummate actress. But she hadn't found happiness, or friends, or herself.

In New York there were too many painful memories. In Hollywood there was Sinatra, film work, and her "Jesus." She saw her salvation in Dr. Ralph Greenson.

And so Marilyn returned to the land of sunshine, swimming pools, and Cadillacs—where she had once walked languorously on the sands of Ocean Park and imagined herself walking "proudly in beautiful clothes and being admired by everyone and overhearing words of praise." It was where dreams took on the illusion of reality, and where loves had been met and lost. It was where Ana Lower and Aunt Grace lay in their graves. And it was where the "night people" took away children who vanished with the dawn.

Zelda Zonk was going home.

Left Coast

If Louis B. Mayer was alive today to see what's happening to Hollywood, he'd turn over in his grave.

—Sam Goldwyn

Hollywood had changed considerably since Marilyn Monroe had last lived there as one of its celebrated residents. She returned as a displaced person at a time when the studio star system was a thing of the past and the industry was in disarray. Many of the great screenwriters had done their last fade-out, tycoons' heads were rolling, and the cinema was being captured from the Hollywood ruling class by Wall Street tyros. More and more of the business was being commissioned by agents with new faces and old cunning.

Zanuck was having a midlife crisis on the Riviera with Juliette Greco, and his replacement at Fox, Buddy Adler, had dropped dead when he saw the dismal second-quarter studio earning reports. The aging Spyros Skouras selected Robert Goldstein to step into Adler's warm executive-elevator shoes. But Goldstein, who had been in charge of Fox's London office for four solid years, had little experience as a Hollywood tycoon. His background had been primarily in exporting the Group Theatre; his claim to fame was producing Clifford Odets's play *Golden Boy* in London with a cast that included Lee J. Cobb and Elia Kazan.

Goldstein was born in Bisbee, Arizona, in 1903, and it was in London that he met displaced fellow traveler and theater buff Henry Weinstein, who ultimately became the producer of Marilyn Monroe's final, uncompleted film *Something's Got to Give*. Henry Weinstein had journeyed to London with his cousin Hannah Weinstein, a Comintern operative who, as chairman of the Arts, Sciences, and Professions Committee in New York, was the organizer of the Waldorf Peace Conference.

Following the HUAC witch-hunts of the mid-fifties, Hannah Weinstein moved to London, where she produced the television series *Robin Hood*. The production company became a haven for many refugees from the Hollywood blacklist. Among the blacklisted writers and directors who found gainful employment on "Little Red *Robin Hood*" were Ring Lardner, Jr., Waldo Salt, Joseph Losey, Cy Endfield, and Walter Bernstein, who would later be called in to bedevil Marilyn with last-minute rewrites on *Something's Got to Give*.

When Robert Goldstein arrived at Fox in mid-July of 1960, David O. Selznick was already in preproduction on *Tender Is the Night*, which was to star his wife Jennifer Jones. F. Scott Fitzgerald's novel about a psychoanalyst whose life is destroyed after he marries a beautiful but deeply disturbed patient had been a pet project of Selznick's for years. But with the arrival of Goldstein at Fox, David O. Selznick—producer of *Gone with the Wind, Rebecca, Spellbound,* and *The Third Man*—was replaced by Goldstein's London comrade, Henry Weinstein, who had never produced a motion picture before.

When Weinstein arrived in Hollywood, he stayed at Shelley Winters's house at 711 Rexford Drive in Beverly Hills, where actress Celeste Holm, a patient of Dr. Ralph Greenson's, was a frequent guest. Greenson and Henry Weinstein had many political and cultural interests in common, and Henry attended "cultural commission" meetings and chamber music recitals at the Greenson house on Franklin Street. Weinstein made Dr. Greenson a technical advisor on *Tender Is the Night*, which nevertheless became a box-office basket case. The Selznick papers include many memos written to Weinstein in a desperate attempt to save the film from Weinstein's "pathetic yessing sessions with Bob Goldstein." At a press conference Goldstein stated, "Money by itself cannot make a successful movie. If it could the studios would never make a bad picture." He then went on to launch Walter Wanger's money-eating monster *Cleopatra*.

In the spring of 1961, when Marilyn returned to the rolling hills of Fox, it looked the same, but the studio would never return to the glory days when Norma Jeane first tripped into the 20th Century-Fox lobby.

When Marilyn arrived, Frank Sinatra was in Hawaii, and she briefly stayed as a guest in his ring-a-ding-ding Coldwater Canyon pad before taking her "Charlies" back to the familiar surroundings of the apartment building at 882 North Doheny Drive. Visitors to the modern white-on-white triplex apartment building at the corner of Doheny Drive and Cynthia Street perceived it as a place of transition. Ralph Roberts and Susan Strasberg described Marilyn's apartment as resembling a hotel room, with modern, utilitarian furnishings and no personal touches—no photographs, no awards—just a few books, suitcases, and clothes.

It was well known within the Sinatra crowd that the apartment was managed by Sinatra's accountant, Harry Ziegler, and for years it was a way station for Sinatra's pals, broads, and business associates. Angie Dickinson and Betsy Duncun had been residents along with actor Brad Dexter, who had once saved Sinatra from drowning.

When Marilyn returned in 1961, Sinatra's secretary, Gloria Lovell, was living in one of the Doheny units and Jeanne Carmen, one of Sinatra's preferred blondes, was living in the other. According to Brad Dexter, Jeanne Carmen had known Sinatra and Johnny Rosselli for a number of years. Dexter, who first met Marilyn when he played a role in *The Asphalt Jungle*, recalled seeing Marilyn and Jeanne Carmen together at the apartment on several occasions.

"They were friends," Dexter recently stated. "I'd see them at Pucini's with Frank, and sometimes at Palm Springs. Frank stayed in Marilyn's apartment for a while after she moved out, and Jeanne was still there in 1964."

Marilyn and Jeanne Carmen had been acquainted since the early fifties. Carmen, like Marilyn, had started her career as a model and cover girl for girlie magazines, and she occasionally was cast in B movies, like *The Monster from Piedras Blancas* for Republic in 1959.

Jeanne Carmen was a night person, and when Marilyn couldn't sleep and Carmen wasn't busy they'd while away the night talking and drinking. They often talked about men, sex and drugs, and sex and men. "We became barbiturate buddies," Carmen stated, and it was on one such occasion, she remembered, that Marilyn talked about the baby girl who had been taken from her. "We were having a drink together and talking one night, and I told Marilyn I had once become pregnant with Frankie's child and had an abortion. I was afraid it might happen again. And Marilyn said if I became pregnant I should have the baby no matter what Frankie said. Then she told me about the baby girl she had when she was nineteen or twenty. The baby was taken away from her and she said she had always suffered from guilt. She'd see young girls on the street or children in the park that would be about the age of her daughter and she'd wonder where her baby was and what she was doing. . . . She wouldn't say who the father was. I was so astonished when she told me the story, and I think she must have seen the look of utter amazement on my face, because she suddenly stopped talking about it. We never discussed it again. . . . Marilyn had the characteristics a woman takes on around the tummy when she's given birth, and I'm sure she was telling me the truth. Marilyn just wouldn't make up things—not like that."

At Marilyn's request, Ralph Roberts had followed her to the West Coast, and she leased a room for him at the nearby Chateau Marmont. "Rafe" helped her move in and installed the blackout curtains on her bedroom windows. She had learned the benefit of blackout curtains from Montgomery Clift, who found he couldn't sleep without them. Allegedly they kept out extraneous noise and light, but the curtains also fulfilled a sensitive celebrity's need for absolute retreat from the horrific monster that lurked just outside—the public.

Roberts became her companion as well as masseur, and because Marilyn no longer drove a car, Ralph drove her to Dr. Greenson's two or three times a week. Now that she was a Los Angeles resident again, the analyst extended himself in a doctor-patient arrangement that was unusually accommodating. Greenson told her that he would place himself on call, day or night, and gave her a special fee of fifty dollars per session. Frequently the sessions would be of two or three hours' duration. Later, as her problems seemed to grow worse, he saw her almost daily, sometimes twice daily. His final bill to Marilyn's estate, which was rendered prior to her funeral, was $1,450 for the month of July and the four days of August.

Greenson didn't approve of her relationship with Sinatra. In May 1961, he wrote to Dr. Kris: "Above all, I try to help her not to be lonely, and therefore to escape into the drugs or get involved with very destructive people, who will engage in some sort of sado-masochistic relationship with her. . . . This is the kind of planning you do with an adolescent girl who needs guidance, friendliness, and firmness, and she seems to take it very well. . . . She said, for the first time, she looked forward to coming to Los Angeles, because she could speak to me. Of course, this does not prevent her from canceling several hours to go to Palm Springs with Mr. F. S. She is unfaithful to me as one is to a parent. . . ."

Marilyn's thirty-fifth birthday was June 1, 1961. That day she sent a telegram to Greenson stating "Dear Dr. Greenson: In this world of people I'm glad there's you. I have a feeling of hope though today I'm Three Five."

Marilyn also became increasingly close to Patricia Kennedy Lawford and frequented the Lawford beach house in the company of Frank Sinatra and Dean and Jeanne Martin. Neighbors of the Lawfords reported seeing Marilyn at the Lawfords' during Jack Kennedy's visit in June 1961. Ralph Roberts recalled her speaking of a visit with the president and saying, "I made his back feel a lot better."

In mid-June, when Sinatra performed at the Sands in Las Vegas, Marilyn was there along with Peter and Pat Lawford and Jean Kennedy Smith. Eddie Fisher, who was there with Elizabeth Taylor, recalled, "Elizabeth and I sat in the audience with Dean and Jeanne Martin and Marilyn Monroe, who was having an affair with Sinatra, to watch his act. But all eyes were on Marilyn as she swayed back and forth to the music and pounded her hands on the stage, her breasts falling out of her low-cut dress. She was so beautiful—and so drunk. She came to the party later that evening, but Sinatra made no secret of his displeasure at her behavior, and she vanished almost immediately."

She had become ill, and Sinatra may have attributed her illness to the mortal sin of not being able to hold her liquor. But Sinatra didn't know that the pain Marilyn suffered in her side for over a year had become tormenting. No amount of barbiturates or alcohol helped. Dr. Hyman Engelberg had been unsuccessful in diagnosing the problem until it became acute. She was finally told she had an inflamed gallbladder, and in the last week of June, Ralph Roberts and Pat Newcomb returned with her to New York, where she entered the Manhattan Polyclinic Hospital. Doctors discovered that she had impacted gallstones, and on June 29 she went into surgery for a cholecystectomy.

Marilyn was released from the hospital on July 11, and outside a crush of reporters, photographers, and fans waited with their questions, flashbulbs, and autograph books—screaming, trying to touch her, shouting questions, tugging at her sweater. *How are you feeling? . . . Smile . . . Sign this to David! . . . Do you miss Arthur Miller? . . . You killed Gable! . . . Please sign this, Miss Mansfield! . . . What's your next picture? . . . Is it true that you and Joe are getting back together? . . . Look over here!*

There was an animalism and cruelty to the crowd Marilyn hadn't sensed before. "It was scary," Marilyn said. "I felt for a few minutes as if they were just going to take pieces out of me. Actually, it made me feel a little sick. I mean, I appreciated the concern and their affection and all that, but—I don't know—it was like a nightmare. I wasn't sure I was going to get into that car safely and get away."

While she was recuperating in her New York apartment, Berniece Miracle arrived for a visit.

"For several months I had been aware of a transition in Marilyn's attitude," Berniece stated. "New problems were coming at her from every direction. In our telephone conversations, her usual wistfulness about getting together had changed to strong invitations. 'I need you to be with me,' Marilyn had said. 'I *need* to talk to you, Berniece, and not over the telephone!'"

Though they had spoken on the phone and written frequently, Marilyn hadn't seen her half sister since the California visit in 1946, and the urgency mystified Berniece. There was an ecstatic reunion at Marilyn's apartment. Joe DiMaggio and his friend George Solotaire joined them for dinner. There was a lot of catching up to do, and late-night discussions about Gladys.

Following her separation from John Eley, Gladys had been confined for eight years in Rockhaven Sanitarium in Verdugo City, California, where she was officially diagnosed as a paranoid schizophrenic. She had tried to escape several times, and there had been suicide attempts.

Through the years Marilyn had paid for her mother's care, and Gladys frequently wrote Marilyn letters of complaint that Rockhaven wasn't operated by members of the Christian Science faith. Marilyn received one of her mother's letters during Berniece's visit, and Berniece noted that Marilyn had difficulty reading it.

"I can't finish this letter now," Marilyn said with tears in her eyes. "I just can't finish Mother's letter. I'll just put it away for a while." With her eyes firmly closed, Marilyn continued, "I just get angry. I know it's irrational. I know that she didn't mean to turn her back on me. She didn't purposely get sick. I try and try, but I still get angry—even when she was with me, she wasn't *there*. God, poor Mother . . ."

Berniece recalled that she kept waiting for Marilyn to reveal the matter that was so important she couldn't discuss it over the phone. "I kept listening, trying to figure out what she wanted to say, and trying to figure out how I could help. I kept waiting for her to get around to exactly what was troubling her." According to Lena Pepitone, Marilyn had invited Berniece to New York in order to give her a large sum of money, "so they can live better and educate their kids."

In the later part of July, before Berniece was to return to her home in Florida, Ralph Roberts drove Marilyn and Berniece to the Roxbury farm to retrieve some of Marilyn's possessions. Knowing that Marilyn was coming, Miller absented himself. Roberts recalled that Marilyn smelled *eau de bourgeoisie* perfume on a fur coat she had left in a closet, and à la Goldilocks she said, "Some Magnum madam has been sleeping in my bed and wearing my coat." She then promptly dropped the fur into a trash can.

That Miller had made a point of not being there bothered Marilyn, and she complained to Norman Rosten, "I told him [Miller] I'd be there, but when I arrived he wasn't. It was sad. I thought maybe he'd ask me in for coffee or something. We spent some happy years in that house. But he was away, and then I thought, 'Maybe he's right'—what's over is over, why torment yourself with hellos? Still, it would have been polite, sort of, don't you think, if he'd been there to greet me? Even a little smile would do."

Before returning to Hollywood, Marilyn told Lena Pepitone that she thought Frank Sinatra was going to marry her. Though he hadn't asked her yet, Marilyn's intuition told her "he's almost ready." Unlike Joe DiMaggio, who didn't want her to be in the movies, Sinatra was in the same business as she was. "Frankie wouldn't expect me to be a housewife. We can both have our careers. It'll be perfect . . . I hope." Crossing the fingers of both hands and holding them in the air, she then closed her eyes, and said, "Let me be lucky—just once!"

During the summer of 1961 Marilyn socialized a great deal with Sinatra and the Rat Pack. In August she spent a weekend with Sinatra on his yacht, and Dean Martin's wife Jeanne said, "I remember going up to Frank's house before we got on the boat and he said, 'Will you please go in and get Marilyn dressed so we can get in the limo and go?' She couldn't get herself organized, but she was the one person Frank was patient with."

Dr. Greenson, who felt that Marilyn's relationship with Sinatra was destructive, wrote to a colleague at this time, "She was terribly, terribly lonely" and she expressed a "feeling of mistreatment, which had paranoid undertones." Greenson went on to state that he felt Marilyn was reacting to her current involvement with "people who only hurt her."

In September, Lena Pepitone received an excited call from Marilyn. "You're coming out to California. I'm going to show you Hollywood!" Marilyn had asked Pepitone to bring her a special dress that she wanted to wear to a Democratic Party fund-raiser she was going to attend at the Hilton Hotel with Frank Sinatra. It was a green sequined dress that Marilyn had Jean-Louis design at a cost of three thousand dollars. Pepitone recalled that Pat Newcomb made the arrangements, and she was flown out to California in first class. Marilyn's chauffeur, Rudy Kautzky, was waiting at the airport. When Pepitone arrived at the apartment, Marilyn threw her arms around her in a warm greeting, exclaiming, "Baby lamb, you're here! You made it!"

Pepitone remembered Sinatra arriving in full evening dress to take Marilyn to the Hilton and being surprised to find Marilyn actually ready on time. "Marilyn flew into the room like an exotic tropical bird; with her platinum hair and green-sequined gown, she electrified the apartment. Frank's face lit up. He was clearly thrilled by the way she looked. With a breathless 'Frankie,' she embraced him. Then, after telling Marilyn to close her eyes, Sinatra pulled out of his pocket a gorgeous pair of emerald and diamond earrings and clipped them to her ears. Marilyn exclaimed how beautiful they were and Frank said, 'They oughtta be. They cost thirty-five-thousand dollars!' "

One of the guests at the fund-raiser was Philip Watson, the Los Angeles County assessor, who was invited to a more intimate gathering in the Kennedy suite at the Hilton later in the evening. "She was there in the room with him [JFK]," Watson recalled. "I had heard stories about them, and it came as no particular surprise. I was introduced to them both, I spoke to her, too, and I thought her a beauty—she was in a skintight sequined dress."

By 1961, Marilyn's affair with the president wasn't much of a secret in Hollywood. Associated Press columnist James Bacon revealed that Marilyn had told him of the relationship during the campaign. "She was very open about her affair with JFK," Bacon stated. "In fact, I think Marilyn was in love with JFK." Marilyn's friend Jeanne Carmen was present at a number of Jack Kennedy's visits to the star. According to Carmen, Marilyn's affair with the president wasn't a well-kept secret. "It was known in the industry. I don't think the public would have believed it then if they heard it. They would have closed their minds to it. The public didn't want to hear stuff like that. I wonder if they want to hear it now? But the industry knew. I mean they were very brazen. I'm amazed it didn't get out."

Edwin Guthman, Robert Kennedy's former press secretary, recalled being at several parties at the Lawford beach house with Robert Kennedy when Marilyn and the president's brother were together. One of the par-

ties took place in the first week of October 1961, shortly after Guthman
attended a conference in San Francisco with the attorney general. "After
the party at Lawfords'," Guthman recalled, "she had too much to drink
to drive home, and we both drove her to her place, an apartment somewhere around Beverly Hills. Bob asked me to come along too. He didn't
say why, but his reason was pretty obvious. He didn't want to be seen
going off alone in a car at night with Marilyn Monroe."

Look magazine photographer Stanley Tretick remembered seeing Bobby
Kennedy and Marilyn dancing together at a party. "It was in a hotel at a
posh, semiprivate affair, a fund-raiser sort of thing. They were dancing
very closely, with their bodies very close together, and it looked rather
romantic. It just struck me at the time, 'My, they really look like a nice
couple together.' "

Marilyn wrote to Norman Rosten about dancing with Bobby Kennedy
at a party.

He was very nice, sort of boyish and likeable. Of course he kept looking down
my dress, but I'm used to that. I thought he was going to compliment me, but
instead he asked me while dancing who I thought was the handsomest man in
the room. I mean, how was I going to answer that? I said *he* was. Well, in a way
he *was*!

Marilyn needed Dr. Greenson's absolute confidence in telling him
about her relationships, and while he tried to discourage her relationships
with many men, including Frank Sinatra and Joe DiMaggio, he didn't
discourage her relationship with either Jack or Bobby Kennedy. In the
interview conducted after Marilyn's death by Robert Litman of the Suicide Prevention Team, Greenson referred to her relationship with "two
powerful and important men in government." Litman's report stated,
"Greenson had very considerable concern that she was being used in these
relationships. However, it seemed so gratifying to her to be associated
with such powerful and important men that he could not declare himself
to be against it."

Sinatra's secretary, Gloria Lovell, recalled that the "chairman of the
board" often spoke to the Prez on the phone. Whenever the president
called, she would interrupt business meetings to tell Sinatra there was a
call from the White House. "Frank would smile at everybody, pick up the

phone and say, 'Hiya, Prez!' After each one of those calls Frank pranced around, so proud of the fact that the president was ringing him up."

Frank's private life fascinated the president, who had an endless curiosity as to what Frank was doing, and to whom. Judith Campbell Exner recalled that during her visits to the White House, Kennedy always quizzed her about Sinatra. "Almost immediately, Jack started pumping me for gossip, most of it directed at Frank. What was Frank doing? Was it true that he was seeing Janet Leigh? We always went through the same routine."

Peter Lawford recalled, "During one of our private dinners, Jack brought up Sinatra and said, 'I really should do something for Frank.' Jack was always so grateful to him for all the work he'd done in the campaign. He said, 'Maybe I'll ask him to the White House for dinner or lunch.' I said that Frank would love that, but then Jack said, 'There's only one problem, Jackie hates him and won't have him at the White House.' But the president brightened up a few minutes later and said, 'I'll wait until Jackie goes to Middleburg, and I'll have Eunice be the hostess.' So that's what he did. When Jackie left, JFK's secretary Evelyn Lincoln called Frank and invited him to the White House. He flew to Washington for the day and a car drove him up to the southwest gate. Even without Jackie there, the president still wouldn't let him come in the front door," Peter Lawford continued. "I don't think he wanted reporters to see Frank Sinatra going into the White House. That's why he never flew on Air Force One, and was never invited to any of the Kennedy state dinners or taken to Camp David for any of the parties there. He got to Hyannis, once."

On September 23, 1961, Sinatra was given the grand tour of the White House family quarters and taken out to the Truman Balcony for Bloody Marys. Presidential aide Dave Powers observed, "Sinatra sat on the balcony sipping his drink and looking out at the sun streaming in and the wonderful view of Washington we got from there. He turned to me and said, 'Dave, all the work I did for Jack—sitting here like this makes it all worthwhile.' " The following day Frank boarded the *Caroline* on a flight to Hyannisport with Pat Lawford, Ted Kennedy, Porfirio Rubirosa, and Rubirosa's wife, Odile. When they landed, Sinatra strolled off the Kennedy plane holding a glass of champagne, followed by twelve pieces of luggage, a case of wine, a dozen bottles of champagne, three cartons of ice cream, and two loaves of Italian bread.

On September 25, they all went cruising with Jack on the *Honey Fitz*, and the president listened to Sinatra talk about his trip to Italy and his audience with Pope John XXIII. Sinatra also put in a good word for his Italian friends in Chicago.

But his Italian friends in Chicago weren't happy about their own relationship with the Kennedys. Shortly after Sinatra's visit, Sam Giancana telephoned Johnny Roselli with a litany of complaints. There was a third party on the line—the FBI:

> ROSELLI: He [Frank Sinatra] was real nice to me. . . . He says: "Johnny, I took Sam's name, and wrote it down, and told Bobby Kennedy, 'This is my buddy, this is what I want you to know, Bob.'" Between you and I, Frank saw Joe Kennedy three different times—Joe Kennedy, the father. He called him three times. . . . He [Frank] says he's got an idea that you're mad at him. I says: "That, I wouldn't know."
>
> GIANCANA: He must have a guilty conscience. I never said nothing. . . . Well, I don't know who the fuck he's [Frank's] talking to, but if I'm gonna talk to . . . after all, if I'm taking somebody's money, I'm gonna make sure that this money is gonna do something, like, do you want it or don't you want it. If the money is accepted, maybe one of these days the guy will do me a favor.
>
> ROSELLI: That's right. He [Frank] says he wrote your name down. . . .
>
> GIANCANA: Well, one minute he [Frank] tells me this and then tells me that and then the last time I talked to him was at the hotel in Florida a month before he left, and he said, "Don't worry about it. If I can't talk to the old man [Joseph Kennedy], I'm gonna talk to the man [President Kennedy]." One minute he says he's talked to Robert, and the next minute he says he hasn't talked to him. So, he never did talk to him. It's a lot of shit. . . . Why lie to me? I haven't got that coming. . . . When he says he's gonna do a guy a little favor, I don't give a shit how long it takes. He's got to give you a little favor."

For several months Ralph Roberts had taken on the routine of driving Marilyn on errands after her massage sessions, and in the afternoon he would drive her to Dr. Greenson's several days a week. Marilyn had become quite dependent on Roberts and sometimes referred to him as her "brother."

On a Saturday in the latter part of October, Roberts recalled Marilyn emerging from Dr. Greenson's deeply upset. She was weeping. "Dr. Greenson thinks you should go back to New York," she cried. "He's chosen someone else to be a companion for me. He said that two Ralphs in my life are one too many. I told him I call you *Rafe*. 'He's Rafe,' I said, over and over. But he says, no—that I need someone else!" The next day Ralph Roberts checked out of the Marmont and went to the Doheny apartment to collect his massage table and say a tearful good-bye before returning to New York.

Several days later, a middle-aged, birdlike woman with gray hair and impish eyes entered the patio in front of the Doheny apartment just below Sunset Strip. As she walked by the ornamental fountain near the tall iron security gates, she stopped at the building directory, where she had been instructed to press the buzzer for apartment number three. Behind the black enameled door of the apartment she would find Marilyn Monroe. "Marilyn Monroe" was only a film star's name to her. She had never seen a Monroe movie or followed the celebrity's career.

She pressed the buzzer, and there was a long wait before the door was opened by the platinum blonde with the incredible blue eyes and the radiant glow. Marilyn Monroe stood at the door barefooted, wearing a red Chinese kimono, her hair tousled with sleep.

"Hello," the middle-aged lady said softly. "My name is Eunice Murray. Dr. Greenson said you'd be expecting me."

The Lady of Shalott

The shackles of an old love straightened him:
His honour rooted in dishonour stood,
And faith unfaithful kept him falsely true.
     Alfred, Lord Tennyson, *Idylls of the King*

Eunice Murray stated in her book, *Marilyn: The Last Months*, that she had been hired "primarily to drive Marilyn Monroe to and from her apartment and the psychiatrist's office, and carry out such things as answering the door and phone, cleaning and dusting." Mrs. Murray had other duties as the film star's housekeeper which she never discussed.

Some years after Marilyn's death, when it was learned that Mrs. Murray was a trained psychiatric nurse, it was assumed that Dr. Greenson had placed her in Marilyn's home to monitor her behavior; however, to surreptitiously place a psychiatric nurse in a patient's home was an unprecedented procedure, and there were other aspects of the relationship between Dr. Greenson and Mrs. Murray that proved to be unusual.

Friends of Marilyn's regarded Mrs. Murray as peculiar. Whitey Snyder described her as "a very strange lady. She was put into Marilyn's life by Greenson, and she was always whispering—whispering and listening. She was this constant presence, reporting everything back to Greenson."

Jeanne Carmen sensed that Mrs. Murray wasn't the simple housekeeper-companion she pretended to be. "I wasn't crazy about Mrs. Murray. I don't know what I didn't like about her, but I just thought she was rather sneaky. When she was there I tried to avoid going around."

Mrs. Murray treated Marilyn's friends and associates with subtle disdain, and in her condescending way she gained a controlling influence on Marilyn's daily life. The day seemed to revolve around the four o'clock appointment with Dr. Greenson at his office. The "office" was in reality Greenson's home in Santa Monica.

In 1968, Mrs. Murray revealed that she always drove Marilyn to Greenson's home, where the film star was frequently invited to stay on for supper. Dr. Greenson's wife, Hildi, recalled that Marilyn often insisted on helping them cook and clean up afterward, saying, "I do dishes very well. I learned how in the foster homes and the orphanage." In effect, Marilyn became a member of the household. The Greensons' daughter, Joan, a student at the Otis Art Institute, quickly became Marilyn's friend. Dr. Greenson also encouraged his twenty-four-year-old son, Danny, to spend time with his celebrity patient. At the time, Danny was a medical student at the University of California at Berkeley, where he was an active member of SLATE.

The Greenson home was a large Mexican-Monterey-style house on a hill with views of Santa Monica and the distant ocean. The walls were wood-paneled; the ceiling was crossed with hand-hewn beams set in place by studio craftsmen during the prolonged Hollywood strike called by John Murray and Herb Sorrell in the forties. A huge fireplace was embellished with Mexican tiles, which also decorated the stairway and the kitchen. Many of the tiles Marilyn admired had been set in place by Eunice.

The living room had an inviting warmth and elegance. An antique table stood in front of the fireplace, and large bookcases lined the length of one wall. A grand piano was often played by Elizabeth Greenschpoon Rudin, Dr. Greenson's sister. She had become a concert pianist and frequently accompanied the chamber concerts that Marilyn often attended in the Greenson living room. Far from the taunts of the street toughs of Brownsville, Romi would play the violin in his Santa Monica home as friends and appreciative guests listened.

Among the guests who frequented these chamber concerts were Henry Weinstein; Celeste Holm; Dore Schary; writer Leo Rosten; Hannah Weinstein; Lillian Hellman; Otto Fenichel's widow, Hanna Fenichel; and Dr.

Lewis Fielding.* Ralph Greenson's mother, Katharine Greenschpoon, who had once directed the concerts at the Brownsville Labor Lyceum, often held the place of honor at these evenings of cultural pleasures. However, it was a glaring violation of all the traditional tenets of psychoanalysis for Dr. Greenson to have taken his patient into his home. It was a totally antianalytic approach to therapy and was highly criticized by his psychiatric colleagues when it became known years later.

Eleven years after Marilyn's death, Dr. Greenson defended his unorthodox therapeutic procedure in the *Medical Tribune* of October 24, 1973, saying "It is controversial, I know that. Nevertheless, I have practiced for some thirty-five years, and I did what I thought best, particularly after other methods of treatment apparently hadn't touched her one iota." But by making Marilyn a quasi-member of his household, the doctor transgressed one of the rules of analysis stated in his own textbook *The Technique and Practice of Psychoanalysis*, in which he criticized antianalytic technique. On page 37, Dr. Greenson wrote, "The anti-analytic procedures are those which block or lessen the capacity for insight and understanding. The use of any measure or course of action which diminishes the ego function of observing, thinking, remembering and judging belongs in this category. Some obvious examples are the administering of drugs, certain kinds of transference gratifications, diversions, etc." Dr. Greenson admitted that his break with the traditional doctor-patient relationship was an inappropriate procedure. "I did it for a purpose," he told the *Medical Tribune*. "My particular method of treatment for this particular woman was, I thought, essential at that time. But it failed. She died."

Friends and colleagues of Dr. Greenson's related the despondency and anguish the doctor went through in the years following Marilyn's death. The "strange sardonic smirk" that Sergeant Clemmons noted in the doctor's expression when he first arrived at the death scene was but the beginning of a problem of conscience that would haunt Ralph Greenson until his own death in 1979. There were priorities that the doctor had put above the welfare of his patient—priorities that led him to sacrifice the basic tenets of his profession. "I did it for a purpose," he had stated, but "the purpose" in the case of Marilyn Monroe wasn't the welfare of

---

* Lewis Fielding, who was a close friend and associate of Ralph Greenson's along with Norman Leites of the Rand Corporation, became Daniel Ellsberg's psychiatrist and was the object of a break-in by the "Plumbers" during the Nixon administration. It had become a matter of concern that the Pentagon Papers had appeared in Moscow before they appeared in the *New York Times*.

the patient. Dr. Greenson was faced with the dilemma of justifying him-self before distinguished colleagues, while at the same time not revealing the depth of his knowledge concerning the circumstances of Marilyn Mon-roe's death, for in doing so he would have to reveal the nature of his own priorities—the deeply guarded secret of his hidden life.

Dr. Greenson maintained a dual identity within the Communist Party. According to Norman Jefferies and former FBI agent Ernest Phillips Co-hen, Dr. Ralph R. Greenson was an agent of the Comintern. While forty pages of Dr. Greenson's lengthy and highly redacted FBI dossier are still withheld by the FBI under the "Internal Security—C (Communist) 105" ruling, Eunice Murray's son-in-law, Norman Jefferies, stated that Dr. Greenson controlled the Arts, Sciences, and Professions Committee (ASPC), which proved to be a vital force in promoting communist ideology on the West Coast. Fronted by John Howard Lawson, the ASPC had at one time been overtly prominent in promoting communist causes in the Los Angeles area before being forced to go underground by the HUAC inves-tigations and the blacklisting of many of its Hollywood members.

Under Greenson's coordination, in 1947 John Howard Lawson and screenwriter Albert Maltz* organized the Hollywood Film Quarterly and the Hollywood Writers Mobilization for Defense. Designated by the at-torney general as communist front organizations, they had their head-quarters on the campus of UCLA, where Dr. Greenson was a member of the faculty. According to Greenson's FBI file, he moderated some of the Writers Mobilization events and spoke at several of their public forums.

Louis Budenz, a Communist Party leader and one time managing editor of the *Daily Worker*, was the founder of the National Arts, Sciences, and Professions Committee. Budenz defected in 1949 and gave a clear and informative picture of how the committee functioned and its purposes:

> How the Communist writers, scientists and professionals were mobilized and how they obtained the cooperation of scores of non-Communists in this Red-controlled organization is a rather simple story. As a start, small knots of Com-munist writers, artists and scientists in New York and Hollywood asked others, friends and acquaintances to join them on the Committee. As usual, the Com-munist leaders made sure that they had secret control of the apparatus of the organization. That meant having enough concealed Communists on the execu-tive committee and in the key posts to exercise directive power.

* After Dr. Hyman Engelberg's wife, Esther, divorced him in 1963, she married Albert Maltz.

Budenz went on to say that the requirement for party members within the committee was "their prime loyalty to Marxism and to Joseph Stalin, the greatest living Marxist. No other loyalty was tolerated, no matter how pre-eminent they may have been in their own spheres."

Dr. Greenson's priorities, therefore, were beyond the welfare of any one person—even beyond the traditional tenets of his profession.

As the secret leader of the Arts, Sciences, and Professions Committee, Dr. Greenson was in charge of a number of professional groups within the committee. Among them was the Doctors Professional Group, of which Dr. Hyman Engelberg was a prominent member.

Another division within the structure of the Arts, Sciences, and Professions Committee was the People's Educational Center, which was established and funded by Frederick Vanderbilt Field. Among the instructors at this school who taught communist ideology were Dr. Hyman Engelberg and Dr. Frank Davis, a close friend of Dr. Greenson's and head of the UCLA psychology department. Clearly the bond between Greenson and Engelberg went far beyond their professionalism, their family relationships, and their sharing of medical offices. They shared a vision of world order under Marxist ideology.

In 1955, Dr. Oner Barker, Jr., who still practices today at his offices in Hollywood, gave testimony to the Senate Committee that Dr. Engelberg was a member of the Communist Party and belonged to the same professional cell that Dr. Barker had joined within the ASPC. Engelberg had openly used his name in connection with communist front activities, but after the Senate investigations he too went underground.

One of Greenson's contacts within the hierarchy of the Comintern was Frederick Vanderbilt Field. As the director of the American Russian Institute, Field was also associated with Greenson's mother, Katherine Greenschpoon, who was on the board of directors, according to the Senate Fact Finding Committee on Un-American Activities in California bulletin of 1948.

During the 1950s, after Frederick Vanderbilt Field was exposed by Louis Budenz as a Comintern operative, he fled to Mexico City, where he lived with a group of expatriate Americans, including some of the Hollywood Ten who were defended by Gang Tyre Rudin and Brown. One of the expatriates close to Frederick Vanderbilt Field in Mexico was Churchill Murray, Eunice Murray's brother-in-law.

Field was closely monitored by the FBI in Mexico City, and according to Norman Jefferies, continued his links to the United States through the Comintern leader in Los Angeles—Dr. Ralph Greenson.

As early as 1964, Frank Capell wrote in the Addenda of his booklet *The Strange Death of Marilyn Monroe:*

> Dr. Ralph Greenson, Marilyn's psychiatrist, resides at 902 Franklin Street in a home built by the husband of Mrs. Eunice Murray, Marilyn's "housekeeper." Mrs. Murray's husband was a left-wing labor leader and organizer who often came home "messed up" from his strike and organizing activities. Dr. Greenson held meetings in his house for a number of years at which an odd group of people assembled. They consisted of well dressed professional appearing people, Negroes, and laboring type persons. Neighbors got the impression that Greenson's home was used for some type of "cell" meetings. The Greensons were described by neighbors as being strong advocates of a socialist government.

Because Capell was considered something of an extremist who saw a red around every corner, his suspicions were discounted. But Capell's suspicions about the reds around the corner on Franklin Street were correct.

Whenever possible, a cell leader had psychiatric training. It was the responsibility of the cell leader to periodically interview key cell members in order to evaluate their state of mind and dedication. Testimony before the Senate Fact Finding Committee established that psychoanalysts' offices across the United States were used by Soviet espionage agents as havens for the safe transfer of confidential information. The one-on-one situation of the outside visitor in a confidential office setting was quite ideal. Among the members of the Psychoanalytic Institutes established in New York City, Boston, Washington D.C., Topeka, Chicago, San Francisco, and Los Angeles were a wide spectrum of analysts with varied political convictions and loyalties; among them were the close-knit heirs of Freudian-Marxism, such as Otto Fenichel's disciple Dr. Ralph Greenson.

Once Marilyn Monroe became Greenson's patient, he became one of the most important Comintern operatives in America; he had access to the mind of a woman who often shared the bed of the president of the United States and was an intimate of the attorney general.

As Greenson had correctly stated, Marilyn Monroe had a tendency to "get involved with very destructive people, who will engage in some sort of sado-masochistic relationship with her." Ironically, among those people were her psychiatrist, her physician, and her housekeeper, Eunice Murray, who joined in a conspiracy to surround Marilyn Monroe within a sphere of influence designed to gather intelligence from her relationship with the president of the United States and the attorney general.

It wasn't until the last weeks of Marilyn's life that she began to realize that a web of deception had been woven around her. In July 1962, she confided to Ralph Roberts that she had found something disturbing about Dr. Greenson's enveloping influence. Roberts wrote to Susan Strasberg, "She was radically turning on Dr. Greenson and Mrs. Murray, the woman he'd put with her, she felt to spy on her."

In her inimitable way of euphemistically revealing the truth, Eunice Murray cites the Camelot legend of the Lady of Shalott in the conclusion of her book, *Marilyn: The Last Months*. She wrote:

Marilyn lived a myth not unlike the legendary figure in Tennyson's poem "The Lady of Shalott"—a maiden of King Arthur's kingdom. The Lady was imprisoned in a tower, weaving into a tapestry the sights of the road below where people passed on their way to Camelot.

But the Lady of Shalott was under a spell. She could observe life only indirectly, as reflected in the mirror of her room. If she turned and looked directly on the scene below, she would die.

But the Lady of Shalott fell in love with the dashing Sir Lancelot as he rode by. She descended into the world—and died on her way to Camelot.

Zona Rosa

She came under the influence of many whom she allowed, in childish trust, to chart the course of her life and who led her to a premature grave.
—Frank A. Capell

While Marilyn continued to see her psychiatrist on an almost daily basis, a good deal of her time in the fall of 1961 was taken up in legal battles with 20th Century-Fox and preparation for her next motion picture, *Something's Got to Give*. Under her old studio agreement, made in 1955, she was earning only $100,000 a picture. In 1962, that was a bargain-basement price for a top star. Most stars were earning at least $700,000, but Fox was demanding that she fulfill her commitment.

Something's Got to Give was originally made as *My Favorite Wife* in 1940 with Irene Dunne and Cary Grant. It had a dated plot: IRIS IN—Wife becomes shipwrecked on a tropical island with an attractive man. She is eventually declared dead; the bereaved husband remarries, but the wife is miraculously rescued and returns to reclaim her husband. IRIS OUT.

Marilyn didn't want to make *Something's Got to Give*, but Mickey Rudin counseled that Fox could tie up her career in court for some time if she refused. Greenson, who was also now advising her on Hollywood career moves, suggested that she make the film in order to put her Fox commitments behind her. In December 1961, she reluctantly signed to do the film, which was to be directed by George Cukor.

The 20th Century-Fox archives clearly indicate that Marilyn never would have started *Something's Got to Give* if Greenson hadn't persuaded her to do it. He claimed that it was important "for her emotional health." Dr. Greenson was not only responsible for getting Marilyn to do the film, but hundreds of documents in the studio archives show that he was deeply involved in many aspects of the production. Phone transcripts detail numerous late-night discussions between the analyst and key studio officials. Throughout the preproduction phase of the film, Greenson remained in constant contact with the studio lawyers, the producer, and even with Ted Strauss, the story editor. Incredibly, Marilyn's psychiatrist became her de facto agent. She ended her long association with the MCA agency in November 1961, and Greenson and Rudin stepped in to represent her.

Something's Got to Give was originally to be produced by David Brown. Under the Robert Goldstein regime, Brown had nurtured the project from the beginning and worked with screenwriter Nunnally Johnson in preparing the script. But toward the end of November, Brown was shocked to learn that he was being replaced by Robert Goldstein's friend Henry Weinstein, the thirty-seven-year-old tyro of *Tender Is the Night*. Baffled that he was being replaced by a man who had questionable experience as a film producer, Brown delved into the reason for his dismissal and found that the orders came from the New York office, and that the change had been engineered by Dr. Ralph Greenson. Part of the deal to get Marilyn to sign included having Weinstein as the producer. The deal came with an amazing guarantee: if Brown was replaced by Weinstein, Dr. Greenson would guarantee Marilyn Monroe's punctuality and that the production would be completed on time. When questioned about his ability to do this, Greenson was quoted as responding, "Don't worry, I can get her to do whatever I want."

"Cukor was furious that Brown was fired," recalled Ted Strauss. "He needed the most experienced, most talented producer for that film, and Brown was a good choice. It wasn't going to make any difference whether or not Henry Weinstein, the producer, knew Marilyn's psychiatrist." Cukor raged to Weinstein, "So you think you can get Marilyn to the set on time? Let me tell you something, if you placed Marilyn's bed on the set with her in it, and the set was fully lighted, she still wouldn't be on time for the first shot!"

Shortly after Henry Weinstein became the producer of *Something's Got to Give*, his friend Robert Goldstein was replaced by Peter Levathes. Levathes was the appointee of Wall Street lawyers Milton Gould, John Loeb, and Samuel Rosenman. All three were associated with the Kennedys. John Loeb had been named by JFK as the Ambassador to Peru; Judge Samuel Rosenman worked within the Justice Department and as a White House labor consultant; and Gould was a partner of Joe Kennedy's in Rhoades and Company, a real estate investment firm. Gould, Loeb, and Rosenman were less enchanted with the silver screen than with the golden pay dirt beneath the rolling hills of 20th Century-Fox—the land. The back lot, which bordered Beverly Hills and capped an oil field, was worth far more than all the plaster dreams that studded the old Tom Mix ranch. And while the heavily laden barge of *Cleopatra* was sinking in the black lagoon of corporate ineptitude, the barracudas of Wall Street were mapping out Century City, where the streets of Paducah and the railway station where Marilyn bought her ticket to Tomahawk were to be bulldozed to make way for the Marriott, the glittering towers of the ABC Entertainment Center, and the Century Plaza.

Following several meetings with Nunnally Johnson on the script of *Something's Got to Give*, Marilyn flew east and spent a week in New York before returning to Los Angeles before Christmas. The desolation she perennially suffered during the Christmas holidays was accentuated by something that occurred during her New York visit. Dr. Greenson reported that she had fallen into a state of depression resembling her condition when he had first visited her at her Beverly Hills Hotel bungalow in January of 1960. Greenson stated that she couldn't deal with "hurtfulness" from "certain ideal figures in her life." After her return from New York, Greenson wrote, "She went through a severe depressive and paranoid reaction." Without detailing what may have caused the reaction, Greenson continued, "She talked about retiring from the movie industry, killing herself, etc. I had to place nurses in her apartment day and night and keep strict control over her medication, since I felt she was potentially suicidal."

Though Greenson disapproved of Marilyn's association with her ex-husband, Joe DiMaggio, he resorted to calling DiMaggio for help in the situation. Her desolation was alleviated when Joe again arrived for what proved to be a last holiday visit. Together they bought a Christmas tree and strung up the lights to make her apartment look festive. Marilyn and DiMaggio spent the afternoon of Christmas at the Greensons' home. On New Year's Eve, Dr. Greenson's daughter, Joan, recalled dropping in at Marilyn's Doheny apartment for a postmidnight visit, where they drank champagne and roasted chestnuts in the fireplace. "DiMaggio seemed doting, caring, like family," Joan recalled. "As for Marilyn, it seemed to please her to be doing things for him. It was like visiting an old married couple." Jeanne Carmen recalled that long after the holidays had ended and DiMaggio had returned to San Francisco, the Christmas tree stood in Marilyn's living room, the decorations drooping from the dead tree, though Marilyn kept the lights burning.

By the end of the year, Greenson was advising Marilyn on many significant matters: what friends she should keep, whom she should date, what kind of pictures she should make, and even where she should live. The doctor had been urging Marilyn to buy a house, and Marilyn asked Mrs. Murray to find her "a Mexican house—as much like Dr. Greenson's as possible." Mrs. Murray readily agreed, and before long found a Mexican hacienda-style house on Fifth Helena Drive. There were simulated adobe walls, a tile roof, and wrought-iron grills on the windows. The house, which was surrounded by tall trees at the end of a cul-de-sac, offered her privacy. While the home had only one story and the rooms were small, it had a swimming pool. Marilyn swam infrequently but had always wanted a swimming pool for friends to enjoy. With Dr. Greenson's encouragement, she quickly purchased the house with the help of her lawyer, Mickey Rudin, who also felt it was an excellent selection.

The house was purchased in January 1962 for $35,000. Marilyn had to borrow money from Joe DiMaggio to make the down payment.* Reportedly, Marilyn burst into tears when she signed the purchase agreement. She explained later, "I felt badly because I was buying a home all alone." However, she had a friend she could call at any time of day or night, Dr. Ralph Greenson, who lived only minutes away. The house Mrs. Murray had found for Marilyn was in a convenient location. One of Marilyn's neighbors was Otto Fenichel's widow, Hanna Fenichel, who remained a close friend of Ralph and Hildi Greenson. By 1961 Hanna Fenichel had become a prominent West Side psychoanalyst who was also active in the Marxist circle within the Psychoanalytic Institute. From her upstairs win-

---

* Probate records indicated that the money was repaid to DiMaggio from her estate.

dow at 12403 Third Helena Drive, she could look down on the cul-de-sac and the courtyard of Marilyn's home. Hanna Fenichel's property was less than seventy-five yards from Marilyn's bedroom window.

In January, Marilyn was invited to Pat and Peter Lawford's to attend a going-away party for Bobby Kennedy. In his official capacity as attorney general, Kennedy was traveling to the Far East on government business. And as Pat Newcomb was to state in her interview with Donald Spoto regarding Marilyn and Bobby, "Off the record, she came on to him." Newcomb went on to say, "I mean, some people have written that Bobby Kennedy would have left his wife—are they crazy? I knew Bobby very well—better than Marilyn did in a lot of ways, and you'd have to know him to know he never would have left Ethel. I mean, seven children— come on! I mean, she came on to him, but I don't think that would have ever happened."*

Marilyn told Jeanne Carmen and Terry Moore that she was making special efforts to prepare herself for Bobby Kennedy's party at the Lawfords'. Greenson generously gave his time in briefing her on possible items of discussion with the attorney general so that Kennedy would be impressed with her knowledge of current events and political topics.

Not only did Greenson brief her on possible subjects to discuss, but his son, Danny, helped in prepping her. Danny even supplied her with a list of questions to ask the attorney general, which Marilyn carried to the Lawford party in her purse.

In his 1984 interview with Anthony Summers, Danny Greenson remembered that several weeks before the party, Marilyn was at the Greensons' home having dinner and made the remark, "Goddamnit, I'm going to dinner at the Lawfords' place, and Bobby's going to be there. Kim Novak will be talking about her new house near Big Sur, and I want to have something serious to talk to him about."

According to Danny Greenson, she was looking for political issues that would make talking points. "She ended up writing them down," recalled the younger Greenson. "They were left-of-center criticisms—way back then I was worried about our support of the Diem regime in Vietnam—

---

* The Spoto interviews for *Marilyn Monroe: The Biography* are housed at the library of the Academy of Motion Picture Arts and Sciences. Many of the interviews substantiate the relationship between Bobby Kennedy and Marilyn; however, this material was excluded from Spoto's book.

and there were questions about the House Un-American Activities Committee and civil rights, and so on. . . . She wanted to impress him."

There were those at the party who observed Marilyn's success. Gloria Romanoff, one of the guests, recalled Bobby Kennedy and Marilyn dancing that evening. She taught him how to do the twist and "Let's Twist Again" played over and over on the Lawford record player. She added that Bobby Kennedy called his father long-distance and said "Guess who's standing next to me? Marilyn Monroe," and he put Marilyn on the phone to speak to Joe. Joe Kennedy, however, was convalescing from a stroke and could neither speak nor walk.

Journalist James Bacon, who also attended the party, recalled, "Marilyn would follow Bobby around. She was wearing horn-rimmed glasses, and was carrying a notebook, and whenever Bobby said anything about civil rights or whatever, Marilyn took it down. I thought it was strange at the time, but Marilyn always had a kooky sense of humor."

It may have been at this time, early in 1962, that Kennedy's sister Jean Smith wrote the thank-you note to Marilyn that was found among her personal papers by Inez Melson.

Dr. Greenson suggested that Marilyn take a holiday before beginning production on *Something's Got to Give*, which was scheduled to start in April. It was decided that she would go to Mexico to rest and purchase furnishings for her new home. While she was gone, Norman Jefferies and his brother, Keith, would begin refurbishing the house.

In early February 1962, Marilyn flew to Florida, ostensibly to visit Joe DiMaggio, who was wintering there with the New York Yankees. She also called on Arthur Miller's father, Isadore, with whom Marilyn maintained a friendship long after the end of the Miller marriage. Marilyn stayed at the Fountainbleu and visited with Jack Kennedy, who, according to White House records, was in Palm Beach on February 6 and 7.

Mack McSwane, who has worked at the Fountainbleu since 1955 and is now bell captain, recently stated that Marilyn was a frequent visitor to the hotel when the Kennedys were in town, and corroborated that in February 1962, when President Kennedy was a guest at the Fountainbleu, "Marilyn Monroe stayed just down the hall next to the Kennedy suite on the seventeenth floor. Everybody knew about that!"

From Florida, Marilyn flew to Mexico City and checked into the Hilton Hotel, where Frank Sinatra had arranged accommodations. But what was supposed to be a quiet holiday before starting her film turned into a state of siege. Armed guards were required to keep the press at bay, and Marilyn was hounded by photographers. During a press conference hastily called to mollify the riotous paparazzi, Marilyn drank too much champagne, and a photo was taken that proved once and for all that Marilyn didn't wear panties.

Eunice Murray had arrived before Marilyn, and the day after the press conference, Marilyn met Churchill Murray, John Murray's brother. According to Norman Jefferies, "Churchill was a communist if there ever was one. He ran a communist propaganda radio station in Mexico City and had a number of political contacts, including diplomats from the Cuban and Soviet embassies." Churchill drove Marilyn and Eunice Murray to the home of Frederick Vanderbilt Field. Field and his wife, Nieves, a former model and mistress of Diego Rivera, were part of the colorful colony of the Zona Rosa, where the left-wing expatriates lived in virtual exile. More than twenty-five families had fled the United States to avoid the stigma of their communist affiliations. Among those in the Zona Rosa colony were Dalton Trumbo, Herbert Biberman, John Bright, George Pepper, John Howard Lawson, and Albert Maltz.

Field wrote in his autobiography, *From Right to Left*, "Marilyn's companion, Mrs. Eunice Murray, was to arrive in Mexico a week early to line things up. I called on her and arranged to meet Marilyn right after her arrival. Mrs. Murray is an accomplished person in her own right. When she became a widow, she had gone into house decorating and also taken therapy training. She had become Marilyn's part-time companion, chauffeur, housekeeper and sort of M.M. watcher at the suggestion of Marilyn's psychiatrist, Dr. Ralph Greenson."

While Marilyn didn't know of the association between Frederick Vanderbilt Field and Greenson, they took to each other at once. Field found Marilyn "beautiful beyond measure—warm, attractive, bright and witty; curious about things, people, and ideas—also incredibly complicated."

Field soon discovered that Marilyn had become involved with the Mexican screenwriter, José Bolaños, a member of the La Reforma lothario set. Bolaños was dark, lean, and handsome and looked as if he had stepped out of the "Latin lover" list at Central Casting. He played the role well, bombarding Marilyn with gifts and flowers and serenading her with mariachi bands. But Field regarded him with suspicion. Bolaños hung around with Luis Buñuel, Dalton Trumbo, and the blacklisted red refugees in the Zona Rosa, but he had also been a buddy of writer–CIA agent E. Howard Hunt, who was a frequent commuter to the Mexico City CIA station.

Field advised Marilyn to stay away from Bolaños, who Field stated was a "man of left-wing pretensions—deeply distrusted by the real left."

Field spent a number of days in Marilyn's company, driving her to the Toluca Market—often in the company of Eunice Murray and Churchill Murray. They journeyed to the mountain resort of Taxco, where Marilyn was followed by Bolaños. Arriving in the middle of the night at the inn where Marilyn was staying as a guest, Bolaños hired mariachi musicians to serenade her to sleep.

Like most visiting Americans, Marilyn was pounced on by the expatriates for news of home. Field and Marilyn had long conversations about many things. According to Field's own statements, she told him a good deal. They spoke of the excitement of knowing the Kennedys, about civil rights, agrarian reform in China, her anger at McCarthyism, and how the Kennedys hated J. Edgar Hoover. "She said that at a party at the Lawfords' attended by Bobby Kennedy she had asked him directly whether he and the President were going to fire Hoover. His answer, she said, was that 'they would like to, but at that time it was politically impossible.'"

She talked a great deal about her marriage to Arthur Miller, and Field related, "She said she wanted to quit Hollywood and find some guy—a combination of Miller and Joe DiMaggio, as far as I could make out—someone who would be decent to her, but also her intellectual leader and stimulant. She wanted to live in the country and change her life completely. She spoke a lot of her intellectual shortcomings, her inability to keep up with people she admired. She talked of her age, the fact that she would be thirty-six, and of the need to get going."

But there were other things that Marilyn Monroe discussed with Frederick Vanderbilt Field that set off loud alarms in the FBI office in Washington, D.C. Ever since Louis Budenz had identified Frederick Vanderbilt Field as a Comintern operative for the Soviets, Field had been under close surveillance, and electronic listening devices had been placed in his home.

An FBI document dated March 6 and headed "MARILYN MONROE—SECURITY MATTER—C [Communist]" was sent from the Mexico City office to J. Edgar Hoover's desk. The contents are heavily redacted, but an FBI briefing revealed that this report, which was filed several days after Marilyn's departure from Mexico, concerned her conversations with Frederick Vanderbilt Field relating to confidential information she had learned in discussions with the president and attorney general (see FBI document in Appendix, page 468).

While J. Edgar Hoover had been alarmed by Jack Kennedy's flagrant womanizing, he was deeply disturbed to learn that his warnings had again been ignored, and that confidential information had been unwittingly passed by Marilyn Monroe to a suspected Soviet espionage agent, known by the FBI to be in communication with foreign intelligence operatives. According to sources close to Hoover at the time, he became enraged and demonstrated a degree of anger seldom witnessed by his subordinates.

Incredibly, the president of the United States had become a security risk.

The Hand of God

Miss Monroe knows the world, but this knowledge has not lowered her great and benevolent dignity; the world's darkness has not dimmed her goodness.
—Dame Edith Sitwell

Jack Kennedy was planning a political trip to California in March 1962, and in January, Peter Lawford had asked Frank Sinatra if the president could stay at Sinatra's Palm Springs home during his visit. Sinatra not only readily agreed, but he spent over half a million dollars on a massive construction project designed to turn his Palm Springs estate into the western White House. A giant heliport was constructed along with special guest cottages, Secret Service accommodations, and a communications center with over twenty-five extra phone lines. "It had been kind of a running joke with all of us in the family," Peter said later. "He even erected a flagpole for the presidential flag after he saw one flying over the Kennedy compound in Hyannisport. No one asked Frank to do this." Sinatra even ordered a special gold plaque inscribed "John F. Kennedy Slept Here," to be mounted at the front door.

During one of the daily briefings of the attorney general's staff, a zealous young lawyer complained about the president's friendship with Frank Sinatra and said, "We are out front fighting organized crime on every level and here the president is associating with Sinatra, who is associating with all those guys."

Bobby Kennedy responded by saying, "Give me a memorandum and give me facts."

The memorandum and the facts revealed that Sinatra had personal associations with ten of the leading figures in organized crime and listed times and dates when these gangsters had telephoned Sinatra at his private number.

"Sinatra has had a long and wide association with hoodlums and racketeers which seems to be continuing," stated the memorandum. "The nature of Sinatra's work may on occasion bring him into contact with underworld figures, but this cannot account for his friendship and/or financial involvement with people such as Joe and Rocco Fischetti, cousins of Al Capone; Paul Emilio D'Amato, John Formosa, Sam Giancana, all of whom are on our list of racketeers."

Though Bobby Kennedy was well aware of Sinatra's underworld associations, the portion of the memo he found disconcerting was the number of visits that Sam Giancana had made to Sinatra's Palm Springs home.

The cement was barely dry on the new presidential heliport at the Sinatra compound when Bobby Kennedy prevailed on the president not to stay at Sinatra's. "Sam Giancana has been a guest at the same house," complained the attorney general. "How is it going to look? There are too many people who know about Sinatra's ties to those guys. We can't take the risk, Jack."

Though Jack Kennedy didn't want to disappoint his pal Sinatra, after reading the Justice Department's memorandum, he was forced to agree. He told his brother to make different arrangements. Bobby Kennedy telephoned Peter Lawford and told him to let Sinatra know that the president's plans had changed. Lawford panicked when he heard the news. He knew that Sinatra's reaction would be less than pleasant, and he didn't want to take the brunt of his anger. Lawford called the president and pleaded with him to keep the plans unchanged, trying to elicit Kennedy's appreciation for all Sinatra had done for the campaign.

"I can't stay there," Kennedy told Lawford. "Bobby says it's impossible because of Frank's associations. You can handle it, Peter!"

Admittedly frustrated by his unenviable task, Lawford braced himself as he telephoned Sinatra with the news.

"Frank was livid," Lawford recalled. "He called Bobby every name in the book and then rang me up and reamed me out again. He was quite unreasonable, irrational really. George Jacobs [Frank's valet] told me later that when he got off the phone he went outside with a sledgehammer and started chopping up the concrete landing pad of his heliport. He was in a frenzy."

To make matters worse, the president now planned to stay at Bing Crosby's nearby estate. "He felt that I was responsible," Lawford lamented, "for setting Jack up to stay at Bing's—the *other* singer and a Republican to boot. Well, Frank never forgave me. He cut me off like that—just like that!"

Sinatra informed friends that he wanted nothing more than to punch Lawford in the face. He refused Lawford's phone calls and canceled Lawford's appearances in future Rat Pack shows at the Sands and the two upcoming Rat Pack movies. Price was no object when it came to revenge, and it was rumored that Sinatra paid Bing Crosby close to a million dollars to replace Lawford in *Robin and the Seven Hoods*.

Lawford's manager, Milt Ebbins, recalled, "Frank just wrote Peter off, and Peter was destroyed. He loved Frank. He loved being part of the Rat Pack, and all of a sudden he was on the outs. Not only did he lose the Rat Pack movies, but a lot of other opportunities as well."

It became clear to Peter Lawford that he would never be allowed back into the inner sanctum of the "chairman of the board." He grew despondent over the loss of this relationship in his life, and he soon ran up against the stumbling blocks that Sinatra began setting up in the path of his career. At the same time, he knew that his marriage to Patricia was in serious trouble, and he began drinking heavily as his troubles increased.

During the Eisenhower years, the Oval Office had an open door to J. Edgar Hoover. Hoover and Eisenhower frequently had lunch and spoke on a weekly basis, but during the Kennedy years, Hoover was denied his easy access to the president. According to Kenny O'Donnell, JFK's appointment secretary, "Hoover was very unhappy" about the situation. "During the thousand days, Hoover was invited to the White House on less than a dozen of them."

On March 22, 1962, the president and J. Edgar Hoover had one of their rare meetings at the White House. They met privately for lunch in the White House living quarters. It was just two weeks after Hoover had received the alarming document regarding Marilyn Monroe's meeting with the suspected communist espionage agent, Frederick Vanderbilt Field, in

Mexico City. "What actually transpired at that luncheon may never be known," said a Senate report thirteen years later, "as both participants are dead and the FBI files contain no records relating to it."

Reportedly, the meeting concerned JFK and his relationship with Judith Campbell Exner; however, the most important item on the luncheon agenda would have related to Kennedy's affair with Marilyn Monroe and her subsequent association with Field. Hoover certainly made it very clear to the president the imminent danger he had succumbed to. Perhaps for the first time since the days of Inga Arvad, Jack Kennedy no longer had to speculate on just how much information Hoover possessed about his private life.

Kenny O'Donnell reported that Kennedy was very disgruntled after the meeting with Hoover and made the remark, "Someday I'm going to get rid of that bastard. He's the biggest bore!" It is evident, however, that some of Hoover's admonitions had an effect. After more than seventy logged phone calls between the president and Judith Campbell Exner, there were few calls after that date. But perhaps Kennedy resolved merely to be more clandestine. Exner insists that she remained in touch with the president until the summer of 1962, and Kennedy rendezvoused with a disguised Marilyn Monroe soon after the luncheon with Hoover.

On Saturday, March 24, just two days after Kennedy and Hoover met, Marilyn emerged from her new bedroom on Fifth Helena Drive before 9 A.M. Usually she slept until noon, but that day she told Mrs. Murray, "I'm going on a trip, and my hairdresser's going to help me get ready." But at 8 A.M. the plumber had arrived with a crew to install a new hot water heater, so there was no water.

"Never mind," said Marilyn. "I'll go over to the Greensons' to have my hair washed—it's all right."

Several hours later Marilyn returned with her hair done, and her mind prepped for things to discuss with the important men in government she was preparing to visit. At noon, Peter Lawford arrived to pick her up. "Peter paced back and forth," Mrs. Murray recalled, "while Marilyn put the finishing touches on her attire." Over an hour later, she was finally ready. Wearing a brunette wig over her neatly coiffured hair, horn-rimmed glasses, and a severe Norman Norrell suit, and carrying a steno pad and a handful of pencils, Marilyn drove with Lawford to the airport, where Air Force One was waiting. The president's plane had already dropped off the presidential entourage in Palm Springs, and then diverted to Los Angeles, where it waited for over two hours to pick up Peter Lawford and the "president's new secretary."

When Marilyn arrived in Palm Springs, she found that the president was quartered at the sprawling Bing Crosby estate. Marilyn was sequestered in a secluded guest cottage, hidden from the main house by trees and shrubs. Philip Watson, the Los Angeles County assessor, had been invited to the formal affair in Crosby's baronial living room, where the president hosted an exclusive dinner party. Later, according to Watson, there was another, less formal party in the secluded guest cottage. Watson was invited to the smaller gathering and saw that Marilyn Monroe was there. He wasn't particularly surprised. He had seen Marilyn at another party at the presidential suite in the Beverly Hilton the previous November. What astonished him was how little effort either made to disguise their intimacy.

Watson stated, "The president was wearing a turtleneck sweater, and she was dressed in a kind of robe thing. She had obviously had a lot to drink. It was obvious they were intimate, that they were staying there together for the night."

That night Ralph Roberts received a phone call from Marilyn in Palm Springs.

"I've been arguing with a friend," she said mischievously, "and he thinks I'm wrong about those muscles we discussed. I'm going to put him on the phone, and you can tell him."

"A moment later," Roberts recalled, "I was listening to those familiar Boston accents. I told him about the muscles and he thanked me. Of course, I didn't reveal that I knew who he was, and he didn't say."

Marilyn later told Roberts that she had been massaging the president's bad back and discussing the muscle system. "I told him he should get a massage from you, Ralph, but he said, 'It wouldn't really be the same.' "

While the president seemed to be oblivious to the dangers of his private affairs, Marilyn had become talkative. Many of her intimate circle of friends knew of the relationship, and Marilyn continued nurturing the hope that Kennedy would one day divorce Jackie, and that she would become Mrs. Kennedy.

The presidential jaunt to Palm Springs was followed by another glittering fund-raiser in Los Angeles at the Beverly Hilton. Marilyn attended the affair and was seen by several people in the Kennedy suite following the gala. Marilyn wrote to Norman and Hedda Rosten and again told them of dancing with Bobby Kennedy, whom she had begun referring to as "the General." From the days that Marilyn first met him, she and the attorney general spoke frequently on the phone. "He was a wonderful person to tell your troubles to," remembers his press aide, Ed Guthman. "And Marilyn called him a lot . . . but then, so did Judy Garland and a lot of other ladies in trouble."

Oftentimes they would continue the conversation that had begun in the den of the Lawford beach house that February, discussing social issues, politics, the Cuban problem, the "freedom rides" and civil rights, and even the morality of the atomic bomb. Determined to be knowledgeable, Marilyn would research the topics discussed, sometimes using the extensive Greenson library or calling Danny or Joan Greenson to brief her on the issue at hand.

In the spring of 1962, Norman Rosten was in Hollywood working on a screenplay, and the day before he was to return to the East Coast he stopped by Marilyn's to say good-bye. Later he wrote of a curious event that took place, which was inexplicable to him at the time. The incident occurred on the afternoon following the Democratic Party fund-raiser at the Beverly Hilton. The president was flying back to Washington that day, Sunday, March 25. Rosten recalled,

It was noon . . . she stumbled out into the living room buttoning her robe: face heavy-lidded, bloated, drugged with sleep. The love goddess wasn't looking too good. She moved to the window, shading her eyes. "God, it's going to be a real dull Sunday."

I suggested, to cheer her spirits, we drive into Beverly Hills and check some of the art galleries that might be open. She agreed; in fact, it seemed to snap her awake. . . . We found a gallery that featured an exhibition of modern paintings. Marilyn began to relax and enjoy herself. She bought a small oil by Poucette, a red abstract study. Then her eye caught something not in the regular exhibit: a Rodin statue—a bronze copy, one of twelve—no more than two feet high. It depicted the full figure of a man and woman in an impassioned embrace: a lyric, soaring image. The man's posture was fierce, predatory, almost brutal; the woman innocent, responding, human.

Marilyn looked at the statue for a full minute, then decided to buy it. The price was over one thousand dollars. I suggested she think about it. No, she said, if a person thinks too long about something, it means they don't really want it. She wrote out a check.

We drove back with the statue. She held it balanced on her lap and stared at it. Shaking her head, she marvelled aloud, "Look at them both. How beautiful. He's hurting her, but he wants to love her, too." It seemed to confirm some deep feeling of exhilaration and fear. Then I recalled how, years earlier in New York, we had spent an hour in the Rodin section of the Metropolitan Museum of Art. She had been enraptured with the exquisite white marble figures of *The*

Hand of God. The lovers entwined in that hand represented an ecstasy she could dream of and possibly achieve. . . .

For some unexplainable reason, her mood shifted from cheerful to sullen, possibly even hostile. She said abruptly, "We'll stop off at my analyst. I want to show him the statue."

"Now?" I asked. I was worried about this turn of events.

"Sure," she mumbled. "Why not now?"

Dr. Greenson greeted us courteously. Marilyn immediately set the statue on the sideboard adjoining the bar, announcing her purchase with pride. 'What do you think?' she asked, stridently turning toward him. He replied quietly that it was a striking piece of art. Marilyn seemed unusually restless and kept touching the bronze figures. A belligerence crept into her speech. "What about it? What does it mean? Is he just screwing her, is it a fake? I'd like to know. . . ." Marilyn kept repeating, her voice shrill, "What do you think, Doctor? What does it mean?"

To a perplexed Norman Rosten, a hidden drama was exploding. She was demanding an answer. Like a child locked in the dark, she was crying out to the man who held the key.

Later they returned to her home and placed the Rodin on a living room table. The next day Rosten returned to the East Coast. It proved to be the last time he saw her alive.

The White Knight

If you needed to get in touch with Marilyn, you didn't call her secretary, her
agent, or her lawyer. You called her psychiatrist!

—George Cukor

The filming of *Something's Got to Give* was scheduled to start on
April 9, and Marilyn was fully prepared for the start of production; however, director George Cukor insisted on additional rewrites and the start
was delayed until April 23. Marilyn wanted to go to New York during the
delay. Henry Weinstein had a premonition of disaster and pleaded with
Marilyn not to go.

"She went east for one of those superprivate fund-raisers for the rich
and beautiful of Manhattan—a ten-thousand-dollar-a-plate affair," said
publicity consultant Rupert Allan, who dined with Marilyn in New York
on April 14. "The president had promised his well-heeled supporters that
Marilyn would attend."

The affair was a black-tie dinner party in the president's honor given
by socialite Fifi Fell in her Park Avenue penthouse. Among the invited
were Peter Lawford and Milt Ebbins. Around 7 P.M., Ebbins was to pick
up Marilyn at her Fifty-Seventh Street apartment, but when he arrived
she wasn't ready. The dinner was scheduled for eight. At ten minutes
after eight, Marilyn's phone rang and Ebbins picked it up. It was Lawford,
"Where is she? The president's here—everybody's waiting."

"She's not ready yet. I'm sitting here waiting," said Ebbins.

"C'mon," Lawford said. "Get her over here. She's holding up the dinner!"

At eight-thirty, Marilyn's maid, Hazel Washington, announced that she would be out shortly. By nine there was still no Marilyn. Lawford called again. "You son of a bitch!" Lawford screamed. "Get her over here—they're still waiting dinner!"

By nine-thirty, Ebbins couldn't take it anymore. He opened the door to Marilyn's bedroom and pleaded with her to hurry. He saw her sitting at her vanity table, naked, staring at herself in the mirror. "Marilyn, for God's sake," he said. "Come on! The president's waiting—everybody's waiting!"

Marilyn looked at him dreamily. "Oh," she said. "I'm glad you finally showed up. I need someone to help me put on my dress."

Marilyn arrived at the party some time after ten, according to Ebbins, "and did she look sensational—like a princess. Marilyn sashayed over to the president and said, 'Hi Prez!' He turned around, smiled at Marilyn, and said, 'Hi! Come on, I want you to meet some people.' " As they walked away, Marilyn looked back at Ebbins and winked. He later learned that dinner was never served. Everybody feasted on hors d'oeuvres and got blind drunk. Nobody cared about dinner after a while, and Marilyn, of course, was the hit of the party.

Before Marilyn's return to Hollywood, she met with Lee Strasberg. Despite warnings that he was sick with a bad cold, they had several sessions together discussing *Something's Got to Give*, scene by scene. Over dinner on April 18, she convinced Paula Strasberg to return to Hollywood at a salary of three thousand dollars a week and, for the fifth time, become her private coach during production. On the way to the airport on April 19, Marilyn told Paula, "I think I'm coming down with Lee's cold."

When Marilyn returned to Los Angeles, she was met by a surprise. The Nunnally Johnson script she had memorized and gone over scene by scene with Lee Strasberg had been totally rewritten by Walter Bernstein, the blacklisted writer Henry Weinstein had brought back from London.

On Sunday, April 22, one day before her first day of shooting, Marilyn became wracked with chills and fever. Virtually unable to leave her bed, she picked up the phone and called Weinstein. "I wanted to tell you as early as possible," she whispered, "I'm not going to be able to be on the set tomorrow." Weinstein listened with growing alarm. Marilyn's illnesses and problems had caused costly delays on *Some Like It Hot*, *Let's Make Love*, and *The Misfits*, but this would be the first time she had shut down a production on the first day. On Monday morning at Fox on Stage 14, there would be the cast and 104 crew members waiting and ready to roll, and no leading lady.

For several days, George Cukor shot around Marilyn, doing scenes involving Dean Martin, Cyd Charisse, and Tom Tryon. Suffering from high fevers, dizziness, and lethargy, Marilyn complained of "unbearable pain behind my eyes." An acute viral cold had developed into a serious sinus infection. Dr. Engelberg diagnosed it as "sinusitis," and tests at Cedars-Sinai showed that she had contracted "chronic sinusitis," which usually required a month of massive antibiotic treatment to cure.

A parade of studio insurance doctors visited Marilyn's house. "Nobody believed she was really sick," said production secretary Lee Hanna. New York executives were always skeptical of opinions by the private medical community and they sent their own studio doctor, Lee Siegel. Siegel, a tall, handsome man with a suave bedside manner, had been treating the actress off and on since 1951. He recorded her temperature at 101 degrees, described her respiratory tract as "badly occluded," and noted that she had a serious secondary infection of the throat. "It will take weeks to cure this infection," he wrote in a memorandum.

At Fox, the mood was grim. "Everyone knew that unless Marilyn felt in perfect condition, she couldn't come in," said Weinstein. "We were now at the mercy of all these doctors." The frustrated director, George Cukor, thought "she was malingering." But Eunice Murray recalled that "Marilyn woke up each morning at three with a headache and a high fever." Each day she tried to go to the studio, but wasn't able to make it. Studio logs show that Marilyn called for her limousine four times during the first seven days of her illness. On one of those days, chauffeur Rudy Kautzky was told by Mrs. Murray that Marilyn had passed out in the bathtub. "She knew she was sick, but was still guilty about not going in," said masseur Ralph Roberts, who had returned to Hollywood at Marilyn's request, despite Greenson's misgivings.

On April 30, against Dr. Siegel's advice, Marilyn went to the studio and filmed for about ninety minutes before collapsing in her dressing room and being driven home. Though she made repeated efforts to work, she was confined to her bed again from May 5 to 11. While Marilyn tried to regain her health, and Cukor rooted around for sequences to film without her, fear was creeping into the Fox executive building. Fox was concurrently filming the ravenous cash-eating monster *Cleopatra* in Europe. Problems with both productions threatened to bankrupt the studio.

While Greenson had guaranteed Fox that Marilyn would be on the set each day and the film would be finished on schedule, he hadn't anticipated physical illness. Paranoid studio executives called Greenson at frequent intervals, reminding him of his assurances and seeking clues to her possible motivations in destroying the studio. Was she really sick? Was she sabotaging them because she was being underpaid? Had she had a mental collapse? Had she succumbed to drugs?

Inexplicably, Greenson departed from Los Angeles on May 10 for four weeks. His disappearance at this very critical time in Marilyn's life remains a mystery. He told Fox that his wife was ill and needed to be treated at a hospital in Switzerland. But that proved not to be true. He told Marilyn and several associates that he was going to Europe on a speaking engagement. In his absence he designated the analyst who shared his Beverly Hills office, Dr. Milton Wexler, to care for his patient. Dr. Wexler, who still practices from his Santa Monica home, refuses to discuss why Greenson left town, where he went, or anything relating to his own visits to Marilyn during Greenson's absence. But according to an associate who was close to the psychoanalyst at the time, Greenson went to Switzerland and on to Germany, where he attended a conference at the Frankfurt School.

In his textbook *Explorations in Psychoanalysis*, Dr. Greenson discussed Marilyn and the problem of his departure. Without naming the patient, in the chapter "On Transitional Objects and Transference" Greenson wrote about an emotionally immature patient who used a chess piece as a talisman to get over his absence at a time when she was making a public appearance of great importance. Greenson wrote, "The young woman had recently been given a gift of a carved ivory chess set. . . . As she looked at the set through the sparkling light of a glass of champagne, it suddenly struck her that I looked like the white knight of her chess set. The realization evoked in her a feeling of comfort. . . . The white knight was a protector, it belonged to her, she could carry it wherever she went, it would look after her, and I could go on my merry way to Europe without having to worry about her."

The public appearance, of course, was the president's birthday gala.

On May 14, Marilyn was finally feeling better and returned to the studio, but a rumor was spreading through the Fox corporate headquarters that Marilyn was planning to attend President Kennedy's birthday gala scheduled for Saturday, May 19, at Madison Square Garden.

Henry Weinstein had given Marilyn tentative approval to attend, but this had been before the number of production delays caused by Marilyn's illness. Marilyn had spent six thousand dollars on an incredible gown designed by Jean-Louis, and the arrangements for her appearance at the gala had been made through Peter Lawford, who was enthralled with the thought of having Marilyn sing "Happy Birthday" to the president.

Gossip columnist Dorothy Kilgallen had already reported to radio listeners that Marilyn was to be the centerpiece of the president's forty-fifth birthday celebration and that a "spectacular dress" had been created for the star.

Designer Jean-Louis recalled Marilyn asking him to create a dazzling gown for the occasion. He said, "It was made of flesh-colored silk gauze embroidered with rhinestones to reflect the spotlights. Each rhinestone was hand-sewn into place." During one of the fittings Jean-Louis said there was a call from Hyannisport, which Marilyn took in the next room. When she returned she was singing, "Happy Birthday, Mr. Presi . . ."—stopped, and said with a wink, "Oops, I'm not supposed to say that." Norman Jefferies remembered Marilyn letting him hold the gown when it first arrived at her home, and the entire silk gown could be held in the palm of his hand.

But word came from the New York office that Marilyn wasn't to attend the gala. Milton Gould, the lawyer who was head of the Fox executive committee, instructed Frank Ferguson, the studio's chief counsel, to warn Marilyn against leaving the set on Thursday for the flight to New York. Though the event was on Saturday, rehearsals were set for late Friday. While it seemed improbable that a major studio would pass up such a major publicity event for one of its top stars, a two-page letter threatening the star with dismissal if she left the set of *Something's Got to Give* was sent to Mickey Rudin. The letter stated, "In the event that Miss Monroe absents herself, this action will constitute a willful failure to render services. In the event that Miss Monroe returns and principal photography of the motion picture continues—such re-commencement will not be deemed to constitute a waiver of [Fox's] right to fire Miss Monroe as stated in her contract."

When Marilyn heard about the letter from the Fox legal department, she called Bobby Kennedy, who knew Judge Rosenman and the top people on the Fox board of directors. However, Kennedy was concerned that factions within the Democratic Party would disapprove of her appearance, and he tried to discourage her from attending. Some leaders had previously expressed their concerns over JFK's association with Monroe. Soon there were private expressions of outrage. Richard Adler, a coordinator of the event, recalled that key leaders called him the day before the gala and begged him to cut Monroe from the ceremony. Six congressmen and three senators, all Democrats, sent him telegrams to protest her appearance. At the time, Washington was awash with gossip about the president's affair with the Hollywood actress. Former CBS news producer Ted Landreth, who later produced the BBC documentary *Say Goodbye to the President* (1986), said that "highly placed political leaders knew of the affair. The Washington press corps knew about it, as well." But either the president failed to perceive the dangers, or the reckless duality of his nature blinded him to the consequences.

Weinstein felt that Marilyn was determined to go in any event; "I mean, here's a girl who really did come from the streets, who had a mother who wasn't there, and a father who had disappeared, a girl who had known all the poverty in the world. And now, she was going to sing 'Happy Birthday' to the president of the United States in Madison Square Garden. There was no way for her to resist that."

When the production company of *Something's Got to Give* broke for lunch on Thursday, May 17, a deafening whine announced the arrival of an enormous helicopter that set down on the heliport near soundstage 14. Borrowed by Peter Lawford from Howard Hughes, the space-age chariot had arrived to take the Lady of Shalott to Camelot. Leaping from the helicoptor, Lawford hurried to Marilyn's dressing room and escorted her to the waiting royal blue chopper. Following several steps behind them were Pat Newcomb and Paula Strasberg. As they boarded the helicoptor, Lawford glanced behind him, hoping he wouldn't see an enraged Cukor running after them. Before the frustrated director and the executives at the Zanuck building knew what happened, the helicopter rose quickly into the air and headed for the Los Angeles Airport.

Marilyn's appearance at the Madison Square Garden Presidential Gala on May 19, 1962, would be her first performance before a large audience since she had entertained the troops in Korea during her honeymoon with Joe DiMaggio. The gala was to be attended by fifteen thousand people and televised to the nation. In a sense, the event was the apex of a dream—the fulfillment of Norma Jeane's dream of attainment, of being accepted and wanted. One of the most popular and beloved film stars of Hollywood singing "Happy Birthday" to the most important man in the world, the president of the United States.

Mickey Song, Marilyn's hairdresser at the event, stated, "While I was working on Marilyn, she was extremely nervous and uptight. The dressing room door was open and Bobby Kennedy was pacing back and forth outside, glaring at us. Finally, he came into the dressing room and said to me, 'Would you step out for a minute?' When I did, he closed the door behind him, and he stayed in there for about fifteen minutes."

While waiting in the hall outside the dressing room, Mickey Song could hear Kennedy and Marilyn having an argument. The attorney general's voice was growing louder and louder, and he was using expletives. When Kennedy came out he said to Song, "You can go in now," and then unexpectedly grabbed Song by the arm and demanded, "By the way, do you like her?"

Song recalled nodding enthusiastically that he did.

"Well, I think she's a rude fucking bitch!" Kennedy exclaimed as he stormed down the hall.

When Song entered the dressing room he noticed that Marilyn was disheveled. She tried to smile and asked, "Could you help me get myself back together?"

Marilyn grew terrified as showtime approached, and had some champagne to steady her nerves. She had difficulty in remembering a stanza of the birthday song that had been written especially for the president. Richard Adler, the producer of the show, had suggested to Jack Kennedy that Marilyn be cut from the production because he felt she might flub her song lines. "Oh, I think she'll be very good," Kennedy responded.

During the show, the president sat in the presidential box, his feet up on the rail, smoking a cigar. Bobby and Ethel Kennedy sat nearby. Jackie Kennedy had begged off. When she heard that Marilyn was going to be there she elected to go horseback riding in Virginia.

While emcee Peter Lawford built up the running gag that led to her entrance, Marilyn sat in the wings. She had lost her white knight, and as she waited for her cue her terror increased. Milt Ebbins recalled that she was heavily fortified by champagne well before her cue at the finale. At last, Lawford said, "Mr. President, because, in the history of show business, perhaps there has been no one female who has meant so much, who has done more . . . Mr. President—the *late* Marilyn Monroe!" There was a thunderous ovation as the spotlights picked up Marilyn's entrance. The thousands of rhinestones created around her a halo of luminosity, and she seemingly floated toward the microphone. Handing Lawford the white ermine jacket she had secretly borrowed from the Fox wardrobe department, she began softly singing to the president in her inimitable breathless manner—giving each syllable a meaning all its own:

> Happy birthday—to—you
> Happy birthday—to—you,
> Happy Birthday Mr. Pres—i—dent
> Happy Birthday to you.

Singing over the raucous laughter and applause, she then rendered a flawless rendition of the special verse written by Richard Adler to the tune of "Thanks for the Memories!":

> Thanks, Mr. President,
> For all the things you've done,
> The battles that you've won,
> The way you deal with U.S. Steel,
> And our problems by the ton,
> We thank you—so much!

As the giant birthday cake was wheeled onto the stage, Marilyn led the throng in another chorus, then stepped away from the microphone as the president took the stage during an overwhelming ovation and said, "Thank you. I can now retire from politics after having had, ah, "Happy Birthday" sung to me in such a sweet, wholesome way."

After Marilyn's performance, she was literally carried back to her dressing room, where she complained to her maid, Hazel Washington, of feeling dizzy. The stress of the event was exhausting, and she had a recurrence of the sinusitis. Hazel tried to persuade her to return to the apartment, but Marilyn insisted on attending a postgala party at the penthouse of theater magnate Arthur Krim. "I was very worried about her," said Hazel Washington. "From that evening on, Marilyn just kept getting sicker and sicker, but she wouldn't stop."

She was escorted to Arthur Krim's party by her former father-in-law, Isadore Miller, whom Marilyn introduced to the president and the attorney general. She had been the hit of the gala, and she mesmerized the crowd as she moved through the party from group to group receiving congratulations for her stunning performance. Adlai Stevenson, who attended the Krim party, said later, "I don't think I had ever seen anyone so beautiful as Marilyn Monroe that night. She was wearing skin and beads. I didn't see the beads! My encounters with her, however, were only after breaking through the strong defenses established by Robert Kennedy, who was dodging around her like a moth around a flame."

Arthur Schlesinger, Jr., noted, "There was at once something magical and desperate about her. Bobby, with his chivalry, his sympathy and absolute directness of response, got through the glittering mist surrounding Marilyn as few did." But Bobby Kennedy's "directness of response" and backstage maneuvers hadn't gotten through the mist surrounding Marilyn's determination to appear at the gala.

Later during the course of the party, the president and Bobby Kennedy escorted Marilyn to a quiet corner where the three held a private but animated conversation for a quarter of an hour. Although a number of photographs were taken of this occasion, only one photograph survives, the rest having been destroyed by the Secret Service. Dorothy Kilgallen later reported that Marilyn and Bobby Kennedy danced five times during the evening, while an angry Ethel Kennedy looked on. As they walked from the dance floor, they encountered uninvited White House journalist Merriman Smith. Smith was making notations in his notebook, and at two-thirty in the morning, Secret Service agents were banging on Smith's door to interrogate him about his notes. "They wanted to make sure I didn't write about Marilyn and Bobby." Agents also appeared at eight-thirty the next morning in the photo lab of *Time* magazine and demanded the photo negatives showing the Kennedys and Monroe at the Krim party.

In the early hours of Sunday, the president and Marilyn left the party and took a private elevator that descended to the basement of the Krim apartment building. From there they walked through the labyrinth of tunnels that connected it to the Carlyle Hotel and the private elevator to the Kennedy penthouse overlooking Manhattan. It was the denouement of a very special day, and what Marilyn hoped would be the dawn of a new dream. But it proved to be the beginning of a rapid descent into a nightmare.

She never saw Jack Kennedy again.

Thanks for the Memory

What fresh hell is this?
—Dorothy Parker

When Marilyn drove to the airport to fly back to Los Angeles, she decided to dispense with her disguise—her wig and sunglasses—and enjoy her new pinnacle of fame. If the public hadn't seen her singing "Happy Birthday" to the president on the network news, they had undoubtedly seen photos of the gala on page one of the Sunday morning paper. Her arrival at the airport caused a near riot that had to be quelled by an emergency call for police assistance.

Aided by amphetamines, Marilyn reported for work at 6:15 A.M. on Monday, May 21, thirty-three hours after the gala. She sent word to George Cukor that she was prepared to film the scenes scheduled for the day, but close-ups were ruled out. She was obviously ill, and makeup artist Whitey Snyder couldn't hide the evidence of fatigue from her whirlwind weekend. To complicate matters, Dean Martin had reported for work despite a bad cold and a temperature, and studio doctor Lee Siegel advised Marilyn against working with Martin until his fever was gone.

On Tuesday afternoon, Pat Newcomb called photographer Lawrence Schiller at his home. "I would plan to be on the set all day tomorrow if I were you, Larry, and bring plenty of film," advised Newcomb, "Marilyn has the swimming scene tomorrow and, knowing Marilyn, she might slip out of her suit!" The scene was a midnight swimming sequence in which Marilyn, in the nude, would lure Dean Martin from Cyd Charrisse's bed. No actual nudity was planned; normally, a body stocking was worn to create the illusion. But Newcomb knew the film needed a publicity boost and that this could be a photo opportunity not to be missed. That she did the scene *des nuda* took everybody by surprise. "She was aware that she still had a fabulous body," recalled Robert Slatzer, "and this was a way to show the world that she wasn't over the hill at the age of thirty-six."

As Schiller and photographer Billy Woodfield took their photos, Monroe swam to the edge of the pool and put one leg up on the rim. In another sequence she sat on the pool steps, looking over her shoulder in wide-eyed innocence. Word quickly spread on the Fox lot that Marilyn was doing a nude scene.

"The reaction was incredible," recalled Henry Weinstein. "Everyone wanted to get on that set. It became a stampede." The producer called for emergency security guards to bar the stage entrance.

With her fever quelled by amphetamines and her headaches eased by Demerol, Marilyn was in the water for four hours while the shutters clicked and Cukor rolled the cameras. Schiller and Billy Woodfield orchestrated an international bidding war for the photographs and they appeared on covers of seventy magazines in thirty-two countries. Schiller and Woodfield made over $150,000—more than Marilyn's salary on the film.

The next day Fox executives screened the dailies of Monroe's "midnight swim," and they were ecstatic. Marilyn had been on the set all week. On Sunday, Lee Siegel gave Dean Martin a clean bill of health and said he was well enough to work with Monroe. There was reason for optimism.

On Monday, May 28, Cukor had scheduled an eight-minute scene with Marilyn, Dean Martin, Cyd Charisse, and Tom Tryon. But something was wrong with Marilyn that Monday morning. Tom Tryon was one of the first to sense that she was in trouble. "What's the matter with Marilyn?" he whispered to the director. Cukor agreed that something was very wrong. "I've never seen her like this," he said. "She looks like she's falling apart."

"From the moment she came on the set, she looked like a piece of fine crystal about to shatter," said Tom Tryon. "All of her moves were tentative and tenuous. In the first take she only had two words to say, which were 'Nick, darling,' but she couldn't get the words correct no matter how many times we tried it. My heart went out to her."

News of the problems on the set quickly rippled through the Fox rumor mill. A switchboard operator recalled that "Marilyn tried to reach Frank Sinatra." Unable to locate him, Marilyn learned through Mickey Rudin's office that Frank was performing on a world tour.

Following ten agonizing takes, in which Marilyn began stuttering, Cukor began treating her with growing impatience and Marilyn ran from the set. "She almost knocked me over," recalled Hazel Washington. "Cukor was acting like a bully—making a bad situation worse." Running hysterically into her studio bungalow, she grabbed a scarlet lipstick and scrawled several times on the mirror, "Frank, help me! Frank, please help me!" before collapsing.

Weinstein found her behavior quite puzzling. When Marilyn had finished filming on Friday, she was in excellent spirits. She had several glasses of Dom Pérignon with members of the cast and crew she invited to her bungalow. Later she met with Larry Schiller to approve selected stills from her nude scene. She was delighted over the angles caught by Schiller's camera, and he found her "vibrant and excited." As she waved good-bye that Friday night when she drove off to Brentwood in her limousine, the photographer admired her determination and effervescent spirit. She then vanished for seventy-two hours. Appointments were broken. Phone calls weren't returned. Dinner dates were canceled.

"This was perhaps the most mysterious weekend of Marilyn's life," said Weinstein. "It was even more puzzling than the day of her death. Something terrible happened to her that weekend. It was deeply personal, so personal that it shook Marilyn's psyche. I saw it happen, and I blame myself for not immediately calling Dr. Greenson and asking him to return." Weinstein dates the beginning of the events that led to Marilyn's "slide to death" as something that happened to her after she left the studio on Friday, May 25.

It wasn't long before the Hollywood rumor mill started grinding out stories concerning what may have occurred on that fateful weekend. Some said she had an abortion, others said that she had been on a LSD trip with Timothy Leary, still others said she had an episode of the same madness that struck her mother. Every possible combination of tabloid trauma was rumored and even printed as fact.

"I don't think we'll ever know for sure about what happened that weekend," Weinstein said. "I mean, there are a few people who do know. Somebody who I think really knew what happened is Pat Newcomb."

What happened that mysterious weekend related to a chain of circumstances that occurred shortly after the presidential birthday gala. On May 22, the Oval Office received an urgent call from J. Edgar Hoover. He wanted to see the president on a matter of national security. It was to be another one of the rare meetings these powerful adversaries would have during the "Thousand Days." Their battle of wills had skirmished in the subcellars of Pennsylvania Avenue for over two decades of public life, and a meeting was scheduled for Thursday, May 24, just five days after the gala. It is possible that the conversation between the two may be one of the 270 confidential Oval Office conversations secretly recorded by President Kennedy and now secured within the confines of the Kennedy Library. But it is doubtful that the public will ever hear the recording.

Hoover was well aware that the clandestine relationships with Monroe and Judith Campbell Exner had continued despite warnings of the inherent danger. If Kennedy persisted in this pattern of behavior, which went back to the days of Inga Arvad, it could conceivably bring down the presidency in the midst of an escalating cold war crisis over Cuba.

The vehemence of Hoover's warning can be judged only by the effect. On the very day of JFK's meeting with Hoover, May 24, 1962, word went out to the Oval Office switchboard that calls from Marilyn Monroe would no longer be accepted, and the private number the president had given her was disconnected. They never saw or spoke to each other again. Jack Kennedy called Judith Campbell Exner himself to tell her the relationship had to end, but he left the responsibility of telling Marilyn to his brother-in-law, Peter Lawford. Patricia Seaton Lawford confirmed that it was left to Peter to inform Marilyn of the president's decision. On Saturday, May 27, Eunice Murray recalled, "Somebody had called long-distance—somebody close to the Kennedy family." That "somebody" was Peter Lawford calling from Hyannisport. It was a job he didn't relish. He knew how much the liaison with the president meant to Marilyn.

Lawford knew he had to be blunt. He decided to let Marilyn know in no uncertain terms that the relationship was over, according to Patricia Seaton Lawford. "There was no effort to let her down easily. She was told that she'd never be able to speak to the president again—that she was never going to be the First Lady. She was not even a serious affair." When

Marilyn broke down, Peter said, "Look, Marilyn, you're just another one of Jack's fucks."

Pat Newcomb was the logical person to look after Marilyn. Alarmed at Marilyn's state of mind and afraid that in her hysteria the film star might call one of her press friends and reveal her relationship with the president, Newcomb literally moved in that weekend, bringing her own bottle of sedatives to be sure that Marilyn was well supplied. According to Eunice Murray, "Pat Newcomb moved in for a couple of days to take over Marilyn's care. Pat said she knew just what to do. Presumably, bringing her own sedatives along to let Marilyn use until her doctor returned." Murray observed, "The door to her bedroom was closed for two days while Pat kept her sedated." The publicist slept at the foot of Marilyn's bed and seldom left the room. Norman Jefferies, who was working at the home that weekend, stated, "Marilyn seemed to be a prisoner in her own bedroom."

On Monday morning, the studio limousine was at her door at six to drive Marilyn to the studio. "She could hardly stand up," said Hazel Washington, "but she insisted on working." What had happened to Marilyn that weekend remained a mystery to the cast and crew. "We just knew she was shattered and needed help," said Tom Tryon. But Marilyn was an amazingly resilient person. Her whole life had been a question of overcoming obstacles. There was a remarkable spirit within her that would not accept defeat. She returned to the set of *Something's Got to Give* on Tuesday afternoon with a renewed dedication. With the exception of the debacle on Monday, May 28, Marilyn worked nine straight days—May 21 through June 1. If she had lost everything else, she still had her career and her fans and her most constant secret admirer—the camera.

On Friday morning, June 1, 1962, the lights were burning in Marilyn's windows as early as four o'clock. Mrs. Murray was busy brewing coffee in the kitchen. She had already run Marilyn's bath and poured in the ritual one ounce of Chanel No. 5. Outside, her driver, Rudy, stood by the waiting limousine; he could hear a Frank Sinatra album playing on Marilyn's record player. He was to wait over an hour and a half while she bathed and put on her makeup. Murray noted, "she seemed to need all this, the perfume baths, the makeup, the background music, to woo that sensual persona into existence."

Once more, Norma Jeane would conjure up her magic trick for the one-eyed black box that produced the illusion millions would come to know as "Marilyn Monroe." Norma Jeane had no idea that this day, June 1, 1962, would prove to be the last day Marilyn Monroe would ever appear before the motion-picture cameras—the culmination of an astonishing career that had spanned sixteen years.

Ironically, this day was also her birthday. She became thirty-six, a worrisome time for a film star. The mid-thirties had been the turning point in the careers of many Hollywood actresses who were dependent on their looks. But Marilyn never looked better. She had lost some weight for the film and her beauty had acquired a delicacy that was enthralling. "To me, she looked marvelous during *Something's Got to Give*—better than she had in years," said Whitey Snyder.

The scene being shot on June 1 was more complicated than most. Marilyn was to pass off anemic Wally Cox as the man she had shared a desert island with for seven years. She was unhappy with the poorly scripted, wooden quips she was supposed to make, but managed to turn them into something that sounded ingeniously clever on film.

During a break in filming that day, Cukor spied Pat Newcomb crossing the stage with two crystal glasses and a bottle of Dom Pérignon. "He was furious about those few sips of champagne," said stand-in Evelyn Moriarity. "And he was angry that a birthday party was being planned for her later in the day."

"Not on this set. Not now!" stormed Cukor.

Fox spent more than five thousand dollars on Elizabeth Taylor's birthday bash on the set of *Cleopatra* in Rome. But Fox executives, angry about the many delays in production, weren't about to spring for Marilyn's birthday party, especially one that could cause further delay. The crew had collected five dollars for a small cake, Dean Martin supplied the champagne, and the Fox commissary sent over a large urn of coffee, which it later billed to the Monroe estate. With the tawdry celebration awaiting, Marilyn, Dean Martin, and Wally Cox completed the last scene Marilyn Monroe was ever to do before a motion-picture camera. "She was wonderful in those last scenes," recalled editor David Bretherton. "She had never been better, or displayed more perfect timing."

For those few who have seen the entire collection of printed takes from *Something's Got to Give*, Marilyn Monroe's work is astonishing. In over six hours of dailies and edited footage that constitute all of Marilyn's completed scenes, the viewer witnesses the performance of a consummate professional. One is struck by the fact that she never blew a line, never missed a cue, never missed her marks—despite how she may have felt either emotionally or physically. As Gable once said, "When she's there, she's really there."

After the last take on Marilyn's last day before the cameras, Henry Weinstein escorted Marilyn to the dark edges of the soundstage where the cast, with sparklers sputtering in their hands, waited around the pitiable birthday cake. Marilyn displayed an artificial gaiety, and for the camera, she gamely fed a piece of cake to a petulant Cukor. "It was only a pretend celebration," said Weinstein. "There was a real pall over it. I don't know why."

That day, the weather had become unseasonably cold for Southern California, blanketing Los Angeles in clouds and fog. The evening air was damp and chilly. As the birthday party wound down, Marilyn turned to Weinstein and asked if she could borrow the Jean-Louis suit and hat that she wore in the film. "I've got an appearance this evening at Dodger Stadium. I won't have time to go home now, and the suit is the only thing I've got that's warm enough."

Henry Weinstein was immediately concerned. He stated, "I knew if she went out in that weather, she could turn sick." He tried to persuade her to cancel her appearance, but Marilyn insisted, "I have to go. I promised the people from Muscular Dystrophy, and they sold thousands of tickets. Besides, I promised to take Dean Martin's son."

Ignoring the cold descending mist, Marilyn spent an hour on the field that evening at Dodger Stadium while chatting with several children in wheelchairs. A chill wind caught her mink hat and blew it from her head, and the last photograph taken in public of Marilyn shows her waving to the children as she holds her hat in her hand.

As she drove home in her limousine later that night, she began feeling the blinding pain behind her eyes. The insidious sinusitis infection had returned with a vengeance.

Hell Hath No Fury Like...

Marilyn's lifelong problem was basically a problem of rejection.
—Ralph R. Greenson

On the weekend of June 2 and 3, Marilyn telephoned both Jeanne Carmen and Terry Moore from her sickbed and discussed the difficulties she was having in reaching Jack Kennedy. "She was very proud that she was given the president's private number and was devastated when he cut it off," said her friend Terry Moore. Having known Jack Kennedy all her adult life, Marilyn felt he owed her an explanation.

Dr. Greenson's absence contributed to Marilyn's sense of abandonment. Eunice Murray recalled, "Marilyn didn't want to interrupt the doctor's trip with her problems." Greenson's son, Danny, had made a point of requesting that Marilyn let him get through "the speaking engagement in Switzerland" without calling him home.

If Marilyn hoped for help from Peter Lawford, it wasn't forthcoming. He too began avoiding her. "Where the hell is Peter?" she asked Jeanne Carmen. "I haven't been able to reach him for days." Carmen noted that "Peter had a way of making himself scarce when he didn't want to talk to you."

Lawford had informed Jack Kennedy that Marilyn reacted very badly to being cut off from contact with the president. She wrote the president a

number of unanswered letters that became increasingly angry and bellig-
erent in tone. Peter Lawford termed them "rather pathetic letters." With
both Hoover and Monroe to contend with, Kennedy was constrained to
heed the warning of the FBI chief, and at the same time found it expe-
dient to mollify the movie star. While Pat Newcomb could be relied upon
to keep Peter Lawford and the Kennedys apprised of Marilyn's state of
mind on a day-to-day basis, Bobby Kennedy was the logical one to solve
the "Marilyn problem," which had now become an imminent danger.
Bobby Kennedy was the ameliorator for the family. Only he was privy to
the complex personal matters relating to Jack Kennedy and Marilyn.

On Sunday, June 3, Marilyn succumbed to her feelings of rejection in a
haze of Nembutal somnambulence. The Aztec calendar, purchased in
Taxco during happier days, would count the deleterious days and hours.
The chess board sat on the game table, the white knight missing. The
Rodin, which stood on her living room table, silently answered her inde-
finable question, "What does it mean? Does he love her? Or is he just
screwing her? Is it a fake? What do you think, Doctor? What does it
mean?"

On Sunday afternoon, she called Dr. Greenson's children, Joan and
Danny. She sounded heavily drugged and disconsolate. Danny recalled
that they hurried over to her house. "She was in bed naked, with just a
sheet over her, and she was wearing a black sleeping mask, like the Lone
Ranger wore. It was the least erotic sight you could imagine. This woman
was desperate. She couldn't sleep—it was the middle of the afternoon.
She said how terrible she felt about herself—that people were only nice
to her for what they could get from her. She said she had no one—that
nobody loved her. She mentioned not having children. It was a whole
litany of depressing thoughts."

Nothing they said could reassure Marilyn. With their father out of the
country, they called in Dr. Milton Wexler. He saw the array of pill bottles
by the bed and promptly swept them into his medical bag. Though Pat
Newcomb denied ever giving Marilyn prescription drugs, according to Mrs.
Murray, the "spin doctor" came over that evening and brought sedatives
to replace those taken by Wexler.

On Monday morning, June 4, Murray called Henry Weinstein to tell
him that Marilyn's infection had returned, and that she was unable to
report for work. At 8 A.M., the studio doctor, Lee Siegel, drove to Brent-

wood to check on Marilyn's condition. He reported that her temperature was over 100 degrees, and instructed Marilyn to stay home. Rumors began spreading that Fox was going to shut down the production.

Weinstein succeeded in reaching Dr. Greenson in Europe, and apprised him of the deteriorating situation. Greenson agreed to fly home immediately, and promised to have Marilyn back on the set by the next Monday. He arrived in Los Angeles on Wednesday afternoon, June 6, and went directly to Marilyn's home, arriving at the Brentwood house just before dark. After spending two hours with Marilyn and conferring with Dr. Engelberg, Greenson determined that she was strong enough emotionally and physically to complete the film.

On Friday, June 8, Rudin and Greenson met with studio executives Phil Feldman and Milton Gould. Twentieth Century-Fox had a long list of humiliating conditions for Marilyn to agree to when she returned to work. She would lose what little creative control she had over the production, report for work promptly, and observe the time limit for the lunch break, and Paula Strasberg would not be allowed on the set. Rudin thought Marilyn would balk at not having Paula; however, Greenson, who had no love for Paula Strasberg, interrupted with: "I can persuade Marilyn to go along with any reasonable request," he said. "While I don't want to present myself as a Svengali, I can convince Marilyn to do anything I want her to do."

Gould and Feldman were amazed by Greenson's statement, which is included in the Fox memos of this meeting. They then asked him, "Would you then determine what scenes Marilyn will or will not do, and decide which takes were favorable or unfavorable?"

"Yes," Greenson replied. "If necessary, I'll even go into the editing room." The luncheon with Feldman and Gould wound up at 1:45 P.M., and as Rudin and Greenson walked to their cars they were optimistic that the production would go forward. But a decision to fire Marilyn had already been made in New York by Fox's chairman of the board, Judge Samuel Rosenman. On Tuesday, June 4, while Greenson had been in flight to Los Angeles, Rosenman had issued orders to the Fox legal department in New York to prepare a dismissal notice and damage suit against Marilyn Monroe for $1 million. The papers were being filed in the Santa Monica court on Friday afternoon while Rudin and Greenson were still negotiating with Feldman and Gould.

Dr. Greenson heard about the firing on his car radio late Friday and hurried to Marilyn's home. The devastating news took Marilyn by surprise, and Greenson stayed with her for more than an hour. After giving Marilyn a tranquilizer shot, the doctor lashed out at Fox and angrily said to Mrs. Murray, "You know, it isn't as if she was goldbricking or out partying. They have acted in bad faith!"

Whitey Snyder, who visited Marilyn shortly after Greenson left, observed, "She had never been fired before, so she was devastated. She couldn't understand it." The morning editions of newspapers around the world carried the news of Marilyn's dismissal. It was the beginning of a campaign structured by the Fox publicity department in New York to discredit Marilyn as the studio geared up for one of the most negative campaigns against a film star in Hollywood history. Orders had come from New York to destroy the star Fox had helped build to the heights of celebrity. The studio executives were relentless, and the viciousness of their attacks was unprecedented.

On Friday, Charles Endfield, vice president of advertising, sent an exclusive to Sheilah Graham: "When Marilyn shows up for work on Monday she will find that she has been fired and replaced—perhaps with Kim Novak. Marilyn hasn't shown up for days, even though she's been out on the town doing the night spots. Twentieth Century-Fox doesn't want her anymore."

Damaging stories were then sent out by Fox over the Associated Press quoting studio sources: "Miss Monroe is not just being temperamental, she's mentally ill, perhaps seriously," declared studio boss Peter Levathes.

In the *Los Angeles Herald Examiner*, Henry Weinstein was quoted as stating, "By her willful irresponsibility, Marilyn has taken the bread right out of the mouths of men who depend on this film to feed their families."

In Hedda Hopper's column George Cukor was quoted as saying, "The poor dear has finally gone round-the-bend. The sad thing is the little work she did is no good. . . . I think it's the end of her career."

But Cukor, Levathes, and Weinstein later denied ever making such statements. Weinstein insisted, "They simply released these statements in my name. I never talked to anyone about it. In fact, I quit Fox in protest. After June 8, I was gone!"

The Fox publicity department excelled itself in ruthlessness and planted a full-page ad in *Weekly Variety* that stated, "Thank you, Miss Monroe, for the loss of our livelihoods." It was signed, "The crew of *Something's Got to Give*." However, the crew, which had only admiration for Marilyn, had not placed the ad.

The incongruous attempt by a major studio to destroy its own star was puzzling. That the Fox publicity department would release statements questioning their star's sanity and refer to her as "mentally ill" was incomprehensible. Certainly to Marilyn it must have been the cruelest aspect of the strange campaign to discredit her. Some speculated that it was an insurance scam at a time when the studio needed cash. But insurance benefits were based on a star's confirmed illness—not alleged malingering. Others theorized that the campaign to destroy the star was merely bad judgment on the part of the Wall Street lawyers who had taken over the Fox board.

On Saturday, June 9, Marilyn called Spyros Skouras. As president of Fox he had always guided her and protected her interests. When Marilyn reached him, she discovered that he had been ill and was recovering from surgery in a New York hospital. Skouras explained that he had been saddened to hear about her dismissal, but he had nothing to do with it. Skouras was not the power at Fox he had been in the glory days. By 1962 he had become only a figurehead and was preparing to resign his post as president; the power was held by the Wall Street barracudas Milton Gould, John Loeb, and Chairman of the Board Samuel Rosenman. They had acquired enormous blocks of Fox stock in order to seize control of the company.

Marilyn learned that Samuel Rosenman was a close friend of Averell Harriman and the Kennedys. Rosenman had been an aide to Franklin Roosevelt and his key speechwriter. Later he was to become an aide to President Truman and a law partner of Clark Clifford, President Kennedy's White House attorney. JFK appointed Rosenman to several labor-relations panels, and Rosenman was instrumental in settling the prolonged steel industry strikes of the early sixties. It was through Rosenman that Bobby Kennedy set up the film deal at Fox for his book, *The Enemy Within*. It was rumored that Skakel and Kennedy money was involved in the studio takeover.

The Great Lakes Carbon Corporation, owned by Ethel Skakel Kennedy's family, had vast real estate holdings in Southern California. The Skakels had purchased thousands of acres for development in Rancho Palos Verdes, and were constructing the Del Amo Business Center in Orange County. Under the chairmanship of Samuel Rosenman, in 1962, the board sold the back lot of 20th Century-Fox for development as Century City. It was purchased by Alcoa Aluminum, an affiliate of the Skakels' Great Lakes Carbon Corporation.

Today, the pumps and invisible derricks of the Fox Hills oil field beneath the towering skyscrapers of Century City are so well camouflaged that the casual passerby would never know they were there. But the massive slant-drilling operation, which extends well into Beverly Hills and beyond Rodeo Drive, has been the back lot's all-time biggest blockbuster.

Judge Rosenman and the Wall Street barracudas were pumping Fox production money into *Cleopatra*, and this gave the board a rationale for selling off the land where the deep pool of finders' fees and serious cash was well hidden.

The attorney general's telephone records indicate a number of calls to Judge Rosenman just prior to Marilyn's being fired. If Bobby Kennedy was behind Marilyn's dismissal and the ruthless campaign to discredit her in order to ensure her silence, he was holding hostage the one thing that mattered to Marilyn Monroe—her career. Marilyn found an unexpected ally in Darryl F. Zanuck, who was in Europe producing his World War II epic, *The Longest Day*. In a Paris press conference Zanuck had only recently expressed his displeasure with the current Fox management. He first heard about Marilyn's dismissal from Nunnally Johnson, who called him from London with the news.

"You know, I never particularly liked Monroe," Zanuck said to Johnson, "but I've got a hell of a high regard for her box-office value. The treatment of her on this film makes me terribly frightened for the future of Fox."

On the Monday following her dismissal, Marilyn called Zanuck in Paris. Whitey Snyder remembered Marilyn explaining to Zanuck that she had been truly ill, and that she very much wanted to finish *Something's Got to Give*. " I only heard one side of her conversation with Zanuck," Snyder said, "but I got the impression that he agreed to help her engineer her comeback." It was the opening gambit of Marilyn's strategy to outwit Robert Kennedy.

When Marilyn had called Zanuck in Paris, he was already furious over his own problems with Judge Rosenman and the Wall Street barracudas, who were selling off Fox real estate and bulldozing the studio. Ravenous for cash, they were planning to seize *The Longest Day*, slash thirty minutes from its running time, and dump it on the market in a mass release.

The Longest Day had taken over two years to film and featured thirty-five stars, including Richard Burton, Henry Fonda, John Wayne, and Robert Redford. Zanuck expected the film to be presented as a prestige motion picture with a series of glittering premieres and a top-ticket road-show presentation, but Rosenman had informed Zanuck that "under no circumstances would *The Longest Day* have special handling." It would have to take its chances under a blanket release to thousands of neighborhood theaters.

Zanuck soon realized that *The Longest Day* could be rescued from the jaws of the Wall Street lawyers only if he regained control of the 20th Century-Fox board and became president of the company.

While neither Rosenman, Gould, nor the other members of the Fox board knew of Zanuck's plans, the ailing Spyros Skouras joined Zanuck in a secret pact to unseat the Wall Street insurgents. Zanuck controlled 280,000 shares of Fox stock and Skouras owned 100,000 shares—almost enough to dominate the proxy battle that loomed ahead.

It was shortly after Zanuck made his decision to regain control of Fox that Marilyn called him in Paris on Monday, June 11. Telling Marilyn of his plans, Zanuck assured her that when he was back in power *Something's Got to Give* would be completed, and she would be the star.

After her conversations with Skouras and Zanuck, Marilyn sent a Western Union message to Robert and Ethel Kennedy declining an invitation she had received in April to attend a party celebrating the wedding anniversary of Pat and Peter Lawford.

ATTY GENERAL AND MRS. ROBERT F. KENNEDY
1962 JUN 13 PM
    HICKORY HILL MCLEANVIR DEAR ATTORNEY GENERAL AND MRS. ROBERT KEN-
NEDY: I WOULD HAVE BEEN DELIGHTED TO HAVE ACCEPTED YOUR INVITATION
HONORING PAT AND PETER LAWFORD. UNFORUNATELY I AM INVOLVED IN A FREE-
DOM RIDE PROTESTING THE LOSS OF THE MINORITY RIGHTS BELONGING TO THE
FEW REMAINING EARTHBOUND STARS. AFTER ALL, ALL WE DEMANDED WAS OUR
RIGHT TO TWINKLE
    MARILYN MONROE

The Method to the Madness

The truth is I've never fooled anyone. I've sometimes let men fool themselves.
—Marilyn Monroe

Joe DiMaggio was visiting Nunnally and Nora Johnson in London when they received the news of Marilyn's problems with Fox. DiMaggio was working as a public relations representative for the Valmore Monette Corporation, an East Coast firm that supplied American military post exchanges. When the Johnsons told DiMaggio about Marilyn's dismissal, he quit his lucrative job and flew to Los Angeles. He felt it had always been Marilyn's career that stood in the way of their happiness, and by all the newspaper accounts her career was over.

"He loved her a great deal," Valmore Monette stated, "and he told me that he had decided to remarry her. He thought things would be different than they had been before, and that everything would work out well for them now. I knew that was why he had left us and was going back out there."

Norman Jefferies remembered working in the guest cottage when Joe DiMaggio arrived from London. "Marilyn was out, and Mr. DiMaggio sat on a ladder and talked to me while he waited for her to return," Jefferies recalled. "Marilyn had told me a lot about him—how nice he was. . . . He was very friendly, and we talked about baseball, Marilyn, the movies, Italian food—you name it."

According to Jefferies, when Marilyn finally arrived there was a warm and heartfelt greeting. Marilyn showed DiMaggio the herb garden that she had planted herself along the brick path that led from the kitchen to the guest cottage, and they talked of the past and happier times. But when their conversation turned to plans for the future, it ended in a quarrel when DiMaggio learned that Marilyn was more determined than ever to pursue her career.

Joe DiMaggio Jr.'s fiancée, Pamela Reis, remembered having heard that there was "a bitter row" over Marilyn's career and the Kennedys. The disagreement soon turned into a violent argument as DiMaggio saw his hopes for a reunion and a real life together slipping away. It was the last bitter argument between Marilyn and the Slugger.

The next day, Thursday, June 14, Dr. Ralph Greenson drove Marilyn to the Beverly Hills clinic of Dr. Michael Gurdin, who had once been Marilyn's plastic surgeon. Gurdin was startled by Marilyn's appearance. When Marilyn removed her scarf and glasses, Dr. Gurdin noted that the film star's nose was black and blue and there was a large bruise on her left cheekbone. Greenson stated, "Marilyn had a small accident in the shower. She fell and hit the tiling." X rays were taken to see if there were any broken bones.

"Greenson did all the talking," Gurdin recalled. "He didn't seem anxious for Marilyn to speak." However, when the nurse brought in the X rays, Marilyn asked, "If my nose is broken, how quickly can we fix it?" The X rays showed that there were no broken bones or cartilage, and she wrapped her arms around Greenson and said, "Thank goodness!"

Putting on her dark glasses and scarf, Marilyn left by the rear door on Greenson's arm. Gurdin later said that the injuries could have been caused by a fall, but Robert Slatzer always believed that somebody "beat the hell out of her."

"My guess was that Joe still loved her," Nunnally Johnson commented, "But after that Joe was under no more illusions about any sort of reunion. In short, he'd had it. So far as he was concerned, she was a lost lady, and while there might be someone to save her, he wasn't the one."

Between June 20 and July 15, Marilyn launched an unparalleled media blitzkrieg with the world's leading syndicated columnists and a nonstop series of interviews and photo sessions with *Vogue*, *Life*, *Redbook*, and *Cosmopolitan*. Calling in Pat Newcomb, she dictated 104 telegrams to the cast and crew of *Something's Got to Give* lamenting the studio's decision to shut down the film.

Marilyn exclaimed to one interviewer, "I don't look on myself as a commodity, but I'm sure a lot of people have, including one corporation in particular which shall be nameless. If I'm sounding 'picked on,' I think I have been. . . . An actor is supposed to be a sensitive instrument. Isaac Stern takes good care of his violin. What if everybody jumped on his violin?"

For George Barris of *Cosmopolitan* she posed on a windswept beach wearing a Mexican sweater, champagne glass in hand, and stated that at age thirty-six, "As far as I'm concerned, the happiest time is *now*. There's a future, and I can't wait to get to it!"

At an extraordinary session for *Vogue*, photographer Bert Stern was enchanted. "Marilyn had the power," Stern later rhapsodized. "She was the light, and the goddess, and the moon—the space and the dream, the mystery and the danger!"

When Richard Meryman interviewed her for *Life*, he was mesmerized by her enthusiasm and expressiveness, "Her inflections came as surprising twists and every emotion was in full bravura, acted out with exuberant gestures," Meryman reflected. "Across her face flashed anger, wistfulness, bravado, tenderness, ruefulness, high humor and deep sadness. And each idea usually ended in a startling turn of thought, with her laugh rising to a delighted squeak. . . . I felt a rush of protectiveness for her; a wish— perhaps the sort that was at the root of the public's tenderness for Marilyn—to keep her from anything ugly and hurtful."

When Meryman recalled asking her if many friends had called up to rally round when she was fired by Fox, "there was a silence, and sitting very straight, eyes wide and hurt, she answered with a tiny 'no.' " However, she had millions of anonymous friends acquired in the darkness of movie theaters around the world, and Fox was soon bombarded with letters and telegrams protesting the studio's actions. Marilyn received help from another unexpected source: when Dean Martin learned that the studio was replacing Marilyn with Lee Remick, he notified his agent at MCA that he was going to walk off the film if it wasn't completed with Marilyn Monroe. In a series of heated meetings between Fox executives and MCA to force Martin to accept a replacement, the agency supported Martin's position, and much to the Fox publicity department's chagrin, the news of Dean Martin's decision made bigger headlines than Marilyn's dismissal.

In mid-June, Zanuck arrived in New York and conferred with his attorney, Arnold Grant, while secretly buying additional shares of Fox stock to ensure success in his forthcoming boardroom battle to regain control of the studio. "We had no knowledge of what Zanuck was up to," Milton Gould later stated. "He spent weeks buying up thousands of shares of stock in order to win enough votes to unseat us."

During the summer of 1962, the attorney general's helicopter often descended on the Fox lot. Bobby Kennedy would leap out wearing blue jeans and a T-shirt, followed by Secret Service agents wearing blue suits and ties, and they would hurry to Jerry Wald's office for preproduction meetings on *The Enemy Within*. On these visits Kennedy frequently spent the night at the Beverly Hilton Hotel, which was only a few minutes away.

On Saturday, June 23, two weeks after Marilyn's dismissal from Fox, Bobby Kennedy flew to Los Angeles and Peter Lawford arranged for Marilyn and Kennedy to meet. Kennedy was to attend a dinner party at the Lawford beach house, and Marilyn was invited. According to Patricia Seaton Lawford, the purpose of Bobby Kennedy's visit was to stop Marilyn from trying to contact the president. She had been trying to reach him at the Oval Office and at Hyannisport, abandoning her code name, stating, "This is Marilyn Monroe, and I expect to speak with Jack!" If she wanted to save her career, she would have to become cooperative—to remain silent.

Shortly before Marilyn was to meet Bobby Kennedy at the Lawfords', dress designer Jean-Louis's assistant, Elizabeth Courtney, recalled, "I never saw her so nervous about a party. We altered three dresses before Marilyn found the right one." When Marilyn left the room during one of the fittings, Courtney asked Hazel Washington what was going on. "She's seeing the man, honey," Hazel answered.

"Who is it?" asked Courtney.

"Kennedy," Hazel said.

"You mean the president?" wondered Courtney.

"No, the other one—the brother," was the reply.

Marilyn arrived at the Lawfords' party two and a half hours late.

The following day, Sunday, June 24, Bobby Kennedy paid a visit to Marilyn's home. Neighbors saw his arrival in the Fifth Helena cul-de-sac, and Mrs. Murray stated that he arrived alone, driving himself in a convertible. "He was casually dressed," she recalled, "looking boyish in slacks and an open shirt." Norman Jefferies was working on the house that day and had been told he'd have to "clear out before Kennedy came." But he recalled that Kennedy arrived just as he was leaving. Marilyn showed Kennedy her new kitchen, and then they went outside by the pool and spoke for over an hour. "Marilyn did not seem bubbly or excited by his visit," Mrs. Murray said.

While there's no record of what was discussed during the private meeting between the film star and "the General," one can surmise what was discussed by the effects. The next day, Monday, June 25, Bobby Kennedy called Judge Rosenman and, according to Fox archives, studio head Peter Levathes was told to renegotiate Marilyn's contract for the completion of *Something's Got to Give.* "I got word to try and negotiate with Miss Monroe from New York. I don't know whether it was from Milton Gould or Judge Rosenman," stated Levathes.

Sixteen days after her humiliating dismissal, the studio did an amazing about-face and was asking her to return.

On Thursday, June 28, Marilyn Monroe had a meeting with Peter Levathes to discuss her terms for resuming work on *Something's Got to Give.* As he arrived at her home, chilled caviar and trays of canapés and cocktails awaited him, and a punctual Marilyn Monroe emerged to greet him. She was uncharacteristically businesslike. In one of her better offscreen performances, she was the new no-nonsense Monroe. Whitey Snyder and Sidney Guilaroff had worked all afternoon creating a startling, severe look for the actress, who wore a conservative Norman Norell dress of sober beige complemented by her horn-rimmed glasses. Levathes admitted to being impressed by this savvy superstar, who appeared to be the exact antithesis of the image created by his own studio's negative press campaign.

At the time, Levathes was unaware that Pat Newcomb was behind the door, listening to every word and making notes of the meeting. "I found, surprisingly, that she was an astute businesswoman in many ways," Levathes said later, "She was very rational. You couldn't have had a better meeting with an actress. She had a kind of renewed interest in the project that was infectious. I was finally confident that the picture would be made. In fact, I even authorized a new rewrite of the script incorporating Marilyn's ideas."

As June came to an end, an agreement was in the works for the resumption of *Something's Got to Give,* and the studio agreed to renegotiate Marilyn's contract into a million-dollar deal—$500,000 for *Something's*

Got to Give, plus a bonus if it was completed on its new schedule, and another $500,000 or more for a new musical called *What a Way to Go,* to be produced by Arthur Jacobs. It was much more money than Marilyn had ever made in the past. Incredibly, Fox agreed to junk the Walter Bernstein rewrites and revert to the Nunnally Johnson script that Marilyn preferred, and the studio agreed to replace George Cukor with a director approved by the star.

It was an astonishing victory for Marilyn that had been brought about by a call from Bobby Kennedy to Samuel Rosenman—but at what price? Had she agreed to forever refrain from contacting JFK? When she signed the new contract, how much of her heart would be on the dotted line?

In early July, Bobby Kennedy again visited Los Angeles on his way to Nevada, where he was to meet General Maxwell Taylor, chairman of the Joint Chiefs of Staff, and view the first hydrogen bomb test in the continental United States—then a top secret. Exactly one month before Marilyn Monroe's death, a Fourth of July barbecue was held at the Lawfords', which was attended by both Marilyn and Bobby Kennedy. It was a conciliatory gathering. To all appearances the differences between the Kennedys and Marilyn had been mended. Bobby and Marilyn walked on the beach together, and the film star listened attentively as the attorney general discussed sensitive world matters, atomic testing, and politics.*

Fox planned to resume filming *Something's Got to Give,* starring Marilyn Monroe, in the third week of July, but inexplicably, once the new contract had been drawn, Marilyn's attorney, Mickey Rudin, began a delaying tactic. Fox wanted to get the contract signed and the film back into production as quickly as possible, but the contract sat on Rudin's desk unsigned.

Numerous calls to Rudin by Fox attorneys went unreturned. The studio planted an item with columnist Earl Wilson stating, "Mickey Rudin is deliberately dragging his feet on the new pact with Monroe. Once the million-dollar contract was drawn up, Marilyn Monroe's attorney, Rudin, seems to be in no rush to ratify it."

But it was Marilyn who was in no rush to sign the contract. Learning that Zanuck was about to launch his D-Day invasion of the Fox board at

---

* What Bobby Kennedy and Marilyn discussed became the subject of a national "security matter" in the FBI document dated July 13, 1962.

a meeting scheduled for July 25, she was playing her waiting game. However, there was no way to foresee the outcome of what promised to be a formidable boardroom battle. There was no guarantee that Rosenman, Gould, and Loeb wouldn't prevail, or that Marilyn's career wouldn't remain hostage to the Kennedy faction. Until Zanuck made his move on the twenty-fifth, Marilyn remained a Rosenman pawn. And it was Marilyn's gambit to delay signing the contract until the Kennedys were in check.

Checkmate

I now live in my work and in a few relationships with the few people I can really count on. Fame will go by and, so long, I've had you, fame. If it goes by, I've always known it was fickle. So at least it's something I experienced, but that's not where I live.

—Marilyn Monroe

In July 1962, U.S. surveillance satellites photographed newly constructed Cuban long-range ballistic missile installations. Within fifteen weeks the Cuban missile crisis would bring the world to the brink of a nuclear holocaust. At this perilous time in history, J. Edgar Hoover received another confidential memorandum from the FBI office in Mexico City headed "MARILYN MONROE—SECURITY MATTER—C [Communist]."

Dated July 13, 1962—just three weeks prior to Marilyn's death—the document, which was withheld from the FBI's Monroe file, survived in highly censored form in the FBI files of both Peter Lawford and Frederick Vanderbilt Field.

Under the Freedom of Information appeals process, FOI attorney James Lesar was told by the FBI that the source of the censored information in the Monroe memorandum was an informant. The FBI had been requested by another intelligence agency (CIA) not to reveal the informant's name. However, the FBI disclosed to Lesar that the source was someone who knew both Field and Monroe and had recently been in private conversation with both of them.

Only Eunice Murray, José Bolaños, Churchill Murray, and Ralph Green-son fell into that category. The likely informant was Bolaños. Field had claimed that Bolaños was "a man of left-wing pretensions, deeply dis-trusted by the real left," when he warned Marilyn not to have anything to do with him.

In March 1962, Bolaños had followed Marilyn back to the United States from Mexico and was her escort at the Golden Globe Awards. When Anthony Summers interviewed Bolaños in 1983, Bolaños stated that he had visited Marilyn in New York in April 1962, and that he last saw her in Los Angeles in early July.

Bolaños is further confirmed as the source by the FBI's disclosure that the details in the confidential memorandum were "heard directly from Marilyn by the informant." Marilyn is quoted as saying that she "attended a luncheon at Peter Lawford's residence with one of the Kennedy broth-ers." Significant questions were discussed, including political matters. One of the "significant questions" had been "the morality of atomic testing." The FBI indicated that the luncheon at Lawford's home occurred in early July, which was when Bolaños last saw Marilyn.

At this critical juncture of the cold war, the relationship of the Kennedy brothers with Marilyn Monroe became a grave national security matter. American intelligence agencies had become acutely aware of the connec-tion between Monroe and suspected Soviet agent Frederick Vanderbilt Field. The CIA document signed by counterintelligence chief James Jesus Angleton (see page 469) establishes that electronic surveillance had, in-deed, been placed on Marilyn's home. At the same time, Field's FBI file in-dicates that he was under intense surveillance in June and July. Alarms again reverberated down the FBI corridors when agents learned that Field had left Mexico City, crossed the border, and was driving to New York. He arrived on July 10 and was staying as a guest in Marilyn Monroe's apartment at 444 East Fifty-Seventh Street, where he remained for several weeks.

When Bobby Kennedy returned to Washington after viewing the secret hydrogen bomb test, J. Edgar Hoover was waiting with another bomb to explode.

On Tuesday, July 17, Marilyn dialed the attorney general's private number but was unable to speak with him. Monroe's telephone records of July 17 indicate that she tried several times to reach Kennedy through the Justice

Department switchboard but was not put through to the attorney general. Following his meeting with Hoover, Bobby Kennedy suddenly cut off communication with Marilyn. Like Jack Kennedy, he offered no explanation.

Jeanne Carmen observed, "All of a sudden she couldn't get through to Bobby. She had no idea what happened, why she couldn't get through. She was extremely angry."

"Damn it! He owes me an explanation!" Marilyn said to Robert Slatzer. "I want to know what happened, and I want Bobby to tell me himself!"

During July, telephone records indicated that Marilyn tried to reach Kennedy at the Justice Department from her Brentwood home on eight occasions. Marilyn had also tried to reach him at his Hickory Hill home. "Bobby was furious with Marilyn for taking this liberty," related Patricia Seaton Lawford.

From early July until August 4, the doctors' bills show that Marilyn saw Dr. Greenson on twenty-seven of thirty-five days, and her internist, Dr. Hyman Engelberg, on thirteen. On a number of these visits, the records show that Marilyn received injections. The records may reveal not only her own problems, but those of her doctors as well. Her loss of the Kennedy relationship had been, in a sense, their loss too. At the same time they had considerable concern as to why Marilyn had been suddenly shunned. Perhaps they realized it had been discovered that she was a security problem.

The doctors and the Kennedys had a burgeoning common cause—to keep Marilyn quiet. Greenson could keep a daily update on her state of mind and intentions, and both Greenson and Engelberg could see to it that she was sedated when she was overwhelmed by anger. Engelberg's ex-wife, Esther Maltz, recently made the comment, "Hy kept Marilyn sedated for Dr. Greenson." And, of course, there was Mrs. Murray, who could keep an eye on Marilyn from within the house and report danger signs.

Robert Slatzer recalled that shortly before he left for Columbus, Ohio, in late July, Marilyn called him from a Brentwood pay phone. She had become convinced her phones were tapped. Marilyn wanted to see him, and it was later that day they drove up the coast to the beach at Point Dume. Slatzer said Marilyn alternated between tears and anger as she spoke about the Kennedys and their refusal to speak to her.

"She was angry and hurt—totally outraged—that they had both cut her off overnight," Slatzer recalled. "Only two months ago she had been singing happy birthday to the president and was the celebrated guest at the party that followed. That association meant a great deal to her. Suddenly it was over and she felt she had been used, mistreated, and then totally rejected."

While Marilyn and Slatzer were discussing her problems, she pulled out of her large carryall handbag some papers wrapped with a rubber band. They were handwritten notes from Bobby Kennedy—some of them on Justice Department stationery. She also showed Slatzer her red diary and allowed him to browse through it. Inside, he saw notes pertaining to conversations with the Kennedys regarding the Bay of Pigs, Castro, the Mafia, and Jimmy Hoffa. When Slatzer asked Marilyn why she had made the notes, she said, "Because Bobby liked to talk about political things. He got mad at me one day because he said I didn't remember anything he told me."

Slatzer questioned what she was going to do if Jack or Bobby Kennedy continued not speaking with her, and Marilyn angrily responded, "I might just hold a press conference. I've certainly got a lot to say!"

Marilyn Monroe was in a position to bring down the presidency. She was cognizant of Jack Kennedy's marital infidelities and other private matters. She had his notes and letters and was privy to Kennedy's involvement with Sam Giancana. That the Kennedy brothers had discussed national security matters with the film star added to an astonishing array of indiscretions. The Profumo affair, which eventually brought down the British government, was to surface in the following year.

A number of people have questioned just how serious Marilyn may have been about calling a press conference. Marilyn was notable for not speaking ill of anybody. She once said to Sidney Skolsky, "I've never been in a public fight or feud. I have the most wonderful memory for forgetting things." But Jeanne Carmen observed that Marilyn was extremely angry and determined. She believed Marilyn would have told all had she lived. But as long as her career remained hostage to Judge Rosenman and the Kennedy faction on the Fox board, Marilyn had no choice but to remain silent. As the crucial date of the boardroom battle for control neared, Marilyn's million-dollar contract still remained unsigned on Micky Rudin's desk.

It was a hot and humid day in New York City on Wednesday, July 25, when the 20th Century-Fox board gathered for the decisive conflict. With Judge Samuel Rosenman presiding, Darryl F. Zanuck and Spyros Skouras sat opposite their adversaries as Milton Gould launched a vicious verbal assault on Zanuck. Characterized as "a womanizer, a drunk, a prolifigate gambler, and a producer of flops," Zanuck remained calm as his detractors attempted to demean his reputation.

"The bile just poured out of them," Zanuck said later. "It was filthy stuff—mostly about my private life."

When the torrent of invective concluded, Rosenman turned to Zanuck and said, "And now perhaps Mr. Zanuck would tell us what he would do for the company if he *did* become president."

Lighting up a cigar, Zanuck stood and said, "I have nothing to say. If you want me, fine. If not, get somebody else!" He then continued on with a four-hour tirade about the mismanagement of the studio, and the giant financial losses that had accrued in his absence. At the conclusion he was elected president by a vote of eight to three. The three voting against him were Rosenman, Gould, and Loeb. They promptly resigned, and Spyros Skouras, the former president, replaced Rosenman as chairman of the board.

With Zanuck's victory, Marilyn had won. *Something's Got to Give* would resume filming as soon as schedules could be arranged. Marilyn Monroe would be the star under the new million-dollar contract she was now ready to sign. She was no longer hostage to the Kennedys. The "dumb blonde" had outmaneuvered "the General."

The Devil's Weekend

Win at all costs!
—Joseph P. Kennedy

On July 28 and 29, a week prior to her death, Marilyn spent the weekend at the Cal-Neva Lodge in Lake Tahoe. What really happened on this mysterious weekend has been obscured by speculation and the misleading statements of Peter Lawford. Those few who witnessed the events have been loath to say what actually took place.

Paul "Skinny" D'Amato, who managed the Cal-Neva Lodge for owners Frank Sinatra and Sam Giancana, remembered Marilyn's visit well, and though he wouldn't talk about it in great detail, he made the statement to Anthony Summers, "There was more to what happened than anyone has told. It would have been the big fall for Bobby Kennedy, wouldn't it?" Immediately regretting that he said anything at all, D'Amato murmured, "Of course, I didn't say that. . . ."

But Skinny had said enough. The raison d'être for the "mysterious weekend" was to persuade Marilyn, by whatever means, not to go to the press. Not only would it have been "the big fall for Bobby Kennedy," it would have been the "big fall" for the executive branch of the government and a whole coterie of people associated with the Kennedy clan as well as Sam Giancana. Stakes were high. Fates were on the line, and Sinatra and his partner, Giancana, were in it for the big Kennedy marker.

Sinatra orchestrated the sinister occasion, ostensibly inviting Marilyn to Cal-Neva to celebrate her new deal with Fox and discuss her next film, *What a Way to Go,* which was to costar Sinatra. According to Ralph Roberts, Marilyn had no real desire to go, but Dean Martin was headlining in the Celebrity Room that weekend, and Marilyn was hoping to persuade him to rearrange his nightclub schedule so that *Something's Got to Give* could resume filming in the last week of August. But there was a hidden agenda, and the desperate import of the weekend can be surmised by the odd nexus of people that Old Blue Eyes brought together.

Sinatra flew Marilyn to Cal-Neva in his private plane, *Christina,* complete with wall-to-wall carpeting, carved wood paneling, bar salon, piano, and luxurious bathroom with heated toilet seats. Sinatra's plane also picked up Peter Lawford, the man Sinatra had threatened to "punch in the face" after Jack Kennedy had changed his plans about staying at Sinatra's Palm Springs estate. Sinatra and Peter hadn't spoken since that incident, nor were they to speak again, but Lawford and his wife, Pat, had influence over Marilyn, and on this weekend there were other considerations that took priority—even over vindictiveness.

The Lawfords were having marital difficulties. Peter had been drinking heavily and made no pretense about his debauchery. Pat spent most of her time on the East Coast, away from him, but Marilyn had more regard for Pat than for Peter, and they had become friends. Because Pat was able to reason with Marilyn, and had some influence over her, she too flew to Cal-Neva from Hyannisport.

Marilyn's friend Gloria Romanoff was at the lodge when Marilyn arrived, as was another guest whom Marilyn hadn't expected to see, Sam Giancana. Because Giancana was identified by the Nevada Gaming Commission as a guest at Cal-Neva that weekend, Sinatra would later lose his gambling license.

According to Robert Slatzer, Marilyn had been told that Bobby Kennedy might be there. The attorney general had been in Los Angeles the previous day. The Beverly Hills Hotel guest register shows that he had checked in on Thursday, July 26, and departed on Friday, July 27. Though the Kennedy Library retains the attorney general's daily diary and appointment records covering his years in office, portions of the July and August records are not available, their whereabouts unknown.

Arthur Jacobs's secretary, Peggy Randall, recalled that she was working alone at the Sunset Boulevard office on Saturday, July 28, when a call came in from Bobby Kennedy. Randall said that Kennedy was trying to reach Pat Newcomb. Stating that it was urgent, Kennedy left a number for Newcomb to call, but Randall doesn't recall where he was calling from. She stated, "It wasn't unusual for Robert Kennedy to call Pat Newcomb there at the office. He had called her there on a number of previous occasions."

Marilyn's name never appeared on the Cal-Neva register. She was put in bungalow 52, part of a complex reserved for special guests of Sinatra and Giancana. Bellboys who delivered food to her room said that the door was usually answered by Peter Lawford and that they never saw her leave the room.

Mae Shoopman, who at that time was a cashier at Cal-Neva, recalled, "She kept herself disguised pretty much, kept herself covered with a black scarf and dark glasses and stayed in her room most of the time. She would sleep with the telephone at her ear open to the switchboard. I think she was afraid."

It soon became apparent to Marilyn why she had been brought to Cal-Neva. It wasn't a gathering of friends; they wanted her to forget about the Kennedy brothers and to ensure her silence.

Giancana was there to enforce just how important it was to him that Marilyn didn't cause any trouble. Sam was not a man to mince words. If Marilyn became a problem, he undoubtedly made it clear to her that problems could be dealt with.

According to Susan Strasberg, when Marilyn returned from Cal-Neva she told Paula Strasberg she was "afraid of the Mafia," but Strasberg had passed her comment off as paranoia.

Marilyn also spoke to Ralph Roberts about the Cal-Neva weekend: "She told me it was a nightmare, a dreadful weekend. She said she didn't want to go particularly and once she got there, she felt like a prisoner, and that the only friend she had there was Joe DiMaggio, and she wasn't able to see him."

Joe DiMaggio arrived unexpectedly. Had she called him when she became afraid? He was staying in San Francisco, which was less than an hour's flight away. Bell captain Ray Langford recalled that DiMaggio arrived late Saturday night and wasn't allowed to stay at the Lodge. Langford helped him get a room at the nearby Silver Crest Motel. DiMaggio asked where Marilyn was, but Langford didn't know because she wasn't registered. Langford's brother, Joe, who had picked Marilyn up at the airport, later revealed that Sinatra had issued orders that DiMaggio wasn't to enter the hotel or have his calls put through.

A Cal-Neva doorman later told the poignant story of looking down at the pool on Sunday morning as a fog was settling in on the Tahoe shore. He was surprised to see Marilyn standing "at the edge of the pool, barefoot, swaying back and forth. She was staring up at the hill." The doorman followed her gaze up to the foothills above the rustic lodge, and standing there in the mist staring back was Joe DiMaggio. It was the last time DiMaggio would see her alive.

According to DiMaggio's friend Harry Hall, DiMaggio was enraged about what had happened to Marilyn at Cal-Neva that weekend. He was furious with Sinatra, and he was furious with the Kennedys. "He was very upset," stated Hall. "She went up there, they gave her pills, they had sex parties—I don't think he's ever talked to Sinatra again."

Photographer Billy Woodfield, who worked for both Marilyn and Sinatra, saw darker images of the Cal-Neva weekend. Woodfield stated that when Sinatra returned from Cal-Neva, he brought Woodfield a roll of film to be developed. In his darkroom the photographer was shocked to see that the photos were of an unconscious Marilyn Monroe being sexually abused in the presence of Sam Giancana and Sinatra. Marilyn had been drugged in order for the compromising photos to be taken.

When Sinatra was given the negatives and prints, Woodfield suggested that Sinatra burn them, but the pictures were intended to ensure Marilyn's silence.

The FBI's surveillance of Giancana corroborates the appalling story. Agent Bill Roemer, who was working with the Chicago Crime Commission, had Giancana under electronic surveillance in 1962. He reports that shortly after Marilyn's death, Johnny Roselli had gone to Chicago to confer with Giancana. Agent Roemer recorded a conversation between the two Mafia mobsters:

"The conversation was muted," Roemer says, "but what I had gleaned was that Giancana had been at Cal-Neva, the Lake Tahoe resort, with Sinatra and Marilyn the week before she died. There, from what I had been able to put together, she was involved in an orgy. From the conversation I overheard, it appeared she may have had sex with Giancana. Roselli said to Giancana, 'You sure get your rocks off fucking the same broad as the brothers, don't you.'"

Roemer was surprised to learn that Roselli was referring to the brothers Kennedy.

Peter Lawford later gave a false account of the Cal-Neva weekend in order to support the suicide scenario that was promulgated after Marilyn Monroe's death. He supplied various accounts of Marilyn having attempted suicide and overdosed that mysterious weekend. Lawford stated, "She tried to kill herself the night of July 28, and she finally succeeded on August 4." He described the incident at Cal-Neva as an overdose caused by her despondency over being fired by Fox. But Lawford knew that Marilyn had been victorious in her fight with Fox, and had, in fact, been elated by her victory. "When Marilyn left," said Joe Langford, "it was in an awful hurry. I think she was giving them some problems." Barbara Lieto, the widow of Sinatra's pilot, recalled that her husband was ordered to Lake Tahoe on short notice on Sunday afternoon, July 29. According to Mrs. Lieto, Peter Lawford and Marilyn returned together and Marilyn appeared to be intoxicated or drugged. The plane arrived in Los Angeles after midnight, and Mrs. Lieto recalled her husband saying that Lawford argued with him about where they should land. Lawford insisted that they land at the Santa Monica Airport, but Lieto pointed out that the airport was closed after midnight. When the plane finally landed at Los Angeles International, Marilyn was "out of it, a mess." Barefoot, she walked from the plane to her limousine, and the crew gave Lawford a ride to his beach house in their car. Mrs. Lieto remembered that her husband was angry because Lawford insisted on stopping a few blocks from his home to make a twenty-minute telephone call from a pay phone. The pilot wondered why Lawford couldn't have waited a few minutes and made the call from his house. By then, Lawford had undoubtedly learned from Bobby Kennedy that his house was under electronic surveillance. Who would Lawford have telephoned about an imperative confidential matter before dawn that Monday morning?

The White House telephone records indicate that the president received a call of eighteen minutes' duration from Lawford on Monday morning, July 30, at 8:40 A.M., or 5:40 A.M. Pacific time. Clearly, the Marilyn Monroe problem had reached a crucial impasse.

The Ominous Ear

It's my feeling that Marilyn looked forward to her tomorrows.

—Eunice Murray

Telephone records indicate that on the day Marilyn returned from Cal-Neva, Monday, July 30, she placed an eight-minute call to the Justice Department. Only the ominous ear of electronic surveillance may know what Marilyn had to say to Bobby Kennedy.

During the week, Marilyn entered a whirlwind of discussions about new projects. There were conferences at the studio with director J. Lee Thompson about her next Fox production, *What a Way to Go*. She spoke with Gene Kelly about a new musical. There were plans for her to do a musical version of *A Tree Grows in Brooklyn*, and she spoke with composer Jule Styne about the score.

On Tuesday, July 31, she called her East Coast friend Henry Rosenfeld to discuss plans for a three-day New York trip in early September. She was going to give a theater party in Washington, D.C., and wanted Henry to be her escort at the opening night of the new Irving Berlin musical, *Mr. President*, directed by Joshua Logan. *Mr. President* was to open on September 6 at the National Theater in Washington, and the press had reported that President Kennedy and Jackie would be in attendance. Interestingly, Marilyn Monroe was making a point of being there the same night, and she had ordered a new $6,000 evening gown from Jean-Louis for the occasion. It promised to be a memorable night at the theater.

On Tuesday evening, July 31, Marilyn invited Whitey Snyder and wardrobe assistant Marjorie Plecher to her home. They were engaged to be married, and together they celebrated both the wedding plans and Marilyn's new start date for *Something's Got to Give*, which was set for September 16. The Snyders recalled how optimistic and enthusiastic Marilyn was about the future. "She never looked better—she was in great spirits," Plecher commented.

Mrs. Murray didn't stay overnight on Wednesday, and Marilyn spent the evening at home. She had made an appointment with Kennedy hairstylist Mickey Song, who had helped her at the birthday gala. Song arrived at her house assuming Marilyn wanted her hair styled. Instead, she wanted to pump Song for information about the Kennedys. "She figured who else would know more about the Kennedys' private life than their hairdresser?" Song recalled. Marilyn asked him questions about both Bobby and Jack Kennedy—where they had been, and if Song had seen them with "other women."

"I didn't want to get involved, and she knew I was being evasive, so she said, 'Don't you want to help me?' Then she told me that the Kennedys were using me, just as they were using her. She tried to make us comrades against the Kennedys. I just said, 'I'm not being used. They're treating me great!' " Several weeks later, after Marilyn's death, Song said, "I saw Bobby, and he said to me, 'You're always defending the Kennedys, aren't you? That's good. I heard a tape Marilyn made of you a couple of weeks ago.'

"I was stunned. I had no idea she was taping me. I guess she was trying to get something on them. At the time I didn't really care about Marilyn or the Kennedys. Now, I think she was abused. They played with her, and they tired of her, and I think they found her a lot of trouble to get off their hands. She wasn't going to go that easily."

In mid-July, Marilyn went to private investigator Fred Otash and asked him to supply her with electronic equipment to bug her own telephone. Unknown to Marilyn, Otash was already involved with bugging her home and apartment. At the time she hadn't told Otash why she wanted the equipment, but it occurred to him that "maybe she wanted to have something she could hang over Bobby's head."

Some years after Marilyn's death, Otash told the *Los Angeles Times* that he had been hired by the master surveillance expert Bernard Spindel to install electronic listening devices at the homes of Peter Lawford and Marilyn Monroe. Spindel had told him that Jimmy Hoffa was trying to obtain compromising information on the president and the attorney general. However, there is no hard evidence that the surveillance was actually made for Hoffa. If the contents of the tapes were as devastating as Otash claimed, they were never used to effect by Hoffa during his egregious problems with Robert Kennedy. In all probability the surveillance tapes were contracted by the CIA counterintelligence chief, James Jesus Angleton, whose signature is on one of the transcript cover sheets. Domestic surveillance is prohibited under the CIA charter; but, as the Church Committee hearings revealed, CIA domestic surveillance was commonly carried out by contracting private investigators, such as Spindell's B. R. Fox Company, which had a history as a CIA contractee.

According to Eunice Murray, on Thursday, August 2, "Marilyn, who was fascinated by greenery and plants, spent four hours at Frank's Nursery in Santa Monica, and ordered citrus trees and an array of flowering plants for her garden." And Dr. Greenson saw her twice that day. According to his final bill, he saw her once at his residence, and later at her home.

On Thursday evening, Marilyn was invited to the Lawford beach house, where Peter's friend Dick Livingston recalled, "She came in carrying her own bottle of Dom Perignon champagne. She drank it over little ice cubes from Peter's ice cube maker. She had on the damnedest outfit—a pair of hip-huggers with a bare midriff that revealed her gallbladder operation scar—and a Mexican serape, wrapped around her neck. She was absolutely white, the color of alabaster." Livingston said to her, "My God, Marilyn, you ought to get some sun." She looked at him and whispered, "I know. What I need is a tan—and a man."

Bobby Kennedy, along with Ethel and four of the children, jetted into San Francisco on Friday, August 3. The attorney general was scheduled to speak at the opening of the American Bar Association Conference on Monday, August 6, and he planned to spend the weekend at the Bates Ranch, located about sixty miles south of San Francisco. The *San Francisco Chronicle* stated, "He was without his usual flashy smile and shook hands woodenly with those that welcomed him. Perhaps the cares of the administration are weighing heavily on him." Or perhaps Kennedy had read columnist Dorothy Kilgallen's lead item in the *New York Journal-American* that day:

> Marilyn Monroe's health must be improving. She's been attending select Hollywood parties and has become the talk of the town again. In California, they're circulating a photograph of her that certainly isn't as bare as the famous calendar, but is very interesting. . . . And she's cooking in the sex-appeal department, too; she's proved vastly alluring to a handsome gentleman who is a bigger name than Joe DiMaggio in his heyday. So don't write off Marilyn as finished.

Kilgallen had been zeroing in on the Kennedy-Monroe story and had questioned a number of people close to the Kennedys, including Kenny O'Donnell. Kilgallen had called Robert Kennedy at the Justice Department on Wednesday, August 1, to try to verify the rumors. Kilgallen later claimed she had learned about Marilyn's Kennedy affairs through a source close to the film star. The Angleton CIA document inferred that Kilgallen's source was Howard Rothberg. However, while Rothberg was Kilgallen's interior decorator and a social friend, he did not know Marilyn. Rothberg became privy to intimate details of Marilyn Monroe's private life through a complex series of relationships.

Rothberg was a friend of Ron Pataki, a syndicated drama critic for the Scripps-Howard newspaper in Columbus, Ohio, where Pataki was a long-time friend of Robert Slatzer. They had grown up together in Columbus, and it was through Slatzer that Pataki obtained his job with Scripps-Howard. When Anthony Summers was researching *Goddess* in 1984, he interviewed Pataki along with several friends of Slatzer's who had firsthand knowledge of Slatzer's relationship with Marilyn Monroe.

Today Ron Pataki still lives in Columbus, where he has become a therapist with a doctorate in theology. In a recent interview he recalled, "Oh, yes, I was very aware of Bob's long-standing friendship with Marilyn. Whenever Bob was in Columbus we'd get together, and oftentimes Bob spoke to Marilyn on the phone. A few times he'd put me on the phone, and I spoke to her on several of those long, rambling calls. . . . She called me several times looking for Bob when he was staying at my place. She called here once from Reno or Cal-Neva. She knew Bob had a real understanding of her. She could always turn to him with her troubles."

Pataki recalled that Slatzer had returned to Columbus to work on a wildlife television series in the summer of 1962, and he remembers two calls that Slatzer received from Marilyn shortly before she died.

"It may have been the last part of July or the first of August when Marilyn called," Pataki stated. "I was at Bob's and answered the phone. They spoke for a long time. After Bob hung up, I knew he was upset, and I asked him what was wrong. He told me Marilyn was having trouble with the Kennedys. He was very worried about her, and we talked about the problems Marilyn was having with JFK and his brother, the attorney general."

When Pataki was recently asked if he had talked to Dorothy Kilgallen or Howard Rothberg about Marilyn's problems with the Kennedys, Pataki paused before responding, "I may have."

Pataki and Dorothy Kilgallen were lovers. Referred to in Lee Israel's book *Kilgallen* as "the out-of-towner," Pataki was one of the last people to see Kilgallen before her untimely death, and he knew many of Dorothy's friends—including Howard Rothberg.*

On Friday, August 3, Marilyn again called Robert Slatzer in Columbus, Ohio. Slatzer related that Marilyn was anticipating seeing Bobby Kennedy that weekend. When Slatzer told her he had read that Bobby was in San Francisco to attend a conference, she told him she was going to try to find out from Patricia Lawford where he was staying, and said, "I'm going to blow the lid off this whole damn thing! I'm going to tell everything! Everybody has been calling trying to get the story anyway—Winchell, Kilgallen. And it's clear to me now that the Kennedys got what they wanted out of me and then moved on!"

Slatzer related, "I warned her against proceeding with the press conference and advised that she be discreet in revealing her plans to others. She said, 'Well, I've told a couple of people already.' I urged her to keep quiet about it, and wait and see what happened over the weekend." It proved to be the last time they spoke.

Although Bobby Kennedy's family was staying at the Bates Ranch, the American Bar Association had provided accommodations for him at the St. Francis Hotel. After calling Patricia Lawford in Hyannisport and learning that Kennedy had reservations at the St. Francis, Marilyn called the

---

* When Kilgallen later conducted an investigation into the assassination of President Kennedy, she confided to intimates that she had discovered "explosive information" that would be published in her book *Murder One*. Kilgallen had just returned from a Dallas interview with Jack Ruby when she died under questionable circumstances on the night of November 8, 1965. The nearly completed manuscript of her Ruby interview vanished along with her notes. When Ron Pataki was asked if he had seen the manuscript, he indicated that he had. When asked what it revealed, he responded with the strange caveat, "Nothing anybody should know about."

hotel on Friday afternoon. A hotel operator stated that Marilyn unsuccessfully tried to reach the attorney general a number of times, and left several messages.

It must have been disconcerting for Robert Kennedy to note that everywhere one looked that week there were pictures of Marilyn Monroe. She was on the cover of *Life* and *Paris-Match*. *Life* was involved with a special publicity campaign that featured large billboard displays of Marilyn. The *Life* magazine story had hit the newsstands that Friday and contained the Richard Meryman interview, in which an outspoken Marilyn discussed the Hollywood studio system and her thoughts on fame:

> If I am a star, the people made me a star—no studio, no person. The people did.... But fame to me certainly is only temporary and a partial happiness— even for a waif. Fame is not really for a daily diet, that's not what fulfills you. ... It might be kind of a relief to be finished. It's sort of like, I don't know, some kind of yard dash you're running, but then you're at the finish line and you sort of sigh—you've made it! But you never have—you have to start all over again.

And Marilyn was starting all over again. In that last week she had told Slatzer, "I'm cleaning house, and I'm starting with Paula. She's gone!" And in fact Marilyn had already given Paula Strasberg a one-way ticket back to New York.

Marilyn had once said, "I'm not as mature as I should be. There's a part of me that has never developed and keeps getting in the way, getting me in lousy situations, screwing up relationships, stopping my rest. I think about it all the time. My mother wasn't strong-minded. Maybe what I'm talking about is a weak-minded quality I inherited from her."

But things were coming together now. At age thirty-six, the waif was becoming independent. Her battle with Fox and her determination not to let the Kennedys control her were maturing experiences, and had steeled her will. People were no longer going to be able to take advantage of her vulnerability. She had made up her mind to rid herself of people she now realized didn't have her best interests at heart.

She was planning to get rid of Pat Newcomb as well as Dr. Greenson. "That last month she became convinced that Greenson wasn't doing her any good," Ralph Roberts said. "It was only a question of time before she was going to get rid of him, as well as Mrs. Murray. She was radically turning on Greenson and Mrs. Murray the woman he'd put with her, she felt, to spy on her."

Marilyn had learned that her old publicist and friend Rupert Allan was returning from his stay in Monaco, and Marilyn hoped he would replace Newcomb. She commissioned Roberts to find Allan for her. "Tell him this is very important," Marilyn said.

"Ralph did reach me," Allan remembered. "But I had jet lag after the flight from France and a bad case of bronchitis. I knew if I spoke one word to Marilyn, she would insist on coming over with chicken soup and aspirin. And I was really too sick for that." When Allan later learned that the "very important business" may have concerned her press conference regarding the Kennedys, he commented, "I don't know how I would have handled that. . . . I was angry and saddened by the way the Kennedys had treated her, but I think that I could have talked her out of making it public knowledge."

On Friday morning, Marilyn called the Rostens in Brooklyn to ask their opinion concerning the *Life* article. Norman Rosten recalled that he told Marilyn how much he and Hedda had enjoyed reading the interview, and how great she looked in the pictures. Marilyn invited the Rostens to join her theater party at the *Mr. President* gala in September.

Later in the day, Marilyn spoke to Newcomb, who said she was suffering from a bad head cold. According to Newcomb, it was Marilyn who suggested she come by and relax around the pool and use Marilyn's heat lamp. However, Newcomb knew that Dorothy Kilgallen was trying to reach Marilyn, and it was incumbent upon Newcomb to ensure that Kilgallen and Marilyn didn't speak.

Marilyn was led to believe that Bobby Kennedy might arrive at Lawford's on Friday evening for a last-ditch attempt at an understanding, but when he failed to arrive Newcomb and Lawford took Marilyn out to dinner at La Scala in Beverly Hills, one of Marilyn's favorite restaurants. Billy Travilla had a vivid recollection of seeing Marilyn at La Scala with Lawford and Newcomb that night. He recalled that Marilyn appeared to be so intoxicated or drugged that she didn't recognize him when he came over to the table to say hello. "She looked up at me with no recognition at all," Travilla remembered.

Newcomb returned home with Marilyn, where the evening ended in an argument. Still intent on having her confrontation with Bobby Kennedy, Marilyn again called the St. Francis Hotel and left another message. Newcomb slept over in the telephone room, which was near Marilyn's bedroom door. At night, Marilyn went through the ritual of closing the blackout curtains on her windows and placing her private phone near her bedside before retiring.

That weekend the Los Angeles basin was going into one of its hot, dry "Santa Ana" conditions, when the winds blow in from the Mojave Desert. Sometimes Maf, Marilyn's poodle, would bark when wind rustled through the trees, and after dark he was kept out in the guest cottage, where his bark wouldn't interfere with her sleep.

In her last months, Marilyn still suffered from night terrors. Eunice Murray recalled Marilyn frequently "awakening from sleep with a small shriek shortly after falling asleep. . . . She awoke each time shivering with fright and bathed in perspiration. She would then get up and sit in a chair until the bad feeling left."

In a sense, Marilyn's home on Fifth Helena was a bulwark against the outside world and her fears. The walls were made of two-foot-thick cement blocks, and the windows were protected by decorative wrought iron. The thick hand-carved doorways and gates spoke of permanence and protection. Outside, high stucco walls ensured seclusion, and the towering eucalyptus trees served as a curtain of privacy. When Marilyn had moved in, she described her home as "a fortress where I can feel safe from the world." But the enemy was her loveless, terrifying childhood, and no matter what she built around her—her career, her startling success, her accumulated knowledge, or her "fortress"—the night would usher in the demons of her childhood. They came with the dark. When she was alone. When she was afraid. Nobody but Norma Jeane would ever know the remarkable courage it took for her to live each day.

Outside, the antique wind chimes, which had been the gift of Carl Sandburg, tolled in the tall trees as she waited for the prescribed sleeping tablets to have their merciful effect. Norma Jeane needed her sleep so that Marilyn Monroe could be reborn with the dawn.

Eunice Murray said, "It's my feeling that Marilyn looked forward to her tomorrows."

Tomorrow would be her last day.

Night Terrors

Don't cry my doll
Don't cry
I hold you and rock you to sleep
Hush hush I'm pretending now
I'm not your mother who died . . .

Down the walk
Clickety clack
As my doll in her carriage
Went over the cracks—
"We'll go far away"
　　　　　—Marilyn Monroe

The dry desert winds had warmed the L.A. basin and by 9 A.M., August 4, 1962, it was already eighty degrees.

Marilyn got up early, wrapped herself in her robe, and made some coffee in the kitchen. Pat Newcomb was still asleep in the telephone room. Marilyn had been up most of the night. With the blackout curtains closed, her room had been stifling—and then there were a series of disturbing phone calls. Jeanne Carmen related that Marilyn woke her at 6 A.M. to tell her about strange calls she had received during the night. A woman whose voice Marilyn wasn't sure she recognized had called a number of times between midnight and dawn, telling her to "leave Bobby alone" and calling her a "tramp." Carmen wondered if it could have been Ethel Kennedy.

"Marilyn sounded nervous and exhausted," Carmen stated. "She begged me to come over and keep her company." Marilyn had things she needed to talk to Carmen about—things she knew she couldn't say over the phone. But Carmen wasn't fully awake or aware of the anxieties she sensed in Marilyn's voice. She remembered Marilyn saying, "Bring over a bag of pills," and thought Marilyn was referring to "uppers" to help her through the day after a bad night. She told Marilyn she didn't have time to come over that day because it was her birthday, and she had a series of engagements that would keep her busy until late that night. They planned to see each other on Sunday.

Eunice Murray had spent the night at her own apartment on Ocean Avenue and arrived at approximately 8 A.M. Her car was being serviced at the nearby garage of Henry D'Antonio. He had driven her to Marilyn's house and was to deliver her car in the late afternoon. Shortly after Mrs. Murray arrived, Norman Jefferies drove through the newly installed wooden gates and parked his red pickup next to Pat Newcomb's car.

By 8:30 A.M. Jefferies had begun working on the new kitchen floor. He remembered seeing Marilyn walk into the kitchen shortly after nine o'clock. She was wrapped in a huge bath towel, and Jefferies stated that she didn't look well. "She looked sick," he said. "She was pale and looked tired. I thought there must have been something wrong with her."

During the course of Robert Slatzer's interview in 1974 with Eunice Murray, Slatzer asked what Marilyn ate that day, and she replied, "We sat down at the table and had some grapefruit juice. Marilyn liked juice, as you know . . . but she didn't have an appetite that day. She didn't have anything to eat." Slatzer added that Mrs. Murray seemed quite firm about this. She stated, "Marilyn did not consume any food or liquor that day."

Marilyn's lack of appetite on Saturday is in keeping with Dr. Engelberg's comment to Sergeant Clemmons, "I only recently gave her an injection because she was suffering from diarrhea." The autopsy, which revealed an inflamed lower colon, would corroborate the statements of Engelberg, Clemmons, and Murray. The diarrhea Engelberg cited may have been an episode of the colitis diagnosed in 1961 by her New York physician, Dr. Richard Cottrell, who noted that Marilyn suffered from an ulcerated colon. He attributed the problem to "a chronic fear neurosis," and stated that on occasions when his patient was "highly nervous, frightened and confused," her emotions brought on episodes of colitis.

During the morning, Marilyn spoke on the phone to Sidney Skolsky and mentioned that she planned to see Bobby Kennedy later that day. In the mid-morning, Ralph Roberts called to check on a tentative dinner date with Marilyn. He recalled that she wasn't sure if she could make it, and she suggested he call back in the afternoon.

According to Mrs. Murray, around 9:30 or 10 A.M., photographer Larry Schiller stopped by to talk to Marilyn about photographs for *Playboy* magazine. Schiller recalled that from the gate he saw Marilyn kneeling beside the flowers bordering the guest cottage. She was pulling weeds or plucking flowers, he thought. When he called to her, she turned and walked across the lawn. Schiller said that Marilyn was having second thoughts about the value of being on the cover of *Playboy*, where she would again be promoted as a sex object. They decided to talk about it again on Monday.

Mrs. Murray observed that Pat Newcomb, who had spent the night in the telephone room, rose close to noon. She walked into the kitchen, where she encountered Marilyn; an argument ensued. In a rare interview granted to Robert Slatzer in 1974, Newcomb stated, "The small argument that day was because I had been able to sleep all night and Marilyn hadn't." But the "small argument" was a continuation of the quarrel that had begun Friday night when Bobby Kennedy didn't show up, and on Saturday they had a bitter disagreement that led to Newcomb's dismissal.

According to Norman Jefferies, the argument was over Pat Newcomb's loyalty to the Kennedys. It was a loud, vitriolic confrontation that Eunice Murray initially claimed not to have heard. Later, Murray would admit that there had been a major disagreement.

Despite the conflict and being told to leave, Newcomb stayed on at Marilyn's, hovering around the telephone room—the self-appointed Marilyn monitor until Bobby arrived. Newcomb told the press that she had started to leave after the "small argument," but was stopped by Mrs. Murray, who asked her to stay for lunch. However, Murray and Newcomb had never been friendly and scarcely spoke. In fact, they had an intense dislike for one another.

In speaking of Eunice Murray, Newcomb stated, "Marilyn sought her advice because she was supposed to be this wonderful housekeeper Greenson had found for her. But from day one, I did not trust Eunice Murray, who seemed to be always snooping around. I tried to stay out of her way because I just didn't like her. She was sort of a spook, always hovering, always on the fringe of things. . . . I think Mrs. Murray should have been hung up by her thumbs."

In her 1974 interview with Robert Slatzer, Newcomb said, "Mrs. Murray fixed Marilyn and I [sic] lunch. They were [sic] hamburgers."

"But you definitely remember that you and Marilyn ate together?" Slatzer asked.

"Yes," she replied. "About lunchtime."

However, Mrs. Murray clearly stated that Marilyn went to her room and Pat Newcomb ate alone, and she was very firm about the fact that Marilyn didn't eat anything that day—a fact confirmed by the autopsy.

Early Saturday afternoon, the roar of a helicopter echoed off the sound-stage walls at the Fox studios. A Fox security guard squinted into the bright blue sky as it began its descent into the heliport near Stage 14, the same heliport Marilyn had used when she flew off to the president's birthday gala. As noted in the studio's security log, the helicopter had received approval to land shortly after 11 A.M. A dark gray limousine waited in the shade as the helicopter touched down in a whirl of dust. Studio publicist Frank Neill, who was working on the lot that Saturday, knew that Darryl Zanuck had shelved *The Enemy Within*, and he was surprised to see Bobby Kennedy leap from the helicopter and dash to the limousine. As the limousine door opened and Bobby jumped in, Neill caught a glimpse of Peter Lawford. Frank Neill's observation of Bobby Kennedy's arrival was corroborated by former Los Angeles Police Chief Daryl Gates, who stated, "The truth is, we knew Robert Kennedy was in town on August 4."

Former Los Angeles mayor Sam Yorty also confirmed the attorney general's presence in Los Angeles on the day Marilyn died. Yorty stated, "I had a conversation with Chief Parker, and he told me himself that Robert Kennedy had arrived in Los Angeles that day and checked into the Beverly Hilton Hotel."

Retired police chief Tom Reddin, who in 1962 was an assistant to Chief Parker, recently stated, "It was reported to me by security officers that the attorney general was in Los Angeles on the weekend when Marilyn Monroe died."

And after twenty-three years of denials, Eunice Murray admitted in 1985 that Bobby Kennedy was in Los Angeles and visited Marilyn Monroe's home on August 4, 1962. During the interview for the BBC documentary *Say Goodbye to the President*, she said, "I was not supposed to know the Kennedys were a very important part of Marilyn's life, but over a period of time, I was a witness to what was happening." Asked point-blank if Bobby Kennedy had been present at Marilyn's house that Saturday, Murray stated, "Oh sure, yes, I was in the living room when he arrived. She was not dressed."

In 1993 Norman Jefferies also confirmed the attorney general's visit to Marilyn Monroe's residence on Saturday, August 4, 1962. Jefferies revealed that he had never left the vicinity of Marilyn's home that Saturday, and he was at the side of his mother-in-law, Eunice Murray, until she left in her car on Sunday morning. He was a witness to Marilyn Monroe's death and the cover-up that ensued.

Jefferies recalled that on August 4, he had planned on leaving earlier in the day. He was loading tools into his truck when Eunice Murray came out of the house and told him that she had been dismissed: "I wasn't aware of a big disagreement between Eunice and Marilyn, but Eunice said she had been told by Marilyn to pack her things and leave. Marilyn expected Eunice to be gone by the end of the day. So I agreed to stay on and help her pack and get her things together. I asked Eunice if it meant that I had been fired too, and she said I'd have to ask Marilyn, but Marilyn had gone to her room." Murray had called Dr. Greenson, but he wasn't able to come over and mediate the problem until later in the day. Murray's car was being serviced, so Jefferies began putting Eunice's belongings into his truck.

Jefferies stated that sometime between three and four in the afternoon Robert Kennedy arrived with Peter Lawford. Though Marilyn had told Pat Newcomb she was no longer welcome, she was still at the house when the attorney general and Lawford arrived.

"Mr. Lawford made it very clear that he wanted Eunice and I [sic] out of there, and he told us to go to the market. He gave me some money and said to buy some Cokes. When we came back—maybe it was an hour later—their car was gone, and when we went into the house Marilyn was hysterical and looked awful. Something terrible had happened—she was scared out of her mind."

Newcomb tried to calm Marilyn, but there was nothing she could say or do. "It's something I'll never forget," Jefferies stated. "Marilyn was having this hysterical rage. It was like nothing I've ever seen. She was scared and at the same time she was terribly angry." Murray then called Dr. Greenson for the second time that day, conveyed that it was urgent, and Greenson said he'd be right over.

Jefferies's revelations were corroborated by Sidney Guilaroff. In 1984, Guilaroff told Anthony Summers he had spoken to Marilyn on that Saturday, but he refused to reveal the contents of the conversation beyond saying that Marilyn was "upset and depressed." In a 1995 interview he stated for the first time that he had spoken to Marilyn twice on Saturday. The first occasion was in the late afternoon or early evening. "Marilyn telephoned me and was in an absolute state," Guilaroff said. "She was in tears, and I had difficulty understanding her. After I calmed her down and said something like, 'Now, what's the matter, dear?' she said 'Bobby Kennedy was here, and he threatened me, screamed at me, and pushed me around!' I think I said something like 'What was Robert Kennedy doing at your house?' because I couldn't believe my ears. I knew absolutely nothing about her affair with Bobby, and I thought I knew everything. I knew about Jack, but she told me she had an affair with Bobby as well as Jack, and everything had gone wrong. Now she was afraid and felt she was in terrible danger. Bobby felt she had become a problem and had said to her, 'If you threaten me, Marilyn, there's more than one way to keep you quiet.' " After Marilyn had calmed down and became more coherent, Guilaroff suggested she should get some rest and they would talk again later in the evening.

Guilaroff's revelation coincides with statements made by Fred Otash to the *Los Angeles Times* and his suppressed interview on ABC's *20/20*. Otash stated that the surveillance tapes recorded a running quarrel between Marilyn and Bobby Kennedy as they moved from room to room during their violent quarrel: "Marilyn and Bobby had a very violent argument and she told him, 'I feel used; I feel passed around.' " Earl Jaycox, Bernard Spindel's assistant, confirmed that they were shouting at each other. Marilyn was screaming, while Kennedy was yelling, "Where is it? Where is it?" She shouted that she was being treated "like a piece of meat."

In 1985, Anthony Summers was led by NBC News executive Mark Monsky to a government contact who had heard some forty minutes of the Otash-Spindel tapes, all of it covering activity at Marilyn's home on the day she died. The tape recorder had been sound-activated and revealed two visits by Robert Kennedy. On the first visit Summers's source related, "You could hear Marilyn and Kennedy talking. It was kind of echoey and at a distance, as though the sound was in a room next to the site of the transmitter, perhaps in some sort of hallway." The tiled entry of Marilyn's home was in fact just beyond her bedroom. The tape then recorded the conversation turning into a heated argument. "Their voices grew louder and louder," he recalled. "They were arguing about something that had been promised by Robert Kennedy. As they argued, their voices got shriller. If I had not recognized RFK's voice already, I'm not sure that I would have known it was him at this point. He was screeching, high-pitched, like an old lady." It became evident that Kennedy was looking for something: "He was asking again and again, 'Where is it? Where the fuck is it?' "

Summers's source told him he wouldn't have identified the third voice on the tape, but had been told it was the voice of Peter Lawford. Lawford was saying, "Calm down! Calm down!" and he recalled Robert Kennedy saying words to the effect, "We have to know. It's important to the family.

We can make any arrangements you want!" The voices then came closer to the location of the transmitter. "There was a *clack, clack, clack* on the tape which Bernie said he thought was coat hangers being pushed along a rail . . . and there was a banging and flopping sound. . . . Monroe was screaming at them, and ordering them out of the house." The episode ended with the sound of a door slamming.*

Dr. Greenson stated that he arrived at Marilyn's between 4:30 and 5 P.M. Three different stories were given as the reason for his visit: First, Mrs. Murray told the police and the press that she called the doctor because of Marilyn's oxygen inquiry. A second story was told by Greenson in a letter to Norman Rosten. Greenson stated. "I received a call from Marilyn about four-thirty in the afternoon. She seemed somewhat depressed and somewhat drugged. I went over to her place. She was still angry with her girlfriend [Pat Newcomb] who had slept fifteen hours that night, and Marilyn was furious because she had had such a poor sleep. But after I had spent about two and a half hours with her she seemed to quiet down." Greenson told a different story to the suicide squad's Dr. Norman Tabachnick. Greenson related that Marilyn "had been close to some very important men in government and that she had been expecting one of them that night." She had called Greenson when she learned the meeting was off. "Marilyn died," Greenson said, "feeling rejected by some of the people she had been close to."

The truth regarding Greenson's visit was clarified by Norman Jefferies. After being told to leave by Lawford when he had arrived in midafternoon with Bobby Kennedy, Jefferies and Eunice Murray returned at approximately 4:30 P.M. to find Marilyn in a hysterical state. Mrs. Murray then called Dr. Greenson.

Greenson stated he arrived between four-thirty and five, which was confirmed by both Murray and Newcomb. Undoubtedly, Mrs. Murray briefed him on the disturbing events of the afternoon before he entered Marilyn's room. He found Marilyn to be despondent, angry, and afraid.

---

* The tapes, which were made by Fred Otash for Bernie Spindel, were seized during a raid in 1966 by New York District Attorney Frank Hogan. At that time, Hogan was a close associate of New York Senator Robert Kennedy. Kennedy was preparing his run for the presidency, and Spindel told *Life* magazine reporter John Neary, "Hogan really did Kennedy a favor by pulling that raid. They stole my tapes on Marilyn Monroe and my complete file." For years Spindel, and then his widow, tried to have the tapes and other seized material returned through litigation, but without success. According to the New York district attorney's office, the material seized during the raid at Spindel's was destroyed.

According to Mrs. Murray, while Dr. Greenson was in Marilyn's bedroom, she and Newcomb were in the living room. "Then Dr. Greenson came out into the living room and said to Pat, 'Are you leaving, Pat?' And Pat just got up and walked out. I wouldn't even want to guess how to account for this, but that's what I observed. . . . I know that Pat wasn't too happy about it."

George "Bullets" Durgom, a dinner guest that evening at Peter Lawford's, observed Newcomb at Lawford's beach house, where she had apparently driven sometime later. Durgom stated, "The one thing I remember clearly is Pat Newcomb coming in at maybe nine o'clock. She stood on the step and said, 'Peter, Marilyn's not coming. She's not feeling well.' "

Ralph Roberts stated that he called Marilyn's private telephone number at about six-thirty. "A man answered the phone. I knew it was Dr. Greenson; I recognized his voice." Roberts recalled that he sounded strangely intense. "I asked for Marilyn and he said, 'She's not in right now!' " It occurred to Roberts that it was unusual that Marilyn's psychiatrist had answered her phone and then said she wasn't in. He wondered what the doctor was doing there if Marilyn wasn't home. Roberts left his name and a message for Marilyn to call him.

In a letter Greenson wrote to Dr. Marianne Kris on August 20, 1962, he amplified on his visit to Marilyn that afternoon. Dr. Greenson wrote of Marilyn's decision to "terminate her therapy" and stated, "I was aware that she was somewhat annoyed with me. She often became annoyed when I did not absolutely and wholeheartedly agree [with her]. . . . She was angry with me. I told her we would talk more, that she should call me Sunday morning."

Greenson's visit concluded at approximately 7 P.M., and he suggested that she take some Nembutal and get a good night's sleep. He told Mrs. Murray to stay overnight, though her belongings were packed. At Murray's request, Norman Jefferies stayed on into the evening. Jefferies recalled that his mother-in-law was unnerved by the day's events, and he watched television with her, while Marilyn remained in her room.

In her last hours, Marilyn turned to her friend the telephone. She had spoken earlier at some length to Sidney Guilaroff about Bobby's visit, and according to Peter Lawford's guests Joe and Dolores Naar, it was approximately seven-thirty when Marilyn called during dinner, and Peter casually returned to the table and said, "Oh, that's just Marilyn again." Undoubtedly, Marilyn had something to say to Peter other than, "Say good-bye to the president" and "You're a nice guy." Her burning comments may still be smoldering in a CIA surveillance file.

At approximately the same time, Joe DiMaggio, Jr., called and had a lively discussion with Marilyn about his girlfriend. According to DiMaggio, "They spoke for about fifteen minutes and Marilyn seemed quite normal and in good spirits."

"It was between eight and eight-thirty that I spoke once again with Marilyn," Sidney Guilaroff stated. "She was feeling much better and had met with her psychiatrist, Dr. Greenson, who I frankly detested. I tried to diffuse her anxieties about her argument with Robert Kennedy, and I think now that I'd totally misunderstood the situation. I dismissed it then as merely a lover's quarrel. We planned on talking again the next day, and I suggested we drive up to the Holiday Inn and talk the whole thing over. She ended the conversation with the provoking comment, 'You know, Sidney, I know a lot of secrets about the Kennedys.'

'What kind of secrets?' I asked.

'Dangerous ones,' she said, and then hung up.

Jeanne Carmen said that Marilyn called her close to nine o'clock that evening. It was Marilyn's third call that day. "Are you sure you can't come over?" Marilyn inquired. Jeanne Carmen again declined, saying she was tired. She said, "Marilyn sounded nervous and afraid." Jeanne has always regretted not responding to the need she detected in Marilyn's voice in their last conversation.

Marilyn's wealthy New York friend Henry Rosenfeld telephoned her close to 9 P.M., California time. They discussed her projected theater party in September and he said, "She sounded groggy, but that wasn't unusual."

It had been a long and exhausting day. Though she had drawn the blackout curtains, she left the front windows open. Outside, it was still sultry. During the Southern California midsummer, the evening light remains in the sky well after sundown. But soon it would be night and the crescent moon would rise.

Shortly after dusk, three men walked down Fifth Helena Drive. One was carrying a small black satchel similar to a medical bag. Elizabeth Pollard, a neighbor of Marilyn's, often asked a group of friends over on Saturday evening to play cards. Several months after Marilyn's death, they told Police Sergeant Jack Clemmons that "they saw Kennedy go into Marilyn's house just after dusk. They were sitting playing bridge and Bobby Kennedy walked right by the window on his way into Marilyn's house."

The women told Clemmons that the attorney general had two other men with him. However, in 1962, Elizabeth Pollard's story was discredited by the police and the district attorney as an aberration. The official story, backed up by FBI documents, was that Bobby Kennedy was not in Los Angeles that day. Elizabeth Pollard has since passed away, but a recent interview with Betty Pollard, Elizabeth's daughter, reconfirmed her mother's statement.

Marilyn's private phone rang shortly after nine-thirty. It was a welcome voice—José Bolaños. He had recently returned to Los Angeles to see Marilyn and was calling from a bar in Santa Monica Canyon. Revealing only that Marilyn told him "something shocking—something that will one day shock the whole world," Bolaños added that during the conversation Marilyn left the phone. She didn't hang up, but she put the telephone down while he waited for her to return. She never came back.

There was a commotion at the door, and Marilyn went to see what it was.

Norman Jefferies recalled that between 9:30 and 10 P.M., Robert Kennedy, accompanied by two men, appeared at the door. They ordered Jefferies and Murray from the house. "We were told to leave. I mean they made it clear we were to be gone. But this time Eunice and I didn't leave the neighborhood. We went to a neighbor's house. I had no idea what was going on. I mean, this was the attorney general of the United States. I didn't know who the two men were with him. I assumed they were some sort of government men. We waited at the neighbor's house for them to leave." Jefferies may have been referring to the neighbors to the west, Mr. and Mrs. Abe Landau. But the Landaus insist they were out that evening until at least eleven. Jefferies may have been referring to the nearby home of Hanna Fenichel on Third Helena Drive.

According to the Naars, it was approximately ten-thirty when Peter Lawford received Marilyn's alarming call, when she lapsed into unconsciousness. Lawford then called back to find that both lines were off the hook, with no conversation taking place. Lawford then called the Naars in a panic and asked Joe Naar to find out what was wrong.

At about ten-thirty Murray and Jefferies saw Bobby and the two men leave. Jefferies stated that he and Murray then ventured back to Marilyn's. As they entered the open gates and crossed the courtyard toward the kitchen door, they heard Maf barking from the guest cottage, where the light was on and the door was standing open. When they entered the cottage, they discovered Marilyn, unclothed, lying across the daybed.

"I thought she was dead," Jefferies stated. "She was facedown, her hand kind of holding the phone. It didn't look to me like she was breathing, and her color was awful—like she was dead. Eunice took the phone and called an ambulance. Then she put through an emergency call to Dr. Greenson, who was someplace nearby and said he would be right over. He told Eunice to call Dr. Engelberg," Jefferies continued. "I went to the gates to wait for the ambulance, but before the ambulance got there Peter Lawford and Pat Newcomb arrived. Pat became hysterical and started screaming at Eunice. I had to take Eunice into the house. She was a basket case. I think the ambulance arrived before Dr. Greenson."

Jefferies's revelation corroborates the disclosures of Schaefer ambulance driver James Hall, who had stated he was only minutes away when he and his partner Murray Liebowitz received the Code Three call to the Monroe residence. Hall had identified the hysterical woman as Pat Newcomb and placed Peter Lawford and Dr. Greenson at the scene.

Hall confirmed finding Marilyn in a comatose state on the bed in the guest cottage, stating that they placed her on her back on the cottage floor in order to attempt resuscitation. When Dr. Greenson arrived, he ordered the removal of the resuscitator and directed Hall to "apply positive pressure," or CPR. Greenson then attempted to inject adrenaline directly into her heart in order to revive her, but the needle hit a rib. Hall said Marilyn succumbed moments later.

"After that all hell broke loose," Jefferies stated. "It was horrible. I was in the living room with Eunice when Marilyn died, and we could hear Pat Newcomb screaming, and we knew Marilyn was dead. After that there were police cars, fire trucks, more ambulances—you name it! A police helicoptor landed at the golf course and soon they were all over the place."

Dr. Engelberg arrived close to midnight and Marilyn's body was moved from the floor of the guest cottage to her bedroom in the main house. Jefferies stated that the "locked room" suicide scenario was formulated by the plainclothes officials who had arrived soon after Marilyn's death. According to Jefferies, at one time 12305 Helena Drive was swarming with at least a dozen plainclothes officers—then suddenly they were gone. He had no idea who they were.

The officer in charge was later identified by Billy Woodfield and several former LAPD officers as Bobby Kennedy's friend Captain James Hamilton of the Los Angeles Police Department Intelligence Division, and the two men who had accompanied Bobby Kennedy to Marilyn's house that night were identified as two detectives assigned to Kennedy as security officers.

Did they intend to murder Marilyn Monroe? Or was the intent to subdue her with a "hot shot" if she caused any problems while they broke into her file cabinet in the guest cottage; took the notes, letters, and legal documents; and searched for the book of secrets? The evidence points to premeditated homicide. In the presence of Bobby Kennedy, she was injected with enough barbiturate to kill fifteen people.

Before dawn on Sunday, August 5, 1962, a warm wind swept off the Mojave Desert and rushed into the Los Angeles basin, swaying the tall trees that formed a curtain of privacy around the Brentwood home of Marilyn Monroe. Antique wind chimes that had been the gift of poet Carl Sandburg softly tolled in the darkness. Strange sounds had been carried on the wind during the night—shouting and the crash of broken glass. Neighbors reported that a hysterical woman had yelled, "Murderers! You murderers! Are you satisfied now that she's dead?"

Mr. and Mrs. Abe Landau, who lived to the immediate west of Marilyn Monroe, had returned home from a dinner party late Saturday evening and had seen an ambulance and a police car parked in the cul-de-sac in front of the film star's residence. Near midnight neighbors heard a helicopter hovering overhead. There were other strange sights and sounds before dawn as the city slept. In the crush of time and extremity the film star's home was carefully rearranged, telephone records were seized, papers and notes were destroyed—and a frantic phone call was placed to the White House.

Shortly before midnight a dark Mercedes sped east on Olympic Boulevard in Beverly Hills. Estimating the car to be driving in excess of fifty-five miles per hour, Beverly Hills police officer Lynn Franklin flipped on his siren and lights and gave chase. When the Mercedes pulled to a stop, Franklin cautiously walked to the driver's side and directed his flashlight toward the three occupants. He immediately recognized that the driver was actor Peter Lawford. Aiming his flashlight at the two men seated in the rear, he was surprised to see the attorney general of the United States, Robert Kennedy, seated next to a third man he later identified as Dr. Ralph Greenson. Lawford explained that he was driving the attorney general to the Beverly Hilton Hotel on an urgent matter. Reminding Lawford that he was in a thirty-five miles-per-hour zone, Officer Franklin waved them on.

———

At midnight on Saturday, August 4, 1962, Sergeant Jack Clemmons came on duty as watch commander at the West Los Angeles Police Department on Purdue Street. Clemmons's duties proved to be routine until the call that came in shortly before dawn. The caller identified himself as Dr. Hyman Engelberg and said, "Marilyn Monroe has died. She's committed suicide."

APPENDIX

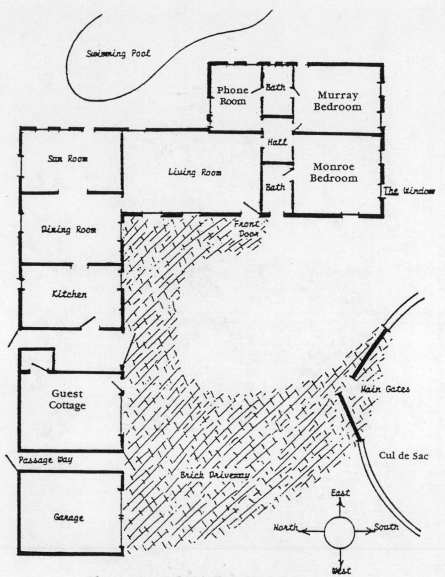

Floor plan of Marilyn Monroe's Brentwood residence in 1962.

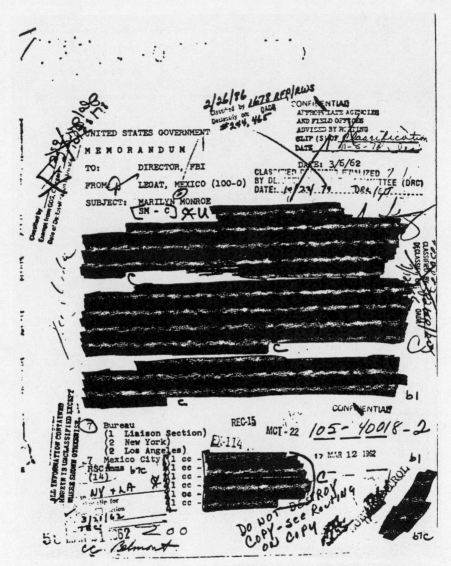

This document, dated March 6, 1962, originated with the FBI in Mexico City. The subject, Marilyn Monroe, has the classification SM-C (Security Matter-Communist). Though the contents are obliterated, the FBI Freedom of Information attorney revealed that the document referred to transcripts of conversations between Frederick Vanderbilt Field and Marilyn Monroe recorded by electronic surveillance placed in Field's residence. The conversation included the discussion of sensitive national security matters.

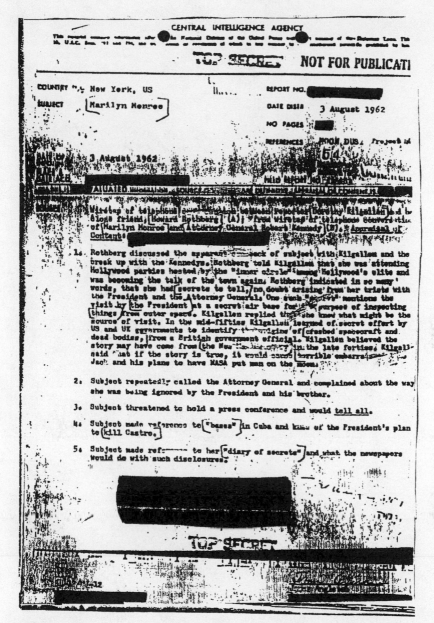

COUNTRY : New York, US

SUBJECT : Marilyn Monroe

REPORT NO.

DATE DISTR   3 August 1962

NO PAGES

REFERENCES   MOON DUST , Project id

3 August 1962

Wiretap of telephone conversation between reporter Dorothy Kilgallen and a close friend, Howard Rothberg (A) from wiretap of telephone conversation of Marilyn Monroe and Attorney General Robert Kennedy (B). Appraisal of Contents.

1. Rothberg discussed the apparent comeback of subject with Kilgallen and the break up with the Kennedys. Rothberg told Kilgallen that she was attending Hollywood parties hosted by the "inner circle" among Hollywood's elite and was becoming the talk of the town again. Rothberg indicated in so many words, that she had secrets to tell, no doubt arising from her trysts with the President and the Attorney General. One such "secret" mentions the visit by the President at a secret air base for the purpose of inspecting things from outer space. Kilgallen replied that she knew what might be the source of visit. In the mid-fifties Kilgallen learned of secret effort by US and UK governments to identify the origins of crashed spacecraft and dead bodies, from a British government official. Kilgallen believed the story may have come from the New ____ in the late forties. Kilgallen said that if the story is true, it would cause terrible embarrassment for Jack and his plans to have NASA put men on the Moon.

2. Subject repeatedly called the Attorney General and complained about the way she was being ignored by the President and his brother.

3. Subject threatened to hold a press conference and would tell all.

4. Subject made reference to "bases" in Cuba and knew of the President's plan to kill Castro.

5. Subject made reference to her "diary of secrets" and what the newspapers would do with such disclosures.

This CIA document, dated August 3, 1962, is an evaluation of wiretaps on the telephones of both Marilyn Monroe and syndicated columnist Dorothy Kilgallen. It discloses that Monroe had learned of top government secrets. Item 1 refers to a discussion between Dorothy Kilgallen and Howard Rothberg regarding Monroe's troubled relationship with the president and the attorney general. Item 2 confirms that she was repeatedly calling Robert Kennedy with complaints about being ignored by JFK. Item 3 verifies her threat to call a press conference. Item 4 reveals that she had been made privy to top secret security matters. Item 5 confirms that Monroe kept a "diary of secrets." The document is signed by James Angleton, CIA chief of counterintelligence.

SOURCE NOTES

NOTE: References to other publications are indicated by authors and titles listed in the bibliography. Unless otherwise indicated, all interviews (int.) were conducted by the author.

Chapter 1

4   Engelberg's call: int., Jack Clemmons, 1993, 1997.

4   Conversations between Clemmons, the doctors, and Eunice Murray were reconstructed in the course of numerous interviews with Clemmons.

4   Description of death scene: Robert Slatzer, *The Life and Curious Death of Marilyn Monroe*, pp. 24–30; int., Clemmons, 1993.

7   Engelberg's comment about Marilyn's injection: *Marilyn Remembered* transcripts of March 22, 1991; int., Clemmons, 1996.

Chapter 2

9   "What day is it?" Norman Rosten, *Marilyn: An Untold Story*, p. 10.

9   Predawn call: int., Don Hockett, 1994.

9   Urgent call to Tommy Thompson: int., Richard Stolley, 1993.

9   Press reactions: int., Joe Hyams, 1994; Billy Woodfield, 1994; James Bacon, 1994.

10   Absence of drinking vessel: int., Clemmons, 1993.

10   Byron's observations: int., Robert Byron, 1993.

10   Chronology of events: Byron's report, August 5, 1962; and follow-up Report, August 6, 1962; int., Clemmons, 1993.

11   Tommy Thompson tape: *Time* and *Life* archives; int., Richard Stolley, 1993.

11   Eunice Murray's statements are taken from police reports and her statements in the *Los Angeles Times* and *Herald Examiner*, August 8, 1962.

12   Murray's Piscean qualities: Murray, *Marilyn: The Last Months*, p. 9.

12   Marilyn's telephones: From phone records reproduced in Anthony
        Summers's, *Goddess: The Secret Lives of Marilyn Monroe*; int.,
        Norman Jefferies, 1993; Ralph Roberts, 1993; Norman Rosten,
        1994.

13   "Mrs. Murray was vague . . .": Armstrong's police report, August 5,
        1962.

13   Pat Newcomb stated . . . : *Los Angeles Times and Herald-Examiner*,
        August 6, 1962; int., Slatzer/Newcomb, 1973.

13   Clemmons didn't see Newcomb or Jacobs: int., Clemmons 1993,
        1994.

13   Newcomb hysterical: Murray, p. 22; int., Jefferies, 1993.

14   "Rigor mortis was advanced . . .": Summers, p. 357; Slatzer, *The Life
        and Curious Death of Marilyn Monroe*, p. 64; int., Don Hockett,
        1994.

14   Hyams's account: int., Hyams, 1994, 1995; Hyams, *Mislaid in Hol-
        lywood; New York Herald-Tribune*, August 6, 1962.

14   Captain James Hamilton's presence at the death scene: int., Billy
        Woodfield, 1994; int., Joe Hyams, 1994, 1995; int., former officer
        of the Intelligence Division who requests anonymity.

15   Marilyn Monroe's body placed in the van: Newsreels and press pho-
        tos; int., Woodfield, Hyams, Hockett, and United Press corre-
        spondent Joe Finegan, 1993, 1994.

15   Incidents at the Westwood Village Mortuary: int., Hyams, Wood-
        field, Hockett, and Alan Abbott, 1993, 1994.

Chapter 3

17   Slatzer was awakened . . . : int., Ron Pataki, 1995; transcript of Sum-
        mers's interview with Dr. Firestone and Ron Pataki, 1983.

18   Arthur Miller quote: *New York Post*, August 6, 1962.

18   Clemmons's call to Dougherty: int., Clemmons, 1993.

18   Strasberg's comment: *New York Herald-Tribune*, August 6, 1962.

19   "Told what was good to tell at the time . . .": Summers, p. 439.

19   "I had arrived at Marilyn's . . .": *New York Journal-American*, August
        12, 1962.

19   "I arrived there about eight-thirty . . .": Murray's statements are
        from police reports; int., Slatzer/Murray, 1972; Summers, p. 348.

21   Lawford's story: Daryl Gates's "in-house" interview conducted by
        the LAPD in 1975; *Los Angeles Times*, 8/6/62, *Los Angeles
        Herald-Examiner*. 8/7/62.

21   "Mr. Rudin stated...": int. of Rudin conducted by Lt. Grover Armstrong and obtained from the files of the LAPD by Robert Slatzer.

23   DiMaggio, Jr., confirmed . . . : Sgt. Byron's police report, August 5, 1962; *New York Post*, August 6, 1962.

23   Murray's statement regarding DiMaggio, Jr.'s call: Sgt. Byron's police report, August 5, 1962.

23   "We won't be going for that drive...": *Los Angeles Herald-Examiner*, August 6, 1962.

Chapter 4

25   "Discovered something strange...": The narrative of Thomas T. Noguchi's assignment to the Monroe case is drawn from Noguchi's *Coroner*; int., Slatzer/Noguchi, 1972.

26   Grandison soon discovered . . . : int., Grandison, 1993; transcript of Slatzer/Grandison interview, 1974.

26   Shortly after 9 . . . : int., Slatzer/Grandison, 1973.

27   Noguchi was joined by . . . : Summers, p. 362.

27   Also attending the autopsy . . . : int., Grandison, 1993.

27   Number of pills: Lieutenant Armstrong's police report, August 5, 1962.

28   Miner's statements about the autopsy: int., Miner, 1993, 1995; Summers, p. 357; int., Slatzer/Miner, 1973.

28   The case of John Belushi: Noguchi, p. 197.

28   livor mortis: int., Dr. Kay Cassell, 1993; int., Robert Cravey, 1993; int., Alan Abbott, 1994.

29   "a slight ecchymotic area . . .": Medical Examiner's report, 1962.

29   Grandison and Miner about the bruises: int., Grandison, 1994; Slatzer, *Marilyn Files*, p. 135.

30   ". . . It is a sign of violence.": Noguchi, *New York Times*, November 13, 1982.

30   The autopsy process is taken from the autopsy report; Noguchi's account in *Coroner*; int., Slatzer/Noguchi, 1972; int., Miner, 1993.

31   Lytess and previous suicide attempt: Lytess, *My Years With Marilyn*, unpublished manuscript in the Zolotow collection, University of Texas, Austin.

31   "odor of pear" as a factor: int., Dr. Kay Cassell, 1993.

31   "Unembalmed blood is taken . . .": autopsy report, p. 6.

32   Wiener photos: int., Leigh Weiner, 1992; Summers, p. 357.

Chapter 5

33   The tests showed . . . : R. J. Abernethy's reports, August 8 and 13, 1962.

34   Correlating the forensic . . . : coroner's report, file #81128.

34   UCLA Toxicological Laboratory: Medical Records Department, UCLA Medical Center, Marilyn Monroe file, 8/6/62.

35   "As I analyze my participation . . .": Slatzer, *The Marilyn Files*, p. 143.

35   Grandison's comments on the autopsy procedure: transcripts of Slatzer/Grandison interview, 1974; int., Grandison, 1994.

35   diary or book of secrets: obtained from the CIA through confidential source.

36   Another witness who viewed . . . : int., Mike Rothmiller, 1998.

36   Jefferies's verification: int., Norman Jefferies, 1993.

36   Grandison and diary: transcripts of Slatzer/Grandison interview, 1974.

37   Curphey's press conference and "Suicide Squad": *Los Angeles Herald-Examiner*, August 6, 1962.

37   Litman, Farberow, and Tabachnik as associates of Greenson and members of the ACLU: documented in Greenson's FBI file.

37   The Los Angeles Suicide Prevention Team receiving a sizable grant from the National Institute of Mental Health: documented in the files of the NIMH.

37   Press conferences of the Suicide Prevention Team were covered by the *Los Angeles Herald-Examiner*, August 7, 8, and 14, 1962.

38   The Greenson/Miner interview: int., Miner, 1993, 1997; Slatzer, *The Marilyn Files*, p. 148; Summers, p. 330.

40   "If Miner's evaluation . . .": Noguchi, p. 87.

40   Grandison's account of signing the death certificate: Slatzer, *The Marilyn Files*, p. 220; int., Grandison, 1993.

40   Curphey's press conference: *Los Angeles Times*, August 22, 1962; *Los Angeles Herald-Examiner*, August 21, 1962; and the files of the coroner's office.

41   Computer analysis of Case #81128 was obtained through the facilities of Dr. Kay Cassell and INFORM.

42   Table 1 prepared by toxicologist Robert H. Cravey.

42   The victim's dying before the fatal concentrations could approach such high blood levels is the opinion of numerous pathologists, including Dr. Sidney Weinberg, and demonstrated by Robert H. Cravey and in cases cited by INFORM.

Chapter 6
44   Brown: Summers, p. 327.
44   scribbled note: int., Slatzer/Grandison, 1978.
45   Slatzer spoke to Marilyn . . . : int., Slatzer, 1994; int., Pataki, 1995.
45   Lawford statements: *Long Beach Star*, February 17, 1976.
45   St. Francis Hotel operator: Slatzer, *The Life and Curious Death of Marilyn Monroe*, p. 27.
46   "Marilyn Mystery Call": *Los Angeles Times*, August 7, 1962.
46   Rosenfeld call: Summers, p. 310.
46   Guilaroff call: int., Sidney Guilaroff, 1996; Guilaroff, *Crowning Glory*, p. 165.
46   Carmen call: int., Jeanne Carmen, 1997; Summers, p. 311.
47   Bolaños call: Summers, p. 310.
47   "Bullets" Durgom confirmed . . . : Summers, p. 343.
47   The Naars' account: James Spada, *The Man Who Kept the Secrets*; Summers, *Goddess*; and Slatzer, *The Marilyn Files*.
49   Marilyn's telephone records: int., Joe Hyams, 1994; Summers, p. 334.
49   Reddin and Yorty statements: Slatzer archives.
49   Hamilton correspondence: The Kennedy Library, Attorney General's personal correspondence.
50   Tobin statement: Summers, p. 337.
50   "Strange pressures . . .": *New York Daily News*, August 8, 1962.
50   "I asked her what . . .": int., Robert Slatzer, 1995.
51   Bates: The Kennedy Library, Attorney General's personal correspondence.
51   Bates statement: Spoto, p. 561.
51   RFK's attendance at mass: *Gilroy Dispatch*, August 6, 1962.
51   Thad Brown discovered . . . : Summers, p. 356.
52   "Where Hamilton and . . .": Ibid., p. 337.

Chapter 7
53   "Mrs. Eley has never . . .": *Los Angeles Herald-Examiner*, August 7, 1962.
54   Snyder and funeral: int., Snyder, 1993.
54   Hockett's assistant: int., Alan Abbott, 1994.
55   "Everybody is always . . .": Meryman int., *Life*, August 3, 1962.
55   Strasberg's eulogy: the collection of Alan Abbott.

Chapter 8

57 Marianne Means interview: *Washington Times-Herald*, August 11, 1962.

58 *Manitou* voyage: Julius Fanta, *Sailing with Kennedy*, p. 53.

58 Wood saw Bobby Kennedy: Ibid., p. 351.

58 Hyams/Woodfield investigation: int., Hyams, 1994; int., Woodfield, 1995; Summers, p. 352.

58 "Look, I cannot explain . . .": Ibid., p. 332; int., Woodfield, 1995.

58 Slatzer and Melson: int., Slatzer, 1994.

59 A-1 Lock and Safe Company: Monroe probate papers.

59 Slatzer and Monroe in Malibu: int, Slatzer, 1994, 1995.

Chapter 9

61 Clemmons returned . . . : int., Clemmons, 1993, 1996.

62 Slatzer . . . returned . . . : int., Slatzer, 1995.

63 "Marilyn's death was . . . : Farber and Green, *Hollywood on the Couch*, p. 107.

63 "There is no way . . .": Ibid., p. 106.

64 "In 1962 Chief Parker . . .": Summers, p. 329.

64 Parker/RFK correspondence: Kennedy Library, Attorney General's correspondence file.

64 Hamilton's reassignment: Daryl Gates, *Chief*, p. 70; int., Gates, 1996.

64 Pat Newcomb's return: Newcomb/RFK correspondence, Kennedy Library, Attorney General's correspondence file; USIA employment records.

Chapter 10

65 Hoover memo: Bureau Chief's personal and confidential file.

66 Guiles and Monroe: int., Fred Guiles, 1994, 1995.

67 Slatzer and Monroe: int., Slatzer, 1994.

67 Quinn/Slatzer: int., Slatzer, 1994; Slatzer, *The Life and Curious Death of Marilyn Monroe*, pp. 248–252.

70 "Every implication of . . .": Mailer interview with Mike Wallace, *60 Minutes*, July 13, 1973.

70 Gates in-house report: int., Daryl Gates, 1995; Gates, *Chief*, p. 142; int., Neil Spotts, 1998.

71 Lawford interview: Gates, p. 143.

72 Greenson: Farber and Green, pp. 83–95.

72 Miner: int., John Miner, 1994, 1997.

Chapter 11

74 Van de Kamp and grand jury: *Los Angeles Times*, August 12, 1982.

75 Van de Kamp's 1982 report: courtesy of Press Relations Office of the Los Angeles District Attorney.

75 "Hot shot": int., Dr. Kay Cassell, 1993; Noguchi, p. 87.

75 Absence of chloral hydrate in liver: Abernethy's toxicology report.

75 Signs of cyanosis: Internationally renowned pathologist Dr. Cyril Wecht states: "When the body is cyanotic, then the pathologist usually looks for the means of death to be other than by an oral overdose"; Milo Speriglio, *Crypt 33*, p. 244.

75 Blue cast of skin: int., Leigh Weiner, 1992.

76 James Hall's account: int., James Hall, 1993, 1996; *Globe*, November 23, 1982; int., Rick Summers, 1993.

78 Ken Hunter's account: District Attorney's report, 1982.

79 "There was no ambulance . . .": int., Clemmons, 1995.

79 Bellonzi on Hunter: int., Carl Bellonzi, 1993.

79 Slatzer and Schaefer: int., Slatzer, 1994.

79 Hunter and Summers: Summers, p. 345.

80 Hall's social security records, payroll, and photo: In 1993 Hall showed the author copies of his social security records and payroll stubs. A photo of Hall wearing a Schaefer uniform appeared in the *Santa Monica Evening Outlook* on September 24, 1962.

80 Polygraph expert and Koder: int., Hall, 1993.

80 Identi-Kit drawing: *Globe*, November 23, 1983.

80 Don Fraser polygraph: int., Fraser, 1993.

81 "It wasn't natural . . .": int., Clemmons, 1993.

81 Liebowitz admission: int., Murray Liebowitz (Leib), 1993.

81 Pilot Bob Neuman's statements: int., 1995.

82 "Arthur absolutely . . .": Summers, p. 286.

Chapter 12

83 Litman's statements: Summers, p. 249.

84 Lawford's death: Spada, *The Man Who Kept the Secrets*, p. 293.

85 "We got the news . . .": Summers, p. 344; int., Natalie Jacobs, 1996.

86 "Had we known of . . .": Carroll's statement was made to Anthony Summers in 1986.

86 Natalie Jacobs maintains . . . : int., Natalie Jacobs, 1996.

88 "I got a call . . . : Rudin interview in the Special Collections Department of the Library of the Academy of Motion Picture Arts and Sciences; Spoto, p. 573.

Chapter 13

89   BBC and Murray: int., Ted Landreth, 1996.

90   Murray and Summers: int., Summers, 1996; BBC's *Say Goodbye to the President* transcript.

91   Canceled *20/20*: Robert Slatzer was a consultant for ABC and the contents of the segment were recounted by Slatzer, Sam Yorty, and Bill Roemer. Other quotes are taken from a transcript.

91   "I just hope . . .": Liz Smith column, New York *Daily News*, October 3, 1985.

91   Arledge—"A sleazy piece of journalism . . .": Liz Smith column, New York *Daily News*, October 4, 1985.

91   Downs—"I am upset . . .": *New York Times*, October 5, 1985.

92   Kennedy links to Arledge: *People*, October 21, 1985; Marc Gunther, *The House That Roone Built*, p. 207.

92   Otash and Chase: transcript of interview from the archives of a private collector.

93   "He [Lawford] said he had . . .": *Los Angeles Times*

94   Schermerhorn/Murray: int., Terry Schermerhorn, 1995; int., Ted Landreth, 1995; *New York Post*, October 16, 1985.

95   Grand jury investigation: *Los Angeles Times*, October 26, 1985.

95   Noguchi/KABC-TV: transcript, October 25, 1985.

95   Reiner announcement: *Los Angeles Times*, October 29, 1985.

96   Cordova's dismissal: Slatzer interview with Sam Cordova, 1997.

96   "The truth is . . .": Gates, p. 144.

97   Carroll's statement and proceedings of the Supervisors' meeting on September 8, 1992, are from the archives of the Los Angeles Board of Supervisors.

98   "The definitive account . . .": HarperCollins, spring catalog, 1993.

Chapter 14

99   "For the first time . . .": STAR, February 1993.

99   "Patricia Newcomb offered . . .": Spoto, p. xv.

100   "Scurrilous accounts . . .": Ibid., p. 489.

100   "In *Goddess* Summers . . .": Ibid., p. 607.

100   Spoto's settlement: "All about Marilyn," #15, July 1994, p. 19; Spoto's retraction appears in the paperback of *Marilyn Monroe— The Biography*.

100   "Please don't make . . .": *Life*, August 3, 1966.

101   Jefferies at MM home: Murray, p. 139; Summers, p. 349.

101   "Murray seemed oddly . . .": Ibid., p. 287.

101   Landreth and Jefferies: int., Landreth, 1993.

101   Jefferies's statements: int., Jefferies, 1993.

Chapter 15

107   "I remember waking . . .": Fred Lawrence Guiles, *Norma Jean: The Life of Marilyn Monroe,* p. 12.

107   The history and genealogy of Marilyn Monroe's family: extensive files of genealogist Roy Turner; Guiles, *Norma Jean* and *Legend*; Miracle, *My Sister Marilyn.*

107   Della's rage: Guiles, p. 14; Roy Turner archives.

Chapter 16

110   "I'm not Mama . . .": Guiles, p. 11.

110   "I used to sit on the edge . . .": Marilyn Monroe, *My Story,* p. 9. Marilyn's quotations from *My Story* are her own words as transcribed by Ben Hecht, and are included in the Ben Hecht papers in the special collections department of the Newberry Library in Chicago. They were serialized in the *London Empire News* in 1954 and published in book form in 1974. Some people have questioned whether the words were Marilyn's. In 1975 Hecht's widow, Rose, confirmed that the account was told to her husband directly by Marilyn Monroe.

111   "She was the pretty woman . . .": Monroe, pp. 9–11.

111   "She seldom spoke . . .": Monroe, pp. 10–11.

112   "Playland of the Pacific . . .": The history of Venice Beach is from the archives of the Venice Historical Society.

112   Gladys's marriage to Baker and the birth dates of the children are contained in Roy Turner's genealogy files; Miracle, chapter 1.

112   "She wouldn't cook . . .": Miracle, p. 12.

113   Trip to Flat Lick: Ibid., p. 13.

113   Divorce papers: Turner archives.

113   "Daddy and my grandmother . . .": Miracle, p. 14.

113   Gladys and Gifford: int., Bebe Goddard, 1993, 1995; unpublished manuscript of Roy Turner; Guiles, *Norma Jean,* pp. 6–7.

113   Divorce action: Turner archives.

114   "They did, as you'd say . . .": Olin Stanley correspondence, Turner archives.

115   "It must have hurt . . .": George Barris, *Marilyn,* p. 5; int., Barris, 1998.

Chapter 17

116 "Nearly everybody I knew . . .": Monroe, p. 15.

116 Jackie's death: Miracle, pp. 16–17.

117 "One day my mother came to call . . .": Monroe, p. 13.

117 Hollywood strikes: *Hollywood Citizen News*, March 13, 1933.

117 Gladys jumped over fence: Olin Stanley correspondence, Turner archives.

118 "I told her not to buy it . . .": Miracle, p. 37.

118 "My mother bought furniture . . .": Monroe, p. 13.

118 Murray Kinnell: Library of the Academy of Motion Picture Arts and Sciences; Guiles, *Norma Jean*, p. 19.

119 The incident with Mr. Kimmell: Monroe, pp. 20–21.

120 The Kimmell incident as told to Barris: Barris, *Marilyn*, pp. 23–24.

121 Custodial records: Roy Turner archives.

121 "When Gladys bought . . .": Miracle, p. 32.

121 "Suddenly there was a terrible noise . . .": Monroe, pp. 13–14.

121 Gladys declared incompetent: Turner archives.

122 "All the furniture disappeared . . .": Monroe, p. 14.

122 "I could hear her friends . . .": Ibid., p. 16.

122 Doc and Grace's marriage: int., Goddard, 1994.

123 Norma Jean taken to orphanage: Guiles, *Norma Jean*, pp. 22–23; Zolotow, *Marilyn Monroe*, p. 17.

Chapter 18

124 a nearby film studio: Zolotow, *Marilyn Monroe*, p. 18.

124 Joseph P. Kennedy and acquisition of RKO: Richard J. Whalen, *The Founding Father*, pp. 87–92.

125 Joe and Gloria: Gloria Swanson, *Swanson on Swanson*, p. 386–387.

125 "Miss Swanson and . . .": Damore, *Cape Cod Years*, p. 21.

126 on board "Aunt Gloria": Madsen, *Gloria and Joe*, p. 241.

126 "My own special interest . . .": Rose Fitzgerald Kennedy, *Times to Remember*, p. 187.

126 "I made him give . . .": Ralph G. Martin, *A Hero for Our Time*, p. 34.

127 "In the orphanage I began . . .": Monroe, p. 17.

127 The stammering problem: Zolotow, p. 18.

128 Outings with Grace: int., Goddard, 1994.

128 "Grace loved and adored . . .": Turner archives.

129   Marilyn's sleeping disorder is described in "Night Terrors," a publication of the UCLA Medical Center's Sleep Disorder Clinic.

130   "Suddenly, I wasn't in . . .": Monroe, pp. 17–19.

Chapter 19

133   "Grace was fun . . .": Turner archives.

133   Goddard's small house: int., Goddard, 1993; *All About Marilyn*, #13, p. 7.

133   "Grace could have . . .": int., Goddard, 1993; *All About Marilyn*, #13, p. 7.

133   "Olin, isn't she pretty? . . .": Turner archives.

133   Doc drank too much: int., James Dougherty, 1995; *All About Marilyn*, #13, p. 7.

134   "I don't think . . .": int., Goddard, 1993.

134   "Norma Jeane and I . . .": Roy Turner interview with Ida Mae, 1981.

135   "The other girls rode . . .": Monroe, p. 22.

135   "In the thirties . . .": Spoto, p. 60.

135   "Norma Jeane was a nice . . .": Wolper documentary, *Legend*.

136   "My body was developing . . .": Monroe, p. 16.

136   "I didn't think of . . .": Ibid., p. 24.

137   "We danced until . . .": Spoto, p. 66.

137   The Anti-Nazi League: Nancy Schwartz, *Hollywood Writers' Wars*, p. 83.

138   Engelberg as number of the Arts Sciences and Professions Council: HUAC report, 1947.

138   The history of the Engelbergs' association with the Communist Party (CP) is documented in the archives of the Los Angeles CP and corroborated in a 1993 interview with Dorothy Healy, who was the Los Angeles CP chairman.

138   Dr. Oner Barker's testimony: HUAC report, 1947.

138   "I remember . . .": Schwartz, p. 89.

138   "The biggest mistake . . .": int., Dorothy Healy, 1993.

139   Niven's yacht party: Otto Friedrich, *City of Nets*, p. 28.

139   "By the summertime . . .": Monroe, p. 24.

Chapter 20

141   Fred Field and Communist Party activities: Field, *From Right to Left*; Klehr and Radosh, *The Amerasia Spy Case*; Howe and Coser, *The American Communist Party*.

141   "All-out aid to the . . .": Howe and Coser, p. 390.

141–42 "Hollywood made three hundred and fifty . . .": Friedrich, p. 34.

142   Dougherty at Lockheed: int., Dougherty, 1997.

142   "I was thirteen when . . .": int., Goddard, 1993.

142   "The dog had got . . .": Dougherty, p. 20.

143   "As I recall . . .": int., Goddard, 1993.

143   "What a Daddy . . .": int., Goddard, 1993.

143   Attack on Peal Harbor: Friedrich, p. 101.

144   "Even Grace and Doc . . .": Spoto, p. 70.

145   "Sometime in the early part of . . .": Dougherty, p. 23; int., Dougherty, 1997.

145   "We were both just . . .": int., Goddard; "Marilyn Remembered," #13, p. 8.

145   The wedding ceremony: Guiles, p. 44; int., Dougherty, 1997.

146   "Norma Jeane was delighted . . .": int., Dougherty, 1997; Dougherty, p. 36.

147   "The most vivid memory . . .": Dougherty, p. 46.

148   Dougherty's attempts to join the services: int., Dougherty, 1997; Dougherty, p. 50.

148   "With friends she . . .": int., Dougherty, 1997.

149   "It was a bad one . . .": Dougherty, pp. 51–52.

149   The move to Avalon: Ibid., pp. 53–55.

150   "Norma Jeane was very . . .": Ibid., p. 63.

150   Dougherty ships out: int., Dougherty, 1997.

Chapter 21

152   Jack and "Inga Binga": Lynne McTaggert, *Kathleen Kennedy—Her Life and Times*, pp. 103–114.

153   Surveillance of JFK and Arvad: J. Edgar Hoover's personal and confidential files—ARVAD.

154   Rear Admiral Wilkinson's concerns: Nigel Hamilton, *J.F.K.—Reckless Youth*, p. 439.

155   First motion picture unit at Roach: Friedrich, p. 154.

155   Conover at Radioplane: Conover, *Finding Marilyn*, pp. 3–12; Guiles, *Legend*, p. 83.

156   Letter to Grace: Bebe Goddard collection.

156   Norma Jeane's visit to Chicago: int., Bebe Goddard, 1993; Miracle, pp. 36–57.

157   "I would rather not . . .": From correspondence in the collection of Bebe Goddard.

158   "Norma Jeane had bought . . .": Dougherty, p. 71.

158   "On one of those last . . .": Dougherty, p. 73.

158   "I could have loved you once . . .": Monroe, *The Observer* (magazine), May 11, 1975.

Chapter 22

159   "They force me into a . . .": David Conover, *Finding Marilyn*, p. 36.

160   "Sundays were the loneliest . . .": Monroe, p. 35.

161   "You don't have to . . .": Ibid., p. 39.

161   Blue Book Modeling: Snively, *Los Angeles Daily News* February 4, 1954; Snively on Wolper documentary, *Legend*; Zolotow, *Marilyn Monroe*, p. 43.

162   Driving problems: int., Dougherty, 1997.

163   The Comintern's focus on Hollywood: Schwartz, pp. 223–227; William Z. Foster, *Toward Soviet America*, pp. 121–213; Harvey Klehr et al., *The Secret World of American Communism*, pp. 71–187.

163   It was Field who financed: HUAC Report, 1947.

163   Lawson, Engelberg, and Sorrell as instructors of the Peoples Education Center: archives of the Los Angeles Communist Party.

163   Another shadowy figure: According to Norman Jefferies, John Murray was a member of the Arts, Sciences, and Professions Council, and he is listed as such in the HUAC Report, 1947.

163   Murray as member of Communist Party, and with Sorrell, organizers of the Conference of Studio Unions: int., Jefferies, 1993; L.A. Civil Case # 446193.

164   Lawson's objective: "As for myself," Lawson wrote in *New Theatre* magazine, "I do not hesitate to say that it is my aim to present the communist position and to do so in the most specific manner"; Otto Friedrich, *City of Nets*, p. 73.

164   Warner Bros. battle: Schwartz, pp. 227–229.

165   "Jack [John] Murray was a strange . . .": int., Jefferies, 1993.

Chapter 23

166   Sigmund Freud was twelve: Ernest Jones, *The Life and Work of Sigmund Freud.* vol. I, p. 22.

166   Dr. Henry Lowenfeld: Otto Friedrich, *Before the Deluge*, p. 371.

167   The history of the Freudian-Marxist immigration to America; Otto Friedrich, pp. 221–224; Russell Jacoby, *The Repression of Psychoanalysis: Otto Fenichel and the Political Freudians*, pp. 118–133; O. Fenichel, *Über die Psychoanalyse als Keim einer Zukunftigen dialektisch-materialistischen Psychologics* (1934), pp. 43–62. (*Psy-*

choanalysis as the Nucleus of a Future Dialectical-Materialistic Psychology).

168 The *Rundbriefe* of Otto Fenichel: Many of the *Rundbriefe* are in the possession of Randi Markowitz and the estate of Hanna Fenichel Pitkin. Some of the Fenichel papers are at the YIVO Institute for Jewish Research in New York. Ernst Simmel's papers are held in the Library of the Los Angeles Psychoanalytic Society and Institute, and in the Special Collections of the UCLA Library.

168 Shortly after he arrived: Albert Kandelin, "The Psychoanalytic Study Group," *Los Angeles Psychoanalytic Society and Institute*, vol. 6, no. 4, February 1970.

169 Another person who: Greenson's memories of the Study Group are included in his oral history, transcribed among the Greenson Papers, Special Collections, UCLA Library.

169 Ralph Greenson's background: Farber and Green, pp. 86–90; Greenson Oral History, Special Collections Department, UCLA Library.

170 Brownsville section of Brooklyn: Alter F. Landesman, *Brownsville: The Birth, Development and Raising of a Jewish Community in New York*; Frommer, *Growing Up Jewish in America*.

171 P.S. 149: archives of the Danny Kaye School.

171 Hurok and Kate Greenschpoon: S. Hurok, *Impresario*, p. 24; Farber and Green, p. 86; Landesman, p. 344.

171 "The Red District . . .": Landesman, p. 7.

172 "large Colonial home . . .": Greenson oral history; Special Collections Department, UCLA Library.

172 Greenson's attendance at Seth Low: Seth Low archives at the Columbia University Library.

172 Greenson's studies in Europe: Farber and Green, p. 87; Greenson oral history, Special Collections Department, UCLA Library.

173 Greenson's army experience: Ibid.

174 "At this time Colonel Murray comes . . .": Greenson papers, Special Collections Department, UCLA Library.

174 "She was drawn . . .": Murray, p. 7.

175 Colonel John M. Murray's background: Boston Psychoanalytic Institute Library.

Chapter 24

176 de Dienes hires Norma Jeane: de Dienes, *Marilyn Mon Amour*, p. 17.

176 "In one fell swoop . . .": Ibid., p. 17.

177 "She still seemed . . .": Snively quoted by Ted Thackrey in *Los Angeles Herald-Examiner*, August 7, 1962.

177 Driving off in de Dienes's: de Dienes, p. 51.

178 The visit with Gladys: Ibid., p. 69.

178 "She was an hour late": int., Dougherty, 1997; Dougherty, pp. 86–87.

179 "She would show me . . .": Ibid., p. 89.

179 "Catalina was wonderful . . .": Ibid., p. 96.

180 Early modeling days: int., Joe Jasqur, 1996; Earl Moran, "A Marilyn for all Seasons," *Life*, vol. 6, no. 7, 1983.

180 By February 1946: int., Bebe Goddard, 1993, 1998.

180 Norma Jeane as blonde: Zolotow, p. 45; Snively interview on Wolper documentary, *Legend*.

Chapter 25

183 "All actors and actresses . . .": Monroe, pp. 39–40.

183 Harry Lipton and MM: Lipton int. on Wolper documentary, *Legend*.

184 "Hey, your old lady's divorcing you . . .": Dougherty, p. 98; int., Dougherty, 1997.

185 Young Robert Slatzer: int., Slatzer, 1996.

185 "What kind of book . . .": int., Slatzer, 1996; Slatzer, *The Life and Curious Death of Marilyn Monroe*, p. 70.

186 Knocking a name: contained in the Chuck Spalding interview among the Nigel Hamilton papers at the Massachusetts Historical Society, Boston.

186 Tierney and JFK: Gene Tierney, *Self-Portrait*, pp. 141–156.

187 "Making it with the ice-skating . . .": Red Fay interview among Nigel Hamilton papers at the Massachusetts Historical Society, Boston.

187 "I first met Norma Jeane . . .": Robert Stack, *Straight Shooting*, p. 84.

187 Hughes escaped death: Zolotow, p. 48.

187 "Howard Hughes is on . . .": *Los Angeles Times*, July 29, 1946.

188 Marilyn Monroe's screen test: Zolotow, p. 49; Monroe, pp. 53–54.

Chapter 26

193 Marilyn Monroe's early days at Fox: Guiles, *Legend*, pp. 85–86; Zolotow, pp. 50–51; int., Whitey Snyder, 1993.

194 Roy Craft interview: Zolotow, p. 53.

194   Gladys at Aunt Ana's: Miracle, pp. 67–75.

194   "I keep telling myself . . .": Ibid., p. 68.

194   Shortly after Berniece: Berniece speaks of a salesman who was a
        tenant in Aunt Ana's apartment, possibly John Stewart Eley, who
        was from West Los Angeles.

195   The visit to Barrymore's: int., Slatzer, 1993, 1997; Slatzer, *The Life
        and Curious Death of Marilyn Monroe,"* p. 106. The author was
        a friend of Hugo Grimaldi, who purchased the Barrymore home
        at auction in 1946. Grimaldi recounted the visit of Marilyn Mon-
        roe and Bob Slatzer to the Barrymore mansion on several occa-
        sions.

195   "One night a bit player . . .": Monroe, p. 56.

196   Feldman knew Joe Kennedy: Blair and Blair, *The Search for J.F.K.*,
        pp. 505–506. The Blairs' interviews with Feldman's wife, Jean,
        Betty Spalding, and Red Fay are contained within the Nigel
        Hamilton papers at the Massachusetts Historical Society, Boston.

197   "What do I do to become . . .": Brown and Barham, *Marilyn*, p. 20.

197   Schenck, Bioff, and Rosselli: Rappleye and Becker, *All American
        Mafioso*, pp. 101–102.

197   Marilyn and Schenck: Guiles, *Norma Jean*, p. 85.

198   "The first fame . . .": Monroe, p. 61.

199   "Now just walk up . . .": Ibid., p. 54.

199   "There were a dozen of us . . .": Ibid., p. 54.

Chapter 27

200   Skolsky and the Schwabadero: Shelley Winters, *Shelley*, p. 93; Ezra
        Goodman, *The Fifty-Year Decline and Fall of Hollywood*, pp. 46–
        47.

201   "That's the Actors Lab . . .": Winters, p. 93.

201   The Group Theatre, Hannah Weinstein, and the Arts, Sciences, and
        Professions Council: Walter Bernstein, *Inside Out* p. 245; Jay
        Williams, *Stage Left*, pp. 203–219.

201   "I never knew what . . .": Zolotow, *Marilyn Monroe*, p. 62.

202   "All I could think . . .": from the Milton Greene papers, folder 16,
        file 4, p. 19.

202   "I got called into . . .": Monroe, p. 61.

203   "That's the way you feel . . .": Ibid., p. 62.

203   Rosselli and Joe Kennedy: Rappleye, pp. 96, 202.

Chapter 28

206   "White Fang": Goodman, p. 177.

207 "She was utterly unsure . . .": Lytess, unpublished memoir, Special Collections Department, University of Texas, Austin.

207 Marilyn and Natasha: Zolotow, p. 64.

207 Much of the background of Natasha Lytess (née Liesl Massary) is drawn from the author's memory as a Lytess student in 1956–1957.

208 In mid-March: Guiles, *Legend*, p. 131.

209 Marilyn attends Lower services: int., Goddard, 1993.

209 "I went and lay down . . .": Miller, *Timebends*, p. 359.

209 Marilyn and Karger: Guiles, *Legend*, p. 126; Monroe, p. 74; Summers, p. 265.

210 For Marilyn the Studio Club: Slatzer, *The Life and Curious Death of Marilyn Monroe*, p. 145; Zolotow, p. 66.

210 *Ladies of the Chorus*: Guiles, *Legend*, p. 136.

211 Marilyn and Cohn: Monroe, pp. 63–66, p. 291.

Chapter 29

214 "I lay in bed . . .": Monroe, p. 72.

214 Nana Karger's advice: Guiles, *Legend*, p. 39.

215 "I sat alone thinking . . .": Monroe, p. 75.

215 "It was while I lay . . .": Ibid., p. 76.

215 Marilyn and Freddy's romance: Summers, p. 42; Zolotow, *Marilyn Monroe*, p. 67.

216 "I've thought of us getting married . . .": Monroe, p. 78.

216 Freddy's gift: Ibid., pp. 82–83.

217 The audition for Groucho: Monroe, pp. 80–81.

Chapter 30

219 Pooled their poverty: int., Slatzer, 1993, 1997.

220 Tom Kelley's calendar photos: Guiles, *Legend*, p. 143.

220 "You're going to be a great star . . .": Monroe, p. 87.

221 "There's a part in John Huston's . . .": Ibid., p. 88.

222 "Johnny Hyde brought me . . .": Ibid., p. 88.

222 "It's a nice sensation . . .": Ibid., 92.

223 Another person whose star was: int., Daryl Gates, 1995; int., Vince Carter, 1995.

223 The Albro story: Carter, pp. 74–76; int., Daryl Gates, 1995; int., Jack Clemmons, 1995.

Chapter 31

225 "The person I wanted . . .": Monroe, p. 107.

226   "When I passed by . . .": Ibid., p. 108.

226   Marilyn's suicide attempt: Summers, p. 48; Lytess, p. 14.

227   "From where I stood . . .": Miller, *Timebends*, p. 303.

227   "Cohn could hardly . . .": Ibid., p. 304.

227   "her hair hung down . . .": Ibid., p. 307.

228   "In the 1950s . . .": Victor Navasky, *Naming Names*, pp. 200–207.

228   When John and Eunice Murray: int., Jefferies, 1993.

228   While Dr. Greenson: archives of the Los Angeles Communist Party;
       int. Dorothy Healy, 1993.

229   "Jews were embracing . . .": Miller, *Timebends*, p. 313.

229   "in strangely meandering . . .": Ibid., p. 328.

230   "There was no hiding . . .": Monroe, p. 109.

230   Marilyn and Chekhov: Guiles, *Legend*, pp. 185–187.

231   Marilyn tracked down her father: Ibid., p. 183; Summers's tran-
       scripts of interviews with Gifford's family, 1989.

Chapter 32

234   *Clash By Night*: Zolotow, *Marilyn Monroe*, pp. 112–115.

234   Harry Brand and the calendar: Slatzer, *Life and Curious Death of
       Marilyn Monroe*. pp. 210–211.

235   "Success came to me in . . .": Monroe, p. 115.

235   "Miss Monroe, this is Joe DiMaggio . . .": Monroe, p. 126.

236   "Would you mind . . .": Ibid., p. 128.

236   "Dear Dr. Rabwin . . .": from the archives of a private collector.

236   Whitey's promise: int., Snyder, 1993.

237   she called Slatzer: int., Slatzer, 1995; Summers, p. 88.

238   "Voice of Broadway," *New York Journal-American*, September 12,
       1952; the fact that Kilgallen cleared Slatzer's column with Mar-
       ilyn was confirmed by a Kilgallen aide, Eddie Jaffe, in a 1996
       interview.

238   In a taped video interview made in 1972, Noble Chissell describes
       his participation in the wedding ceremony; int., Slatzer, 1995.

238   "It was pure chance . . .": Summers, p. 77.

238   On the way back from: int., Slatzer, 1996.

238   "I remember very well . . .": Summers, p. 76.

239   "I was making more . . .": Monroe, p. 116.

239   *How to Marry a Millionaire*: Guiles, *Legend*, pp. 221–224; Zolotow,
       Marilyn Monroe, pp. 176–185.

240   Conflicts with Preminger: Zolotow, *Marilyn Monroe*, pp. 186–191.

241   "I wonder if I can take . . .": Monroe, pp. 136–138.

Chapter 33
242   The honeymoon: Guiles, *Legend*, pp. 237–239.
242   "We took a helicopter": Monroe, pp. 142–143.
243   The injury: Summers, p. 111; *Los Angeles Times*, January 30, 1954.
243   "Sidney, do you know who...": Skolsky, *Don't Get Me Wrong*, p. 213.
244   The DiMaggios and the Kennedys: Summers, pp. 215–216; Slatzer, *The Marilyn Files*, pp. 28–29.
244   When Jack Kennedy was hospitalized: Summers, p. 215.
245   neighbors at the St. Regis: Summers, p. 103; Zolotow, *Marilyn Monroe*, p. 214.
245   News of separation: *Los Angeles Times*, October 4 and 5, 1954.
246   *Itch* party: *Hollywood Citizen-News*, November 9, 1954; *Life*, November 29, 1954.
246   Marilyn and Milton Greene: Guiles, *Legend*, pp. 231, 232, 259, 260.

Chapter 34
251   "This sad and bitter child...": Monroe, p. 31.
252   "She finally did come out": Kotsilibas-Davis, *Milton's Marilyn*, p. 40.
253   Edward R. Murrow: *Person to Person*, April 8, 1955.
253   "We will go into...": *New York Times*, January 8, 1955.
253   The move to the Gladstone: James Haspiel, *Marilyn: The Ultimate Look at the Legend*, p. 47.
254   "Now they reach my...": Rosten, pp. 11–12.
255   "Oh, yes, there is something...": Truman Capote, *Music For Chameleons*, p. 227.
255   Actors Studio and Strasberg: Adams, *Imperfect Genius*, pp. 254–279; Zolotow, *Marilyn Monroe*, p. 265; Summers, p. 129.
256   "I no longer knew...": Miller, *Timebends*, p. 356.

Chapter 35
257   Celebrity Circus: int., Jimmy Haspiel, 1995; Haspiel, p. 54.
258   "She was a...": Miller, *Timebends*, p. 359.
258   Marilyn Monroe's FBI file clearly indicates that she and Arthur Miller were put under surveillance in 1955.
259   "Easily the most curious...": int., Haspiel, 1996.
259   Brando, Rosenfeld, and Karger: Summers, pp. 142–143.
259   "I saw Marilyn...": Summers, p. 223.

260   "It's me . . .": Rosten, pp. 27–28.

Chapter 36
261   The background of Lee Strasberg and the Actors Studio: Cindy
        Adams, *Lee Strasberg: The Imperfect Genius of the Actors Studio*;
        Kazan, *A Life*.
262   "This tousled piece . . .": Summers, p. 130.
262   Marilyn chose "I'll Get By": Strasberg, *Marilyn and Me*, p. 83.
263   Marilyn and Hohenberg: int., Haspiel, 1995; Spoto, p. 384.
264   "Don't talk to me . . .": Guiles, *Legend*, p. 268.
264   "With her open . . .": Miller, *Timebends*, p. 326.
265   *Seven Year Itch* premiere: int., Haspiel, 1995.
265   "We're just good friends . . .": *New York Journal-American*, June 2,
        1955.
265   Marilyn's victory over Fox: Zolotow, *Marilyn Monroe*, p. 266.
266   "Miller was in love . . .": int., Rosten, 1994.
266   "Saw Marilyn M. and . . .": Gerald Clarke, A *Biography—Capote*,
        p. 269.

Chapter 37
267   The press conference: *Time*, vol. 67, no. 8, February 20, 1956, p. 94;
        Summers, p. 146.
268   *Anna Christie*: Zolotow, *Marilyn Monroe*, p. 270; Strasberg, *Marilyn
        and Me*, p. 99.
268   "She was so terrified . . .": Strasberg, *Marilyn and Me*, p. 99.
268   "I couldn't see anything . . .": *Redbook*, February 1958, p. 96.
269   "Very deep and . . .": Kobal, *People Will Talk*, p. 140.
269   Marilyn's return to Hollywood: Summers, p. 167.
269   Dressing room: Dorothy Manning, *Photoplay*, October 1956.
270   When she finally appeared: *Time*, May 14, 1956.
270   Lytess problems: Lytess, p. 27.
271   "It was the last time . . .": Lytess, p. 28.
271   The author was a Lytess student during the difficult years following
        her dismissal from Fox. Lytess lost her Beverly Hills home in fore-
        closure in 1957.
271   "She was begging for . . .": int., Slatzer, 1997.
272   Preparing for Cherie: Zolotow, *Marilyn Monroe*, p. 276; Logan,
        Movie Stars, Real People, and Me, pp. 42–55.

Chapter 38
276   "During the rodeo . . .": Summers, p. 153.

276 Carmen Adams Newcomb: "Who's Who in Washington," 1938.

276 Pat Newcomb's educational background is on file with the Mills College Alumni Association, and Pierre Salinger's credentials at Mills are included in the Salinger oral history at the Kennedy Library.

277 "I shall never forget . . .": Salinger, *With Kennedy*, p. 29.

277 "We arrived in Los Angeles . . .": Robert Kennedy, *The Enemy Within*, p. 20.

277 "At the invitation of . . .": int., Daryl Gates, 1996.

277 Newcomb's dismissal: Summers, p. 154; Allan interview on file at the Library of the Academy of Motion Picture Arts and Sciences, 1992.

278 "His weekend visits to the . . .": Patten, *Life at the Marmont*, p. 160.

278 Arthur Miller's stay at Quail Canyon: Goode, *The Story of the Misfits*, p. 17.

278 "Once a week I . . .": Miller, *Timebends*, p. 378.

279 "Like a child . . .": Guy Trebay, *Interview*, October 1973, p. 21.

280 "I can't do it . . .": Miller, *Timebends*, p. 379.

280 "I suddenly saw that . . .": Miller, *Timebends*, p. 380.

Chapter 39

281 Miller called before HUAC: Guiles, *Legend*, pp. 299–303.

282 "When I opened . . .": Miller, pp. 401–404.

283 Miller and the Committee: *New York Times*, June 22, 1956; *Chicago Tribune*, June 25, 1956.

283 "You can't let those bastards . . .": Summers, p. 158.

284 that damned communist: int., Lena Pepitone, 1994.

284 "Have you heard?": int., Rosten, 1994.

285 "I believe in everything . . .": Strasberg, *Marilyn and Me*, p. 112.

285 Reporters waiting for wedding news: int., Haspiel, 1997; Zolotow, *Marilyn Monroe*, pp. 287–292.

286 Second thoughts: Spoto, p. 365.

287 *After the Fall* excerpt: pp. 60–61.

288 "On this day . . .": Rosten, p. 37.

Chapter 40

289 "First of all . . .": Logan, p. 50.

290 "The camera flashes . . .": Miller, *Timebends*, p. 413.

290 "Cold as a refrigerated . . .": Zolotow, *Marilyn Monroe*, p. 298.

291 "By the end . . .": Olivier, *Confessions of an Actor*, p. 206.

291   Leigh's problems: Alexander Walker, *Vivien: The Life of Vivien Leigh*, pp. 204–217.

293   "Paula's presence alarmed . . .": Olivier, p. 208.

293   "Marilyn was not used to . . .": Ibid., p. 208.

294   "All you have to do is be sexy . . .": Spoto, p. 370; Strasberg, *Marilyn and Me*, p. 117.

294   "Her manner to me . . .": Olivier, *Confessions*, p. 204.

295   "My dear, you mustn't concern . . .": Colin Clark, *The Prince, the Showgirl and Me*, p. 104.

295   "Wednesday, 15 August": Ibid., p. 111.

295   "She came to believe that . . .": Miller, *Timebends*, p. 418.

296   "I refused to . . .": Olivier, p. 209.

297   difficult wives: Walker, pp. 208–210.

297   Miller, Olivier, and Osborne: Miller, *Timebends*, p. 417.

297   "Sunday, 19 August": Clark, p. 116.

298   Sammy Davis, Jr., was: Sammy Davis, Jr., *Hollywood in a Suitcase*, p. 238.

299   Jacqueline Kennedy rushed to hospital: C. David Heymann, *A Woman Named Jackie*, pp. 190–191.

299   The notebook revealed: Bart Mills, *Marilyn on Location*, p. 108; Spoto, p. 371; Strasberg, *Marilyn and Me*, p. 122.

299   *After the Fall*: Miller, p. 75.

300   "Monday, 27 August": Clark, pp. 127, 129.

301   "Wednesday, 19 September": Ibid., pp. 146–147.

301   "Friday, 12 October": Ibid., p. 172.

Chapter 41

304   "Soon there was a routine . . .": Miller, p. 445.

304   "Upon their return . . .": Rosten, p. 45.

304   "The survival of . . .": Rollynson, p. 138.

305   "We walked the empty . . .": Miller, *Timebends*, p. 457.

305   "Marilyn went over . . .": int., Haspiel, 1997; Haspiel, p. 146.

305   "In a bid to . . .": *New York Times*, April 12, 1957; int., Robert Montgomery, 1997.

306   "It seems that Marilyn . . .": *Los Angeles Times*, April 12, 1957.

306   "She gave a star performance . . .": Olivier, *Confessions*, p. 213.

306   "She was ultrasensitive . . .": *Los Angeles Herald-Examiner*, August 5, 1982.

307   Marianne Kris: Gargan, "Tribute to Marianne Kris," *New York Times*, December 8, 1980; Kris obituary, *New York Times*, November 25, 1980.

307   "a crown with a thousand diamonds . . ."; Miller, *Timebends*, p. 457.
308   "She lay there beyond sadness . . .": Ibid. p. 458.

Chapter 42
309   "This farmhouse is . . .": Guiles, *Legend*, p. 325.
310   Lorraine went up in flames: Miller, *Timebends*, p. 326.
311   "What is it, dear?": Rosten, p. 46.
312   "With *The Misfits* . . .": Miller, *Timebends*, p. 460.
312   "There is no word to describe . . .": Guiles, *Legend*, p. 333.
312   *After the Fall*: Miller, *Timebends*, p. 78.
313   "After she was revived . . .": Guiles, *Legend*, p. 333.
313   "She seemed to be . . .": Pepitone, p. 97.

Chapter 43
314   "Another stupid blonde . . .": Pepitone, p. 128.
315   "Money! All he cares about is . . .": Ibid., p. 130.
315   "I've got a real problem . . .": Guiles, *Legend*, p. 339.
316   "Should I do my next . . .": Rosten, p. 76.
317   "She had a tremendous sense of . . .": Guiles, *Legend*, p. 342.
318   "Cut. You still haven't got it . . .": Ibid., p. 343.
318   The author was working at Goldwyn Studios during the production
         of *Some Like It Hot*, and was on the set during the filming of
         the flask sequence.
319   "I never heard such . . .": *The Listener* (London), August 30, 1979.
319   The constant flubs: as observed by author.
319   "Marilyn was constantly late . . .": Spoto, p. 399.
319   "Well, I think that's . . .": Marilyn Monroe to Richard Meryman,
         July 1962.
320   "Where's the bourbon?": I. A. L. Diamond, "The Day Marilyn
         Needed 47 Takes to Remember to Say, 'Where's the Bourbon?' "
         California, vol. 10, no. 12, December 1985, pp. 132–135; Zolo-
         tow, *Marilyn Monroe*, p. 322.
320   The bourbon bit was observed by the author on the set.
321   "Twenty-nine days over . . .": Zolotow, *Marilyn Monroe*, p. 324.
322   "I'm eating better . . .": Ibid., p. 325.
322   "I made *him* sick?": Pepitone, p. 139.
323   It had been another close call: Rosten, p. 75.

Chapter 44
324   "The pupil/student had . . .": Rosten, p. 79.
324   "She would read . . .": Miller, *Timebends*, p. 461.

325　　"Marilyn was getting . . .": Pepitone, p. 119.

325　　"If she was so . . .": Pepitone, p. 132.

325　　"I'm not sure I . . .": Gene Tierney, *Self-Portrait*, p. 147.

326　　that big tease: Pepitone, p. 238.

327　　Carl Sandburg and Marilyn Monroe: *Look*, vol. 26, September 11, 1962, pp. 90–94.

327　　Montand and Signoret: Guiles, *Legend*, p. 362.

328　　When Gregory Peck: Ibid., p. 365.

328　　"She was always on time . . .": Hutchinson, *Marilyn Monroe*, p. 74.

328　　"If I can realize . . .": Georges Belmont, *Marilyn Monroe and the Camera Eye*, p. 21.

329　　At a dinner party: Rosten, p. 55.

329　　Greenson/Kris correspondence: Greenson papers, Special Collections Department, UCLA Library.

329　　"According to . . . Hildi . . .": Lucy Freeman, *Why Norma Jean Killed Marilyn Monroe*, p. 1.

330　　Dr. Greenson found: Summers, p. 188; Farber and Green, *Hollywood on the Couch*, p. 93.

331　　"As she becomes more . . .": Summers, p. 189.

331　　"My Jesus—My Savior": Pepitone, p. 206.

Chapter 45

335　　"She still has . . .": *Hollywood Citizen-News*, Jan., 20, 1960.

335　　"Next to my husband . . .": *Look*, July 5, 1960, p. 96.

335　　"Everything she do is . . .": Ibid.

336　　"If I was thinking of . . .": Montand, p. 316.

336　　"You know, Cukor's not . . .": Ibid., p. 318.

336　　"I would knock . . .": Ibid., p. 319.

336　　"I guess it . . .": Guiles, *Legend*, p. 370.

337　　"She's got so . . .": Montand, p. 311.

337　　"Such a perpetual orphan . . .": Greenson papers, Special Collections Department, UCLA Library.

337　　Another Ralph in . . . : int. Roberts, 1998.

338　　"I'll miss you": Montand, p. 323.

338　　"He's leaving me with Marilyn . . .": Guiles, *Legend*, p. 371.

340　　"I couldn't help her . . .": Guiles, *Legend*, p. 371.

340　　"Montand wasn't the only one . . .": int., Rosten, 1994; Summers, p. 185.

340　　"I was touched . . .": Montand, p. 327.

Chapter 46

342   "He was very taken . . .": Kessler, *The Sins of the Father*, p. 314.

343   "Hell, Janet, Jack isn't . . .": Ibid., p. 377.

343   "I got into the . . .": Ibid., p. 378.

343   Sinatra and Giancana: Kitty Kelley, *His Way*, pp. 263–267.

343   "Frank wanted to be . . .": Ibid., p. 265.

344   "I'm not going to talk about . . .": Ibid., p. 269.

344   "It is a known fact . . .": The statement is included in Peter Lawford's FBI file.

344   Describing the visit: Judith Exner, *My Story*, pp. 80–95.

344   "I sat next to Teddy . . .": Ibid., p. 86.

345   The West Virginia primaries: Kelley, pp. 270–271; Kessler, pp. 375–376; Hersh, *The Dark Side of Camelot*, pp. 95–101.

345   the "Marilyn Monroe problem": Hersh, p. 104.

345   MM joins the Kennedy bandwagon: Summers, pp. 218–220.

346   "he was the mastermind . . .": Kessler, p. 383.

346   Pucini's: int., Detective John St. John, 1993.

347   After the Coliseum: Ibid., p. 211.

347   "I couldn't get the drift . . .": Summers, p. 221.

Chapter 47

350   Marilyn arrives in Reno: James Goode, *The Story of the Misfits*, p. 19.

350   Trouble with the wig: int., Guilaroff, 1996.

351   "Desperately unhappy at . . .": Spoto, p. 533.

351   Rumors quickly spread: Guiles, *Legend*, p. 386.

351   "She was very late . . .": Ibid., p. 380.

351   "Astonishingly beautiful": McIntyre, *Esquire*, March 1961.

352   "*La femme eternelle*": Goode, p. 101.

352   "Why is it that . . . ": Gregory and Speriglio, p. 134.

352   Gable's heart condition: Ibid., pp. 134,135; int., Whitey Snyder, 1994.

352   Clift's problems: Patricia Bosworth, *Montgomery Clift—A Biography*, p. 315.

353   Seeds of discord: Guiles, *Legend*, p. 389.

353   "I told them that . . .": Ibid., p. 383.

353   "I went to Reno . . .": Strasberg, *Marilyn and Me*, p. 215.

354   "I can't tolerate this . . .": Strasberg, *Marilyn and Me*, p. 218.

354   Circled the flagons: int., Ralph Roberts, 1998.

354   "Marilyn sat on a . . .": Strasberg, *Marilyn and Me*, p. 210.

354   Sinatra invited Marilyn: int., Ralph Roberts, 1998.

355   Sinatra's acquisition of Cal-Neva: Kelley, pp. 314–317.

355   The Kennedys at Cal-Neva: int., Bill Roemer, 1994, 1996; Lawford's
       FBI file.

355   "talk to Marilyn Monroe": Hersh, p. 104.

355   Marilyn taken to Westside: Goode, p. 124; Summers, p. 194.

356   "Her incredible resilience . . .": Miller, *Timebends*, p. 485.

356   The last scene at Paramount: Guiles, *Legend*, pp. 391,392.

Chapter 48

357   "Mr. President, with a bit . . .": Bradlee, *Conversations with Ken-
       nedy*, pp. 33, 151; Reeves, *A Question of Character*, p. 214.

358   Bobby's appointment: Reeves, pp. 225–226.

359   "What happened was . . .": Hersh, p. 104.

359   Smathers recalled . . . : Ibid., p. 105.

359   "If anything untoward . . .": Arthur Schlesinger, Jr., *A Thousand
       Days: John F. Kennedy in the White House.* p. 392.

359   Code name: Summers, p. 287.

360   Sinatra and Grace Kelly: Sarah Bradford, *Princess Grace*, p. 393.

360   The imminent divorce . . . Guiles, *Legend*, p. 396.

360   "He really wants to . . .": Pepitone, p. 180.

360   "Oh, God, why . . .": Ibid., p. 181.

361   "She was so gentle . . .": Ibid., p. 182.

361   "No, no—let me die . . .": Ibid., p. 183.

362   "Frank Sinatra and his . . .": Miller, *Timebends*, p. 510.

363   "withdrawing like a sick . . .": Strasberg, *Marilyn and Me*, p. 224.

363   Driven to hospital: Marilyn's stay at Payne Whitney is related in
       Guiles, *Legend*; Spoto, *Marilyn Monroe: The Biography*; Pepitone,
       Marilyn Monroe Confidential; and Norman Rosten, *Marilyn: An Un-
       told Story*.

364   "It was like a . . .": Summers, p. 228.

364   The letter to the Strasbergs is quoted in Guiles, *Legend*, p. 402.

364   "take the hospital apart . . .": Rosten, p. 93.

364   "Marilyn began screaming . . .": int., Ralph Roberts, 1993, 1998;
       Strasberg, *Marilyn and Me*, p. 227.

365   "he was under terrific . . .": Reeves, p. 260.

365   "I remember that he . . .": George Smathers, Oral History, JFK Li-
       brary.

365   "the least covert military operation . . .": Pierre Salinger, Oral History, JFK Library.

366   Castro assassination plot: Reeves, p. 277; Church Committee, Interim Report, pp. 149–176.

366   Another person who: int., Robert Slatzer, 1994, 1997; Slatzer, *The Marilyn Files*, pp. 53,55.

366   Marilyn's note-taking: int., James Bacon, 1994; Summers, p. 123. Amy Greene told Summers: "Marilyn bought a small leather-covered diary, one with a clasp and a tiny key. She would carry it around the house making notes on conversations and magazine articles that caught her interest."

366   of concern to CIA: It was counterintelligence chief Angleton who signed the CIA Monroe surveillance document. (See page 469.)

366   "completely dependent upon . . .": Pepitone, p. 208.

367   "As a great intellect . . .": Freeman, p. 67.

367   "This is my baby . . .": Pepitone, p. 193.

Chapter 49

370   Hannah Weinstein and "Little Red Robin Hood": Bernstein, p. 249.

370   Fox and Selznick and Weinstein: Rudy Behlmer, *Memo from David O. Selznick*, pp. 444–468.

370   When Weinstein arrived: Winters II, p. 430.

370   "pathetic yessing sessions": Behlmer, p. 463.

370   "Money by itself . . .": *New York Times*, July 18, 1960.

371   Brad Dexter and Sinatra: Kelley, pp. 334, 355.

371   "They were friends . . .": int., Dexter, 1998.

371   "We were having . . .": int., Carmen, 1998.

372   Roberts became: int., Roberts, 1993, 1997.

372   The doctor/patient relationship: Slatzer, *The Life and Curious Death of Marilyn Monroe*, pp. 146–147.

373   "I made his back feel . . .": int., Roberts, 1993, 1998; Roberts interview on canceled 20/20 segment.

373   "Elizabeth and I . . .": Fisher, p. 203.

374   "For several months . . .": Miracle, p. 148.

374   "I can't finish this . . .": Ibid., p. 164.

375   "I told him . . .": Rosten, p. 91.

375   "Frankie wouldn't expect . . .": Pepitone, p. 227.

376   "Marilyn flew into the room . . .": Ibid., p. 228.

376   "She was very open . . .": int., Carmen, 1997.

377   "After the party . . .": Summers, p. 266.

377   "He was very nice . . .": Rosten, p. 119.

377   "Frank would smile . . .": Kelley, p. 291.

378   Sinatra's visit to the White House: Kelley, pp. 291–293.

379   Rosselli/Giancana wiretap: From the Giancana files of the FBI.

379   "Dr. Greenson thinks you . . .": int., Roberts, 1993, 1998.

380   "My name is Eunice Murray": Murray, p. 12.

Chapter 50

381   "primarily to drive Marilyn . . .": Murray, p. 13; Spoto, p. 592.

382   "I wasn't crazy about . . .": Slatzer, *Marilyn Files*, p. 69.

382   "I do dishes very well . . .": Freeman, p. 16.

382   Danny as a member of SLATE: Capell, p. 71; Report of Un-American Activities in Calif., 1961.

383   Cultural pleasures: Freeman, p. 18; Greenson Oral History, Greenson Papers, Special Collections Dept. UCLA Library.

383   Unorthodox therapeutic procedure: Freeman, pp. 25, 26.

384   Dr. Greenson maintained: int., Jefferies, 1993.

384   Several appeals have been filed over a period of years with the FBI Freedom of Information Act to review the highly redacted Greenson File. Thus far the FBI has not responded to the appeal process.

384   Under Greenson's coordination: Greenson's involvement in the Hollywood Writers Mobilization was confirmed by an associate of Greenson's who attended many of the Writers Mobilization meetings. Noted in Greenson's FBI file.

384   At a hearing of the Un-American Activities Committee, Louis Budenz, former editor of the *Daily Worker*, named Frederick Vanderbilt Field as a Soviet agent and the fund-raiser for the Arts, Sciences, and Professions Committee. On pages 219–220 of his book, *Men Without Faces*, Budenz describes the organization of the Writers Mobilization at UCLA, stating, "They had ordered the comrades in the Writers Mobilization, led by John Howard Lawson, to work out a Writers Congress. Under the direction of Trachtenberg, Jerome and the Politburo, the comrades of the Coast had persuaded Dr. Robert Sproul, president of the University of California, to lend them the campus for a meeting place and let them use the university's name as a co-sponsor. . . ."

384   the National Arts, Sciences, and Professions: Budenz, p. 219.

385   Dr. Oner Barker's testimony regarding Dr. Engelberg is found on

page 266 of the Un-American Activities in California Report of 1948. Dr. Engelberg is named as a principal speaker at the Thought Control Conference, held on July 11, 1947, by the Hollywood Arts, Sciences, and Professions Committee; HUAC 1948 Report, p. 346.

385 One of the expatriates: Norman Jefferies stated that the association between the Murrays and Field began sometime in the forties and that Eunice Murray corresponded with Field during the fifties and for several years after Marilyn's death. In a letter to genealogist Roy Turner, dated in 1968, Eunice Murray talks about a recent correspondence with "Fred Field." Field discusses his association with Churchill and Eunice Murray in his book *From Right to Left*, pp. 295–305.

386 The Capell quotation: Capell, *The Strange Death of Marilyn Monroe*, addenda, p. 71.

386 Testimony regarding psychoanalysts: Senate Fact Finding Committee Report, 1947.

387 "Marilyn lived a myth . . .": Murray, p. 152.

Chapter 51

388–89 Fox commitments behind her: Summers, pp. 267, 268.

389 Greenson's involvement with production: Brown and Barham, p. 47; Fox memos from the Brown Archives.

389 David Brown and Weinstein: D. Brown, *Let Me Entertain You*, pp. 54, 55.

389 "So you think you can get . . .": D. Brown, p. 55.

390 The Kennedy Library retains the correspondence file of John Loeb and Samuel Rosenman; Rosenman obituary, *New York Times*, June 25, 1973.

390 In the Manhattan Corporate Records Department of the State of New York, Joe Kennedy is listed as one of the founding partners, and Gould is listed as an officer of Rhoades and Company.

390 "She went through a severe . . .": Summers, p. 243.

391 "DiMaggio seemed doting . . .": Ibid., p. 243.

391 House hunting with Murray: Murray, p. 33; *Redbook*, August 1962.

391 Hanna Fenichel's address and phone number at 12403 Third Helena Drive were accidentally discovered in a book from the Greenson Library donated to the San Diego Psychoanalytic Institute. That she was living there in 1962 was confirmed by neighbors.

392   "Off the record . . .": Newcomb tape in the Special Collections Department of the Academy of Motion Picture Arts and Sciences Library.

392   "Goddamnit, I'm going . . .": Summers, p. 244.

393   "Guess who's standing next . . .": Ibid., p. 247.

393   "Marilyn would follow . . .": int., Bacon.

393   "Marilyn Monroe stayed just . . .": int., Mack McSwane, 1998.

393   MM's visit to Mexico: Murray, chapters 6 and 7; Field, chapter 29.

394   "Marilyn's companion, Mrs. Eunice . . .": Field, p. 295.

394   Bolaños as friend of E. Howard Hunt: Dalton Trumbo papers, Special Collection Department, UCLA Library.

395   "man of left-wing pretensions . . .": Summers (Signet ed.), p. 458.

395   "She said that at a party . . .": Field, p. 302.

395   FBI document: In 1986 Anthony Summers obtained a copy of the FBI's "105C" file. ("105" designating "foreign counterintelligence matters," and "C" designating "communist.") Under the Freedom of Information appeals process the document was reviewed for Summers by the chief of the FBI's Appeals Unit. He informed Summers and FOIA Attorney James Lesar that the Marilyn Monroe file was voluminous and that the file contained thirty-one "105C" files that were totally redacted. Thirteen heavily censored pages were shown to Lesar, including the document dated March 6, which concerned her conversations with Frederick Vanderbilt Field relating to confidential information she had learned in conversations with the president and attorney general.

Chapter 52

397   "It had been kind of . . .": Spada, p. 326.

397   "We are out front . . .": Kelley, p. 300.

398   "Sam Giancana has been a guest . . .": Ibid., p. 326.

398   "Frank was livid . . .": Spada, p. 327.

399   It was rumored: The story of the Sinatra/Lawford feud was widely circulated in Harry Drucker's Beverly Hills barbershop where Drucker was the barber to Sinatra, Johnny Rosselli, Lawford, and the author.

399   "Frank just wrote Peter off . . .": Spada, p. 327.

399   Hoover was denied: The Presidential appointment logs at the Kennedy Library indicate only nine meetings between JFK and the Bureau Chief. One such meeting is logged on March 22, 1962.

400   Marilyn emerged from: Murray, p. 86.

400   "Peter paced back and forth . . .": Ibid., p. 87.

401   "The president was wearing . . .": Summers, p. 228; Brown, p. 72.

401   "I've been arguing with . . .": Ralph Roberts on canceled 20/20; Summers, p. 72; Brown, p. 73.

401   "He was a wonderful person to . . .": Brown, p. 252.

402   "It was noon . . .": int., Rosten, 1994; Rosten, pp. 113–115.

Chapter 53

404   "She went East for . . .": Brown, p. 67.

405   "She's not ready yet . . .": Spada, pp. 335–336.

405   "I wanted to tell you . . .": Brown, p. 77, from transcripts of his Weinstein interviews.

405   Details of MM's illness: Found by Peter Brown on microfilm in the Fox Studio Archives.

406   "Everyone knew that unless Marilyn . . .": Brown interview with Weinstein.

406   "Marilyn woke up each . . .": Murray, p. 91.

406   Marilyn's illness: Slatzer, *The Marilyn Files*, pp. 87–91.

406   "She knew she was sick . . .": int., Roberts, 1993, 1998.

407   Greenson's departure: Spoto, pp. 514, 515; Murray, p. 107.

407   The White Knight: Greenson, *Explorations in Psychoanalysis*, pp. 493–495.

408   "It was made of . . .": int., Jean Louis, 1993.

408   Norman Jefferies remembered: int., Jefferies, 1993.

408   "In the event that . . .": Brown, p. 133.

409   "highly placed political leaders . . .": int., Landreth, 1997.

409   "I mean, here's a girl . . .": Brown, p. 135.

409   a deafening whine announced: Brown, p. 131; Bernstein, "Monroe's Last Picture Show," *Esquire,* July 1973.

409   "While I was working . . .": int., Song, 1994; Spada, p. 336.

410   "By the way . . .": Brown, p. 147.

410   "Oh I think she'll . . .": Spada, p. 338.

410   The gala was replayed in the Wolper television documentary, *The Legend of Marilyn Monroe.*

411   "I was very worried about . . .": Brown, p. 150.

412   "There was at once something . . .": Schlesinger, *Robert Kennedy*, p. 590.

Chapter 54

413   "I would plan . . .": int., Schiller, 1993; Brown, p. 156.

414   "She was aware that . . .": int., Slatzer, 1994, 1997.

414   "The reaction was incredible . . .": Ibid., p. 159.

414   "What's the matter with . . .": Ibid., p. 163.

415   News of the problems: Ibid., p. 164.

415   "This was perhaps the most . . .": Ibid., p. 165.

416   "I don't think we'll ever . . .": Summers, p. 281.

416   Thursday, May 24: The meeting between Hoover and the President
        is logged in the Presidential Appointment Calendar at the Ken-
        nedy Library.

416   Calls from MM no longer accepted: Brown, p. 168; int., Slatzer,
        1994, 1997; Murray interview on canceled 20/20.

416   "There was no effort to . . .": Patricia Seaton Lawford, *The Peter
        Lawford Story*, p. 161.

417   "Pat Newcomb moved in for . . .": Murray, p. 107.

417   "She could hardly stand . . .": Brown, p. 169.

417   "she seemed to need all . . .": Murray, p. 106.

418   "To me, she looked . . .": int., Snyder, 1994.

418   "She was wonderful . . .": Brown, p. 177.

418   The entire collection of printed takes from *Something's Got to Give*
        is included in the archives of a prominent Monroe collector who
        kindly allowed the author to view them.

419   "I've got an appearance . . .": Brown, p. 180.

Chapter 55

420   "She was very proud . . .": Brown, p. 70.

420   "Marilyn didn't want to . . .": Murray, p. 107.

420   "Where the hell is Peter? . . . ": Spada, p. 341.

421   "rather pathetic letters": Ibid., p. 342.

421   "She was in bed naked . . .": Summers, pp. 273–274.

422   Greenson's return: Summers, p. 274; Brown, pp. 201–202.

422   "I can persuade Marilyn . . .": Brown, p. 203, Feldman phone logs,
        Fox Archives.

423   "You know, it isn't . . .": Brown, p. 207; Brown interview with Ru-
        din, 1992.

423   The morning editions: *Los Angeles Times* and *Los Angeles Herald-
        Examiner*, June 9, 1962; *New York Times*, June 10, 1962.

423   The crew had not placed the ad: Assistant director Buck Hall stated,
        "It came from somewhere else. Believe me, I would have known
        if the crew placed that ad."

424   Marilyn's calls to Skouras are documented in the Skouras Papers in
        the Special Collections Department, Stanford University; Brown,
        p. 232.

424 Rosenman's background and association with the Kennedys are out-
     lined in his obituary in the *New York Times*, June 25, 1973.

424 Great Lakes Carbon Corporation: Jerry Oppenheimer, *The Other
     Mrs. Kennedy*, pp. 170–173.

425 Bobby Kennedy's calls to Rosenman: Brown, p. 233; the Skouras
     Papers in the Special Collections Department, Stanford Univer-
     sity; Zanuck Papers, American Film Institute, Los Angeles.

425 "You know I never . . .": Leonard Mosley, *Zanuck*, p. 339.

425 "I only heard one side . . .": Brown, p. 233.

425 Zanuck's problems with Fox: Mosley, pp. 238–244.

426 Western Union message: Private Correspondence File of the At-
     torney General, Kennedy Library.

Chapter 56

427 "He loved her a . . .": N.Y. *Daily News*, August 14, 1962.

427 "Marilyn was out . . .": int., Jefferies, 1993.

428 "a bitter row": Summers, p. 296.

428 Visit to Dr. Gurdin: Ibid., p. 274; Brown, p. 244, Brown's interview
     with Gurdin, 1992.

428 "My guess was that . . .": "Marilyn Remembered," July 1993.

429 "Her inflections came . . .": Meryman, *Life*, November 4, 1966.

429 Dean Martin learned: *Los Angeles Herald-Examiner*, June 8, 1962;
     New York Times, June 9, 1962.

430 Zanuck arrived in New York: Mosley, p. 342.

430 "I never saw her so . . .": Brown, p. 254.

430 "He was casually dressed . . .": Murray, p. 112; Murray interview on
     canceled 20/20.

431 "I got word to . . .": Brown, p. 247.

431 "I found, surprisingly, that . . .": Ibid., 248.

432 "Mickey Rudin is deliberately . . .": Earl Wilson, *The Show Business
     Nobody Knows*, pp. 297, 298.

Chapter 57

434 105 File: FBI releases of File 105–40018 on Monroe.

435 Bolaños had followed: Summers, pp. 254, 255; Bolaños was photo-
     graphed as MM's escort at the Golden Globes: see Summers,
     Goddess paperback, pp. 454–461.

435 "heard directly from Marilyn . . .": Summers, *Goddess* paperback,
     p. 459.

435 as a guest in MM's apartment: Summers's interview with Field,
     1986; Field, p. 304.

436   "All of a sudden . . .": int., Carmen, 1997.

436   "Bobby was furious . . .": Lawford, p. 161.

436   The doctors' bills were entered into probate.

436   "Hy kept Marilyn sedated . . .": int., Maltz, 1996.

436   Robert Slatzer recalled: int., Slatzer, 1993, 1998; Slatzer, *The Life and Curious Death of Marilyn Monroe*, pp. 9–15.

437   Would have told all: int., Carmen, 1997.

437   20th Century-Fox Board: Mosley, p. 343.

438   They promptly resigned: Ibid., p. 344.

Chapter 58

439   "There was more to . . .": Summers, p. 297.

440   According to Ralph Roberts: int., Roberts, 1993, 1998.

440   Sinatra flew Marilyn: int. Julius Bengston, 1993: Bengston, a friend of Pat Newcomb's, went to Cal-Neva on the *Christina* as Marilyn's hairdresser and was helpful in filling in the details and itinerary of the Cal-Neva weekend.

440   Giancana at Cal-Neva: int., Bill Roemer, 1994, 1995. Former FBI agent Roemer had placed Giancana under constant surveillance, and he stated that the FBI was aware of Giancana's presence at Cal-Neva that weekend.

440   Bobby Kennedy might be there: int., Slatzer, 1993, 1998.

441   Bobby trying to reach Newcomb: int., Peggy Randall, 1993.

441   "She kept herself . . .": Summers, p. 283.

441   ". . . afraid of the Mafia": Strasberg, *Marilyn and Me*, p. 249.

441   "She told me it . . .": int., Roberts, 1993, 1998.

442   "at the edge of . . .": Summers, p. 295.

442   "He was very upset . . .": Ibid., p. 295.

442   Woodfield stated: int., Woodfield, 1995.

442   "The conversation was . . .": int., Roemer, 1994, 1995; Roemer, p. 184.

443   "When Marilyn left . . .": Summers, p. 293.

443   "out of it, a mess . . .": Ibid., p. 294.

443   White House telephone records: The president's phone logs, Kennedy Library.

Chapter 59

444   She called Rosenfeld: Summers, p. 301.

445    $6,000 evening gown: int., Jean Louis, 1993.

445   "She never looked better . . .": Summers, p. 301.

445   "She figured who else . . .": Spada, pp. 346–347.

445   Otash told the *Los Angeles Times*: *Los Angeles Times*, October 8, 1985.

446   History as CIA contractee: Jim Hougan, *Spooks*, pp. 99–112.

446   "Marilyn, who was fascinated . . .": Murray, p. 120.

446   "She came in carrying . . .": Spada, p. 350.

446   "He was without . . .": *San Francisco Chronicle*, August 4, 1962.

447   "Marilyn Monroe's health . . .": "The Voice of Broadway," *New York Journal-American*, August 3, 1962. Kilgallen never identified the "interesting" photograph being circulated in California.

447   Rothberg became privy: int., Howard Rothberg, 1995; Lee Israel, *Kilgallen*, pp. 338–340.

447   "Oh, yes, I was . . .": int., Ron Pataki, 1995.

448   "It may have been . . .": Ibid.

448   Pataki and Kilgallen: int., Lee Israel, 1995; Israel, pp. 431–439.

448   Marilyn called Slatzer: int., Slatzer, 1993, 1998.

449   A hotel operator: Summers, p. 304.

449   "If I am a star . . .": Meryman interview, *Life*, August 3, 1962.

449   "I'm cleaning house . . .": int., Slatzer, 1993, 1998.

449   "I'm not as mature . . .": Weatherby, p. 184.

455   "That last month . . .": int., Roberts, 1993, 1998; Strasberg, *Marilyn and Me*, p. 251.

450   "Tell him this is . . .": int., Roberts, 1993.

450   "Ralph did reach me . . .": Ibid.

450   Marilyn called the Rostens: int., Rosten, 1993, 1994.

450   Travilla at La Scala: Spada, p. 351.

451   "awakening from sleep . . .": Murray, p. 41.

451   "It's my feeling that . . .": Ibid., p. 156.

Chapter 60

452   Strange calls: Summers, p. 305; Spada, pp. 351–352; int., Carmen, 1997.

453   Murray spent the night: Murray, p. 123.

453   Jefferies had begun: int., Jefferies, 1993.

453   "We sat down at . . .": transcript of Slatzer interview with Murray, 1971.

453   "I only recently . . .": Clemmons lecture, "Marilyn Remembered," March 22, 1991.

453   "a chronic fear neurosis": Cottrell, *Ladies Home Companion*, January 1965.

453   Call to Skolsky: Summers, pp. 306–307.

453   Schiller recalled: int., Schiller, 1993.

454   "The small argument . . .": Slatzer, p. 221.

454   Newcomb's loyalty to the: int., Jefferies, 1993.

454   "Mrs. Murray fixed Marilyn . . .": Slatzer, p. 222.

455   Roar of a helicopter: Summers, p. 350; Brown, p. 303.

455   "The truth is, we . . .": Gates, p. 144.

455   "I was not supposed to . . .": Murray, from the transcript of BBC's
       Say Goodbye to the President.

455   Norman Jefferies confirmed: int., Jefferies, 1993.

456   "Mr. Lawford made it . . .": Ibid.

456   "Marilyn telephoned me . . .": int., Guilaroff, 1995; Guilaroff,
       Crowning Glory, pp. 165–167; transcript of Peter Brown interview
       with Guilaroff.

457   Otash's suppressed interview: from the canceled 20/20 transcripts.

457   "Where is it? Where is it?": Summers, p. 263.

457   two visits by Robert Kennedy: Summers, *Goddess* (Signet ed.),
       pp. 442–445.

458   "I received a call from . . .": int., Rosten, 1994.

458   Marilyn in hysterical state: int., Jefferies, 1993.

458   "Are you leaving, Pat?": Slatzer, p. 224.

459   "A man answered the phone . . .": Summers, p. 309.

459   "Terminate her therapy": Greenson to Kris, August 20, 1962.

459   At Murray's request . . . : int., Jefferies, 1993.

460   "It was between eight and eight-thirty . . .": int., Guilaroff, 1995.

460   "Are you sure you can't . . .": int., Carmen, 1998; Summers, p. 311.

460   Rosenfeld call: Ibid., p. 310.

460   Shortly after dusk: int., Clemmons, 1993, 1997; int., Slatzer, 1993,
       1997; Summers, p. 351. During Summers's research for *Goddess*,
       he interviewed Betty Pollard, who confirmed that Robert Kennedy
       was seen entering the Monroe gate on the evening Marilyn died.

461   The Bolaños call is documented in the transcripts of an interview
       with Anthony Summers in 1983. Bolaños stated that Marilyn
       didn't hang up, but she never came back to the phone.

461   "We were told to leave . . .": int., Jefferies, 1993.

462   "I thought she was dead": Ibid.

462   Hall confirmed . . . : int., Hall, 1993, 1994. Though the *Globe* article
       regarding the ambulance call implied that Dr. Greenson may
       have been responsible for Marilyn Monroe's death when he ad-
       ministered the heart needle, the administration of Adrenalin to
       the heart as a last-ditch lifesaving procedure was common prac-
       tice in 1962.

BIBLIOGRAPHY

Adams, Cindy. *Lee Strasberg: The Imperfect Genius of the Actors Studio*. Garden City, N.Y.: Doubleday, 1980.

Allen, Maury. *Where Have You Gone, Joe DiMaggio?* New York: Dutton, 1975.

Bacall, Lauren. *By Myself*. New York: Knopf, 1979.

Barris, George. *Marilyn: Her Life in Her Own Words*. New York: Birch Lane Press, 1995.

Behlmer, Rudy (editor). *Memo From David O. Selznick*. New York: Viking, 1972.

Belmont, Georges (interviewer). *Marilyn Monroe and the Camera Eye*. Boston: Bulfinch/Little, Brown, 1989.

Bernstein, Walter. *Inside Out*. New York: Knopf, 1996.

Blair, Joan, and Clay, Jr. *The Search for J. F. K.* New York: Berkeley, 1976.

Bosworth, Patricia. *Montgomery Clift—A Biography*. New York: Harcourt Brace Jovanovich, 1978.

Brown, David. *Let Me Entertain You*. New York: Morrow, 1990.

Brown, Peter, and Patte Barham. *Marilyn: The Last Take*. New York: Penguin, 1992.

Budenz, Louis Francis. *Men Without Faces*. New York: Harper, 1948.

Capell, Frank. *The Strange Death of Marilyn Monroe*. The Herald of Freedom, 1964.

Carpozi, George, Jr. *Marilyn Monroe: Her Own Story*. New York: Belmont, 1961.

Carter, Vincent A. *L.A.P.D.'s Rogue Cops*. Lucerne Valley, CA: Desert View, 1993.

Chekhov, Michael. *To the Actor: On the Technique of Acting*. New York: Harper, 1953.

Clark, Colin. *The Prince, the Showgirl, and Me*. New York: St. Martin's, 1996.

Conover, David. *Finding Marilyn*. New York: Grosset & Dunlap, 1981

Davis, Sammy, Jr. *Hollywood in a Suitcase*. New York: Morrow, 1980.

de Dienes, Andre, *Marilyn Mon Amour*. New York: St. Martin's, 1985.

Dougherty, James E. *The Secret Happiness of Marilyn Monroe*. Chicago: Playboy, 1976.

Draper, Theodore. *The Roots of American Communism*. New York: Viking, 1957.

Exner, Judith, and Ovid Demaris. *My Story*. New York: Grove, 1977.

Farber, Stephen, and Marc Green. *Hollywood on the Couch*. New York: Morrow, 1993.

Field, Frederick Vanderbilt. *From Right to Left*. Connecticut: Lawrence Hill, 1983.

Freeman, Lucy. *Why Norma Jean Killed Marilyn Monroe*. Chicago: Global Rights, 1992.

Friedrich, Otto. *City of Nets*. New York: Harper, 1986.

Gates, Daryl F. *Chief: My Life in the L.A.P.D.* New York: Bantam, 1992.

Gentry, Curt. *J. Edgar Hoover: The Man and the Secrets*. New York: Penguin, 1991.

Goode, James. *The Story of the Misfits*. Indianapolis: Bobbs-Merrill, 1961.

Goodman, Ezra. *The Fifty-Year Decline and Fall of Hollywood*. New York: Simon & Schuster, 1961.

Goodman, Walter. *The Committee*. New York: Farrar, Straus & Giroux, 1964.

Greenson, Ralph R. *The Technique and Practice of Psychoanalysis*. New York: International Universities Press, 1967.

Gregory, Adela, and Milo Speriglio. *Crypt 33*. New York: Carol, 1993.

Guiles, Fred Lawrence. *Legend: The Life and Death of Marilyn Monroe*. New York: Stein and Day, 1984.

———. *Norma Jean: The Life of Marilyn Monroe*. New York: McGraw-Hill, 1969.

Gunther, Marc. *The House That Roone Built*. New York: Little, Brown and Company, 1994.

Hamilton, Nigel. *J. F. K.—Reckless Youth*. New York: Random House, 1992.

Haspiel, James. *Marilyn: The Ultimate Look at the Legend*. New York: Holt, 1991.

Hersh, Seymour M. *The Dark Side of Camelot*. New York: Little, Brown, 1997.

Howe, Irving, and Lewis Coser. *The American Communist Party*. Boston: Beacon, 1957.

Hoyt, Edwin P. *Marilyn: The Tragic Venus*. New York: Duell, Sloan and Pearce, 1965.

Hurok, S., and Ruth Goode. *Impresario*. Canada: Random House, 1946.

Huston, John. *An Open Book*. New York: Knopf, 1980.

Israel, Lee. *Kilgallen*. New York: Delacorte, 1979.

Jacoby, Russell. *The Repression of Psychoanalysis: Otto Fenichel and the Political Freudians*. Chicago, Ill.: University of Chicago Press, 1983.

Johnson, Dorris, and Ellen Leventhal (editors). *The Letters of Nunnally Johnson*. New York: Knopf, 1981.

Johnson, Nora. *Flashback: Nora Johnson on Nunnally Johnson*. New York: Doubleday, 1979.

Kahn, Roger. *Joe and Marilyn: A Memory of Love*. New York: Morrow, 1986.

Kazan, Elia. *A Life*. New York: Knopf, 1988.

———. *People Will Talk*. New York: Knopf, 1985.

Kelley, Kitty. *His Way: The Unauthorized Biography of Frank Sinatra*. New York: Bantam Books, 1986.

Kennedy, Robert F. *The Enemy Within*. New York: Harper, 1960.

Kessler, Ronald. *The Sins of the Father*. New York: Warner, 1996.

Klehr, Harvey. *The Heyday of American Communism*. New York: Basic, 1984.

———, John Earl Haynes, and Fridrikh Igorevich Firsov. *The Secret World of American Communism*. New Haven, Conn.: Yale University Press, 1995.

———. and Ronald Radosh: *The Amerasia Spy Case*. Chapel Hill: University of North Carolina Press, 1996.

Koch, Stephen. *Double Lives*. New York: Macmillan, 1994.

Lambert, Gavin. *On Cukor*. New York: Putnam, 1972.

Lawford, Patricia Seaton, and Ted Schwarz. *The Peter Lawford Story*. New York: Carroll & Graf, 1988.

Logan, Joshua. *Movie Stars, Real People and Me*. New York: Delacorte, 1978.

Mailer, Norman. *Marilyn*. New York: Grosset & Dunlap, 1973; Galahad, 1988.

——— (with photographs by Milton H. Greens). *Of Women and Their Elegance*. New York: Simon & Schuster, 1980.

Mankiewicz, Joseph L. *More About All About Eve*. New York: Random House, 1972.

Masters, George, and Norma Lee Browning. *The Masters Way to Beauty*. New York: NAL/Signet, 1978.

McCann, Graham. *Marilyn Monroe*. New Brunswick, N.J.: Rutgers University Press, 1988.

Miller, Arthur. *After the Fall*. New York: Dramatists Play Service, 1964.

———. *Timebends*. New York: Grove, 1987.

Miracle, Berniece Baker, and Mona Rae Miracle. *My Sister Marilyn*. Chapel Hill: Algonquin Books, 1994.

Monroe, Marilyn. *My Story*. New York: Stein and Day, 1974.

Montand, Yves, with Herne Hamon and Patrick Rotman. *You See I Haven't Forgotten*. New York: Alfred A. Knopf, Inc., 1992.

Morphos, Evangeline (editor). *Lee Strasberg: A Dream of Passion*. Boston: Little, Brown, 1987.

Mosley, Leonard. *Zanuck*. Boston: Little, Brown. 1984.

Murray, Eunice. *Marilyn: The Last Months*. New York: Pyramid, 1975.

Negulesco, Jean. *Things I Did . . . and Things I Think I Did*. New York: Linden/ Simon & Schuster, 1984.

Noguchi, Thomas T. *Coroner*. New York: Pocket, 1983.

Olivier, Laurence. *Confessions of an Actor*. New York: Penguin, 1984.

———. *On Acting*. New York: Touchstone/Simon & Schuster, 1986.

Oppenheimer, Jerry. *The Other Mrs. Kennedy*. New York: St. Martin's, 1994.

Otash, Fred. *Investigation Hollywood*. Chicago: Regnery, 1976.

Parsons, Louella O. *Tell It to Louella*. New York: Putnam, 1961.

Pepitone, Lena, and William Stadiem. *Marilyn Monroe Confidential*. New York: Simon & Schuster, 1979.

Preminger, Otto. *Preminger: An Autobiography*. New York: Doubleday, 1977.

Rappleye, Charles, and Ed Becker. *All American Mafioso*. New York: Doubleday, 1991.

Riese, Randall, and Neal Hitchens. *The Unabridged Marilyn: Her Life from A to Z*. New York: Congdon & Weed, 1987.

Roemer, William F. *Man Against the Mob*. New York: Donald I. Fine, Inc., 1989.

Rollynson, Carl E., Jr. *Marilyn Monroe: A Life of the Actress*. Ann Arbor: University of Michigan Research Press, 1986.

Rose, Frank. *The Agency*. New York: HarperCollins, 1995.

Rosten, Norman. *Marilyn: An Untold Story*. New York: NAL/Signet, 1973.

Russell, Jane. *Jane Russell: My Paths and My Detours*. New York: Franklin Watts, 1985.

Schlesinger, Arthur M., Jr. *Robert Kennedy and His Times*. Boston: Houghton Mifflin, 1978.

Schwartz, Nancy Lynn. *The Hollywood Writers' Wars*. New York: Knopf, 1982.

Shaw, Sam, and Norman Rosten. *Marilyn Among Friends*. London: Bloomsbury, 1987.

Signoret, Simone. *Nostalgia Isn't What It Used to Be*. New York: Penguin, 1979.

Skolsky, Sidney. *Don't Get Me Wrong—I Love Hollywood*. New York: Putnam, 1975.

———. *Marilyn*. New York: Dell, 1954.

Slatzer, Robert. *The Life and Curious Death of Marilyn Monroe*. New York: Pinnacle, 1974.

———. *The Marilyn Files*. New York: S.P.I., 1992.

Spada, James, and George Zeno. *Monroe: Her Life in Pictures*. New York: Doubleday, 1982.

————. *Peter Lawford: The Man Who Kept the Secrets*. New York: Bantam, 1991.

Speriglio, Milo. *The Marilyn Conspiracy*. New York: Pocket, 1986.

Spindel, Bernard B. *The Ominous Ear*. New York: Award House, 1968.

Spoto, Donald. *Marilyn Monroe: The Biography*. New York: HarperCollins, 1993.

Stack, Robert, with Mark Evans. *Straight Shooting*. New York: Macmillan, 1980.

Steinem, Gloria (with photographs by George Barris). *Marilyn*. New York: Henry Holt, 1986.

Strasberg, Susan. *Bittersweet*. New York: Putnam, 1980.

————. *Marilyn and Me: Sisters, Rivals, Friends*. New York: Warner, 1992.

Sullivan, William C., and Bill Brown. *The Bureau: My Thirty Years in Hoover's FBI*. New York: Norton, 1979.

Summers, Anthony. *Goddess: The Secret Lives of Marilyn Monroe*. New York: Macmillan, 1985; Signet, 1986.

Swanson, Gloria. *Swanson on Swanson*. New York: Random House, 1980.

Theoharis, Athan (editor). *From the Secret Files of J. Edgar Hoover*. Chicago: Dee, 1991.

Tierney, Gene, and Mickey Herskowitz. *Self-Portrait*. New York: Wyden, 1979.

Walker, Alexander. *Vivien: The Life of Vivien Leigh*. New York, Grove, 1987.

Weatherby, W. J. *Conversations with Marilyn*. New York: Mason/Charter, 1976.

Whalen, Richard J. *The Founding Father: The Story of Joseph P. Kennedy*. New York: N.A.L. World, 1964.

Williams, Jay. *Stage Left*. New York: Scribner, 1974.

Wilson, Earl. *Show Business Laid Bare*. New York: Putnam, 1974.

Winters, Shelley. *Shelley II*. New York: Simon & Schuster, 1989.

Young-Bruehl, Elisabeth. *Anna Freud*. New York: Summit, 1988.

Zolotow, Maurice. *Billy Wilder in Hollywood*. New York: Putnam, 1977.

————. *Marilyn Monroe*. New York: Harcourt Brace, 1960.

Grateful acknowledgment is made for permission to quote from the following:

After the Fall by Arthur Miller. Copyright 1964 by Arthur Miller. Reprinted by permission of Viking Penguin, a division of Penguin Putnam, Inc.

Goddess: The Secret Lives of Marilyn Monroe by Anthony Summers (U.S. reprint). Copyright 1984 by Anthony Summers. Reprinted by permission of Sterling Lord Literistic, Inc.

The Life and Curious Death of Marilyn Monroe by Robert F. Slatzer. Copyright 1974, 1975 by Robert F. Slatzer. Reprinted by permission of Robert F. Slatzer.

Marilyn: An Untold Story by Norman Rosten. Copyright 1967, 1972, 1973 by Norman Rosten. First published by New American Library. Reprinted by permission of Harold Ober Associates, Inc., and Patricia Rosten Filan.

Marilyn: The Last Take by Patte B. Barham and Peter Harry Brown. Copyright © 1992 by Patte B. Barham and Peter Harry Brown. Used by permission of Dutton, a division of Penguin Putnam Inc.

My Sister Marilyn: A Memoir of Marilyn Mornoe by Berniece Baker Miracle and Mona Rae Miracle. Copyright 1994 by Berniece Baker Miracle. Reprinted by permission of Algonquin Books, Chapel Hill, a division of Workman Publishing.

My Story edited by Milton H. Greene. Copyright 1998 by the Archives of Milton H. Greene, LLC. Reprinted by permission of The Archives of Milton H. Greene, LLC. *www.archivesmhg.com.*

The Prince, the Showgirl, and Me by Colin Clark. Copyright 1995 by Colin Clark. Reprinted by permission of St. Martin's Press, Inc.

The Secret Happiness of Marilyn Monroe by James Dougherty. Copyright by James Dougherty. Reprinted by permission of James Dougherty.

INDEX